The Earth and Its Peoples:

A Global History

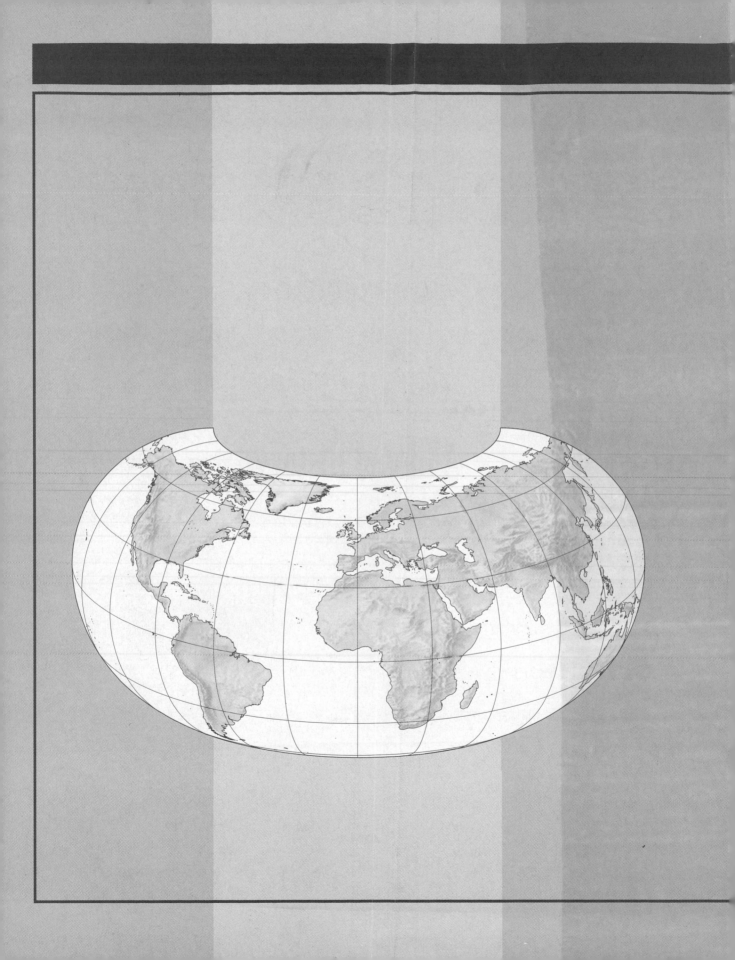

THE EARTH AND ITS PEOPLES:

A GLOBAL HISTORY

Volume I: to 1500

Richard W. Bulliet   COLUMBIA UNIVERSITY

Pamela Kyle Crossley   DARTMOUTH COLLEGE

Daniel R. Headrick   ROOSEVELT UNIVERSITY

Steven W. Hirsch   TUFTS UNIVERSITY

Lyman L. Johnson   UNIVERSITY OF NORTH CAROLINA—CHARLOTTE

David Northrup   BOSTON COLLEGE

Houghton Mifflin Company   BOSTON   NEW YORK

Senior Sponsoring Editor: *Patricia A. Coryell*
Senior Basic Book Editor: *Elizabeth M. Welch*
Senior Project Editor: *Susun Westendorf*
Senior Production/Design Coordinator: *Jill Haber*
Senior Manufacturing Coordinator: *Priscilla Bailey*

Cover designer: *Anthony Saizon*

Cover image research: *Rose Corbett Gordon*

Cover image: *Rollout photograph of Maya Codex-style vase painting, 600–900* © *Justin Kerr.*

Printed in the U.S.A.

Library of Congress Catalog Card Number: 96-76875

ISBN: 0-395-53492-5

Examination Copy ISBN: 0-395-84296-4

23456789—VH—00 99 98 97

BRIEF CONTENTS

CONTENTS

MAPS

ENVIRONMENT & TECHNOLOGY

VOICES & VISIONS

PREFACE

History is not easy. We met in a conference room at Houghton Mifflin: six professional historians seated around a table hammering out our ideas on what a global history textbook at the start of a new millennium should be. Together we brought to the project a high level of knowledge about Africa, the Americas, Asia, Europe, the Middle East. We argued; we made up over dinner; we debated some more.

But there was no short cut. Though not by nature contentious people, we were determined to write the best global history we could. And that necessarily meant testing ideas aloud; considering alternatives put forward by smart, articulate colleagues; and bargaining over what to include and what, with regret, to pass over. We believe the result was worth the sweat.

Our goal was to write a textbook that would not only speak for the past but speak to today's student and today's teacher. By the time a class has completed it, students and instructor alike should have a strong sense that the history of the human species, throughout the globe, follows a particular trajectory: from sparse and disconnected communities reacting creatively to their individual circumstances; through ever more intensive stages of contact, interpenetration, and cultural expansion and amalgamation; to a twenty-first century world situation in which people increasingly visualize a single global community.

This trajectory of human development is not a fixed road map, however. Different parts of the world have moved or paused at different points in time and have followed their own paths. The chronology of the transition from the first domesticated plants and animals to broad territorial empires in the Western Hemisphere, for example, is unconnected with that of the Eastern Hemisphere, just as the industrialization of Western Europe and North America preceded by a century or two industrialization elsewhere. Yet the world all comes together in the late twentieth century, a paradoxical period of global political and economic forces confronting intensified reassertions of particular national and cultural identities. As in ages past, however large and encompassing social, cultural, and political systems become, human diversity persists. Those people who speak today of an emerging global community are answered by others who insist on their own distinctive identities.

The keynote of this book is not progress but process: a steady process of change over time, at first differently experienced in various regions of the world but eventually entangling peoples from all parts of the globe. Students should come away from this book with a sense that the problems and promises of their world are rooted in a past in which people of every sort, in every part of the world, confronted problems of a similar character and coped with them as best they could. We believe our efforts will help students see where their world has come from and learn thereby something useful for their own lives.

Central Theme

We have subtitled *The Earth and Its Peoples* "A Global History" because the book explores the common challenges and experiences that unite the human past. Although the dispersal of early humans to every livable environment resulted in myriad economic, social, political, and cultural systems, all societies displayed analogous patterns in meeting their needs and exploiting their environments. Our challenge was to select the particular data and episodes that would best illuminate these global patterns of human experience.

To meet this challenge, we adopted a central theme to serve as the spinal cord of our history. That theme is "technology and environment," the commonplace bases of all human societies at all times and a theme that grants no special favor to any cultural or social group even as it em-

braces subjects of the broadest topical, chrono-
logical, and geographical range.

It is vital for students to understand that technology, in the broad sense of experience-based
knowledge of the physical world, underlies all
human activity. Writing is a technology, but so is
oral transmission from generation to generation
of lore about medicinal or poisonous plants. The
magnetic compass is a navigational technology,
but so is the Polynesian mariners' hard-won
knowledge of winds, currents, and tides that
made possible the settlement of the Pacific
islands.

All technological development, moreover, has
come about in interaction with environments,
both physical and human, and has, in turn, affected those environments. At the most basic
level, concern with technology and the environment arises from the reality that all humans must
eat. Yet less material cultural attainments are encompassed as well. Quite apart from such facilitating technologies as writing, papermaking, and
printing, philosophies and religions have started
from and sought to explain real world phenomena. Technological skills like stonecutting, paint
mixing, and surveying have enabled creative
artists to frame their works in response to specific environments: the indestructible rock paintings and engravings of the Sahara and Kalahari
Desert, the Greek temple of Sounion on a high
cliff by the sea, the grand mosques of Istanbul
atop the city's seven hills, Daoist Chinese landscape painting capturing the mists of the Yangtze
River gorges. Cultural achievements of these sorts
reflect changing understandings of human relations to one another and to the world they live in.
Thus they belong in this book, evidence of the
technology and environment theme as a constant
in human society and a solid basis for comparing
different times, places, and communities.

Organization

The Earth and Its Peoples uses eight broad chrono-
logical divisions to define its conceptual scheme
of global historical development. In **Part I: The
Emergence of Human Communities, to 500
B.C.E.,** we examine important patterns of human

communal organization. Early human communities were small, and most parts of the world were
populated sparsely, if at all. As they spread
worldwide, men and women encountered and
responded to enormously diverse environmental
conditions. Their responses gave rise to many
technologies, from implements for meeting daily
needs to the compilation of exhaustive lore about
plants, animals, the climate, and the heavens.
This lore, in turn, fueled speculations about the
origin of the world and humanity, the nature of
the gods or forces they felt controlled the world
around them, the purpose of life, and the meaning of death. Though scarcity of written sources
limits what we know about the world's first societies, the evolution of their technologies tells us
much about gender relations, specialization of
work activities, and patterns of everyday life—in
short, about the growing complexity of human
communities.

**Part II: The Formation of New Cultural Com-
munities, 1000 B.C.E.–500 C.E.,** introduces the
concept of a "cultural community," in the sense
of a coherent pattern of activities and symbols
pertaining to a specific human community.
While all communities have distinctive cultures,
the advances and conquests of some communities in this period magnified the geographical
and historical imprint of their cultures.

In the geographically contiguous African-
Eurasian landmass, the cultures that proved to
have the most enduring influence traced their
roots to the second and first millennia B.C.E. The
long-term impact of these cultural communities
involved competition with other cultures that
did not prove so enduring. This frequently violent competition, culminating in the extensive
empires of the Assyrians, Persians, Romans, and
Han Chinese, was often marked by technological
mixing across contested frontiers. Thus, non-
Greek elements in Greek culture (such as the use
of an alphabet invented by Phoenicians), the influence of non-Chinese steppe nomads on Chinese culture (as with the introduction of
horse-related technologies), and other such examples are used to show how all cultural traditions become amalgams as they grow.

**Part III: Growth and Interaction of Cultural
Communities, 300 B.C.E.–1200 C.E.,** deals with

early episodes of technological, social, and cultural exchange and interaction on a continental scale outside the framework of imperial expansion. These are so different from earlier interactions arising from conquest or extension of political boundaries that they constitute a distinct era in world history, an era that set the world on the path of increasing global interaction and interdependence that it has been following ever since.

Exchange along long-distance trade routes and migrations by peoples equipped with advanced technologies played an especially important role in the coming together of the world's peoples. The Silk Road, for example, put China into contact with Mesopotamia and the Mediterranean lands, leading to a stimulating exchange of products and ideas and to the emergence of urban society in central Asia. In Africa, the Bantu migrations spread iron-working and cultivation of yams and other crops throughout most of the sub-Saharan region, while in the Americas a similar diffusion of corn, potatoes, and other domestic plants made possible the sophisticated states of the Mayas, Incas, and Aztecs. And throughout Europe, Asia, and much of Africa the universal religions of Buddhism, Christianity, and Islam gained so many adherents that they became defining elements of entire civilizations.

In **Part IV: Interregional Patterns of Culture and Contact, 1200–1500**, we take a look at the world during three centuries that saw both intensified cultural and commercial contact and increasingly confident self-definition of cultural communities in Europe, Asia, and Africa. The Mongol conquest of a vast empire extending from China to Iran and eastern Europe greatly stimulated trade and interaction while Chinese civilization itself extended its influence. Muslim religious expansion brought new cultural values and societal contacts to India, West Africa, and the Balkans and promoted trading networks around the Indian Ocean and across the Sahara. In the West, strengthened European kingdoms began maritime expansion in the Atlantic, forging direct ties with sub-Saharan Africa and laying the base for expanded global contacts after 1500.

Part V: The Globe Encompassed, 1500–1700, treats a period dominated by the global effects of European expansion and continued economic growth. European ships took over, expanded, and extended the maritime trade of the Indian Ocean, coastal Africa, and the Asian rim of the Pacific Ocean.

This maritime commercial enterprise had its counterpart in European colonial empires in the Americas and a new Atlantic trading system. In Asia, the Middle East, and Africa powerful new states emerged in this period that limited, challenged, or simply ignored the growing European dominance elsewhere. The contrasting capacities and fortunes of land empires and maritime empires, along with the exchange of domestic plants and animals between the hemispheres, underline the technological and environmental dimensions of this first era of complete global interaction.

In **Part VI: Revolutions Reshape the World, 1750–1870**, the word *revolution* is used in three senses: in the political sense of governmental overthrow, as in France and the Americas; in the metaphorical sense of radical transformative change, as in the Industrial Revolution; and in the broadest sense of a profound change in circumstances and world-view, as in the abolitionist movement, which in time completely destroyed an instrument of oppression that had been part of human life for thousands of years. These three senses of the word make it possible to integrate the experiences of a Western Europe intoxicated by the enormous power triggered by industrialization; a Western Hemisphere consumed with a passion for freedom from European domination; and Ottoman, Chinese, and Japanese states that saw their earlier conceptions of the world rapidly dissolve even as they struggled to adapt to the currents of change.

Technology and environment lie at the core of these developments. With the ascendancy of the Western belief that science and technology could overcome all challenges, environmental or otherwise, technology became not only an instrument of transformation but also an instrument of domination, threatening the integrity and autonomy of cultural traditions in nonindustrial lands. At the same time, other aspects of technology intensified social diversity by accentuating the difference between rich and poor, slave and free, and male and female.

Part VII: Global Dominance and Diversity, 1850–1945, examines the development of a world arena in which people conceived of events on a global scale. Imperialism, world war, international economic connections, and world-encompassing ideological forces, like nationalism and socialism, present the picture of an increasingly interconnected globe. European dominance took on a worldwide dimension, at times seeming to threaten permanent subordination to European values and philosophies while at other times triggering strong political or cultural resistance. The accelerating pace of technological change deepened other sorts of cleavages as well. Economic class divisions, for example, became part of the ideological struggle between socialism and capitalism; and a spreading desire for political participation led to demands by women for voting rights.

For **Part VIII: The Perils and Promises of a Global Community, 1945 to the Present**, we chose a thematic structure in keeping with how many people perceive the past half century. Countries throughout the world experienced more or less similar challenges in the era of Cold War and decolonization that culminated in 1991. In large measure, these challenges derived from global economic, technological, and political forces that limited the options for political and economic development open to the scores of new nations that emerged at the start of this period.

In a world contest for resources, the difference between growth and prosperity or overpopulation and poverty often hinged on technological and environmental factors, such as the development of high-yielding strains of rice and other crops. Yet even as the world faced the prospect of deepening gulfs between its rich and its poor regions, technological development simultaneously brought its peoples into closer contact than ever before. With the dimensions and the values of an increasingly globalized economy and society up for debate, issues such as gender equality, racial justice, human rights, and the demise or revitalization of human cultural diversity remained for the next century to resolve.

Distinctive Features

Learning and teaching aids are especially important in a book that extends its scope to all of human history. The pedagogical framework for *The Earth and Its Peoples* seeks to make the text accessible and memorable by reinforcing its theme and highlighting its subject matter.

To keep the technology and environment theme and the structural linkage between the parts clear, each part begins with an opening essay that sets the following chapters into the broad context of the book as a whole. A unique "geographic locator" map accompanies this opener to help the student visualize the world areas and developments that will be discussed in the part.

"Environment and Technology" boxes in each chapter further emphasize our central theme. Each feature expands on a particular topic in technological history—for example, ship design, camel saddles, coinage, military technology, writing systems, Indian mathematics, Copernican astronomy, the McCormick reaper, and compact disks. Accompanying illustrations enhance student understanding of the far-reaching impact of technological and environmental developments on human experience.

"Voices and Visions" features likewise accompany each chapter. These consist of excerpts from primary written, or occasionally visual, sources. While encouraging close study of historical evidence, they also enhance our narrative by giving clear voice to an array of individual viewpoints and cultural outlooks. Slavery in different periods and places receives attention, for example, as do witchcraft accusations and prosecutions, a Chinese official's views on the opium trade, a Nigerian woman's recollection of her childhood at the turn of the twentieth century, and Arthur Ashe's struggle against AIDS. Questions for analysis designed to stimulate critical interpretation of primary sources close each "Voices and Visions" feature.

Each chapter opens with a thematic introduction intended to engage the reader's interest while previewing what will follow. Extensive maps and illustrations serve to reinforce and complement, not merely ornament, surrounding discussion, while numerous charts and timelines help to organize and review major developments. Careful chapter conclusions draw together major topics and themes and link the present chapter to the one that follows. An annotated list of Suggested Reading at the end of each chapter contains a wide range of up-to-date references to help students pursue their interests.

For further assistance, *The Earth and Its Peoples* is issued in three formats to accommodate different academic calendars and approaches to the course. There is a one-volume hardcover version containing all 35 chapters, along with a two-volume paperback edition: Volume I, To 1500 (Chapters 1–16), and Volume II, Since 1500 (Chapters 17–35). For readers at institutions with the quarter system, we offer a three-volume paperback version: Volume A, To 1200 (Chapters 1–12); Volume B, From 1200 to 1870 (Chapters 13–27); and Volume C, Since 1750 (Chapters 23–35).

At the end of each volume, an extensive pronunciation guide shows the reader how to pronounce the many foreign terms and names necessary to a book of this scope.

Supplements

We have assembled with care an array of text supplements to aid students in learning and instructors in teaching. These supplements, including a *Study Guide*, a *Computerized Study Guide*, an *Instructor's Resource Manual*, *Test Items*, *Computerized Test Items*, *Map Transparencies*, and a *Power Presentation Manager*, are tied closely to the text, to provide a tightly integrated program of teaching and learning.

The *Study Guide*, authored by Michele G. Scott James of MiraCosta College, contains learning objectives, chapter outlines (with space for students' notes on particular sections), key-term identifications, multiple-choice questions, short-answer and essay questions, and map exercises. Included too are distinctive "comparison charts," to help students organize the range of information about different cultures and events discussed in each chapter. The *Study Guide* is published in two volumes, to correspond to Volumes I and II of the text: Volume I contains Chapters 1–16 and Volume II Chapters 17–35.

The *Study Guide* is also available in a computerized version for use with IBM PC and compatible computers. This *Computerized Study Guide* contains text references for all questions and rejoinders to each multiple-choice question that explain why the student's response is or is not correct.

The *Instructor's Resource Manual*, prepared by Rosanne J. Marek, Ball State University, provides useful teaching strategies for the global history course and tips for getting the most out of the text. Each chapter contains instructional objectives, a detailed chapter outline, discussion questions, individual learning activities, and audio-visual resources.

Each chapter of the *Test Items*, written by John Cashman of Boston College, offers 20 to 25 key-term identifications, 5 to 10 essay questions with answer guidelines, 35 to 40 multiple-choice questions, and 3 to 5 history and geography exercises. We also provide a computerized version of the *Test Items*, to enable instructors to alter, replace, or add questions. Each entry in the *Computerized Test Items* is numbered according to the printed test items to ease the creation of customized tests. The computerized test item file is available for use with both IBM PC and compatibles and Macintosh computers.

In addition, a set of *Transparencies* of all the maps in the text is available on adoption.

We are also pleased to offer the *Power Presentation Manager*, a software tool that enables teachers to prepare visual aids for lectures electronically, using both textual and visual material. Instructors can customize their lectures by incorporating their own material onto the PPM and combining it with the electronic resources provided, including adaptable chapter outlines as well as tables, illustrations, and maps from the text.

Acknowledgments

From our first to final draft, we have benefited from the critical readings of many colleagues. Our sincere thanks in particular to the following instructors: Kathleen Alaimo, St. Xavier University; Kenneth Andrian, Ohio State University; Norman Bennett, Boston University; Fritz Blackwell, Washington State University; Steven C. Davidson, Southwestern University; John E.

Davis, Radford University; Chandra de Silva, Indiana State University; Keven Doak, University of Illinois at Urbana-Champaign; Ellen Eslinger, DePaul University; Allen Greenberger, Pitzer College; Frances Harmon, College of Mount Saint Joseph; Janine Hartman, University of Cincinnati; Michele G. Scott James, MiraCosta College; Charles R. Lee, University of Wisconsin—La Crosse; Rosanne J. Marek, Ball State University; Peter Mellini, Sonoma State University; Shirley Mullen, Westmont College; Patricia O'Neill, Central Oregon College; William Parsons, Eckerd College; John P. Ryan, Kansas City Kansas Community College; Abraham Sherf, North Shore Community College; Steven R. Smith, Savannah State University; Sara W. Tucker, Washburn University; Sarah Watts, Wake Forest University; and Kenneth Wolf, Murray State University.

We would like to extend our collective thanks as well to Lynda Shaffer for her early conceptual contributions. Individually, Richard Bulliet thanks Jack Garraty and Isser Woloch for first involving him in world history; Pamela Crossley wishes to thank Gene Garthwaite, Charles Wood, and David Morgan; Steven Hirsch extends his gratitude to Dennis Trout; Lyman Johnson his to Kenneth J. Andrien, Richard Boyer, Grant D. Jones, William M. Ringle, Hendrik Kraay, Daniel Dupre, and Steven W. Usselman; and David Northrup thanks Mrinalini Sinha, Robin Fleming, Benjamin Braude, Alan Rogers, and John Tutino.

Over the years it took to bring this project to fruition, we worked with an excellent editorial and publishing team at Houghton Mifflin. Our hearts belong especially to Elizabeth M. Welch, Senior Basic Book Editor, who with unfailing good humor and sympathy (at least in our presence) guided us around every pitfall. At a somewhat earlier stage, Sean W. Wakely, our former Sponsoring Editor, and Jane Knetzger, Senior Associate Editor and our former Basic Book Editor, bore with remarkable aplomb the burden of listening to our lengthy debates while keeping us headed toward the final goal.

The rest of the Houghton Mifflin team, to each of whom we extend our deepest thanks, consisted of: Jean L. Woy, Editor-in-Chief for History and Political Science; Patricia A. Coryell, Senior Sponsoring Editor; Jeff Greene, Senior Associate Editor; Jeanne Herring, Assistant Editor; Susan Westendorf, Senior Project Editor; Charlotte Miller, map editor; Carole Frohlich, photo researcher; Jill Haber, Senior Production and Design Coordinator; Ron Kosciak, interior designer; Anthony L. Saizon, cover designer; and Rose Corbett-Gordon, cover image researcher.

We thank also the many students whose questions and concerns shaped much of this work, and we welcome all our readers' suggestions, queries, and criticisms. Please contact us at our respective institutions or at this e-mail address: history@hmco.com

Richard W. Bulliet   A professor of Middle Eastern history at Columbia University and director of its Middle East Institute, Richard W. Bulliet received his Ph.D. from Harvard University. He has written scholarly works on a number of topics: the social history of medieval Iran (*The Patricians of Nishapur*), the historical competition between pack camels and wheeled transport (*The Camel and the Wheel*), the process of conversion to Islam (*Conversion to Islam in the Medieval Period*), and the overall course of Islamic social history (*Islam: The View from the Edge*). He has also published four novels, co-edited *The Encyclopedia of the Modern Middle East*, and hosted an educational television series on the Middle East.

Pamela Kyle Crossley   Pamela Kyle Crossley received her Ph.D. in Modern Chinese History from Yale University and is Professor of History at Dartmouth College. Her research has been supported in recent years by the American Council of Learned Societies, the Marion and Jasper Whiting Foundation, the Woodrow Wilson International Center for Scholars, and the John Simon Guggenheim Memorial Foundation. She is author of the books *A Translucent Mirror: History and Identity in Qing Ideology*, *The Manchus*, and *Orphan Warriors: Three Manchu Generations and the End of the Qing World*, as well as articles in the *American Historical Review*, the *Journal of Asian Studies*, and the *Harvard Journal of Asiatic Studies*.

Daniel R. Headrick   Daniel R. Headrick received his Ph.D. in History from Princeton University. Professor of History and Social Science at Roosevelt University in Chicago, he is the author of several books on the history of technology, imperialism, and international relations, including *The Tools of Empire: Technology and European Imperialism in the Nineteenth Century*, *The Tentacles of Progress: Technology Transfer in the Age of Imperialism*, and *The Invisible Weapon: Telecommunications and International Politics*. His articles have appeared in the *Journal of World History* and the *Journal of Modern History* and he has been awarded fellowships by the National Endowment for the Humanities and the John Simon Guggenheim Memorial Foundation.

Steven W. Hirsch   Steven W. Hirsch holds a Ph.D. in Classics from Stanford University and is currently Associate Professor of Classics and History at Tufts University and Chair of the Department of Classics. He has received grants from the National Endowment for the Humanities and the Massachusetts Foundation for Humanities and Public Policy. His research and publications include *The Friendship of the Barbarians: Xenophon and the Persian Empire*, as well as articles and reviews in the *Classical Journal*, the *American Journal of Philology*, and the *Journal of Interdisciplinary History*.

Lyman L. Johnson   Professor of History at the University of North Carolina at Charlotte, Lyman L. Johnson earned his Ph.D. in Latin American history from the University of Connecticut. A two-time Senior Fulbright-Hays Lecturer, he has also received fellowships from the Tinker Foundation, the Social Science Research Council, the National Endowment for the Humanities, and the American Philosophical Society. His recent books include *The Problem of Order in Changing Societies*, *Essays on the Price History of Eighteenth-Century Latin America* (with Enrique Tandeter), and *Colonial Latin America* (with Mark A. Burkholder). The current President of the Conference on Latin American History (1997–1998), he has also published in journals, including the *Hispanic American Historical Review*, the *Journal of Latin American Studies*, the *International Review of Social History*, *Social History*, and *Desarrollo Económico*.

David Northrup   Professor of History at Boston College, David Northrup earned his Ph.D. from the University of California, Los Angeles. He has twice been awarded Fulbright-Hays Research Abroad Grants and National Endowment for the Humanities Summer Stipends, along with an African Studies Grant from the Social Science Research Council. He is the author of *Trade Without Rulers: Pre-Colonial Economic Development in South-Eastern Nigeria*, *Beyond the Bend in the River: A Labor History of Eastern Zaire, 1870–1940*, *Indentured Labor In the Age of Imperialism, 1834–1922*, and he compiled and edited *The Atlantic Slave Trade*. His research has appeared in the *Journal of African History*, the *Journal of Interdisciplinary History*, *History in Africa*, the *International Journal of African Historical Studies*, and the *Journal of Church and State*.

NOTE ON SPELLING AND USAGE

Where necessary for clarity, dates are followed by the letters C.E. or B.C.E. C.E. stands for "Common Era" and is equivalent to A.D. (*Anno Domini*, Latin for "in the year of the Lord"). B.C.E. stands for "Before the Common Era" and means the same as B.C. ("Before Christ"). In keeping with their goal of approaching world history without special concentration on one culture or another, the authors chose these neutral abbreviations as appropriate to their enterprise. Because many readers will be more familiar with English than with metric measurements, however, units of measure are generally given in the English system, with metric equivalents following in parentheses.

In general, Chinese has been romanized according to the *pinyin* method. Exceptions include proper names well established in English (e.g., Canton, Chiang Kai-shek) and a few English words borrowed from Chinese (e.g., kowtow). Spellings of Arabic, Ottoman Turkish, Persian, Mongolian, Manchu, Japanese, and Korean names and terms avoid special diacritical marks for letters that are pronounced only slightly differently in English. An apostrophe is used to indicate when two Chinese syllables are pronounced separately (e.g., Chang'an).

For words transliterated from languages that use the Arabic script—Arabic, Ottoman Turkish, Persian, Urdu—the apostrophe indicated separately pronounced syllables may represent either of two special consonants, the *hamza* or the *ain*. Because most English speakers do not hear distinction between these two, they have not been distinguished in transliteration, and they are not indicated when they occur at the beginning or end of a word. As with Chinese, some words and commonly used placenames from these languages are given familiar English spellings (e.g., Quran instead of Qur'an, Cairo instead of al-Qahira). Arabic romanization has normally been used for terms relating to Islam, even where the context justifies slightly different Turkish or Persian forms, again for ease of comprehension.

There is lively scholarly debate on how best to render Amerindian words in English letters. Nahuatl and Yacatec Maya words and placenames are given in familiar, conventional forms that some linguists now challenge. Thus terms like Tenochtitlán and Chichén Itzá contain accented vowels, contrary to some scholarly recommendations. Similarly, like most North American historians, we have not followed recent proposals for a new system of transliterating Aymara and Quechua words from the Andean region. Thus we retain Inca instead of Inka and *quipu* instead of *khipu*.

To help clarify placenames that have changed over time, the modern form of the name is often put in parentheses after the form appropriate to the period of history under discussion. Thus, Annam, an ancestor state of Vietnam, is referred to as such where appropriate historically, with its relationship to modern Vietnam noted in parentheses. In some cases, consideration of the reader has demanded careful anachronisms (e.g., "Inner China" and "Outer China" in discussion of the early history of territories that only much later became part of empires based in China, and eventually of China itself). Anachronisms of this sort are explained in the text.

The Earth and Its Peoples:

A Global History

The Emergence of Human Communities,

TO 600 B.C.E.

Though remote from the present, the global events that we examine in the first part of *The Earth and Its Peoples* are fundamental for understanding the origins of human nature, culture, and society. These chapters examine two aspects of the earliest human interactions with the natural world: how environmental forces affected humans' physical evolution and how evolving humans gradually devised tools and acquired technical knowledge that enabled them to reshape environments to meet their needs. These chapters also detail how the movement of humans across the planet gave rise to cultural differences in language, customs, and beliefs and how the development of increasingly complex societies led to social distinctions based on occupation and status as well as on gender and age.

An unusually cool climate dominated the long era during which human beings first appeared on the earth. Great masses of ice slowly expanded and contracted over much of northern Eurasia and North America, soaking up so much water that sea levels and rainfall were affected even in tropical regions. During this "Great Ice Age," which lasted until about 10,000 years ago, the pace of change in human development was also glacially slow. Like other creatures, members of the human species *Homo* evolved physically in ways that improved their species' chances for survival.

During the later millennia of the Ice Age, a unique capacity for cultural change gave humans a survival strategy that unfolded more quickly and more easily than physical evolution. As physically modern people gradually evolved, their mental capacities enabled them to adapt to various environmental situations by devising new tools and strategies. Because many of the earliest tools that have been discovered are made of stone, researchers have named the expanse of time extended from 2 million years ago to 4,000 years ago the "Stone Age."

Those tools and learning ability enabled humans to fan out to the far reaches of the planet. Arriving in different environments, they learned how to hunt the local animals, gather native plants for food, make clothing, and build dwellings from materials at hand. They also used their mental powers to develop languages, create works of art, and speculate about the meaning of life.

The value of humans' ability to adapt their way of life to new environments became evident when the Ice Age ended and generally warmer temperatures returned. Humanity entered a new stage in its relationship with nature, and the pace of historical change quickened. No longer entirely dependent on wild plants and animals for food, people began to cultivate edible plants and to domesticate animals such as wild cattle, pigs, and water buffalo. In arid lands people depended on herds of domesticated animals for their livelihood. Their way of life is known as pastoralism. In places where water was more abundant, people established permanent communities where they cultivated food crops and improved their ability to manage and shape their environment. A series of "agricultural revolutions" occurring in Eurasia, Africa, and the Americas between 10,000 and 5,500 years ago supported a steady rise in populations. Some agricultural settlements grew into towns and cities.

The growth and concentration of population intensified humans' manipulation of the environment around 3500 B.C.E. (Before the Common Era)—that is, some fifty-five hundred years ago. In the floodplains of great river valleys in Egypt, Mesopotamia, India, and, later, China, communities constructed complex systems of irrigation to increase crop yields. Under the direction of powerful rulers, they built cities distinguished by monumental buildings, and they waged large-scale wars to defend and extend their territories.

One of the striking changes apparent in these river-valley civilizations was social stratification—the emergence of a class structure. At the top were powerful and wealthy kings who directed and controlled the lives of ordinary people, defending them from invaders, collecting taxes in goods and labor, and issuing and enforcing laws. Claiming to be far more than mere administrators, rulers enhanced their authority by taking on the attributes of gods. For example, a ruler might attribute a bountiful harvest to his mystical powers over nature rather than to his administrative skills.

Priests, who headed the state religion, were another exalted class. They performed religious rites, offered sacrifices to the gods, communicated the god's wishes, and conducted public festivals. At the bottom of the social ladder were the people conquered and enslaved in the course of frequent wars. In general, women seem to have lost standing to men in the social hierarchy of these civilizations.

Striking changes also appeared in the material culture of the river-valley civilizations, especially in architecture, writing, and recordkeeping. The cities and their outlying areas boasted splendid temples, palaces, and royal tombs, designed by master architects and built by armies of conscripted laborers. Stone became an important construction material. The development of tools made of bronze (an alloy of copper and tin) enabled builders to shape building stones with exquisite care. Bronze also was used in weapons and other implements. Just as the characteristic stone tools gave their name to the "Stone Age," so the "Bronze Age" that began about 3500 B.C.E., was named for its key technology.

Technology

2,000,000 B.C.E.—Stone tools (Africa)

1,000,000 B.C.E.—Controlled use of fire (Africa)

ca. 10,500 B.C.E.—First pottery in China

9000 B.C.E.—Domestication of animals and plants

7000 B.C.E.—Early metalworking (Middle East)

4000 B.C.E.—Bronze casting (Middle East)

3500 B.C.E.—Invention of wheel and plow (Mesopotamia)

3100 B.C.E.—First writing (Sumer)

3000 B.C.E.—Domestication of the camel (Arabia)

2500 B.C.E.—Domestication of the horse (Central Asia)

Environment

2,000,000–12,000 B.C.E.—Great Ice Age

32,000–12,000 B.C.E.—Last glacial period;
     animal extinctions

12,000 B.C.E.—Warming trend melts glaciers

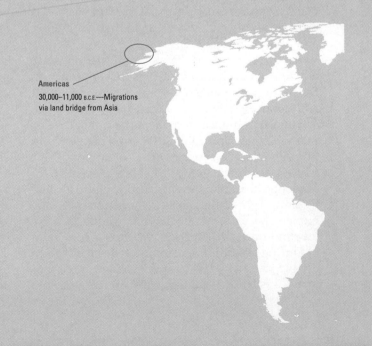

Americas
30,000–11,000 B.C.E.—Migrations via land bridge from Asia

The invention of writing was another achievement of enduring importance. Rulers employed a small number of specially trained writing specialists—scribes—to keep track of the collection of taxes, to record royal laws, and to memorialize military victories and other royal achievements. Temple scribes also began to record myths and other religious lore. At this time writing consisted of stylized pictures (pictographs) of the objects being represented; later, scribes developed simplified phonetic alphabets.

The influence of the river-valley civilizations extended beyond their borders, because members of the royal and priestly classes of these states traded with people living in distant parts of their realm. They used their wealth to trade for precious metals such as gold and silver; for the copper and other metals that went into bronze; for exotic jewels, animal skins, feathers, and other items of personal adornment; and for special woods, stones, and other materials for construction. Specialized artisans using various systems of counting kept accounts of these transactions.

In the Middle East merchants helped to spread aspects of their culture beyond the areas of conquest. Egyptian culture influenced Nubia to the south. The development of a sophisticated culture around the Aegean Sea in the eastern Mediterranean owed much to influence from Egypt and other parts of the middle East.

Yet on the whole, most of the world was little affected by the development of the river-valley civilizations. Most people continued to practice pastoralism, hunting, and gathering, and small-scale farming. Although their ways of life left no spectacular ruins, such societies did produce significant achievements. For example, in the third millennium B.C.E., pastoralists in Arabia domesticated the camel and other pastoralists in Central Asia domesticated the horse. Both animals became important for warfare, trade, and communication.

During the Late Bronze Age of the second and first millennia B.C.E., the reach, complexity, and sophistication of the civilizations in the eastern Mediterranean, Middle East, and East Asia grew. Building on earlier achievements, these civilizations also extended their influences by new conquests and trade. Despite disrupting invasions in the eastern Mediterranean and in Mesopotamia around 1200 B.C.E., these communities left enduring legacies.

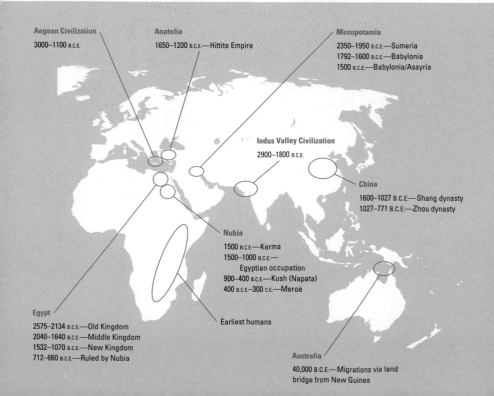

Aegean Civilization
3000–1100 B.C.E.

Anatolia
1650–1200 B.C.E.—Hittite Empire

Mesopotamia
2350–1950 B.C.E.—Sumeria
1792–1600 B.C.E.—Babylonia
1500 B.C.E.—Babylonia/Assyria

Indus Valley Civilization
2900–1800 B.C.E.

China
1600–1027 B.C.E.—Shang dynasty
1027–771 B.C.E.—Zhou dynasty

Nubia
1500 B.C.E.—Kerma
1500–1000 B.C.E.—
    Egyptian occupation
900–400 B.C.E.—Kush (Napata)
400 B.C.E.–300 C.E.—Meroë

Earliest humans

Egypt
2575–2134 B.C.E.—Old Kingdom
2040–1640 B.C.E.—Middle Kingdom
1532–1070 B.C.E.—New Kingdom
712–660 B.C.E.—Ruled by Nubia

Australia
40,000 B.C.E.—Migrations via land
bridge from New Guinea

Society

1,000,000 B.C.E.—Gathering and
    hunting bands
9000 B.C.E.—Agricultural communities
ca. 8000 B.C.E.—First walled town
    (Jericho)
ca. 3500 B.C.E.—First religious elites
ca. 3100 B.C.E.—First kingdoms
ca. 3000 B.C.E.—First major cities
    (Mesopotamia)
237 B.C.E.—First empires (Middle East)

Culture

First languages
First music and dance
First religious practices
30,000 B.C.E.—Earliest known cave art
4000 B.C.E.—Megalithic tombs
2590 B.C.E.—Great Pyramid at Giza
1750 B.C.E.—Hammurabi's Law Code

CHAPTER ONE

Nature, Humanity, and History: The First Four Million Years

African Genesis • History and Culture in the Ice Age

The Agricultural Revolutions • Life in Neolithic Communities

According to a story handed down by the Yoruba people of West Africa, at one time there was only water below the sky. Then the divine Owner of the Sky let down a chain by which his son Oduduwa descended along with sixteen male companions. Oduduwa scattered a handful of soil across the water and set down a chicken that scratched the soil into the shape of the land. A palm nut that he planted in the soil grew to became the bountiful forest that is the home of the Yoruba people. Oduduwa was their first king.

At some point in their history most human societies began telling similar stories about their origins. In some the first humans came down from the sky; in others they emerged out of a hole in the ground. Historical accuracy was not the point of such creation myths. Like the story of Adam and Eve in the Hebrew Bible, their primary purpose was to define the moral principles that a society thought should govern humans' dealings with the supernatural world, with each other, and with the rest of nature. In addition, they provided an explanation of how a people's way of life, social divisions, and cultural system arose.

In the absence of any contradictory evidence, creation myths became embedded in the identities and beliefs of peoples throughout the world. However, in the nineteenth century evidence started to accumulate that human beings and ways of life based on farming and herding domesticated animals had quite different origins. Natural scientists were finding remains of early humans who resembled apes rather than gods. Other evidence suggested that the familiar ways of life based on farming and herding did not arise within a generation or two of creation, as the myths suggest, but after humans had been around for many hundreds of thousands of years.

Although such evidence has long stirred controversy, a careful consideration of it reveals insights into human identity that may be as meaningful as those propounded by the creation myths. First, humans began their existence not with the ability to control and manipulate nature but as part of the natural world, subject to its laws. Second, the physical and mental abilities humans gradually acquired in response to changes in the natural world gave them a unique capacity to adapt to new environments by altering their way of life rather than by evolving physically as other species did. Finally, after nearly 2 million years of physical and cultural development, human communities in different parts of the world opened up extraordinary possibilities for change when they learned how to manipulate the natural world, domesticating plants and animals for their food and use. In short, one of the fundamental themes of human history concerns how people have interacted with the environment.

AFRICAN GENESIS

The discovery in the mid-nineteenth century of the remains of ancient creatures that were at once humanlike and apelike generated both excitement and controversy. The evidence upset many because it challenged accepted beliefs about human origins. Others welcomed the new evidence as proof of what some researchers had long suspected: the physical characteristics of modern humans, like those of all other creatures, had evolved over incredibly long periods of time. But until recently the evidence was too fragmentary to be convincing.

Interpreting the Evidence

In 1856 in the Neander Valley of what is now Germany workmen discovered fossilized bones of a creature with a body much like that of modern humans but with a face that, like the faces of apes, had heavy brow ridges and a low forehead.

Although we now know these "Neanderthals" were a type of human common in Europe some 40,000 years ago, in the mid-nineteenth century the idea that earlier forms of humans could have existed was so novel that some scholars who first examined them argued they must have been deformed individuals from recent times.

Another perspective on human links to the distant past was already gaining ground. Three years after the Neanderthal finds, Charles Darwin, a young English naturalist (student of natural history), published *On the Origin of Species*. In this work he argued that the time frame for all biological life was far longer than most persons had supposed. Darwin based his conclusion on pioneering naturalists' research and on his own investigations of fossils and living plant and animal species in Latin America. He proposed that the great diversity of living species and the profound changes in them over time could be explained by *natural selection*, the process by which biological variations that enhanced a population's ability to survive became dominant in that species and over very long periods led to the formation of distinct new species.

Turning to the sensitive subject of human evolution in *The Descent of Man* (1871), Darwin summarized the growing consensus among naturalists that, by the same process of natural selection, humans were "descended from a hairy, tailed quadruped" (four-footed animal). Because humans shared so many physical similarities with African apes, he proposed that Africa must have been the home of the first humans, even though no evidence then existed to substantiate this hypothesis.

As it happened, the next major discoveries pointed to Asia, rather than Africa, as the original human home. On the Southeast Asian island of Java in 1891 Eugene Dubois uncovered an ancient skullcap of what was soon called "Java man," a find that has since been dated to between 1 million and 1.8 million years ago. In 1929 W. C. Pei discovered near Peking (Beijing), China, a similar skullcap that became known as "Peking man."

By then, even older fossils had been found in southern Africa. In 1924, while examining fossils from a lime quarry, Raymond Dart found the skull of an ancient creature that he named *Australopithecus africanus* (African southern ape), which he argued was transitional between apes and early humans. For many years most specialists disputed Dart's idea, because, while *Australopithecus africanus* walked upright like a human, its brain was ape-size. Such an idea went against their expectations that large brains would have evolved first and that Asia, not Africa, was the first home of humans. Biologists classify australophithecines as members of a family of primates known as *hominids*. Primates are members of a family of warm-blooded, four-limbed, social animals known as *mammals* that first appeared about 65 million years ago.

Since 1950, Louis and Mary Leakey, their son Richard, along with many others, have discovered a wealth of other hominid fossils in the exposed sediments of the Great Rift Valley of eastern Africa. These finds strongly support Dart's hypothesis and Darwin's guess that the tropical habitat of the African apes was the cradle of humanity. Although new discoveries could alter these conclusions, most researchers now believe that tropical Africa was the home of the earliest human ancestors.

The development of precise archaeological techniques has enhanced the quantity of evidence currently available. Rather than collect isolated bones, modern researchers literally sift the neighboring soils to extract the remains of other creatures existing at the time, locating fossilized seeds and even pollen by which to document the environment in which the humans lived. They can also determine the age of most finds by using dating the rate of molecular change in potassium, in minerals in lava flows, or in carbon from wood and bone.

As the result of this new work, is it now possible to trace the evolutionary changes that produced modern humans during a period of 4 million years. As Darwin suspected, the earliest transitional creatures have been found only in Africa; the later human species (including Java man and Peking man) had wider global distribution. By combining that evidence with the growing understanding of how other species adapt to their natural environments, scientists can describe with some precision when, where, and how early human beings evolved and how they lived.

"Rather Odd African Apes"?

The accumulating evidence that humans evolved gradually over millions of years has led to much debate about how our species should be defined. Some researchers focus on our similarities to other living creatures; others look at what makes us different. Each approach yields different and important insights. As close as humans are to other primates, small genetic oddities are responsible for immense differences in our capacities. Indeed, humans are unique in being able to contemplate the meaning of life and consider the question we are grappling with here: what is a human being?

Within the primate kingdom humans are most closely related to the African apes—chimpanzees and gorillas. Since Darwin's time it has been popular (and controversial) to say that we are descended from apes. Modern research has found that over 98 percent of human DNA, the basic genetic blueprint, is identical to that of the great apes. For this reason anthropologist David Philbeam has called human beings "rather odd African apes."[1]

From a biological perspective, three major traits distinguish humans from other primates. As Dart's australopithecines demonstrated, the earliest of these traits to appear was *bipedalism* (walking upright on two legs). This frees the forelimbs from any necessary role in locomotion and enhances an older primate trait: a hand that has a long thumb that can work with the fingers to manipulate objects skillfully. Modern humans' second trait, a very large brain, distinguishes us more profoundly from the australopithecines than does our somewhat more upright posture. Besides enabling humans to think abstractly, experience profound emotions, and construct complex social relations, this larger brain controls the fine motor movements of the hand and of the tongue, increasing humans' tool-using capacity and facilitating the development of speech. The physical possibility of language, however, depends on a third distinctive human trait: the

Fossilized footprints Archaeologist Mary Leakey (shown at top) found these remarkable footprints of a hominid adult and child at Laetoli, Tanzania. The pair had walked through fresh volcanic ash that solidified after being buried by a new volcanic eruption. Dated to 3.5 million years ago, the footprints are the oldest evidence of bipedalism yet found. (John Reader/Photo Researchers, Inc.)

human larynx (voice box) lies much lower in the neck than does the larynx of any other primate. This trait is associated with many other changes in the face and neck.

How and why did these immensely important biological changes take place? Scientists still employ Darwin's concept of natural selection, attributing the development of distinctive human

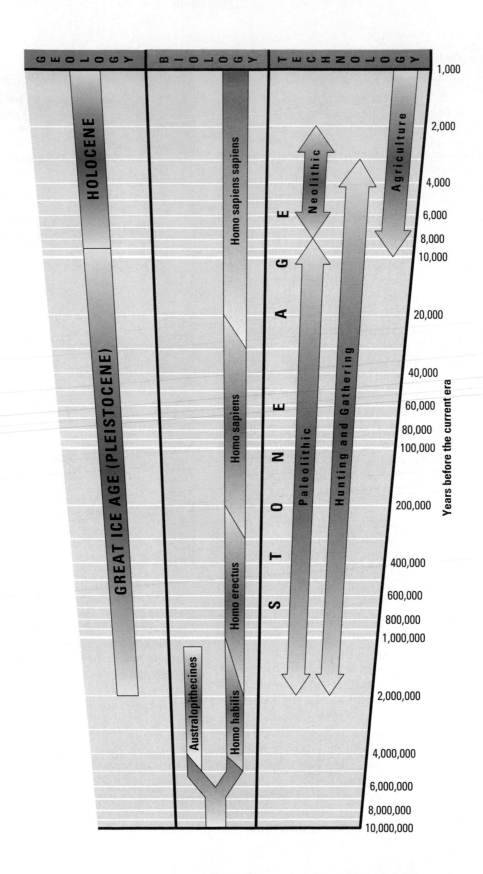

traits to the preservation of genetic changes that enhanced survivability. Although the details have not been fully worked out, it is widely accepted that major shifts in the world's climate led to evolutionary changes in human ancestors and other species. About 10 million years ago the earth entered a period of lower average temperatures that culminated in the Great Ice Age, or Pleistocene epoch, from about 2 million to about 11,000 years ago (see Figure 1.1). The Pleistocene epoch included more than a dozen very cold periods, each spanning several thousand years, separated by warmer periods. The changes that these climate shifts produced in rainfall, vegetation, and temperature imposed great strains on existing plant and animal species. As a result, large numbers of new species evolved during the Pleistocene.

In the temperate regions of the earth during the Pleistocene, massive glaciers of frozen water spread out from centers of snow accumulation. At their peak such glaciers covered a third of the earth's surface and contained so much frozen water that ocean levels were lowered by over 450 feet (140 meters), exposing land bridges between many places now isolated by water.

Unlike the frozen lands to the north and south, the equatorial regions of the world were not touched by the glaciers, but during the Pleistocene they probably experienced cooler and drier climates that led to the growth of open savanna grasslands in places once dominated by tropical forests. According to one popular theory, as the forests shrank, some tree-dwelling apes were forced to search for more of their food on the ground. Gradually the new family of primates—the hominids—evolved with a more upright way of walking.

Some recent evidence of ancient vegetation casts doubt on that scenario, but it is well established that between 3 million and 4 million years ago several new species of bipedal australopithecines inhabited eastern Africa. In a remarkable find in northern Ethiopia in 1974, Donald Johanson unearthed a remarkably well pre-

Figure 1.1 Human Biological Evolution and Technological Development in Geological and Historical Context

served skeleton of a twenty-five-year-old female, whom he nicknamed "Lucy." In northern Tanzania in 1977, Mary Leakey discovered fossilized footprints that provide spectacular visual evidence of how australopithecines walked.

Bipedalism evolved because it provided australopithecines with some advantage for survival. Some studies suggest that a decisive advantage of bipedalism may have come from its energy efficiency in walking and running. Another theory is that bipeds survived better because they could fill their arms with food to carry back to mates and children. Whatever its decisive advantage, bipedalism led to other changes.

Climate changes between 2 million and 3 million years ago led to the evolution of a new species, the first to be classified in the same genus (*Homo*) with modern humans. At Olduvai Gorge in northern Tanzania in the early 1960s Louis Leakey discovered the first fossilized remains of this creature, which he named *Homo habilis* (handy human). What most distinguished *Homo habilis* from the australopithecines was a brain that was nearly 50 percent larger. A larger brain would have added to the new species' intelligence. What was happening in this period that favored greater mental capacity? Some scientists believe that the answer had to do with food. Greater intelligence enabled *Homo habilis* to locate a vast number of different kinds of things to eat throughout the seasons of the year. They point to seeds and other fossilized remains in ancient *Homo habilis* camps that indicate the new species ate a greater variety of more nutritious seasonal foods than the australopithecines ate.

By about 1 million years ago *Homo habilis* and all the australopithecines had become extinct. In their habitat lived a new hominid, *Homo erectus* (upright human), which had first appeared in eastern Africa about 1.8 million years ago. These creatures possessed brains a third larger than those of *Homo habilis*, which presumably accounted for their better survivability. A nearly complete skeleton of a twelve-year-old male of the species discovered by Richard Leakey in 1984 on the shores of Lake Turkana in Kenya shows that *Homo erectus* closely resembled modern people from the neck down. *Homo erectus* was very successful in dealing with different environ-

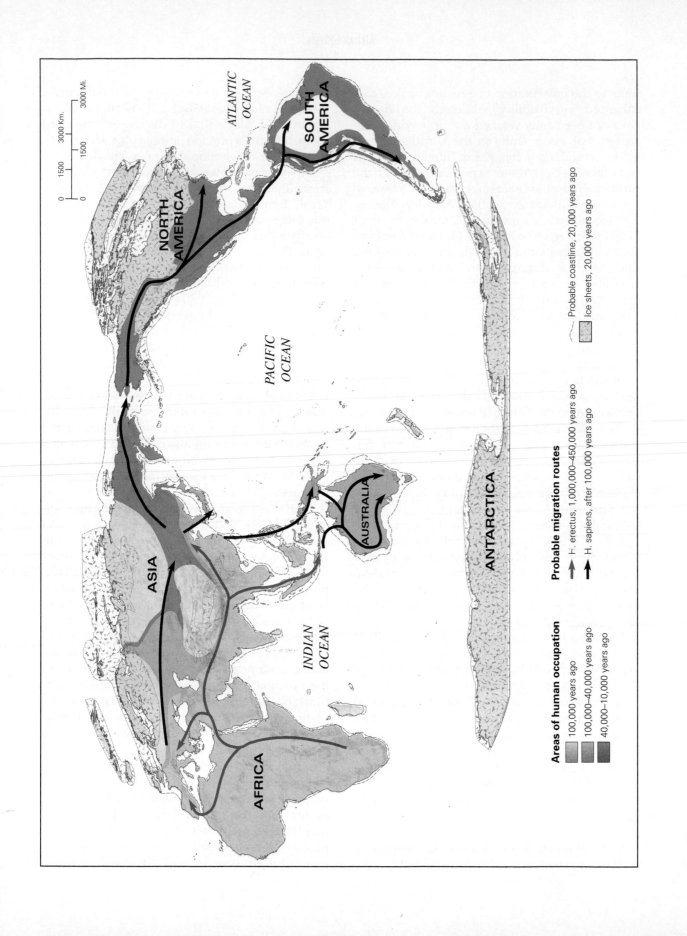

Areas of human occupation

100,000 years ago

100,000–40,000 years ago

40,000–10,000 years ago

Probable migration routes

H. erectus, 1,000,000–450,000 years ago

H. sapiens, after 100,000 years ago

Probable coastline, 20,000 years ago

Ice sheets, 20,000 years ago

NORTH AMERICA

SOUTH AMERICA

ATLANTIC OCEAN

PACIFIC OCEAN

INDIAN OCEAN

ASIA

AFRICA

AUSTRALIA

ANTARCTICA

3000 Mi.

3000 Km.

1500

1500

0

0

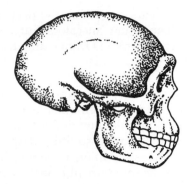 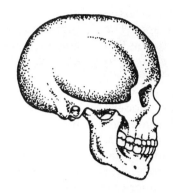 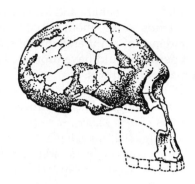

Evolution of the human brain   These drawings of skulls show the extensive cranial changes associated with the increase in brain size during the 3 million years from *Homo habilis* to *Homo sapiens sapiens.* (Left, middle: From *Origins Reconsidered* by Richard Leakey. Copyright © 1992 B. V. Sherma. Used by permission of Doubleday, a division of Bantam Doubleday Dell Publishing Group, Inc.; Right: Courtesy of A. Walker and Richard Leakey/*Scientific American,* 1978, all rights reserved.)

ments and underwent hardly any biological changes during a million years.

However, by a long, imperfectly understood evolutionary process between 400,000 and 100,000 years ago, a new human species emerged: *Homo sapiens* (wise human). The brains of *Homo sapiens* were a third larger than those of *Homo erectus,* whom they gradually superseded. *Homo sapiens* also had greater speech capacity.

This slow but remarkable process of physical evolution that distinguished humans by a small but significant degree from other primates was one part of what was happening. Equally remarkable was the way in which humans were extending their habitat.

Migrations from Africa

Early humans gradually expanded their range in eastern and southern Africa. Then they ventured out of Africa, perhaps following migrating herds of animals or searching for more abundant food

Map 1.1   Human dispersal to 10,000 years ago   Early migrations from Africa into southern Eurasia were followed by treks across land bridges during cold spells when giant ice sheets had lowered ocean levels.

supplies in time of drought. The details are unsettled, but the end result is vividly clear: humans learned to survive in every part of the globe from the arctic to the equator, from deserts to tropical rain forests. This dispersal demonstrates early humans' talent for adaptation (see Map 1.1).

Homo erectus was the first human species to inhabit all parts of Africa and the first to be found outside Africa. By migrating overland from Africa across southern Asia, *Homo erectus* reached Java as early as 1.8 million years ago. At that time sea levels caused by water being trapped in ice-age glaciers were so low that Java was not an island but was joined to the Southeast Asian mainland. Although Java's climate would have been no colder than East Africa's, Java's dense forests would have been very different from the open grasslands of eastern Africa. Even more challenging was adaptation to the harsh winters of northern Europe and northern China, where *Homo erectus* settled between 700,000 and 300,000 years ago.

Scientists disagree whether *Homo sapiens* also spread outward from Africa or evolved separately from *Homo erectus* populations in different parts of the world. If, as most scientists suppose, *Homo sapiens* first evolved in Africa, their migrations to the rest of the world would have been made easier by a wet period that transformed the normally arid Sahara and Middle East into fertile grasslands until about 40,000 years ago. The abundance of plant and animal food during this wet period would have promoted an increase in human populations.

By the end of that wet period further evolutionary changes had produced fully modern humans (*Homo sapiens sapiens*), which some evidence suggests may have originated in Africa. This new species displaced older human populations, such as the Neanderthals in Europe, and penetrated for the first time into the Americas, Australia, and the Arctic.

During the last glacial period, between 32,000 and 13,000 years ago, when the sea levels were low, hunters were able to cross a land bridge from northeastern Asia into North America. As these pioneers and later migrants moved southward (penetrating southern South America by 27,000 years ago), they passed through lands teeming with life, including easily hunted large animal species. Meanwhile, traveling by boat from Java, other *Homo sapiens sapiens* colonized New Guinea and Australia when both were part of a single landmass, and they crossed the land bridge then existing between the Asian mainland and Japan. Despite the generally cool climate of this period, human bands also followed reindeer even into northern arctic environments during the summer months.

As populations migrated, they may have undergone some minor evolutionary changes that helped them adapt to extreme environments. One such change was in skin color. The deeply pigmented skin of today's indigenous inhabitants of the tropics (and presumably of all early humans who evolved there) is an adaptation that reduces the harmful effects of the harsh tropical sun. At some point, possibly as recent as 5,000 years ago, especially pale skin became characteristic of Europeans living in northern latitudes with far less sunshine especially during winter months. The loss of pigment enabled their skins to produce more vitamin D from sunshine, though it exposed Europeans to a greater risk of sunburn and skin cancer when they migrated to sunnier climates. This was not the only possible way to adapt to the arctic. Eskimos who began moving into northern latitudes of North America

no more than 5,000 years ago retain the deeper pigmentation of their Asian ancestors but are able to gain sufficient vitamin D from eating fish and sea mammals.

As distinctive as skin color is in a person's appearance, it represents a very minor variation biologically. What was far more remarkable about the widely dispersed populations of *Homo sapiens sapiens* was that they varied so little. Despite a global dispersal and adaptation to many diverse environments, all modern human beings are members of the same species. Instead of needing to evolve physically like other species in order to adapt to new environments, modern humans were able to change their eating habits and devise new forms of clothing and shelter. As a result, human communities became culturally diverse while remaining physically homogeneous.

HISTORY AND CULTURE IN THE ICE AGE

E vidence of early humans' splendid creative abilities first came to light in 1940 near Lascaux in southern France. Examining a newly uprooted tree, youths discovered the entrance to a vast underground cavern. Once inside, they found that its walls were covered with paintings of animals, including many that had been extinct for thousands of years. Other collections of cave paintings have been found in Spain and elsewhere in southern France, including an enormous cavern near Vallon-Pont-d'Arc, discovered in 1994, containing hundreds of paintings from 20,000 years ago.

Observers of these cave paintings have been struck not only by the great age of this art but also by its high artistic quality. To even the most skeptical person, such rich finds are awesome demonstrations that thousands of years before the first "civilizations" (see Chapter 2), there existed individuals with richly developed imaginations and skill. Though less strikingly visible, great talent also can be perceived in the production of ever more specialized tools and in the development of complex social relations.

The fact that similar art and tools were produced over wide areas and long periods of time demonstrates that skills and ideas were not simply individual but were deliberately passed along within societies. These learned patterns of action and expression constitute *culture*. Culture includes material objects, such as dwellings, clothing, tools, and crafts, along with nonmaterial values, beliefs, and languages. Although it is true that some other species also learn new ways, all other species' activities are determined primarily by inherited instincts. Uniquely, among humans the proportions are reversed: instincts are less important than the cultural traditions that each new generation learns. The development, transmission, and transformation of cultural practices and events are the subject of *history*. All living creatures are part of natural history, which traces their biological development, but only human communities have a history that traces their varied cultural development over time.

Food Gathering and Stone Technology

Most early human activity centered on gathering food. Like the australopithecines, early humans depended heavily on vegetable foods such as leaves, seeds, and grasses, but one of the changes evident in the Ice Age is the growing consumption of highly nutritious animal flesh. Moreover, unlike australopithecines, humans regularly made tools. The first crude tools made their appearance with *Homo habilis*, later human species made much more sophisticated tools. These two changes—increased meat-eating and toolmaking—appear to be closely linked.

When archaeologists examine the remains of ancient human sites, the first thing that jumps out at them is the abundant evidence of human toolmaking—the first recognizable cultural activity. Because the tools that survive are made of stone, the extensive period of history from the appearance of the first fabricated stone tools around 2 million years ago until the appearance of metal tools around 4 thousand years ago has been called the Stone Age.

The name Stone Age can be quite misleading.

In the first place, not all tools were made of stone. Early humans would also have made useful objects and tools out of bone, skin, wood, and other natural materials less likely to survive the ravages of time. In the second place, as this period of nearly 2 million years has been better studied, it has become evident that there were so many distinct periods and cultures during the

Making stone tools About 35,000 years ago the manufacture of stone tools became highly specialized. Small blades, chipped from a rock core, were mounted in a bone or wooden handle. Not only were such composite tools more diverse than earlier all-purpose hand-axes, but the small blades required fewer rock cores—an important consideration in areas where suitable rocks were scarce. (From Jacques Bordaz, *Tools of the Old and New Stone Age.* Copyright 1970 by Jacques Bordaz. Redrawn by the permission of Addison-Wesley Educational Publishers, Inc.)

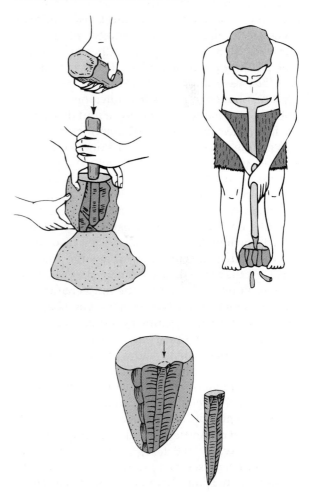

Stone Age that the old division into a Paleolithic (Old Stone) Age down to 10,000 years ago and a Neolithic (New Stone) Age is no longer adequate. Modern research scientists have largely abandoned the use of *Paleolithic* in favor of particular labels, but *Neolithic* remains in current usage.

Most stone tools made by *Homo habilis* have been found in the Great Rift Valley of eastern Africa, whose sides expose sediments laid down over millions of years. One branch of this valley, the Olduvai Gorge in Tanzania, explored by Louis and Mary Leakey, has been a particularly important source. The earliest tools were made by chipping flakes off the edges of volcanic stones. Modern experiments show that the razor-sharp edges of such flakes are highly effective in skinning and butchering wild animals.

The small-brained *Homo habilis*, however, probably lacked the skill to hunt large animals successfully and probably obtained animal protein by scavenging meat from kills made by animal predators or by accidents. There is evidence that they used large stone "choppers" for cracking open bones to get at the nutritious marrow. The fact that many such tools are found together far from the outcrops of volcanic rock suggests that people carried them long distances for use at killsites and camps.

Homo erectus were also scavengers, but their larger brains would have made them cleverer at it—capable, for example, of finding and stealing the kills of leopards and other large predators that drag their kills into trees. They also made more effective tools for butchering large animals, although the stone flakes and choppers of earlier eras continued to be made. The most characteristic stone tool used by *Homo erectus* was a hand ax formed by removing chips from both sides of a stone to produce a sharp outer edge.

Modern experiments show the hand ax to be an efficient multipurpose tool, suitable for skinning and butchering animals, for scraping skins clean for use as clothing and mats, for sharpening wooden tools, and for digging up edible roots. Since a hand ax can also be hurled accurately for nearly 100 feet (30 meters), it might also have been used as a projectile to fell animals. From sites in Spain there is evidence that *Homo*

erectus even butchered elephants, which then ranged across southern Europe, by driving them into swamps where they became trapped and died.

Homo sapiens were far more skillful hunters. They tracked and killed large animals (including mastodons, mammoths, and bisons) throughout the world. Their success depended on their superior intelligence and on an array of finely made tools. Sharp stone flakes chipped from carefully prepared rock cores were often used in combination with other materials. A spear could be made by attaching a stone point to a wooden shaft. Embedding several sharp stone flakes in a bone handle produced a sawing tool.

Indeed, *Homo sapiens* were so skillful and successful as hunters that they may have caused or contributed to a series of ecological crises. Between 40,000 and 13,000 years ago the giant mastodons and mammoths gradually disappeared, first from Africa and Southeast Asia and then from northern Europe. In North America the sudden disappearance around 11,000 years ago of highly successful large-animal hunters known as the Clovis people was almost simultaneous with the extinction of three-fourths of the large mammals in the Americas, including giant bisons, camels, ground sloths, stag-moose, giant cats, mastodons, and mammoths. In Australia there was a similar event. Since these extinctions occurred during the last series of severe cold spells at the end of the Great Ice Age, it is difficult to measure which effects were the work of global and regional climate changes and which resulted from the excesses of human predators. Whichever the case, 10,000 years ago major changes in human food strategies were under way that would have far greater impact on the planet and its life forms (as the next section shows).

Finds of fossilized animal bones bearing the marks of butchering tools clearly attest to the scavenging and hunting activities of Stone Age peoples, but anthropologists do not believe that early humans depended primarily on meat for their food. Modern food-gathering peoples in the Kalahari Desert of Southern Africa and Ituri Forest of central Africa all derive the bulk of their day-to-day nourishment from wild vegetable foods; meat is the food of feasts. It is likely that Stone Age peoples would have done the same, even though the tools and equipment for gathering and processing vegetable foods have left few traces for they were made of materials too soft to survive for thousands of years.

Like modern hunter-gatherers, ancient humans would have used skins and mats woven from leaves for collecting fruits, berries, and wild seeds. They would have dug edible roots out of the ground with wooden sticks. Archaeologists believe that the donut-shaped stones often found at Stone Age sites may have been weights placed on wooden digging sticks to increase their effectiveness.

The evidence of early food preparation is also scarce and largely indirect. Modern societies pound and grind roots and seeds to make them more palatable, but this can be done with ordinary stones that would not appear distinctive in the archaeological remains. Both meat and vegetables become tastier and easier to digest when they are cooked. The first cooked foods were probably found by accident after wildfires, but there is new evidence from East and South Africa that humans were setting fires deliberately between 1 million and 1.5 million years ago. The wooden spits and hot rocks that would have been used for roasting, frying, or baking are not distinctive enough to stand out in an archaeological site. Only with the appearance of clay cooking pots some 12,500 years ago in East Asia is there hard evidence of cooking.

Gender Divisions and Social Life

To bring the mute material remains of Ice Age humans to life, anthropologists have studied the few surviving present-day hunter-gatherer societies. Although in many ways such societies must be quite different from hunting and gathering communities thousands of years earlier, in other ways they provide models of what such early societies could have been like.

For example, the gender division of labor in present-day hunting and gathering societies suggests that in the Ice Age women would have done most of the gathering and cooking (which can be performed while caring for small children). Men, with stronger arms and shoulders, would have been more suited than women to hunting, particularly for large animals. Some early cave art shows males in hunting activities.

Other aspects of social life in the Ice Age are suggested by studies of modern peoples. All modern hunter-gatherers live in small groups or bands. The community has to have enough members to defend itself from predators and to divide responsibility for the collection and preparation of animal and vegetable foods. However, if it has too many members, it risks exhausting the food available in its immediate vicinity. Even a band of optimal size has to move at regular intervals to follow migrating animals and take advantage of seasonally ripening plants in different places. Archaeological evidence from Ice Age campsites suggests early humans were organized in highly mobile bands.

Other researchers have studied the organization of nonhuman primates for clues about very early human society. Gorillas and chimpanzees live in groups consisting of several adult males and females and their offspring. Status varies with age and sex, and a dominant male usually heads the group. Sexual unions between males and females generally do not result in long-term pairing. Instead, the strongest ties are those between a female and her children and among siblings. Adult males are often recruited from neighboring bands.

Very early human groups likely shared some similar traits, but by the time of *Homo sapiens sapiens* the two-parent nuclear family would have been characteristic. How this change from a mother-centered family to a two-parent family developed over the intervening millennia can only be guessed at, but it is likely that physical and social evolution were linked. Larger brain size was a contributing factor. Big-headed humans have to be born in a less mature state than other mammals so they can pass through the narrow birth canal, and thus they take much longer to mature outside the womb. Other large mammals are mature at two or three years of age; humans at from twelve to fifteen. Human infants' and children's need for much longer nurturing makes care by mothers, fathers, and other relatives a biological imperative.

The human reproductive cycle also became unique at some point. In other species sexual contact is biologically restricted to a special mating season of the year or to the fertile part of the female's menstrual cycle. As well, among other primates the choice of mate is usually not a matter for long deliberation. To a female baboon in heat (estrus) any male will do, and to a male baboon any receptive female is a suitable sexual partner. In contrast, adult humans can mate at any time and are much choosier about their partners. Once they choose their mates, frequent sexual contacts promote deep emotional ties and long-term bonding.

An enduring bond between parents made it much easier for vulnerable offspring to receive the care they needed during the long period of their childhood. In addition, human couples could nurture dependent children of different ages at the same time, unlike other large mammals whose females must raise their offspring nearly to maturity before beginning another reproductive cycle. Spacing births close together also ensured offspring a high rate of survival and would have enabled humans to multiply more rapidly than other large mammals. The gender specialization in hunting and gathering food discussed earlier would also have maximized band members' chances for survival.

Hearths and Cultural Expressions

Because frequent moves were necessary to keep close to migrating herds and ripening plants, hunting and gathering peoples usually did not lavish much time on housing. Natural shelters under overhanging rocks or in caves in southern Africa and southern France are known to have been favorite camping places to which bands returned at regular intervals. Where the climate was severe or where natural shelters did not

Mammoth-bone architecture   Composed of the different bones of giant mammoths, this reconstructed framework of a 15,000-year-old communal hut in the Ukraine would have been covered with hides to provide a durable shelter against the weather. (Novosti)

exist, people erected huts of branches, stones, bones, skins, and leaves as seasonal camps. More elaborate dwellings were common in areas where protection against harsh weather was necessary.

An interesting camp dating to 15,000 years ago has been excavated in the Ukraine southeast of Kiev. Its communal dwellings were framed with the bones of elephant-like mammoths, then covered with hides. Each oblong structure, measuring 15 to 20 feet (4.5 to 6 meters) by 40 to 50 feet (12 to 15 meters), was capable of holding fifty people and would have taken several days to construct. The camp had five such dwellings, making it a large settlement for a hunting-gathering community. Large, solid structures were common in fishing villages that grew up along rivers and lake shores where the abundance of fish permitted people to occupy the same site year-round.

Making clothing was another necessary technology in the Stone Age. Animal skins were an early form of clothing, and the oldest evidence of fibers woven into cloth dates from about 26,000 years ago. An "Iceman" from 5,300 years ago, whose frozen remains were found in the European Alps in 1991, was wearing many different garments made of animal skins sewn together with thread fashioned from vegetable fibers and rawhide.

Although accidents, erratic weather, and disease took a heavy toll on a hunting and gathering band, there is reason to believe that day-to-day existence was not particularly hard or unpleasant. Some studies suggest that under the conditions operating on the African savannas and other game-rich areas, securing the necessities of food, clothing, and shelter would have occupied only from three to five hours a day. This would have left a great deal of time for artistic endeavors as well as for toolmaking and social life.

Although the foundations of what later ages called science, art, and religion are harder to detect and interpret, they were established during the Stone Age. Basic to human survival was extensive and precise knowledge about the natural environment. Gatherers needed to know which local plants were best for food and the seasons when they were available. Successful hunting re-

The "Iceman" A 5,300-year-old body found frozen in the Alps preserved remarkable evidence of clothing and tools. Dressed for cold weather, he wore a fur hat, tailored deer-skin vest, and leather leggings. His tools included a copper-headed ax, a long bow and quiver of arrows, a flint knife in a string sheath, a flint scraper, a flint awl, and fire-starting tools. The Iceman also carried a birch bark cup. (New York Times Picture Sales)

quired intimate knowledge of the habits of game animals. People learned how to use plant and animal parts for clothing, twine, and building materials, as well as which natural substances were effective for medicine, consciousness altering, dyeing, and other purposes. Knowledge of the natural world included identifying minerals suitable for paints, stones for making the best tools, and so forth. Given humans' physical capacity for speech, it is likely that the transmission of such prescientific knowledge involved verbal communication, even though direct evidence for language appears only in later periods.

Early manifestations of music and dance have left no traces, but the evidence of painting and drawing is vivid and abundant. The use of pigment for painting or personal adornment is very old. Red-ochre sticks found at the site of Terra Amata on the French Riviera have been dated to between 200,000 and 300,000 years ago, for example. Cave paintings were being made in Europe and north Africa by 32,000 years ago and at later times in other parts of the world. Cave art that features wild animals such as oxen, reindeer, and horses, which were hunted for food, has led to speculation that the art was meant to record hunting scenes or that it formed part of some magical and religious rites to ensure success. However, the newly discovered cave at Vallon Pont-d'Arc features rhinoceroses, panthers, bears, owls, and a hyena, which probably were not the objects of hunting. Still other drawings include people dressed in animal skins and smeared with paint. In many caves there are large numbers of stencils of human hands. Are these the signatures of the artists or the world's oldest graffiti? Some scholars suspect that other marks in cave paintings and on bones from this period may represent efforts at counting or writing.

Theories about cave and rock art emphasize concerns with fertility, efforts to educate the young, and elaborate mechanisms for time reckoning. These different interpretations do not exclude each other, for there is no reason to think that a single purpose was in the minds of all the artists during several thousands of years and in distant parts of the world. Another way to view such art is from the perspective of living peoples. The San have been hunters, gatherers, and artists in southern Africa since time immemorial. Archaeologist David Lewis-Williams has argued that much, if not all, of the cave art of southern Africa can be interpreted in terms of potency and

trance—that is, it represents visions hallucinated by people in altered physical states brought on by meditation or psychoactive drinks and smokes (see Voices and Visions: Interpreting Rock Art).

Stone Age people possessed sufficiently well-developed brains to have wondered about the majesty of the heavens, the mystery of success in the hunt, and the fate of the dead. In other words, they could have devised the first religions. But without written religious texts it is very difficult to know exactly what early humans believed. Sites of deliberate human burials from about 100,000 years ago give some hints. The fact that an adult was often buried with stone implements, food, clothing, and red-ochre powder suggests that early people revered their leaders enough to honor them after death and may imply a belief in an afterlife.

It is likely that future discoveries will add substantially to the understanding of Stone Age life. Already this vast era, whose existence was scarcely dreamed of two centuries ago, can be recognized as a period of formative importance. Important in its own right, the period was also a necessary preparation for the major changes ahead as human communities passed from being food gatherers to being food producers.

THE AGRICULTURAL REVOLUTIONS

Like all other species, early humans depended on wild plants and animals for their food. But around 10,000 years ago some humans began to meet their food needs by raising domesticated plants and animals. Gradually over the next millennium most people became food producers, although hunting and gathering continued to exist in some places. This transition to food production was a major milestone in humans' manipulation of nature and had myriad implications for the human species and their planet (see Map 1.2).

The change from food gathering to food production at the end of the Stone Age has been called the "Neolithic revolution." The name can

Interpreting Rock Art

The drawings of animals and people found in caves or in rock shelters in many parts of the world are spectacular visually but hard to interpret. Some of the drawings seem to record common activities, such as hunting. Others are puzzling mixtures of realistic and fantastic shapes in odd configurations. Archaeologist David Lewis-Williams has extracted rich meaning from one school of cave art by connecting it with the beliefs and rituals of a southern African hunting and gathering people now known as the San.

The last San groups to create such paintings died out a century ago, but Lewis-Williams believes the records of their beliefs, customs, and symbols provide a way to interpret a tradition of rock art that extends back thousands of years. As he reconstructs it, the rock drawings were made by *shamans*, men and women in San society who acquired the power to cure sickness, control antelope herds, and make rain while in trances. He believes much of San art depicts trance scenes when the shamans shook, sweated, and fell into a deep sleep during which they had out-of-body experiences.

Lewis-Williams reads the scene reproduced here as representing a shaman's efforts to control the rain by leading a mystical animal across a parched landscape. The figure marked (1) is a shaman entering a trance,

holding his body characteristically bent over with his arms thrown back. Figure (2) is a shaman fully in a trance, lying down; the lines represent his spirit leaving his body. The partially obscured figure (3) above the rain animal has his hand to his nose in depiction of "snoring," which the San associated with curing illness. The line of small dots above the animal (4) are bees, whose swarming the San believed marked a particularly potent time for trance medicine.

Unfortunately, nowhere else in the world has rock art been connected to a recorded system of beliefs. However, Lewis-Williams's reconstructions do suggest how much symbolic belief and mystical lore may lie behind the cave art of these early periods.

If you had only the drawing to go by, could you make sense of it? Why is it important to understand the cultural context in which a work of art is made? What do you know about the San that helps explain why they attached such importance to animals? Why might they prize personal mystical experiences?

Source: Adapted from Martin Hall, *Farmers, Kings, and Traders: The People of Southern Africa, 200–1860* (Chicago: University of Chicago Press, 1990), 62. The illustration is reproduced by permission of David Lewis-Williams, "Introductory Essay. Science and Rock Art," *South African Archaeological Society, Goodwin Series* 4 (1983): 3–13.

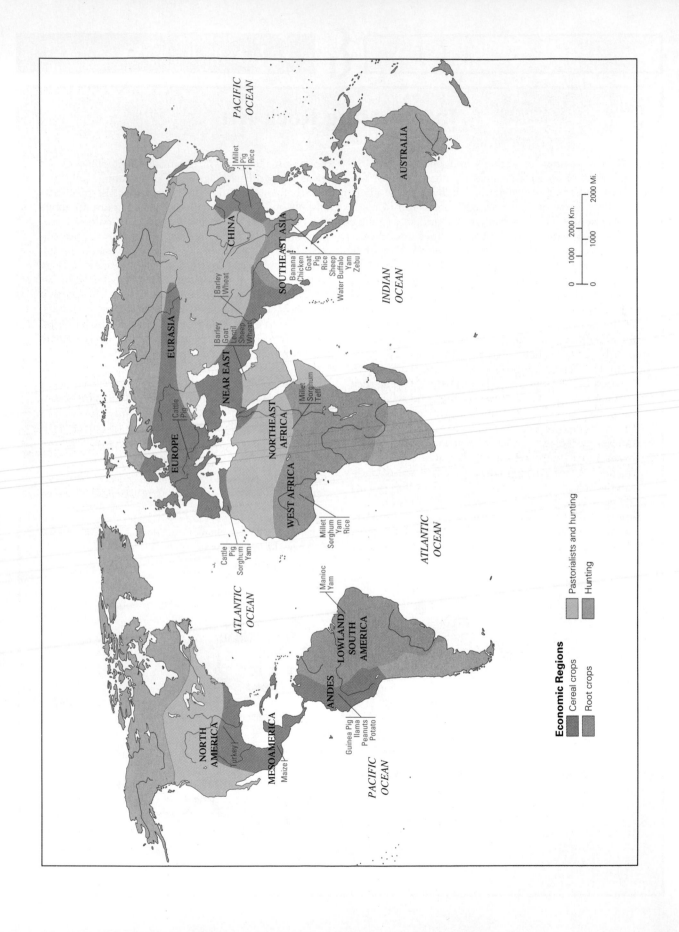

PACIFIC
OCEAN

AUSTRALIA

Millet
Pig
Rice

CHINA

SOUTHEAST ASIA

Barley
Wheat

Banana
Chicken
Goat
Pig
Rice
Sheep
Water Buffalo
Yam
Zebu

INDIAN
OCEAN

EURASIA

Barley
Goat
Lentil
Sheep
Wheat

NEAR EAST

2000 Km.

1000   2000 Mi.

0   1000

0

Cattle
Pig

EUROPE

NORTHEAST
AFRICA

Millet
Sorghum
Teff

WEST AFRICA

Cattle
Pig
Sorghum
Yam

ATLANTIC
OCEAN

Millet
Sorghum
Yam
Rice

ATLANTIC
OCEAN

Manioc
Yam

LOWLAND
SOUTH
AMERICA

ANDES

NORTH
AMERICA

Turkey

MESOAMERICA

Guinea Pig
Llama
Peanuts
Potato

Maize

PACIFIC
OCEAN

Economic Regions

Cereal crops

Root crops

Pastorialists and hunting

Hunting

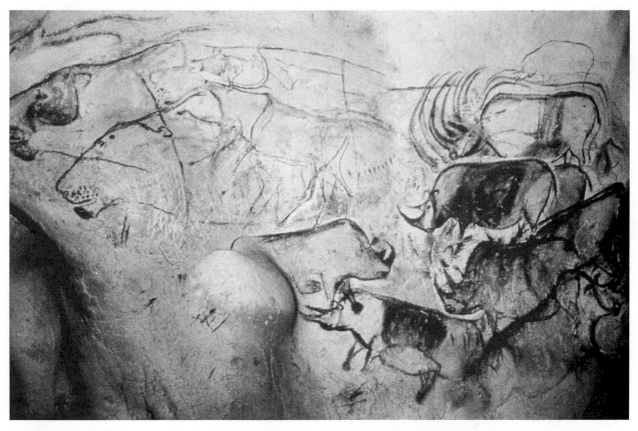

Cave art   Remarkable paintings and engravings of 300 animals were discovered in cave at Vallon-Pont-d'Arc in southern France in 1994. Dated to about 20,000 years ago, the depictions in black and red include bison, rhinoceros, reindeer, lions, horses, oxen, and bears, as well as the only known portrayal of a panther. (Jean Clottes/Ministère de la Culture/Sygma)

be misleading because stone tools were not its essential component and because it was not a single event but a series of separate transformations in different parts of the world. "Agricultural revolu-

tions" is a more precise label, stressing that the central change was in food production and that this momentous transformation occurred independently in many different parts of the world. In most cases agriculture included the domestication of animals for food as well as the cultivation of new food crops. Changes in global climate appear to have caused this transformation.

The Transition to Plant Cultivation

Map 1.2 Centers of plant and animal domestication Many different parts of the world made original contributions to domestication during the "agricultural revolutions" that began about 10,000 years ago. Later interactions helped spread these domesticated animals to new locations. In lands less suitable for crop cultivation, pastoralism and hunting predominated.

Food gathering gave way to food production in stages spread over hundreds of generations. The process may have begun when hunter-gatherer bands returning year after year to the same seasonal camps took measures to encourage the nearby growth of the foods they liked. They deliberately scattered the seeds of desirable plants in locations where they would thrive, and they discouraged the growth of competing plants by clearing them away. Such techniques of semicultivation could have supplemented food gathering for many generations. Families willing to devote their energies principally to food production, however, had to settle permanently in their formerly seasonal camp.

One component of settled agriculture was the production of new specialized tools and the development of techniques to enhance success. Indeed, the abundant evidence of new tools first alerted archaeologists to the significance of the food production revolutions. Many specialized stone tools were developed or improved for agricultural use, including sickle blades of small, sharp stone chips imbedded in bone or wooden handles, polished or ground stone heads used to work the soil, and stone mortars in which grain was pulverized.

However, stone axes were not very efficient in clearing shrubs and trees. For that a much older technology was used: fire. Farmers set fires to get rid of unwanted undergrowth, and from the ashes they received a bonus: natural fertilizer. After the burn-off they could use blades and axes to trim away the regrowth before it got too large.

More fundamental to the success of agriculture than new tools was the new technique of selecting the highest-yielding strains of wild plants, which over time led to the development of valuable new domesticated varieties. Because women were the principal gatherers of wild plant foods, they are likely to have played a major role in this transition to plant cultivation. The success of a farming community also would have required extensive male labor, especially to clear fields for planting.

The transition to agriculture has been traced in greatest detail in the Middle East. By 8000 B.C.E. (Before the Common Era) human selection had transformed certain wild grasses into higher-yielding domesticated grains now known as emmer wheat and barley. Communities there also discovered that alternating the cultivation of grains and pulses (plants yielding edible seeds such as lentils and peas) helped to maintain soil fertility.

Crops that were first domesticated in the Middle East were later grown elsewhere, but the spread of agriculture was not essentially a process of diffusion. Agriculture arose independently in many parts of the world. Over time much borrowing occurred, but it was societies that already had begun to practice agriculture on their own that were most likely to borrow new plants, animals, and farming techniques from their neighbors.

The oldest traces of food production in northern Africa are in the eastern Sahara, which was able to support farming during a particularly wet period after 8000 B.C.E. As in the Middle East, emmer wheat and barley became the principal crops and sheep, goats, and cattle the main domesticated animals. The return of drier conditions about 5000 B.C.E. led many Saharan farmers to move to the Nile Valley, where the annual flooding of the Nile River provided moisture for cereal farming.

In Europe cultivation of wheat and barley began as early as 6000 B.C.E. in Greece, combining local experiments and Middle Eastern borrowings. Shortly after 4000 B.C.E. farming developed in the light-soiled plains of Central Europe and along the Danube River. As forests receded because of climate changes and human clearing efforts, agriculture spread to other parts of Europe over the next millennium.

Early farmers in Europe and elsewhere practiced shifting cultivation, also known as *swidden agriculture*. After a few growing seasons, the fields were left fallow (abandoned to natural vegetation), and new fields were cleared nearby. Between 4000 and 3000 B.C.E., for example, communities of from 40 to 60 people in the Danube Valley of Central Europe supported themselves on about 500 acres (200 hectares) of farmland, cultivating a third or less each year while leaving the rest fallow to restore its fertility. From around 2600 B.C.E. people in Central Europe began using ox-drawn wooden plows to till heavier and richer soils.

Although the lands around the Mediterranean seem to have shared a complex of crops and farming techniques, there were major geographical barriers to the spread of this complex. Wheat and barley were unsuited to the rainfall patterns

Agricultural Revolutions in Asia and the Americas

astern and southern Asia were major centers of plant domestication, although the details and dates are not so clearly documented as in the Middle East. Rice was one important food that was first domesticated in southern China, the northern half of Southeast Asia, or northeastern India, possibly as early as 10,000 B.C.E., but more likely closer to 5000 B.C.E. Rice cultivation thrived in the warm and wet conditions of southern China. The cooler, drier climate of northern China favored locally domesticated cereals, such as foxtail millet. In India several pulses (including hyacinth beans, green grams, and black grams) domesticated about 2000 B.C.E. were cultivated along with rice.

At the same time as food production was spreading in Eurasia and Africa, the inhabitants of the isolated American continents were creating another major center of crop domestication. As game animals declined in the Tehuacán Valley of Mexico after 8000 B.C.E., wild vegetable foods became increasingly important to the diet. New dating techniques indicate that agriculture based on maize (corn) developed there after 3500 B.C.E. and spread to what is now the southwestern United States about 500 B.C.E. About the same time as maize-based agriculture was emerging in Mexico, the inhabitants of Peru were developing a food production system based on squash and quinoa, a protein-rich seed grain. In the more tropical regions of Mesoamerica, tomatoes, peppers, and potatoes were cultivated.

It is significant for their own early history that Asia and the Americas were able to develop distinctive domesticated plants quite independent of outside influences. In later centuries many of their crops were carried to other lands, adding to the variety and abundance of the world's food supply.

south of the Sahara. Instead, farming in sub-Saharan Africa came to be based on a wide variety of locally domesticated grains, including sorghums, millets, and (in Ethiopia) teff. Grains could not be grown at all in the very humid regions of equatorial West Africa, where there is early evidence of indigenous domestication of root crops such as yams. Eastern Asia and the Americas were also major centers of food plant domestication (see Environment and Technology: Agricultural Revolutions in Asia and the Americas).

Animal Domestication and Pastoralism

The revolution in food production was not confined to plants; the domestication of animals also expanded rapidly during these same millennia. The first domesticated animal was probably the dog, tamed to assist early hunters in tracking game. Later animals were domesticated to provide meat, milk, and energy. Like the domestication of plants, this process is best known in the Middle East.

By studying the refuse dumped outside some Middle East villages during the centuries after 7000 B.C.E., archaeologists have been able to document a gradual decline in the quantity of wild gazelle bones. This finding probably reflects the depletion of such wild animals through overhunting by the local farming communities. Meat eating, however, did not decline; the deposits show sheep and goat bones gradually replacing gazelle bones. It seems likely that wild sheep and goats had learned to scavenge for food scraps around agricultural villages and that people began to feed the tamer sheep and goats and protect them from wild predators in order to provide themselves with a ready supply of food. At first the biological differences between tame and wild species are too slight to date domestication precisely. Distinct domesticated species evolved as people controlled the breeding of their sheep and goats to produce desirable characteristics such as high milk production and long wool.

Elsewhere in the world other animal species were being domesticated during the centuries before 3000 B.C.E. Wild cattle were domesticated in northern Africa; pigs and water buffalo in

China; and humped-back Zebu cattle, buffalo, and pigs in India. As in the case of food plants, varieties of domesticated animals from abroad sometimes replaced the species initially domesticated. For example, the Zebu cattle originally domesticated in India first became important in sub-Saharan Africa about 2000 years ago.

In most parts of the world, farming populations depended on domesticated plants and animals for food and also used domesticated oxen, cattle, or (in China) water buffalo as draft animals. Animal droppings were important for fertilizing the soil and their wool and hides for clothing. However, there were two notable deviations from this pattern of mixed agriculture and animal husbandry.

One variation was in the Americas. There, comparatively few species of wild animals were suitable for domestication, other than llamas (for transport and wool) and guinea pigs and some fowls (for meat). No species could be borrowed from elsewhere because the Americas' land bridge to Asia had submerged as melting glaciers raised sea levels. Hunting remained an important source of meat for Amerindians, but perhaps their exceptional contributions to the world's domesticated plant crops were partly in compensation for the shortage of domesticated meat animals (see Chapter 12).

The other notable variation from mixed farming occurred in more arid parts of Africa and Central Asia. There, pastoralism, a way of life dependent on large herds of small and large stock, predominated. For example, pastoralists had replaced farmers in the Sahara as it became drier, up until about 2500 B.C.E., when desert conditions forced them to migrate southward. The necessity of moving their herds to new pastures and watering places throughout the year meant that pastoralists needed to be almost as mobile as hunter-gatherers and thus could accumulate little in the way of bulky possessions and substantial dwellings. Like modern pastoralists, early cattle-keeping people were probably not great meat eaters but relied heavily on the milk from their animals for their diet. During seasons when grasses for grazing and water were plentiful, they could also have done some hasty crop cultivation or bartered meat and skins for plant foods with nearby farming communities.

Agriculture and Ecological Crisis

Why in the Neolithic period did societies in so many parts of the world gradually abandon a way of life based on food gathering? Some theories assume that people were drawn to food production by its obvious advantages. For example, it has recently been suggested that people settled down in the Middle East so they could grow enough grains to ensure themselves a ready supply of beer. Beer drinking is frequently depicted in ancient Middle Eastern art and can be dated to as early as 3500 B.C.E.

However, most researchers today believe that some ecological crisis during the period of global warming after the ice age drove people to abandon hunting and gathering in favor of pastoralism and agriculture. Such a crisis would explain why so many places adopted food production during the same period. Although the precise nature of the crisis has not been identified, some scholars think food production may have been a response to shortages of wild food. In some places a warmer, wetter climate could have promoted rapid forest growth in former grasslands, reducing the supplies of game and wild grains. Or, because a warmer climate made it easier for more people to survive, rising population could have depleted supplies of wild food.

Additional support for an ecological explanation comes from the fact that in many drier parts of the world, where wild food remained abundant, agriculture was not adopted. The inhabitants of Australia continued to rely exclusively on hunting and gathering until recent centuries, as did some peoples in all the other continents. Many Amerindians in the arid grasslands from Alaska to the Gulf of Mexico hunted bison, while in the Pacific Northwest others took up salmon-fishing. Abundant supplies of fish, shellfish, and aquatic animals permitted food gatherers east of the Mississippi River in North America to become increasingly sedentary. In the equatorial rain forest and in the southern part of Africa conditions favored retention of the older ways. The reindeer-based societies of northern Eurasia were also unaffected by the spread of farming.

Whatever the causes, the effects of the gradual adoption of food production in most parts of the world between 12,000 and 2,000 years ago were momentous. A hundred thousand years ago there probably were fewer than 2 million humans, and their range was largely confined to the temperate and tropical regions of Africa and Eurasia. During the last glacial epoch, between 32,000 and 13,000 years ago, human population may have fallen even lower. As the glaciers retreated, humans expanded into new land and adopted agriculture, and their numbers gradually rose to 10 million by 5000 B.C.E. Then human population mushroomed, reaching from 50 million to 100 million by 1000 B.C.E. and 200 million or more a millennium later. This increase in numbers brought momentous changes to social and cultural life.

LIFE IN NEOLITHIC COMMUNITIES

The evidence that people were driven to food production by a crisis rather than drawn to it has led researchers to reexamine the disadvantages and advantages of agriculture compared to those of hunting and gathering. Modern studies suggest that food producers have to work much harder and for much longer periods than do food gatherers. In return for modest harvests, early farmers needed to put in long days of arduous labor clearing and cultivating the land. Pastoralists had to guard their herds from wild predators, guide them to fresh pastures, and tend to their many needs.

There is also evidence that even though the food supply of early farmers was more secure than that of food-gathering peoples and pastoralists, the farmers' diet was less varied and nutritious. Skeletal remains show that on average Neolithic farmers were shorter than earlier food-gathering peoples. Farmers were also likely to die at an earlier age because permanent villages and towns were unhealthier than temporary camps. Contagious diseases could establish themselves more readily in densely settled communities because human waste contaminated drinking water, disease-bearing vermin and insects infested persons and buildings, and new diseases migrated to humans from their domesticated animals (especially pigs and cattle).

The most notable benefit of agriculture was a more dependable supply of food that could be stored between harvests to tide people over seasonal changes and short-term climate fluctuations such as droughts. Over several millennia, permanent settlements experienced slow but steady population growth. There were also profound changes in culture and the emergence of towns and craft specialization.

Rural Population and Settlement

Researchers have long wondered exactly how farmers displaced hunter-gatherers. Some have envisioned a violent struggle between practitioners of the two ways of life; others believe there was a more peaceful transition. Some violence was likely, especially as the amount of cleared land reduced the wild foods available to hunter-gatherers. Probable too were conflicts among farmers for control of the best land. A growing body of evidence, however, suggests that in most cases farmers displaced hunter-gatherers by a process of gradual infiltration rather than by rapid conquest.

The key to the food producers' expansion may have been the simple fact that their small surpluses gave them a long-term advantage in population growth, by ensuring slightly higher survival rates during times of drought or other crisis. The respected archaeologist Colin Renfrew argues, for example, that over a few centuries farming-population densities in Europe could have increased by from fifty to one hundred fold. According to his scenario, as population densities rose, those individuals who had to farm at a great distance from their native village eventually formed a new farming settlement.

Renfrew finds it consistent with the archaeological evidence for a steady nonviolent expansion of agricultural peoples—moving only 12 to 19 miles (20 or 30 kilometers) a generation—to have repopulated the whole of Europe from Greece to Britain between 6500 and 3500 B.C.E.[2] The process would have been so gradual that it need not have provoked any sharp conflicts with existing hunter-gatherers, who simply could have stayed clear of the agricultural frontier or gradually adopted agriculture themselves and been absorbed by the advancing farming communities. This hypothesis of a gradual spread of agricultural people across Europe from southeast to northwest is also supported by new studies that map similar genetic changes in the population.[3]

Like hunter-gatherer bands, the expanding farming communities were organized around kinship and marriage. Nuclear families (parents and their children) probably did not become larger, but people traced kinship relations back over more generations so that distant cousins were clearly aware of their membership in the same kin network. This was important because landholding was likely to be vested in large kinship units, known as *lineages* and *clans*.

Even if one assumes stable marriage patterns, tracing descent is a complex matter. Because each person has two parents, four grandparents, eight great-grandparents, and so on, each individual has a bewildering number of ancestors. Societies tend to trace descent primarily through a single parent. Some trace descent through mothers (*matrilineal societies*) and some through fathers (*patrilineal societies*).

Some scholars have argued that ancient peoples may have traced descent through women and may have been ruled by women. For example, the traditions of Kikuyu farmers on Mount Kenya in East Africa relate that women once ruled them, but the Kikiyu men conspired to get all the women pregnant at once and then overthrew them while the women were unable to fight back. No specific evidence can prove or disprove legends such as this, but it is important not to confuse tracing descent through women (*matrilineality*) with the rule of women (*matriarchy*). In both patrilineal and matrilineal societies today, men, particularly older men, are dominant.

Cultural Expressions

The importance of their kinship systems influenced early agricultural people's outlook on the world. Reverence for departed ancestors was an important part of group solidarity, and the deaths of old persons tended to be marked by elaborate burials. The existence of a plastered skull from Jericho in the Jordan Valley of modern Israel may be evidence of an early ancestor cult. (A cult is a system of religious rituals expressing reverence or worship.)

The religion of food producers also reflected their awareness of their relationship to nature. In contrast to food gatherers, whose religions tended to center on sacred groves, springs, and wild animals, many farming communities centered their religious activities on the Earth Mother, a female deity who was the source of all new life, along with other gods and goddesses representing fire, wind, and rain. Beliefs in an all-powerful (and usually) male Sky God were also common.

The story in an ancient Hindu text about the burning of a large forest near modern India's capital, New Delhi, may preserve a memory of the conflict between old and new beliefs. In the story the gods Krishna and Arjuna are picnicking in the forest when Agni, the fire-god, appears in disguise and asks them to satisfy his hunger by burning the forest along with every creature in it. As interpreted by some scholars, this story represents both the clearing of the land for cultivation and the destruction of the wildlife on which food gatherers depended.[4]

Religions placed different emphasis on the role of ancestors, the Sky God, and the Earth Mother, but most seem to have included all three in their religious practices, along with older rituals and deities. Large chambers called *megaliths* (meaning "big stones") dating from 4000 B.C.E. provide some evidence of an ancestor cult in western Europe. The early ones appear to have been communal burial chambers, which descent groups may have erected to mark their claims to farmlands. Megaliths were also built on eastern Mediterranean (Aegean) islands. In the Middle East, the Americas, and other parts of the world, giant earth burial mounds and ziggurats (mounds on which temples were later built) may have served similar functions.

Another fundamental cultural contribution of Neolithic period was the dissemination of the large language families that form the basis of most languages spoken today. Renfrew has suggested that the spread of the western half of the giant Indo-European language family (from which Germanic, Romance, and Celtic languages are derived) was the work of the pioneering agriculturalists who gradually moved across Europe. The age of the language family and its differentiation into many related but distinct languages are indeed more consistent with a pattern of gradual infiltration than with rapid conquest. Similarly, the Afro-Asiatic language family that spans the Middle East and northern Africa might have been the result of the food producers' expansion, as might the spread of the Sino-Tibetan family in East and Southeast Asia.

These interpretations of language diffusion must be considered speculative because there is no physical evidence of what languages were actually spoken during the Neolithic period. Indisputable instances of language and an agricultural population spreading together do exist from somewhat later times. One example is the great wave of Malayo-Polynesian colonization of the East Indies and the thousands of islands in the Pacific Ocean between 4000 B.C.E. and 1000 C.E. Everywhere they went, Pacific mariners introduced their principal crops—breadfruit, taro, coconut, yams, and bananas—along with the current version of their spoken language. Another example of agricultural and linguistic expansion, the spread of the Bantu-speaking people across central and southern Africa, occurred from about 500 B.C.E. to 1000 C.E. (see Chapter 8).

Early Towns and Specialists

Most early farmers lived in small villages, but in some parts of the world a few villages grew into towns, which were centers of trade and craft specialization. These larger communities were most notable in river valleys where rich soils and regular water supplies provided high agricultural

Neolithic goddess Many versions of a well-nourished and pregnant female figure were found at Çatal Hüyük. Here she is supported by twin leopards whose tails curve over her shoulders. To those who inhabited the city some 8,000 years ago the figure likely represented fertility and power over nature. (C.M. Dixon)

yields that could support denser populations (see Chapters 2 and 3). Towns and cities had elaborate dwellings and ceremonial buildings made of mud brick, stone, and wood, as well as many large structures for storing the surplus production until the next harvest. Baskets and other woven containers held dry foods; pottery jugs, jars, and pots stored liquids.

Most of these structures and objects could be made by the agriculturalists in their spare time, but larger communities had craft specialists, who devoted their full energies to making products of unusual complexity or beauty. Such specialization was possible because the community produced a surplus of food and other necessities.

Two towns in the Middle East that have been extensively excavated are Jericho on the west bank of the Jordan River and Çatal Hüyük in central Anatolia (modern Turkey).

The excavations at Jericho revealed an unusually large and elaborate early agricultural settlement. Around 8000 B.C.E. dwellings at Jericho were round, mud-brick structures, perhaps imitating the shape of the tents of hunters who once had camped near Jericho's natural spring. A millennium later there were rectangular rooms with finely plastered walls and floors and wide doorways that opened on a central courtyard. Around the 10-acre (4-hectare) settlement extended a massive stone wall, to which tall towers were added about 7000 B.C.E. The walls were clearly for defense against invasion, presumably by local pastoralists.

Çatal Hüyük, an even larger Neolithic town, dates to between 7000 and 5000 B.C.E. and covered 32 acres (13 hectares) at its height. Its residents also occupied plastered mud-brick rooms that were elaborately decorated. Unlike Jericho, Çatal Hüyük had no defensive fortifications. But the outer walls of the houses formed a continuous barrier without doors or large windows, so invaders would have found it difficult to break in. Residents entered their house by climbing down a ladder through a hole in the roof.

Çatal Hüyük was a bustling town that prospered from long-distance trade in obsidian, a hard volcanic rock that craftspeople skillfully chipped, ground, and polished into tools, weapons, mirrors, and ornaments. Other residents made fine pottery and practiced many other crafts, including weaving baskets and woolen cloth, making stone and shell beads, and working leather and wood. House sizes varied, but there is no evidence that Çatal Hüyük had a dominant class or a centralized political structure.

Although the amount and the importance of craftwork in towns like Jericho and Çatal Hüyük were quite new in history, the two towns displayed many close links with older ways of living. The very extensive representational art at Çatal Hüyük makes it clear that hunting retained a powerful hold on people's minds. Elaborate wall paintings depict hunting scenes remarkably similar to those of earlier cave paintings, and men were buried with weapons of war and hunting, not with the tools of farming. Moreover, many of the wall scenes depict persons, both males and females, adorned with the skins of wild leopards.

Discarded bones are proof that wild game featured prominently in the diet of Çatal Hüyük residents, but, however neglected in their art, agriculture was the basis of their existence. Fields around the town produced crops of barley and emmer wheat, as well as legumes and other vegetables. A species of pig was kept along with goats and sheep. Wild foods such as acorns and wild grains were also important in the diet.

Perhaps the most striking finds at Çatal Hüyük are concerned with religious practice. There is a religious shrine for every two houses. At least forty rooms contained shrines with depictions of horned wild bulls, female breasts, goddesses, leopards, and handprints. There are dishes where grains, legumes, and meat were burned as offerings, but there is no evidence of live animal sacrifice. The fact that statues of plump female deities far outnumber statues of male deities persuaded the principal excavator of Çatal Hüyük that a cult of the goddess was central to the town's religion. He further concluded that the large number of females who had received elaborate burials in the shrine rooms were priestesses of this cult. In his view, although male priests were also present, "It seems extremely likely that the cult of the goddess was administered mainly by women."[5]

Whether male or female, religious leaders were a specialized occupation in many Neolithic communities. Spectacular evidence is provided by the growing number of large stone structures constructed after 3000 B.C.E., including the stone circles of western Europe (of which Stonehenge is the most famous), the ziggurats of Mesopotamia and Mesoamerica, the pyramids of Egypt, and the citadels of the Indus Valley. There is no reason to think these widely scattered structures had any connection to each other. Like agriculture, each arose in its own cultural context as an expression of human communal ties, fears, and aspirations.

Metalworking was another important specialized occupation in the late Neolithic period. At Çatal Hüyük objects of copper and lead, metals that occur naturally in a fairly pure form, can be dated to about 6400 B.C.E. Silver and gold were also worked at an early date in many parts of the world. Because of their rarity and their softness these metals did not replace stone tools and weapons but instead were used primarily to make decorative or ceremonial objects. The discovery of many such objects in graves suggests they were symbols of status and power.

The growth of towns, specialized crafts, and elaborate religious shrines added to the workload of agriculturalists, who already had to work hard to till the soil. The towns' permanent houses needed much labor to build, as did Jericho's defensive walls and towers. Extra food had to be produced for the nonfarming full-time priests and craft specialists. Building religious monuments in stone must have occupied much time during the less busy season of the agricultural year. It is estimated, for example, that even a fairly small structure like Stonehenge took 30,000 person-hours to build. No evidence from this period indicates whether these tasks were performed freely or coerced. But after 3500 B.C.E. it is clear that political authorities coerced labor for large building projects (see Chapter 2).

CONCLUSION

The span of time that this chapter covers is immense, far longer than the combined time span of all the rest of the chapters in the book. Compressing so long a period into a single chapter highlights the fundamental and gradually evolving relationships between humans and their natural environment—relationships that underlie human history. In the first stage the struggle to survive in the changing environments of the early Ice Age gave rise to the physical evolution of human beings. Next, distinctive physical and mental abilities enabled humans to adapt culturally to many different natural environments. Since the Neolithic period, people

consciously and deliberately have modified parts of the natural world to suit their needs. These events suggest several themes that have been important throughout human history.

First, the fact that human nature and human cultures have been profoundly shaped by the struggle to survive the rigors of their environments strongly suggests that we humans must respect our place in nature. However much we use our unique abilities to reshape the land and develop new domesticated species by artificial selection, we must be careful not to upset the ecological balance on which our own existence depends.

Second, the use of tools, techniques, and specialized technical knowledge that societies passed down from one generation to the next enabled humans to exploit many natural environments. Technology enabled cultural change to become the alternative to biological change.

A third theme concerns diversity. Although many distinct species of humans once existed, by the late Neolithic period humans were the least varied biologically of any living organism. Yet they were also the earth's most widely dispersed mammals. A single species, *Homo sapiens sapiens*, had developed many diverse cultures and learned how to thrive in all the habitable continents.

The transition from food collection to food production brought the greatest modification of the natural environment and the greatest cultural changes since the first people walked our planet. Indeed, the agricultural revolution was one of the most momentous changes in all of human history. Agriculture brought many toils and hardships, but it enabled people to exercise over the natural environment a degree of control that no other species had ever attained. The transition to farming and settled life opened the way to still greater changes in technology and population size as well as in social and cultural diversity. The patterns of language and belief, of diet, dress, and dwelling, that emerged in the Neolithic period shaped the next several millennia. As Chapters 2 and 3 detail, specialization made possible by settled life gave rise to significant advances in architecture and metallurgy, to artistic achievements, and to the growth of complex religious and political systems.

SUGGESTED READING

Useful reference works for this period are Ian Tattersall, Eric Delson, and John Van Couvering, eds., *Encyclopedia of Human Evolution and Prehistory* (1988), and *The World Atlas of Archaeology* (1985). Reliable surveys for interested students are Brian Fagan's *People of the Earth: An Introduction to World Prehistory*, 8th ed. (1995), and Bernard G. Campbell, *Humankind Emerging*, 6th ed. (1992). Fagan has also written a popular survey, *The Journey from Eden: The Peopling of Our World* (1990).

Accounts of the discoveries of early human remains, written for the nonspecialist by eminent researchers, include Donald Johanson, Leorna Johanson, and Blake Edgar, *In Search of Human Origins* (1994), based on the *Nova* television series of the same name; Richard Leakey and Roger Lewin, *Origins Reconsidered: In Search of What Makes Us Human* (1992); and Donald C. Johanson and Maitland A. Edey, *Lucy: The Beginnings of Mankind* (1981). Other useful books that deal with this subject include George D. Brown, Jr., *Human Evolution* (1995), for a precise biological and geological perspective; Adam Kuper, *The Chosen Primate: Human Nature and Cultural Diversity* (1994), for an anthropological analysis; Glyn Daniel and Colin Renfrew, *The Idea of Prehistory*, 2d ed. (1988), detailing the development of the discipline and relying primarily on European examples; Robert Foley, *Another Unique Species: Patterns in Human Evolutionary Ecology* (1987), a thoughtful and readable attempt to bring together archaeological evidence and biological processes in the development of early humans.

More analytical overviews of the evolutionary evidence are Richard G. Klein, *The Human Career: Human Biological and Cultural Origins* (1989); and Paul Mellars, ed., *The Emergence of Modern Humans* (1991). Provocative and speculative explorations of key issues are Colin Renfrew, *Archaeology and Language: The Puzzle of Indo-European Origins* (1988); Ronald K. Siegel, *Intoxication: Life in Pursuit of Artificial Paradise* (1989); and Marija Gimbutas, *The Civilization of the Goddess: The World of Old Europe* (1991). Margaret Ehrenberg, *Women in Prehistory* (1989), and M. Kay Martin and Barbara Voorhies, *Female of the Species* (1975), provide

interesting, though necessarily speculative, discussions of women's history.

Cave and rock art and their implications are the subject of many works. A broad, global introduction is Hans-Georg Bandi, *The Art of the Stone Age: Forty Thousand Years of Rock Art* (1961); Ann Sieveking, *The Cave Artists* (1979), provides a brief overview of the major European finds. Other specialized studies are Robert R. R. Brooks and Vishnu S. Wakankar, *Stone Age Painting in India* (1976); R. Townley Johnson, *Major Rock Paintings of Southern Africa* (1979); J. D. Lewis-Williams, *Believing and Seeing* (1981) and *Discovering Southern African Rock Art* (1990); Mario Ruspoli, *The Cave Art of Lascaux* (1986); and N. K. Sanders, *Prehistoric Art in Europe* (1968).

For the transition to food production see Allen W. Johnson and Timothy Earle, *The Evolution of Human Societies: From Foraging Group to Agrarian State* (1987), and J. D. Clark and Steven A. Brandt, eds., *From Hunters to Farmers: The Causes and Consequences of Food Production in Africa* (1984). James Mellaart, the principal excavator of Çatal Hüyük, has written an account of the town for the general reader: *Çatal Hüyük: A Neolithic Town in Anatolia* (1967). A pioneering work on human ecology, whose early sections are about this period, is Madhav Gadgil and Ramachandra Guha, *This Fissured Land: An Ecological History of India* (1992).

NOTES

1. Quoted in Richard Leakey and Roger Lewin, *Origins Reconsidered: In Search of What Makes Us Human* (New York: Doubleday, 1992), 81.

2. Colin Renfrew, *Archaeology and Language: The Puzzle of Indo-European Origins* (New York: Cambridge University Press, 1988), 125, 150.

3. Luigi Cavalli-Sforza, L. Luca, Paolo Menozzi, and Alberto Piazza, *The History and Geography of Human Genes* (Princeton, NJ: Princeton University Press, 1994).

4. Madhav Gadgil and Ramachandra Guha, *This Fissured Land: An Ecological History of India* (Berkeley: University of California Press, 1992), 79.

5. James Mellaart, *Çatal Hüyük: A Neolithic Town in Anatolia* (New York: McGraw-Hill, 1967), 202.

CHAPTER TWO

The First River-Valley Civilizations,

3500–1500 B.C.E.

Mesopotamia · Egypt · The Indus Valley Civilization

The Challenges and Opportunities of Great River Valleys

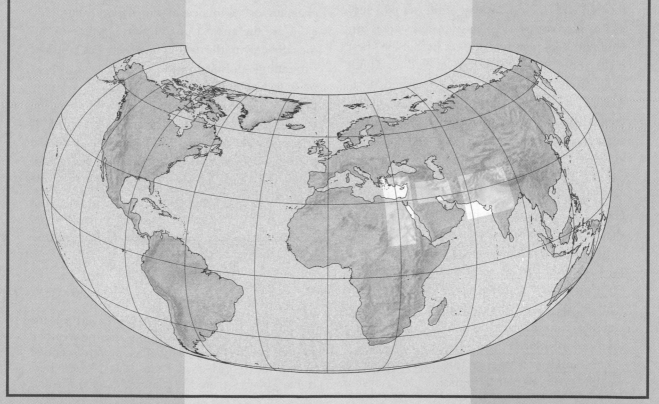

The *Epic of Gilgamesh*, whose roots date to some time before 2000 B.C.E., making it perhaps the oldest surviving work of literature in the world, provides a definition of *civilization* as the people of ancient Mesopotamia (present-day Iraq) understood it. Gilgamesh, an early king, sends a priestess to tame Enkidu, a wild man who lives like an animal in the grasslands. After using her sexual charms to win Enkidu's trust, she says to him:

> "Come with me to the city, to Uruk,
> to the temple of Anu and the goddess Ishtar . . .
> to Uruk, where the processions are and music,
> let us go together through the dancing
> to the palace hall where Gilgamesh presides."[1]

She then clothes Enkidu and teaches him to eat cooked food, drink brewed beer, and bathe and oil his body. By her actions she indicates some of the behavior and choices that ancient Mesopotamians associated with civilized life.

The tendency of the Mesopotamians, like other peoples throughout history, to equate civilization with their own way of life, should serve as a caution for us. What assumptions are hiding behind the frequently made claim that the "first" civilizations, or the first "advanced" or "high" civilizations, arose in western Asia and northeastern Africa sometime before 3000 B.C.E.? Given that *civilization* is a loaded and ambiguous concept, the idea that the "first" civilizations emerged in ancient Mesopotamia and Egypt needs to be explained carefully.

What we can say is that certain political, social, economic, and technological phenomena that scholars agree are indicators of civilization appeared in the Middle East before 3000 B.C.E.: (1) cities that served as administrative centers, (2) a political system based on territory rather than on kinship, (3) specialization of labor and a significant number of people engaged in non-food-producing activities, (4) class divisions and a substantial increase in the accumulation of wealth, (5) monumental building, (6) a system for keeping permanent records, (7) long-distance trade, and (8) major advances in science and the arts.

We also know that the earliest societies in which those features are apparent developed in the floodplains of great rivers in Asia and Africa: the Tigris and Euphrates in Mesopotamia, the Indus in Pakistan, the Yellow (Huang He) in China, and the Nile in Egypt (see Map 2.1). The periodic flooding of the rivers brought benefits—deposits of fertile silt and irrigation for the fields—but also threatened lives and property. To protect themselves and channel these powerful forces of nature, people living near these rivers created new technologies and forms of political and social organization.

In this chapter, we trace the rise of civilization in Mesopotamia, Egypt, and the Indus River Valley from approximately 3500 to 1500 B.C.E. Our starting point roughly coincides with the origins of writing, so we can observe aspects of human experience that scholars cannot deduce from archaeological evidence alone. Events after 1500 B.C.E. are the subject of Chapter 3, which examines the new patterns that emerged as a result of expanding political and economic networks, new technologies, and the activities of new groups of people. Because the independent emergence of civilization based on river floods and irrigation occurred somewhat later in China than in Mesopotamia, Egypt, and the Indus Valley, early China is also taken up in the next chapter.

MESOPOTAMIA

Because of the unpredictable nature of the Tigris and Euphrates Rivers and the weather, the peoples of ancient Mesopotamia tended to see the world as a hazardous place where human beings were the playthings of fickle and uncompassionate gods who were personifications of natural forces. One of their explanations for the origins and nature of their world is what we know as the Babylonian Creation Myth (Babylon was the most powerful city in southern Mesopotamia in the second and first millennia B.C.E.). The high point of the myth is a cosmic battle between Marduk, the chief god of Babylon, and Tiamat, a female figure who personifies the salt sea. Marduk cuts up Tiamat and from her body fashions the earth and sky. He then creates the divisions of time, the celestial bodies, rivers, and weather phenomena, and from the blood of a defeated rebel god he creates human beings. Creation myths of this sort provided the ancient inhabitants of Mesopotamia with a satisfactory explanation for the environment in which they were living.

Settled Agriculture in an Unstable Landscape

Mesopotamia is a Greek word meaning "land between the rivers." It reflects the centrality of the Euphrates and Tigris Rivers to the way of life in this region. Mesopotamian civilization developed in the plain alongside and between the Tigris and Euphrates, which originate in the mountains of eastern Anatolia (modern Turkey) and empty into the Persian Gulf. This is an alluvial plain, built up over many millennia by silt that the rivers deposited.

Mesopotamia lies mostly within modern Iraq. Certain natural features establish its boundaries: to the north and east, the arc of mountains extending from northern Syria and southeastern Anatolia to the Zagros Mountains, which cut off the plain of the Tigris and Euphrates from the Iranian Plateau; to the west and southwest, the Syrian and Arabian deserts; and to the southeast, the Persian Gulf. This region is subject to unpredictable extremes of weather. Floods can be sudden and violent and tend to come at the wrong time for grain agriculture—in the spring when the crop is ripening in the field. There also is the ever-present danger of the rivers changing course, suddenly cutting off fields and population centers from water resources and avenues of communication.

Periods of Mesopotamian History

3000–2350 B.C.E.	Early Dynastic (Sumerian)
2350–2200 B.C.E.	Akkadian (Semitic)
2112–2004 B.C.E.	Third Dynasty of Ur (Sumerian)
1900–1600 B.C.E.	Old Babylonian (Semitic)
1500–1150 B.C.E.	Kassite

The first domestication of plants and animals took place not far away, in the "Fertile Crescent" region of northern Syria and southeastern Anatolia, around 8000 B.C.E. Agriculture did not come to Mesopotamia until approximately 5000 B.C.E. Agriculture that depends on rain requires annual rainfall of at least 8 inches (20 centimeters). In hot, dry southern Mesopotamia, agriculture depended on irrigation. At first, people probably took advantage of the occasional flooding of the rivers over their banks and into the nearby fields, but shortly after 3000 B.C.E. they learned to construct canals to supply water as needed and to carry water to more distant parcels of land.

Barley was the main cereal crop in southern Mesopotamia. It was better able to withstand the effects of the salt drawn to the surface of the soil when the fields were flooded than the wheat grown in northern Mesopotamia. By 4000 B.C.E. farmers were using plows pulled by cattle to turn over the earth. A funnel attached to the plow dropped a carefully measured amount of seed. Fields were left fallow (unplanted) every other year, to replenish the nutrients in the soil. Date palms provided food, fibers, and some wood. Small garden plots produced vegetables. Reed plants, which grew on the river banks and in the marshy southern delta, could be woven into mats, baskets, huts, and boats. Fish from the rivers and marshes were an important part of people's diet. Herds of sheep and goats, which grazed on the fallow land and beyond the zone of cultivation, provided wool and milk. Cattle and donkeys carried or pulled burdens, joined in the third and second millennia B.C.E. by newly introduced camels and horses.

The earliest people living in Mesopotamia in the "historical period"—that is, the period for

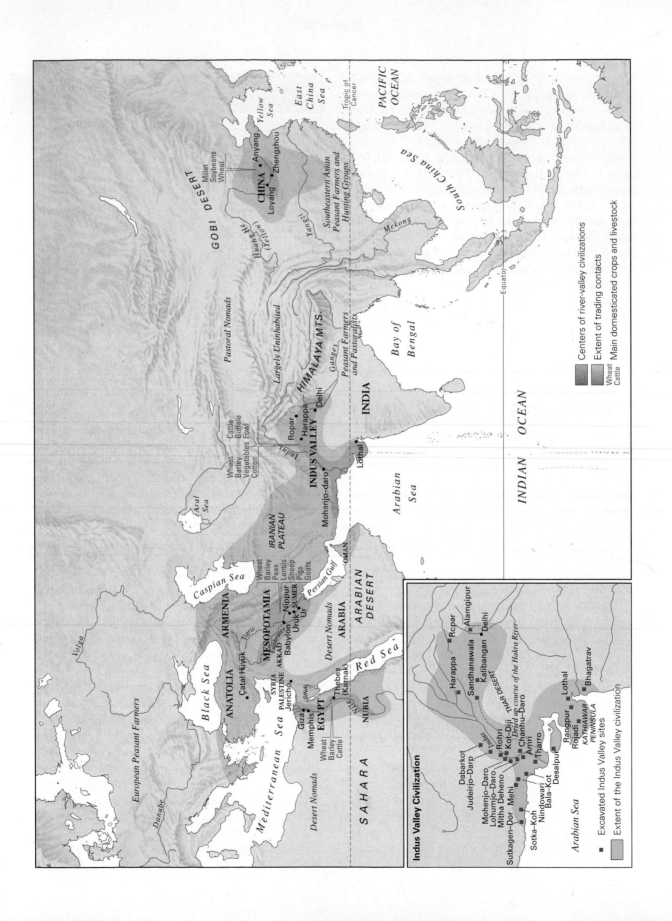

PACIFIC
OCEAN

East
China
Sea

Tropic of Cancer

*Millet
Soybeans
Wheat*

CHINA • Anyang
Loyang• •Zhengzhou

*Huang He
(Yellow)*

Yangzi

*Southeastern Asian
Peasant Farmers and
Hunting Groups*

Mekong

South China Sea

*Yellow
Sea*

GOBI DESERT

Pastoral Nomads

Largely Uninhabited

HIMALAYA MTS.

Peasant Farmers and Pastoralists

Ganges

Bay of
Bengal

*Cattle
Buffalo
Fowl*

Ropar• •Harappa
Delhi•

*Wheat
Barley
Vegetables
Cotton*

INDUS VALLEY
Mohenjo-daro•

INDIA

•Lothal

Aral
Sea

*IRANIAN
PLATEAU*

INDIAN   OCEAN

Caspian Sea

*Wheat
Barley
Peas*
*Lentils
Sheep
Pigs
Goats*

ARMENIA

Tigris

Arabian
Sea

Equator

ANATOLIA

MESOPOTAMIA
Çatal Hüyük• •Nippur SUMER
AKKAD•Uruk
Babylon• •Ur
Euphrates
Persian Gulf

OMAN

Desert Nomads
ARABIA

**ARABIAN
DESERT**

Volga

Black Sea

SYRIA
PALESTINE
Jericho• SINAI
Thebes
•(Karnak)
Memphis•
Giza• **EGYPT**

Red Sea

NUBIA

European Peasant Farmers

Mediterranean Sea

*Wheat
Barley
Cattle*

Nile

Danube

Desert Nomads

S A H A R A

Centers of river-valley civilizations
Extent of trading contacts
Main domesticated crops and livestock
Wheat
Cattle

Indus Valley Civilization

Rcpar•
•Alamgipur

Harappa■ Sandhanawala■ ■Kalibangan
•Delhi

THAR DESERT

Dried up course of the Hakra River

Dabarkot■
Judeirjo-Darp■
Mohenjo-Daro■
Lohumjo-Daro■
Mitha Deheno■
Rohri■ Kot-Diji■
Amri■ Chanhu-Daro■
Tharro■

Indus

Sotka-Koh■
Nindowari■ Bala-Kot■
Desalpur■
Mehi■

Lothal■ •Bhagatrav
Rangpur■
Rojadi■
*KATHIAWAR
PENINSULA*

Arabian Sea

■ Excavated Indus Valley sites
  Extent of the Indus Valley civilization

which we have some written evidence—are the Sumerians. There is mounting archaeological evidence that they were in southern Mesopotamia at least by 5000 B.C.E. and perhaps even before then. The Sumerians created the main framework of civilization in Mesopotamia—a framework adopted and adapted by other ethnic groups that later rose to dominance in the region. The third millennium B.C.E. was primarily a Sumerian epoch. However, even in this period the Sumerians were not the only ethnic and linguistic group inhabiting the Tigris-Euphrates Valley. From as early as 2900 B.C.E. the names of individuals recorded in inscriptions from northerly cities in the southern plain suggest the presence of Semites—people who spoke a Semitic language. (The term *Semitic* refers to a family of related languages that have long been spoken across parts of western Asia and north Africa. In antiquity these languages included Hebrew, Aramaic, and Phoenician; the most widespread modern member of the Semitic family is Arabic.)

Historians believe that these Semites descended from nomadic peoples who had migrated into the Mesopotamian plain from the western desert. There is little indication of ethnic conflict between Sumerians and Semites. The Semites assimilated to Sumerian culture and sometimes gained positions of wealth and power.

By 2000 B.C.E. the Semitic peoples had become politically dominant, and from this time forward Akkadian, a Semitic language, was the primary language in Mesopotamia. Much of the Sumerian cultural legacy, however, was preserved. Sumerian-Akkadian dictionaries were compiled, Sumerian literature was translated, and from these stories we know that the Semitic gods borrowed characteristics and adventures of the Sumerian gods. This cultural synthesis parallels a biological merging of Sumerian and Semitic stocks through intermarriage. Other ethnic groups, including mountain peoples such as the

Map 2.1 River Valley Civilizations, 3500–1500 B.C.E. The earliest complex societies arose in the flood plains of large rivers: in the fourth millennium B.C.E. in the valley of the Tigris and Euphrates Rivers in Mesopotamia and the Nile River in Egypt, in the third millennium in the valley of the Indus River in Pakistan, and the second millennium in the valley of the Yellow River in China.

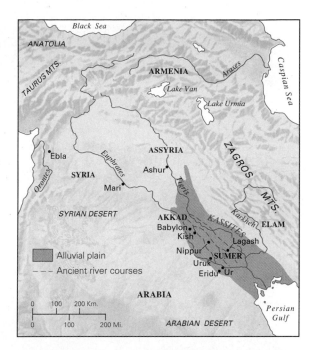

Map 2.2 Mesopotamia The Sumerians of southern Mesopotamia developed new technologies, complex political and social institutions, and distinctive cultural practices, responding to the need to organize labor resources to create and maintain an irrigation network in the Tigris-Euphrates Valley, a land of little rain.

Kassites as well as Elamites and Persians from Iran, played a part in Mesopotamian history. But not until the arrival of Greeks in the Middle East in the late fourth century B.C.E. would the Sumerian/Semitic cultural heritage of Mesopotamia be fundamentally altered.

Cities, Kings, and Trade

Mesopotamia was a land of villages and cities. Villages—groups of families that live close to one another—are common in agricultural societies. By banding together, families can protect each other, share farming implements and facilities such as barns and threshing floors, and help each other at key times in the agricultural cycle. Villages also serve human social needs, providing a pool of potential marriage partners and a variety of people to talk to.

Cities also depend on agriculture; indeed, the earliest known urban centers in the Middle East,

Lagash, Ur-Nanshe Stone wall plaque depicting the twenty-fifth century B.C.E. Sumerian ruler of Lagash, Ur-Nanshe. In the upper register the king carries on his head a basket with mud bricks, symbolizing his role as a builder. The figures to his right may be his wife and sons. In the lower register he is seated on a throne and approached by subjects or members of court. Note how the king's superior status is indicated by his greater size. (Louvre © R.M.N.)

such as Jericho and Çatal Hüyük, sprang up shortly after the first appearance of agriculture (see Chapter 1). In nonurban societies almost everyone engages in the basic tasks of subsistence, gathering or growing enough food to feed themselves and their families. Cities, however, depend on the ability of farmers to produce surplus food to feed people who are not engaged in food production but instead specialize in other kinds of activities, such as metallurgy (creating useful objects from metal), crafts, administration, and serving the gods. Even so, many people living in early Mesopotamian cities went out each day to labor in nearby fields.

Most cities evolved from villages. As a successful village grew, smaller satellite villages developed nearby, and eventually the main village and its satellites coalesced into an urban center.

Cities and villages continued to be linked in a relationship of mutual dependence. A city controlled the agricultural land and villages in its vicinity, requiring the surplus foodstuffs of the countryside to feed its population of specialists. At the same time the city provided the rural districts with military protection against bandits and raiders and a market where villagers could trade surplus products, often for manufactured goods produced by specialists in the city.

We use the term *city-state* to refer to independent ancient urban centers and the agricultural hinterlands they controlled. Early Mesopotamia was a land of many small city-states. Stretches of open and uncultivated land, whether desert or swamp, lay between the territories controlled by the various communities and served as buffers. However, disputes over land, water rights, and movable property often sparked hostilities be-tween neighboring cities and prompted most to build protective walls of sun-dried mud bricks. But cities also cooperated in various ways, shar-ing water and allowing safe passage of trade goods through their territories.

The production of food surpluses in the Tigris-Euphrates Valley required new land to be opened up to agriculture by the construction and maintenance of an extensive irrigation network. Canals brought water to fields distant from the rivers. Drainage ditches carried water away from flooded fields before a damaging layer of salt and minerals was drawn to the surface of the soil. Dikes protected young plants emerging in fields near the riverbanks from being destroyed in flood season. Gravity moved the water through the network. Dams raised the water level of the river so that water could flow into the irrigation channels. A machine with counter-weights was invented to lift water—for example, up from the river and over the dike to the land beyond. Because the rivers carried so much silt, channels got clogged and needed constant dredging.

The successful operation of such a sophisticat-ed irrigation infrastructure depended on the emergence of individuals or groups wielding sufficient political power to compel and organize large numbers of people to work together. Other projects also relied on the cooperation of many people: the harvest, sheep shearing, the construc-tion of fortification walls, the construction of monuments, and waging war. Little is known about the political institutions of early Mesopo-tamian city-states, although there are traces of some sort of citizens' assembly that may have evolved from the traditional village council. The two centers of power for which there are written records are the temple and the king.

Each Mesopotamian city contained one or more temples housing the cult of the deity or deities who watched over the community. The temples owned extensive tracts of agricultural land and stored the gifts that worshipers donat-ed. The importance of the cults is confirmed by the central location of the temple buildings. The leading members of the priesthood, who con-trolled the shrine and managed the deity's con-

siderable wealth, appear to have been the dominant political and economic force in early Mesopotamian communities.

In the third millennium B.C.E. another kind of leadership developed in the Sumerian cities. A figure who is referred to in Sumerian documents as *lugal*, or "big man"—what we would call a "king"—emerged. How this position evolved is not clear, but it may have been related to an in-crease in the frequency and scale of warfare as ever-larger communities quarreled over limited quantities of land, water, and raw materials. Ac-cording to one plausible theory, certain men cho-sen by the community to lead the armies in time of war found ways to extend their authority into peacetime and to assume key judicial and ritual functions. The position of lugal was not automat-ically hereditary, but capable sons had a good chance of succeeding their fathers.

The later development of this secular authori-ty is often reflected in the position of the palace, the seat of the king's power. The palace tends not to be as centrally located as the temple, having emerged after the heart of the city had been es-tablished. There must have been considerable jockeying for wealth and power between priests and kings, and the process of political evolution must have varied from community to communi-ty. The overall trend, however, favored the king, presumably because he had the army behind him. Though still influential because of their wealth and religious mystique, the priests and temples became dependent on the palace. By the late third millennium B.C.E. royal officials were supervising the temples. Some Mesopotamian kings claimed to be gods on earth, but this con-cept did not take root, and the normal pattern was for the king to portray himself as the earthly representative of the god.

Appointed and favored by the divinity, the king assumed responsibility for the upkeep and building of temples and the proper performance of ritual. Other key responsibilities of the king in-cluded maintenance of the city walls and defens-es, upkeep and extension of the network of irrigation channels, preservation of property rights, and protection of the people from outside attackers and from perversions of justice at home. Some kings even took steps to correct economic inequalities, by setting prices and cancel-ing debts.

We catch glimpses of the unchecked power, restless ambition and value to the community of this new breed of rulers in the epic of Gilgamesh. While the story, as we now have it, has gone through various changes over the centuries and relates many supernatural events in an other-worldly landscape, it is based on a historical fig-ure who was king of Uruk. Gilgamesh is depict-ed as the strongest man in his community. His subjects resent his prerogative to demand sexual favors from new brides, but they depend upon his wisdom and courage to protect them. In his quest for everlasting glory, Gilgamesh built mag-nificent walls around the city and stamped his name on all the bricks. And his journey to the faraway Cedar Mountains reflects the king's role in bringing valuable resources to the community.

Over time certain political centers became powerful enough to extend their control over other city-states. Sargon, ruler of the city of Akkad around 2350 B.C.E., was the first to unite many cities under the control of one king and capital. His title, "King of Sumer and Akkad," became symbolic of this claim to universal do-minion ("Sumer" and "Akkad" denoted, respec-tively, the southern and central portions of the Tigris-Euphrates Valley). Sargon and the four members of his family who succeeded him over a period of one hundred twenty years secured their power in a number of ways. They razed the walls of conquered cities, installing governors backed by garrisons of Akkadian troops. Soldiers received land to ensure their loyalty. Because Sargon and his people were of Semitic stock, the cuneiform system of writing used for Sumerian (discussed later in the chapter) was adapted to express their language. A uniform system of weights and measures and standardized formats for official documents facilitated tasks of admin-istration such as the assessment and collection of taxes, recruitment of soldiers, and organization of large labor projects.

For reasons that are not completely clear to modern scholars, the Akkadian state fell around 2230 B.C.E. The so-called Sumerian King List, which claimed to catalog the rulers of

Mesopotamia since the time of creation, wryly referred to the period after the fall of Akkad (a period in which the various cities regained their independence) by asking, "Who was King? Who was not King?" A last resurgence of Sumerian language and culture in the cities of the southern plain was seen under the Ur III Dynasty, (2112–2004 B.C.E.). Based on a combination of campaigns of conquest and alliances cemented by marriage, the dynasty encompassed five kings who ruled for a century. The Ur III state did not control territories as extensive as those of its Akkadian predecessor, but a rapidly expand-ing bureaucracy of government administrators led to tight government control of a wide range of activities and an obsessive degree of record keeping. A corps of messengers and well-maintained road stations facilitated rapid communication, and an official calendar, stan-dardized weights and measures, and uniform scribal practices enhanced the effectiveness of the central administration. As the southern plain came under increasing pressure from Semitic Amorites in the northwest, the kings erected a great wall 125 miles (201 kilometers) in length to keep out the nomadic invaders. In the end, though, the Ur III state succumbed to the com-bined pressure of nomadic incursions and an at-tack of Elamites coming from the southeast.

The Amorites founded a new city at Babylon, not far from Akkad. During the reign of the ag-gressive Hammurabi (r. 1792–1750 B.C.E.), Baby-lon became the capital of what historians have named the "Old Babylonian" state, which ex-tended its control not only over Sumer and Akkad but also far to the north and northwest from 1800 to 1600 B.C.E. Hammurabi is best known for his Law Code, inscribed on a polished black stone tablet. Though not a comprehensive list of all the laws of the time, Hammurabi's Code provided judges with a lengthy set of ex-amples illustrating the principles they were to employ when deciding cases. Some of its formu-lations call for physical punishments to be inflict-ed on the body of an offender to compensate for a crime. Such laws are precursors of the Is-raelites' principle of "an eye for an eye, a tooth for a tooth" (see Chapter 4). When we compare them to the monetary penalties in the earlier Ur III codes, we see that the Amorites introduced their own principles of justice.

The far-reaching conquests of some Mesopotamian states were motivated, at least in part, by the need to obtain access to vital resources. The alternative was to trade for raw materials, and long-distance commerce did flourish in most periods. Evidence of boats used in sea trade goes back as far as the fifth millennium B.C.E. Wood, metals, and stone had to be imported from afar. In exchange, wool, cloth, barley, and oil were exported. Wood was acquired from cedar forests covering the slopes of mountain ranges in Lebanon and Syria. Silver came from Anatolia, gold from Egypt, copper from the eastern Mediterranean and Oman (on the Arabian peninsula), tin from Afghanistan (in south-central Asia). Chlorite, a greenish stone from which bowls were carved, came from the Iranian Plateau; black diorite, from the Persian Gulf; lapis lazuli, from eastern Iran and Afghanistan; and carnelian, from Pakistan (in south-central Asia) for jewelry and carved figurines.

In the third millennium B.C.E. merchants were in the employ of the palace or temple. Those were the only two institutions that had the financial resources and long-distance connections to organize the collection, transport, and protection of goods. Merchants exchanged the surplus from the agricultural estates of kings or priests for vital raw materials and luxury goods. In the second millennium B.C.E. commerce came more and more into the hands of independent merchants, and merchant guilds became powerful forces in the community and even assumed some official functions in periods of political crisis or decline.

Modern scholars do not know where in the Mesopotamian city the most important commercial activities took place. There does not appear to have been an open public area dedicated to this function. Two possible locations are the area just inside the city gates and in the vicinity of the docks. Wherever it occurred, all this commercial activity was accomplished without the benefit of money. Coins—that is, pieces of metal whose value the state guarantees—were not invented until the sixth century B.C.E. (see Chapter 5, Envi-

ronment and Technology: The Origins and Early Development of Coinage) and did not reach Mesopotamia until several centuries later. For most of Mesopotamian history, items could be bartered for one another or valued in relation to fixed weights of precious metal, primarily silver.

Mesopotamian Society

One of the persistent features of urbanized civilizations is the development of social divisions— that is, significant variation in the status and privileges of different groups of people due to differences in wealth, in social functions, and in legal and political rights. The rise of cities, specialization of function, centralization of power, and the use of written records enabled certain groups of people to accumulate wealth on an unprecedented scale. As we have seen, the temple leadership and the kings controlled large agricultural estates, and the palace administration also collected various kinds of taxes from its subjects. It is less apparent how certain other people, who made up what we might call an elite class, acquired large holdings of land, for the sale of land was rare. Debtors who could not pay back what they owed forfeited their land, and soldiers and religious officials received plots of land in return for their services.

Social divisions in Mesopotamian society must have varied considerably over time and place, but the situation that historians can infer from the Law Code of Hammurabi for Babylon in the eighteenth century B.C.E. may reveal fundamental distinctions valid for other places and times. There were three classes: (1) *awilum*, the free, landowning class, which included royalty, high-ranking officials, warriors, priests, merchants, and some artisans and shopkeepers; (2) *mushkenum*, the class of dependent farmers and artisans, who were legally attached to land that belonged to king, temple, or elite families and thus provided the bulk of the work force for the rural estates and temple complexes; and (3) *wardum*, the class of slaves, primarily employed in domestic service. In the Old Babylonian period, the awilum—the class of people who were not dependent on the great institutions of temple or palace—grew in numbers and importance, and the amount of land and other property in private hands increased. Penalties for crimes prescribed in the Law Code differed, depending on the class of the offender.

Slavery existed but was not as prevalent and fundamental to the economy as it would be in the later societies of Greece and Rome (see Chapters 5 and 6). Many of the slaves came from mountain tribes and either had been captured in war or sold by slave traders. There was a separate category of slavery for those who were unable to pay off a debt. Under normal circumstances slaves were not chained or otherwise constrained, but they had to wear a distinctive hairdo. If they were given their freedom, a barber shaved off the telltale mark. In the surviving documents it is often hard to distinguish slaves or dependent workers from free laborers, because both were paid in commodities such as food and oil and the quantities varied according to a person's age, gender, and task. There seems to be a trend toward the use of free labor in the second millennium B.C.E., when a larger percentage of the population was no longer dependent on the institutions of temple or palace.

It is difficult to reconstruct the life experiences of ordinary Mesopotamians, especially those who lived in villages or on large estates in the countryside, since they leave little trace in the archeological or literary record. Rural peasants built their houses out of materials such as mud-brick and reed, which quickly disintegrate, and they possessed little in the way of metals. Being illiterate, they were not able to write about their lives.

It is particularly difficult to discover very much about the experiences of women in ancient Mesopotamia. The written sources are the product of male scribes (trained professionals who applied their skills in reading and writing to tasks of administration) and, for the most part, reflect elite male activities. Archaeological remains provide only limited insight into attitudes, status, and gender roles.

Anthropologists theorize that women lost social standing and freedom as part of the transition from hunter-gatherer to agricultural

societies (see Chapter 1). Women previously had provided the bulk of the community's food from their gathering activities. But agricultural labor in a place like Mesopotamia depended on the hard physical work of dragging around a plow and digging irrigation channels and tended to be done by men. At the same time, the generation of a food surplus permitted families to have more children, and bearing and raising children became the primary occupation of many women. The amount of time given to the care of children made it hard for women to acquire the specialized skills of the scribe or artisan, though in rare instances women did fill these roles. Non-elite women who stayed at home must have been engaged in other tasks—helping with the harvest, planting vegetable gardens, milking cattle, cooking and baking, cleaning the house, fetching water, tending the household fire, and weaving baskets and textiles. Some women worked outside the household, in textile factories and breweries or as prostitutes, tavern keepers, bakers, or fortunetellers. Women had no apparent political role, but they had important economic rights and were able to own property, maintain control of their dowry, and even engage in trade.

There is evidence for a decline in the standing of women in the Semitic second millennium B.C.E. This development may be linked to the rise of an urbanized middle class and an increase in private wealth. Women could be used by their families to preserve and increase wealth through tactics such as (1) arranged marriages, which created alliances between families, and (2) the avoidance of marriage—and the resulting loss of a dowry—by dedicating certain girls to the service of a deity as "god's brides." The husband became more dominant in the household and had greater latitude in the laws relating to marriage and divorce. Although Mesopotamian society was generally monogamous, a man could obtain a second wife if the first gave him no children, and in the later stages of Mesopotamian history kings and others who could afford to do so had several wives. Some scholars believe that from the second millennium B.C.E. may originate the constraints on women that eventually became part of the Islamic tradition, such as the expectation that they confine themselves to

The impression made by a Mesopotamian cylinder seal   Seals indicated the identity of an individual and were impressed into wet clay or wax to "sign" legal documents or to mark ownership of an object. Here the owner of the seal stands before the goddess Ishtar, recognizable by her characteristic star symbol and lion. Ishtar (Sumerian Inanna), whose domains encompassed both love and violence, is dressed as a warrior. (Courtesy, Trustees of the British Museum)

the household and go veiled in public (see Chapter 10).

Gods, Priests, and Temples

The ancient Mesopotamians believed in a multitude of gods who embodied the forces of nature. For the Sumerians the god Anu was the sky, Enlil the air, Enki the water, Utu the sun, Nanna the moon. The emotional impulses of sexual attraction and violence were the domain of the goddess Inanna. People believed these gods were *anthropomorphic*—that is, like humans in form and conduct. They thought their gods had bodies and senses, sought nourishment from sacrifice, enjoyed the worship and obedience of humanity, and were driven by lust, love, hate, anger, and all the other emotions that motivated human beings. Generally speaking, the Mesopotamians feared their gods, who they believed were responsible for the changes that occurred without warning in the unpredictable

landscape in which they lived, and they sought to appease their deities by any means.

When the Semitic peoples became dominant, they equated their deities with those of the Sumerians. For example, the Sumerian gods Nanna and Utu became the Semitic Sin and Shamash, and the goddess Inanna became Ishtar. The myths of the Sumerian deities were transferred to their Semitic counterparts, and many of the same rituals continued to be practiced.

Particularly visible in the archaeological record is the public, state-organized religion. Each city contained temples to one or more patron divinities who protected the community and were given special devotion. Nippur, with its temple of the air-god Enlil, was especially venerated as a religious center for all the peoples of Sumer. The temple was regarded as the residence of the god, and the cult statue, which was located in a special interior shrine, was believed to be occupied by the life-force of the deity. Priests literally waited on this physical image of the divinity, anticipating and meeting its every need in a daily cycle of waking, bathing, dressing, feeding, moving around, entertaining, soothing, and revering. These efforts reflected the emphatic claim of the Babylonian Creation Myth that humankind had been created to be the servants of the gods. Several thousand priests may have staffed a large temple, such as the temple at Babylon of the chief god Marduk.

The office of priest was hereditary; fathers passed along sacred lore to their sons. Priests were paid in food taken from the crops raised on the deity's estates. The amount an individual received depended on his rank. Within the priesthood there was a complicated hierarchy of status and specialized function. The high priest performed the central acts in the great rituals. Certain priests made music to please the gods. Others knew the appropriate incantations for exorcising evil spirits. Still others were seers who interpreted dreams and divined the future by methods such as examining the organs of sacrificed animals, reading patterns in the rising incense smoke, or casting dice.

The temple precinct was surrounded by a high wall. The enclosed area contained the shrine of the chief deity, as well as open-air plazas, chapels for other gods, housing, dining facilities and offices for the priests and other members of the temple staff, and craft shops, storerooms, and service buildings to meet the needs of a large and busy organization. The most visible part of the temple precinct was the *ziqqurat*, a multistoried tower approached by ramps and stairs and built of mud brick. Modern scholars are not entirely certain of the ziqqurat's function and symbolic meaning.

Even harder to determine are the everyday beliefs and religious practices of the common people. Modern scholars do not know how accessible the temple buildings were to the general public. Individuals did place votive statues in the sanctuaries. They believed that these miniature replicas of themselves could continually beseech and seek the favor of the deity. The survival of many amulets (small charms meant to protect the bearer from evil) and representations of a host of demons suggest a widespread belief in the value of magic—the use of special words and rituals that allow people to manipulate and control the forces of nature. A headache was believed to be caused by a demon that could be driven out of the ailing body. Lamashtu, who was held responsible for miscarriages, could be frightened off if a pregnant woman wore an amulet with the likeness of the hideous but beneficent demon Pazuzu. In return for an appropriate gift or sacrifice, a god or goddess might be prevailed on to reveal information about the future.

The religion of the elite and the religion of ordinary people came together in great festivals such as the twelve-day New Year's Festival held each spring in Babylon to mark the beginning of a new agricultural cycle. The Babylonians believed that the world went through a cycle from birth to death each year, but they did not assume that the cycle would automatically recur every year. The New Year's Festival was a virtual restaging of the act of creation, an effort by all members of society to ensure the victory of life over death and the restarting of time.

Technology and Science

The ancient Mesopotamians, like all complex societies, developed a set of technologies which allowed them to exert some degree of control over their environment. The term "technology" comes from the Greek word *techne,* meaning "skill" or "specialized knowledge." Technology in the broadest sense can encompass both tools and machinery to manipulate the physical world and ideas that can influence the intellectual, emotional, and spiritual spheres in which human beings also operate, as, for instance, the religious knowledge of the priests.

A particularly important example of the latter type of technology is writing, which first appeared in Mesopotamia before 3300 B.C.E. The earliest inscribed tablets were found in the chief temple at Uruk and date from a time when the temple was the most important economic institution in the community. According to a plausible recent theory, writing originated from a system of tokens used to keep track of property—sheep, cattle, wagon wheels, and the like—as increases in the amount of accumulated wealth and the volume and complexity of commercial transactions strained the capacity of people's memory to preserve an accurate record. These tokens were made in the shape of the commodity and were inserted and sealed in a clay envelope. Pictures of the tokens were incised on the outside of the envelope as a reminder of what was inside. Eventually people realized that the incised pictures were an adequate record of the transaction, rendering the tokens inside redundant. These pictures became the first written symbols.

The earliest symbols were thus pictures of the objects they represented, but they could also stand for the sound of that word if it was part of a longer word. For example, the symbols *shu* for "hand" and *mu* for "water" could be combined to form *shumu* for "name." The commonest method of writing was with a sharpened reed on a moist clay tablet. Because the reed made wedge-shaped impressions, the early pictures were increasingly stylized into a combination of strokes and wedges that evolved into the *cuneiform* (Latin for "wedge-shaped") system of writing. Mastering this system of writing required years of training and practice. Several hundred signs were in use at any one time, as compared to the twenty-five or so signs required for an alphabetic system. In the "tablet-house," which may have been attached to a temple or palace, students were taught writing and mathematics by a headmaster and were tutored by older students called "big brothers." Members of the scribal class had prestige and regular employment because of their skill and thus may have been reluctant to simplify the cuneiform system. In the Old Babylonian period, the growth of the private commercial sector was accompanied by an increase in the number of people who could read and write. Nevertheless, only a small percentage of the population was literate. Kings and commanders normally did not know how to read and write and paid scribes to exercise this skill on their behalf.

Cuneiform is not a language but a system of writing. Developed originally for the Sumerian language, it was later adapted to express the Akkadian language of the Mesopotamian Semites as well as other languages of western Asia such as Hittite, Eblaite (see Voices and Visions:

Baked clay model of a sheep's liver (about 1700 B.C.E.) A diviner who examined the physical appearance of the liver of a sacrificed animal could deduce valuable information about the future or will of the gods. The cuneiform inscriptions on this model, which was probably used to teach divination, explain the significance of markings in different areas of the organ. (Courtesy, Trustees of the British Museum)

Ebla), Elamite, and Persian. The earliest documents are economic, but cuneiform is an outstanding example of a technology that had wide-ranging uses beyond the use for which it was originally conceived. In the early period, legal acts had been validated by the recitation of oral formulas and the performance of symbolic actions. After the development of cuneiform, written documents that were marked with the seal of the participants became the primary indicator of validation. In similar fashion the system of writing also came to be used for political, literary, religious, and scientific purposes.

Other technologies enabled the Mesopotamians to meet the challenges of their environment. As we have seen, irrigation was indispensable to agriculture and called for the construction and maintenance of canals, dams, and dikes. Appropriate means of transportation were developed for different terrains. Carts and sledges drawn

Ebla

One of the most exciting archaeological discoveries of the past half century was at Tell Mardih, near Aleppo in northern Syria, where, since the 1960's, Italian archaeologists have been unearthing the ancient city of Ebla (see Map 2.2). Excavation has focused both on the elevated citadel, where several palaces and temples have been found, and on the lower town. Besides the remains of buildings and artifacts, excavators stumbled upon the palace archives, several rooms filled with tablets. Approximately two thousand tablets were intact and many thousands more in fragmentary condition, the result of a fiery destruction of the palace. The tablets were inscribed with cuneiform symbols in two languages, Sumerian and the local Semitic dialect now called Eblaite. The tablets are mostly records of the palace economy, keeping track of the harvesting and distribution of food stocks, flocks of sheep, shearing of wool, manufacture of cloth, and collection of gold and silver tribute. There are also official letters and treaties between Ebla and other states, literary texts, and Sumerian-Eblaite dictionaries.

The pinnacle of its wealth and power occurred in the period from 2400 to 2250, when it controlled an extensive territory in northwest Syria and derived wealth from agriculture, sheepraising, and manufacturing cloth. Ebla played an important role in the trade routes between Mesopotamia and the Mediterranean, involving the exchange of timber, copper, and silver, available in the nearby mountains of Lebanon, Syria, and southwest Anatolia, and even blocks of lapis lazuli from distant Afghanistan.

This interstate commerce is illuminated by the following excerpts from a treaty between Ebla and the northern Mesopotamian city-state of Ashur:

Thus says Ebla's king to Ashur: Without my consent there will be no movement of emissaries in the country; you, Ja-dud, [will not authorize any movement of emissaries]; (only) I issue orders regarding commercial traffic. In case emissaries who have undertaken a journey of 20 days have exhausted all their supplies, you must, graciously, procure provisions for their stay at the trading post at market-price.

. . . In cases where emissaries go on a journey, their goods must not be touched; silver, oxen, sheep, son, daughter, wife, must not be taken, and you must not appropriate them.

The city-state of Kablul and (its) trade centers belong to Ebla's ruler; the city-state of Za-ar in Uziladu and (its) trade centers belong to Ebla's ruler; the city-state of Guttanum [and its trade centers] belong to Ebla's ruler. The subjects of Ebla's ruler in all the (aforesaid) trade centers are under the jurisdiction of Ebla's ruler, (whereas) the subjects of Ashur's ruler are under the jurisdiction of Ashur's ruler.

If an Eblaite fights with an Assyrian and the latter dies, then 50 rams will be given as penalty; [if an Assyrian fights with an Eblaite] and the latter dies, then 50 rams will be given as penalty.

(If) Ebla has received either a male or female citizen as a slave, and Ashur [requests] the house of Ebla for [their liberation], then Ebla will free the slaves, (but Ashur) must give 50 rams as compensation (to Ebla).

In case he (Ashur's ruler) does wrong, then the sun god, the storm god, and Venus, who are witnesses, will scatter his "word" on the steppe. Let there be no water for (his) emissaries who undertake a journey. You will have no permanent residence, but (on the contrary) you, Ja-dud, will begin a journey to perdition.

The discoveries at Ebla demonstrate the cultural vitality of third millennium Syria and the complexity of the relationships between various peoples in western Asia, as well as providing a wealth of detail about life in an early Middle Eastern city-state. What is the relationship between the kings of Ebla and Ashur? What common interests do they share? What kinds of problems and disputes are anticipated in this treaty, and how are they to be resolved? How are the terms of the treaty to be enforced?

Source: Giovanni Pettinato, *Ebla: A New Look at History* (1991), pp. 230–237.

by cattle were common in some locations. Boats and barges were more effective in the south, where numerous water channels cut up the landscape. In northern Mesopotamia, donkeys were the chief pack animals for overland caravans in the centuries before the advent of the camel (see Chapter 8).

Although the Mesopotamians had to import raw metal ore, they became quite skilled in metallurgy, mixing copper with arsenic or tin to make bronze. The stone implements of earlier eras continued to be produced in this period, for the poorest members of the population usually could not afford metal. Bronze, however, has the advantage of being more malleable than stone. Liquid bronze can be poured into molds, and hardened bronze takes a sharper edge than stone, is less likely to break, and is more easily repaired.

Resource-poor Mesopotamians possessed one commodity in abundance: clay. Mud bricks, whether dried in the sun or baked in an oven for greater durability, were their primary building material. Construction on a monumental scale—whether city walls, temples, or palaces—required considerable practical knowledge of architecture and engineering. For example, the reed mats that Mesopotamian builders laid between the mud-brick layers of ziqqurats served the same stabilizing purpose as girders in modern high-rise construction. The abundance of good clay also meant that pottery was the most common form of dishware and storage vessel. The potter's wheel was in use by 4000 B.C.E.

In the military sphere as well there were innovative developments—in organization, tactics, and weapons and other machinery of warfare. Early military forces were rallied when needed by calls for the able-bodied members of the community. The powerful states of the later third and second millennia B.C.E. built up professional armies. In the early second millennium B.C.E. horses appeared in western Asia, and the horse-drawn chariot came into vogue, carrying close to enemy lines a driver and an archer who could unleash a volley of arrows. Using increasingly effective siege machinery, Mesopotamian soldiers could climb over, undermine, or knock down the walls protecting the cities of their enemies.

In many other ways the Mesopotamians sought to gain control of their physical environment. They used a base-60 number system (the origin of the seconds and minutes we use today) in which numbers were expressed as fractions or multiples of 60, in contrast to our base-10 system. Advances in mathematics and careful observation of celestial phenomena made the Mesopotamians sophisticated practitioners of astronomy. Mesopotamian priests compiled lists of omens or unusual sightings on earth and in the heavens together with a record of the events that coincided with them. They consulted these texts at critical times, for they believed that if, at some future time, a similar omen appeared, the event that originally occurred with the omen would occur again. The underlying premise here was that material phenomena, from the macrocosmic to the microscopic, were interconnected in mysterious but undeniable ways.

EGYPT

Nowhere is it more apparent how profoundly natural environment shapes the history and culture of a society than in ancient Egypt. Located at the intersection of Asia and Africa, Egypt is protected by surrounding barriers of desert and a harborless seacoast. Mesopotamia was open to migration or invasion and was dependent on imported resources. In contrast, natural isolation and essential self-sufficiency allowed Egypt to develop a unique culture that for long periods of time had relatively little to do with other civilizations.

The Land of Egypt: "Gift of the Nile"

The fundamental geographical feature of Egypt, ancient and modern, is the Nile River. The world's longest river, the Nile originates from Lake Victoria and from several large tributaries in the highlands of tropical Africa and flows northward, carving a narrow valley between the

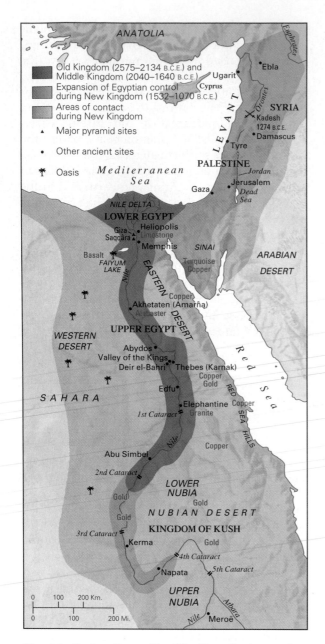

Map 2.3 Ancient Egypt The Nile River, flowing south to north, carved out of the surrounding desert a narrow green valley which became heavily settled in antiquity.

the Mediterranean the river breaks up into a number of channels to form a triangular delta. Virtually the entire population of the region lives in that twisting, green ribbon alongside the river or in the Nile Delta. The rest of the country, 90 percent or more, is a bleak and inhospitable desert of mountains, rocks, and dunes. The ancient Egyptians recognized this stark dichotomy between the low-lying, life-sustaining "Black Land" with its dark soil alongside the river and the elevated, deadly "Red Land" of the desert. With justification and insight did the fifth-century B.C.E. Greek traveler Herodotus call Egypt the "gift of the Nile."

The river was the main means of travel and communication. In antiquity, boats sailed southward, upriver, propelled by the perpetual following wind, and were rowed northward, downriver. The orientation of the country was along the axis of the river. The most important cities were located considerably upstream. Because the river flows from south to north, the Egyptians called the southern part of the country "Upper Egypt," the northern part "Lower Egypt." The southern boundary of Egypt in most periods was the First Cataract—the northernmost of a series of impassable rocks and rapids below Aswan (about 500 miles [800 kilometers] south of the Mediterranean)—though at times Egyptian control extended farther south into what they called "Kush" (later Nubia, the southern part of the modern state of Egypt and northern Sudan). The Egyptians also settled a number of large oases—green and habitable "islands" in the midst of the desert—which lay some distance west of the river.

The hot climate with plenty of sunshine was favorable for agriculture, but south of the delta there is virtually no rainfall. Thus agriculture was entirely dependent on river water. Throughout Egyptian history great efforts were made to increase the amount of land suitable for planting by digging irrigation channels to carry water out into the desert. And in the basin of Lake Faiyum, a large depression west of the Nile, successful drainage techniques rendered the lake smaller and allowed more land to be reclaimed for agriculture.

Each September, with considerable regularity, the river overflowed its banks, spreading water

chain of hills on either side, until it reaches the Mediterranean Sea (see Map 2.3). The land through which it flows is mostly desert, but the river makes green a narrow strip on either side of its banks. About 100 miles (160 kilometers) from

Limestone relief of an Egyptian cargo boat, from a tomb at Saqqara, ca. 2300 B.C.E. The large sail, used when going upstream, is rolled up at the moment as the vessel floats downstream with the current (northwards). The steersman uses the rudder at the rear (right), while men with long poles watch out for shallows. This vessel is carrying a large block of stone from one of the quarries upriver for use in a monumental construction project. (Egyptian Museum, Cairo)

out into the depressed basins. Unlike the Mesopotamians, the Egyptians did not need to construct dams and mechanical devices to lift river water to channels and fields. And unlike the Tigris and Euphrates, whose flood came at a disadvantageous time, the Nile flooded at just the right time for grain agriculture. When the waters receded, they left behind a fertile layer of mineral-rich silt, and farmers could easily plant their crops in the moist soil. The Egyptians had many versions of the Creation Myth, but it always involved the emergence of life from a primeval swamp.

The height of the river when it crested was crucial to the prosperity of the country. "Nilometers"—stone staircases with incised units of measure—were placed along the river's edge to gauge the flood surge. When the flood was too high, dikes were washed out and much damage resulted. When the flood was too low for a series of years, the country was plunged into famine and decline. Indeed, the ebb and flow of successful and failed regimes seems to be linked to the cycle of floods. Nevertheless, in most eras there was a remarkable stability to this landscape, and Egyptians viewed the universe as an orderly and beneficent place.

Egypt was well endowed with natural resources. Egyptians used reeds that grew in marshy areas and along the banks of the river to make sails, ropes, and a kind of paper. Hunters pursued the wild animals and birds that abounded in the marshes and on the edge of the desert, and fishermen lowered their nets into the river. Building stone could be quarried and floated downstream from a number of locations in southern Egypt. Clay for mud bricks and pottery could be found almost everywhere. Copper and turquoise deposits in the Sinai desert to the east and gold from Nubia to the south were within reach and the state organized armed expeditions and mustered forced labor to exploit these resources. Thus Egypt was self-sufficient to a much larger degree than Mesopotamia.

Farming villages appeared in Egypt as early as 5500 B.C.E. as inhabitants of the Nile Valley borrowed and adapted knowledge of how to domesticate various species of plants and animals that had emerged several millennia earlier in western Asia. However, the circumstances that led to Egypt becoming a focal point of civilization were due, at least in part, to a change in climate that took place gradually from the fifth to the third millennium B.C.E. Until that time, the Sahara, the vast region that is now the world's largest desert, had a relatively mild and wet climate and lakes and grasslands that supported a variety of plant and animal species as well as populations of hunter-gatherers (see Chapter 8). As the climate changed and the Sahara began to dry up and become a desert, some displaced groups migrated into the Nile Valley.

Divine Kingship

The increase in population produced new, more complex levels of political organization, including a form of local kingship. The pivotal event, in the view of later generations of Egyptians, was the conquest of these smaller units and the unification of all Egypt by Menes, a ruler from the south, around 3100 B.C.E. Although some scholars question whether Menes was a historical or mythical figure, many authorities equate him with Narmer, a historical ruler who is represented on a decorated slate palette that shows a king exulting over defeated enemies. Later kings of Egypt were referred to as "Rulers of the Two Lands"—Upper and Lower Egypt—and were depicted with two crowns and implements symbolizing the unification of the country. In contrast to Mesopotamia, Egypt was unified early in its history.

The system that historians use to organize Egyptian history is based on thirty dynasties (sequences of kings from the same family) identified by Manetho, an Egyptian from the third century B.C.E. The rise and fall of dynasties often reflects the dominance of different parts of the country. At a broader level of generalization, scholars refer to the "Old," "Middle," and "New Kingdoms," each a period of centralized political power and brilliant cultural achievement, punc-

tuated by "Intermediate Periods" of political fragmentation and cultural decline. Although experts disagree about specific dates for these periods, the chronology (see page 49) is representative of current opinion.

The central institution in the Egyptian state was the *pharaoh*, or king. From the period of the Old Kingdom if not earlier, the principle was established that the king was the son of the sun-god, Re. Egyptians believed that their king was sent to earth by the gods and that his function on earth was to maintain *ma'at*, the divinely authorized order of the universe. He was the indispensable link between his people and the gods, and through his benevolent rule he ensured the welfare and prosperity of the country. The Egyptians' conception of a divine king who was the source of law and authority may explain the apparent lack of efforts to publish in Egypt an impersonal code of law comparable to Hammurabi's Code in Mesopotamia.

In a very real sense, all of Egypt belonged to the king, and everyone served him. When the monarchy was strong, it controlled the country and virtually every facet of people's lives. An extensive administrative apparatus began at the village level and progressed to the districts into which the country was divided and, finally, to the central government based in the capital city.

Various cities served as the royal capital at different times, for the capital was usually the original power base of the dynasty that occupied the throne. Memphis, on the Lower Nile near the apex of the Delta (close to Cairo, the modern capital), held this central position during the Old Kingdom. Thebes, far to the south, came to prominence during much of the Middle and New Kingdom periods.

The royal bureaucracy used writing to keep track of land, labor, products, and people. It enabled the ruler to extract as taxes a substantial portion of the annual revenues of the country—at times as much as 50 percent. The income was used to subsidize the palace, bureaucracy, and army, to build and maintain temples, and to raise great monuments of the ruler's reign. Because the villages lined up along the river, it was easy for the government to monitor their activities and extract their surplus resources.

The royal administration maintained a monopoly over key sectors of the economy and controlled long-distance trade. Private enterprise was almost nonexistent. Everyone worked in some capacity for the state, though independent exchanges of goods surely took place on a small scale at the local level. This was quite different from Mesopotamia, where commerce increasingly fell into the hands of an acquisitive urban middle class.

This system of kingship and administration crystallized relatively quickly after the unification of the country. Early rulers may have been influenced by the emergent civilization of Mesopotamia, for in the late fourth millennium B.C.E. trading linked Egypt and western Asia. Nevertheless, they adapted what they borrowed and gave such institutions a uniquely Egyptian form. After this early rush of innovation, Egyptian civilization remained relatively static and resistant to change for nearly three millennia, in large part because of the natural isolation of the country.

The death of the king was a critical moment in the life of the country, because so much depended on him. Every effort was made to ensure the well-being of his soul on its perilous journey to rejoin the company of the gods. Massive resources were poured into the construction of royal tombs, the celebration of elaborate funerary rites, and the sustenance of kings' souls in the afterlife by perpetual offerings in funerary chapels attached to the royal tombs. Early rulers were buried in flat-topped, rectangular tombs made of mud brick. But around 2630 B.C.E., Djoser, a Third Dynasty king, ordered the construction for himself at Saqqara, about 20 miles south of the Delta, of a spectacular stepped pyramid consisting of a series of stone platforms laid one on top of the other. Rulers in the Fourth Dynasty filled in the steps to create the smooth-sided, limestone pyramids that have become the most memorable symbol of ancient Egypt. Between 2550 and 2490 B.C.E., the pharaohs Khufu and Khefren erected huge pyramids at Giza, several miles to the north of Saqqara, the largest stone structures ever built by human hands. Khufu's pyramid originally reached a height of 481 feet (147 meters).

Periods of Egyptian History

3100–2575 B.C.E.	Early Dynastic
2575–2134 B.C.E.	Old Kingdom
2134–2040 B.C.E.	First Intermediate Period
2040–1640 B.C.E.	Middle Kingdom
1640–1532 B.C.E.	Second Intermediate Period
1532–1070 B.C.E.	New Kingdom

Egyptians accomplished all this construction with bronze tools and no machinery other than simple levers, pulleys, and rollers. What really made it possible was almost unlimited human muscle power. Calculations of the human resources needed to build a pyramid within the lifetime of the ruler suggest that large numbers of people must have been pressed into service for part of each year, probably during the flood season, when no agricultural work could be done. Although this labor was compulsory, the Egyptian masses probably regarded it as a kind of religious service that helped to ensure the continuity of their beneficent environment. Virtually all the surplus resources of the country went into the construction of these artificial mountains of stone. In the end, the outlay was more than the country could sustain for long. The age of the great pyramids lasted only about a century, although pyramids continued to be built on a smaller scale for two millennia afterward.

Administration and Communication

The need for extensive records of the resources of the country led to the creation of a complex administrative bureaucracy. Officials received grants of land from the king and were supported by dependent peasants who worked the land.

The hallmark of this administrative class was literacy. A system of writing had been developed by the beginning of the Old Kingdom, perhaps under the influence of Mesopotamia but with distinctively Egyptian qualities. *Hieroglyphics,* the earliest form of this writing system, were picture symbols standing for words, syllables, or individual sounds. Our ability to read ancient Egyptian writing is due to the decipherment, in the early nineteenth century C.E., of the Rosetta Stone, a document from the second century B.C.E. that gave both hieroglyphic and Greek versions of the same text.

Hieroglyphic writing long continued in use on monuments and ornamental inscriptions. By 2500 B.C.E., however, a cursive script, in which the original pictorial nature of the symbol was less readily apparent, had been developed for the everyday needs of administrators and copyists working with ink on a writing material called *papyrus*, after the reed from which it was made. The stems of the papyrus reed were laid out in a vertical and horizontal grid pattern and then pounded with a soft mallet until the moist fibers merged to form a sheet of writing material. The plant grew only in Egypt but was in demand throughout the ancient world and was exported in large quantities. Indeed, the word *paper* is derived from Greek and Roman words for papyrus.

Writing came to be used for many purposes other than administrative recordkeeping. A large written literature developed—tales of adventure and magic, love poetry, religious hymns, and manuals of instruction on technical subjects. Workshops attached to the temples produced copies of traditional texts.

When the monarchy was strong, officials were appointed and promoted on the basis of merit and accomplishment. Lower-level officials were assigned to work in villages and district capitals; high-ranking officials served in the royal capital. When Old Kingdom officials died, they were buried in tombs laid out around the monumental tomb of the king so that they could serve him in death as they had done in life.

One sign of the breakdown of centralized power in the late Old Kingdom and First Intermediate Period was the presence of officials' tombs in their home districts, where they spent much of their time and exercised power more or less independently. Another sign was the tendency of administrative posts to become hereditary. Throughout Egyptian history there is an underlying tension between the centralizing power of the monarchy and the decentralizing forces created by the Egyptian bureaucracy. The early monarchs of the Middle Kingdom responded to the fragmentation of the preceding period by reducing the power and prerogatives of the old elite and creating a new middle class of administrators.

It has often been said that Egypt was a land of villages and did not have any real cities, because the political capitals were really extensions of the palace and central administration. In Mesopotamia, in contrast, cities were not only the basic political units but also centers of economic activity in which many people produced wealth through specialized, nonagricultural tasks. It is true that, in comparison with Mesopotamia, a far larger percentage of the Egyptian population lived in rural villages and engaged in agriculture, and that the essential wealth of Egypt resided to a higher degree in the land and its products. But there were towns and cities in ancient Egypt, although they were less crucial than Mesopotamian urban centers to the economic and cultural dynamism of the country. Unfortunately, archaeologists for the most part have been unable to excavate them, because many ancient urban sites in Egypt have been continuously inhabited and lie beneath modern communities.

During the Old and Middle Kingdoms, Egypt was isolationist in its foreign policy. The king maintained limited contact with the other advanced civilizations of the region but did not actively seek to expand beyond Egypt's natural boundaries. When necessary, local militia units backed up a small standing army of professional soldiers. The nomadic tribes living in the eastern and western deserts and the Libyans in the northwest were a nuisance rather than a real danger to the Nile Valley and were readily handled by the Egyptian military. Egypt's interests abroad focused primarily on maintaining access to valuable resources rather than on acquiring territory. Trade with the coastal towns of the Levant (modern Israel, Lebanon, and Syria) brought in cedar wood. In return, Egypt exported grain, papyrus, and gold.

In all periods the Egyptians had a particularly strong interest in goods that came from the

The pyramid of Khephren at Giza, ca. 2500 B.C.E. With a width of 704 feet (214.5 meters) and a height of 471 feet (143.5 meters), it is only eight feet shorter than the nearby Great Pyramid of Khufu. The construction of these massive edifices depended on relatively simple techniques of stonecutting, transport (the stones were floated downriver on boats and rolled out to the site on sledges), and lifting (the stones were dragged up the face of the pyramid on mud brick ramps). However, the surveying and engineering skills required to level the platform, lay out the measurements, and securely position the blocks were very sophisticated and have withstood the test of time. (Werner Forman/Art Resource, NY)

south. Nubia contained rich sources of gold (in Chapter 3 we examine the rise of a civilization in Nubia that, though heavily influenced by Egypt, created a vital and original culture that lasted for more than two thousand years). The southern course of the Nile offered the only easily passable corridor to sub-Saharan Africa.

In the Old Kingdom, Egyptian noblemen living at Aswan on the southern border led donkey caravans south to trade for gold, incense, and products of tropical Africa such as ivory, ebony, and exotic animals. A line of forts along the southern border protected Egypt from attack. In the second millennium B.C.E., Egyptian forces struck south into Nubia, extending the Egyptian border as far as the Third Cataract and taking possession of the gold fields. Still farther to the south, perhaps in the northern coastal region of present-day Somalia, lay the fabled land of Punt, source of the fragrant myrrh resin that priests burned on the altars of the Egyptian gods. Normally this commodity passed through the hands of a series of intermediaries before reaching Egypt, but in the fifteenth century B.C.E. a naval expedition sailed down the Red Sea to initiate direct contacts between Punt and Egypt (see Chapter 3).

The People of Egypt

The population of ancient Egypt—perhaps between 1 million and 1½ million people—was physically heterogeneous, ranging from dark-skinned people related to the populations of sub-Saharan Africa to lighter-skinned people akin to the Berber and Arab populations of North Africa and western Asia. Although Egypt was not subject to the large-scale migrations and invasions that Mesopotamia experienced, throughout the historical period various groups of settlers trickled into the Nile Valley and assimilated with the people already living there.

Social stratification clearly existed in Egypt: some people possessed more status, wealth, and power than others. But it does not appear that a rigid class structure emerged. At the top of the social hierarchy were the king and high-level officials. In the middle were lower-level officials, local leaders, priests and other professionals, artisans, and well-to-do farmers. At the bottom were peasants, the vast majority of the population. Peasants lived in rural villages. Their lives were filled with the seasonally changing tasks of agriculture—plowing, sowing, tending emerging shoots, reaping, threshing, and storing grain or other products of the soil. Plowing was relatively easy in the soft, silt-laden soil left behind after the departure of the floodwaters. The irrigation network of channels, basins, and dikes had to be maintained, improved, and extended. Domesticated animals—cattle, sheep, goats, and fowl—and fish supplemented their diet. Inhabitants of the same village must have shared implements, work animals, and storage facilities, as well as helped one another at peak times in the agricultural cycle and in the construction of houses and other buildings. They also prayed and feasted together at festivals to the local gods and other public celebrations. Villagers periodically were required to contribute labor to state projects, such as construction of the pyramids. If the burden of taxation or compulsory service proved too

great, few avenues of resistance were available to villagers other than running away into the inhospitable desert.

This account of the lives of ordinary Egyptians is largely conjectural because the numerous villages of ancient Egypt, like those of Mesopotamia, left few traces in the archaeological or literary record. Tomb paintings of the elite sometimes depict the lives of common folk. The artists employed pictorial conventions to indicate status, such as obesity for the possessors of wealth and comfort, baldness and deformity for members of the working classes. Poetry frequently uses metaphors of farming and hunting, and legal documents on papyruses preserved in the hot, dry sands tell of property transactions and the disputes of ordinary people.

Slavery existed on a limited scale but was of little significance for the economy. Prisoners of war, condemned criminals, and debtors could be found on the country estates or in the households of the king and the upper classes. Treatment of slaves was relatively humane, and they could be given their freedom.

Obstacles also deprive us of any vivid sense of the experiences of women in ancient Egypt. Some information is available about the lives of women of the upper classes, but it is filtered through the brushes and pens of male artists and scribes. Egyptian women had rights over their dowry in case of divorce, they could own property, and they could will their property to whomever they wished. Historical evidence suggests that at certain times queens and queen-mothers played a significant behind-the-scenes role in the politics of the royal court. Tomb paintings show women of the royal family and elite classes accompanying their husbands and engaging in typical activities of domestic life. They are depicted with dignity and affection, though clearly in a subordinate position to the men. The artistic convention of depicting men with a dark red and women with a yellow flesh tone implies that the elite woman's proper sphere was assumed to be indoors, away from the searing sun.

In the beautiful love poetry of the New Kingdom the lovers address each other in terms of apparent equality and express emotions akin to our own ideal of romantic love. We cannot be sure how accurately this poetry represents the prevalent attitude in other periods of Egyptian history or among groups other than the educated elite. The limited evidence, however, does suggest that women in ancient Egypt were treated more respectfully and had more social freedom than women in other ancient societies such as Mesopotamia.

Belief and Knowledge

The religion of the Egyptians was rooted in the physical landscape of the Nile Valley and in the vision of cosmic order that this environment evoked. The consistency of their environment— the sun rose every day into a clear and cloudless sky, and the river flooded on schedule every year, ensuring a bounteous harvest—persuaded the Egyptians that the natural world was a place of recurrent cycles and periodic renewal. The sun-god, Re, was said to journey in a boat through the Underworld at night, fighting off the attacks of demonic serpents so that he could be born anew each morning. The story of Osiris, a god who once ruled the land of Egypt, was especially popular. Osiris was slain by his adversary Seth, who then scattered the dismembered pieces. Isis, Osiris's devoted wife, found the remnants and Horus, his son, took revenge on Seth. Osiris was restored to life and installed as king of the Underworld, and his example gave people hope of a new life in a world beyond this one.

In normal times the king—himself the son of Re, the sun-god—was the chief priest of Egypt, intervening with the gods on behalf of his land and people. When a particular town attained special significance as the capital of a ruling dynasty, the chief god of that town became prominent across the land. Thus did Ptah of Memphis, Re of Heliopolis, and Amon of Thebes become gods of all Egypt, serving to unify the country and strengthen the monarchy.

Egyptian rulers took a special interest in building new temples, refurbishing old ones, and making lavish gifts to the gods, as well as overseeing the construction of their own monumental tombs. Thus a considerable portion of the wealth of Egypt was used for religious purposes as part of a ceaseless effort to win the gods' favor, maintain the continuity of divine kingship, and ensure the renewal of the life-giving forces that sustained the world.

The many gods of ancient Egypt were diverse in origin and nature. Some deities were normally depicted with animal heads; others were always given human form. Few myths about the origins and adventures of the gods have survived, but there must have been a rich oral tradition. Many towns had temples in which locally prominent deities were thought to reside. Cult activities were carried out in the privacy of the inner reaches of the temples, where priests daily served the needs of the deity by attending to his or her statue. As in Mesopotamia, some temples came to possess extensive landholdings worked by dependent peasants, and the priests who administered the deity's wealth played an influential role locally and sometimes even throughout the land.

During great festivals, a boat-shaped litter carrying the shrouded statue and cult items of the deity was paraded around the town. Such occasions allowed large numbers of people to have contact with the deity and to participate in a mass outpouring of devotion and celebration. Little is known about the day-to-day beliefs and practices of the common people, however. In the household family members revered and made small offerings to Bes, the grotesque god of marriage and domestic happiness, to local deities, and to the family's ancestors. Amulets and depictions of demonic figures reflect the prevalence of magical practices. In later times Greeks and Romans regarded Egypt as a place where the devotion to magic was especially strong.

Egyptians believed fervently in the reality of the afterlife and made extensive preparations for a safe and successful passage to the next world and a comfortable existence once they arrived there. One common belief was that death was a journey beset with hazards along the way. The Egyptian Book of the Dead, which has been found in many excavated tombs, provided guidance for those making the journey. It contained rituals and prayers to protect the soul of the deceased at each point of the trip. The final and most important challenge was the weighing of the deceased's heart in the presence of the judges of the Underworld to determine whether the traveler had led a good life and deserved to reach the ultimate blessed destination.

Along with Egyptians' obsession with the afterlife went great concern about the physical condition of the cadaver. The Egyptians perfected techniques of mummification to preserve the dead body. The idea probably derived from the early practice of burying the dead in the hot, dry sand on the edge of the desert, where bodies decomposed slowly. The elite classes utilized the most expensive kind of mummification. The brain and certain vital organs were removed, preserved, and stored in stone jars laid out around the corpse. Body cavities were filled with

A scene from the Egyptian Book of the Dead, ca. 1300 B.C.E. The mummy of the deceased, a royal scribe named Hunefar, is approached by members of his household before being placed in the tomb. Behind Hunefar is Anubis, the jackal-headed god, who will conduct the spirit of the deceased to the afterlife. The Book of the Dead provided Egyptians with the necessary instructions to complete this arduous journey and gain a blessed existence in the afterlife. (Courtesy, Trustees of the British Museum)

various packing materials. The cadaver was immersed for long periods in dehydrating and preserving chemicals and eventually was wrapped in linen cloth. The mummy was then placed in one or more decorated wooden caskets and was entombed.

Tombs usually were placed at the edge of the desert so as not to tie up valuable farmland. They were filled with pictures and samples of food and the objects of everyday life, so that the deceased would have whatever he or she might need in the next life. From this practice of stocking the tomb with utilitarian and luxury household objects we have gleaned much of what we know about ancient Egyptian life. Small figurines called *shawabtis* were included to play the part of servants and to take the place of the deceased in case the regimen of the afterlife included periodic calls for compulsory labor. The elite classes, at least, had chapels attached to their tombs and left endowments to subsidize the daily attendance of a priest and offerings of foodstuffs to sustain their souls for all eternity.

The form of the tomb also reflected the wealth and status of the deceased. Common people had to make do with simple pit graves or small mud-brick chambers. The privileged classes built larger tombs and covered the walls with pictures and inscriptions. Kings erected pyramids and other grand edifices, employing subterfuges to hide the sealed chamber containing the body and treasures, as well as curses and other magical precautions, to foil tomb robbers. Rarely did they succeed, however. Nearly all the tombs that archaeologists have discovered had been plundered.

The ancient Egyptians made remarkable advances in many areas of knowledge and developed an array of advantageous technologies. They learned much about chemistry through their experiments to find ever better methods for preserving the dead body. The process of mummification also provided ample opportunities to learn about human anatomy, and as a result Egyptian doctors were in high demand in the courts of western Asia because of their relatively advanced medical knowledge and techniques.

The centrality of the Nile flood to their way of life spurred the Egyptians to find ways to better control and profit from this critical event. They devoted much effort to constructing, maintaining, and expanding the network of irrigation channels and holding basins. They needed mathematics to survey and measure the dimensions of fields and calculate the quantity of agricultural produce owed to the state. Sophisticated astronomical knowledge resulted from their efforts to calculate the time when the Nile would rise.

The construction of pyramids, temple complexes, and other monumental building projects called for great skill in engineering and architecture. Vast quantities of earth had to be moved. Large stones had to be quarried, dragged on rollers, floated downstream on barges, lifted into place, then carved to the exact size needed and made smooth. Long underground passageways were excavated to connect the mortuary temple by the river with the tomb near the desert's edge, and on several occasions Egyptian kings dredged out a canal more than 50 miles (80 kilometers) long in order to join the Nile Valley to the Red Sea and expedite the transport of goods.

Archaeologists recently discovered an 8-mile-long road (13 kilometers), made of slabs of sandstone and limestone and connecting a rock quarry with Faiyum Lake. Dating to the second half of the third millennium B.C.E., it is the oldest known paved road in the world. Relatively simple technologies facilitated the transportation of goods and people: carts pulled by draft animals, river barges for floating huge stones from the quarries, and lightweight ships equipped with sails and oars—well suited for travel on the peaceful Nile and sometimes used for voyages on the Mediterranean and Red Seas.

THE INDUS VALLEY CIVILIZATION

Civilization arose almost as early in India as it did in Mesopotamia and Egypt. Just as each of the Middle Eastern civilizations was centered on a great river valley, civilization in India originated on a fertile floodplain. In the valley of the Indus River, settled farming created the agricultural surplus essential to urbanized society.

Natural Environment

In the central portion of the Indus river valley, in the Sind region of modern Pakistan, a plain of more than 1 million acres (400,000 hectares) lies between the mountains to the west and the Thar Desert to the east (see Map 2.1). Because the Indus River carries a great load of silt, over the ages the riverbed and its containing banks have risen above the level of the plain. Twice a year the river overflows its banks and spreads for as much as 10 miles (16 kilometers). In the spring, in March and April, melting snow feeds the river's sources in the Pamir and Himalaya mountain ranges. Then in August, the great monsoon (seasonal wind) blowing off the ocean to the southwest brings rains that swell the streams flowing into the Indus. As a result, farmers in this region of little rainfall are able to plant and harvest two crops a year. In ancient times, the Hakra River, which has since dried up, ran parallel to the Indus about 25 miles (40 kilometers) to the east and provided a second area suitable for intensive cultivation.

Several adjacent regions were also part of this fertile zone. To the northeast is the Punjab, where five rivers converge to form the main course of the Indus. Lying beneath the shelter of the towering Himalaya range, the Punjab receives considerably more rainfall than the central plain but is less prone to flooding. From this region settlements spread as far as Delhi in northwest India. Another zone of settlement extended south into the great delta where the Indus empties into the Arabian Sea, and southeast into India's hook-shaped Kathiawar Peninsula, an area of alluvial plains and coastal marshes. The territory covered by the Indus Valley civilization is roughly equivalent in size to modern France—much larger than the zone of Mesopotamian civilization.

Material Culture

The Indus Valley civilization flourished from approximately 2900 to 1800 B.C.E. Although archaeologists have located several hundred sites, the culture is best known from the archaeological remains of two great cities first discovered nearly eighty years ago. The ancient names of these cities are unknown, so they are referred to by modern names: Harappa and Mohenjo-Daro. Unfortunately, a rise in the water table at these sites has made excavation of the lowest and earliest levels of settlement virtually impossible.

The identity, origins, and fate of the people who created and maintained this advanced civilization for more than a thousand years are in dispute. Until recently, scholars assumed that they were dark-skinned speakers of the Dravidian languages whose descendants were later pushed out of the north into central and southern India by invading Indo-European nomads around 1500 B.C.E. Studies of skeletal evidence, however, indicate that the population of these lands remained stable from ancient times to the present. Scholars now think that settled agriculture in this part of the world dates back to at least 5000 B.C.E. The precise relationship between the Indus Valley civilization and several earlier cultural complexes in the Indus Valley and in the hilly lands to the west is unclear. Also unclear are the forces giving rise to the urbanization, population increase, and technological advances that occurred in the early third millennium B.C.E. Nevertheless, the case for continuity seems stronger than the case for a sudden migration due to the movement of new peoples into the valley.

Like the Mesopotamians and Egyptians, the people of the Indus Valley had a system of writing. They used more than four hundred signs to represent syllables and words. Archaeologists have recovered thousands of inscribed seal stones and copper tablets. Unfortunately, these documents have not yet provided us with a picture of the society, because no one has been able to decipher them.

This society produced major urban centers. Harappa, the smaller of the major urban centers excavated so far, was 3½ miles (506 kilometers) in circumference and may have housed a population of 35,000. Mohenjo-Daro was several times larger. There are marked similarities in the planning and construction of these cities. High, thick brick walls surrounded each. The streets were laid out on a grid pattern. Covered drainpipes carried away waste. The regular size of the streets and length of the city blocks, as well as the uniformity of the mud bricks used in construction, may be evidence of a strong central authority. The seat of this authority may have been located in the citadel—an elevated, enclosed compound containing large buildings. Nearby stood well-ventilated structures that scholars think were storehouses of grain for feeding the urban population and for export. The presence of barracks may point to some regimentation of the skilled artisans.

A common assumption has been that these urban centers dominated the rural hinterland around them, though there is no proof that they did. Various factors may account for the location of the chief centers, and different centers may have had different functions. Mohenjo-Daro seems to dominate the great floodplain of the Indus. Harappa, which is nearly 500 miles (805 kilometers) from Mohenjo-Daro, seems to be on a kind of frontier between farmland and herding land, for no other settlements have been found west of its location. Harappa may have served as a "gateway" to the natural resources of the northwest, such as copper, tin, and precious stones. Seaports to the south would also have had a commercial function, expediting seaborne trade with the Persian Gulf.

Mohenjo-Daro and Harappa have received the most attention from archaeologists, and published accounts of the Indus Valley civilization have tended to treat those urban centers as the norm. Most people, however, lived in smaller settlements. Two intriguing features of the Indus Valley civilization are the considerable standardization of styles and shapes for many kinds of artifacts and the fact that the full range of materials, as well as the types and styles of artifacts, is found not only in the large cities but also in the smaller settlements. Some scholars suggest that this standardization may be due not to a strong and authoritarian central government but rather to extensive exchange and trading of goods within the zone of this civilization.

There is a greater abundance of metal in the Indus Valley than in Mesopotamia or Egypt, and most of the metal objects that archaeologists have found in the Indus Valley are utilitarian—

tools and other useful objects. In contrast, metal objects unearthed in Mesopotamia and Egypt tend to be decorative—jewelry and the like. Moreover, these metal objects were available to a large cross-section of the Indus Valley population, but in the Middle East metals were primarily reserved for the elite classes.

The civilization of the Indus Valley possessed impressive technological capabilities. These people were adept in the technology of irrigation. They used the potter's wheel, and they laid the foundations of large public buildings with mud bricks baked in a kiln, because sun-dried bricks exposed to floodwaters would quickly dissolve. Smiths worked skillfully with various metals—gold, silver, copper, and tin. The varying ratios of tin to copper in their bronze objects suggest that they were acutely aware of the hardness of different mixtures and conserved the relatively rare tin by using the smallest amount necessary, since, for example, knives need not be as hard as axes.

Archaeological evidence proves the people of the Indus Valley had widespread trading contacts. Thanks to passes through the mountains in the northwest, they had ready access to the valuable resources found in eastern Iran and Afghanistan, as well as to ore deposits in western India. These resources included metals (such as copper and tin), precious stones (lapis lazuli, jade, and turquoise), building stone, and timber. Rivers served as major thoroughfares for the movement of goods within the zone of Indus Valley culture. It has been suggested that the undeciphered writing on the many seal stones that have been found may convey the names of merchants who stamped their wares.

The inhabitants of Mesopotamia and of the Indus Valley obtained raw materials from some of the same sources, and Indus Valley seal stones have been found in the Tigris-Euphrates Valley. Thus some scholars believe that Indus Valley merchants served as middlemen in the long-distance trade, obtaining raw materials from the lands of west-central Asia and shipping them to the Persian Gulf.

We know little about the political, social, economic, and religious structures of Indus Valley society. Attempts have been made to demon-

Bronze statuette from the Indus Valley   Found in a house in Mohenjo-Daro, it represents a young woman whose only apparel is a necklace and an armful of bracelets. Appearing relaxed and confident, she has been identified by some scholars as a dancer. (National Museum, New Delhi)

strate the presence at this early date of many cultural features that are characteristic of later periods of Indian history (see Chapter 7), including sociopolitical institutions (a system of hereditary occupational groups, the predominant political role of priests), architectural forms (bathing tanks like those later found in Hindu temples, private interior courtyards in houses), and religious beliefs and practices (depictions of gods and sacred animals on the seal stones, a cult of the mother-goddess). Much of this work is highly speculative, however, and further knowledge about this society can only come from additional archaeological finds and decipherment of the Indus Valley script.

Transformation of the Indus Valley Civilization

The Indus Valley cities were abandoned sometime after 1800 B.C.E. Archaeologists once thought that invaders destroyed them, but now they believe that this civilization suffered "systems failure"—the breakdown of the fragile interrelationship of the political, social, and economic systems that sustain order and prosperity. The precipitating cause may have been one or more natural disasters, such as an earthquake or massive flooding. Gradual ecological changes may also have played a role.

The Hakra river system dried up, and salinization (an increase in the amount of salt in the soil, inhibiting plant growth) and erosion may have taken their toll (see Environment and Technology: Environmental Stress in the Indus Valley). Towns no longer on the river, ports no longer by the sea, and regions suffering a loss of fertile soil and water would have necessitated the relocation of large portions of the population and a change in the livelihood of those who remained. The causes, patterns, and pace of change probably varied in different areas; urbanization is likely to have persisted longer in some regions than in others. But in the end, the urban centers could not be sustained, and village-based farming and herding took their place. As the interaction between regions lessened, the standardization of technology and style of the previous era was replaced by distinct regional variations.

Historians can do little more than speculate about the causes behind the changes and the experiences of the people who lived in the Indus

Valley around 1800 B.C.E. But it is important to keep two tendencies in mind. In most cases like this, the majority of the population adjusts to the new circumstances. But members of the political and social elite, who depended on the urban centers and complex political and economic structures, lose the source of their authority and are merged with the population as a whole.

===

THE CHALLENGES AND OPPORTUNITIES OF GREAT RIVER VALLEYS

I t is surely no accident that the first civilizations to develop high levels of political centralization, urbanization, and technology were situated in river valleys where rainfall was insufficient for dependable agriculture. Although the theories of earlier generations of scholars overstated the necessity of those three conditions for the emergence of powerful political centers, the combination of need and opportunity does seem to have spurred political and technological development in Mesopotamia, Egypt, and the Indus Valley as well as in other river valleys.

Dependent as they were on river water to irrigate the cultivated land that fed their populations, Mesopotamia, Egypt, and the Indus Valley civilization channeled significant human resources into the construction and maintenance of canals, dams, and dikes. This work required expertise in engineering, mathematics, and metallurgy, as well as the formation of political centers that could organize the necessary labor force. Failure to contain the forces of nature and to maintain a viable ecological balance led to immediate disaster or to gradual degradation of the environment, whether in the form of deadly floods, rivers changing course, meager harvests and attendant famines, or excess salinization of the soil.

Agriculture constituted the economic base of these societies, and agricultural labor was the chief activity of most of the people. Surpluses

Environmental Stress in the Indus Valley

All three river valley civilizations covered in this chapter were located in arid or semiarid regions with little rainfall. Such regions are particularly vulnerable to changes in the environment. The debates of scholars of the Indus Valley Civilization over the existence and impact of changes in the climate and landscape of that region illuminate some of the potential factors at work, as well as the difficulties of proving and interpreting such changes for the distant past.

One of the points at issue is climatic change. An earlier generation of scholars made a series of arguments to show that the climate of the Indus Valley must have been considerably wetter during the height of that civilization. They pointed to the amount of wood from extensive forests that would be needed to bake the millions of mud bricks used to construct the cities (see photo below), the distribution of human settlements on land that is now unfavorable for agriculture, and the representation of jungle and marsh animals on decorated seals. Other experts were skeptical about a dramatic climatic change, and countered with refined calculations of the amount of timber needed, instances of utilization of unbaked brick, the evidence of plant remains, and the growing of barley, a grain which is tolerant of dry conditions. Radiocarbon-dated samples of ancient pollen have been used to argue both for continuity and for change in the climate. Recent studies of the stabilization of sand dunes, which occurs in periods of greater rainfall, and analysis of the sediment deposited by rivers and winds, have been used to revive the claim that the Indus Valley zone used to be wetter, and entered a period of drier conditions in the early-to-mid second millennium that have persisted till the present day.

A much clearer case can be made for changes in the landscape caused by shifts in the courses of rivers. These shifts are due, in many cases, to tectonic forces such as earthquakes. Dry channels, whether detected in satellite photographs or on-the-ground inspection, reveal the location of old river beds. It appears that a second major river system once ran parallel to the Indus some distance to the east. Either the Sutlej, which now feeds into the Indus, or the Yamuna, which

Source: D. P. Agrawal and R K. Sood in Gregory L. Possehl (ed.), *Harappan Civilization: A Contemporary Perspective*, p. 229. Photo from *The Cambridge History of India: The Indus Civilization*, Sir Mortimer Wheeler. With permission of the Syndics of the Cambridge University Press.

now pours into the Ganges basin, may have been the main source of water for this system. As for the Indus itself, the present-day course of the lower reaches of the river has shifted 100 miles to the west since the arrival of the Greek conqueror Alexander the Great in the late fourth century, and the deposit of massive volumes of silt has pushed the mouth of the river fifty miles further south.

As a recent study concludes: "It is obvious that ecological stresses, caused both climatically and technically, played an important role in the life and decay of the Harappan Civilization."

that the ruling class siphoned off made possible the emergence of towns and cities—crowded and lively urban environments inhabited by specialists of various sorts engaged in the work of administration, war, commerce, religion, arts, and crafts.

We have reached the limit of what we can say in our comparison of the three river-valley civilizations described in this chapter. Because of our limited information about the people of the Indus Valley, we must focus any further comparison on the better-documented civilizations of Mesopotamia and Egypt.

In both regions kingship emerged as the dominant political form. The monarch was assisted by a privileged administrative bureaucracy that used the technology of writing, known only to a relative few, to record, manage, and exploit the resources of the country.

The religious outlook of both cultures was polytheistic (believing in more than one god). There was a hierarchy of gods, ranging from protective demons and local deities that people worshiped in their homes to the gods of the state, whose importance rose or fell with the power of the political centers with which they were associated. The priests who administered major temples controlled vast sums of wealth and were politically influential, sometimes challenging the authority of the monarchy.

In both Egypt and Mesopotamia the population was ethnically heterogeneous, yet both regions experienced a remarkable tradition of cultural continuity over centuries and millennia, because the various groups of peoples who migrated into the central cultural zone were readily assimilated to the dominant language, belief system, and lifeways. Culture, not physical appearance, was the criterion by which people were identified.

So much for the similarities. There were also telling differences, beginning with the landscapes in which these civilizations were rooted. The unpredictable and violent floods of the Tigris-Euphrates Basin were a constant source of alarm for the people of Mesopotamia. In contrast, the predictable, opportune, and gradual Nile floods were eagerly anticipated events in Egypt. The relationship with nature stamped the

world-view of both peoples. Mesopotamians nervously tried to appease their harsh deities so as to survive in a perverse world. Egyptians confidently trusted in, and nurtured, the supernatural powers, which they believed guaranteed orderliness and prosperity.

In Egypt, political unification and centralization of power were the norm. Both were weakened from time to time by economic crises and challenged by the autonomy of high-level administrators and priests, but they were restored as soon as conditions permitted. The central authority of the king and court may have inhibited the process of urbanization outside the capital. In Mesopotamia, urbanization reached a more advanced stage. The city was the central political, social, and economic unit. The proliferation of independent-minded cities made it hard for any one center of power to be dominant for long. The temporary nature of centralized power in Mesopotamia may help to explain why private enterprise was given relatively free reign there, whereas the economy of Egypt was largely controlled by the state.

Although both societies developed a form of kingship, the ideology of each was different. In Egypt, particularly during the Old Kingdom, the king's divine origins made him central to the welfare of the entire country and gave him a religious monopoly superseding the authority of the temples and priests. Egyptian monarchs lavished much of the wealth of the country on their tombs because proper burial helped to ensure the continuity of kingship and the attendant blessings that it brought to the land and people. Mesopotamian rulers, who were not normally regarded as divine, had to justify their position on other grounds. They built new cities, towering walls, splendid palaces, and religious edifices as advertisements of their power to contemporaries and reminders to posterity of their greatness.

The somewhat different position of women in these societies may be related to the higher degree of urbanization and class stratification in Mesopotamia. Constraints on women often are related to the emergence of a highly property-conscious urban and commercial middle class. And in general, women appear to have lost freedom and legal privilege in Mesopotamia in the second millennium B.C.E., whereas Egyptian pictorial documents, love poems, and legal records indicate an attitude of respect and a higher degree of equality for women in the valley of the Nile.

Cheered by the essential stability of their environment, the Egyptians tended to have a more positive conception of the gods' designs for humankind, both in this life and beyond the grave. The Egyptian imagination devised several different versions of paradise, and although the journey to the next world was beset with hazards, the righteous soul that overcame them could look forward to a blessed existence that included all the pleasures of life on earth. In contrast, Gilgamesh, the hero of the Mesopotamian epic, is tormented by terrifying visions of the afterlife: disembodied souls of the dead stumbling around in the darkness of the Underworld for all eternity, eating dust and clay, and slaving for the heartless gods of that realm.

CONCLUSION

In sum, the demands of their respective environments sometimes evoked similar organizational and technological responses from the first advanced civilizations of the ancient world. However, each of these societies met the challenges of daily life with a particular spirit deriving from its own distinctive outlook on life and death, nature and the supernatural, and the individual and the state.

In the second millennium B.C.E., as the societies of Mesopotamia and Egypt consolidated their cultural achievements and entered new phases of political expansion, and as the Indus Valley centers went into irreversible decline, a new and distinctive civilization, based likewise on the exploitation of the agricultural potential of a floodplain, was emerging in the valley of the Yellow River in eastern China. It is to that area that we turn our attention in Chapter 3.

SUGGESTED READING

Jack M. Sasson (ed.), *Civilizations of the Ancient Near East*, 4 vols. (1993) contains up-to-date articles and bibliography on a wide range of topics. An excellent starting point for geography, chronology, and basic institutions and cultural concepts in ancient western Asia is Michael Roaf, *Cultural Atlas of Mesopotamia and the Ancient Near East* (1990). General historical introductions can be found in A. Bernard Knapp, *The History and Culture of Ancient Western Asia and Egypt* (1988); Hans J. Nissen, *The Early History of the Ancient Near East, 9000–2000 B.C.* (1988); H. W. F. Saggs, *Civilization Before Greece and Rome* (1989); and Georges Roux, *Ancient Iraq*, 3d ed. (1992). Joan Oates, *Babylon* (1979), focuses on the most important of all the Mesopotamian cities. J. N. Postgate, *Early Mesopotamia: Society and Economy at the Dawn of History* (1992), offers deep insights into the political, social, and economic dynamics of Mesopotamian society.

The most direct and exciting introduction to the world of early Mesopotamians is through the epic of Gilgamesh, in the attractive translation of David Ferry, *Gilgamesh* (Noonday Press, New York, 1992). Thorkild Jacobsen, *The Treasures of Darkness: A History of Mesopotamian Religion* (1976), is a classic study of the evolving mentality of Mesopotamian religion. Stephanie Dalley, *Myths from Mesopotamia* (1989), and Henrietta McCall, *Mesopotamian Myths* (1990), deal with the mythical literature. Jeremy Black and Anthony Green, *Gods, Demons and Symbols of Ancient Mesopotamia* (1992), is a handy illustrated encyclopedia of myth, religion, and religious symbolism.

C. B. F. Walker, *Cuneiform* (1987), is a concise guide to the Mesopotamian system of writing. James B. Pritchard, *Ancient Near Eastern Texts Relating to the Old Testament*, 2d ed. (1955), contains an extensive collection of translated documents and texts from western Asia and Egypt. Attitudes, roles, and the treatment of women are taken up by Barbara Lesko, "Women of Egypt and the Ancient Near East," in *Becoming Visible: Women in European History*, 2d ed., Renata Bridenthal, Claudia Koonz, and Susan Stuard (1994), and by Guity Nashat, "Women in the Ancient Middle East," in *Restoring Women to History* (1988). The significance of Ebla and ancient Syria is taken up in Harvey Weiss, ed., *Ebla to Damascus: Art and Archaeology of Ancient Syria* (1985), and Giovanni Pettinato, *Ebla: A New Look at History* (1991).

John Baines and Jaromir Malek, *Atlas of Ancient Egypt* (1980), and T. G. H. James, *Ancient Egypt: The Land and Its Legacy* (1988), are primarily organized around the sites of ancient Egypt and provide general introductions to Egyptian civilization. Historical treatments include B. G. Trigger, B. J. Kemp, D. O'Connor, and A. B. Lloyd, *Ancient Egypt: A Social History* (1983); Barry J. Kemp, *Ancient Egypt: Anatomy of a Civilization* (1989); and Nicholas-Cristophe Grimal, *A History of Ancient Egypt* (1992). John Romer, *People of the Nile: Everyday Life in Ancient Egypt* (1982); Miriam Stead, *Egyptian Life* (1986); and Eugen Strouhal, *Life of the Ancient Egyptians* (1992), emphasize social history. For women see the article by Lesko cited above; Barbara Watterson, *Women in Ancient Egypt* (1991); and Gay Robins, *Women in Ancient Egypt* (1993).

Stephen Quirke, *Ancient Egyptian Religion* (1990), is a highly regarded treatment of a complex subject. George Hart, *Egyptian Myths* (1990), gathers the limited written evidence for what must have been a thriving oral tradition. Pritchard's collection, cited above, and Miriam Lichtheim, *Ancient Egyptian Literature: A Book of Readings, Vol. 1, The Old and Middle Kingdoms* (1973), provide translated original texts and documents.

For the Indus Valley civilization, there is a brief treatment in Stanley Wolpert, *A New History of India*, 3d ed. (1989). More detailed are Mortimer Wheeler's *Civilizations of the Indus Valley and Beyond* (1966) and *The Indus Civilization*, 3d ed., (1968). Gregory L. Poschl has edited two collections of articles by Indus Valley scholars: *Ancient Cities of the Indus* (1979) and *Harappan Civilization* (1982).

NOTE

1. David Ferry, *Gilgamesh* (Noonday Press, New York, 1992).

The Late Bronze Age in the Eastern Hemisphere, 2200–500 B.C.E.

Early China · The Cosmopolitan Middle East · Nubia

The Aegean World · The Fall of Late Bronze Age Civilizations

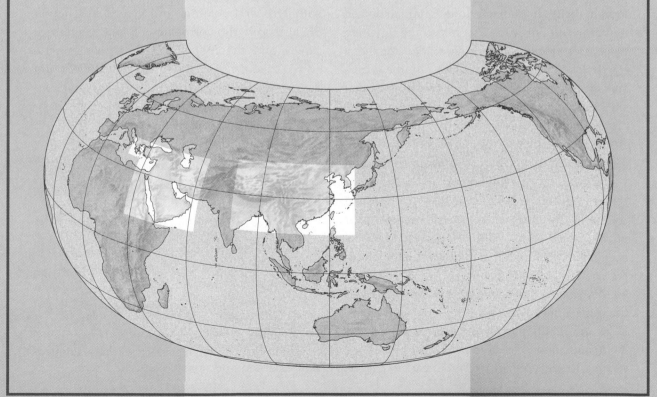

Around 1450 B.C.E. Queen Hatshepsut of Egypt sent a naval expedition down the Red Sea to the fabled land that the Egyptians called "Punt." Historians believe Punt was in the northern coastal region of modern Somalia. Myrrh exported from Punt usually passed through the hands of several intermediaries before reaching Egypt. Hatshepsut hoped to bypass the middlemen and establish direct trade between Punt and Egypt.

A fascinating written and pictorial record of this expedition and its aftermath is preserved in the mortuary temple of Hatshepsut at Deir el-Bahri, near Thebes. Besides bringing back myrrh resin and various sub-Saharan luxury goods—ebony and other rare woods, ivory, cosmetics, live monkeys, panther skins—the ships also carried young myrrh trees, probably to create a home-grown source of this precious substance which the Egyptians burned on the altars of their gods. These items are represented in the royal Egyptian tomb as tribute given by the people of Punt to their Egyptian overlord. Egyptian power, however, did not reach that far, so the Egyptian emissaries actually must have traded for them. Hatshepsut staged public displays of these treasures from southern lands and emphasized that she had accomplished what none of her predecessors had been able to do.

Hatshepsut's highly touted expedition to Punt reveals much that is important about the ancient world in the second millennium B.C.E. The major centers resolutely pursued access to important resources, by trade or conquest, because their power, wealth, and legitimacy depended on the acquisition of these commodities. A hallmark of this period in northeastern Africa, the eastern Mediterranean, western Asia, and East Asia was the interconnectedness of regions and states, large and small, in complex webs of political relationships and economic activities. Embassies, treaties, trade agreements, political marriages, and scribes utilizing widely recognized languages and writing systems were but some of the links connecting the heterogeneous peoples of these regions. Commerce over long distances, centering on the trade in metals, was vital to the power and prosperity of the ruling classes.

The movement of goods across long distances promoted the flow of ideas and technologies. These included concepts of kingship, methods of administration, systems of writing, religious beliefs and rituals, artistic tastes, metallurgical skills, and new forms of transportation. By the standards of the ancient world, the Late Bronze Age was a cosmopolitan and comfortable era, a time of stability and prosperity, of technological progress and cultural accomplishments.

The spread of ideas and technologies sparked important political changes across the Eastern Hemisphere (the vast landmass comprising the joined continents of Asia, Africa, and Europe). This period, which witnessed the last flourishing of the ancient centers of civilization in Egypt and southern Mesopotamia (introduced in Chapter 2), also saw the formation of new centers of power and the first stirrings of peoples who would take center stage in the first millennium B.C.E.:—Assyrians in northern Mesopotamia, Nubians in northeastern Africa, Greeks in the eastern Mediterranean, and the Shang and Zhou in northeastern China.

EARLY CHINA

On the eastern edge of the great Eurasian landmass, Chinese civilization evolved in the second millennium B.C.E. Under the political domination of the Shang and Zhou monarchs many of the characteristic institutions, patterns, and values of classical Chinese civilization emerged and spread south and west. As in

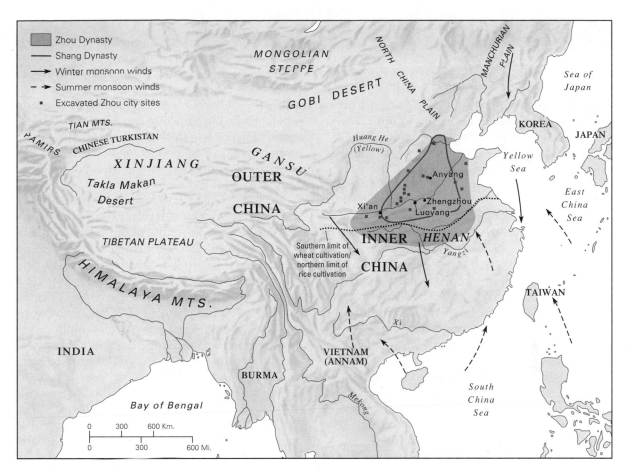

Map 3.1   China under the Shang and Zhou Dynasties, 1750–221 B.C.E.   A complex civilization arose in the second millennium B.C.E. in the floodplain of the Yellow River. While southern China benefits from the monsoon rains, northern China depends on irrigation. As population increased, the Han Chinese migrated to other parts of Inner China, carrying their technologies and cultural practices. Other ethnic groups predominated in Outer China, and the nomadic peoples of the northwest constantly challenged Chinese authority.

Mesopotamia, Egypt, and the Indus Valley, the rise of a complex society possessing cities, specialization of labor, bureaucratic government, writing, and other advanced technologies depended on the marshaling of human labor and exploitation of the waters of a great river system—the Yellow River (Huang He) and its tributaries—to support intensive agriculture in the plains. Although there is archaeological evidence of some movement of goods and ideas between western and eastern Asia, these developments were largely independent of the rise of complex societies in the Middle East and the Indus Valley.

Geography and Resources

China is isolated from the rest of the Eastern Hemisphere by formidable natural barriers: to the southwest the Himalayas, the highest mountains on the planet; to the west the Pamir and Tian Mountains and the Takla Makan Desert; to the northwest the Gobi Desert and the treeless and grassy hills and plains of the Mongolian steppe (see Map 3.1). To the east lies the vastness of the Pacific Ocean. Although China's separation was not total—trade goods, people, and ideas moved back and forth between China,

India, and Central Asia—its development in many instances was unique.

Most of the East Asian subcontinent is covered with mountains, making overland travel, transport, and communications difficult and slow. The great river systems of eastern China, however—the Yellow River, the Yangzi River, and their tributaries—facilitate internal movement along an east-west axis. It is useful to distinguish between Inner China and Outer China. Intensive agriculture was practiced and the population clustered in the eastern river valleys of Inner China. In Outer China—the steppe lands of Mongolia, the deserts and oases of Xinjiang, and the high plateau of Tibet—sparser populations practiced quite different forms of livelihood. The topographical diversity of East Asia is matched by climatic zones ranging from the dry, subarctic reaches of Manchuria in the north to the lush, subtropical forests of the south, and by rich variation in the plant and animal life adapted to these zones.

Even within Inner China there is a fundamental distinction between north and south. The same forces that create the great monsoon of India and Southeast Asia (see Chapter 2) also drench southern China with substantial amounts of rainfall in the summer months, the most beneficial time for agriculture. Northern China, in contrast, receives a much more erratic and restricted amount of moisture. As a result, in north and south there are different patterns for the use of land, the kinds of crops that can flourish, and the organization of agricultural labor. As in Mesopotamia, the Indus Valley, and southern Greece (see below), where technological and social developments also sprang up in a relatively adverse environment, the early history of China centered on the demanding environment of the northern plains. In that region arose important technologies, political traditions, and a set of philosophical and religious views that have been the hallmark of Chinese civilization. From the third century C.E. on, because of the gradual flow of population toward the warmer southern lands, the political and intellectual center of gravity also moved south.

The eastern river valleys and North China Plain contained timber, stone, and scattered deposits of metals. Above all, this region offered potentially productive land. Since prehistoric times, winds rising over the vast expanse of Central Asia have deposited a yellowish-brown silt called *loess* (silt in suspension in the water has given the Yellow River its distinctive hue and name). Over the ages this annual sprinkling has accumulated into a thick mantle of soil that is extremely fertile and soft enough to be worked with wooden digging sticks. The very lack of compactness of this soil is the reason why the region has been hit by catastrophic earthquakes.

In this landscape agriculture, which first appeared in the fourth millennium B.C.E., demanded immense human labor. In parts of northern China forests had to be cleared to open up land for planting. The Yellow River was prone to devastating floods, necessitating the construction of earthen dikes and channels to carry off the overflow. The region was equally vulnerable to prolonged droughts, for which the best defense was the digging of catch basins (reservoirs) to store river water and rainfall.

The staple crops in the northern region were millet, indigenous to China, and wheat, which spread to East Asia from the Middle East. The cultivation of rice in the Yangzi River Valley and the south required an even greater outlay of labor. The reward for this effort was a spectacular yield—rice can feed a larger number of people per cultivated acre than can any other grain. Rice prospered in the south because it requires a relatively high air temperature. Rice paddies must be absolutely flat and surrounded by water channels to bring and lead away water according to a precise schedule. Seedlings sprout in a nursery and then are transplanted one by one into the paddy and are flooded for a time. The flooding eliminates weeds and other rival plants and supports microscopic organisms that keep the soil fertile. When the crop is ripe, the paddy must be drained, the rice stalks harvested with a sickle, and the edible kernels separated out. As the population of ancient China expanded, people claimed more land for cultivation by building retaining walls to partition the hillsides into tiers of flat terraces. Thus, in both northern and southern China, agriculture required the coordinated efforts of large groups of people.

The Shang Period

Archaeologists have distinguished among several early cultural complexes in China, primarily on the basis of styles of pottery and forms of burial. These early populations grew millet and raised pigs and chickens. They made pottery on a wheel and fired it in high-temperature kilns. They mastered the techniques of silk-cloth production, fostering the growth of silkworms, which gorged on the leaves of mulberry trees and spun cocoons, which people carefully unraveled to produce silk thread. The early Chinese built walls of pounded earth by hammering the soil inside temporary wooden frames until it became hard as cement. By 2000 B.C.E. they had acquired bronze metallurgy.

Later generations of Chinese told stories about the dynasty of the Xia, who are said to have ruled the core region in the centuries before and after 2000 B.C.E. The validity of those stories, however, is difficult to gauge. For all practical purposes Chinese history begins with the rise to power of the Shang clans, coinciding with the earliest written records in the early second millennium B.C.E.

According to tradition, Tang, a subordinate of the last Xia monarch, overthrew his decadent master around 1750 B.C.E. The prominent class among the Shang was a warrior aristocracy whose greatest pleasures in life were warfare, hunting (both for recreation and to fine-tune the skills required for war), exchanging gifts, feasting, and wine-filled revelry. The Shang originated in the part of the Yellow River Valley that lies in the present-day province of Henan. Between approximately 1750 and 1027 B.C.E. they extended their control across a large swath of territory extending north into Mongolia, west as far as Gansu, and south into the Yangzi River Valley. Various cities served as the capital of the Shang Empire. The last and most important of them was near modern Anyang (see Map 3.1).

The core area of the empire was ruled directly by the king and his administrators, who were members of the aristocracy and served, as needed, as generals, ambassadors, and supervisors of public projects. Members of the royal family and

A bronze vessel with rams and dragons from the Shang Period Such vessels were used in the rituals which allowed the Shang ruling class to make contact with its ancestors. As both the source and proof of the authority of this elite, these vessels were often buried in their tombs. The complex shape and elaborate decoration testify to the high level of artisans' skills. (Seth Joel/Laurie Platt Winfrey, Inc.)

high-ranking nobility managed provinces farther out. The most distant regions were governed by native rulers bound by ties of allegiance to the Shang king. The king was often on the road, traveling to the courts of his subordinates to reinforce their ties of loyalty.

Military campaigns were frequent. They provided the warrior aristocracy with a theater for brave achievements, and they yielded considerable plunder. The "barbarians," as the Chinese called the nomadic peoples who occupied the steppe and desert regions to the north and west, periodically were rolled back and given a reminder of Shang power. (The word *barbarian* reflects the language and view of Chinese sources.

Modern readers should be wary of the Chinese claim that these nomads were culturally backward and morally inferior to the Chinese.) The campaigns against peoples in the north and west produced large numbers of prisoners of war who were carried off to the Shang capital and used as slaves.

Far-reaching networks of trade sprang up across China, bringing to the core area of the Shang domain valued commodities such as jade, ivory, and mother of pearl (a hard, shiny substance from the interior of mollusk shells) used for jewelry, carved figurines, and decorative inlays. There are indications that Shang China was in contact with the civilization of Mesopotamia and that these centers exchanged goods and ideas with one another.

The Shang kings devised an ideology of kingship that reinforced their power. They presented themselves as indispensable intermediaries between their people and the gods. The Shang aristocracy worshiped the spirits of their male ancestors and believed that these ancestors were intensely interested in the fortunes of their descendants and had special influence with the gods. Before taking any action, the Shang used divination to ascertain the will of the gods (see Environment and Technology: Chinese and Mesopotamian Divination). Court ritual also called for sacrifices to gods and to ancestors in order to win divine favor. Burials of kings also entailed sacrifices, not only of animals but also of humans, including noble officials of the court, women, servants, soldiers, and prisoners of war.

Possession of bronze objects was a sign of authority and legitimacy and was mostly confined to members of the elite. Rural peasants were still using stone tools. Bronze was used in warfare and ritual, which, according to ancient sources, were the primary purposes of the state. Bronze weapons allowed the state to assert its authority, and the use of bronze ritual vessels was the best way to gain the support of ancestors and gods. The sheer quantity of bronze objects found in tombs of the Shang ruling class is very impressive, especially since copper and tin (the principal ingredients of bronze) were not plentiful in northern China. Clearly the Shang elite expended a huge effort on finding and mining deposits of those elements, refining the mixed ores into pure metal, transporting the precious cargo to the capital, and commissioning the creation of skillfully made and beautifully decorated objects.

When the copper and tin had been mixed in the right proportions, artisans poured the molten bronze into clay molds. Separate hardened pieces were later joined together as necessary. The foundries were located outside the walls of the main cities. Artisans were sufficiently well rewarded to enjoy a comfortable lifestyle. They made weapons, chariot fittings, musical instruments, and, most important of all, the ritual vessels that held the liquids and solids used in religious ceremonies. Many of these elegant bronze vessels were vividly decorated with the stylized forms of real and imaginary animals. The decorations may indicate a belief that these creatures served as intermediaries between heaven and earth.

The Shang period was a time of other significant technological advances as well. The horse-drawn chariot, which the Shang may have adapted from the contemporary Middle East, was a formidable instrument of war. Domestication of the water buffalo provided additional muscle power. Growing knowledge of the principles of engineering and an effective administrative organization for mobilizing human labor led to the construction of cities, massive defensive walls of pounded earth, and monumental royal tombs.

A key to effective administration was the form of writing developed in this era. The original pictograms (pictures representing objects and concepts) were combined with phonetic symbols representing the sounds of syllables to form a complex system requiring scribes to memorize hundreds of signs. Because of the time needed to master this system, writing was the hallmark of the educated, elite class. The Chinese system has endured for thousands of years. Other ancient systems of writing that also were difficult to learn and brought special status and opportunities to those who did so—such as the cuneiform of Mesopotamia and the hieroglyphics of Egypt—were replaced by simpler alphabetic approaches.

Chinese and Mesopotamian Divination

The inhabitants of China and Mesopotamia and many other peoples of the ancient world believed that the gods controlled the forces of nature and foresaw events. Starting from this premise, they considered natural phenomena to be signs of the gods' will, and they tried to interpret these signs. Using various techniques of divination, the ancients sought to communicate with the gods and thereby anticipate, and even influence, the future.

The Shang ruling class in China frequently sought information from shamans, individuals who claimed to have the ability to make direct contact with ancestors and other higher powers (the king himself often functioned as a shaman). Chief among the tools of divination used by a shaman was oracle bones. The shaman touched a tortoise shell or the shoulder bone of an animal with the heated point of a stick. The shell or bone would crack, and the cracks could be "read" as a message from the spirit world.

Tens of thousands of oracle bones survive. They are a major source of information about Shang life, because usually the question that was being posed and the resulting answer were inscribed on the back side of the shell or bone. The rulers asked about the proper performance of ritual, the likely outcome of wars or hunting expeditions, the prospects for rainfall and the harvest, and the meaning of strange occurrences.

In Mesopotamia in the third and second millennium B.C.E. the most important divination involved the close inspection of the form, size, and markings of the organs of animals sacrificed. Archaeologists have found models of sheeps' livers accompanied by written explanations of the meaning of various features. Two other techniques of divination were following the trail of smoke from burning incense and examining the patterns that resulted when oil was thrown on water.

From about 2000 B.C.E. Mesopotamian diviners also foretold the future from their observation of the movements of the Sun, Moon, planets, stars, and constellations. In the centuries after 1000 B.C.E. celestial omens were the most important source of predictions about the future, and specialists maintained precise records of astronomical events. Mesopotamian mathematics, essential for calculations of the movements of celestial bodies, was the most sophisticated math in the ancient Middle East. A place-value system, in which a number stands for its value multiplied by the value of the particular column in which it appears (such as our ones, tens, and hundreds columns, moving from right to left), made possible complex operations with large numbers and small fractions.

Astrology, with its division of the sky into the twelve segments of the zodiac and its use of the position of the stars and planets to predict an individual's destiny, developed out of long-standing Mesopotamian attention to the movements of celestial objects. Horoscopes—charts with calculations and predictions based on an individual's date of birth—have been found from shortly before 400 B.C.E. In the Hellenistic period (323–30 B.C.E.), Greek settlers flooded into western Asia, built on this Mesopotamian foundation, and greatly advanced the study of astrology.

Chinese divination shell (Institute of History and Philology, Academia Sinica)

Women beating chimes   This scene, from a bronze vessel of the Zhou era, illustrates the important role of music in festivals, religious rituals, and court ceremonials. During the politically fragmented later (Eastern) Zhou era, many small states marked their independence by having their own musical scales and distinctive arrangement of orchestral instruments. (Courtesy, Imperial Palace Museum, Beijing)

The Zhou Period

Shang domination of central and northern China lasted more than six centuries. In the eleventh century B.C.E. the last Shang king was defeated by one of his dependents from the Wei River Valley, Duke Wu of Zhou. The Zhou line of kings (ca. 1027–221 B.C.E.) would prove to be the longest-lasting and most revered of all dynasties in Chinese history. As the Semitic peoples in Mesopotamia had adopted and adapted the Sumerian legacy (see Chapter 2), the Zhou preserved the foundations of culture created by their predecessors, adding important new elements of ideology and technology.

The positive image of Zhou rule, in many respects accurate, was skillfully constructed by propagandists for the new regime. The early Zhou monarchs had to formulate a new ideology of kingship to justify their seizure of power to the restive remnants of the Shang clans, as well as to their other subjects. The chief deity was now referred to as "Heaven," the monarch was called the "Son of Heaven," and his rule was called the "Mandate of Heaven." According to the new theory, the ruler would retain the backing of the gods as long as he served as a wise,

principled, and energetic guardian of his people. His mandate could be withdrawn if he misbehaved, as the last Shang ruler had done.

Although elements of Shang ritual were allowed to continue, there was a marked decline in the practice of divination and in the extravagant and bloody sacrifices and burials that had been hallmarks of Shang court ceremonial. The priestly power of the ruling class, which alone during the Shang period had been able to make contact with the powerful spirits of ancestors, was largely removed. The resulting separation of religion from political dealings allowed China to develop important secular philosophies in the Zhou period. The beautifully crafted bronze vessels that had been sacred implements in the Shang Period became family treasures.

The early period of Zhou rule—the eleventh through ninth centuries B.C.E.—is sometimes called the Western Zhou era. These centuries saw the development of a sophisticated administrative apparatus. The Zhou built a series of capital cities with pounded earth foundations and walls. The major buildings all faced south, beginning a long Chinese fascination with the orientation of structures. The king was supposed to be a model of morality, fairness, and concern for the welfare of the people—qualities that were expected of all imperial officials. The Zhou regime was highly decentralized. More than a hundred subject territories were ruled with considerable autonomy by members and allies of the royal family. The court was the scene of elaborate ceremonials, embellished by music and dance, which impressed on observers the glory of Zhou rule and reinforced the bonds of obligation between rulers and ruled. Standing armies were supplemented by local militias.

By around 800 B.C.E., Zhou power began to wane. Proud and ambitious local rulers operated ever more independently and waged war on one another, and nomadic peoples began to press on the borders from the northwest. Moreover, the center had lost its technological advantages over outlying regions. Knowledge of how to forge bronze tools and weapons and build sturdy city walls had spread to the subjects of the Zhou Empire and even to some of the "barbarian" groups.

The subsequent epoch of Chinese history is sometimes called the Eastern Zhou era. Members of the Zhou lineage who in 771 B.C.E. had relocated to a new, more secure, eastern capital near Luoyang continued to hold the imperial title and to receive at least nominal homage from the real power brokers of the age. This was a time of political fragmentation, rapidly shifting centers of power, and rampant competition and warfare among numerous small and independent states. The Eastern Zhou is also conventionally subdivided. The years between 771 and 481 B.C.E. are called the "Springs and Autumns Period," after a collection of chronicles that give annual entries for those two seasons. The period from 480 B.C.E. to the unification of China in 221 B.C.E. is called the "Warring States Period."

The many states of the Eastern Zhou era, when not paralyzed by internal power struggles, contended with one another for leadership. Cities, some of them quite large, spread across the Chinese landscape. Long walls of pounded earth, the ancestors of the Great Wall of China, protected the kingdoms from suspect neighbors and northern nomads. By 600 B.C.E. iron began to replace bronze as the primary metal for tools and weapons, and the Chinese had learned from the steppe nomads to put fighters on horseback.

In each of the states bureaucrats expanded in number and function. Codes of law were written down. The government collected taxes from the peasants directly, and people's lives were regimented and regulated by the great rituals of court. The ruling class both justified its position and was steered toward right conduct by its claim that its actions were in accordance with a high standard of morality.

For those who lived through the political flux and social change, this was an anxious time. Their experiences led some to question old assumptions and begin to think in new ways. This was the historical setting for the life of Kong Fu Zi (Confucius 551–479 B.C.E.), an official and philosopher whose doctrine of duty and public service was to become one of the most influential strains in Chinese thought (see Chapter 6).

This era also saw the decline of the clan-based kinship structures that had characterized the Shang and early Zhou periods. Taking their place was the three-generation family—grandparents, parents, and children—which became the fundamental social unit. Related to this development was the emergence of the concept of private property. Land was considered to belong to the men of the family and was divided equally among the sons when the father died.

Very little is known about the conditions of life for women in early China. Some scholars believe that women may have had an important role as shamans, entering into trance states to communicate with supernatural forces, make requests on behalf of their communities, and receive predictions of the future. By the time written records begin to illuminate our knowledge of their experiences, however, women were in a subordinate position in the strongly patriarchal family.

The disparity in male and female roles was rationalized by the concept of *yin* and *yang*, which represented the complementary nature of male (yin) and female (yang) roles in the natural order. Male toughness was to be balanced by female gentleness, male action and initiation by female endurance and need for completion, male leadership by female willingness to follow. Only men were allowed to conduct the all-important rituals and make offerings to the ancestors; women helped to maintain the ancestral shrines in the household. Fathers held authority over the women and children, arranged marriages for

Periods of Early Chinese History

8000–2000 B.C.E.	Neolithic Cultures
1750–1027	Shang Dynasty
1027–772	Western Zhou
771–221	Eastern Zhou
771–481	Springs and Autumns Period
480–221	Warring States Period

their offspring, and were free to sell the labor of family members. A man was supposed to have only one wife but was permitted additional sexual partners, who had the lower status of concubines. Among the elite classes marriages were used to create political alliances, and it was common for the groom's family to offer a substantial "bride-gift" to the family of the prospective bride. A man whose wife died had a virtual duty to remarry in order to produce male heirs to keep alive the cult of the ancestors. Widows, however, were under considerable pressure not to remarry as proof of their devotion to their husbands.

In sum, during the long centuries of Zhou rule the classical Chinese patterns of family, property, and bureaucracy took shape. All that remained was for a strong central power to unify all the Chinese lands. This outcome would be achieved by the state of Qin, whose aggressive tendencies and disciplined way of life had made it the premier power among the warring states by the third century B.C.E. (see Chapter 6).

THE COSMOPOLITAN MIDDLE EAST

Both Mesopotamia and Egypt succumbed to outside invaders in the seventeenth century B.C.E. (see Chapter 2). Eventually the outsiders were either ejected or assimilated, and a new political equilibrium was achieved. In the period between 1500 and 1200 B.C.E. a number of large territorial states dominated the Middle East (see Map 3.2). Those centers of power controlled the smaller city-states, kingdoms, and kinship groups as they competed with, and sometimes fought against, one another for control of valuable commodities and trade routes.

Historians have called the Late Bronze Age in the Middle East a "cosmopolitan" era, meaning one in which elements of culture and lifestyle were widely shared among different groups. Extensive diplomatic relations and commercial contacts between states fostered the flow of ideas, and throughout the region one could find among the elite groups a relatively high standard of living and similar products and concepts. The majority of the population, peasants in the countryside, may have seen some improvement in their standard of living, but they reaped far fewer of the benefits deriving from increased contacts and trade among different societies.

Western Asia

By 1500 B.C.E. Mesopotamia was divided into two distinct political zones: Babylonia in the south and Assyria in the north (see Map 3.2). The city of Babylon had gained political and cultural ascendancy over the southern plain under the dynasty of Hammurabi in the eighteenth and seventeenth centuries B.C.E. Subsequently there was a persistent inflow of Kassites, peoples from the Zagros Mountains to the east who spoke a non-Semitic language, and by 1460 a Kassite dynasty had come to power in Babylon. The Kassites retained names in their native language but otherwise embraced Babylonian language and culture and intermarried with the native population. During their 250 years in power, the Kassite lords of Babylonia did not actively pursue territorial conquest and were content to defend their core area and trade for vital raw materials.

The Assyrians of the north had a more expansionist destiny. Back in the twentieth century B.C.E. the city of Ashur had become one pole of a busy trade route that crossed the northern Mesopotamian plain and ascended the Anatolian plateau, where representatives of Assyrian merchant families maintained trade settlements out-

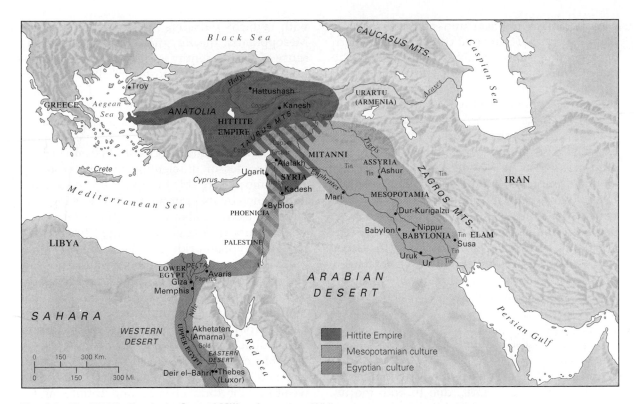

Map 3.2 The Middle East in the Second Millennium B.C.E.   While wars were not uncommon, treaties, diplomatic missions, and correspondence in Akkadian cuneiform helped relations between states. All were tied together by extensive networks of exchange centering on the trade in metals, and peripheral regions, such as Nubia and the Aegean Sea, were drawn into the web of commerce.

side the walls of important Anatolian cities. This commerce brought tin and textiles to Anatolia in exchange for silver. In the eighteenth century B.C.E. an Assyrian dynasty gained control of Mari, a key city-state on the upper Euphrates River near the present-day border of Syria and Iraq. Although this "Old Assyrian" kingdom, as it is now called, was short-lived, it illustrates the importance of the cities that lay astride the trade routes connecting Mesopotamia to Anatolia and the Syria-Palestine coast. After 1400 B.C.E. a resurgent "Middle Assyrian" kingdom was once again engaged in campaigns of conquest and economic imperialism.

Other ambitious states emerged on the periphery of the Mesopotamian heartland, including Elam in southwest Iran and Mitanni in the broad plain lying between the upper Euphrates

and Tigris Rivers. Most formidable of all were the Hittites, speakers of an Indo-European language who became the foremost power in Anatolia from around 1700 to 1200 B.C.E. From their capital at Hattushash, near present-day Ankara in central Turkey, they employed the fearsome new technology of horse-drawn war chariots. The hills of Anatolia contained rich deposits of some of the metals that were so prized in this age—copper, silver, and iron—and the Hittites came to play an indispensable role in international commerce. The Hittite king laid down a standardized code of law, demanded military service and labor in exchange for grants of land, and supported artists and craftsmen engaged in the construction and decoration of palaces and temples.

A distinctive feature of western Asia during the second millennium B.C.E. was the diffusion of

Mesopotamian political and cultural concepts from the original Sumerian core area in southern Mesopotamia across much of the region. The cuneiform system of writing was employed to communicate in Elamite, Hittite, and other languages. Mesopotamian myths and legends were taken over by other peoples, and Mesopotamian styles of art and architecture were imitated. In this new regional order the old center was often hard-pressed by newcomers who had learned well and improved on the lessons of Mesopotamian civilization. The small, fractious, Mesopotamian city-states of the third millennium B.C.E. had been concerned with their immediate neighbors in the southern plain. In contrast, the larger states of the second millennium B.C.E. interacted politically, militarily, and economically in a geopolitical sphere extending across western Asia.

New Kingdom Egypt

With the decline of the Middle Kingdom in the seventeenth century B.C.E., due to both the increased independence of high-level officials and the pressure of new groups migrating into the Nile Valley, Egypt entered a period of political fragmentation, economic regression, and cultural disruption. Around 1640 B.C.E. it came under foreign rule for the first time—at the hands of the Hyksos, or "Princes of Foreign Lands." Historians are uncertain about the precise identity of the Hyksos and how they came to power. Semitic peoples from the Syria-Palestine region to the northeast (today the countries of Israel, Palestine, Jordan, Lebanon, and Syria) had been migrating into the eastern Nile Delta for centuries, and it is likely that in the chaotic conditions of this time other peoples joined them and were able to establish control, first in the delta and then throughout lower Egypt (see Map 3.2). This process may not have been different from that by which the Amorites and Kassites first settled in and gained control in Babylonia.

The Hyksos intermarried with the Egyptian population and largely assimilated to native ways. They used the Egyptian language and maintained Egyptian institutions and culture. Nevertheless, in contrast to the relative ease with which outsiders were assimilated in Mesopotamia, the Egyptians, with their strong sense of ethnic identity and long tradition of political unity, continued to regard the Hyksos as "foreigners."

As with the formation of the Middle Kingdom approximately five hundred years earlier, the reunification of Egypt under a native dynasty again came from the princes of Thebes. Through three decades of unrelenting fighting, Kamose and Ahmose were able to expel the Hyksos from Egypt, thereby inaugurating the New Kingdom, which lasted from about 1532 to 1070 B.C.E.

A century of foreign domination had been a blow to Egyptian pride and shook the new leaders of Egypt out of the isolationist mindset of earlier eras. New Kingdom Egypt was an aggressive and expansionist state, engaging in frequent campaigns of conquest and extending its territorial control north into Syria-Palestine and south into Nubia. In this way Egypt won access to valuable commodities—including timber, copper, and gold—and to a constant infusion of wealth in the form of taxes and tribute, and a buffer zone of occupied territory protected Egypt against foreign attack. The mechanisms of Egyptian control in the Syria-Palestine region included strategically placed forts and garrisons of Egyptian soldiers and support for local rulers who were willing to collaborate. In Nubia, in contrast, Egypt imposed control directly and pressed the native population to adopt important elements of Egyptian language and culture.

At the same time, Egypt became a full-fledged participant in the network of diplomatic and commercial relations that linked the large and small states of western Asia. Egyptian soldiers, administrators, diplomats, and merchants spent much time outside Egypt. Their travels abroad exposed Egypt to new technologies, including improved potter's wheels and looms for weaving, new fruits and vegetables, new musical instruments, and the war chariot. In sum, the New Kingdom was a period of great innovation.

During this period at least one woman laid claim to the throne of Egypt. Hatshepsut was the queen of Pharaoh Tuthmosis II. When he died, she served at first as regent for her young stepson but soon claimed the royal title for herself

(r. 1473–1458 B.C.E.). In the inscriptions which she commissioned for her mortuary temple at Deir el-Bahri, she often used the male pronoun to refer to herself, and drawings show her wearing the long, conical beard symbolic of the king of Egypt. It was Hatshepsut who dispatched the naval expedition to Punt, described at the beginning of this chapter, to open up direct trade between Egypt and the source of the prized myrrh resin. She used the success of this expedition to bolster her claim to the throne. After her death, in a reaction that reflected simmering opposition in some official quarters to having a woman as ruler, her picture was defaced and her name blotted out wherever it appeared.

The reign of another ruler also saw sharp departures from the ways of the past. Originally called Amenhotep IV, this ruler began to refer to himself as Akhenaten (r. 1353–1335 B.C.E.) which means "beneficial to the *Aten* (the disk of the sun)." Changing his name was just one of the ways in which he emphasized the primacy of the Aten. He closed the temples of the other gods, directly challenging the long-standing supremacy of Amon among the gods and the temporal power and influence of the priests of Amon.

Scholars have drawn various conclusions about the spiritual impulses behind these changes, but it is likely that Akhenaten's motives were at least partly political and that he was attempting to reassert the superiority of the king over the priests and to renew belief in the divinity of the king. The worship of Aten was actually confined to the royal family in the palace. The population of Egypt was pressed to revere the divine ruler.

Akhenaten built a new capital at modern-day Amarna, halfway between Memphis and Thebes. He and his artists created a new style of realism: the king, his wife Nefertiti, and the family were depicted in fluid, natural poses. The discovery at Amarna of an archive containing correspondence between the Egyptian government and various local rulers in the Syria-Palestine dependencies illuminates the diplomatic currents of this so-called Amarna period (see Voices and Visions: The Amarna Letters).

Painting on a wooden casket from the tomb of Tutankhamun   The light, wooden chariot drawn by a pair of horses introduced into warfare a fearsome new level of speed and mobility. While Tutankhamun, here shown riding in a war chariot and slaughtering Nubian enemies, was pharaoh during the New Kingdom, a period in which Egypt abandoned its traditional isolation and extended its control over neighboring peoples in Nubia and Syria-Palestine, it is unlikely that this represents a real event in the brief reign of the boy-king (r. 1333-1323). (Griffiths Institute, Ashmokan Museum, Oxford)

The Amarna Letters

The Amarna Letters are nearly four hundred documents discovered in 1887 C.E. at modern Tell el-Amarna (ancient Akhetaten), the capital of the Egyptian pharaoh Akhenaten. The documents date from approximately 1355 to 1335 B.C.E.—from the last years of Akhenaten's father, Amenhotep III, through the reign of Akhenaten. Primarily they are correspondence between the Egyptian monarch and various subordinate local rulers within the territory of modern Israel, Palestine, Lebanon, and Syria.

Using Akkadian cuneiform, the vehicle for international communication at the time, the scribes sometimes betray their origins as Canaanites (the indigenous Semitic people of Syria-Palestine) by linguistic slips.

This archive reveals the complex and shifting political dynamics of the Egyptian empire, as can be seen in this letter from Lab'ayu, the Canaanite ruler of Shechem in central Israel, to Amenhotep III:

To the king, my lord and my Sun-god: Thus Lab'ayu, thy servant, and the dirt on which thou dost tread. At the feet of the king, my lord, and my Sun-god, seven times and seven times I fall.

I have heard the words which the king wrote to me, and who am I that the king should lose his land because of me? Behold, I am a faithful servant of the king, and I have not rebelled and I have not sinned, and I do not withhold my tribute, and I do not refuse the requests of my commissioner. Now they wickedly slander me, but let the king, my lord, not impute rebellion to me!

The opening language of abject subordination to the divine king is a formula that appears in almost every document. Apparently Lab'ayu had been accused of disobedience by some of his neighbors and was writing to protest his innocence. In fact, Lab'ayu is frequently accused in the Amarna Letters of attacking the territory and robbing the caravans of other Egyptian subjects.

What can we deduce from this document about the relationship of the Egyptian government to the complex patchwork of subordinate local rulers in Syria-Palestine? What were the duties of Egyptian subjects? Why might the Egyptian government have tolerated quarreling and competition among the local chiefs?

Other documents in the archive provide glimpses of the goods (including human beings) traded through this region, a crossroads between Egypt, Syria, the Mediterranean, and Mesopotamia:

To Milkilu, prince of Gezer. Thus the king. Now I have sent thee this tablet to say to thee: Behold, I am sending to thee Hanya, the commissioner of the archers, together with goods, in order to procure fine concubines (i.e.) weaving women: silver, gold, linen garments, turquoise, all sorts of precious stones, chairs of ebony, as well as every good thing, totalling 160 deben. . . . So send very fine concubines in whom there is no blemish.

The appearance of Canaanite, Egyptian, and Indo-European names in the letters reveals the diverse mix of ethnic groups living in this region. There are also frequent references to the troubles caused by the Apiru, characterized as backward, nomadic peoples prone to prey on the farmlands and towns, as in this appeal to Akhenaten from Shuwardata, a local ruler from the Hebron region:

Let the king, my lord, learn that the chief of the Apiru has risen in arms against the lands which the god of the king, my lord, gave me; but I have smitten him. . . . So let it be agreeable to the king, my lord, and let him send Yanhamu, and let us make war in earnest, and let the lands of the king, my lord, be restored to their former limits!

What common interests bind together the Egyptian monarchy and the local rulers in Syria-Palestine? What forms might cooperation between these groups take?

The reforms of Akhenaten stirred resistance from the administration, the priesthood, and other groups whose privileges and wealth were linked to the traditional system. After his death the old ways were restored with a vengeance: the temples were reopened, Amon was returned to his position of primacy in the pantheon, and the institution of kingship was weakened to the advantage of the priests. The boy-king Tutankhamun (r. 1333–1323), one of the immediate successors of Akhenaten and famous solely because his is the only royal tomb found by archaeologists that had not been pillaged by tomb robbers, reveals both in his name (meaning "beautiful in life is *Amon*") and his insignificant reign the ultimate failure of Akhenaten's revolution.

Shortly thereafter the general Haremhab took possession of the throne for his family, the Ramessides, and this dynasty renewed the policy of conquest and expansion that had been neglected in the Amarna period. The greatest monarch of this line, Ramesses II—Ramesses the Great, as he is sometimes called—ruled for sixty-six years (r. 1290–1224) and dominated his age.

Early in his reign Ramesses II commanded Egyptian forces in a major battle against the Hittites at Kadesh in northern Syria (1285). Although Egyptian scribes presented this encounter as a great victory for their side, other evidence suggests that it was essentially a draw. In subsequent years Egyptian and Hittite diplomats negotiated a series of territorial agreements, which were strengthened by the marriage of Ramesses to a Hittite princess. Ramesses also looms large in the archaeological record because he undertook building projects all over Egypt, including the rock-cut temple at Abu Simbel, with its four colossal images of the seated king, and the two tall, needle-shaped obelisks at Luxor.

Commerce and Diplomacy

At issue in the great rivalry between Egypt and the Hittite kingdom was control of the region lying between them—Syria-Palestine—the pivot in the trade routes that bound together this part of the globe. Lying at a crossroads between the great powers of the Middle East and at the end of the east-west land route across Asia, the inland cities of Syria-Palestine—such as Mari on the upper Euphrates and Alalakh in western Syria—were meeting places where merchants from different lands could exchange goods. The coastal port towns—particularly Ugarit on the Syrian coast and the up-and-coming Phoenician towns of the Lebanese seaboard—served as transshipment points for products going to or coming from the lands ringing the Mediterranean Sea.

In the eastern Mediterranean, northeastern Africa, and western Asia in the Late Bronze Age, access to metal resources was vital for any state with pretensions to power. Indeed, commerce in metals energized the long-distance trade that bound together the economies of the various states of the time. We have seen the Assyrian traffic in silver from Anatolia, and later in this chapter we discuss the Egyptian passion for Nubian gold. The sources of the most important *utilitarian* metals—copper and tin to make bronze—lay in different directions. Copper came from Anatolia and Cyprus; tin came from Afghanistan and possibly the British Isles. Both ores had to be carried long distances and pass through a number of hands before arriving in the political centers where they were melded and shaped.

New modes of transportation expedited communications and commerce across great distances and inhospitable landscapes. Horses arrived in western Asia around 2000 B.C.E. Domesticated by nomadic peoples in Central Asia, they were brought into Mesopotamia from the northeastern mountains. They reached Egypt by about 1500 B.C.E. Horse-drawn chariots became the premier instrument of war, giving a terrifying advantage over soldiers on foot. The speed of travel and communication made possible by the horse opened up new opportunities for the creation of large territorial states and empires, because soldiers and government agents on horseback could cover great distances in a relatively short time.

Sometime after 1500 B.C.E., but not for another thousand years in Egypt, people began to make common use of camels, though the animal may have been domesticated a millennium earlier in southern Arabia. Thanks to their strength and ca-

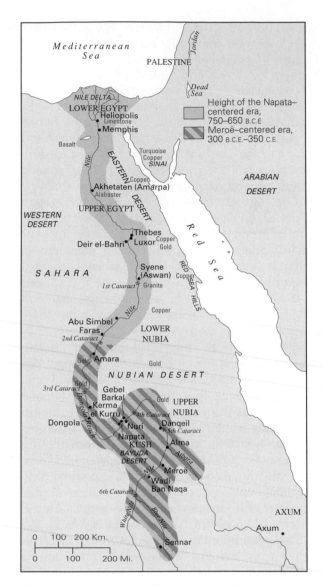

Map 3.3 Ancient Nubia   The land route alongside the Nile River as it flows through Nubia (modern-day northern Sudan and southern Egypt) has long served as a corridor connecting sub-Saharan Africa with North Africa. The centuries of Egyptian occupation, as well as time spent in Egypt by Nubian hostages, mercenaries, and merchants, led to a marked Egyptian cultural influence in Nubia.

pacity to go long distances without water, camels were able to travel across barren terrain. Their fortitude led, eventually, to the emergence of a new desert nomad and to the creation of cross-desert trade routes (see Chapter 8).

NUBIA

The long-distance commerce in precious goods that flourished in the second millennium B.C.E. in western Asia and the eastern Mediterranean had repercussions to the south. Of even greater importance to Egypt than myrrh and other products from southern lands was the gold of Nubia.

Since the first century B.C.E. the name "Nubia" has been applied to a thousand-mile (1,600-kilometer) stretch of the Nile Valley lying between Aswan and Khartoum (see Map 3.3). The ancient Egyptians called it "Ta-sety," "Land of the Bow," after the favorite weapon of its warriors, and "Kush." This region straddles the southern part of the modern nation of Egypt and the northern part of Sudan. Nubia is the only continuously inhabited stretch of territory connecting the lands south of the vast Sahara with North Africa. For thousands of years it has served as a corridor for trade between tropical Africa and the Mediterranean. It also was richly endowed with coveted natural resources—gold, copper, and semiprecious stones like diorite—which it exported.

Nubia's vital intermediary position and natural wealth explain the early rise there of a civilization with a complex political organization, social stratification, metallurgy, monumental building, and writing. Egyptian efforts to secure control of Nubian gold sparked the emergence of this vital and long-lived civilization. Nubia traditionally has been considered a periphery of Egypt and its culture regarded as derivative. Now, however, most scholars emphasize the interactions between Egypt and Nubia and the mutually beneficial borrowings and syntheses that took place.

Early Cultures and Egyptian Domination

The central geographical feature of Nubia, as of Egypt, is the Nile River. In this part of its course the Nile flows through a landscape of rocky desert, grassland, and fertile plain. Water from

Wall painting of Nubians arriving in Egypt with rings and bags of gold This scene was depicted in the fourteenth-century B.C.E. tomb of an Egyptian chief administrator in Nubia. Drawn by its rich gold deposits, during the New Kingdom Egyptian control extended deep into Nubia. Many Nubians also spent time in Egypt as emissaries, hostages, and soldiers. In this period Egypt exerted great influence on Nubian culture. (Courtesy of the Trustees of the British Museum)

the river was essential for agriculture in a climate that was severely hot and virtually without rainfall. Because of six cataracts—large boulders and threatening rapids—it was not possible for boats to follow the river continuously. Nevertheless, commerce and travel were made possible by boats operating over shorter distances between the cataracts and by tracks for walking and riding alongside the river or across the desert.

In the fourth millennium B.C.E. bands of people in northern Nubia—labeled the "A-Group" by archaeologists—made the transition from seminomadic hunting and gathering to a settled life based on grain agriculture and cattle herding. Peoples migrating into southern Nubia from the western desert around 2300 B.C.E. created the "C-Group" culture along similar lines. Egypt already must have been trading with Nubia before 3000 B.C.E., for Egyptian craftsmen of that period were working in ivory and in dark ebony wood—products of tropical Africa that had to come through Nubia.

Nubia first enters the historical record around 2300 B.C.E., in Old Kingdom Egyptian accounts of trade missions dispatched to southern lands. At that time Aswan, just north of the First Cataract,

was the southern limit of Egyptian control. Egyptian noblemen stationed there led donkey caravans south in search of gold, incense, ebony, ivory, slaves, and exotic animals from tropical Africa. This was dangerous work, requiring delicate negotiations with local Nubian chiefs in order to secure protection, but it brought substantial rewards to those who succeeded. The following account was left by Harkhuf, who made several voyages south around 2250:

His majesty sent me a second time alone; I went forth upon the Elephantine road, and I descended . . . an affair of eight months. When I descended I brought gifts from this country in very great quantity. Never before was the like brought to this land. . . . Never had any companion or caravan-conductor who went forth to Yam before this, done (it). . . . His majesty now sent me a third time to Yam; I went forth. . . . and I found the chief of Yam going to the land of Temeh to smite Temeh. . . . I went forth after him . . . and I pacified him, until he praised all the gods for the king's sake. . . . I descended with 300 asses laden with incense, ebony, heknu, grain, panthers, ivory (throw sticks) and every good product. [Yam and Temeh were regions in Nubia.][1]

During the Middle Kingdom (ca. 2040–1640 B.C.E.) Egypt adopted a more aggressive stance toward Nubia. Egyptian rulers were eager to secure direct control of the gold mines located in the desert east of the Nile and to cut out the Nubian middlemen who drove up the cost of luxury goods from the tropics. The Egyptians erected a string of mud-brick forts on islands and riverbanks south of the Second Cataract. These forts and the garrisons residing within them protected the southern frontier of Egypt against Nubians and desert raiders and regulated the flow of commerce. There seem to have been peaceable relations but little interaction between the occupying Egyptian forces and the native population of northern Nubia, which continued to practice its age-old farming and herding ways.

Farther south, where the Nile makes a great U-shaped turn in the fertile plain of the Dongola Reach, a more complex political entity was evolving from the chiefdoms of the third millennium B.C.E. The Egyptians gave the name "Kush" to the kingdom whose capital was located at Kerma, one of the earliest urbanized centers in tropical Africa. The kings of Kush mustered and organized the labor to build monumental walls and structures of mud brick, and they were accompanied to the grave by dozens or even hundreds of servants and wives. These human sacrifices as well as the rich objects found in the tombs prove the wealth and power of the kings and suggest a belief in some sort of afterlife where attendants and possessions would be useful. Kushite craftsmen were skilled in metalworking, whether for weapons or jewelry, and their pottery surpassed in skill and beauty anything produced in Egypt.

During the expansionist New Kingdom (ca. 1532–1070 B.C.E.) the Egyptians penetrated even more deeply into Nubia. They destroyed the kingdom of Kush and its capital at Kerma, and they extended their frontier to the Fourth Cataract. The Egyptians built a new administrative center at Napata, near Gebel Barkal, "the Holy Mountain," believed to be the abode of a local god. A high-ranking Egyptian official called "Overseer of Southern Lands" or "King's Son of Kush" ruled Nubia. In an era of intense commerce among the states of the Middle East, when everyone was looking to Egypt as the prime source of gold, Egypt extensively exploited the mines of Nubia at considerable human cost. Fatalities were high among native workers in the brutal desert climate, and the army had to ward off attacks from the desert tribes.

Five hundred years of Egyptian domination in Nubia left many marks. The Egyptian government imposed Egyptian culture on the native population. The children of high-ranking natives were brought to the Egyptian royal court, simultaneously serving as hostages to ensure the good behavior of their families back in Nubia and absorbing Egyptian language, culture, and religion, which they later carried home with them. Many Nubians went north to serve as archers in the Egyptian armed forces. The manufactured goods that they brought back to Nubia have been found in their graves. The Nubians built towns on the Egyptian model and erected stone temples to Egyptian gods, particularly Amon. The frequent depiction of Amon with the head of a ram, however, may reflect a blending of the chief Egyptian god with a Nubian ram deity.

The Kingdom of Meroë

Egyptian weakness after 1200 B.C.E. led to the collapse of Egypt's authority in Nubia (see below). In the eighth century B.C.E. a powerful new native kingdom emerged in southern Nubia. The story of this civilization, which lasted for over a thousand years, can be divided into two parts. During the early period, between the eighth and fourth centuries B.C.E., Napata, the former Egyptian headquarters, was the primary center. During the later period, from the fourth century B.C.E. to the fourth century C.E., the center of gravity shifted farther south to the site of Meroë, near the Sixth Cataract.

For half a century, from around 712 to 660 B.C.E., the kings of Nubia ruled all of Egypt as the Twenty-fifth Dynasty. They conducted themselves in the age-old manner of Egyptian rulers. They were addressed by the royal titles, depicted in traditional costume, and buried according to Egyptian custom. However, they kept their Nubian names and were depicted with Nubian physical features. They inaugurated an artistic and cultural renaissance, building on a monumental scale for the first time in centuries and reinvigorating Egyptian art, architecture, and religion by drawing selectively on practices and motifs of various periods. In this period each Nubian king resided at Memphis, the Old Kingdom capital. Thebes, the capital of the New Kingdom, was the residence of a female member of the king's family who remained celibate and was titled "God's Wife of Amon."

The Nubian dynasty overextended itself beginning in 701 B.C.E. by assisting local rulers in Palestine in their resistance to the Assyrian Empire. The Assyrians retaliated by invading Egypt and driving the Nubian monarchs back to their southern domain by 660 B.C.E. Napata again became the chief royal residence and the religious center of the kingdom, and Egyptian cultural influences remained strong. Egyptian hieroglyphs were the medium of written communication. Pyramids of modest size made of sandstone blocks were erected over the subterranean burial chambers of royalty. Royal bodies were mummified and the tombs filled with *shawabtis*, human figurines intended to play the role of servants in the next life.

By the fourth century B.C.E. the center of gravity had shifted south to Meroë, perhaps because Meroë was better situated for both agriculture

Temple of the lion-headed god Apedemak at Naqa in Nubia, first century C.E. Queen Amanitore (right) and her husband, Natakamani, are shown here slaying their enemies. While the architectural forms are Egyptian, the deity is Nubian. The costumes of the monarchs and the important role of the queen also reflect the trend in the Meroitic era to draw upon sub-Saharan culture practices. (P. L. Shinnie)

and trade, the economic mainstays of the Nubian kingdom. One consequence was a movement in cultural patterns away from Egypt and toward sub-Saharan Africa. A clear sign is the abandonment of Egyptian hieroglyphs and the adoption of a new set of symbols to write the Meroitic language. This form of writing is still essentially undeciphered. People continued to worship Amon as well as Isis, an Egyptian goddess connected to fertility and sexuality. But those deities had to share the stage with Nubian deities like the lion-god Apedemak, and elephants had some religious significance. Meroitic art was an eclectic mixture of Egyptian, Greco-Roman, and indigenous traditions.

Women of the royal family played an important role in the Meroitic era, another reflection, perhaps, of the influence of cultural concepts from sub-Saharan Africa. The Nubians employed a matrilineal system in which the king was succeeded by the son of his sister. In a number of cases Nubia was ruled by queens, either by themselves or in partnership with their husbands. Greek, Roman, and biblical sources refer to a queen of Nubia named Candace. However, these sources relate to different times, so "Candace" was most likely a title borne by a succession of rulers rather than a proper name. At least seven of these queens can be dated to the period between 284 B.C.E. and 115 C.E. Few details of their reigns are known, but they played a part in warfare, diplomacy, and the building of great temples and pyramid tombs.

Meroë itself was a huge city for its time, more than a square mile in area, overlooking a fertile stretch of grasslands and dominating a converging set of trade routes. Great reservoirs were dug to catch precious rainfall. The city was a major center for iron smelting (after 1000 B.C.E. iron had replaced bronze as the primary metal for tools and weapons). The Temple of Amon was approached by an avenue of stone rams, and the enclosed "Royal City" was filled with palaces, temples, and administrative buildings. The ruler, who may have been regarded as divine, was assisted by a professional class of officials, priests, and army officers.

Weakened by shifts in the trade routes when profitable commerce with the Roman Empire was diverted to the Red Sea and to the rising kingdom of Axum (in present-day Ethiopia), Meroë collapsed in the early fourth century C.E. Nomadic tribes from the western desert who had become more mobile because of the advent of the camel in North Africa may have overrun Meroë. In any case, the end of the Meroitic kingdom, and of this phase of civilization in Nubia, was as closely linked to Nubia's role in long-distance commerce as had been its beginning.

THE AEGEAN WORLD

Parallels between the rise of Nubian civilization in the second millennium B.C.E.—sparked by contact with the already ancient civilization of Egypt but striking out on its own path of cultural evolution—and concurrent developments in the lands of the Aegean Sea, a gulf of the eastern Mediterranean, are intriguing. The emergence of the Minoan civilization on the island of Crete and the Mycenaean civilization of Greece is another manifestation of the fertilizing influence of older centers on outlying lands and peoples.

The landscape of southern Greece and the Aegean islands is mostly rocky and arid, with small plains lying between the ranges of hills. The limited arable land is suitable for grains, grapevines, and olive trees. Flocks of sheep and goats graze the slopes. Sharply indented coastlines, natural harbors, and small islands lying virtually within sight of one another made sea travel the fastest and least costly mode of travel and transport. This region is resource-poor, having few deposits of metals and little timber. Those vital commodities, as well as surplus food for a large population, had to be imported from abroad. Thus the facts of geography and the lack of resources drew the inhabitants of the Aegean to the sea and brought them into contact with other peoples.

The Aegean peoples learned from the older, advanced civilizations of Mesopotamia, Syria, and Egypt and joined the diplomatic and economic networks of this "international" age. Indeed, because of their deficiency in important raw materials, the rise, success, and eventual fall of these societies was closely connected to their commercial and political relations with other peoples in the region.

The Minoan Civilization of Crete

Well before 2000 B.C.E. the island of Crete, which forms the southern boundary of the Aegean Sea (see Map 3.4), was the home of the first civilization in Europe to have complex political and social structures and advanced technologies such as were found in western Asia and northeastern Africa. These features include centralized government, monumental building, bronze metallurgy, writing, and recordkeeping. Archaeologists labeled this civilization "Minoan" after Greek legends about King Minos. The King ruled a vast naval empire and kept the monstrous Minotaur—half-man, half-bull—beneath his palace in a mazelike labyrinth built by the ingenious inventor Daedalus. Thus later Greeks recollected a time when Crete was home to many ships and sophisticated technologies.

Little is known about the ethnicity of the Cretans of this period, and their writings still cannot be translated. But archaeology has revealed sprawling palace complexes at the sites of Cnossus, Phaistos, and Mallia, and the distribution of Cretan pottery and other artifacts around the Mediterranean and Middle East testifies to widespread trading connections. The layout and architectural forms of the Minoan palaces, the methods of centralized government, and the system of writing all seem to owe much to the influence of the older civilizations of Egypt, Syria, and Mesopotamia. The absence of identifiable representations of the Cretan ruler, however, contrasts sharply with the grandiose depictions of the king in the Middle East and suggests a different conception of authority.

If small statues of women with elaborate headdresses and serpents trailing around their limbs have been correctly interpreted, we may say that the Cretans apparently worshiped female deities embodying the forces of fertility.

Gold cup with relief image of a young man capturing a wild bull Produced ca. 1500 B.C.E., by an artist from Crete but found in a tomb in southern Greece, this cup testifies both to the wealth of the ruling classes in the Bronze Age civilizations of the Aegean, who acquired precious and utilitarian metals from other parts of the Mediterranean and western Asia, and to the cultural influence of Minoan Crete on the Mycenaean Greeks. The elite seems to have enjoyed such idealized depictions of peasant life in romantic natural landscapes. (National Archaeological Museum Athens/Archaeological Receipts Fund)

Colorful fresco paintings applied to still-wet plaster on the walls of Cretan palaces portray groups of women in frilly, layered skirts enjoying themselves in conversation and observation of rituals or entertainments. We do not know whether pictures of young acrobats vaulting over the horns and back of an onrushing bull show a religious activity or mere sport. Scenes of servants briskly carrying jars and fishermen throwing nets and hooks from their boats suggest a joyful attitude toward work, though this portrayal may say more about the sentimental tastes of the elite classes than about the reality of daily toil for the masses. The stylized depictions of flora and fauna on painted vases—plants with swaying leaves and playful octopuses whose tendrils wind around the surface of the vase—reflect a delight in the beauty and order of the natural world.

Other than Cnossus, all the Cretan palaces, and even houses of the elite and peasant villages in the countryside, were deliberately destroyed

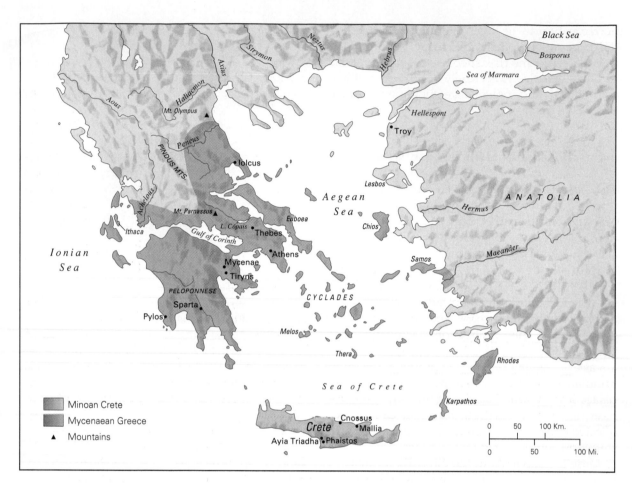

Map 3.4   Minoan and Mycenaean Civilizations of the Aegean   The earliest complex civilizations in Europe arose in the Aegean Sea. The Minoan civilization on the island of Crete evolved in the later third millennium B.C.E., and had a major cultural influence on the Mycenaean Greeks. Palaces decorated with fresco paintings, a centrally controlled economy, and the use of a system of writing for record-keeping are among the most conspicuous features of these societies.

around 1450 B.C.E. Because Mycenaean Greeks took over at Cnossus, most historians regard them as the likely culprits.

The Rise of Mycenaean Civilization

The standard view of Greek origins is that speakers of an Indo-European language ancestral to Greek migrated into the Greek peninsula around 2000 B.C.E., although some scholars argue for a much earlier date. A synthesis—through intermarriage, blending of languages, and melding of religious concepts—must have taken place be-

tween the indigenous population and the newcomers. Out of this mix emerged the first Greek culture. For centuries this society was simple and static. Farmers and shepherds lived in essentially Stone Age conditions, wringing a bare living from the land. Then, sometime around 1600 B.C.E. life on the Greek mainland changed relatively suddenly.

More than a century ago a German businessman, Heinrich Schliemann, set out to prove the historical veracity of the *Iliad* and the *Odyssey*, two great epics attributed to a poet named Homer, who probably lived shortly before 700 B.C.E. Homer's Greeks were led by Agamemnon, the king of Mycenae in southern Greece. In 1876 Schliemann stunned a skeptical scholarly world by his discovery at Mycenae of a circle of graves at the base of deep, rectangular shafts. These shaft graves, containing the bodies of men, women, and children, were filled with gold jewelry and ornaments, weapons, and utensils. Clearly, some people in this society had acquired a new level of wealth, authority, and the capacity to mobilize human labor. Subsequent excavation at Mycenae uncovered a large palace complex, massive fortification walls, another circle of shaft graves, and other components of a rich and technologically advanced civilization that lasted from around 1600 to 1150 B.C.E.

How is the sudden rise of Mycenae and other centers in mainland Greece to be explained? Greek legends later spoke of the arrival of immigrants from Phoenicia (modern Lebanon) and Egypt, but archaeology provides no confirmation. Another legend recalled the power of King Minos of Crete, who demanded from the Greek city of Athens an annual tribute of ten maidens and ten young men. The Athenian hero Theseus went to Crete, entered the labyrinth, and slew the Minotaur, thereby liberating his people.

Although there is no archaeological evidence for Cretan political control of the Greek mainland, there is much evidence of the powerful cultural influence exerted by Crete. From the Minoans the Mycenaeans borrowed the idea of the palace, the centralized economy, the administrative bureaucracy, and their writing system. Also from the Minoans they learned styles and techniques of architecture, pottery making, and fresco and vase painting. This explains where the Mycenaean Greeks got their technology. But how did they suddenly accumulate power and wealth? Most historians look to the profits from trade and piracy and perhaps also to the pay and booty brought back by mercenaries (soldiers who served for pay in foreign lands).

This first advanced civilization in Greece is called "Mycenaean" largely because Mycenae was the first site excavated. Other centers have been excavated since Schliemann's day—including Tiryns, about 10 miles (16 kilometers) from Mycenae; Pylos, in the southwest; Athens and Thebes in central Greece; and Iolcus in northern Greece.

Mycenae exemplifies the common pattern of these citadels: a commanding location on a hilltop surrounded by high, thick fortification walls made of stones so large that later Greeks believed the giant, one-eyed Cyclopes lifted them into place. Within the fortified perimeter were the palace and administrative complex. The large central hall with an open hearth and columned porch was surrounded by courtyards, by living quarters for the royal family, courtiers, and servants, and by offices, storerooms, and workshops. The palace walls were covered with brightly painted frescoes depicting scenes of war, the hunt, and daily life, as well as decorative motifs from nature. The fortified perimeter served as a place of refuge for the entire community in time of danger.

Nearby lay the tombs of the rulers and other leading families—shaft graves and later, much grander, beehive-shaped tombs made of rings of stone and covered with a mound of earth. Large houses, probably belonging to the aristocracy, lay just outside the walls. The peasants lived on the lower slopes and in the plain below, close to the land that they worked.

Additional information about Mycenaean life is provided by over four thousand baked clay tablets. The writing found on the tablets, today known as "Linear B," uses pictorial signs to represent syllables, like the earlier, still undeciphered system employed on Crete, but it is recognizably an early form of Greek. An unwieldy system of writing, it was probably known only to the palace administrators. These tablets are essentially lists: of chariot wheels piled up in palace storerooms, of rations paid to textile workers, of gifts dedicated to a particular deity, of ships stationed along the coasts. An extensive palace bureaucracy kept track of people, animals, and objects in exhaustive detail and exercised a high degree of control over the economy of the kingdom. Well-organized grain production supported large populations in certain regions, such as the territory controlled by Pylos in the southwest. (Archaeologists can make a rough estimate of population through surface surveys in which they tabulate the number of pieces of broken pottery from a given period that are visible on the ground.)

Certain industries seem to have been state monopolies. For instance, the state controlled the wool industry from raw material to finished product. Scribes kept track of the flocks in the field, the sheared wool, the distribution of raw wool to spinners and weavers, and the production, storage, and disbursal of cloth articles.

The view of this society that modern researchers can extract from the archaeological evidence and from the texts of the tablets is very limited. We know almost nothing about individual personalities—not even the name of a single Mycenaean king—very little about the political and legal systems, social structures, gender relations, and religious beliefs, and nothing about particular historical events and relations with other Mycenaean centers or peoples overseas.

The limited evidence for the overall political organization of Greece in this period is contradictory. In Homer's *Iliad* Agamemnon, the king of Mycenae, is in charge of a great expedition of Greeks from different regions against the city of Troy in northwest Anatolia. To this can be added the cultural uniformity to be found in all the Mycenaean centers: a remarkable similarity in the shapes, decorative styles, and production techniques of buildings, tombs, utensils, tools, clothing, and works of art. Some scholars argue that such cultural uniformity can be understood only within a context of political unity. The plot of the *Iliad*, however, revolves around the difficulties Agamemnon has in asserting control over other Greek leaders, such as the indomitable warrior Achilles. And the archaeological remains and contents of the Linear B tablets give strong indications of independent centers of power at Mycenae, Pylos, and elsewhere. Given this evidence, cultural uniformity might best be explained by extensive contacts and commerce between the various Greek kingdoms.

Overseas Commerce, Settlement, and Aggression

Long-distance contact and trade were made possible by the seafaring skill of Minoans and Mycenaeans. Two sources provide evidence of the appearance and functioning of Aegean vessels:

(1) wall paintings from Egypt and from Thera, an Aegean island, and (2) the excavation of vessels buried in sand at the bottom of the Mediterranean. Freighters depended entirely on wind and sail; the crews of warships could take down the mast and use oars when necessary. In general ancient sailors preferred to keep the land in sight and sail in daylight hours. Their sleek, light, wooden vessels had little decking, so the crew had to go ashore for food and sleep every night. With their low keels the ships could run right up onto the beach.

The wide dispersal of Cretan and Greek pottery and crafted goods indicates that Cretans and Greeks engaged in trade not only within the Aegean but with other parts of the Mediterranean and Middle East. At certain sites, where the quantity and range of artifacts suggest a settlement of Aegean peoples, an interesting pattern is evident. The oldest artifacts are Minoan, then Minoan and Mycenaean objects are found side by side, and eventually Greek wares replace Cretan goods altogether. The physical evidence seems to indicate that Cretan merchants opened up commercial routes and established trading posts in the Mediterranean, then admitted Mycenaean traders to these locations, and were supplanted by the Greeks in the fifteenth century B.C.E.

What commodities formed the basis of this widespread commercial activity? The numerous Aegean pots found throughout the Mediterranean and Middle East must once have contained products such as wine or oil. Other possible exports include weapons and other crafted goods, as well as slaves and mercenary soldiers, which leave no trace in the archaeological record. Minoan and Mycenaean sailors may also have served as middlemen along long-distance trading networks, making a tidy profit by carrying goods from and to other places.

As for imports, amber (a hard, translucent, yellowish-brown fossil resin used for jewelry) from northern Europe and ivory from Syria have been discovered at Aegean sites, and it seems likely that the large population of southwest Greece and other regions necessitated imports of grain. Above all, the Aegean lands needed metals, both the gold so highly prized by the rulers and the copper and tin needed to make bronze.

Fresco from the Aegean island of Thera, ca. 1600 B.C.E. This fresco depicts the arrival of a fleet in a harbor as people watch from the walls of the town. The Minoan civilization of Crete was famous in later legend for its naval power. This picture, originally painted on wet plaster, reveals the appearance and design of ships in the Bronze Age Aegean. The island of Thera was devastated by a massive volcanic explosion in the seventeenth century B.C.E., thought by many to be the origin of the myth of Atlantis sinking beneath the sea. (Archaeological Receipts Fund, Athens)

A number of sunken ships carrying copper ingots recently have been excavated on the floor of the Mediterranean. Scholars believe these ships probably carried metals from the island of Cyprus, in the northeast corner of the Mediterranean, to the Aegean. As in early China, members of the elite classes were virtually the only people who possessed things made of metal, and their near monopoly of metals may have had symbolic significance, working to legitimate their power. The bronze tripods piled up in the storerooms of Homer's heroes bring to mind the bronze vessels buried in Shang tombs.

In an unsettled world, the flip side of trade is piracy. Mycenaeans were tough, warlike, and acquisitive. They traded with those who were strong enough to hold their own and took from those who were too weak to resist. There is reason to believe that they became a thorn in the side of the Hittite kings of the fourteenth and thirteenth centuries B.C.E. A number of documents found in the archives at Hattusha, the Hittite capital, refer to the king and land of "Ahhijawa," most likely a Hittite rendering of *Achaeans*, the term used most frequently by Homer for the Greeks. The documents indicate that relations were sometimes friendly, sometimes strained, and they give the impression that the people of Ahhijawa were aggressive and taking advantage of Hittite preoccupation or weakness. Homer's tale of the ten-year Greek siege and eventual destruction of Troy, a city located on the fringes of Hittite territory and controlling an important commercial route connecting the Mediterranean and Black Seas, should be seen against this backdrop of Mycenaean belligerence and opportunism. Archaeology has confirmed a destruction at Troy around 1200 B.C.E.

THE FALL OF LATE BRONZE AGE CIVILIZATIONS

Hittite difficulties with Ahhijawa and the Greek attack on Troy foreshadow the troubles that culminated in the destruction of many of the old centers of the Middle East and Mediterranean around 1200 B.C.E. This was a momentous period in human history when, for reasons that historians do not completely understand, large numbers of people were on the move. As migrants or invaders swarmed into one region, they displaced other peoples, who then became part of the tide of refugees.

Around 1200 B.C.E. invaders from the north destroyed Hattusha, and the Hittite kingdom came crashing down (see Map 3.3). The tide of destruction moved south into Syria, and the great coastal city of Ugarit was swept away. Egypt managed to beat back two attacks. Around 1220 B.C.E., Pharaoh Merneptah, the son and successor of Ramesses II, repulsed an assault on the Nile Delta by "Libyans and Northerners coming from all lands," and about thirty years later Ramesses III checked a major invasion of "Peoples of the Sea" in Palestine. The Egyptian pharaoh claimed to have won a great victory, but the Philistines occupied the coast of Palestine. Egypt survived, barely, but gave up its territories in Syria-Palestine and lost contact with the rest of western Asia. The Egyptians also lost their foothold in Nubia, opening the way for the emergence of the native kingdom centered on Napata.

Among the invaders listed in the Egyptian inscriptions are the Ekwesh, a group that could be Achaeans—that is, Greeks. In this time of troubles it is easy to imagine opportunistic Mycenaeans taking a prominent role. Whether or not the Mycenaeans participated in the destructions elsewhere, in the first half of the twelfth century B.C.E. their own centers collapsed. The rulers apparently had seen trouble coming, for at some sites they began to build more extensive fortifications, and they took steps to guarantee the water supply of the citadels. But their efforts were in vain, and virtually all the palaces were destroyed. The Linear B tablets survived only because they were baked hard like pottery in the fires that consumed the palaces.

Scholars used to attribute the Mycenaean destruction to foreign invaders, but the archaeological record contains no trace of outsiders, and later Greek legends portrayed this as a time of internal dynastic struggles and wars between rival Greek kingdoms. A compelling explanation has been advanced that combines external and internal factors, since it is likely to be more than coincidence that the collapse of Mycenaean civilization occurred at roughly the same time as the fall of other great civilizations in the region. If the ruling class in the Mycenaean centers depended for their wealth and power on the import of vital commodities and the profits from trade, then the annihilation of major trading partners and disruption of trade routes would have weakened their position. Competition for limited resources may have led to the growth of internal unrest and, ultimately, political collapse.

The end of Mycenaean civilization illustrates the degree to which the major centers of the Late Bronze Age were interdependent. It also serves as a case study of the consequences of political and economic collapse. The destruction of the palaces meant the end of the political and economic domination of the ruling class. The massive administrative apparatus revealed in the Linear B tablets disappeared, and the technique of writing was forgotten, having no function outside the context of palace administration. People were displaced and on the move. Surface studies in various parts of Greece indicate depopulation in some regions and an inflow of people to other regions that had escaped the destruction. The Greek language, however, persisted, and a thousand years later people were still worshiping certain gods mentioned in the Linear B tablets. There was also continuity in material culture: people continued to make and use the vessels and implements that they were familiar with. But this society was much poorer, and there was a marked decline in artistic and technical skill. Different regions developed local shapes, styles, and techniques. This change from the uniformity of the Mycenaean Age was a consequence of the isolation of different parts of Greece from one another in this period of limited travel and communication.

Thus perished the cosmopolitan world of the Late Bronze Age in the Mediterranean and Middle East. The fragile infrastructure of civilization was shattered by a combination of external violence and internal weaknesses. Societies that had become interdependent through complex links of trade, diplomacy, and shared technologies, and had long prospered together, now fell together into a "Dark Age"—a period of poverty, isolation, and loss of knowledge—that lasted for four centuries. (The advent of the Iron Age and revival of complex and interdependent societies will be taken up for western Asia in Chapter 4, and for the eastern Mediterranean in Chapter 5.)

CONCLUSION

This chapter traces the development of a number of civilizations in Africa, Europe, and Asia in the second and first millennium B.C.E. Just as bronze metallurgy began at different times in different parts of the Eastern Hemisphere (in western Asia around 2500 B.C.E., in East Asia around 2000, in northeastern Africa around 1500), so too did the Bronze Age end at different times in different societies. The transition to iron as the primary metal came around 1000 B.C.E. in the eastern Mediterranean, northeastern Africa, and western Asia, and about five hundred years later in East Asia.

The acquisition of copper and tin to make bronze was a priority of Bronze Age elite classes. To a significant degree, political, military, and economic strategies reflected the demand for this commodity. Bronze was acquired in various ways in different parts of the hemisphere. In early China the state largely controlled the prospecting, mining, refining, alloying, and manufacturing processes. In western Asia long-distance networks of exchange were built up to

Important Events for the Late Bronze Age Civilizations of Western Asia, Northeastern Africa, and Southeastern Europe

1750 B.C.E.	Rise of Kingdom of Kush
1700	Hittites Become Dominant Power in Anatolia
1532	Hyksos Expelled from Egypt
1500	Egyptian Conquest of Nubia
1460	Kassites Assume Control of Southern Mesopotamia
1450	Queen Hatshepsut, Ruler of Egypt, Dispatches Expedition to Punt
1450	Destruction of Minoan Palaces in Crete
1353	Akhenaten Launches "Revolution" in Egypt
1285	Pharaoh Ramesses II Battles Hittites at Kadesh
1200–1150	Destruction of Late Bronze Age Centers in Anatolia and Greece

facilitate the trade in metals. Cities sprang up and achieved great prosperity as a result of their location on trade routes. Commercial crossroads became targets of military and diplomatic activity for the major powers of the time, as, for instance, the Syria-Palestine region was for the Egyptian and Hittite states.

The uses to which bronze was put also varied in different societies. Normally this costly metal was available only to the elite classes. Possession of bronze weapons with their hard, sharp edges enabled the warriors of the Mycenaean and Shang ruling classes, as well as the royal armies of Egypt and Mesopotamia, to dominate the peasant masses. In the poems of Homer, Greek aristocrats hoard bronze weapons and utensils in their heavy-gated storerooms and give them to one another in rituals of gift exchange that create bonds of friendship and obligation. In Shang China the most important use of bronze was to craft the bronze vessels that played a vital role in the rituals of contact with the spirits of ancestors.

The period from 2200 to 500 B.C.E. saw the rise of complex societies with social stratification, powerful governments, large bureaucracies, strong armies, systems of writing, and impressive technologies of manufacture and monumental building, in China, Iran, Syria-Palestine, Anatolia, Nubia, and the Aegean. Many of these new civilizations learned much from the already ancient centers in Mesopotamia and Egypt. At the same time, the old centers could hardly afford to remain static. In the competitive circumstances of this increasingly interconnected world, new means had to be found to expedite travel, transport, and communication. So, for instance, Akkadian cuneiform writing was used throughout western Asia, even in correspondence between the Egyptian throne and dependent rulers in Syria-Palestine. The use of horses speeded up communication between central governments and their outlying areas and facilitated the projection of power through fearsome squadrons of war chariots.

The interdependence of the societies of the eastern Mediterranean and western Asia promoted prosperity, development, and the spread of ideas and technologies in the Late Bronze Age. Ironically, that interdependence became a source of weakness at the end of the era, during the time of migrations and invasions around 1200 B.C.E. The disruption of trading networks weakened ruling classes accustomed to easy access to metals and other valuable commodities, and the attacks of invaders and the wanderings of displaced peoples brought down swollen bureaucracies.

In East Asia at roughly the same time there was no "fall," because China was far away and not tightly linked by trade relations to the eastern Mediterranean and western Asia. The Zhou replaced the Shang, but there was much continuity in political, religious, and cultural traditions. In contrast, in the eastern Mediterranean and western Asia the destruction was so great that the old centers did not survive or were severely weakened, and this part of the world entered a Dark Age. Within a few centuries new peoples

would come to the fore—in particular the Assyrians, Phoenicians, and Hebrews, whose story unfolds in the next chapter.

SUGGESTED READING

Caroline Blunden and Mark Elvin, *Cultural Atlas of China* (1983), contains general geographic, ethnographic, and historical information about China through the ages, as well as many maps and illustrations. Conrad Schirokauer, *A Brief History of Chinese Civilization* (1991), and John King Fairbank, *China: A New History* (1992), offer useful chapters on early China. John Hay, *Ancient China* (1973), and Kwang-chih Chang, *The Archaeology of Ancient China*, 4th ed. (1986), go into greater depth and emphasize archaeological evidence. W. Thomas Chase, *Ancient Chinese Bronze Art: Casting the Precious Sacral Vessel* (1991), contains a brief but useful discussion of the importance of bronzes in ancient China, as well as a detailed discussion of bronze-casting techniques. Robert Temple, *The Genius of China: 3,000 Years of Science, Discovery, and Invention* (1986), explores many aspects of Chinese technology, using a division into general topics such as agriculture, engineering, and medicine. Sharon L. Sievers, in *Restoring Women to History* (1988), and Patricia Ebrey, "Women, Marriage, and the Family in Chinese History," in *Heritage of China: Contemporary Perspectives on Chinese Civilization*, ed. Paul S. Ropp (1990), address the very limited evidence for women in early China.

Many of the books recommended in the Suggested Reading list for Chapter 2 are useful for Mesopotamia, Syria, and Egypt in the Late Bronze Age. In addition see Miriam Lichtheim, *Ancient Egyptian Literature: A Book of Readings, Vol. 2, The New Kingdom* (1973); Donald B. Redford, *Egypt, Canaan, and Israel in Ancient Times* (1992), which explores the relations of Egypt with the Syria-Palestine region in this period; and H. W. F. Saggs, *Babylonians* (1995), which devotes several chapters to this more thinly documented epoch in the history of southern Mesopotamia. On the Hittites see O. R. Gurney, *The Hittites*, 2d ed., rev. (1990), and J. G. Macqueen, *The Hittites and Their Contemporaries in Asia Minor* (1975). Tamsyn Barton, *Ancient Astrology* (1994), devotes her first chapter to early manifestations of astrology in Mesopotamia and Egypt.

After a long period of scholarly neglect—with an occasional exception such as Bruce G. Trigger, *Nubia Under the Pharaohs* (1976)—the study of ancient Nubia is beginning to receive considerable attention. David O'Connor, *Ancient Nubia: Egypt's Rival in Africa* (1993); Joyce L. Haynes, *Nubia: Ancient Kingdoms of Africa* (1992); Karl-Heinz Priese, *The Gold of Meroë* (1993)—all reflect the new interest of major museums in the art and artifacts of this society, as does John H. Taylor, *Egypt and Nubia* (1991), which also emphasizes the fruitful interaction of the Egyptian and Nubian cultures.

R. A. Higgins, *The Archaeology of Minoan Crete* (1973), O. Krzysz Kowska and L. Nixon, *Minoan Society* (1983), and N. Marinatos, *Minoan Religion* (1993), examine the archaeological evidence for the Minoan civilization. The brief discussion of M. I. Finley, *Early Greece: The Bronze and Archaic Ages* (1970), and the much fuller accounts of Emily Vermeule, *Greece in the Bronze Age* (1972), and J. T. Hooker, *Mycenaean Greece* (1976), are still useful treatments of Mycenaean Greece, based primarily on archaeological evidence.

For the evidence of the Linear B tablets see John Chadwick, *Linear B and Related Scripts* (1987) and *The Mycenaean World* (1976). J. V. Luce, *Homer and the Heroic Age* (1975), and Carol G. Thomas, *Myth Becomes History: Pre-Classical Greece* (1993), examine the usefulness of the Homeric poems for reconstructing the Greek past. For the disruptions and destructions of the Late Bronze Age in the eastern Mediterranean, see N. K. Sandars, *The Sea Peoples: Warriors of the Ancient Mediterranean* (1978), and Trude Dothan and Moshe Dothan, *People of the Sea: The Search for the Philistines* (1992).

NOTES

1. J. H. Breasted, *Ancient Records of Egypt*, vol. 1 (1906), pp. 153–154.

2. William L. Moran, *The Amarna Letters* (1992), pp. xxx.

The Formation of New Cultural Communities, 1000 B.C.E. – 500 C.E.

For a number of reasons, the fifteen centuries from 1000 B.C.E. to 500 C.E. may be seen as a new chapter in the story of humanity, involving a vast expansion in the scale of human institutions and activities. First, new ethnic groups—Assyrians in northern Mesopotamia and Iranians in the high plateau to the east, Israelites at the crossroads between Asia and Africa, the Phoenicians of Lebanon and their Carthaginian offspring, Greeks and Romans in the Mediterranean, Aryans in India—arose to challenge the primacy of the old centers. These peoples occupied lands watered by rainfall rather than by river-water irrigation. Such environments sustained small farms worked by independent individuals and families, in contrast to the strong central authority and mass mobilization of dependent laborers required by the river-

Technology

Iron metallurgy in western Asia/eastern Mediterranean
Cavalry in Middle East and China
Shipbuilding and navigation (Phoenician, Greek, Indian Ocean, Polynesian)
Road networks, aqueducts, and watermills
Astronomy
Alphabetic system of Phoenicians and Greeks
700 B.C.E.—Hoplite infantry in Greece
700 B.C.E.—Coinage in Anatolia
500 C.E.—Mathematics (zero and place-value system) in India
300 B.C.E.—Horse-collar harness in China

Environment

Rainwater agriculture
Slash-and-burn agriculture in Southeast Asia
Polynesian settlement of Pacific islands
500 B.C.E.—Persian "paradise" (ancestor of Western garden)

valley civilizations. This difference led to new social structures, political traditions, religious institutions, and conceptions of humanity and of the gods.

The political and social traditions of these peoples discouraged exploitation of members of their own community, so elite groups devised new ways of gaining wealth and power. Thus, a second key phenomenon of the period was the formation of empires in which one ethnic group controlled the territory and taxed the surplus wealth of other groups. Technological innovations in metallurgy, military tactics, engineering, transportation, and communications made possible large political entities with diverse populations. Networks of cities connected by well-built roads permitted effective administration of far-flung territories. Greatly expanded trade over long distances brought essential raw materials and luxury goods to the ruling classes and facilitated the spread of new ideas—political ideologies explaining the relationship of individuals to the state and religious ideas promising knowledge and salvation.

Essential to empire formation was a third major development: significant enhancement of

old technologies and the development of new ones. In many parts of the world iron replaced bronze as the preferred metal for tools and weapons. Political changes often reflected advances in military technology and tactics. In the Middle East and China soldiers on horseback replaced charioteers. The success of Greek armored infantrymen fighting in tight formations inspired Macedonian (northern Greek) and Roman foot soldiers, who forged empires of unprecedented size. Advances in siege and fortification techniques, ship design, and naval tactics accompanied these developments.

Utilizing new materials and techniques and mobilizing large pools of labor, governments undertook construction projects on unprecedented scales. To move troops, expedite communication, and protect frontier areas, the Roman and Chinese governments built thousands of miles of paved roads, long walls, and chains of forts. The technology of communication also underwent profound change. The development of an alphabetic system by Phoenicians and Greeks removed writing from the control of specialists. New, written literature emerged. Simplified writing systems also made possible the extensive

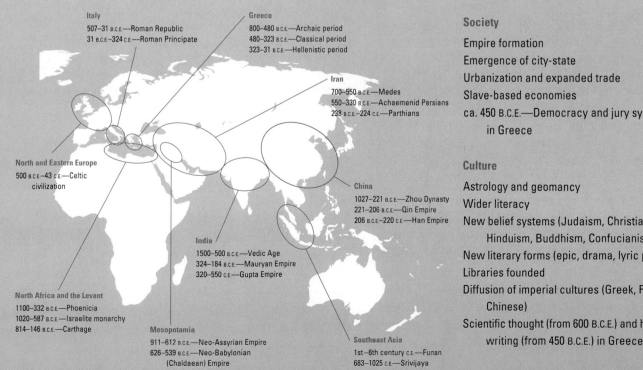

Italy
507–31 B.C.E.—Roman Republic
31 B.C.E.–324 C.E.—Roman Principate

Greece
800–480 B.C.E.—Archaic period
480–323 B.C.E.—Classical period
323–31 B.C.E.—Hellenistic period

Iran
700–550 B.C.E.—Medes
550–330 B.C.E.—Achaemenid Persians
238 B.C.E.–224 C.E.—Parthians

North and Eastern Europe
500 B.C.E.–43 C.E.—Celtic civilization

China
1027–221 B.C.E.—Zhou Dynasty
221–206 B.C.E.—Qin Empire
206 B.C.E.–220 C.E.—Han Empire

India
1500–500 B.C.E.—Vedic Age
324–184 B.C.E.—Mauryan Empire
320–550 C.E.—Gupta Empire

North Africa and the Levant
1100–332 B.C.E.—Phoenicia
1020–587 B.C.E.—Israelite monarchy
814–146 B.C.E.—Carthage

Mesopotamia
911–612 B.C.E.—Neo-Assyrian Empire
626–539 B.C.E.—Neo-Babylonian (Chaldaean) Empire

Southeast Asia
1st–6th century C.E.—Funan
683–1025 C.E.—Srivijaya

Society

Empire formation

Emergence of city-state

Urbanization and expanded trade

Slave-based economies

ca. 450 B.C.E.—Democracy and jury system in Greece

Culture

Astrology and geomancy

Wider literacy

New belief systems (Judaism, Christianity, Hinduism, Buddhism, Confucianism)

New literary forms (epic, drama, lyric poetry)

Libraries founded

Diffusion of imperial cultures (Greek, Roman, Chinese)

Scientific thought (from 600 B.C.E.) and historical writing (from 450 B.C.E.) in Greece

record keeping so important to the survival of large empires such as those of the Romans and Chinese, as well as new kinds of propaganda to bolster the position of the ruling classes.

Fourth, this period saw the emergence of cities with populations in the hundreds of thousands or more—Alexandria in Egypt, Rome in Italy, Chang'an in China, Pataliputra in India. Imperial capitals dotted with palaces, temples, monuments, storehouses, market centers, and places for public entertainment advertised the glory and power of the rulers, while stretching to the limit the capacities of ancient technology to carry water into crowded urban centers and carry sewage away. These giants were but the most extreme products of a process of urbanization that brought into being many smaller cities and towns. Most people, however, lived in the countryside and labored on the land. Without the agricultural surplus that the farming population was able to produce, city dwellers would not have been able to engage in specialized tasks of manufacture, trade, and services on such a large scale.

Fifth, trade took on a new character. The land and sea routes that expedited imperial control also became the highways by which long-distance trade expanded. Like writing, commerce was no longer the exclusive preserve of elite groups; emerging middle classes also sought imported goods. The advent of coinage in the first millennium B.C.E. further stimulated local and regional economies, making it easier for people to store wealth and facilitating exchanges.

The routes used for trade also carried ideas. Religious beliefs different from the largely localized cults of earlier times sprang up. Mystery religions that promised salvation after death and religions that taught belief in one universal god and demanded high ethical standards had broad appeal. The Zoroastrian religion of the Persians, one of the great ethical creeds of the ancient world, spread during the period of Persian rule and may have exerted considerable influence on Judaism. Jews dispersed far beyond their home-land, paving the way for the spread of Christianity, itself an offshoot of Judaism. Hinduism evolved to become a cultural force unifying many political, social, and ethnic divisions in South Asia. Buddhism spread from its point of origin in northern India and began to make its way into central, southeast, and east Asia.

Sixth, this era saw dramatic movements of peoples. Members of *dominant* ethnic groups moved from the core area of empires, carrying with them their language, beliefs, technologies, and customs. The attractions of the Greek, Roman, and Chinese cultures, as well as the opportunities those cultures offered to ambitious members of *dominated* populations, led to the creation of large cultural zones in which elite groups participated in a luxurious way of life, while most members of the peasant population of the countryside retained their ancestral languages and cultures. Phoenicians, Greeks, and Italians moved to new homes all over the Mediterranean, attracted by the familiar climate, seasonal rhythms, and plants and animals of the region. Celts spread out from eastern Europe to occupy most of Europe north of the Alps. Aryans moved south and east from the Indus River Valley to occupy the Ganges basin and all but the southern portion of the Indian subcontinent.

In an inversion of this phenomenon, the Assyrians and, to a lesser extent, the Persians carried out forcible relocations of entire populations, usually rebellious groups. They were taken to strategic locations in the heart of the empire, where their labor was utilized to promote agriculture or construct imperial showplaces. The huge inflow of enslaved prisoners-of-war to Italy in the period of Roman expansion similarly altered the ethnic composition of Italy.

The end result of the interaction of these six forces was the creation of large cultural communities, some of them persisting to modern times. In the later second and first millennium B.C.E. in Israel, Greece, Iran, Rome, China, and India, cultural traditions sprang up that directly helped to shape the modern world.

CHAPTER FOUR

The Early Iron Age in Western Eurasia, 1000–300 B.C.E.

Celtic Europe · The First Empire: The Rise of Assyria

Israel · Phoenicia and the Mediterranean

The End of an Era: The Fall of Assyria

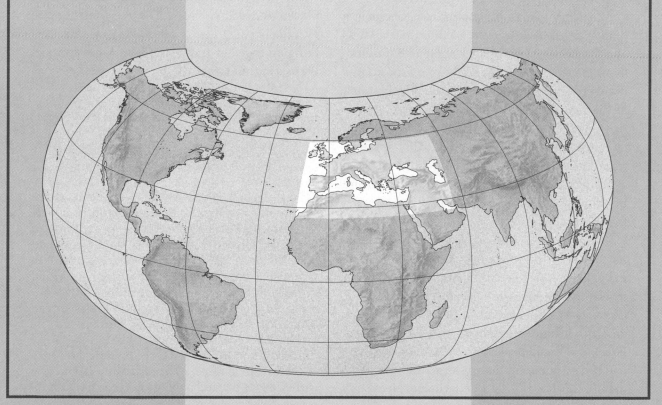

A ncient peoples were very interested in the origins of their communities. One famous story concerned the great city of Carthage in present-day Tunisia, which for centuries dominated the waters and commerce of the western Mediterranean. Tradition held that Dido, a member of the royal family of the Phoenician city-state of Tyre in southern Lebanon, fled in 814 B.C.E. with her supporters to the western Mediterranean after her husband had been viciously murdered by her brother, the king of Tyre. Setting ashore on the North African coast, these refugees made friendly contact with the local population, who agreed to give them as much land as a cow's hide could cover. By cleverly cutting the hide into narrow strips, they were able to mark out a substantial piece of territory for their new foundation: Kart Chadasht, or "the New City" (*Carthago* on the tongues of their Roman enemies). At a later time, faithful to the memory of her dead husband, Dido committed suicide rather than marry a local chieftain.

This story evokes an important phenomenon of the Early Iron Age in the Mediterranean lands and western Asia: the migration and resettlement of peoples. For a variety of reasons, large numbers of people relocated during the first half of the first millennium B.C.E. Some populations fled when conquerors occupied their territories. Other conquered peoples were forcibly removed from their ancestral homes. Still others chose to settle in distant lands in response to political and military pressures or in the hope of improving their lot in life.

This chapter examines the history of Europe north of the Alps, western Asia, and North Africa in the Early Iron Age but carries the story farther forward when necessary. The focus is on four societies: the Celtic peoples of Europe; the Assyrians of northern Mesopotamia; the Israelites of Israel; and the Phoenicians of Lebanon and Syria and their colonies in the western Mediterranean, mainly Carthage. After the decline or demise of the ancient centers dominant throughout the third and second millennia B.C.E., these four societies evolved into new political, cultural, and commercial centers.

Of primary concern are the causes, means, and consequences of large-scale movements of people. But this chapter also focuses on how these societies developed different forms of political, social, and economic organization. In Celtic Western Europe an elite class of warriors and priests, operating out of hilltop fortresses, were the leaders of society. Under the direction of a powerful centralized monarchy, the Assyrians forged the first real empire in world history. The Israelites evolved from seminomadic herders belonging to a set of loosely federated tribes to settled agriculturalists in a small monarchic state in which the priests of their god Yahweh wielded considerable power and influence. The Phoenicians inhabited a string of autonomous city-states in which the leading merchant families, in concert with the monarch, played a dominant role. The Assyrian Empire eventually ruled nearly all of western Asia, thus bringing together the histories of Mesopotamia, Phoenicia, and Israel.

CELTIC EUROPE

T o this point we have taken little note of Europe except for the emergence on its southeast fringe of the Late Bronze Age cultures of Crete and Greece (see Chapter 3). Humans had been living in Europe for a very long time (see Chapter 1), but the lack of any system of writing severely limits our knowledge of the earliest Europeans. Around 500 B.C.E. Celtic peoples spread across a substantial portion of Europe and, by coming into contact with the literate societies of the Mediterranean, entered the historical record.

Our main source of information about the early Celts is the archaeological record, which re-

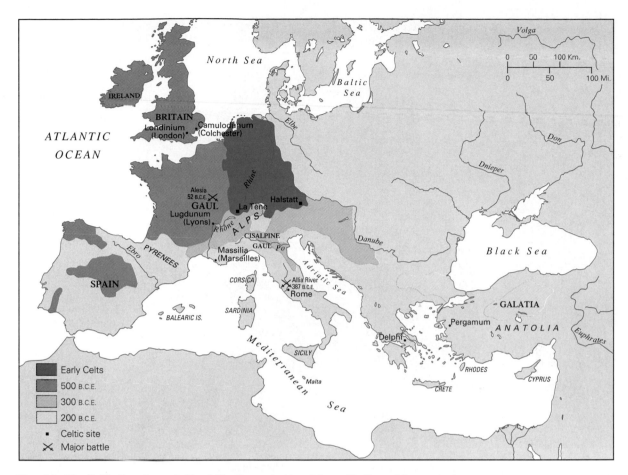

Map 4.1 The Celtic Peoples Celtic civilization probably originated in Central Europe in the early part of the first millennium B.C.E. Around 500 B.C.E. Celtic peoples began to migrate, making Celtic civilization the dominant cultural style in Europe north of the Alps. The Celts' interactions with the peoples of the Mediterranean, including Greeks and Romans, encompassed both wars and trade.

veals a lot about the objects they made and used and the spaces in which they lived. The accounts of Greek and Roman travelers and conquerors also provide information about political and social organization, religion, and some historical personalities and events, although those outside observers sometimes may have been misinformed or biased. Another useful source is Celtic literature from Wales and Ireland that was written down centuries later during the European Middle Ages, and though colored by the Christianity of that era, probably descends from earlier oral traditions preserved by the bards, specialists who composed and transmitted stories of the legendary past.

The Spread of the Celts

The term *Celtic* is a linguistic designation referring to a branch of the Indo-European family of languages. Archaeologists link this language group to two cultural complexes, each named after an important site: (1) Hallstatt, in present-day Austria, which began in the eighth century B.C.E., and (2) La Tène, in Switzerland, dating from the fifth century B.C.E. Celtic civilization originated in Central Europe, in parts of present-day Germany, Austria, and the Czech Republic, in the early first millennium B.C.E. (see Map 4.1). The early Celts lived in or near hill forts—lofty

A Celtic hill fort in England   Such fortresses, of which hundreds have been found across Europe, served a variety of purposes: as centers of administration, gathering points for Celtic armies, manufacturing centers, storage depots for food and trade goods, and places of refuge. The natural defenses of a hill could be improved, as here, with elaborate sequences of ditches and earthwork walls. Particularly effective was the so-called "Gallic Wall," which combined earth, stone, and timber to create both strength and enough flexibility to absorb the pounding from siege engines. (Royal Commission for Historic Monuments)

natural locations made even more defensible by earthwork fortifications. Elite members of Celtic society were buried in wagons filled with extensive grave goods, suggesting belief in some sort of afterlife. By 500 B.C.E. these elites were trading with the Mediterranean lands, seeking crafted goods and wine. The contact may have stimulated the new styles of manufacture and art that launched the La Tène period.

The development of those new features coincides with a rapid expansion of Celtic groups in several directions. Moving to the west, Celtic groups occupied virtually all of France, much of Britain, and Ireland, and Celts and indigenous peoples merged to create the Celtiberian culture of northern Spain. Celts also migrated east and south. They overran northern Italy in the fifth century B.C.E. They made destructive raids into central Greece, and one group—Galatians— settled in central Anatolia (modern Turkey). By 300 B.C.E. Celtic peoples were spread across Europe north of the Alps, from present-day Hungary to Spain and Ireland. Their traces remain in the names of many places: rivers (Danube,

Rhine, Seine, Thames, and Shannon); countries (Belgium); regions (Bohemia, Aquitaine), and towns (Paris, Bologna, Leiden). They shared elements of language and culture, but there was no Celtic "state," for they were grouped into hundreds of small, loosely organized kinship groups.

Greeks and Romans were struck by the physical appearance of male Celts—their burly size, long red hair (which they often made stiff and upright by applying a cementlike solution of lime), shaggy mustaches, and loud, deep voices—as well as by their strange apparel— pants (usually an indication of horse-riding peoples) and twisted gold collars around their necks. Particularly terrifying were the warriors who fought naked and eagerly made trophies of the heads of defeated enemies. Their Mediterranean neighbors characterized the Celts as wildly fond of war, courageous, childishly impulsive and emotional, overly fond of boasting and exaggeration, yet quick-witted and eager to learn.

Celtic Society

Our greatest source of information about Celtic social and political organization is the Roman military commander Gaius Julius Caesar, who composed a detailed account of his eight-year conquest of Gaul (present-day France) between 58 and 51 B.C.E. Many of the Celtic groups in Gaul had been ruled by kings at an earlier time, but by about 60 B.C.E. they periodically chose public officials, perhaps under Greek and Roman influence.

Celtic society was divided into an elite class of warriors, professional groups of priests and bards, and the largest group of all: the common people. The warriors owned land and flocks of cattle and sheep and monopolized both wealth and power. The common people labored on their land. The warriors of Welsh and Irish legend reflect a stage of political and social development less complex than that of the Celts whom the Romans encountered in France. They bring to mind the heroes of Homer's *Iliad* and *Odyssey* (see Chapter 3), and the Indian *Mahabharata* (Chapter 7), raiding one another's flocks, reveling in

drunken feasts, and engaging in impromptu contests of strength and wit. At a banquet the bravest warrior could help himself to the choicest part of the animal, the "hero's portion," and men would fight to the death to win this privilege.

The priests, called Druids, belonged to a well-organized fraternity. Trainees received their knowledge of prayers, rituals, legal precedents, and traditions through a long program of memorization. The Druids were the teachers of Celtic society as well as the religious leaders. The priesthood was the one Celtic institution that crossed tribal lines. Sometimes the Druids were able to head off warfare between feuding groups, and they served as judges in cases that involved Celts from more than one group. In the first century C.E. the Roman government methodically set about stamping out the Druids, probably because of concern that they might serve as a rallying point for Celtic opposition to Roman rule, rather than because of their alleged involvement in bloody human sacrifices and forms of divination repugnant to Roman sensibilities.

Celtic women engaged primarily in child rearing, food production, and some crafts. Although they did not have true equality with men, their situation was superior to that of women in the Middle East or in the Greek and Roman Mediterranean. Marriage was a partnership to which both parties contributed property, and each party had the right to inherit the estate if the other died. Celtic women also had greater freedom in their sexual relations than did their southern counterparts.

Greek and Roman sources depict Celtic women as strong and proud. This portrayal corresponds to the representation of women in Welsh and Irish tales, where self-confident wives sit at banquet with their husbands, engage in witty conversation, and often provide ingenious solutions to vexing problems. Although women were not regular combatants, they might be present in the vicinity of the battlefield, and they would defend themselves fiercely if cornered.

Some of the Celtic burial chambers that archaeologists have excavated contain rich collections of clothing, jewelry, and furniture for use in the next world, identifying them as the tombs of elite women. Daughters of the elite were married to leading members of other tribes to create alliances. When the Romans invaded Celtic Britain in the first century C.E., they sometimes were opposed by Celtic tribes headed by queens (some experts see this as an abnormal circumstance created by the Roman invasion itself).

Belief and Knowledge

The condescending attitude of Greek and Roman sources gives a misleading impression of Celtic belief and knowledge. Historians know the names of more than four hundred Celtic gods and goddesses. Most of them are associated with particular localities and kinship groups, although certain deities have wider currency. Lug, for example, is the god of light, crafts, and inventions. Some are associated with animals or even depicted with animal features, such as the horse-goddess Epona or the horned god Cernunnos. "The Mothers," a set of three goddesses always depicted together and holding symbols of prosperity, must have played a part in some kind of fertility cult. The traditions of Halloween and May Day preserve the ancient Celtic holidays of Samhain and Beltaine, which took place at key moments in the growing cycle.

The early Celts did not build temples (later Celts learned to do so from the Mediterranean peoples). Instead, they worshiped at special places where they felt the presence of divinity, such as springs, groves, and hilltops. At the sources of the Seine and Marne Rivers, archaeologists have found huge caches of wooden statues thrown into the water by hopeful devotees.

In Irish and Welsh legends the barriers between the natural and supernatural worlds are far more permeable than they are in the mythology of other cultures. Celtic heroes and divinities pass back and forth from one to the other with relative ease, and magical occurrences are commonplace. Celtic priests set forth a doctrine of reincarnation—the rebirth of the soul in a new body.

The Celts were successful agriculturalists, able to support large populations by tilling the heavy but fertile soils of continental Europe. Their metallurgical skills probably surpassed those of the Mediterranean peoples. Celts living on the Atlantic shore of France built solid ships that could withstand ocean waves, winds, and currents. They used the large, navigable rivers as thoroughfares for extensive commerce, and by the first century B.C.E. some of the old hill-forts were evolving into urban centers.

The Roman conquest of many of the Celtic lands—Spain, southern Britain, France, and parts of Central Europe—from the second century B.C.E. to the first century C.E. curtailed the evolution of Celtic society, replacing it with an Italian model. The peoples in these lands were in large part assimilated to Roman ways (see Chapter 6). That is why the inhabitants of modern Spain and France speak languages that are descended from Latin. Germanic invaders from the third century C.E. on all but finished the job, and present-day inhabitants of Britain speak a language with a Germanic base. Only on the western fringes of the European continent—in Brittany (northwest France), Wales, Scotland, and Ireland—did Celtic peoples maintain their language, art, and culture into modern times.

THE FIRST EMPIRE: THE RISE OF ASSYRIA

Far to the south and east of the Celtic lands of continental Europe, the peoples of western Asia also were experiencing momentous changes in the first millennium B.C.E. The chief force for change was the rise of the powerful and aggressive Neo-Assyrian Empire. Although historians sometimes apply the term *empire* to earlier regional powers—such as the Akkadian state ruled by Sargon, the Babylonian kingdom of Hammurabi, and the expansionist New Kingdom in Egypt—the Assyrians of the early first millennium B.C.E. were the first to rule over far-flung lands and diverse peoples (see Map 4.2).

As we saw in Chapter 3, the Assyrian homeland in northern Mesopotamia differs in essential respects from the flat expanse of Sumer and Akkad to the south—hillier, more temperate in climate, with greater rainfall, and more exposed to raiders from the mountains to the east and north and from the arid steppe and desert to the west. Sturdy peasant farmers, accustomed to defending themselves against marauders, provided the military base for a revival of Assyrian power in the ninth century B.C.E. The rulers of the Neo-Assyrian Empire (911–612 B.C.E.) struck out in a ceaseless series of campaigns: westward across the steppe and desert as far as the Mediterranean, north into mountainous Urartu (modern Armenia), east across the Zagros range onto the Iranian plateau, and south along the Tigris River to Babylonia.

It is no accident that these tracks largely coincided with the most important long-distance trade routes in western Asia. These campaigns provided immediate booty and the prospect of tribute and taxes. They also guaranteed access to vital resources such as iron and silver and brought the Assyrians control of profitable international commerce.

What started out as an aggressive program of self-defense soon took on a far more ambitious agenda. Driven by pride, greed, and religious conviction, the Assyrians defeated all the rival great kingdoms of the day—Elam (southwest Iran), Urartu, Babylon, and Egypt. At its peak their empire stretched from Anatolia, Syria-Palestine, and Egypt in the west, across Armenia and Mesopotamia, as far as western Iran. In the end the Assyrians created a new kind of empire, larger in extent than anything seen before and dedicated to the enrichment of the imperial center at the expense of the subjugated periphery.

God and King

The king was both literally and symbolically the center of the Assyrian universe. Technically all the land belonged to him, and all the people—even the highest-ranking officials—were his "servants." Assyrians believed that the gods chose the king to rule as their earthly representative and instrument. Normally the sitting king chose one of his sons to be his successor, and the choice was confirmed both by divine oracles and by the Assyrian elite. The crown prince lived in the "House of Succession," where he was trained

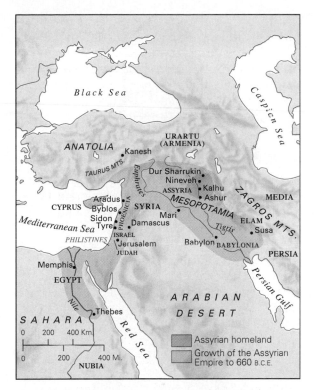

Map 4.2 The Assyrian Empire From the tenth to the seventh century B.C.E. the Assyrians of northern Mesopotamia created the largest empire the world had yet seen, extending from the Iranian plateau to the eastern shore of the Mediterranean and containing an array of peoples.

in the duties of the monarch and gradually given administrative and military responsibilities. In the ancient capital city of Ashur the high priest anointed the new king by sprinkling his head with oil and gave him insignia of kingship; a crown and scepter. The kings were buried in Ashur.

The duties of the king were enormous. Every day he received information carried by messengers and spies from all corners of the empire. He made decisions, appointed officials, heard complaints, corresponded with subordinates by dictating his wishes to an army of scribes, and received and entertained foreign envoys and high-ranking government figures. He was the military leader, responsible for the strategic planning of campaigns and often on tour inspecting the troops and commanding important operations. (Shalmaneser, who reigned from 858 to 824

Stone statue of Ashurnasirpal II, the ninth century B.C.E. Assyrian king This statue was found in a temple at Kalhu, the new royal capital which Ashurnasirpal built to advertise his greatness to contemporaries and posterity. Assyrian kings had themselves depicted in various guises. Here the scepter and flail in the king's hands are symbols of royal power, while the shawl indicates his role as a high priest. (Courtesy of the Trustees of the British Museum)

B.C.E., led his army in battle in thirty-one of the thirty-five years of his reign.) Hunting, the Assyrian kings' passion, whether shooting a bow from a chariot or stalking lions in a private preserve, was both recreation and preparation for the rigors of war.

Among the king's chief responsibilities was to fulfill his role as head of the state religion. He devoted much of his time to elaborate public and private rituals as well as to overseeing the upkeep of the temples. The king made no decisions of state without first consulting and gaining the approval of the gods through elaborate rituals of divination. All the decisions made by the king and central government were carried out under the banner of Ashur, the chief god, and were justified as being in accordance with Ashur's wishes. All victories were cited as proof of Ashur's superiority over the gods of the conquered peoples.

A relentless tide of government propaganda secured the acquiescence and participation of the Assyrian people in military campaigns that mostly benefited and enriched the king and nobility. Assyrian priests revised the Babylonian Creation Myth (see Chapter 2), replacing Marduk with Ashur as king of the gods, victor over the forces of evil and chaos, and creator of the world in its present form. Royal inscriptions cataloging the accomplishments of recent campaigns and harping on the power of Assyrian arms, the charisma and relentless will of the king, the backing of the all-powerful gods, and the ruthless punishments that would be given to those who resisted were put on public display (and presumably read aloud since most people were not literate) throughout the empire.

Art also served the Assyrian state. This use of art as political propaganda was an innovative departure in the ancient Middle East from the almost exclusive dedication of art to the worship of the gods. The walls of the royal palaces at Kalhu and Nineveh were covered with relief sculptures depicting hunts, battles, sieges, executions, and deportations. Looming over most scenes was the king, larger than anyone else, muscular and fierce, having the very visage of the gods. The purpose of these images was to overawe visitors to the court. The private, interior portions of the palace, probably off-limits to all but the royal family and high-ranking courtiers, contained a broader range of subjects, including many scenes of peaceful and pleasant pursuits.

Exploitation and Administration of the Empire

The Assyrians exploited to the maximum the wealth and resources of their subjects. The cost of military campaigns and administration had to be covered by the plunder the victors captured and the tribute they imposed. The wealth of the periphery was funneled to the center, where the king and nobility grew rich. As a result, proud kings seeking to display their magnificence to contemporaries and to leave a grand monument to posterity expanded the ancestral capital and religious center at Ashur and built magnificent new royal cities—Dur Sharrukin, Kalhu, and Nineveh—and adorned them with walls, palaces, and temples. Dur Sharrukin, "the Fortress of Sargon," was completed in a mere ten years, proof of the enormous human resources dedicated to the task. The labor force for these projects was drawn from prisoners of war transferred to the core zone, as well as from Assyrian citizens who owed periodic service to the state.

What made possible the Assyrians' conquest of their extensive and heterogeneous empire? A fundamental factor was their superior military organization and technology. Early Assyrian armies were put together one campaign at a time. They consisted not only of men who were obligated to give military service as part of the terms by which they held grants of land but also of peasants and slaves whose service was contributed by large landowners. Tiglathpileser (r. 744–727 B.C.E.) added a core army of professional soldiers drawn from both Assyrians and the most formidable subject peoples. At its peak the Assyrian state could mobilize a half-million troops, divided into contingents of light-armed bowmen and slingers who launched stone projectiles, spearmen with body armor, cavalry equipped with bow or spear, and four-man chariots.

Iron weapons gave Assyrian soldiers an advantage over opponents, and cavalry provided unprecedented speed and mobility. Assyrian engineers developed machinery and tactics for besieging fortified towns. They dug tunnels under the walls, built mobile towers to put their archers above the height of defenders, and brought up rams to batter weak points. The Assyrians destroyed some of the most ancient and best-fortified cities of the Middle East—Egyptian Thebes, Phoenician Tyre, Elamite Susa, and Babylon. Couriers and signal fires made communication across vast distances possible, and a network of spies gathered intelligence.

The Assyrian state also frequently used terror tactics—swift retribution, harsh punishments, brutal examples—to discourage resistance. The Assyrian state found in the practice of mass deportation—the forcible uprooting of entire communities from their homes in order to transport and resettle them—a means to accomplish a number of objectives simultaneously (see Voices and Visions: Mass Deportation in the Neo-Assyrian Empire). The deployment of deportees was also part of a grand economic strategy to shift human resources from the periphery to the center, where the deportees were employed as mass labor on the estates of king and nobility, to open up additional lands for agriculture, and to build the new palaces and cities. Skilled craftsmen and soldiers among the deportees could be assigned to units of the Assyrian army.

One particularly refined ploy involved exchanging two troublesome populations—that is, settling each people on the land of the other. Both groups were immediately rendered docile and even loyal to the interests of the very state that had removed them because submission was their only protection in an often hostile new environment. In addition to these concrete and immediate aims, the abrupt removal of a community also served as a conspicuous warning to others who might be contemplating resistance.

The need to control their empire posed enormous problems of organization and communication for the Assyrians. They had to contend with vast distances and diverse landscapes within which lived an array of peoples who differed in language, customs, religion, and political organization. Nomadic and sedentary kinship groups,

Wall relief from the Palace at Nineveh, depicting the Assyrian king Sennacherib's forces laying siege to the Israelite town of Lachish (701 B.C.E.)   The Assyrians have built ramps, covered with wooden planks, to drag their equipment up close to the walls of the town. A long spear projecting from a tank-like siege machine is dislodging blocks from an enemy tower, while archers fire volleys of arrows to pin down the defenders. At right, we see the outcome of the battle. Prisoners from the captured town are marching into exile carrying but few possessions. (Courtesy of the Trustees of the British Museum)

temple-states, city-states, and, in a few instances, kingdoms composed the Assyrian domain.

Yet the Assyrians never found a single, enduring solution to the problem of how to govern such an empire. Control tended to be tight and effective at the center and in lands closest to the core area, less so as one moved outward. The Assyrian kings waged many campaigns to reimpose control on territories subdued in a previous campaign or reign. In the early days the Assyrians often backed a local ruler or faction willing to collaborate with them, but this arrangement made their position vulnerable whenever local authority changed hands. And some subject states chafing under Assyrian rule sought the protection of Egypt, Elam, or Urartu. As part of his plan to reshape the state apparatus, Tiglath-pileser extended direct Assyrian control over more outlying regions.

Towns and villages were headed by a council of elders who were responsible to a district commander and provincial governor. The primary duties of Assyrian provincial officials were to ensure payment of tribute and taxes, to maintain

Mass Deportation in the Neo-Assyrian Empire

We can gain some insight about the mentality of Assyrian rule by examining one of the most characteristic aspects of Assyrian imperial policy: mass deportation. This practice already had a long history in the ancient Middle East—in Sumer, Babylon, Urartu, Egypt, and the Hittite Empire. But the Neo-Assyrian monarchs employed it on an unprecedented scale. Surviving documents record the relocation of over 1 million people, and historians estimate the true figure exceeds 4 million.

The following entries from a set of inscriptions recording the year-by-year achievements of King Sargon II (r. 721–705 B.C.E.) reveal the fate of the people and territory of the northern Israelite kingdom and of several coastal cities:

[F]irst Year] I besieged and conquered Samaria [the capital of the northern kingdom], led away as booty 27,290 inhabitants of it. I formed from among them a contingent of 50 chariots and made the remaining inhabitants resume their social positions. I installed over them an officer of mine and imposed upon them the tribute of the former king. . . . [Seventh Year] Upon a trust-inspiring oracle given by my lord Ashur, I crushed the tribes of Tamud, Ibadidi, Marsimanu, and Haiapa, the Arabs who live, far away, in the desert [and] who know neither overseers nor officials and who had not yet brought their tribute to any I deported their survivors and settled them in Samaria. . . . [Eleventh Year] I besieged and conquered the cities Ashdod, Gath, Asdudimmu; I declared his [the ruler of Ashdod's] images, his wife, his children, all the possessions and treasures of his palace as well as the inhabitants of his country as booty. I reorganized the administration of these cities and settled therein people from the regions of the East which I had conquered personally. I installed an officer of mine over them and declared them Assyrian citizens and they pulled the straps of my yoke.

To what uses did the Assyrian government put deportees? What was the legal status of deportees? Looking at the deportations chronicled in Years 1 and 7, do you see any evidence of a master plan for where deportees were resettled? What might have been the emotional impact on deportees of being separated from the familiar environment in which they had grown up?

Source: Excerpt of translation of entries from transcriptions recording the year-by-year achievements of King Sargon II: James B. Pritchard, ed., *The Ancient Near East: An Anthology of Texts and Pictures*, 1958, pp. 195–197. Reprinted with permission of Princeton University Press.

---

law and order, to raise troops, and to undertake necessary public works. The central government intervened directly in provincial affairs, and local ruling classes and Assyrian provincial governors were subject to frequent inspections by royal overseers.

A large administrative bureaucracy was needed to carry out these multifaceted duties. At the top of the ladder was a group of dignitaries with titles like "commander-in-chief," "great chancellor," and "chief cup-bearer"; they served as advisers to the king and were dispatched on special missions. An army of courtiers, supervisors, scribes, and servants maintained the palace and the various offices of the central government. High-ranking officials had their own courts and estates worked by peasants tied to the land. This elite class was bound to the monarchy by oaths of obedience, by fear of punishment for misbehavior, and by the expectation of rewards, such as grants of land and a share in booty and taxes, for loyalty and good performance. The support of the class of professionals—priests, diviners, scribes, doctors, and artisans—was also vital to the functioning of the state, and they too were bound to the monarchy by oaths and rewards.

When the ruling class grew too arrogant and abusive, an uprising of the rural nobility and free citizens of Assyria occurred in the late ninth and early eighth centuries B.C.E. This action led to Tiglathpileser's reforms, which strengthened the powers of the king and weakened the old aristocracy by breaking up provinces and administrative offices into numerous small jurisdictions.

Assyrian Society and Culture

The extant sources primarily shed light on the deeds of kings, victories of armies, and workings of government. Nevertheless, a certain amount is known about the lives and activities of the millions of subjects of the Assyrian Empire. In the core area people were assigned to the same three classes that had existed in Hammurabi's Babylon a millennium before (see Chapter 2): (1) free, landowning citizens, (2) farmers and artisans attached to the estates of the king or other rich landholders, and (3) slaves. Slaves—drawn from debtors who had failed to make good and from prisoners of war—had legal rights and, if sufficiently talented, could rise to positions of influence.

The government normally did not distinguish between native Assyrians and the increasingly large number of subjects and deportees residing in the Assyrian homeland. All were referred to as "human beings," entitled to the same legal protections and liable to the same obligations of labor and military service. Over time this inflow of outsiders led to changes in the ethnic makeup of the population of Assyria.

Agriculture constituted the economic foundation of the Assyrian Empire. The vast majority of subjects worked on the land, and the agricultural surpluses that they produced allowed a substantial number of people to engage in specialized activities—including the standing army, government officials, religious experts, merchants, artisans, and all manner of professionals in the towns and cities.

Individual artisans and small workshops in the towns manufactured goods. Most trade took place at the local level and involved foodstuffs and simple crafted goods like pottery, tools, and clothing. The state fostered long-distance trade, for imported luxury goods brought in substantial customs revenues and ultimately found their way into the possession of the royal family and elite classes. These included metals, fine textiles, dyes, gems, and ivory. Silver was the basic medium of exchange, weighed out for each transaction in a time before the invention of coins.

The Assyrian era saw both the preservation of old knowledge and the acquisition of new knowledge. When archaeologists excavated the palace of Ashurbanipal (r. 668–627 B.C.E.), one of the last Assyrian kings, at Nineveh, they discovered more than twenty-five thousand tablets or fragments of tablets. This "Library" contained official documents and an array of literary and scientific texts. Some were originals that had been brought to the capital; others were copies made at the king's request. Ashurbanipal was clearly an avid collector of the literary and scientific heritage of Mesopotamia, and the "House of Knowledge" referred to in some of the documents may have been an academy that attracted learned men to the imperial center. There is also evidence that libraries may have been attached to temples in various Assyrian cities.

Assyrians devoted much effort to the creation and preservation of lists covering all manner of subjects, such as plant and animal names, geographic terms, and astronomical occurrences. Building on the achievements of their Mesopotamian ancestors (see Environment and Technology: Chinese and Mesopotamian Divination, in Chapter 3), the Assyrians continued to make original contributions in mathematics and astronomy. Their assumption that gods or demons caused disease obstructed the investigation of natural causes, but in addition to the specialists whose job was to exorcise the demons thought to be possessing a sick person, another type of physician experimented with medicinal and surgical treatments to relieve symptoms.

The Assyrians preserved many of the achievements of Mesopotamian art, literature, and science, and much of what we know about earlier eras in Mesopotamian history comes to us through discoveries at Assyrian sites. Similarly, the Roman Empire later served as the conduit by which the achievements of Greek civilization were preserved in the West (see Chapter 6).

ISRAEL

On the western edge of the Assyrian Empire, in a land bordering on "the Upper Sea" as the Assyrians called the Mediterranean,

Ancient Textiles and Dyes

Throughout human history the production of textiles—cloth for clothing, blankets, carpets, and coverings of various sorts—may have required an expenditure of human labor second only to the amount of work necessary to provide food. Despite its importance, however, rather little is known about textile production in antiquity because it leaves so few traces in the archaeological record. The plant fibers and animal hair used for cloth are organic and quickly decompose except in rare and special circumstances. Some textile remains have been found in the hot, dry conditions of Egypt and adjacent desert locales, and others have been preserved in ice in the tombs of Siberian nomads and in the peat bogs of northern Europe. Most of our knowledge of ancient textiles, however, depends on the discovery of instruments used in textile production—such as spindles, loom weights, and dyeing vats—and on pictorial representations and descriptions in texts.

The production of cloth has usually been the work of women, for a simple but important reason. Women nearly always have the major responsibility for child rearing because only they can breast-feed the infant, often for several years. This responsibility limits their ability to participate in other activities but does not consume all their time, energy, and productive potential. In many societies textile production has been complementary to child-rearing activities, for it can be done in the home, is relatively safe, does not require great concentration, and can be interrupted and resumed without consequence. For many thousands of years cloth production has been one of the great common experiences of women around the globe.

The growing and harvesting of plants such as cotton or flax (from which linen is made) and the shearing of wool from sheep are outdoor activities, but the subsequent stages of production can be carried out indoors in the household environment. Various technological innovations improved the efficiency and quality of textile production. The basic methods, however, did not change much from early antiquity until the mid-eighteenth century C.E., when the fabrication of textiles was transferred to mills and mass production began.

When textile production has been considered "women's work," most of the output has been for domestic consumption. Men typically have become involved in commercial production, which increases the possibility of significant profit. One of these situations was in ancient Phoenicia, where fine textiles with bright, permanent colors became a major export product. These striking colors were produced by dyes derived from several species of snail: a blue-purple from the banded dye-murex and a red-purple from the spiny dye-murex. Most prized of all, the red-purple was known as Tyrian purple because Tyre was the major source. Robes dyed in this color were worn by Persian and Hellenistic kings, and a white toga with a purple border was the sign of a Roman senator.

The production of Tyrian purple was an exceedingly laborious process. The spiny dye-murex snail lives on the sandy Mediterranean bottom at depths ranging from 30 to 500 feet (10 to 150 meters). Nine thousand snails were needed to produce 1 gram (0.035 ounce) of dye. Particular techniques for the production of the best dyes were, no doubt, secrets carefully guarded by the Phoenician manufacturers. A Roman naturalist of the first century C.E., the elder Pliny, described the process of dye production as it existed in his day. The dye was made from a colorless liquid in the snail's hypobranchial gland. The gland sacs were removed, crushed, soaked with salt, and exposed to sunlight and air for some days; then they were subject to controlled boiling and heating.

Huge mounds of broken shells on the Phoenician coast are testimony to the ancient industry. It is likely that the snail was rendered virtually extinct at many locations, and some scholars have speculated that Phoenician colonization in the Mediterranean may have been motivated in part by the search for new sources of snails. The production of purple cloth in this region began before 1700 B.C.E. and continued until the seventh century C.E., when it fell victim to the destruction accompanying the Muslim conquest of Syria-Palestine.

Clothing of the Bog Body   (The National Museum, Copenhagen)

lived a people who probably seemed of no great significance to the masters of western Asia but were destined to play an important role in world history. The history of ancient Israel is marked by two grand and interconnected dramas that played out over more than fifteen hundred years, from around 2000 to 500 B.C.E.: (1) a loose collection of tribes of nomadic herders and caravan drivers became a sedentary, agricultural people, developed complex political and social institutions, and became integrated into the commercial and diplomatic networks of the Middle East; and (2) the austere cult of a desert god evolved into a unique concept of deity and the exacting way of life of the Jewish people. Both the land and the people at the heart of this story have gone by various names: Canaan, Israel, Palestine; Hebrews, Israelites, Jews. For the sake of consistency, the people are referred to here as *Israelites*, the land they occupied in antiquity as *Israel*.

Israel is a crossroads, linking Anatolia, Egypt, Arabia, and Mesopotamia (see Map 4.3). This accident of geography has given the place an importance in history, both ancient and modern, out of all proportion to its size and economic or political potential. Its natural resources are few. The Negev Desert and the vaster wasteland of the Sinai lie to the south. The Mediterranean coastal plain was usually in the hands of others, particularly the Philistines throughout much of the biblical period. At the center are the rock-strewn hills of the Shephelah. Galilee to the north, with its sea of the same name, was a relatively fertile land of grassy hills and small plains. The narrow ribbon of the Jordan River runs down the eastern side of the region into the Dead Sea, so named because of its high salt content.

Israelite Origins

Information about the history of ancient Israel comes from several sources, including archaeological excavation and references in documents from other Middle Eastern societies, particularly Egyptian and Assyrian royal annals. However, the fundamental source is the extraordinarily rich yet problematic collection of writings preserved in the Hebrew Bible (called the Old Testament by Christians). The text of the Hebrew Bible is like a layer cake, having several collections of material superimposed on one another and choices made at each stage about what to include and exclude. Many traditions about the Israelites' early days were long transmitted orally. Not until the tenth century B.C.E. did they begin to be written down, by means of an alphabet borrowed from the nearby Phoenicians. The canonical text that we have today was compiled in the fifth century B.C.E. and reflects the point of view of the priests who controlled the Temple in Jerusalem. The Hebrew language of the Bible reflects the speech of the Israelites until about 500 B.C.E. It is a Semitic language, most closely related to Phoenician and to Aramaic (the language that later supplanted Hebrew in Israel), more distantly related to the Akkadian language of Mesopotamia and to Arabic. This linguistic affinity probably parallels the Israelites' ethnic relationship to the neighboring peoples.

In some respects the history of the ancient Israelites is unique, the primary source of the Judaeo-Christian tradition so central to Western civilization. But in another sense that history reflects a familiar pattern in the ancient Middle East. It is the story of nomadic pastoralists who occupied marginal land between the inhospitable desert and the settled agricultural areas. Early on, these nomads periodically raided the farms and villages of the settled peoples, but eventually they settled down to an agricultural way of life and at a somewhat later stage developed a state apparatus.

The Hebrew Bible preserves vivid traditions about the Patriarchs—the male leaders of the early Israelite groups—Abraham, Isaac, and Jacob. Abraham was born in the city of Ur in southern Mesopotamia, probably in the twentieth century B.C.E. He left the city of his birth, disgusted by the idol worship that predominated there, and moved with his herd animals (sheep, cattle, donkeys) and his extended family through the Syrian desert. Eventually he arrived in the land of Israel, which, according to the biblical account, had been promised to him and his descendants as part of a "covenant," or pact, with the Israelite god, Yahweh.

These "recollections" of the journey of Abraham may compress the experience of generations of pastoralists who moved through the grazing lands between the upper reaches of the Tigris and Euphrates Rivers and the Mediterranean coastal plain. Abraham, his family, and companions were following the usual pattern in this part of the world. They camped by a permanent water source in the dry season, then drove the herds of domesticated animals to a well-established sequence of grazing areas during the rest of the year. The animals provided for most needs—milk, cheese, meat, and cloth.

The early Israelites and the settled peoples of the region were suspicious of one another. This friction between nomadic herders and settled farmers, as well as the Israelites' view of their ancestors as being on the nomadic side of the equation, comes through in the story of the innocent shepherd Abel, who was killed by his farmer brother Cain, and in the story of Sodom and Gomorrah, two cities that Yaweh destroyed because of their wickedness.

Abraham's son and grandson, Isaac and Jacob, succeeded him as leaders of this wandering group of herders. In the next generation the story of Jacob's son Joseph, who was sold to passing merchants by his brothers, reveals the tensions that could arise within a leading family between children of different mothers. Through luck and ability Joseph became a high official at the court of the Egyptian king. Thus he was in a position to help his people when drought swept the land of Israel and the Israelites and their flocks migrated to Egypt. The sophisticated Egyptians, however, both feared and looked down on these rough herders and eventually reduced the Israelites to the status of slaves and put them to work on the grand building projects of the pharaoh.

That is the version of events given in the Hebrew Bible. Several points need to be made about it. First, the biblical account glosses over the very centuries (1700–1500 B.C.E.) during which Egypt was dominated by the Hyksos, who generally are identified as Semitic groups that infiltrated the Nile Delta from the northeast (see Chapter 3). The Israelites' migration to Egypt and their later enslavement may have been connected to the rise and fall of the Hyksos. Second, although extant Egyptian sources do not refer to Israelite slaves, they do complain about *Apiru*, a derogatory term applied to nomads, caravan drivers,

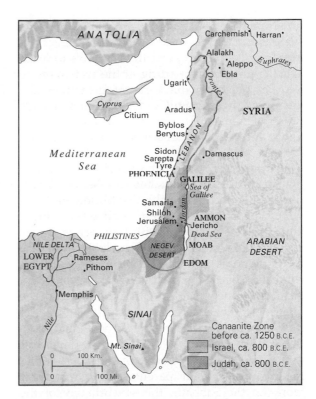

Map 4.3 Phoenicia and Israel The lands along the eastern shore of the Mediterranean Sea—sometimes called the Levant or Syria-Palestine—have always been a crossroads, traversed by migrants, nomads, merchants, and armies moving between Egypt, Arabia, Mesopotamia, and Anatolia.

bandits, and other marginal and stateless groups. The word seems to designate a class of people rather than a particular ethnic group, but some scholars have suggested an etymological connection between *Apiru* and *Hebrew* (see Voices and Visions: The Amarna Letters, in Chapter 3). Third, the period of Israelite slavery coincided with the Ramesside era of Egyptian history—1400 to 1200 B.C.E., during which pharaohs Sethos I and Ramesses II engaged in ambitious building programs (see Chapter 3).

Exodus from Egypt and Settlement in Canaan

According to the Hebrew Bible, the Israelite slaves were led out of captivity by Moses, an Israelite with connections to the Egyptian royal family. The narrative of the Exodus—the departure from Egypt—is overlaid with folktale motifs such as the ten plagues visited upon Egypt before the pharaoh allowed the Israelites to leave and the miraculous parting of the waters of the Red Sea, which enabled the refugees to escape the Egyptian army. Still, oral tradition may have preserved memories of an emigration from Egypt and years of wandering in the wilderness of Sinai.

During their forty-year sojourn in the desert the Israelites became devoted to a stern and warlike god. According to the Old Testament, Yahweh, who may have been localized at Mount Sinai, made a covenant with the Israelites: they promised to worship Yahweh exclusively, and he made them his "Chosen People." This pact was confirmed by tablets that Moses brought down from the top of Mount Sinai. Written on the tablets were the Ten Commandments, which laid down the basic tenets of Jewish belief and practice. This document prohibited murder, adultery, theft, lying, and envy, and demanded that the Israelites respect their parents and refrain from work on the Sabbath, the seventh day of the week.

In the later thirteenth century B.C.E. the Israelites came from the east into the land of Canaan (modern Israel and Palestine). Led by Joshua, Moses' successor, they attacked and destroyed Jericho and other Canaanite cities. The biblical account is confirmed by the evidence of archaeology. It shows the destruction of Canaanite towns at this time, followed shortly thereafter by the resettlement of lowland sites and the establishment of new sites in the hills—thanks in part to the development of cisterns for holding rainwater. The new settlers were a population with a cruder material culture than that of the Canaanites. This is yet another manifestation of the age-old pattern: nomadic pastoralists settle down and are assimilated into an agrarian economy.

It is unlikely that all members of the later Israelite population were descendants of the people who escaped from Egypt. The newcomers may have linked up with related peoples who had remained behind in Israel at the time of the migration into Egypt. And initial successes against the Canaanites probably attracted other nomad groups to join the Israelite rampage.

Throughout history, nomadic groups have formed new coalitions and then invented a common ancestry.

At this time there was no Israelite "state" as such. The "Children of Israel"—that is, descendants of the Patriarch Jacob—were members of twelve tribes that took their names from the sons of Jacob and Joseph. Each tribe installed itself in a different part of the conquered territory, and each tribe looked for guidance to one or more chiefs. Such leaders usually had limited coercive authority and were primarily responsible for mediating disputes and seeing to the welfare and protection of the group. Certain charismatic figures, famed for their daring in war or their genius in arbitration, were called "Judges" and (like the Celtic Druids) had a special standing that transcended tribal boundaries. The tribes were also bound together by their common access to a shrine in the hill country at Shiloh. The shrine housed the holy Ark of the Covenant, a chest containing the tablets of commandments that Yahweh had given to Moses.

Rise of the Israelite Monarchy

The Israelites were not the only triumphant newcomers in this region. The years around 1200 B.C.E. were a time of troubles throughout the eastern Mediterranean (see Chapter 3). In the early twelfth century B.C.E. the Philistines, who may be connected to the pre-Greek population of the island of Crete, occupied the coastal plain of Israel. Israelites and Philistines fought frequently in this period. Their wars were memorialized in the biblical traditions about the long-haired strongman Samson, who pulled down the walls of a Philistine temple, and the bravery of young David, whose slingshot felled the towering warrior Goliath.

An influential religious leader named Samuel, recognizing the need for a stronger central authority if the Israelites were to contend successfully against the Philistine city-states, anointed Saul as first king of Israel around 1020 B.C.E. Saul had mixed success, and when he perished in battle, the throne passed to David (r. ca. 1000–960 B.C.E.).

Gifted musician, brave warrior, and adroit politician, David completed the transition from tribal confederacy to unified monarchy. He strengthened royal authority by making the recently captured hill city of Jerusalem, which lay outside tribal boundaries, his new capital. Soon after, the Ark was brought to Jerusalem, making that city the religious as well as political center of the kingdom. To curtail the disorder caused by blood feuds, David designated "cities of refuge"—places to which those guilty of certain crimes could flee and escape retribution. A census was taken to facilitate the collection of taxes by the central government, and a standing army, with soldiers paid by and loyal to the king, was insti-

tuted. These innovations gave David the resources to win a string of military victories and substantially expand Israel's borders.

The reign of David's son Solomon (r. ca. 960–920 B.C.E.) marked the high point of the Israelite monarchy. Alliances and trade linked Israel with near and distant lands. Solomon and Hiram, the king of Phoenician Tyre, together commissioned a fleet that sailed south into the Red Sea and brought back gold, ivory, jewels, sandalwood, and exotic animals from distant Ophir. The story of the fabulous visit to Solomon by the queen of Sheba, who brought gold, precious stones, and spices, may be mythical, but it reflects the reality of trade with Saba (biblical

A model of the ancient city of Jerusalem, with the Temple at the center Strategically located in the middle of lands occupied by the Israelite tribes and on a high plateau overlooking the central hills and the Judaean desert, Jerusalem was captured c. 1000 B.C.E. by King David and made into his capital. The next king, Solomon, built the First Temple to serve as the center of the worship for the Israelite god, Yahweh. Solomon's Temple was destroyed during the Neo-Babylonian sack of the city in 587 B.C.E., but a modest structure was soon rebuilt and later replaced by the magnificent Second Temple was built by King Herod in the last decades of the first century B.C.E. This model represents the city in Second Temple times. (Private collection)

Sheba) in south Arabia (present-day Yemen) or the Horn of Africa (present-day Somalia). Considerable wealth flowed into the royal coffers, subsidizing the lavish lifestyle of Solomon's court, the expanding administrative bureaucracy, and a standing chariot army that made Israel into a regional power. Solomon undertook an ambitious building program employing slaves and the compulsory labor of citizens. To further link religious and secular authority, he built the First Temple in Jerusalem. Henceforth, the Israelites had a central shrine and an impressive set of rituals that could compete with the attractions of pagan cults.

The Temple priesthood, which carried out animal sacrifices to Yahweh on behalf of the community, received a percentage of the annual agricultural yield and evolved into a powerful and wealthy class. The expansion of Jerusalem, new commercial opportunities, and the increasing prestige of the Temple hierarchy began to change the social composition of Israelite society. A gap emerged between urban and rural, rich and poor, polarizing a people that previously had been relatively homogeneous.

The Israelites lived in extended families—the "house of the father" it was called; several generations lived together under the authority of the eldest male. Marriages, usually arranged between families, were an important economic as well as social institution. The groom gave a substantial gift to the father of the bride. Her entire family participated in the ceremonial weighing out of the silver or gold. Monogamy was the norm. The wife brought into the marriage a dowry that included a slave girl who attended her for life. Male heirs were of paramount importance. Firstborn sons received a double share of the inheritance. If no son was forthcoming from the marriage, the couple could adopt a son, or the husband could have a child by the wife's slave attendant. If a man died childless, his brother was expected to marry the widow and provide an heir.

Women suffered from certain legal disadvantages. They could not inherit, and they could not initiate divorce. Men could have extramarital relations, but equivalent behavior by wives was punishable by death. Women of the working classes labored with other family members in agriculture or herding, in addition to maintaining the household and raising the children. As the society became more urbanized, some women worked outside the home as cooks, bakers, perfumers, wet nurses (usually recent mothers, still producing milk, who were hired to provide nourishment to another person's child), prostitutes, and singers of laments at funerals. On occasion women reached positions of influence. For example, Deborah the Judge, a prophet and arbitrator of disputes, led troops in battle against the Canaanites. Women known collectively as "wise women" appear to have been educated and composed sacred texts in poetry and prose.

Fragmentation and Diaspora

After the death of Solomon around 920 B.C.E., resentment over the demands of the crown and royal neglect of tribal prerogatives led to the split of the monarchy into two kingdoms: Israel in the north, with its capital at Samaria; and Judah in the southern territory around Jerusalem. The two kingdoms were sometimes at war, sometimes in alliance with one another.

This period saw the crystallization of *monotheism*, the absolute belief in Yahweh as the one and only god. Nevertheless, religious leaders had to contend with the appeal of polytheistic (involving belief in multiple gods) cults. Many Israelites were attracted to the ecstatic rituals of the Canaanite storm-god, Baal, and the fertility goddess, Astarte. Fiery prophets claiming to convey messages from Yahweh, rose up to oppose the adoption of foreign ritual and to castigate the monarchs and aristocracy for their corruption, impiety, and neglect of the poor.

In response to the rise of the aggressive and brutal Neo-Assyrian Empire, the small states of Syria and Israel lay aside their rivalries and resisted together, but to no avail. In 721 B.C.E. the Assyrians destroyed the northern kingdom of Israel and deported a substantial portion of its population to the east (see Voices and Visions: Mass Deportation in the Neo-Assyrian Empire). New settlers were brought in, altering the ethnic composition, culture, and religious practices of this land and removing it from the mainstream of Jewish history. The southern kingdom of Judah hung on for over a century, at times paying tribute to the Neo-Assyrian Empire and then to the Neo-Babylonian kingdom that succeeded it, at other times breaking into rebellion. When the Neo-Babylonian monarch Nebuchadrezzar captured Jerusalem in 587 B.C.E., he destroyed the Temple and deported to Babylon the leading elements of the society—royal family, aristocracy, and workers with useful skills such as blacksmiths and scribes.

The deportees adapted quickly and prospered in their new home "by the waters of Babylon," and half a century later most of their descendants refused the offer of the Persian monarch Cyrus (see Chapter 5) to return to their homeland. This was the origin of the Jewish *Diaspora*—a Greek word meaning "dispersal" or "scattering"—which continues today. The communities of the Diaspora began to develop institutions that allowed them to maintain their religion and culture outside the homeland. One such institution was the *synagogue* (a Greek term meaning "bringing together"), a communal meeting place that came to serve religious, educational, and social functions.

Several groups of Babylonian Jews—as we may now begin to call these people, since an independent Israel no longer existed—did make the long trek back to Judah, where they met a cold reception from the local population. Nevertheless, the Temple was rebuilt in modest form and a new set of regulations, the Deuteronomic Code (*deuteronomic* is Greek for "second code of laws"), became the basis of law and conduct for the Jewish community. The fifth century B.C.E. also saw the compilation of the Hebrew Bible in roughly its present form.

The loss of political autonomy and the experience of exile had sharpened the Jewish identity and put an unyielding monotheism at the core of that identity. Jews lived by a rigid set of rules. Dietary restrictions forbade the eating of pork and shellfish and insisted that meat and dairy products not be consumed together. Rules of purity required women to take ritual baths to remove the taint of menstruation. The need to venerate the Sabbath (the seventh day of the week) meant

"Hezekiah's Tunnel" and the Pool of Siloam Anticipating an Assyrian siege in 701 B.C.E., the Israelite king Hezekiah constructed an underground tunnel through the rock of the hillside to bring water from a nearby spring to the city. Excavation began from both ends and a surviving inscription tells of the moment when the two crews met in the middle. (Garo Nalbandian)

refraining from work and from fighting, in imitation of their god, who rested on the seventh day according to the biblical story of the creation of the world (this is the origin of the concept of the weekend). There also was a ban on marrying non-Jews. These strictures tended to isolate the Jews from other peoples, but they also yielded a powerful sense of community and belief in the protection of a watchful and beneficent deity.

PHOENICIA AND THE MEDITERRANEAN

While the Assyrians were recovering from the disorders at the end of the Bronze Age and laying the foundation for future expansion, and the Israelite tribes were being forged into a united kingdom, important transformations also were taking place among another people who occupied the eastern shore of the Mediterranean. The ancient inhabitants of present-day Syria, Lebanon, and Israel (sometimes called the Levant or Syria-Palestine), are commonly designated Phoenicians, though they referred to themselves by the ethnic designation "Can'ani"—Canaanites. Their story is complicated by inconsistent terminology, sparse written evidence, and frequent migrations and invasions, which complicate the archaeological picture.

Yet, we can draw some insights into the history of this ethnic group. When western Asia and the eastern Mediterranean entered a period of violent upheavals and mass movements of population around 1200 B.C.E. (see Chapter 3), many settlements in Syria-Palestine were destroyed. Aramaeans migrated into the interior portions of Syria. Israelite tribes under the command of Joshua wandered into Canaan, destroyed

Wall relief of a Phoenician warship, ca. 700 B.C.E. This depiction in an Assyrian palace reflects the reliance of the Assyrians, and the Persians after them, on the Phoenicians for the core of their navy. The mast and broad square sail which these vessels used for cruising would be deposited on shore before battle. Manned by fifty rowers on two levels, the upper deck was protected by a screen of shields. The long, projecting "ram" at right was used to open a hole below the water line in an enemy vessel. (Courtesy, Trustees of the British Museum)

Canaanite cities, and settled down as herders and farmers. At the same time, the Philistines occupied the coast of much of present-day Israel and introduced iron-based metallurgy to this part of the world.

The Phoenician City-States

As a result of those invasions and migrations, by 1100 B.C.E. the zone that the Canaanites occupied was no more than a narrow strip of land lying between the mountains and the sea in present-day Lebanon (see Map 4.3). The inhabitants of this densely populated area adopted new political forms and sources of livelihood, particularly in manufacture and seaborne commerce. Rivers and rocky spurs of Mount Lebanon sliced the coastal plain into a series of small city-states. The most important were Aradus, Byblos, Berytus, Sidon, Sarepta, and Tyre. This region was the homeland of the Phoenicians, as the Canaanites came to be called by Greeks who encountered them in the early first millennium B.C.E. The Greek term *Phoinikes* may mean "red men" and have something to do with the color of the Canaanites' skin, or it may refer to the purple pigment that they produced from the murex snail and used to dye expensive garments (see Environment and Technology: Ancient Textiles and Dyes).

Thriving commerce brought in considerable wealth and gave the Phoenician city-states an important role in the international politics of the age. This commercial activity centered on raw materials, foodstuffs, and crafted luxury products: cedar and pine, metals, papyrus, wine, spices, salted fish, incense, textiles, carved ivory, and glass.

The Phoenicians developed earlier Canaanite models into the first alphabetic system of writing. In such a system each symbol stands for a sound, and only about two dozen symbols are needed. This technology was a considerable advance over cuneiform and hieroglyphics, which required hundreds of signs. Little indigenous written material survives from this period, however. Whatever "historical" records the Phoenicians may have had are lost, probably because

they were written on perishable papyrus, though some information in Greek and Roman sources may be based on them. Equally regrettably, the archaeological remains from Phoenicia are very limited.

In the second millennium B.C.E. Byblos was the most important Phoenician city-state. It was a distribution center for cedar wood from the slopes of Mount Lebanon and for Egyptian papyrus, the precious writing medium of the age (the Greek word *biblion*, meaning "book written on papyrus," comes down as our word *bible*). In the early centuries of the first millennium B.C.E. Tyre, in southern Lebanon, came to play an ever more dominant role. King Hiram, who lived in the tenth century B.C.E., was responsible for Tyre's initial rise to prominence. According to the Hebrew Bible, he formed a close friendship and alliance with the Israelite king Solomon. When Solomon built the temple at Jerusalem, he used cedar from Lebanon and drew upon the skills of Phoenician craftsmen. In return, Tyre gained access to silver, surplus food, and trade routes to the east and south. In the ninth century B.C.E. Tyre extended its territorial control over nearby Sidon and monopolized the Mediterranean coastal trade.

The city itself was virtually impregnable because of its location on an island directly offshore. It had two harbors—one facing north, the other south—connected by a canal. It also had a large marketplace, a magnificent palace complex with treasury and archives, temples to the gods Melqart and Astarte, suburbs spilling onto the adjacent mainland, and a population of thirty thousand or more. Its one weakness was its dependence on the mainland for food and fresh water.

Little is known about the internal affairs of Tyre and the other Phoenician cities. The names of a series of kings are preserved, and the scant evidence suggests that leading merchant families dominated the political arena. Between the ninth and seventh centuries B.C.E. the Phoenician city-states had to contend with Assyrian aggression, followed in the sixth century B.C.E. by the expansion of the Neo-Babylonian kingdom and later the Persian Empire (see Chapter 5). Just as in the previous millennium, these small states of the

Levantine coast had to be adept at diplomacy, preserving their autonomy by playing the great powers off against one another when possible, accepting a subordinate relationship to a distant master when necessary.

Expansion into the Mediterranean

In the ninth century B.C.E. Tyre began to turn its attention westward into the Mediterranean. The colony of Citium was established on Cyprus, a large island 100 miles (161 kilometers) west of the Syrian coast (see Map 4.4). Phoenician merchants sailing into the Aegean Sea are mentioned in the *Iliad* and *Odyssey* of the Greek poet Homer (ca. 700 B.C.E.), and the Greeks imitated the Phoenicians by adapting the alphabet to their own language and sailing out into the Mediterranean in search of farmland and raw materials. In the ninth and eighth centuries B.C.E. a string of settlements in the western Mediterranean gradually formed a "Phoenician triangle" composed of the stretch of North African coast that today lies in western Libya, Tunisia, and Morocco, the south and southeast coast of Spain (including Gades—modern Cadiz—located astride the Strait of Gibraltar and controlling access into and out of the Mediterranean), and the major islands of Sardinia, Sicily, and Malta off the coast of Italy. Many of these new foundations were situated on promontories or offshore islands in imitation of Tyre. The result was a Phoenician trading network that spanned the entire Mediterranean.

Tyrian expansion westward in the Mediterranean was made possible by a combination of state enterprise and private initiative. It probably was a response both to the frequent and destructive invasions of the Syria-Palestine region by the Neo-Assyrian Empire and to the shortage of arable land to feed Tyre's swelling population. Overseas settlement provided an outlet for excess population, new sources of valuable trade commodities, and new trading partners. For a time Tyre maintained its autonomy by providing the considerable sums of money and goods that the Assyrian kings demanded as tribute. By the early seventh century B.C.E., however, the Assyrians conquered Tyre and stripped it of much of its territory and population, and the leading place

in Phoenicia was taken over by Sidon in the sixth and fifth centuries B.C.E.

The Phoenicians' activities in the western Mediterranean often brought them into conflict with the Greeks, who at this time were also seeking out valuable resources in the western Mediterranean and colonizing southern Italy and Sicily. The focal point of this rivalry was Sicily. Phoenicians occupied the western end of the island, and Greeks colonized the eastern and central sectors. For centuries Greeks and Phoenicians fought for control of Sicily in some of the most savage wars in the history of the ancient Mediterranean. The sources contain many stories of atrocities, massacres, wholesale enslavements, and removals of populations. The unusual level of brutality must reflect the fact that each side felt its very existence to be at stake. In the end both communities survived, but the Carthaginians, who led the coalition of Phoenician communities in the western Mediterranean, had gained the upper hand and by the mid-third century B.C.E. controlled all of Sicily.

Carthage

Historians know far more about the new foundations in the western Mediterranean—particularly Carthage—than they know about the cities in the Phoenician homeland. Much of this knowledge comes from the Greeks' and Romans' reports of their wars with the western Phoenician communities.

This chapter opens with an account of the origins of Carthage—an account preserved by Roman sources but probably derived from a Carthaginian original. However much truth may lie behind the legend of Dido, archaeological excavation has roughly confirmed the traditional foundation date of 814 B.C.E. Carthage was established at a strategic location, very near the present-day city of Tunis in Tunisia, at that point in the middle portion of the Mediterranean where the sea crossing from Europe to Africa is narrowest. The new foundation prospered and grew rapidly, soon coming to dominate other Phoenician colonies in the west.

The city of Carthage was located on a narrow promontory jutting out into the Mediterranean

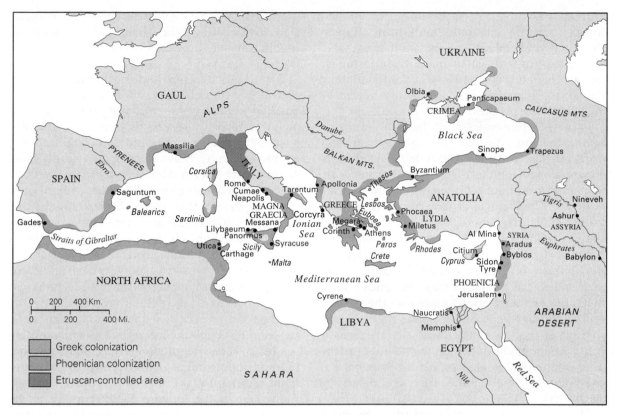

Map 4.4 Colonization of the Mediterranean In the ninth century B.C.E, the Phoenicians of Lebanon began to explore and colonize parts of the western Mediterranean, including the coast of North Africa, southern and eastern Spain, and the islands of Sicily and Sardinia. The Phoenicians were primarily interested in access to valuable raw materials and trading opportunities.

from the North African mainland. The crowded heart of the city stretched between Byrsa, the original fortified hilltop citadel of the community, and a double harbor. The inner harbor could accommodate up to 220 warships. Naval command headquarters were situated on an island in the middle of it. A watchtower allowed surveillance of the surrounding area, and high walls made it impossible to see in from the outside. The outer commercial harbor was filled with docks for merchant ships and with sheds and yards for shipbuilding and refitting. In a crisis the mouth of the harbor could be closed off by a huge chain.

Around the perimeter of a large central square lay government office buildings. Open space in the square itself was used by magistrates to hear legal cases outdoors. The inner city was a maze of narrow, winding streets, multistory apartment buildings, and sacred enclosures of the gods. Out from the center was Megara, a sprawling suburban district where fields and vegetable gardens separated the spacious houses of the well-to-do. This entire urban complex was enclosed by a wall 22 miles (35 kilometers) in length. At the most critical point—the 2½-mile-wide (4-kilometer-wide) isthmus connecting the promontory to the mainland—the wall was over 40 feet high (13 meters) and 30 feet thick (10 meters), and had high watchtowers at intervals.

With a population of roughly four hundred thousand, Carthage was one of the largest cities in the world in the mid-first millennium B.C.E. Given the limitations of ancient technology, the provision of food, water, and sanitation must have posed substantial challenges. The city housed an ethnically diverse population, including people of Phoenician stock, indigenous people likely to have been the ancestors of modern-day Berbers, and immigrants from all over the Mediterranean and sub-Saharan Africa who had come to Carthage to make their fortunes. Despite the reluctance of Dido in the foundation legend, the Phoenicians quite readily intermarried with other peoples.

Each year two *suffetes*, or "judges" (a word having the same Semitic root as the Israelites' word for their early leaders), were elected from the upper-class families. They served as heads of state and carried out administrative and judicial functions. The real seat of power was the Senate, made up of members of the leading merchant families, who sat for life, formulating policy and directing the affairs of the state. Within the Senate, an inner circle of heads of the thirty or so most influential families made the crucial decisions. Occasionally an Assembly of the people was called together to elect public officials and vote on important issues. Normally the Senate and officials made decisions, but if the leaders were divided or wanted to stir up popular enthusiasm for some venture, they would turn to the people as a whole.

There is little evidence at Carthage of the kind of social and political unrest that later plagued Greece and Rome (see Chapters 5 and 6). This perception may be due in part to the limited information in our sources about internal affairs at Carthage. However, a merchant aristocracy, unlike an aristocracy of birth, was not a closed circle, and in a climate of economic and social mobility ambitious and successful new families and individuals could push their way into the circle of politically influential citizens. The ruling class also saw to it that all benefited from the riches of empire, and the masses usually were ready to defer to those who made that prosperity possible.

A Commercial "Empire"

The most important arm of Carthaginian power was the navy. With citizens of Carthage playing an important role as rowers and navigators, the Carthaginian navy ruled the seas of the western

Mediterranean for centuries. The many Phoenician towns along the shores of the western Mediterranean provided a chain of friendly ports.

Expert in the design and construction of ships and highly proficient as sailors, the Carthaginians had a large number of fast and maneuverable warships. These vessels were outfitted with a sturdy pointed ram in front that could be driven into an enemy vessel to open up a deadly hole at the water line. A deck allowed marines (soldiers onboard a ship) to take their positions and fire weapons at the enemy. Innovations in the placement of benches and oars made room for 30, 50, and eventually as many as 170 rowers to propel the ship at high speed. The Phoenicians of the eastern and western Mediterranean and their rivals the Greeks contributed to these technological advances and used similar vessels.

The foreign policy of the Carthaginian state reflected its economic interests. Protection of the sea lanes, access to raw materials, and fostering of trade opportunities mattered most to the dominant merchant class. Indeed, Carthage claimed the waters of the western Mediterranean as its own. Merchant vessels of other peoples were free to sail to Carthage to market their goods, but if they tried to operate on their own, they risked being sunk by the Carthaginian navy. Treaties between Carthage and other states included formal recognition of this maritime commercial monopoly.

Carthaginian merchants were active all around the Mediterranean, but the archaeological record provides little evidence of which commodities they traded. This commerce may have included perishable goods—for example, foodstuffs, textiles, and animal skins, as well as slaves, which would not survive in the archaeological record—and raw metals (silver, lead, iron, and tin) whose Carthaginian origin would not be evident. Goods manufactured elsewhere were carried by Carthaginian ships, and products brought to Carthage by foreign traders were re-exported for a profit.

There is also evidence for some form of trade with sub-Saharan Africans. Hanno, an eminent Carthaginian of the fifth century B.C.E., claimed to have sailed out of the Strait of Gibraltar, stopping at various points to found small settlements and explore the West African coast. A surviving Greek version of his adventure-filled official report includes descriptions of ferocious savages, drums in the night, and rivers of fire. Scholars have had difficulty matching up Hanno's topographic descriptions and distances with the actual geography of the Atlantic coast of Africa. Some regard the document as an outright fiction. Others surmise that Hanno purposely altered distances and exaggerated the dangers so that other explorers would not dare to follow in his tracks and compete in this new commercial sphere.

The Greek historian Herodotus describes a form of silent barter in which the Carthaginians deposited items on the beach and returned at a later time to pick up the gold that the local inhabitants left in exchange. Other Carthaginian commanders explored the Atlantic coast of Spain and France and secured control of an important source of tin (a component of bronze, still important in the Iron Age) in the "Tin Islands," as Greek sources call them, probably Cornwall in the British Isles.

It is important to be precise about the goals and methods of the Carthaginian "empire" in the western Mediterranean between the sixth and third centuries B.C.E. Unlike Assyria, Carthage did not seek direct rule of a large amount of territory. A belt of fertile land in northeastern Tunisia, owned by Carthaginians but worked by native peasants and imported slaves, provided a secure food supply. Indigenous groups in this territory were subject to taxation and military service.

Beyond this core area Carthaginian domination was usually indirect. Other Phoenician communities in the western Mediterranean were essentially independent. However, because of Carthage's superior economic and military resources and the shared interests of all the Phoenician communities of the west, they normally looked to Carthage for military protection, and they followed Carthage's lead in foreign policy. Sardinia and southern Spain were provinces under the direct control of a Carthaginian governor and garrison, probably because they contained vital agricultural, metal, and manpower resources.

Carthage's overarching emphasis on commerce may explain an unusual feature of the state: citizens were not required to serve in the military, because they were of more value in a civilian capacity. Carthage had little to fear from potential enemies close to home. The indigenous North African population was not well organized politically or militarily and thus was easily controlled. Carthage did need armies for military operations overseas, and it engaged in a series of fierce and destructive wars with Greeks and Romans from the fifth through third centuries B.C.E. For these conflicts it came to rely on mercenaries, soldiers hired from the most warlike peoples in their dominions or in neighboring areas—such as Numidians from North Africa, Iberians from Spain, Gauls from France, and various Italian peoples. These well-paid mercenaries were under the command of professional Carthaginian officers.

Another sign that the conduct of war was not seen as the primary business of the state was the separation of military command from civilian government. Generals were chosen intermittently by the Senate and kept in office for as long as they were needed. This practice led to the rise of a professional class of military experts, men who studied the art of war and gained experience and a high level of skill over the course of long commands. There is a telling contrast with Assyria and the other major states of the ancient Middle East, whose kings normally led the campaigns.

Gods and Cult

Carthaginian religion fascinated Greek and Roman writers. Like the deities of Mesopotamia (see Chapter 2), the gods of the Carthaginians—chief among them Baal Hammon, a male-storm god, and Tanit, a female fertility figure—were powerful and capricious entities whose worshipers sought to appease them at any price.

It was reported, for example, that members of the Carthaginian elite sacrificed their own male children at times of crisis. Excavations at Carthage and other Phoenician towns in the west have turned up *tophets*—walled enclosures in

The "Tophet" of Carthage   This is where the cremated bodies of sacrificed children were buried from the seventh to second centuries B.C.E. The claim in ancient sources that the Carthaginians sacrificed children to their gods at times of crisis has been confirmed by archaeological excavation. The stone markers, decorated with magical signs and symbols of divinities as well as the name of the family, were placed over ceramic urns containing the ashes and charred bones of one or more infants or, on occasion, older children. (Martha Cooper/Peter Arnold, Inc.)

which were buried thousands of small, sealed urns containing the burned bones of children. Some scholars see these compounds as the final resting place of infants born prematurely or taken by childhood illnesses. Most experts, however, maintain that the western Phoenicians practiced child sacrifice on a more or less regular basis.

The motivation behind this activity and the meanings that it held for its practitioners are not well understood. Presumably it was intended to win the favor of the gods at critical moments, such as the eve of decisive battles with Greek and Roman foes. Originally practiced by the upper classes, child sacrifice was later taken over by broader elements of the population and became increasingly common in the fourth and third centuries B.C.E.

Plutarch, a Greek who lived around 100 C.E., long after the demise of Carthage, but who had access to earlier sources, wrote the following about the Carthaginians:

> The Carthaginians are a hard and gloomy people, submissive to their rulers and harsh to their subjects, running to extremes of cowardice in times of fear and of cruelty in times of anger; they keep obstinately to their decisions, are austere, and care little for amusement or the graces of life.[1]

We should not take at face value what was said about the Carthaginians by their Greek and Roman enemies, but it is important to recognize that the Carthaginians were perceived as different and that cultural barriers, leading to misunderstanding and prejudice, played a significant role in the encounters of these peoples of the ancient Mediterranean. In Chapter 6 we follow the protracted and bloody struggle between Rome and Carthage for control of the western Mediterranean.

THE END OF AN ERA: THE FALL OF ASSYRIA

The extension of Assyrian power over the entire Middle East had enormous consequences for all the peoples of this region and caused the stories of Mesopotamia, Israel, and Phoenicia to converge. As we have seen, in 721 B.C.E. the

New Cultural Communities in Western Eurasia, ca. 1200–500 B.C.E.

	Israel	Phoenicia/Carthage	Mesopotamia
1250–1200 B.C.E.	Israelite conquest of Canaan		
1000	David establishes Jerusalem as capital		
969		Hiram of Tyre comes to power	
960	Solomon builds First Temple		
920	Division into two kingdoms		
911			Rise of Neo-Assyrian empire
814		Foundation of Carthage	
744–727			Reforms of Tiglath-Pileser
721	Assyrian conquest of northern kingdom		
701		Assyrian humiliation of Tyre	
668–627			Reign of Ashurbanipal
612			Fall of Assyria
626–539			Neo-Babylonian Kingdom
587	Neo-Babylonian capture of Jerusalem		
465		Voyage of Hanno the Carthaginian to West Africa	

Assyrians destroyed the northern kingdom of Israel and deported a substantial portion of the population, and for over a century the southern kingdom of Judah was exposed to relentless pressure (see Voices and Visions: Mass Deportation in the Neo-Assyrian Empire). Assyrian threats and demands for tribute spurred the Phoenicians to explore, colonize, and commercially exploit the western Mediterranean. The humiliation of Tyre, the leading Phoenician state, by the Assyrians in the seventh century B.C.E. accelerated the decline of the Phoenician homeland, but the western colonies, especially Carthage, lying far beyond Assyrian reach, flourished for centuries.

Even Egypt, for so long impregnable behind its desert barriers, was conquered and occupied for a time by Assyrian forces in the mid-seventh century B.C.E. Thebes, its ancient capital, was damaged beyond recovery. The southern plains of Sumer and Akkad, the birthplace of Mesopotamian civilization, were reduced to a protectorate. The venerable old metropolis at Babylon was alternately razed and rebuilt by Assyrian kings of differing dispositions. Urartu and Elam, Assyria's great power rivals close to home, were ultimately destroyed.

By the mid-seventh century B.C.E. Assyria stood seemingly unchallenged in western Asia. But the cost had been high. The arms race with Urartu, the frequent expensive campaigns, and protection of lengthy borders had overextended Assyrian resources. The brutality of Assyrian conduct and the exploitation of the conquered peoples had aroused the hatred of many subjects and neighbors. And changes in the ethnic composition of the army and in the population of the homeland had rendered both soldiers and civilians less committed to the interests of the Assyrian state.

Two dynamic new political entities spearheaded resistance to Assyria: a resurgent Babylonia under the Neo-Babylonian, or Chaldaean, dynasty, and the kingdom of the Medes, an Iranian people who by the seventh century B.C.E. were extending their control eastward across the Iranian plateau. These two powers launched a series of attacks on the Assyrian homeland, and by 612 B.C.E. the chief Assyrian cities had been destroyed. The rapidity of the Assyrian decline and fall is stunning. The destruction systematically carried out by the victorious attackers led to the depopulation of northern Mesopotamia. Two centuries later, when a corps of Greek mercenaries passed by mounds that concealed the ruins of the Assyrian capitals, the Athenian chronicler Xenophon had no inkling of the existence of the Assyrians and their once-mighty empire.

The Medes took over the Assyrian homeland and the northern steppe as far as eastern Anatolia, but most of the immediate benefits went to the Neo-Babylonian kingdom. Kings Nabopolassar (r. 625–605 B.C.E.) and Nebuchadrezzar (r. 604–562 B.C.E.), both energetic campaigners, took over much of the territory of the old empire. Babylonia underwent a cultural renaissance. The city of Babylon was enlarged and adorned, becoming the greatest urban complex in the world in the sixth century B.C.E. Old cults were reactivated, temples rebuilt, festivals resurrected. The related pursuits of mathematics, astronomy, and astrology reached new heights.

CONCLUSION

The history of Europe, North Africa, and western Asia shared two main themes in the first millennium B.C.E. First, this epoch witnessed the rise to prominence of peoples who had played a less significant role earlier—in particular the Assyrians of northern Mesopotamia and the Phoenicians (Canaanites) of the eastern Mediterranean coast—or whose way of life had undergone such significant changes as to constitute a new culture—as in Israel and among the Celts of Europe.

In each of those cases we can follow the evolution of new, more complex political, social, and economic structures. The Assyrians, using land-based military technologies, created an empire on a scale that never before had been seen in the world, extending over vast distances and encompassing many different ethnic groups. The distances involved and the slowness of communications made it difficult to maintain control. The Assyrian response was to employ and advertise brute force and terror in order to cow opponents into submission and keep reluctant subjects obedient. The Carthaginians, the most successful of the Phoenician colonists in the western Mediterranean, created an "empire" of a different sort, based on naval dominance of the waters of the western Mediterranean and commercial exploitation of the resources of adjacent lands. In both cases great wealth was funneled into the center. The Assyrian royal family and aristocracy were enriched by the booty, taxes, and labor exacted from conquered peoples. The Carthaginian merchant families grew prosperous from trade and manufacture.

The second main theme of this chapter is population movements and the relocation of large numbers of people to new homes. Other historical periods may be better known as eras of mass migration—the prehistoric diffusion of the human species across all the habitable regions of the planet (see Chapter 1), the eruption of the new religion of Islam across western Asia and North Africa in the seventh century C.E. (see Chapter 10), and our own highly mobile century, for example. But the population movements of the first millennium B.C.E., though less well documented, also sparked profound political, social, cultural, and economic changes in the lands of Europe, North Africa, and western Asia.

The Assyrians, with their military conquest of most of western Asia, exemplify a pattern of coerced population movements. Large numbers of prisoners of war were deported from outlying subject territories to the core area in northern Mesopotamia. The Phoenician colonization of the nearby island of Cyprus and the more distant shores of North Africa, Spain, and the islands off Italy was at least partially a response to Assyrian aggression but also exemplifies a different pattern: citizens voluntarily left their overpopulated homeland to make better lives for themselves in new settlements. And, as the next chapter discusses, while the Phoenicians were exploring and settling in the western Mediterranean, Greeks from the Aegean Sea region were colonizing and occupying coastal points in southern

Italy, Sicily, southern France, western Libya, and the lands bordering the Black Sea.

The story of the Israelite settlement of Canaan and the radiation of Celtic peoples from a Central European point of origin across a wide swath of Europe north of the Alps describes yet another pattern of mass migration. Phoenician colonists largely duplicated in their new homes the forms they had been using in the old country. Celts and Israelites, in contrast, underwent a more profound political, social, and cultural transformation as they adapted to new zones of settlement.

It is no accident that several of the peoples featured in this chapter who settled in large numbers outside their places of origin had long and glorious destinies ahead of them. In the first millennium B.C.E., as in later historical eras, diasporas proved to be both fertile sources of innovation and safety valves for the preservation of culture. The Carthaginian enterprise was eventually cut short by the Romans, but Jews and Celts survive into our own time. Ironically the Assyrians, for a time the most powerful of all these societies, suffered the most complete termination of their way of life. Because Assyrians did not settle outside their homeland in significant numbers, when their state was toppled in the late seventh century B.C.E. their culture also fell victim.

The Neo-Babylonian kingdom that arose on the ashes of the Neo-Assyrian Empire would prove to be the last revival of the ancient Sumerian and Semitic cultural legacy in western Asia. The next chapter relates how the destiny of the peoples of the Middle East became enmeshed in the stories of Iran and Greece.

SUGGESTED READING

The best concise introduction to Celtic civilization is Simon James, *The World of the Celts* (1993). Also of use are T. G. E. Powell, *The Celts* (1980), and Barry Cunliffe, *The Celtic World* (1979). Miranda J. Green, *The Celtic World* (1995) is a large and comprehensive collection of articles on many aspects of Celtic civilization.

On Celtic religion and mythology see Proinsias Mac Cana, *Celtic Mythology* (1983); and two books by Miranda Green: *The Gods of the Celts* (1986) and *Dictionary of Celtic Myth and Legend* (1992). Celtic art is covered by Ruth and Vincent Megaw, *Celtic Art: From Its Beginnings to the Book of Kells* (1989), and I. M. Stead, *Celtic Art* (1985). For translations and brief discussion of Celtic legends see Patrick K. Ford, *The Mabinogi and Other Medieval Welsh Tales* (1977), and Jeffrey Gantz, *Early Irish Myths and Sagas* (1981).

Fundamental for all periods in the ancient Middle East is Jack M. Sasson, ed., *Civilizations of the Ancient Near East*, 4 vols. (1995). This collection, containing nearly two hundred articles with bibliography by contemporary experts, is divided into sections covering environment, population, social institutions, history and culture, economy and trade, technology and artistic production, religion and science, language, writing and literature, and visual and performing arts. Barbara Lesko, ed., *Women's Earliest Records: From Ancient Egypt and Western Asia* (1989), is a collection of papers on the experiences of women in the ancient Middle East. John Boardman, I. E. S. Edwards, N. G. L. Hammond, and E. Sollberger, *The Cambridge Ancient History*, 2d ed., vols. 3.1–3.3 (1982–1991), provides extremely detailed historical coverage of the entire Mediterranean and western Asia.

For general history and cultural information about the Neo-Assyrian Empire and Mesopotamia and western Asia in the first half of the first millennium B.C.E. see Michael Roaf, *Cultural Atlas of Mesopotamia and the Ancient Near East* (1990); H. W. F. Saggs, *Civilization Before Greece and Rome* (1989); and A. Bernard Knapp, *The History and Culture of Ancient Western Asia and Egypt* (1988). Jeremy Black and Anthony Green, *Gods, Demons and Symbols of Ancient Mesopotamia: An Illustrated Dictionary* (1992), is valuable for religious institutions and conceptions, mythology, and artistic representation.

H. W. F. Saggs, *Babylonians* (1995), has coverage of the fate of the old centers in southern Mesopotamia during this era in which the north attained dominance.

Julian Reade, *Assyrian Sculpture* (1983), provides a succinct introduction to the informative relief sculptures from the Assyrian palaces. Andre Parrot, *The Arts of Assyria* (1961), provides full coverage of all artistic media.

Primary texts in translation for Assyria and other parts of western Asia can be found in James B. Pritchard, ed., *Ancient Near Eastern Texts Relating to the Old Testament*, 3d ed. (1969).

For general historical introductions to ancient Israel see Michael Grant, *The History of Israel* (1984); J. Maxwell Miller and John H. Hayes, *A History of Ancient Israel and Judah* (1986); and J. Alberto Soggin, *A History of Israel: From the Beginnings to the Bar Kochba Revolt, A.D. 135* (1984). Amihai Mazar, *Archaeology of the Land of the Bible, 10,000–586 B.C.E.* (1990), provides an overview of the discoveries of archaeological excavation in Israel. For the Philistines see Trude Dothan, *The Philistines and Their Material Culture* (1982).

Donald Harden, *The Phoenicians* (1962), and Gerhard Herm, *The Phoenicians: The Purple Empire of the Ancient World* (1975), are general introductions to the Phoenicians in their homeland. Maria Eugenia Aubet, *The Phoenicians and the West: Politics, Colonies and Trade* (1993), is a sophisticated investigation of the dynamics of Phoenician expansion into the western Mediterranean. Lionel Casson, *The Ancient Mariners: Seafarers and Sea Fighters of the Mediterranean in Ancient Times*, 2d ed. (1991), 75–79, discusses the design of warships and merchant vessels. For Carthage, David Soren, Aicha Ben Abed Ben Khader, and Hedi Slim, *Carthage: Uncovering the Mysteries and Splendors of Ancient Tunisia* (1990), fills a long-standing void. Aicha Ben Abed Ben Khader and David Soren, *Carthage: A Mosaic of Ancient Tunisia* (1987), includes articles by American and Tunisian scholars as well as the catalog of a museum exhibition. R. C. C. Law, "North Africa in the Period of Phoenician and Greek Colonization, c. 800 to 323 B.C.," Chapter 2 in *The Cambridge History of Africa*, vol. 2 (1978), places the history of Carthage in an African perspective.

Elizabeth Wayland Barber, *Women's Work: The First 20,000 Years: Women, Cloth, and Society in Early Times* (1994), is an intriguing account of textile manufacture in antiquity, with emphasis on the social implications and primary role of women. I. Irving Ziderman, "Seashells and Ancient Purple Dyeing," *Biblical Archaeologist* 53 (June 1990): 98–101, is a convenient summary of Phoenician purple-dyeing technology.

NOTE

1. Plutarch, *Moralia* 799 D, translated by B. H. Warmington, *Carthage* (Penguin, Harmondsworth, 1960), 163.

Greece and Iran, 1000–30 B.C.E.

Ancient Iran • The Rise of the Greeks

The Struggle of Persia and Greece • The Hellenistic Synthesis

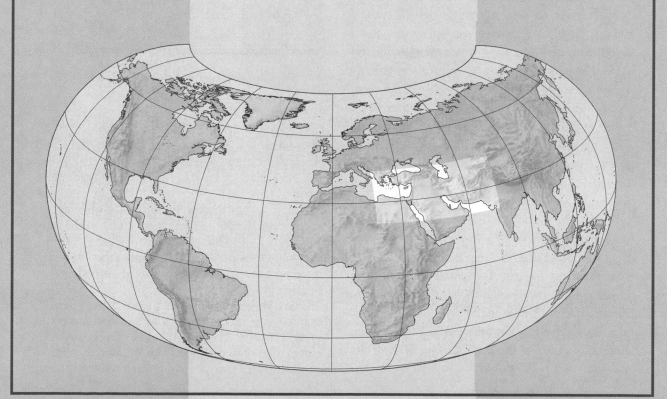

The Greek historian Herodotus (ca. 485–425 B.C.E.), chronicler of the struggles of Greece with the Persian Empire in the sixth and fifth centuries B.C.E., tells a revealing story about cultural differences. The Persian king Darius I, who ruled an empire stretching from eastern Europe to northwest India, summoned the Greek and Indian wise men who served him at court. He first asked the Greeks whether under any circumstances they would be willing to eat the bodies of their deceased fathers. The Greeks, who cremated their dead, recoiled at the impiety of such an act. Darius then asked the Indians whether they would be prepared to burn the bodies of their dead parents. The Indians were repulsed, because it was their practice to ritually partake of the bodies of the dead. The point, as Herodotus wryly points out, was that different peoples have very different practices but each regards its own way as "natural" and superior.

The effort of some thinkers to distinguish between what was natural and what was mere cultural convention was creating much discomfort among Greeks in Herodotus's lifetime, since it called into question their fundamental assumptions. Herodotus's story also reminds us that the Persian Empire (and the Hellenistic Greek kingdoms that succeeded it) brought together in Europe and in Asia lands, peoples, and cultural systems that previously had known little direct contact, and that this new cross-cultural interaction had the potential to be alarming and to stimulate new and exciting cultural syntheses.

In this chapter we look at the eastern Mediterranean and western Asia in the first millennium B.C.E., emphasizing the experiences of the Persians and the Greeks. The rivalry and wars of Greeks and Persians from the sixth to fourth centuries B.C.E. are traditionally seen as the first act of a drama that has continued intermittently ever since: the clash of the civilizations of East and West, of two peoples and two ways of life that

were fundamentally different and thus almost certain to come into conflict.

Ironically, Greeks and Persians had far more in common than they realized. They both spoke in tongues belonging to the same Indo-European family of languages found throughout Europe and western and southern Asia. Many scholars believe that all the ancient peoples who spoke languages belonging to this family inherited fundamental cultural traits, forms of social organization, and religious outlooks from their shared past.

By tracing the rise of Persian and Greek civilizations in very different physical landscapes and historical circumstances, and by looking at the characteristic institutions and values of each people, we can see how two centuries of rivalry and warfare affected the development of both peoples, and we can see what impact Persian and Greek domination made on the lands and other peoples of the eastern Mediterranean and western Asia from the sixth to second centuries B.C.E.

ANCIENT IRAN

The location of Iran, "the land of the Aryans," makes it a link between western Asia and southern and Central Asia, and its history has been marked by this mediating position (see Map 5.1). In the sixth century B.C.E. the vigorous Persians of southwest Iran created the largest empire the world had yet seen. Heirs to the long legacy of Mesopotamian history and culture, they fused it with distinctly Iranian elements and introduced new forms of political and economic organization in western Asia.

Relatively little written material from within that empire has survived, so we are forced to view it mostly through the eyes of Greeks—outsiders who were ignorant at best, usually hostile, and interested only in events that affected them-

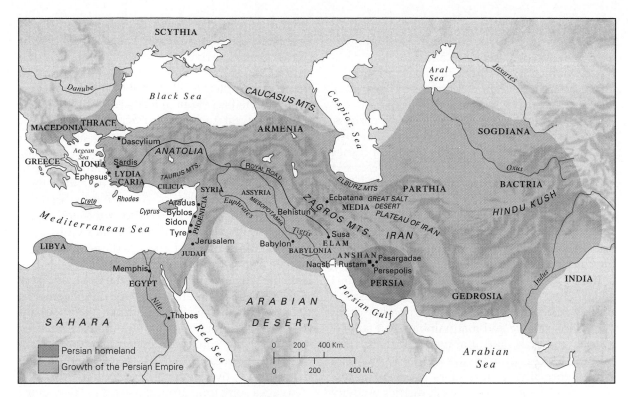

Map 5.1 The Persian Empire Between 550 and 522 B.C.E., the Persians of southwest Iran, under their kings Cyrus and Cambyses, conquered each of the major states of western Asia— Media, Babylonia, Lydia, and Egypt. The third king, Darius I, extended the boundaries as far as the Indus Valley in the east and the European shore of the Black Sea in the west. The first major setback came when the fourth king, Xerxes, failed in his invasion of Greece in 480 B.C.E. For their empire, which was considerably larger than its recent predecessor, the Assyrian Empire, the Persian rulers developed a system of provinces, governors, regular tribute, and communication via royal roads and couriers that allowed for efficient operations for almost two centuries.

selves. This Greek perspective leaves us unaware of developments in the central and eastern portions of the Persian Empire. Nevertheless, recent archaeological discoveries and close analysis of the limited written material from within the empire can be used to supplement and correct the perspective of the Greek sources.

Geography and Resources

Iran is bounded by the Zagros Mountains to the west, the Caucasus Mountains and Caspian Sea to the northwest and north, the mountains of

Afghanistan and the desert of Baluchistan to the east and southeast, and the Persian Gulf to the southwest. The northeast is less protected by natural boundaries, and Iran has always been open to attacks from the nomads of Central Asia through that corridor.

The fundamental topographical facts about Iran are that there are high mountains at the edges, salt deserts in the interior depressions, and mountain streams traversing the sloping plateau and draining into seas or interior salt lakes and marshes. For humans to survive in these harsh lands, they must find ways to exploit limited water resources. Unlike the valleys of the Nile, Tigris-Euphrates, Ganges, and Yellow Rivers, ancient Iran never had a dense population. The most well-watered and populous parts of the country lie to the north and west; aridity increases and population decreases as one moves south and east. On the interior plateau, oasis settlements sprang up beside streams or springs. The Great Salt Desert, which covers most of eastern Iran, and Baluchistan in the southeast corner were extremely inhospitable, and the scattered settlements in the narrow plains beside the Persian Gulf were cut off by mountain barriers from the interior plateau.

The advent of irrigation in the first millennium B.C.E. enabled people to move down from the mountain valleys and open up the plains to agriculture. To prevent evaporation of precious water in the hot, dry climate, they devised a unique system of underground irrigation channels. Constructing and maintaining these subterranean channels and the vertical shafts that provided access at intervals was labor-intensive work. Normally, local leaders oversaw the expansion of the network in each district. Activity accelerated during periods when a strong central authority was able to organize large numbers of laborers. The connection between royal authority and prosperity is evident in the ideology of the first Persian Empire (see below). Even so, human survival depended on a delicate ecological balance, and increased levels of salt in the soil or a falling water table sometimes forced the abandonment of settlements.

Iran's mineral resources—copper, tin, iron, gold, and silver—were exploited on a limited scale in antiquity. Mountain slopes, more heavily wooded than they are now, provided fuel and materials for building and crafts. Since this austere land could not generate much of an agricultural surplus, minerals and crafted goods (such as textiles and carpets) tended to be the objects of trade.

Rise of the Persian Empire

In antiquity many groups of people, whom historians refer to collectively as Iranians because they spoke related languages and shared certain cultural features, spread out across a wide expanse of western and Central Asia, comprising not only the modern nation of Iran but also Turkmenistan, Afghanistan, and Pakistan. Several of these groups arrived in western Iran near the end of the second millennium B.C.E. The first to reach a complex level of political organization was the Medes (Mada in Iranian)[*] who settled in the northwest and came under the influence of the ancient centers in Mesopotamia and Urartu (modern Armenia). The Medes played a major role in the destruction of the Assyrian Empire in the late seventh century B.C.E. and extended their control westward across Assyria into Anatolia (modern Turkey). They also projected their power southeast toward the Persian Gulf, a region occupied by Persian tribes (Parsa).

The Persian rulers of the region of Anshan—called Achaemenids because they traced their lineage back to an ancestor named Achaemenes (Hachamanish)—cemented their relationship with the Median court through marriage. Cyrus (Kurush), the son of a Persian chieftain and a Median princess, united the various Persian tribes and overthrew the Median monarch Astyages sometime around 550 B.C.E. His victory should perhaps be seen less as a conquest than as an alteration of the relations between groups within the framework of the Median kingdom, for Cyrus placed both Medes and Persians in positions of responsibility. The differences between these two Iranian peoples were not great—principally dialectical differences in the way they spoke and variations in dress. The Greeks could not readily tell the two apart and used the term *Medoi* to refer to both Persians and Medes.

Like most Indo-European peoples, the early inhabitants of western Iran had a patriarchal organization: the male head of the household had virtually absolute authority over family members. Society was divided into three social and occupational castes: warriors, priests, and peasants. Warriors were the dominant element. A land owning aristocracy, they took pleasure in hunting, fighting, and gardening, and the king was the most illustrious member of this group. The Magi (*magush*) were ritual specialists who

---

[*]Iranian groups and individuals are known in the Western world by Greek approximations of their names; thus these familiar forms are used here. The original Iranian names are given in parentheses.

supervised the proper performance of sacrifices. The common people were primarily village-based farmers and shepherds.

The rise of the Persians was breathtakingly sudden. Cyrus, by his conquests, thrust his relatively backward society into the role of an imperial people. At first they retained the framework of Median rule. The Persians were always willing to adapt to local circumstances, to learn from those with more experience, and to employ non-Persians who had valuable skills.

Over the course of two decades the energetic Cyrus (r. 550–530 B.C.E.) redrew the map of western Asia. In 546 B.C.E. he prevailed in a cavalry battle outside the gates of Sardis, the capital of the kingdom of Lydia in western Anatolia, because the smell of his camels disconcerted his opponents' horses. All Anatolia, including the Greek city-states on the western coast, came under Persian control. In 539 he swept into Mesopotamia, where the Chaldaean, or Neo-Babylonian, dynasty had ruled since the collapse of Assyrian power (see Chapter 4). Cyrus made a deal with disaffected elements within Babylon, and when he and his army approached, the gates of the city were thrown open to him without a struggle. A skillful propagandist, Cyrus showed respect to the Babylonian priesthood and had his son crowned king in accordance with native traditions.

After Cyrus lost his life in 530 B.C.E. while campaigning against a coalition of nomadic Iranians in the northeast, his son Cambyses (Kambujiya r. 530–522 B.C.E.) set his sights on Egypt, the last of the great ancient kingdoms of the Middle East. The Persians prevailed over the Egyptians in a series of bloody battles, after which they sent exploratory expeditions south to Nubia and west to Libya. Greek sources depict Cambyses as a cruel and impious madman, but contemporary documents from Egypt show him operating in the same practical vein as his father, cultivating local priests and notables and respecting native traditions.

The manner in which Cambyses' eventual successor, Darius I (Darayavaush), came to the throne is shrouded in mystery. By birth he was from a junior branch of the ruling clan. Our primary account of the events that led to his accession is the great cuneiform inscription that he ordered to be carved into a cliff face at Behistun

Relief of two Persian magi   A stone relief from Dascylium, the headquarters of the Persian governor in northwest Anatolia, showing two Iranian magi. The magi, who conducted religious rituals, are here seen wearing veils over their mouths and holding bundles of sticks used in the ceremony of sacrifice. The Persian kings and their subordinates were Zoroastrians, and it is likely that Zoroastrian religion spread to the provinces, where significant numbers of Persians lived, and influenced the beliefs of other peoples. (Courtesy, Archaeological Museums of Istanbul)

in Western Iran. According to Darius, Cambyses had secretly murdered his own brother and heir, Bardiya. When Cambyses died in 522 B.C.E., the throne was seized by a Median priest who claimed to be the surviving son of Cyrus. Darius and six other leading Persians discovered the masquerade and slew the impostor. Darius's account has struck commentators as improbable, and many believe that Darius and his fellow conspirators killed the real Bardiya. The choice of a Median scapegoat may have been an attempt to justify the dominance of Persians over Medes within the ruling class. Medes subsequently played a more junior role than they had enjoyed in the first two reigns, and all the major posts went to members of leading Persian families.

The elevation of Darius (r. 522–486 B.C.E.) was not well received everywhere. The rest of the Behistun inscription recounts how the new king and his deputies had to put down nine pretenders to the throne and fight nineteen battles across the length and breadth of the empire. The fact that Darius ultimately prevailed over all comers is testimony to his skill, energy, and ruthlessness. In the ensuing decade he extended Persian control eastward as far as the Indus Valley and westward into Europe, where he bridged the Danube River and chased the nomadic Scythian peoples north of the Black Sea. The Persians erected a string of forts in Thrace (modern-day northeast Greece and Bulgaria) and by 500 B.C.E. were on the doorstep of Greece. Darius also promoted the development of maritime routes, dispatching the Anatolian mariner Scylax to explore the waters from the Indus Delta to the Red Sea and completing a canal that linked the Red Sea with the Nile.

Imperial Organization and Ideology

The empire of Darius I was the largest the world had yet seen (see Map 5.1). Stretching from eastern Europe to Pakistan, from southern Russia to the Sudan, it encompassed a multitude of ethnic groups and every form of social and political organization, from nomadic tribe to subordinate kingdom to city-state. Darius can rightly be considered a second founder of the Persian Empire, after Cyrus, because he created a new organizational structure that was maintained throughout the remaining two centuries of the empire's existence.

Darius divided the empire into twenty provinces. Each one was under the supervision of a Persian *satrap*, or governor, who was often related or connected by marriage to the royal family. In his province the satrap was not just a representative but a replica of "the Great King"; the satrap's court was a miniature version of the royal court. The tendency for the position of satrap to become hereditary meant that satraps' families lived in the province governed by their

leader, acquired a fund of knowledge about local conditions, and formed connections with the local native elite. The farther a province was from the center of the empire, the more autonomy the satrap had, because slow communications made it impractical to refer most matters to the central administration.

One of the satrap's most important duties was to collect and then send tribute to the king. Darius had prescribed how much precious metal each province was to contribute annually (only in the western provinces were coins in circulation; see Environment and Technology: Origins and Early Development of Coinage). This amount was forwarded to the central treasury. Some of it was disbursed for necessary expenditures, but most of it was hoarded. As more and more precious metal was taken out of circulation, the price of gold and silver rose, and it became increasingly difficult for the provinces to meet their quotas. Evidence from Babylonia indicates a gradual economic decline setting in by the fourth century B.C.E. The increasing burden of taxation and official corruption worsened the economic downturn.

Royal roads connected the outlying provinces to the heart of the empire. Well maintained and patrolled, they had stations at intervals to receive important travelers and couriers carrying official correspondence. Garrisons were installed at strategic points, such as mountain passes, river crossings, and important urban centers. The administrative center was Susa, the ancient capital of Elam, in southwest Iran near the present-day border with Iraq. It was to Susa that Greeks and others went with requests and messages for the king. It took a party of Greek ambassadors at least three months to make the journey to Susa. Altogether, travel time, time spent waiting for an audience with the Persian king, delays due to weather, and the duration of the return trip probably kept the ambassadors away from home a year or more.

The king lived and traveled with his numerous wives and children. The little information that we have about the lives of Persian royal women comes from foreign sources and is thus suspect. The Book of Esther in the Hebrew Bible tells a romantic story of how King Ahasuerus

Origins and Early Development of Coinage

Numismatics, the study of coins, is a valuable source of information for historians. Coins from the ancient world survive in large numbers and can be used to trace commercial and political relations as well as the changing programs and slogans of the governments that issued them. Coins were invented in the early sixth century B.C.E., probably in Lydia. They soon spread throughout the Greek world and beyond. In the ancient world a coin was a piece of metal whose weight and purity, and thus value, were guaranteed by the state. Silver, gold, bronze, and other metals were an attractive choice for a medium of exchange: sufficiently rare to be perceived as valuable, relatively lightweight and portable (at least in the quantities available to most individuals), seemingly indestructible and therefore permanent, yet easily divided. Other items with similar qualities have been used as money in various historical societies, including beads, hard-shelled beans, and cowrie shells.

All such materials have no absolute value. They have only the value that a particular society attributes to them, based on rarity, desirability, and convention. In the modern world, paper money and even some coins lack any intrinsic value and only represent objects of value (such as the gold stored at Fort Knox) that underlie the collective wealth of the society.

Prior to the invention of coinage, people in the lands of the eastern Mediterranean and western Asia had to weigh out quantities of gold, silver, or bronze and exchange pieces of those metals for items they wanted to buy. Coinage allowed for more rapid exchanges of goods as well as for more efficient record keeping and storage of wealth. It stimulated trade and increased the total wealth of the society. However, international commerce could still be confusing because different states used different weight standards, which had to be reconciled.

At the height of their power, the Athenians required all the states in their maritime empire to use Athenian coins, weights, and measures. They probably argued that this standardization would promote commerce and be of benefit to all, and there would have been a degree of truth to this claim. However, besides being a blatant statement of Athenian domination, because the right to issue coins was a mark of sovereignty, the imposition of an Athenian monetary standard brought the lion's share of commerce to the ships and warehouses of Athens. The Athenian "owl" shown here—so called because of the portrait of Athena on one side of the coin and her symbol, the owl, on the other—became the standard for international exchange and was welcomed everywhere.

In the eastern parts of the Persian Empire coinage did not gain a foothold in the sixth to fourth centuries B.C.E. The Persian administration, however, did issue its own coin, the Daric, with a picture of Darius I, for use in the western regions that were, by then, accustomed to coinage. Several of the western satraps also issued coins with their own portraits, probably to pay Greek mercenary soldiers working for them. Later, in the Hellenistic period, Greek-style coins spread across the lands of western Asia.

Athenian coin (Courtesy, Trustees of the British Museum)

(Xerxes) picked the Jewish woman Esther to be one of his wives because of her great beauty and how the courageous and clever queen later saved the Jewish people from a plot to massacre them. Greek sources make clear that women of the royal family could become pawns in the struggle for power. Darius strengthened his claim to the throne by marrying a daughter of Cyrus, and the Greek ruler Alexander the Great would later marry a daughter of the last Persian king. Greek sources portray Persian queens as vicious intriguers, poisoning rival wives in the

king's large harem and plotting to win the throne for their sons.

Besides the royal family, the king's large entourage included other groups: the sons of the Persian aristocracy, who were educated at court and also served as hostages for their parents' good behavior; many noblemen, who were expected to attend the king when they were not otherwise engaged; the central administration, including officials and employees of the treasury, secretariat, and archives; the royal bodyguard; and countless courtiers and slaves. Long gone was the simplicity of the days when the king hunted and caroused with his warrior companions. Inspired by Mesopotamian conceptions of monarchy, the king of Persia had become an aloof figure of majesty and splendor: "The Great King, King of Kings, King in Persia, King of countries." He referred to everyone, even the Persian nobility, as "my slaves," and those who approached were required to bow down before him. In sculptured reliefs he is larger than all the figures around him, and hovering overhead is a winged figure that represents *farna*, the charisma, glory, and fortune of kingship.

The king owned vast tracts of land throughout the empire. Some of this land he gave to his supporters. Donations called "bow land," "horse land," and "chariot land" in Babylonian documents obliged the recipient to provide military service. Scattered around the empire were gardens, orchards, and hunting preserves belonging to the king and the high nobility. The *paradayadam* (meaning "walled enclosure"—the term has come into English as *paradise*), a green oasis in an arid landscape, advertised the prosperity

Stone relief in Hall of 100 Columns   A stone relief from Persepolis, ca. 500 B.C.E., showing the Persian king on a throne supported by his subjects. Above the king hovers the *farna*, a winged figure representing the glory of kingship. Persian art, architecture, documentary language, and administrative methods often show the influence of the Assyrians, their imperial predecessors in this part of the world. Yet the Persians represented themselves as a new kind of master, concerned with the welfare of their subjects and tolerant of local practices. Persian artists have here transformed an Assyrian motif, depicting the subjects upright and happy to support the monarchy. (Courtesy, Trustees of the British Museum)

that the king and empire could bring to those who loyally served them.

Surviving administrative records from the Persian homeland give us a glimpse of how the complex tasks of administration were managed. The Persepolis Treasury and Fortification Texts, inscribed in Elamite Cuneiform on baked clay tablets show that government officials distributed food and other essential commodities to large numbers of workers of many different nationalities. Some of these workers may have been prisoners of war brought to the center of the empire to work on construction projects, maintain and expand the irrigation network, and farm on the royal estates. Workers are broken down into groups of men, women, and children. Women receive less than men of equivalent status, but pregnant women and women with babies receive more. Men and women performing skilled jobs receive more than their unskilled counterparts.

Tradition remembered Darius as a lawgiver who created a body of "laws of the King" and a system of royal judges operating throughout the empire and encouraged the codification and publication of the laws of the various subject peoples. In a manner that typifies the decentralized character of the Persian empire, he allowed each people to live in accordance with its own traditions and ordinances.

The central administration was based not in the Persian homeland (present-day Fars, directly north of the Persian Gulf) but farther west in Elam and Mesopotamia. This location was closer to the geographical center of the empire and allowed the kings to employ the trained administrators and scribes of these ancient civilizations. However, on certain occasions the king returned to one special place back in the homeland.

Darius began construction of a ceremonial capital at Persepolis (Parsa), an artificial platform on which were built a series of palaces, audience halls, treasury buildings, and barracks. Here, too, Darius (and his son Xerxes, who completed the project) was inspired by Mesopotamian traditions, for each of the great Assyrian kings had created a fortress-city as an advertisement of his wealth and power. Darius's approach can be seen in the luxuriant relief sculpture that covers the foundations, walls, and stairwells of the buildings at Persepolis.

Representatives of all the peoples of the empire—recognizable by their distinctive hair, beards, dress, hats, and footwear—are depicted in the act of of bringing gifts to the king. Historians used to think that the sculpture was a pictorial representation of a real event that transpired each year at Persepolis. In recent years this interpretation has lost support, and according to the new consensus the sculpture at Persepolis was an exercise in what today we would call public relations or propaganda: it is Darius's carefully crafted vision of an empire of vast extent and abundant resources in which all the subject peoples willingly cooperate. In one telling sculptural example, Darius subtly contrasted the character of his rule with that of the Assyrian Empire, the Persians' predecessors in these lands (see Chapter 4). The Assyrian kings had gloried in their raw power and depicted subjects staggering under the weight of a giant platform that supported the throne. Darius's artists altered the motif to show erect subjects shouldering the burden voluntarily and without strain.

What actually took place at Persepolis? This opulent retreat in the homeland probably was the scene of events of special significance for the king and his people: the New Year's Festival, coronation, marriage, death and burial. The kings, from Darius on, were buried in elaborate tombs cut into the cliffs at nearby Naqsh-i Rustam.

Another perspective on what the Persian monarchy claimed to stand for is provided by the several dozen inscriptions that have survived. At Naqsh-i Rustam Darius makes the following claim:

> Ahuramazda [god], when he saw this earth in commotion, thereafter bestowed it upon me, made me king. . . . By the favor of Ahuramazda I put it down in its place . . . I am of such a sort that I am a friend to right, I am not a friend to wrong. It is not my desire that the weak man should have wrong done to him by the mighty; nor is that my desire, that the mighty man should have wrong done to him by the weak.[1]

As this inscription makes clear, behind Darius and the empire lies the will of god. Ahuramazda made Darius king and gave him a mandate to

View of the east front of the Apadana (Audience Hall) at Persepolis, ca. 500 B.C.E.   To the right lies the Gateway of Xerxes. Persepolis, in the Persian homeland, was built by Darius I and his son Xerxes, and it was used for ceremonies of special importance for the Persian king and people—coronations, royal weddings, funerals, and the New Year's festival. The stone foundations, walls, and stairways of Persepolis are filled with sculpted images of members of the court and embassies bringing gifts, offering a vision of the grandeur and harmony of the Persian Empire. (Courtesy of the Oriental Institute, University of Chicago)

bring order to a world in turmoil, and, despite his sweet reasonableness, the king will brook no opposition. Ahuramazda is the great god of the Zoroastrian religion, and it is virtually certain that Darius and his successors were Zoroastrians.

The origins of this religion are shrouded in uncertainty. The Gathas, hymns in an archaic Iranian dialect, are said to be the work of Zoroaster (Zarathushtra). The dialect and the physical setting of the hymns indicate that Zoroaster lived in eastern Iran, but scholarly guesses about when he lived range from 1700 to 500 B.C.E. He revealed that the world had been created by Ahura Mazda, "the wise lord," but was threatened by the malevolent designs of Angra Mainyu, "the hostile spirit," backed by a host of demons. In this dualist universe the struggle between good and evil plays out over a period of twelve thousand years. At the end of this period, good is destined to prevail, and the world will return to the pure state of creation. In the meantime, humanity is a participant in this cosmic struggle, and individuals are rewarded or punished in the afterlife for their actions.

The tenets of Zoroastrianism are best known from later periods, and it is difficult to determine how much the beliefs and practices of the Achaemenid period (550–331 B.C.E.) differed from later orthodoxy. Besides the teachings of Zoroaster, the Persians drew on moral and metaphysical conceptions with deep roots in the Iranian past. They were sensitive to the beauties of nature and venerated beneficent elements, such as water, which was not to be sullied, and fire, which was worshiped at fire altars. They were greatly concerned about the purity of the body. Corpses were exposed to wild beasts and the elements to prevent them from putrifying in the earth or tainting the sanctity of fire. The Persians still revered some of the major deities from the pagan past, such as Mithra, associated with the sun and defender of oaths and compacts. They were expected to keep promises and tell the truth. Darius castigated evildoers in his inscriptions as followers of "the Lie."

Zoroastrianism was one of the great religions of the ancient world. It believed in one supreme deity, held humans to a high ethical standard, and promised salvation. It traveled across western Asia with the advance of the Persian Empire, and it may have exerted a major influence on Judaism and thus, indirectly, on Christianity. God and the Devil, Heaven and Hell, reward and punishment, the Messiah and the End of Time, all appear to be legacies of this profound belief system, which, because of the accidents of history, has all but disappeared (except for a relatively small number of Parsees, as Zoroastrians are now called, in Iran and India).

THE RISE OF THE GREEKS

Because Greece was a relatively resource-poor region, the cultural features that emerged there in the first millennium B.C.E. came into being only because the Greeks had access to foreign sources of raw materials and to markets abroad. Greeks were in contact with other peoples, and Greek merchants and mercenaries brought home not only raw materials and crafted goods but also ideas. Under the pressure of population, poverty, war, or political crisis, Greeks moved to other parts of the Mediterranean and western Asia, carrying with them their language and culture and exerting a powerful influence on other societies. Awareness of the different practices and beliefs of other peoples stimulated the formation of a Greek identity and created an interest in geography, ethnography,

and history. The two-century-long rivalry with the Persian Empire also played a large part in shaping the destinies of the Greek city-states.

Geography and Resources

Greece is part of a large ecological zone that encompasses the Mediterranean Sea and the lands surrounding it (see Map 4.4). This zone is bounded by the Atlantic Ocean to the west, the several ranges of the Alps to the north, the Syrian Desert to the east, and the Sahara to the south. The lands lying within this zone have a roughly uniform climate, experience a similar sequence of seasons, and are home to similar plants and animals. In the summer a weather front stalls near the entrance of the Mediterranean, impeding the passage of storms from the Atlantic and allowing hot, dry air from the Sahara to creep up over the region. In winter the front dissolves, and the ocean storms roll in, bringing waves, wind, and cold. Within this ecological zone, it was relatively easy for people to move around, whether driven by the pressures of war, the need for land, or the pursuit of trade.

Greek civilization arose in the lands bordering the Aegean Sea: the Greek mainland, the islands of the Aegean, and the western coast of Anatolia (see Map 5.2). As we saw in Chapter 3, southern Greece is a dry and rocky land with small plains carved up by low mountain ranges. There are no navigable rivers to ease travel or the transport of commodities across this difficult terrain. The small islands dotting the Aegean were inhabited from early times. People could cross the water from Greece to Anatolia almost without losing sight of land. From about 1000 B.C.E. Greeks began to settle on the western edge of Anatolia. Rivers that formed broad and fertile plains near the coast made Ionia, as the ancient Greeks called this region, a comfortable place. The interior of Anatolia is rugged plateau, and the Greeks of the coast were in much closer contact with their fellows across the Aegean than with the native peoples of the interior. The sea was always a connector, not a barrier.

Without large rivers, Greek farmers on the mainland depended entirely on rainfall to water

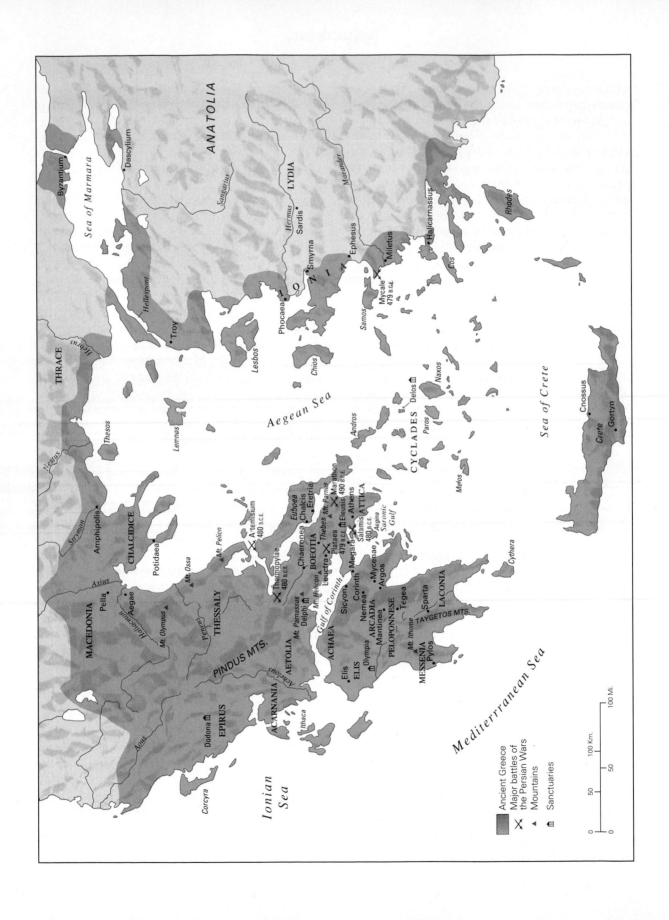

ANATOLIA

Sea of Marmara

Byzantium

Dascylium

Sangarius

LYDIA

Hermus

Sardis

Smyrna

Ephesus

Maeander

Halicarnassus

Rhodes

Miletus

Mycale
479 B.C.E.

Cos

Samos

THRACE

Hebrus

Phocaea

Troy

Hellespont

Lesbos

Chios

Aegean Sea

Sea of Crete

CYCLADES Delos

Naxos

Paros

Andros

Cnossus

Gortyn

Crete

Melos

Thesos

Lemnos

Nestus

Strymon

Amphipolis

CHALCIDICE

Potidaea

Mt. Pelion

A·temisium
480 B.C.E.

Euboea

Chaeronea   Chalcis

Eretria

Mt. Parnes   Marathon
490 B.C.E.

Thebes   Eleusis   Athens
Plataea   479 B.C.E.   ATTICA
Salamis   480 B.C.E.
Aegina   *Saronic*
Megara   *Gulf*

BOEOTIA   *Mt. Helicon*   Leuctra

Thermopylae
480 B.C.E.

Mt. Ossa

MACEDONIA

Pella

Aegae

Axius

Haliacmon

Mt. Olympus

Peneus

THESSALY

Mt. Parnassus
Delphi

AETOLIA

Achelous

PINDUS MTS.

Gulf of Corinth

Sicyon

Corinth

ACHAEA

Nemea

Mycenae

Argos

Cythera

ARCADIA

Mantinea

Tegea

Sparta

TAYGETOS MTS.

PELOPONNESE

LACONIA

Elis

ELIS

Olympia

Mt. Ithome

MESSENIA

Pylos

ACARNANIA

Ithaca

EPIRUS

Dodona

Aous

Corcyra

Ionian Sea

Mediterrranean Sea

O   N   I   A

Ancient Greece
Major battles of
the Persian Wars
Mountains
Sanctuaries

their crops. The limited arable land, thin topsoil, and sparse rainfall could not sustain large populations. In the historical period it was common practice to plant grain (mostly barley, which was hardier than wheat) in the flat plain, olive trees at the edge of the plain, and grapevines on the terraced lower slopes of the foothills. Sheep and goats were grazed in the hills during the growing season. In northern Greece, where the rainfall is greater and the land opens out into broad plains, cattle and horses were more abundant. These Greek lands had virtually no metal deposits and little timber, although both building stone, including some fine marble, and clay for the potter were abundant.

A glance at the map reveals a deeply pitted coastline with many natural harbors. A combination of circumstances—the difficulty of overland transport, the availability of good anchorages, and the need to import metals, timber, and grain—drew the Greeks to the sea. They would obtain timber from the northern Aegean, gold and iron from Anatolia, copper from Cyprus, tin from the western Mediterranean, and grain from the Black Sea, Egypt, and Sicily. Sea transport was much cheaper and faster than overland transport. To give a concrete example, a pair of oxen pulling a cart filled with grain will eat all the grain before traveling 50 miles (80 kilometers). Thus, though never comfortable with "the wine-dark sea," as Homer called it, the Greeks had no choice but to embark upon it in their small, frail ships, hugging the coastline or island-hopping where possible.

Map 5.2 Ancient Greece   By the early first millennium B.C.E., Greek-speaking peoples were dispersed throughout the Aegean region, occupying the Greek mainland, most of the islands, and the western coast of Anatolia. The rough landscape of central and southern Greece, with small plains separated by ranges of mountains, and the many islands in the Aegean favored the rise of hundreds of small, independent communities. The presence of adequate rainfall meant that agriculture was organized on the basis of self-sufficient family farms. As a result of the limited natural resources of this region, the Greeks had to resort to sea travel and trade with other lands in the Mediterranean to acquire metals and other vital raw materials.

The Emergence of the *Polis*

The first flowering of Greek culture in the Mycenaean civilization of the second millennium B.C.E. is described in Chapter 3. For several centuries after the destruction of the Mycenaean palace-states, c. 1150–800 B.C.E., Greece lapsed into a "Dark Age": dark for those who lived through it because of depopulation, poverty, and backwardness; dark for us because it left few traces in the archaeological record. One of the hallmarks of the Dark Age was isolation. Greece and the Aegean as a whole were isolated from the wider world. The importation of raw materials had been the chief source of Mycenaean prosperity. Lack of access to vital resources lay behind the poverty of the Dark Age. Within Greece, regions that had little contact with one another developed distinct regional styles in pottery and other crafts.

The isolation of Greece ended around 800 B.C.E. when Phoenician sailors arrived in the Aegean (see Chapter 4). The Phoenician city-states were dominated by a merchant class that was making ever more distant voyages west in search of valuable commodities and trading partners. By reestablishing contact between the Aegean and the Middle East, the Phoenicians gave Greek civilization an important push and inaugurated what scholars now term the "Archaic" period of Greek history (ca. 800-480 B.C.E.). Soon Greek ships were also plying the waters of the Mediterranean in search of raw materials, trade opportunities, and fertile farmland. The appearance of lifelike human and animal figures and imaginative mythical beasts on painted Greek pottery reveals the influx of new ideas from the east.

The most auspicious gift of the Phoenicians was a writing system. The Phoenicians used a set of twenty-two symbols to represent the consonants in their language, leaving the vowel sounds to be inferred by the reader. The Greeks utilized some of the symbols for which there was no equivalent sound in the Greek language to represent the vowel sounds, thus producing the first true alphabet. An alphabet has tremendous advantages over systems of writing employing ideographic and syllabic signs, such as cuneiform and hieroglyphics. Because they required years of training and the memorization of several hundred signs, cuneiform and hieroglyphics remained the preserve of a scribal class whose elevated social position stemmed from their mastery of this technology. An alphabet opens the door for more widespread literacy, because it requires only a few dozen signs to represent all the possible statements in a language and people can learn an alphabet in a relatively short period of time.

There is controversy over the first uses of the Greek alphabet. Some scholars maintain that it was first used for economic purposes, such as to keep inventories. Others propose that it originated as a vehicle for preserving the oral poetic tradition. Whatever its first use was, the new technology was soon being used to produce new forms of literature, law codes, religious dedications, and epitaphs on gravestones. This does not mean, however, that Greek society immediately became literate in the modern sense. For centuries to come, Greece remained a primarily oral culture in which people used oral means such as storytelling, rituals, and dramatic performances to preserve and transmit information.

One indicator of the powerful new forces at work was a veritable explosion of population. Studies of cemeteries in the vicinity of Athens show that there was a dramatic increase (perhaps as much as five- or sevenfold) during the eighth century B.C.E. The reasons for it are not fully understood, but it probably reflects a more intensive use of land as farming replaced herding, as well as increasing prosperity based on the importation of food and raw materials. Rising population density led to the merging of villages into urban centers. It also created the potential for specialization of labor: freed from agricultural tasks, some members of the society were able to develop skills in other areas, such as crafts, commerce, and religion.

Greece at this time consisted of hundreds of independent political entities, reflecting the facts of Greek geography—small plains separated from each other by mountain barriers. The Greek *polis* (usually translated "city-state") consisted of an urban center and the rural territory that it

controlled. City-states came in various sizes, having populations as small as several thousand or as large as several hundred thousand in the case of Athens.

Most urban centers had certain characteristic features. An *acropolis* ("top of the city") offered a place of refuge in an emergency. The town spread out around the base of this fortified high point. An *agora* ("gathering place") was an open area where the citizens came together to ratify the decisions of their leaders or to line up with their weapons before military ventures. Government buildings were located there, but the agora soon developed into a marketplace as well, since vendors everywhere are eager to set out their wares wherever crowds gather. Fortified walls surrounded the urban center; but as the population expanded, new buildings sprang up beyond the perimeter. City and country were not so sharply distinguished as in our society. The urban center depended on its agricultural hinterland to provide food, and many of the people living within the walls of the city went out to work nearby farms during the day.

Each polis was fiercely jealous of its independence and suspicious of its neighbors, and this state of mind led to frequent conflict. By the early seventh century B.C.E. the Greeks had developed a new kind of warfare, based on the *hoplite*, a heavily armored infantryman who fought in a close-packed formation called a *phalanx*. Protected by a helmet, a breastplate, and leg guards, each hoplite held a small round shield over his own left side and the right side of the man next to him and brandished a thrusting spear, with a sword in reserve. The key to victory in this style of combat was maintaining the cohesion of one's own formation while breaking open the enemy's line. Most of the casualties were suffered by the defeated army in flight.

Recent studies have emphasized the close relationship of hoplite warfare to the agricultural basis of Greek society. When a hoplite army marched into the fields of another community, the enraged farmers of that community, who had expended so much hard labor on their land and buildings, could not fail to meet the challenge. And, brutal and terrifying as the clash of two hoplite lines might be, it did offer a quick decision.

The Acropolis at Athens   This steep, defensible plateau jutting up from the Attic plain served as a Mycenaean fortress in the second millennium B.C.E., and the site of Athens was continuously occupied from that time. In the mid-sixth century B.C.E. the tyrant Pisistratus built a temple to Athena, the patron goddess of the community, which was destroyed by the Persians when they invaded Greece in 480 B.C.E. The Acropolis was left in ruins for three decades as a reminder of what the Athenians had sacrificed in defense of Greek freedom, but in the 440s Pericules initiated a building program, using funds from the naval empire, which Athens now headed. These construction projects, including a new temple to Athena—the Parthenon— brought glory to the city and popularity to Pericles and the new democracy which he championed. (Robert Harding Picture Library)

Battles rarely lasted more than a few hours, and the survivors could promptly return home to tend their farms.

The expanding population soon surpassed what the small plains could support. Many communities were forced to send away their surplus population to establish independent "colonies" in distant lands. Not every colonist went willingly. Sources tell of people being chosen by lot and forbidden to return on pain of death. After obtaining the approval of the god Apollo, who spoke through a priestess at Delphi, the colonists set out, carrying with them fire from the communal hearth of the "mother-city," a symbol of the kinship and religious ties that would connect the two communities. They settled by the sea in the vicinity of a hill or other natural refuge. The "founder," a prominent member of the mother-city, allotted parcels of land and drafted laws for the new community. In some cases the indigenous population was driven away or reduced to a semiservile status; in other cases there was some intermarriage and mixing between colonists and natives.

A wave of colonization in the eighth through sixth centuries B.C.E. spread Greek culture far beyond the land of its origins. New settlements sprang up in the northern Aegean area, around the Black Sea, and on the Libyan coast of North Africa. In southern Italy and on the island of Sicily (see Map 4.4) a whole second Greek world was established. Not only did the colonies become trading partners for their mother-cities, but new developments first appearing in the colonial world traveled back to the Greek homeland— urban planning, new forms of political organization, and, as we shall see shortly, new intellectual currents. (See "Voices and Visions: Conceptions of Identity in Greece and Persia" for the impact of the frontier experience on Greek cultural identity.)

Conceptions of Identity in Greece and Persia

Most people in the ancient world were under the authority of a particular political entity, but their sense of relationship and obligation was far different from modern notions of citizenship. What were the components of Greek and Persian identity, and what was the significance of being inside or outside these groups?

During the early Archaic period Greeks began to use the term Hellenes (Graeci is what the Romans later called them) to distinguish themselves from barbaroi, the other peoples they were encountering on the frontiers created by exploration, colonization, and the expansion of long-distance commerce. Increasing interaction with new peoples and exposure to their different practices made the Greeks aware of the factors that bound them together: their language, religion, and life-style.

At first barbaroi was a descriptive, non-judgmental term meaning "non-Greeks." The struggle with Persia in the early fifth century B.C.E. strengthened the Greek sense of identity and caused a change in attitude, with the contrast between Hellenes and barbaroi beginning to take on a moral dimension that is still felt in our word "barbarian."

The Greek historian Herodotus, in his narrative of Xerxes' invasion, explicitly contrasts Greek and Persian characters. He reports a dialogue (whose historical accuracy is impossible to determine) between Xerxes and Demaratus, an exiled Spartan king, over whether the Spartans and other Greeks will stand their ground in the face of the Persians' overwhelming numerical advantage. Demaratus says:

P overty has always been native in Greece, but the courage they have comes imported, and it is achieved by a compound of wisdom and the strength of their laws. By virtue of this Greece fights off poverty and despotism. . . . Fighting singly, they [the Spartans] are no worse than any other people; together, they are the most gallant men on earth. For they are free—but not altogether so. They have as despot over them Law, and they fear him much more than your men fear you.

The Athenians make similar claims when an envoy from the Persians offers them terms of peace if they will abandon the Greek alliance:

We know of ourselves that the power of the Mede is many times greater than our own. . . . Yet we have such a hunger for freedom that we will fight as long as we are able. . . . There is not enough gold in the world anywhere, nor territory beautiful and fertile enough, that

we should take it in return for turning to the Persian interest and enslaving Greece. . . . We are one in blood and one in language; those shrines of the gods belong to us all in common, and the sacrifices in common, and there are our habits, bred of a common upbringing.

What qualities do the Greeks particularly value? In what ways do they claim to be fundamentally different from barbarians? What might be the causes of these differences?

The lack of sources makes it more difficult to gauge the Persian sense of identity. Our best glimpse of the qualities that Persians valued comes from several inscriptions of Darius I:

I am Darius the Great King, King of Kings, King of countries containing all kinds of men, King in this great earth far and wide, son of Hystaspes, an Achaemenian, a Persian, son of a Persian, an Aryan, having Aryan lineage.

What is right, that is my desire. I am not a friend to the man who is a Lie-follower. I am not hot-tempered. What things develop in my anger, I hold firmly under control by my thinking power. I am firmly ruling over my own impulses. . . . Trained am I both with hands and with feet. As a horseman I am a good horseman. As a bowman I am a good bowman both afoot and on horseback. As a spearman I am a good spearman both afoot and on horseback.

What claims is Darius making here for a Persian character? Which qualities are especially valued?

Herodotus reports another story which, if true, might represent how the Persians viewed the Greeks. Cyrus allegedly said of the Greeks:

I never yet feared men who have a place set apart in the midst of their cities where they gather to cheat one another and exchange oaths, which they break.

Why might Zoroastrian Persians have looked down on the commercial and legal practices of the Greeks?

Sources: The first, second, and fourth quotations are from Herodotus, The History, trans. David Grene (Chicago: University of Chicago Press, 1988), 502–504, 610–611, 103 (=Herodotus 7.102–104, 8.143–144, 1.153). The third translation is from Roland G. Kent, Old Persian: Grammar, Texts, Lexicon, 2nd ed. (New Haven, CT: American Oriental Society, 1953), 138, 140.

By reducing surplus population, colonization helped to relieve pressures building within the Archaic Greek world. Nevertheless, it was an era of political instability. Kings ruled the Dark Age societies depicted in the great epic poems of Homer, the *Iliad* and the *Odyssey*, but at some point councils composed of the heads of noble families superseded the kings. This aristocracy derived its wealth and power from ownership of large tracts of land. The land was worked by peasant families who were allowed to occupy a plot and keep a portion of what they grew, or by debt-slaves, men who had borrowed money or seed from the lord and lost their freedom when unable to repay. A typical community also contained free peasants who owned small farms and urban-based craftsmen and merchants who began to constitute a growing "middle class."

In the seventh and sixth centuries B.C.E. in one city-state after another, an individual "tyrant"—by which the Greeks meant someone who held power contrary to the established traditions of the community—gained control. The individuals who seized power—often disgruntled members of the aristocracy—were backed by the emerging middle class. New opportunities for economic advancement and the declining cost of metals meant that a larger number of people could acquire arms. This group was playing an ever more important role as hoplite soldiers in the local militia and thus could put force at the disposal of their leader. Weary of the corruption and arrogance of the aristocrats who monopolized political power, this class must have demanded some political prerogatives as the price of their cooperation.

Ultimately, the tyrants of this age were unwitting catalysts in a process of political evolution. Although some were able to pass their position on to the next generation, sooner or later the tyrant-family was ejected, and authority in the community developed along one of two lines: toward *oligarchy*, in which only the wealthier members exercised political privilege; or toward *democracy*, in which all free, adult males could play a role.

Greek religion encompassed a wide range of cults and beliefs. The ancestors of the Greeks had brought a pantheon of sky-gods with them when they entered the Greek peninsula at the end of the third millennium B.C.E. Male gods predominated, but a number of female deities had important roles. These gods often represented forces in nature: Zeus sent storms and lightning, and Poseidon was master of the sea and earthquakes. The *Iliad* and the *Odyssey*, which Greek schoolboys memorized and professional performers recited, put a distinctive stamp on the personality and character of these deities. The gods that Homer portrayed were anthropomorphic, that is, conceived as humanlike in appearance and emotion. Indeed, the chief thing that separated them from humans was humans' mortality.

The worship of these gods at state-sponsored festivals was as much an expression of civic identity as of personal piety. Sacrifice was the central ritual of Greek religion. Carried out at altars in front of the temples that were the gods' places of residence in the town, it reveals how the Greeks thought about the relationship of humans and gods. The gods were given gifts, which could be as humble as a small cake deposited on the altar or a cup of wine poured out on the ground. In return the gods were expected to favor and protect the donor. Spectacular forms of ritual involved a group of people in the act of killing one or more animals, spraying the altar with the victim's blood, and burning parts of its body so that the aroma would ascend to the gods on high. The Greeks created a sense of community out of shared participation in the taking of life.

Greek individuals and poleis (the plural of polis) sought information, advice, or predictions of the future from oracles, sacred sites where the gods communicated with humans, especially from the prestigious oracle of Apollo at Delphi in central Greece. The god responded at Delphi through his priestess, the Pythia, whose obscure poetic utterances were interpreted by the male priests who administered the sanctuary. Because most Greeks were farmers, fertility cults, which worshiped and sought to enhance the productive forces in nature (for obvious reasons usually conceived of as female), were popular though often hidden from modern view because of our dependence on literary texts expressing the values of an educated, urban elite.

Vase painting depicting a sacrifice to the god Apollo, ca. 440 B.C.E.   For the Greeks, who believed in a multitude of gods who looked like humans and behaved in a similar fashion, the central act of worship was the sacrifice, the ritualized offering of a gift. This created a relationship between the human worshipper and the deity, with the expectation that the god would bestow favors in return. Here we see a number of male devotees, in their finest clothing with garlands in their hair, near the sacred outdoor altar and statue of Apollo holding his characteristic bow and laurel branch. The man on the right is offering to the god bones wrapped in fat, while the human celebrants will feast on the meat carried by the boy. (Museum für Vor-u. Frühgeschichte, Frankfurt)

New Intellectual Currents

The material changes taking place in Greece in the Archaic Period—new technologies, increased prosperity, and social and political development—led to distinctive innovations in the intellectual and artistic outlook of the Greeks. One distinctive feature of the age was a growing emphasis on the individual. In early Greek communities, the individual was enveloped by the family, and land belonged collectively to the family, including ancestors and descendants. Ripped out of this communal network and forced to establish a new life on a distant frontier, the colonist became a model of the rugged individualist, as was the tyrant who seized power for himself alone. These new patterns of activity led toward a concept of *humanism*, of the uniqueness, potentialities, and prerogatives of the individual, which has remained a central tenet of western civilization.

We see signs of individualism clearly in the new *lyric poetry*, short compositions in which the subject matter is intensely personal, drawn from the immediate experience of the poet and highlighting his or her loves, hates, and views. Archilochus, a soldier and poet living in the first half of the seventh century B.C.E. made a surprising admission:

Some barbarian is waving my shield, since I was
    obliged to
leave that perfectly good piece of equipment
    behind
under a bush. But I got away, so what does it
    matter?
Let the shield go; I can buy another one equally
    good.[2]

Here Archilochus is making fun of the heroic ideal that scorned a soldier who ran away from the enemy.

Sappho, one of the few Greek women poets whose work has partially survived, composed exquisite poetry reflecting the lives and loves of the circle of young women whom she mentored on the Aegean island of Lesbos around 600 B.C.E. For example:

> She was like the sweetest apple
> That ripened highest on the tree,
> That the harvesters couldn't reach,
> And pretended they forgot.
> Like the mountain hyacinth trod underfoot
> By shepherd men, its flower purple on the ground.[3]

In challenging traditional values and exploiting the medium to disseminate personal feeling and opinion, lyric poets like Archilochus and Sappho paved the way for the modern Western conception of poetry.

There were also challenges to traditional religion, as when certain thinkers known as pre-Socratic philosophers called into question the kind of gods that Homer had popularized. Xenophanes, living in the sixth century B.C.E. protested:

> But if cattle and horses or lions had hands, or were able to draw with their hands and do the works that men can do, horses would draw the forms of the gods like horses, and cattle like cattle, and they would make their bodies such as they each had themselves.[4]

The pre-Socratic philosophers rejected traditional religious explanations for the origins and nature of the world and sought to explain things rationally. They were primarily concerned with questions of natural science: How was the world created? What is it made of? Why does change occur? (The term *pre-Socratic* reflects the the fact that Socrates, in the later fifth century B.C.E., turned the focus of philosophy to ethical questions.) Their science is theoretical rather than experimental, for the pre-Socratics developed conceptual models to account for the phenomenal world but did not test their validity.

Certain pre-Socratic thinkers postulated various combinations of earth, air, fire, and water as the primal elements that combine or dissolve to form the numerous substances found in nature. One advanced the theory that the world is composed of microscopic atoms (from a Greek word meaning "indivisible") moving through the void of space, colliding randomly, and combining in various ways to form the many substances of the natural world. In some respects startlingly similar to modern atomic theory, this model was merely a lucky intuition, but it is a testament to the sophistication of these thinkers. Espousing such views took courage, because more conventional Greeks regarded the pre-Socratics as impious. It is probably no coincidence that most of these theorists came from Ionia and southern Italy, two zones in which Greeks were in close contact with non-Greek peoples. The shock of encountering people with very different ideas may have stimulated new lines of inquiry.

Another important intellectual development also took place in Ionia in the sixth century B.C.E. A group of men later referred to as *logographers* ("writers of prose accounts") set about gathering information on a wide range of topics, including the geography and ethnography (description of the physical characteristics and cultural practices of a group of people) of Mediterranean lands and peoples, the foundation of important cities, and the origins of famous Greek families. They called the method they employed to collect, sort, and select information *historia*, "investigation/research." In the mid-fifth century B.C.E. Herodotus (ca. 485–425 B.C.E.), from Halicarnassus in southwest Anatolia, published his *Histories*. Early parts of the work are filled with the geographic and ethnographic reports, legends, folktales, and marvels dear to the logographers, but in later sections Herodotus focuses on the great event of the previous generation: the wars between the Greeks and the Persian Empire.

Herodotus declared his new conception of his mission in the first lines of the book:

> I, Herodotus of Halicarnassus, am here setting forth my history, that time may not draw the color from what man has brought into being, nor those great and wonderful deeds, manifested by both Greeks and barbarians, fail of their report, and, together with all this, the reason why they fought one another.[5]

When he states that he wants to find out *why* Greeks and Persians came to blows, he is a historian who is seeking the causes behind historical events. Herodotus directed the all-purpose techniques of *historia* to the service of *history* in the modern sense of the term, thereby narrowing the meaning of the word. For this achievement he is known as "the father of history."

Athens and Sparta

The two preeminent city-states of the later Archaic and Classical periods were Athens and Sparta. The remarkably different character of these two communities, both of which arose under the umbrella of Greek culture, underscores the immense potential for diversity in the evolution of human societies.

The ancestors of the Spartans had migrated into the Peloponnese, the southernmost part of the Greek mainland, around 1000 B.C.E. For a time Sparta followed a typical path of development, participating in trade and fostering the arts. Then in the seventh century B.C.E. something happened to alter the destiny of the Spartan state.

Like many other parts of Greece, the Spartan community was feeling the effects of rising population and a shortage of arable land. However, instead of sending out colonies, the Spartans crossed their mountainous western frontier and invaded the fertile plain of Messenia. Hoplite tactics may have given the Spartans the edge they needed to prevail over fierce Messenian resistance. The result was the takeover of Messenia and the virtual enslavement of the native population, who descended to the status of *helots*, the most abused and exploited population on the Greek mainland.

Fear of a future helot uprising led to the evolution of the unique Spartan way of life. The Spartan state became a military camp in a permanent state of preparedness. Territory in Messenia and Laconia (the Spartan homeland) was divided into several thousand lots and assigned to Spartan citizens. The helots worked the land and turned over a portion of what they grew to their Spartan masters, who were thereby freed from food production and able to spend their lives in military training and service.

The professional Spartan soldier was the best in Greece, and the Spartan army was superior to all others, since the other Greek states relied on citizen militias called out in time of crisis. The Spartans, however, paid a huge personal price for their military readiness. At age seven, boys were taken from their families and put into barracks, where they were toughened by a severe regimen of discipline, beatings, and deprivation. A Spartan male's whole life was subordinated to the demands of the state.

Sparta essentially stopped the clock, refusing to participate in the economic, political, and cultural revival taking place in the Archaic Greek world. There were no longer any poets or artists at Sparta. In an attempt to maintain equality among citizens, precious metals and coinage were banned, and Spartans were forbidden to engage in commerce. The fifth-century B.C.E. historian, Thucydides, a native of Athens, remarked that in his day Sparta appeared to be little more than a large village and that no future observer of the ruins of the site would be able to guess its power.

Other Greeks admired the Spartans for their courage and commitment but were put off by their arrogance, ignorance, and cruelty. The Spartans purposefully cultivated a mystique by rarely putting their reputation to the test. Under the leadership of a Council of Elders and two kings who commanded troops in the field, Sparta practiced a foreign policy that was cautious and isolationist. Reluctant to march far from home for fear of a helot uprising, the Spartans sought to maintain peace in the Peloponnese through the Peloponnesian League, a system of alliances between Sparta and its neighbors.

Athens followed a strikingly different path. By the standards of Greek city-states it possessed an unusually large and populous territory: the entire region of Attica. By the fifth century B.C.E. it had a population of approximately 300,000 people. Attica contained a number of moderately fertile plains and was ideally suited for cultivation of the olive tree. In addition to the urban center of Athens, located some 5 miles (8 kilometers) from the sea where the sheer-sided Acropolis towered above the Attic Plain, the peninsula was dotted with villages and a few larger towns.

The large land area of Attica provided a buffer against the initial stresses of the Archaic period, but by the early sixth century B.C.E. things had reached a critical point. In 594 B.C.E. Solon, a member of the aristocracy with ties to the merchant community, was appointed lawgiver with extraordinary powers to avert a looming crisis. He divided Athenian citizens into four classes based on the annual yield of their farms. Those in the top three classes could hold state offices. Members of the lowest class, who had little or no property, could not hold office but were allowed to participate in meetings of the Assembly. This arrangement, which made rights and privileges a function of wealth, was a far cry from democracy, but it broke the absolute monopoly on power of a small circle of aristocratic families, and it allowed for social and political mobility. And by abolishing the practice of enslaving individuals for failure to repay their debts, Solon guaranteed the freedom of Athenian citizens.

Despite Solon's efforts to defuse the crisis, political turmoil continued until 546 B.C.E., when an aristocrat named Pisistratus seized power. At this time most Athenians still lived in villages in the Attic countryside, identified primarily with their district, and were under the thumb of local lords, who lived in strongly constructed manor houses. To strengthen his position and weaken the aristocracy, Pisistratus tried to shift the allegiance of the rural population to the urban center of Athens, where he was the dominant figure. He undertook a number of monumental building projects, including a Temple of Athena on the Acropolis. He also instituted or expanded several major festivals: the City Dionysia, which was to become the setting for dramatic performances, and the Panathenaea, which drew people to Athens for a religious procession and athletic and poetic competitions.

Pisistratus passed the tyranny on to his sons, but with Spartan assistance the tyrant family was turned out in the last decade of the sixth century B.C.E. In the 460s and 450s B.C.E. Ephialtes and Pericles took the last steps in the evolution of democracy, transferring all power to popular organs of government: the Assembly, Council of 500, and People's Courts. Henceforth it was possible for men of moderate or little means to hold office and engage in the political process. In sensitive areas, such as managing public money and commanding military forces, offices were filled by means of election, to guarantee the ability of those chosen. But men were selected by lot to fill even the highest offices in the state, and they were paid for public service so they could afford to take time off from their work.

Henceforth, the focal point of political life was the Assembly of all citizens. Several times a month proposals were debated there, decisions were openly made, and anyone could speak to the issues of the day. There was no strong executive office; members of the Council took turns presiding and representing the Athenian state. Pericles (ca. 495–429 B.C.E.), who seems to have dominated Athenian politics for three decades, must have created an effective political organization that got out the vote on every important occasion.

In tandem with this century-and-a-half process of internal political evolution, Athens's economic clout and international reputation rose steadily. From the time of Pisistratus, Athenian pottery is increasingly prominent in the archaeological record at sites all around the Mediterranean, crowding out the products of former commercial powerhouses such as Corinth and Aegina. These pots often contained olive oil, Athens's chief export, but the elegant painted vases must have been desirable luxury commodities in their own right. Extensive trade increased the numbers and wealth of a burgeoning middle class and helps to account for why Athens took the path of increasing democratization.

THE STRUGGLE OF PERSIA AND GREECE

For the Greeks of the fifth and fourth centuries B.C.E., Persia was the great enemy of their civilization, and the wars with Persia were the decisive historical event of the era. No doubt Persians would have viewed these events differently, would have located the center of gravity farther to the east, and would not have seen the wars with the Greeks in the early fifth century B.C.E. as being so consequential. Nevertheless, the encounter with the Greeks over a period of two centuries was, in the end, of profound importance for the history of the eastern Mediterranean and western Asia.

Early Encounters

Cyrus's conquest of Lydia in 546 B.C.E. led to the subjugation of the Greek cities of the Anatolian seaboard. In the years that followed the Greek cities were ruled by local individuals or factions willing to collaborate with the Persian government so as to maintain themselves in power and allow their city to operate with minimal Persian interference. All this changed when the Ionian Revolt, a great uprising of Greeks and other subject peoples on the western frontier, broke out in 499 B.C.E. The Persians needed five years and a massive infusion of troops and resources to stamp out the insurrection.

This failed revolt led to the Persian Wars, two Persian attacks on Greece in the early fifth century B.C.E. In 490 B.C.E. Darius dispatched a naval fleet to punish Eretria and Athens, two states on the Greek mainland that had given assistance to the Ionian rebels, and to warn others about the foolhardiness of crossing the Persian king. After Eretria had been betrayed to the Persians by several of its own citizens, the survivors were marched off to permanent exile in southwest Iran. In this, as in many things, the Persians took over the practices of their Assyrian predecessors, although they resorted to mass deportation less often and were more reticent to advertise it. The Athenians were next on the list and no doubt would have had a similar fate, but their hoplites defeated the lighter-armed Persian troops in a short, sharp engagement at Marathon, 26 miles (42 kilometers) from Athens.

Xerxes (Khshayarsha r. 486–465 B.C.E.) succeeded his father on the Persian throne in 486 B.C.E. and soon turned his attention to the troublesome Greeks. He probably was moved by a desire to prove himself the equal of his predecessors, all of whom had made major acquisitions of territory for the empire. He and his advisers also must have recognized that the Aegean Sea did not provide a satisfactory boundary for the empire as long as Greeks under Persian control were in easy contact with independent Greeks across the waters.

In 480 B.C.E. Xerxes set out with a huge invasionary force. The Persian core army was supported by contingents summoned from all the peoples of the empire and by a large fleet of ships drawn from maritime subjects. Crossing the Hellespont (the narrow strait at the edge of the Aegean separating Europe and Asia) and journeying across Thrace, they descended into central and southern Greece (see Map 5.2). Xerxes sent messengers ahead to most of the Greek states, bidding them to offer up "earth and water," the tokens of submission.

Many Greek communities did indeed acknowledge Persian overlordship. But in southern Greece an alliance of states bent on resistance was formed under the leadership of the Spartans. This Hellenic League, as modern historians call it, failed to halt the Persian advance at the pass of Thermopylae in central Greece, where three hundred Spartans and their king gave their lives to buy time for their fellows to escape. However, after seizing and sacking the city of Athens in 480 B.C.E., the Persians allowed their navy to be lured into the narrow straits of nearby Salamis, where they gave up their advantage in numbers and maneuverability and suffered a devastating defeat. The following spring (479 B.C.E.), the Persian land army was routed at Plataea and the immediate threat to Greece receded.

For contemporary Greeks the victory over Xerxes' army and navy was a miracle. It was, to be sure, the first major setback for Persian arms after seventy years of expansion. A number of factors help to account for the outcome: the Persians' difficulty in provisioning a very large army in a distant land; the serious tactical error made by the Persian high command in being drawn into the narrow waters off Salamis; and the superiority of heavily armed and well-drilled Greek hoplite soldiers over lighter-armed Asiatic infantry.

The collapse of the threat to the Greek mainland did not mean the end of the war. The Greeks now went on the offensive. Athens's stubborn refusal to submit to the Persian king, even after the city had been sacked twice in two successive years, and the vital role played by the Athenian navy, which made up fully half of the allied Greek fleet, had earned the city a large measure of respect. The next phase of the war—the aim of which was to drive the Persians away from the Aegean and liberate Greek states still under Persian control—was naval. Thus Athens replaced isolationist and land-based Sparta as leader of the campaign against Persia.

In 477 B.C.E. the Delian League was formed. It was a voluntary alliance of Greek states eager to prosecute the war against Persia. Within less than twenty years, League forces, led by Athenian generals, had swept the Persians from the waters of the eastern Mediterranean and freed all Greek communities except those in distant Cyprus.

The Height of Athenian Power

By scholarly convention, the Classical period (480–323 B.C.E.) of Greek history begins with the successful defense of the Greek homeland against the forces of the Persian Empire. Ironically the Athenians, who had played such a crucial role, exploited these events to become an imperial power. Success and the passage of time led many of their Greek allies to assume an increasingly passive stance and, instead of contributing ships and men, to contribute money. The Athenians used this money to build and man an ever larger navy. Eventually they saw the other members of the Delian League as their empire. The Athenians demanded annual contributions and other signs of submission. States that tried to leave the League were brought back by force, stripped of their defenses, and rendered subordinate to Athens.

Athens's mastery of naval technology transformed Greek warfare and politics and brought power and wealth to Athens itself. Greek commercial ships were powered by wind and sail. They used a single square-rigged sheet, which was effective for sailing downwind but of little use in a headwind. Almost round in shape for stability and to allow maximum space for cargo,

these vessels could carry 100 tons or more. For the relatively small crews there was room on board to cook and sleep. Greek sailors were reluctant to go to sea in the winter months, both because of the increased danger of storms and because of the difficulty of navigating in cloudy weather, when they could see neither landmarks ashore nor the sun.

Unlike commercial ships, military vessels could not be left to drift if the wind failed. Thus they relied on large numbers of rowers. Having little deck room or storage space, these ships needed to hug the coastline and go ashore nightly to replenish food supplies and to give the crew a chance to sleep. For centuries the primary warship in Greek waters had been the *pentekonter*, a sturdy vessel powered by fifty oars in two tiers. Naval battles fought in pentekonters were crude engagements. Warriors from each side launched volleys of spears and arrows to clear the decks of the enemy ship before boarding and fighting hand to hand. By the late sixth century B.C.E. experimentation had begun with the *trireme*, a sleeker, faster vessel powered by 170 rowers.

The design of the trireme has long been a puzzle, but the unearthing at Athens of the slips where these vessels were moored, and recent experiments with full-scale replicas manned by international volunteers, have revealed much about the design of the trireme and the battle tactics that it made possible. The Greek trireme was sleek (approximately 115 by 15 feet or 35 by 6 meters) and fragile. Rowers using oars of differing lengths and carefully positioned on three levels so as not to run afoul of one another were able to achieve short bursts of speed of up to 7 knots. Athenian crews, by constant practice, became the best in the eastern Mediterranean. They could disable enemy vessels by sheering off their oars, smashing in their sides below the water line with an iron-tipped ram, or forcing them to collide with one another by running around them in ever-tighter circles.

The effectiveness of the new Athenian navy had significant consequences, both at home and abroad. The emergence at Athens of a democratic system in which each male citizen had, at least in principle, an equal voice is connected to the new primacy of the fleet. Hoplites were members of the middle and upper classes (they had to provide their own protective gear and weapons). Rowers, in contrast, came from the lower classes, and because they were providing the chief protection for the community and were the source of its power, they could insist on full rights.

Possession of a navy allowed Athens to project its power farther than it could have done with a citizen militia (which could be kept in arms for only short periods of time). In previous Greek wars, the victorious state had little capability to occupy a defeated neighbor permanently (with the exception, as we have seen, of Sparta's takeover of Messenia). Usually the victor satisfied itself with booty and, perhaps, minor adjustments to boundary lines. Athens was able to continually dominate and exploit other, weaker communities in an unprecedented way.

Athens did not hesitate to use political power to promote its commercial interests (see Environment and Technology: Origins and Early Development of Coinage). Athens's port, the Piraeus, grew into the most important commercial center in the eastern Mediterranean. The money collected each year from the subject states helped to subsidize the increasingly expensive Athenian democracy as well as underwrite the construction costs of the beautiful buildings on the Acropolis, including the majestic new temple of Athena, the Parthenon. Many Athenians worked on the construction and decoration of these monuments. Indeed, the building program was a means by which the Athenian leader, Pericles, redistributed the profits of empire to the Athenian people and gained extraordinary popularity. When his political enemies protested against the use of Delian League funds for the building program, Pericles replied: "They [Athens's subjects] do not give us a single horse, nor a soldier, nor a ship. All they supply is money. . . . It is no more than fair that after Athens has been equipped with all she needs to carry on the war, she should apply the surplus to public works, which, once completed, will bring her glory for all time."[6]

In other ways as well Athens's cultural achievements were dependent on the profits of empire. The economic advantages that empire brought to Athens subsidized indirectly the festivals at which the great dramatic tragedies of Aeschylus, Sophocles, and Euripides, and the comedies of Aristophanes, were performed. Money and power are a prerequisite for support of the arts and sciences, and the brightest and most creative artists and thinkers in the Greek world were drawn to Athens. Traveling teachers, called *Sophists*, or "wise men," provided advanced instruction in logic and public speaking to pupils who could afford their fees. The new discipline of *rhetoric*—the construction of attractive and persuasive arguments—gave those with training and quick wits a great advantage in politics and the courts. The Greek masses became connoisseurs of oratory, eagerly listening for each innovation yet so aware of the power of words that *sophist* came to mean one who uses cleverness to distort and manipulate reality.

These new intellectual currents came together in 399 B.C.E., when the philosopher Socrates (ca. 470–399 B.C.E.) was brought to trial on charges of corrupting the youth of Athens and not believing in the gods of the city. A sculptor by trade, Socrates spent most of his time in the company of young men who enjoyed conversing with him and observing him deflate the pretensions of those who thought themselves wise. He wryly commented that he knew one more thing than everyone else: that he knew nothing.

In an Athenian trial there was no guarantee that anyone involved had any legal expertise. Complainants and defendants spoke for themselves. The presiding magistrate was an ordinary citizen assigned to office by lot. Large juries of scores, or even hundreds, of citizens decided guilt and punishment, often motivated more by emotion than by legal principles.

At his trial, Socrates was easily able to dispose of the actual charges, because he was a deeply religious man and had the support of the families of the young men who had associated with him. He recognized that the real basis of the hostility he faced was twofold: (1) He was being held responsible for the actions of several of his aristocratic students who had badly harmed the state. (2) He was the target of popular prejudice against the Sophists and other intellectuals who raised questions about traditional religious beliefs and morality. The vote that found him guilty of the charges was fairly close. But his lack of

A segment of the marble frieze from the Parthenon, ca. 440 B.C.E. A continuous band of sculptured relief ran around the upper edge of the walls of the temple. Most scholars believe that it represents the great procession which was a central component of the most important civic festival in Athens, the Panathenaea, which celebrated the new year and the birthday of Athena. Here we see pairs of women carrying trays, as well as several cloaked men. Festivals were among the few occasions when Athenian women of the middle and upper classes would be out in public. Other scenes on the frieze depict young horsemen, priests with animals about to be sacrificed, and several gods looking on. Surviving records of the construction of the Parthenon indicate that the sculptors took two months to make each figure. (Giraudon/Art Resource, NY)

contrition in the penalty phase, in which he proposed that he be rewarded for his services to the state, led a larger majority of the jury to condemn him to death by drinking hemlock.

The trial of Socrates reveals a number of fault lines in Athens: between democrats and oligarchs, between members of the upper classes and commoners, and between the conservative majority and new-style intellectuals. Sophocles' disciples regarded his execution as a martyrdom. In response to it, smart young men such as Plato, who normally would have devoted their energies to political careers, withdrew from public life and dedicated themselves to the philosophical pursuit of knowledge and truth.

This period also encompasses the last stage in Greece of the transition from orality to literacy. Socrates himself wrote nothing, preferring to converse with people he met in the street. Plato (ca. 428–347 B.C.E.) may represent the first generation to be truly literate. He gained much of his knowledge from books and habitually wrote down his thoughts. Plato founded a school on the outskirts of Athens. In his Academy young men pursued a course of higher education. Yet even Plato retained vestiges of the orality of the world in which he had grown up. He wrote dialogues—an oral form—in which his protagonist, Socrates, uses the "Socratic method" of question and answer to reach a deeper understanding of the meaning of values such as justice, excellence, and wisdom. Plato refused to write down the most advanced stages of the philosophical and spiritual training that took place at his Academy. He believed that full apprehension of a higher reality, of which our own sensible world is but a pale reflection, was available only to "initiates" who had completed the earlier stages.

Inequality in Classical Greece

It is important to keep in mind that Athenian democracy, the inspiration for the concept of democracy in the Western tradition, was a democracy only for the relatively small percentage of the inhabitants of Attica who were truly citizens—free, adult males of pure Athenian ancestry. Excluding women, children, slaves, and foreigners, this came to only 10 or 15 percent—30,000 or 40,000 people out of a total population of approximately 300,000. Other democratic Greek poleis, less well known to us than Athens, were, no doubt, equally exclusive.

Slaves, mostly of foreign origin, constituted perhaps a third of the population of Attica in the fifth and fourth centuries B.C.E., and the average Athenian family owned one or more. Slaves were needed to run the shop or work on the farm while the master was attending meetings of the Assembly or serving on one of the countless boards that oversaw the day-to-day activities of the state. The slave was a "living piece of property," required to do any work, submit to any sexual acts, and receive any punishments that the owner ordained (some communities did prohibit arbitrarily killing a slave). For the most part, however, Greek slaves were not subjected to the extremes of cruelty and abuse that occurred in other places and times.

In the absence of huge estates there were no rural slave gangs, and the condition of Greek slaves was like that of the favored domestic servants in other slave-owning societies. Slaves were regarded as members of the household, and they often worked together with the master or mistress on the same tasks. The close daily contact between owners and slaves meant, in many cases, that a relationship developed, and this made it hard for Greek slave owners to deny the essential humanity of their slaves. Still, Greek thinkers rationalized the institution of slavery by arguing that *barbaroi* (non-Greeks; see Voices and Visions: Conceptions of Identity in Greece and Persia) lacked the capacity to reason and thus were better off under the direction of rational Greek owners. The social stigma attached to slavery was so great that most Athenians refused

to work as wage laborers for another individual because following the orders of an employer was akin to being his slave.

Equally essential to providing Athenian men with the freedom to engage in political and social life were women. The position of women varied across Greek communities. The women of Sparta, because they were expected to bear and raise strong children, were encouraged to exercise and enjoyed a level of public visibility and outspokenness that shocked other Greeks. Athens—the case historians know best because of the abundance of written sources and vase paintings—may have been on the extreme end of Greek communities as regards the confinement and oppression of women. This situation, ironically, is linked to the high degree of freedom for men in a democratic state.

Athenian marriages were patently unequal affairs. The man might be thirty, reasonably well educated, a veteran of war, experienced in business and politics. Under law he had virtually absolute authority over the members of his household. He arranged a marriage with the parents of his prospective wife, who was likely to be a teenager who had been brought up in the women's quarters of her parents' house and had no formal education and only minimal training in weaving, cooking, and household management. Coming into the home of a husband she hardly knew, she had no political rights and limited legal protection. Given the differences in age, social experience, and authority, the relationship between husband and wife was in many ways similar to that of father and daughter.

The primary function of marriage was to produce children, preferably male. It is impossible to prove the extent of infanticide—the killing through exposure of unwanted children—because the ancients were sufficiently ashamed to say little about it. But it is likely that more girls than boys were abandoned.

Husbands and wives had limited contact in the daily round of activities. The man spent the day outdoors attending to work or political responsibilities; he dined with male friends at night; and usually he slept alone in the men's quarters. The closest relationship in the family was likely to be between the wife and her slave attendant—women of roughly the same age who spent enormous amounts of time together. The servant could be sent into town on errands while the wife stayed in the house, except to attend funerals and certain festivals and to make discreet visits to the houses of female relatives. Greek men justified the confinement of women by claiming that they were naturally promiscuous and likely to introduce other men's children into the household—an action that would threaten the family property and violate the strict regulation of citizenship rights. Athenian law allowed a husband to kill an adulterer caught in the act with his wife.

The wife's normal duties included the production of clothing, cooking, and cleaning, as well as raising the children and directing the household slaves. In wealthy families with many possessions and a large contingent of slaves, those duties might amount to extensive supervisory responsibilities.

Without any documents written by women in this period, we cannot tell the extent to which Athenian women resented their situation or accepted it because they knew little else. Women's festivals, such as the Thesmophoria, provided a rare opportunity to get out. During this three-day festival the women of Athens lived together and managed their own affairs in a great encampment, carrying out mysterious rituals meant to enhance the fertility of the land. The appearance of bold and self-assertive women on the Athenian stage is also suggestive: the defiant Antigone of Sophocles' play, who buried her brother despite the injunction of the king; and the wives of Aristophanes' comedy *Lysistrata*, who refused to have sex with their husbands until the men ended a war. Although these plays were written by men and probably reflect a male fear of strong women, the playwrights must have had models in their mothers, sisters, and wives.

The inequality of men and women also posed obstacles to creating a meaningful relationship between the sexes. To find his intellectual and emotional "equal," a man often looked to other men. Bisexuality was common in ancient Greece, as much a product of the social structure as of biological inclinations. A common pattern was that of an older man serving as admirer, pursuer, and men-

Vase painting depicting women at an Athenian fountain house, ca. 520 B.C.E. The paintings on Greek vases provide the most vivid pictorial record of ancient Greek life. The subject matter usually reflects the interests of the aristocratic males who purchased them—warfare, athletics, mythology, and drinking parties—but sometimes we are given glimpses into the lives of women and the working classes. These women are presumably domestic servants sent to fetch water for the household from a public fountain. On their heads they balance large water jars, like the one on which this scene is depicted. (William Francis Warden Fund. Courtesy, Museum of Fine Arts, Boston)

tor of a youth. Bisexuality became part of a system by which young men were educated and initiated into the community of adult males. At least this was true of the elite, intellectual groups that loom large in the written sources. It is hard to say how prevalent bisexuality and the confinement of women were among the Athenian masses.

Failure of the City-State and Triumph of the Macedonians

The emergence of Athens as an imperial power in the half-century after the Persian invasion aroused the suspicions of other Greek states and led to open hostilities between former allies. In the year 431 B.C.E. the Peloponnesian War broke out. This nightmarish struggle for survival between the Athenian and Spartan alliance systems encompassed most of the Greek world. It was a war unlike any previous Greek war because the Athenians had used their naval power to insulate themselves from the dangers of an attack by land. In mid century they had built three long walls connecting the city with the port of Piraeus and the adjacent shoreline. As long as Athens controlled the sea lanes and was able to provision itself, it could not be starved into submission by a land-based siege.

At the start of the war, Pericles formulated an unprecedented strategy, refusing to engage the Spartan-led armies that invaded Attica each year. Pericles knew that the enemy hoplites must soon return to their farms. Instead of being a short, sharp conflict typical of Greek hoplite warfare, the Peloponnesian War dragged on for nearly three decades with great loss of life and squandering of resources. It severely sapped the morale of all of Greece. The war ended only with the defeat of Athens in a naval battle in 404 B.C.E. The Persian Empire had bankrolled construction of ships by the Spartan alliance that were able to take the conflict into Athens's own element, the sea.

The Spartans, who had entered the war championing "the freedom of the Greeks," took over Athens's overseas empire until their own increasingly highhanded behavior aroused the opposition of other city-states. Indeed, the fourth century B.C.E. was a time of continuous skirmishing or warfare among Greek states. It is the tragedy of Greek history that this people, despite all its creativity and brilliance of intellect, failed to solve the problem of how to achieve peace. One can make the case that the independent *polis*, from one point of view the glory of Greek culture, was also the fundamental structural flaw.

Internal conflict in the Greek world had given the Persians their chance to recoup old losses. By the terms of the King's Peace of 387 B.C.E., to which most of the states of war-weary Greece subscribed, all of western Asia, including the Greek communities of the Anatolian seaboard, were conceded to Persia. The Persian king became the guarantor of a status quo that kept the Greeks divided and weak. Why, then, did the Persian kings of the fourth century B.C.E. not undertake another invasion of the Greek mainland? Luckily for the Greeks, rebellions in Egypt,

Cyprus, and Phoenicia as well as trouble with some of the satraps in the western provinces demanded the Persians' attention.

Meanwhile, in northern Greece developments were taking place that would irrevocably alter the balance of power in the eastern Mediterranean and western Asia. Philip II (r. 359–336 B.C.E. was transforming his previously backward kingdom of Macedonia into the premier military power in the Greek world. (Although southern Greeks had long doubted the "Greekness" of the rough and rowdy Macedonians, modern scholarship is inclined to regard their language and culture as Greek at base, though much influenced by contact with non-Greek neighbors.) Philip had made a number of improvements to the traditional hoplite format. He increased the striking power and mobility of his phalanx by equipping his soldiers with longer thrusting spears and less armor and experimenting with the coordinated use of infantry and cavalry (horses thrived in the broad, grassy plains of the north). He and his engineers had also developed new kinds of siege equipment, including the first catapults—machines using the power of twisted cords which, when relaxed, hurled arrows or stones great distances.

In 338 B.C.E. Philip defeated a coalition of southern states and established the Confederacy of Corinth as an instrument for controlling the Greek city-states. Philip was elected military commander for a planned all-Greek campaign against Persia, and his generals established a bridgehead on the Asiatic side of the Hellespont. It appears that Philip was following the advice of the Athenian educator Isocrates, who had pondered the lessons of the Persian Wars of the fifth century B.C.E. and urged a crusade against the national enemy as a means of unifying his quarrelsome countrymen.

We will never know how far Philip's ambitions extended, for an assassin killed him in 336 B.C.E. When Alexander (356–323 B.C.E.), his son and heir, crossed over into Asia in 334, his avowed purpose was to exact revenge for Xerxes' invasion a century and half before. Alexander defeated the Persian forces in three pitched battles—against the satraps of the western provinces at the Granicus River in northwest Anatolia and against King Darius III (r. 336–330

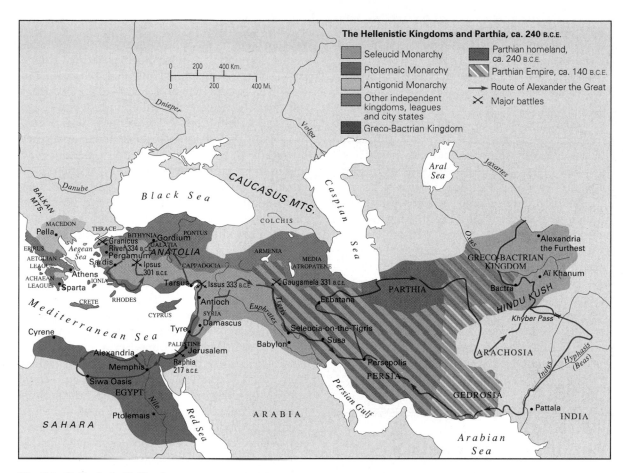

Map 5.3 Hellenistic Civilization   After the death of Alexander the Great in 323 B.C.E., his vast empire soon split apart into a number of large and small political entities. A Macedonian dynasty was established on each continent: the Antigonids ruled the Macedonian homeland and endeavored, with varying success, to extend their control over southern Greece; the Ptolemies ruled Egypt; and the Seleucids inherited the majority of Alexander's conquests in Asia, though they lost control of the eastern portions due to the rise of the Parthians of Iran in the second century B.C.E. This period saw Greeks migrating in large numbers from their overcrowded homeland to serve as a privileged class of soldiers and administrators on the new frontiers, where they replicated the life style of the city-state.

B.C.E.) himself at Issus in southeast Anatolia and at Gaugamela, north of Babylon (see Map 5.3).

From the beginning Alexander the Great, as he came to be called, maintained the framework of Persian administration in the lands he conquered, recognizing that it was well adapted to local circumstances and reassuringly familiar to the subject peoples. But he replaced Persian officials with his own Macedonian and Greek comrades. As a way of controlling strategic points in

his expanding empire, Alexander also established a series of Greek-style cities, beginning with Alexandria in Egypt, and settled wounded and aged ex-soldiers in them. After his victory at Gaugamela (331 B.C.E.), he began to experiment with leaving cooperative Persian officials in place. He also admitted some Persians and other Iranians into the army and the circle of his courtiers, and he adopted elements of Persian dress and court ceremonial. Finally, he married several Iranian women who had useful royal or aristocratic connections, and he pressed his leading subordinates to do the same.

Scholars have reached widely varying conclusions about why Alexander adopted policies that were so unexpected and so fiercely resented by the Macedonian nobility. It is probably wisest to see Alexander as operating from a combination of motives, both pragmatic and idealistic. He set off on his Asian campaign with visions of glory, booty, and revenge. But the farther east he traveled, the more he began to see himself as the legitimate successor of the Persian king (a claim facilitated by the death of Darius III at the hands of subordinates). Alexander may have recognized that he had responsibilities to all the diverse peoples who fell under his control, and he may also have realized the difficulty of holding down so vast an empire by brute force and without the cooperation of important elements among the conquered peoples. In this, too, he was following the example of the Achaemenids.

THE HELLENISTIC SYNTHESIS

At the time of his sudden death in 323 B.C.E. at the age of thirty-two, Alexander apparently had made no plans for the succession. Thus his death ushered in a half-century of chaos, as the most ambitious and ruthless of his officers struggled for control of the vast empire. When the dust cleared, the empire had been broken up into three major kingdoms, each ruled by a Macedonian dynasty—the Seleucid, Ptolemaic, and Antigonid kingdoms (see Map 5.3). Each major kingdom faced a unique set of problems, and although they frequently were at odds with one another, a rough balance of power prevented anyone from gaining the upper hand and enabled smaller states to survive by playing off the great powers.

Historians call this new epoch ushered in by the conquests of Alexander the "Hellenistic Age" (323–30 B.C.E.), reflecting the tendency for the lands in northeastern Africa and western Asia that came under Greek rule to be *Hellenized*—

powerfully influenced by Greek culture. This was an age of large kingdoms with heterogeneous populations, great cities, powerful rulers, pervasive bureaucracies, and vast disparities in wealth between rich and poor—a far cry from the small, homogeneous, independent city-states of Archaic and Classical Greece. It was a cosmopolitan age of long-distance trade and communications, which saw the rise of new institutions like libraries and universities, new kinds of scholarship and science, and the cultivation of sophisticated tastes in art and literature. In many respects, it was a world much more like our own than like the preceding Classical era.

Of all the successor states, the Seleucids, who took over the bulk of Alexander's conquests, faced the greatest challenges. The Indus Valley and Afghanistan soon split off, and over the course of the third century B.C.E. Iran was lost to the Parthians. What remained for the Seleucids was a core in Mesopotamia, Syria, and parts of Anatolia, which the Seleucid monarchs ruled from their capital at Syrian Antioch. Their sprawling territories were open to attack from many directions, and, like the Persians before them, they had to administer lands inhabited by many different ethnic groups organized under various political and social forms. In the countryside, where the bulk of the native population resided, they maintained an administrative structure modeled on the Persian system. The Seleucids also continued Alexander's policy of founding Greek-style cities throughout their domains. These cities served as administrative centers and were also the lure that the Seleucids used to attract colonists from Greece, for many were willing to desert their economically depressed homeland for opportunities on the new frontier—as long as they could maintain a Greek way of life. The Seleucids desperately needed Greek soldiers, engineers, administrators, and other professionals.

The dynasty of the Ptolemies ruled Egypt and sometimes laid claim to adjacent Palestine. It faced a straightforward task. Natural boundaries of sea, mountains, and desert protected the Ptolemies' kingdom. The people of Egypt belonged to only one ethnic group and were fairly easily controlled because the vast majority of them were farmers living in villages alongside the

Nile. The Ptolemies were able to take over much of the administrative structure of the pharaohs, a system that had been perfected over the millennia to efficiently extract the surplus wealth of this populous and productive land. The Egyptian economy was centrally planned and highly controlled. Vast revenues poured into the royal treasury from rents (the king owned most of the land), taxes of all sorts, and royal monopolies on olive oil, salt, papyrus, and other key commodities.

The Ptolemies ruled from Alexandria, the first of the new cities laid out by Alexander himself. The orientation and status of this city says much about Ptolemaic policies and attitudes. The capitals of ancient Egypt, Memphis and Thebes, had been located upriver, reflecting the internal orientation of Egypt under the pharaohs. Alexandria was situated near to where the westernmost branch of the Nile runs into the Mediterranean Sea and clearly was meant to be a link between Egypt and the Mediterranean world. In the language of the Ptolemaic bureaucracy, Alexandria was technically "beside Egypt" rather than in it, as if to emphasize the gulf between rulers and subjects.

The Ptolemies, like the Seleucids, actively encouraged the immigration of Greeks from the homeland and, in return for their skills and collaboration in the military or civil administration, gave them land and a privileged position in the new society. But the Ptolemies did not seek to scatter Greek-style cities throughout the Egyptian countryside, and they made no effort to encourage the adoption of Greek language or ways by the native population. In fact, so separate was the Greek ruling class from the subject population that only the last Ptolemy, Queen Cleopatra (r. 51–30 B.C.E.), even bothered to learn the language of the Egyptians. For the Egyptian peasant population laboring on the land, life was little changed by the advent of new masters. Yet from the early second century B.C.E., periodic native insurrections in the countryside, which government forces in cooperation with Greek and Hellenized settlers quickly stamped out, were signs of Egyptians' growing resentment of the exploitation and arrogance of the Greeks.

Back in Europe the Antigonid dynasty ruled the Macedonian homeland and adjacent parts of northern Greece. This was a compact and ethni-

cally homogeneous kingdom, so there was little of the hostility and occasional resistance that the Seleucid and Ptolemaic ruling classes faced. Macedonian garrisons at strongpoints gave the Antigonids a toehold in central and southern Greece, and the shadow of Macedonian intervention always hung over the south. The southern states met the threat by banding together into

A copy of a Hellenistic sculpture, ca. 300 B.C.E., depicting the head of the god Serapis. The cult of Serapis was created by Ptolemy I, the founder of the Macedonian dynasty in Egypt, to legitimize his rule. Meant to be accessible to both his Greek and Egyptian subjects, it was a syntheses of Greek religious conceptions with the mythology and ritual of the Egyptian god of the dead, Osiris. A great sanctuary was built to the new deity in Alexandria. In the art of the Hellenistic Period, the naturalism of the Classical Period was preserved but the style became more ornate, as seen here in the folds of the robe and the treatment of the hair. (Alinari/Art Resources, NY)

confederations, such as the Achaean League in the Peloponnese, in which the member-states maintained local autonomy but pooled resources and military power.

Athens and Sparta, the two leading cities of the Classical period, stood out from these confederations. The Spartans never quite abandoned the myth of their own invincibility and made a number of heroic but futile stands against Macedonian armies. Athens, which held a special place in the hearts of all Greeks because of the artistic and literary accomplishments of the fifth century B.C.E., pursued a foreign policy of neutrality. The city became a large museum, filled with the relics and memories of a glorious past, as well as a university town that attracted the children of the well-to-do from all over the Mediterranean and western Asia.

In an age of cities, the greatest city of all was Alexandria, with a population of nearly half a million. At the heart of this city was the royal compound. This precinct contained the palace and administrative buildings for the ruling dynasty and its massive bureaucracy. The centerpiece was the magnificent Mausoleum of Alexander. The first Ptolemy had stolen the body of Alexander while it was being brought back to Macedonia for burial. The theft was a move aimed at gaining legitimacy for Ptolemaic rule by claiming the blessing of the great conqueror, who was declared to be a god.

Alexandria gained further luster from its famous Library, which had several hundred thousand volumes, and from its Museum, or "House of the Muses" (the divinities presiding over the arts and sciences), a research institution that supported the work of the greatest poets, philosophers, doctors, and scientists of the day. Two harbors served the needs of the many trading ventures that linked the commerce of the Mediterranean with the Red Sea and Indian Ocean network. A great lighthouse—the first of its kind, a multistory tower with a fiery beacon visible at a distance of 30 miles (48 kilometers)—was one of the wonders of the ancient world.

Greek residents of Alexandria enjoyed citizenship in a Greek-style polis with Assembly, Council, and officials who dealt with purely local affairs, and they took advantage of public works and institutions that signified the Greek way of life. Pub-

lic baths and shaded arcades were places to relax and socialize with friends. Ancient plays were revived in the theaters, and musical performances and demonstrations of oratory took place in the concert halls. The *gymnasium* offered facilities for exercise and fitness and also was the site where young men of the privileged classes were schooled in athletics, music, and literature. Jews had their own civic corporation, officials, and courts and predominated in two of the five main residential districts. Other quarters were filled with the sights, sounds, and smells of ethnic groups from Syria, Anatolia, and the Egyptian countryside.

In all the Hellenistic states, ambitious members of the indigenous populations learned the Greek language and adopted elements of the Greek way of life, because doing so put them in a position to become part of the privileged and wealthy ruling class. For the ancient Greeks, to be Greek was primarily a matter of language and lifestyle rather than physical traits. Now there was a spontaneous synthesis of Greek and indigenous ways. Egyptians migrated to Alexandria, and Greeks and Egyptians intermarried in the villages of the countryside, where their children were likely to grow up speaking and acting more Egyptian than Greek. Greeks living amid the monuments and descendants of the ancient civilizations of Egypt and western Asia were exposed to the mathematical and astronomical wisdom of Mesopotamia, the elaborate mortuary rituals of Egypt, and the many attractions of foreign religious cults. With little official planning or blessing, stemming for the most part from the day-to-day experiences and actions of ordinary people, this age saw a great multicultural experiment as Greek and Middle Eastern cultural traits clashed and merged in numerous ways.

CONCLUSION

P rofound changes took place in the lands of the eastern Mediterranean and western Asia in the first millennium B.C.E., with pivotal roles played by Persians and Greeks. Let us compare the impacts of these two peoples and assess the broad significance of these centuries.

The empire of the Achaemenid Persians was the largest empire yet to appear in the world. It also was a new kind of empire because it encompassed such a wide variety of landscapes, peoples, and social, political, and economic systems. How did the Persians manage to hold together so diverse a collection of lands for more than two centuries?

The answer did not lie entirely in brute force. The Persians lacked the manpower to install garrisons everywhere, and communication between the central administration and provincial officials was sporadic and slow. They managed to co-opt leading elements of the subject peoples, who were willing to collaborate in return for being allowed to retain a dominant position among their own people. The Persian government demonstrated flexibility and tolerance in dealing with the laws, customs, and beliefs of subject peoples, and the Persian administration was superimposed on top of local structures, allowing a considerable role to local institutions.

The Persians also displayed a flair for public relations. The Zoroastrian religion underlined the authority of the king as the appointee of god and upholder of cosmic order. In their art and inscriptions, the Persian kings broadcast an image of a benevolent empire in which the dependent peoples contributed to the welfare of the realm.

Certain peoples with long and proud traditions, such as the Egyptians and Babylonians, revolted from time to time. But most subjects found the Persians to be decent enough masters and a great improvement over earlier Middle Eastern empires such as that of the Assyrians.

Western Asia underwent a number of significant changes in the period of Persian supremacy. First, the early Persian kings put an end to the ancient centers of power in Mesopotamia, Anatolia, and Egypt. Second, by imposing a uniform system of law and administration and by providing security and stability, the Persian government fostered commerce and prosperity, at least for some. Some historians have argued that this period was a turning point in the economic history of western Asia. The Achaemenid government possessed an unprecedented capacity to organize labor on a large scale, for the purposes of constructing an expanded water distribution network and working the extensive estates of the Persian royal family and nobility. The Persian "paradise" was not only the symbol but also the proof of the connection between political authority and the productivity of the earth.

Most difficult to assess is the cultural impact of Persian rule. The long dominant culture of Mesopotamia was fused with some Iranian elements to form a new synthesis, most visible in the art, architecture, and inscriptions of the Persian monarchs. The lands east of the Zagros Mountains as far as northwest India were brought within this cultural sphere. It has been suggested that the Zoroastrian religion spread across the empire and influenced other religious traditions, such as Judaism, but it does not appear that Zoroastrianism had a broad, popular appeal. Because the Persian administration relied heavily on the scribes and written languages of its Mesopotamian, Syrian, and Egyptian subjects, and because literacy remained the preserve of a small, professional class, the Persian language does not seem to have been widely adopted by the inhabitants of the empire. And even if there was a greater degree of Persianization in the provinces than is suggested by the extant evidence, it was so thoroughly swamped by Hellenism in the succeeding era that few traces are left.

Nearly two centuries of trouble with the Greeks on their western frontier were a vexation for the Persians but probably not their first priority. It appears that Persian kings were always more concerned about the security of their eastern and northeastern frontiers, where they were vulnerable to attack by the nomads of Central Asia. The technological differences between Greece and Persia were not great. The only difference that seems to have been of much significance was a set of arms and a military formation used by the Greeks that often allowed them to prevail over the Persians. The Persian king's response in the later fifth and fourth centuries B.C.E. was to hire Greek mercenaries to employ these hoplite tactics for his benefit. The claim is sometimes made that the Persian Empire was weak and crumbling by the time Alexander invaded, but no one could have anticipated the charismatic leadership and boundless ambition of Alexander of Macedonia.

The shadow of Persia loomed large over the affairs of the Greek city-states for more than two centuries, and even after the repulse of Xerxes' great expeditionary force there was a perpetual fear of another Persian invasion. The victories in 480 and 479 B.C.E. did allow the Greek city-states to continue to evolve politically and culturally at a critical time. Athens, in particular, vaulted into power, wealth, and intense cultural creativity as a result of its role in the Greek victory. It evolved into a new kind of Greek state, upsetting the rough equilibrium of the Archaic period by threatening the autonomy of other city-states and changing the rules of war. The result was the Peloponnesian War, which squandered lives and resources for a generation, raised serious doubts about the viability of the city-state, and diminished many people's allegiance to it.

Alexander's conquests brought to the Greek world changes virtually as radical as those suffered by the Persians. Greeks spilled out into the sprawling new frontiers in northeastern Africa and western Asia, and the independent city-state became inconsequential in a world of large kingdoms. The centuries of Greek domination had a far more pervasive cultural impact on the Middle East than did the Persian period. Alexander had been inclined to preserve the Persian administrative apparatus, leaving native institutions and personnel in place. His successors relied almost exclusively on a privileged class of Greek soldiers, officers, and administrators.

Equally significant were the foundation of Greek-style cities, which exerted a powerful cultural influence on important elements of the native populations, and a system of easily learned alphabetic Greek writing accompanied by frequent and diverse uses of the written medium, which led to more widespread literacy and far more effective dissemination of information. The end result of all this was that the Greeks had a profound impact on the peoples and lands of the Middle East, and Hellenism persisted as a cultural force for a thousand years. As we shall see in the next chapter, when the Romans arrived in the eastern Mediterranean in the second century B.C.E., they would be greatly influenced by the cultural and political practices of the Hellenistic kingdoms.

SUGGESTED READING

The most accessible treatment of the Persian Empire is J. M. Cook, *The Persian Empire* (1983). Richard N. Frye, *The History of Ancient Iran* (1984), and volume 2 of *The Cambridge History of Iran*, ed. Ilya Gershevitch (1985), are written by Iranian specialists and have abundant bibliography. John Curtis, *Ancient Persia* (1989), emphasizes the archaeological record. Roland G. Kent, *Old Persian: Grammar, Texts, Lexicon*, 2d ed. (1953), contains translations of the royal inscriptions.

William W. Malandra, *An Introduction to Ancient Iranian Religion: Readings from the Avesta and Achaemenid Inscriptions* (1983), contains documents in translation pertaining to religious subjects. Vesta Sarkhosh Curtis, *Persian Myths* (1993), is a concise, illustrated introduction to Iranian myths and legends.

The fullest treatment of Greek history and civilization in this period is in *The Cambridge Ancient History*, 3d ed., vol. 3–7 (1970–). Among the many standard one-volume histories of Greece are J. B. Bury and Russell Meiggs, *A History of Greece* (1975), and Nancy Demand, *A History of Ancient Greece* (1996). For the Archaic period see Oswyn Murray, *Early Greece*, 2d ed. (1993).

Social history is emphasized by Frank J. Frost, *Greek Society*, 3d ed. (1987). Peter Levi, *Atlas of the Greek World* (1980), is filled with maps and pictures. Michael Grant and Rachel Kitzinger, ed., *Civilization of the Ancient Mediterranean* (1987), is a three-volume collection of essays by contemporary experts on virtually every aspect of ancient Greco-Roman civilization and includes up-to-date bibliographies.

We are fortunate to have an abundant written literature from ancient Greece, and the testimony of the ancients themselves should be the starting point for any inquiry. Herodotus, Thucydides, and Xenophon chronicled the history of the Greeks and their Middle Eastern neighbors from the sixth through fourth centuries B.C.E. Arrian, who lived in the second century C.E., provides the most useful account of the career of Alexander the Great. Among the many collections of documents in translation, see Michael Crawford and David Whitehead, eds., *Archaic and Classical Greece: A Selection of Ancient Sources in Translation* (1983). David G. Rice and John E. Stambaugh, eds., *Sources for the Study of Greek Religion* (1979); Mary R. Lefkowitz and Maureen B. Fant, eds., *Women's Life in Greece and Rome: A Source Book in Translation* (1982); and Thomas

Wiedemann, ed., *Greek and Roman Slavery* (1981), are specialized collections.

Some of the most valuable treatments of particular topics include Elaine Fantham, Helene Peet Foley, Natalie Boymel Kampen, Sarah B. Pomeroy, and H. Alan Shapiro, *Women in the Classical World;* Yvon Garlan, *Slavery in Ancient Greece* (1988); Walter Burkert, *Greek Religion* (1985); Victor Davis Hanson, *The Western Way of War: Infantry Battle in Classical Greece* (1989); Lionel Casson, *The Ancient Mariners: Seafarers and Sea Fighters of the Mediterranean in Ancient Times,* 2d ed. (1991); Joint Association of Classical Teachers, *The World of Athens: An Introduction to Classical Athenian Culture* (1984); N. G. L. Hammond, *The Macedonian State: The Origins, Institutions and History* (1989); Joseph Roisman, ed., *Alexander the Great: Ancient and Modern Perspectives* (1995); and William R. Biers, *The Archaeology of Greece: an Introduction* (1990). Jack Martin Balcer, *Sparda by the Bitter Sea: Imperial Interaction in Western Anatolia* (1984), is a study of the interaction of Greeks and Persians.

For the Hellenistic world see F. W. Walbank, *The Hellenistic World,* rev. ed. (1993) and Michael Grant, *From Alexander to Cleopatra: The Hellenistic World* (1982). M. M. Austin, ed., *The Hellenistic World from Alexander* to the Roman Conquest: A Selection of Ancient Sources in Translation* (1981) provides sources in translation.

NOTES

1. Quoted in Roland G. Kent, *Old Persian: Grammar, Texts, Lexicon,* 2d ed. (New Haven, CT: American Oriental Society, 1953), 138, 140.

2. Richmond Lattimore, *Greek Lyrics,* 2d ed. (Chicago, University of Chicago Press, 1960), 2.

3. Guy Davenport, *Sappho: Poems and Fragments* (Ann Arbor, University of Michigan Press, 1965), fragment 40.

4. G. S. Kirk and J. E. Raven, *The Presocratic Philosophers: A Critical History with a Selection of Texts* (Cambridge, Cambridge University Press, 1957), 169.

5. Herodotus, *The History,* trans. David Grene (Chicago: University of Chicago Press, 1988), 33. (Herodotus 1.1)

6. Plutarch, *Pericles* 12, translated by Ian Scott-Kilvert, *The Rise and Fall of Athens: Nine Greek Lives by Plutarch* (Harmondsworth, Penguin Books, 1960, 178.

CHAPTER SIX

An Age of Empires: Rome and Han China, 753 B.C.E.–330 C.E.

Imperial Parallels

Rome's Creation of a Mediterranean Empire, 753 B.C.E.–330 C.E.

The Origins of Imperial China, 221 B.C.E.–220 C.E.

A ccording to Chinese sources, in the year 166 C.E. a group of travelers identifying themselves as delegates from An-tun, the king of distant Da Qin, arrived at the court of the Chinese emperor Huan, who belonged to the Han dynasty. An-tun was Marcus Aurelius Antoninus, the emperor of Rome.

As far as we know, these men were the first "Romans" to reach China, although they probably were not natives of the Italian peninsula but residents of one of the eastern provinces, perhaps Egypt or Syria. They may have stretched the truth in claiming to be official representatives of the Roman emperor. More likely they were merchants hoping to set up a profitable trading arrangement at the source of the silk so highly prized in the West. Chinese officials, however, were in no position to disprove their claim, since there was no direct contact between the Roman and Chinese empires.

We do not know what became of these travelers, and their mission apparently did not lead to any more direct or regular contact between the emperors at opposite ends of the vast Eurasian landmass. Even so, the episode raises some interesting points. First, it is clear that in the early centuries C.E. Rome and China were linked by far-flung international trading networks encompassing the entire Eastern Hemisphere, and that they were dimly aware of each other's existence. Second, the period of the last centuries B.C.E. and the first centuries C.E. saw the emergence of two manifestations of a new kind of empire.

As we noted in Chapter 4, historians apply the term empire to political entities differing greatly in size, wealth, power, institutions, and longevity. The Roman and Han Chinese empires were both quantitatively and qualitatively different from earlier empires. The Roman Empire encompassed all the lands surrounding the Mediterranean Sea as well as substantial portions of continental Europe and the Middle East. The Han Empire stretched from the Pacific Ocean to the oases of Central Asia. They were the largest empires the world had yet seen, extending over a greater diversity of lands and peoples than the Assyrian and Persian Empires in the Middle East and the Mauryan Empire in India. Yet they were able to centralize control to a greater degree than the earlier empires, their cultural impact on the lands and peoples they dominated was more pervasive, and they were remarkably stable and lasted for many centuries.

Thousands of miles separated the empires of Rome and Han China; neither one influenced the other. Why, then, did two such unprecedented political entities flourish at the same time? Historians have put forth theories stressing supposedly common factors operating in both places— such as climatic change or the pressure of nomadic peoples from Central Asia on the Roman and Chinese frontiers—but none of them has won the support of most scholars. In this chapter, we examine why the Roman and Han Empires came into being, the sources of their stability or instability, and the benefits and liabilities that these empires brought to the dominant and the dominated parties.

We explore striking parallels between the Roman and Chinese Empires. These parallels suggest that rulers facing similar problems— problems that, perhaps, are bound to afflict empires of this magnitude—devise similar solutions. At the same time, we need to account for the equally important differences between the empires of East and West, to understand the unique cultural traditions that have evolved in these two parts of the world.

IMPERIAL PARALLELS

The similarities between ancient Rome and China begin at the level of the family. In both cultures the family comprised the living generations and was headed by an all-powerful patriarch. It was a tightly knit unit to which individual members were bound by strong loyalties and obligations. The family inculcated values—obedience, respect for superiors, piety, and a strong sense of duty and honor—that individuals carried with them into the wider social and political world, creating a pervasive social cohesion.

For each civilization, agriculture was the fundamental economic activity and source of wealth. The revenues of both imperial governments derived primarily from a percentage of the annual agricultural yield. Each empire depended on a free peasantry—sturdy farmers who could be pressed into military service or other forms of compulsory labor. Conflicts over who owned the land and how the land was to be used were at the heart of the political and social evolution that occurred in both places. The autocratic rulers of the Roman and Chinese states secured their positions by breaking the power of the old aristocratic families, seizing the excess land that they had amassed, and giving some land back to small farmers. The later reversal of this process, as wealthy noblemen once again gained control of vast tracts of land and reduced the peasants to dependent tenant farmers, signaled the erosion of the authority of the state.

Both empires spread out from an ethnically homogeneous core to encompass widespread territories having diverse ecosystems, populations, and ways of life. Both brought to those regions a cultural unity that has persisted, at least in part, to the present day. This development involved far more than military conquest and political domination. The skill of Roman and Chinese farmers and the high yields that they produced led to a dynamic expansion of population. As the population of the core areas outstripped the available resources, Italian and Han settlers moved into new regions, bringing their

languages, beliefs, customs, and technologies with them. Many people in the conquered lands were attracted to the culture of the ruler nation and chose to adopt these practices and to attach themselves to a "winning cause."

Both empires found similar solutions to the problems of administering far-flung territories and large populations in an age in which travel and communications were slow. Technologies that facilitated imperial control also fostered cultural unification and improvements in the general standard of living. Roads built to expedite the movement of troops became the highways of commerce and the thoroughfares by which imperial culture spread. A network of cities and towns served as the nerve center of each empire, providing local administrative bases, further promoting commerce, and radiating imperial culture out into the surrounding countryside.

Cities and towns modeled themselves on the capital cities—Rome and Chang'an. Travelers throughout each empire could find in outlying regions the same types and styles of buildings and public spaces, as well as other attractive features of urban life, that they had seen in the capital, though on a smaller scale. The majority of the population still resided in the countryside, but most of the advantages of empire were enjoyed by people living in urban centers.

In an age when a message could not be transmitted faster than a man on horseback or on foot could carry it, the central government had to delegate considerable autonomy to officials at the local level. In both empires a kind of civil service developed. It was staffed by educated and capable members of a prosperous middle class.

The empires of Rome and Han China faced similar problems of defense: long borders located far from the administrative center and aggressive neighbors who coveted the prosperity of the empire. Both empires had to build walls and maintain a chain of forts and garrisons to protect against incursions. The cost of frontier defense was staggering and eventually eroded the economic prosperity of the two empires. Rough neighbors gradually learned the skills that had given the empires an initial advantage and were able to close the "technology gap." Eventually, both empires were so weakened that their borders were overrun and their central governments collapsed. Ironically, the new peoples who migrated in and took over political control had been so deeply influenced by imperial culture that they maintained it to the best of their abilities.

ROME'S CREATION OF A MEDITERRANEAN EMPIRE, 753 B.C.E.–330 C.E.

Rome's central location contributed to its success in unifying first Italy and then all the lands ringing the Mediterranean Sea (see Map 6.1). The second of three peninsulas that jut from the European landmass into the Mediterranean, the boot-shaped Italian peninsula and the large island of Sicily constitute a natural bridge almost linking Europe and North Africa. Italy was a crossroads in the Mediterranean, and the site of Rome was a crossroads within Italy. Rome lay at the midpoint of the peninsula, about 15 miles (24 kilometers) from the western coast, where a north-south road intersected an east-west river route. The Tiber River on one side and a double ring of seven hills on the other afforded natural protection to the site.

The burgeoning Roman state drew on the considerable natural resources of the peninsula. Italy is a land of hills and mountains. The Apennine range runs along its length like a spine, separating the eastern and western coastal plains. The arc of the Alps serves as a shield to the north. Many of the rivers of Italy are navigable, and passes through the central range and even through the snow-capped Alps allowed merchants and armies to travel overland. The mild Mediterranean climate affords a long growing season and conditions suitable for a wide variety of crops. The hillsides, largely denuded of cover today, were well forested in ancient times, providing timber for construction and fuel. The region of Etruria in the northwest was rich in iron and other metals.

Even though as much as 75 percent of the total area of the Italian peninsula is hilly, there is still ample arable land in the coastal plains and river valleys. Much of this land has extremely fertile volcanic soil and sustained a much larger population than was possible in Greece. While expanding within Italy, the Roman state created effective mechanisms for tapping the human resources of the countryside.

According to popular legend, the city of Rome was founded in 753 B.C.E. by Romulus, who, as a baby, had been cast adrift on the Tiber River and nursed by a she-wolf. Archaeological research, however, shows that the earliest occupation of the Palatine Hill—one of the seven hills on the site of Rome—took place as early as 1000 B.C.E. The merging of several hilltop communities to form an urban nucleus, made possible by the draining of a swamp on the site of the future Roman Forum (civic center), took place shortly before 600 B.C.E.

A Republic of Farmers

Agriculture was the essential economic activity and land was the basis of wealth in the early Roman state. As a consequence, social status, political privilege, and fundamental values were related to landownership. The vast majority of early Romans were self-sufficient independent farmers owning small plots of land. A relatively small number of families managed to acquire large tracts of land. The elders of these wealthy families were members of a council—the *senatus*, or Senate—that played a dominant role in the politics of the Roman state. These wealthy families constituted the senatorial class.

According to tradition, between 753 and 507 B.C.E. there were seven kings of Rome. The first was Romulus; the last was the tyrannical Tarquinius Superbus. In 507 B.C.E. members of the senatorial class, led by Brutus "the Liberator," deposed Tarquinius Superbus and instituted a *res publica*, a "public possession" or republic.

The Roman Republic, which lasted from 507 to 31 B.C.E., was hardly a democracy. In principle sovereign power resided in several assemblies that male citizens were eligible to attend, but the

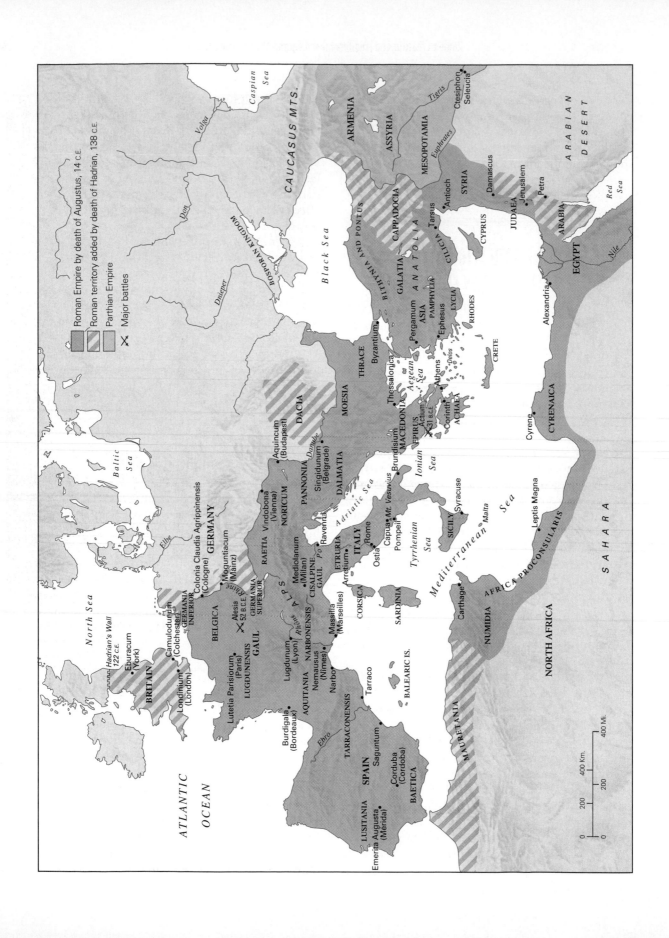

Roman Empire by death of Augustus, 14 C.E.

Roman territory added by death of Hadrian, 138 C.E.

Parthian Empire

X Major battles

ATLANTIC OCEAN

North Sea

Baltic Sea

Caspian Sea

Black Sea

Mediterranean Sea

Adriatic Sea

Ionian Sea

Tyrrhenian Sea

Aegean Sea

Red Sea

CAUCASUS MTS.

SAHARA

ARABIAN DESERT

Volga

Don

Dnieper

Elbe

Rhine

Rhône

Danube

Po

Ebro

Tigris

Euphrates

Nile

BOSPORAN KINGDOM

BRITAIN

Hadrian's Wall
122 C.E.

Eburacum
(York)

Camulodunum
(Colchester)

Londinium
(London)

GERMANIA INFERIOR

Colonia Claudia Agrippinensis
(Cologne)

GERMANY

Moguntiacum
(Mainz)

GERMANIA SUPERIOR

BELGICA

Alesia
52 B.C.E.

GAUL

Lutetia Parisiorum
(Paris)

LUGDUNENSIS

Lugdunum
(Lyon)

AQUITANIA

Burdigala
(Bordeaux)

NARBONENSIS

Nemausus
(Nîmes)

Narbo

Massilia
(Marseilles)

RAETIA

Vindobona
(Vienna)

NORICUM

ALPS

Mediolanum
(Milan)

CISALPINE GAUL

Ravenna

ETRURIA

Arretium

ITALY

Rome

Ostia

Capua

Pompeii

Mt. Vesuvius

Brundisium

PANNONIA

Aquincum
(Budapest)

DACIA

Singidunum
(Belgrade)

DALMATIA

MOESIA

THRACE

Byzantium

BITHYNIA AND PONTUS

GALATIA

CAPPADOCIA

ARMENIA

ASSYRIA

MESOPOTAMIA

Ctesiphon

Seleucia

ANATOLIA

Pergamum

ASIA

Ephesus

LYCIA

PAMPHYLIA

CILICIA

Tarsus

SYRIA

Antioch

Damascus

JUDAEA

Jerusalem

Petra

ARABIA

EGYPT

Alexandria

CYPRUS

RHODES

CRETE

Delos

Athens

ACHAEA

Corinth

Actium
31 B.C.E.

EPIRUS

MACEDONIA

Thessalonica

Cyrene

CYRENAICA

Leptis Magna

AFRICA PROCONSULARIS

Carthage

NUMIDIA

NORTH AFRICA

MAURETANIA

Malta

SICILY

Syracuse

SARDINIA

CORSICA

BALEARIC IS.

SPAIN

Saguntum

Tarraco

TARRACONENSIS

Corduba
(Cordoba)

BAETICA

LUSITANIA

Emerita Augusta
(Mérida)

0   200   400 Mi.

0   200   400 Km.

system of voting was rigged so that the votes of the wealthiest classes counted for more than the votes of poorer citizens. A slate of civic officials was elected each year, and a hierarchy of state offices evolved. The culmination of a political career was to be selected as a *consul,* or chief magistrate. Each year two men were tapped to serve as consuls. When at home, the consuls presided over meetings of the Senate and assemblies. Often they were away from the city, commanding the army on military campaigns.

The real center of power was the Senate, the one permanent body in the Roman state (members sat for life). Technically an advisory council, first to the kings and later to the annually changing Republican officials, the Senate increasingly made policy and governed. The Senate nominated the sons of senators for lower-level public offices and filled vacancies in the Senate from the ranks of former officials. This self-selected body was the repository of wealth, influence, and political and military experience in the state and had both the competence and the will to rule.

The basic unit of Roman society was the family, consisting of several generations as well as the family slaves. Every member of the family was under the absolute authority of the oldest living male, the *paterfamilias.* The head of the family and the most important members of society as a whole—all men—were invested with *auctoritas,* the quality that enabled a man to inspire and demand obedience from his inferiors.

Roman society was unashamedly hierarchical. When a Roman man went for a walk, virtually everyone he met was of inferior or superior social status and expected to be treated accordingly. In this stratified society individuals and families were connected by complex ties of obligation. A fundamental social relationship existed

Map 6.1 The Roman Empire   The Roman Empire came to encompass all the lands surrounding the Mediterranean Sea, as well as parts of continental Europe. When Augustus died in 14 C.E., he left behind instructions to his successors not to expand beyond the limits he had set, but Claudius invaded southern Britain in the mid-first century and the soldier-emperor Trajan added Romania early in the second century. Deserts and seas provided solid natural boundaries, but the long and vulnerable river border in Central and Eastern Europe would eventually prove expensive to defend and vulnerable to invasion by Germanic and Central Asian peoples.

Statue of a Roman carrying busts of his ancestors, first century B.C.E.   Roman society was extremely conscious of status, and an elite Roman family's status was determined, in large part, by the public achievements of ancestors and living members. A visitor to a Roman home would find portraits of distinguished ancestors in the entry hall, along with labels listing the offices they held, and portrait heads were carried in funeral processions. (Alinari/Art Resource, NY)

between a *patron,* a man of wealth and influence, and a *client,* a man who sought a patron's help and protection.

At Rome a senator might be the patron of dozens or even hundreds of men. He could provide his clients with legal advice and representation, physical protection, and loans of money in tough times. In turn, the client was expected to follow his patron out to battle, to support him in the political arena, to work on his land, and even to contribute toward the dowry of his daughter. A throng of clients awaited their patron in the morning and accompanied him from his house to the Forum for the day's business. A man with an especially large retinue enjoyed great prestige. Middle-class clients of the aristocracy might be patrons of poorer men. In sum, at Rome inequality was accepted, institutionalized, and turned into a system of mutual benefits and obligations.

Our sources do not often permit us to observe the activities of Roman women, largely because they played no public role. Virtually all our information about Roman women pertains to those in the upper classes. In a legal sense, a woman never ceased to be a child. She started out under the absolute authority of her paterfamilias. When she married, she came under the jurisdiction of the paterfamilias of her husband's family. Unable to own property or represent herself in legal proceedings, she had to depend on a male guardian to advocate her interests.

However, despite all the limitations put on them, Roman women seem to have been less constrained than their counterparts in the Greek world (see Chapter 5). New forms of marriage allowed them greater personal protection and economic independence. There are many stories of strong women who had great influence on their husbands or sons and thereby helped to shape Roman history. Roman poets confess their love for women who appear to be educated and outspoken, and the accounts of the careers of the early emperors are filled with tales of self-assured and assertive queen mothers and consorts.

How did the early Romans view the natural world and their place in it? Like other Italian peoples, they believed the world was filled with *numina*—invisible, shapeless forces. Vesta, the living, pulsating energy of fire, was in the hearth. Janus guarded the door. The Penates watched over food stored in the cupboard. Other deities resided in nearby hills, caves, grottoes, and springs. Small offerings of cakes and liquids were made to win the favor of these spirits. Certain gods had a larger sphere of operations—for example, Jupiter, the god of the sky, and Mars, initially a god of agriculture as well as war.

The Romans were especially concerned to maintain the *pax deorum* (peace of the gods), a covenant between the gods and the Roman state. Boards of priests drawn from the aristocracy performed sacrifices and other rituals to win the gods' favor. In return, the gods were expected to bring success to the undertakings of the Roman state. When the Romans came into contact with the Greeks of southern Italy (see Chapter 5), they equated their major deities with gods from the Greek pantheon, such as Zeus (Jupiter) and Ares (Mars), and took over the myths attached to the Greek gods.

Expansion in Italy and the Mediterranean

At the dawn of the Roman Republic, around 500 B.C.E., Rome was a relatively insignificant city-state among many in the region of central Italy called Latium. Three-and-a-half centuries later Rome was the center of a huge empire encompassing virtually all the lands surrounding the Mediterranean Sea. Expansion began slowly but picked up momentum, reaching a peak in the third and second centuries B.C.E.

Scholars have long debated the forces that propelled this expansion. Some credit the greed and aggressiveness of a people fond of war. Others observe that the very structure of the Roman state encouraged recourse to war, because consuls had only one year in office in which to gain glory through a military command. The Romans themselves, as part of the elaborate ceremonial accompanying their declarations of war, invariably claimed that they were only defending themselves. A strong case can be made that fear drove the Romans to expand the territory under their control in order to provide a buffer against attack: each new conquest became vulnerable, and a sense of insecurity led to further expansion. In any event, the Romans were quick to seize opportunities as they presented themselves.

Rome's conquest of Italy was sparked by ongoing friction between the hill tribes of central Italy—pastoral groups whose livelihood depended on driving their herds to seasonal grazing grounds—and the agriculturalists of the coastal plains. In the fifth century B.C.E. Rome rose to a position of leadership within a league of central Italian cities organized for defense against the nearby hill tribes. In the fourth century B.C.E. the Romans were called in to defend the wealthy and sophisticated cities of Campania, the region on the Bay of Naples possessing the richest farmland in the peninsula. By 290 B.C.E., in the course of three wars with the tribes of Samnium, in central Italy, the Romans had extended their "protection" over nearly the entire peninsula.

One key to the Romans' success in consolidating their hold over Italy was their willingness to extend Roman citizenship—with its attendant political, legal, and economic privileges—to conquered populations. In this they contrasted sharply with the Greeks, who were reluctant to share the privileges of citizenship with outsiders (see Chapter 5). In essence, the Romans co-opted the most influential elements within the conquered communities and made Rome's interests their interests. Rome demanded of its Italian subjects that they provide soldiers for the Roman military. A seemingly inexhaustible reservoir of manpower was another key to Rome's military success. In a number of crucial wars Rome was able to endure higher casualties than the enemy and to prevail by sheer numbers.

In the mid- and late third century B.C.E. Rome fought two protracted and bloody wars against the Carthaginians, those energetic descendants of Phoenicians from Lebanon who had settled in present-day Tunisia and dominated the waters and commerce of the western Mediterranean (see Chapter 4). In the end, the Roman state emerged as the unchallenged master of the western Mediterranean and acquired its first overseas colonies in Sicily, Sardinia, and Spain. Between 200 and 146 B.C.E. a series of wars pitted the Roman state against the major Greek kingdoms in the eastern Mediterranean. The Romans were at first reluctant to occupy such distant territories and withdrew their troops at the conclusion of several wars. But when the settlements that they imposed failed to hold up, a frustrated Roman government took over direct administration of these turbulent lands.

Initially the Romans did not find it feasible to extend to the overseas provinces the system of governance and the extension of citizenship rights that they had employed in Italy. Considerable autonomy, including responsibility for local administration and tax collection, was given to indigenous elite groups willing to collaborate with the Roman authorities. In addition, every year a member of the Senate, usually someone who recently had held a high public post, was dispatched to each province to serve as governor. The governor took with him a surprisingly small retinue of friends and relations to serve as advisers and deputies. The governor's primary responsibilities were to defend the province against outside attack and internal disruption, to oversee the collection of taxes and other revenues due Rome, and to decide legal cases.

Over time this system of provincial administration proved inadequate. Officials were chosen because of their political connections at Rome, not their competence or experience, and yearly changes of governor meant that the incumbent had little time to gain experience or make local contacts. Although many Roman governors were honest, some were notoriously unscrupulous and put all their ingenuity into discovering new ways to extort money from the provincial populace. While governing an ever-larger Mediterranean empire, the Romans maintained the institutions and attitudes which had developed when Rome was merely a city-state.

The Failure of the Republic

The spectacular achievement of Rome in creating an empire of unprecedented proportions unleashed powerful forces that eventually brought down the Republican system of government. As a result of the frequent wars and territorial expansion of the third and second centuries B.C.E., profound changes were taking place in the Italian landscape. Two factors were driving this complex process: Italian peasant farmers were away from home on military service for long periods of time, and most of the wealth acquired by conquest and control of new provinces ended up in the hands of members of the upper classes.

The upper classes naturally preferred to funnel the profits of empire into the purchase of Italian land. Because the soldier-farmers were away for long periods of time, it was relatively easy for investors to get possession of their farms by purchase, deception, or intimidation. As a result, the small, self-sufficient peasant farms of the Italian countryside, from which had come the soldiers who were the backbone of the Roman legions (units of 6,000 soldiers), were replaced by *latifundia*, literally "broad estates" or ranches.

The owners of these estates found it more lucrative to graze herds of cattle or to grow crops, such as grapes for wine, that brought in a big profit than to grow wheat, the staple food of ancient Italy. Thus large segments of the population of Italy, especially in the burgeoning cities, became dependent on expensive imported grain. Meanwhile, displaced peasants, who had lost their farms and could not find work in the countryside because of the cheapness of slave labor, moved to cities such as Rome (see Voices and Visions: Slavery in Rome and China). But there was no work for them in the cities, and they found themselves living in dire poverty. The growing urban masses, idle and prone to riot, would play a major role in the political struggles of the late Republic.

A critical factor contributing to the Senate's loss of authority was a change in the composition of the Roman army. One consequence of the decline of peasant farmers in Italy was a shortage of men who owned the minimum amount of property required for eligibility to serve in the legions. This shortage was felt acutely during a war that the Romans fought in North Africa at the end of the second century B.C.E.

Gaius Marius, a "new man" not from the traditional ruling class, reached a position of unprecedented political prominence by accepting into the legions poor, propertyless men and promising to give them farms when they retired from military service. These troops became devoted to the man who guaranteed their future. In the decades that followed, a series of ambitious

individuals—Sulla, Pompey, Julius Caesar, and Mark Antony—commanded armies whose primary loyalties were to their generals rather than to the state. These men did not hesitate to use the Roman legions to increase their personal power and influence. A number of bloody civil wars pitted Roman army against Roman army. The city of Rome itself was taken by force on several occasions, and victorious commanders executed their political opponents and exercised dictatorial control of the state.

Julius Caesar's grandnephew and heir, Octavian (63 B.C.E.–14 C.E.), eliminated all rivals by 31 B.C.E. and painstakingly set about refashioning the Roman system of government. He fundamentally altered the realities of power but was careful to maintain the forms of the Republic—the offices, the honors, and the social prerogatives of the senatorial class. A military dictator in fact, he never called himself king or emperor, claiming merely to be *princeps*, "first among equals" in a restored Republic. For this reason it is conventional to refer to the period following the Republic as the Principate.

Augustus, one of the many honorific titles that the Roman Senate gave Octavian, combines connotations of reverence, prosperity, and piety and became the name by which he is best known to posterity. Augustus succeeded thanks to a combination of ruthlessness, patience, and his intuitive grasp of the psychology of all elements of Roman society, which enabled him to manipulate each group in turn. He also had the good sense to live a long time. When he died in 14 C.E., after forty-five years of carefully veiled rule, almost no one was still alive who could remember the Republic. During his reign Egypt, parts of the Middle East, and Central Europe were added to the empire (the only significant later additions were the southern half of Britain and modern Romania).

So popular was Augustus when he died that four members of his family succeeded to the position of "emperor" (as we may call it) despite their serious personal and political shortcomings. The emperorship was never automatically regarded as a hereditary privilege, and after the mid-first century C.E. other families obtained the post. In theory, the early emperors were affirmed by the Senate. In reality they were chosen by the

Slavery in Rome and China

Although slaves were to be found in most ancient societies, Rome, was one of the few historical societies in which slave labor became the indispensable foundation of the economy. In the course of the frequent wars of the second century B.C.E., *large numbers of prisoners were carried into slavery. Landowners and manufacturers found they could compel slaves to work longer and harder. Periodically, the harsh working and living conditions resulted in slave revolts.*

The following excerpt comes from one of several surviving manuals on agriculture which give ample advice on the subject of controlling and efficiently exploiting slaves:

When the head of a household arrives at his estate, after he has prayed to the family god, he must go round his farm on a tour of inspection on the very same day, if that is possible. . . . On the next day after that he must call in his manager. . . . If the work doesn't seem to him to be sufficient, and the manager starts to say how hard he tried, but the slaves weren't any good, and the weather was awful, and the slaves ran away, and he was required to carry out some public works, then when he has finished mentioning these and all sorts of other excuses, you must draw his attention to your calculation of the labor employed and time taken. . . . There are all sorts of jobs that can be done in rainy weather—washing wine-jars, coating them with pitch, cleaning the house, storing grain, shifting muck, digging a manure pit, cleaning seed, mending ropes or making new ones. . . . The head of the household . . . should sell any old oxen, cattle or sheep that are not up to standard, wool and hides, an old cart or old tools, an old slave, a sick slave—anything else that is surplus to requirements. (Cato the Elder, *Agriculture* 2—second century B.C.E.)

What is the attitude of this Roman writer toward slaves, and how does he treat slaves? What forms of resistance do slaves put up? What precautions and punitive measures do slaveowners take to minimize the resistance and maximize the productivity of their slaves? What incentives exist for slaves to be productive?

Slavery was far less prominent in ancient China. During the Warring States Period, the large holdings of the landowning aristocracy were worked by slaves as well as by dependent peasants. The Qin government sought to abolish slavery, but the institution persisted into the Han period, although it involved only a small fraction of the population. The relatives of criminals could be seized and enslaved, and
poor families sometimes sold unwanted children into slavery. In China, whether they belonged to the state or to individuals, slaves generally performed domestic tasks.

Wang Ziyuan of Shu Commandery went to the Jian River on business, and went up to the home of the widow Yang Hui, who had a male slave named Bianliao. Wang Ziyuan requested him to go and buy some wine. Picking up a big stick, Bianliao climbed to the top of the grave mound and said: "When my master bought me, Bianliao, he only contracted for me to care for the grave and did not contract for me to buy wine for some other gentleman."

Wang Ziyuan was furious and said to the widow: "Wouldn't you prefer to sell this slave?". . . Wang Ziyuan immediately settled on the sale contract. . . .

The slave again said: "Enter in the contract everything you wish to order me to do. I, Bianliao, will not do anything not in the contract."

Wang Ziyuan said: "Agreed."

The text of the contract said: . . . The slave shall obey orders about all kinds of work and may not argue. He shall rise at dawn and do an early sweeping. After eating he shall wash up. Ordinarily he should pound the grain mortar, tie up broom straws, carve bowls and bore wells, scoop out ditches, tie up fallen fences, hoe the garden, trim up paths and dike up plats of land, cut big flails, bend bamboos to make rakes, and scrape and fix the well pulley . . . [the list of tasks continues for two-and-a-half pages]. . . .

The reading of the text of the contract came to an end. The slave was speechless and his lips were tied. Wildly he beat his head on the ground, and beat himself with his hands. He said: "If it is to be exactly as master Wang says, I would rather return soon along the yellow-soil road, with the grave worms boring through my head. Had I known before I would have bought the wine for master Wang." (Wang Bao—first century B.C.E.)

How does the situation of slaves in China seem to be somewhat different from that of Roman slaves? In what ways do the tasks of slaves and the relations between master and slave in China seem similar to those in Rome?

Sources: Thomas Wiedemann, *Greek and Roman Slavery* (1981), pp. 139–141, 183–184; C. Martin Wilbur, *Slavery in China During the Former Han Dynasty, 206* B.C.–A.D. *25* (1943), pp. 383, 388.

armies. By the second century C.E. a new mechanism of succession had been worked out by the so-called Good Emperors of that era: each designated as his successor a mature man of proven ability whom he adopted as his son and with whom he shared offices and privileges.

Augustus had allied himself with the *equites*, the class of well-to-do Italian merchants and landowners second in wealth and social status only to the senatorial class. This body of competent and self-assured individuals became the core of a new civil service that helped to run the Roman Empire. At last Rome had an administrative bureaucracy up to the task of managing a large empire with considerable honesty, consistency, and efficiency.

An Urban Empire

The Roman Empire of the first three centuries C.E. was an *urban empire*. This term does *not* mean that most people were living in cities and towns. Perhaps 80 percent of the 50 million or 60 million people living within the borders of the empire were engaged in agriculture and lived in villages or on isolated farms in the countryside. The empire, however, was administered through a network of towns and cities and brought the greatest benefits to the urban populace, and for that reason we characterize it as "urban."

The number of people living in urban centers varied widely. Numerous small towns had perhaps several thousand inhabitants. A handful of major cities—Alexandria in Egypt, Antioch in Syria, and Carthage—had populations of several hundred thousand. Rome itself had approximately a million residents. The largest cities put a huge strain on the limited technological capabilities of the ancients. Providing adequate supplies of food and water and removing sewage were always problems.

At Rome the upper classes lived in elegant townhouses on one or another of the seven hills. The house was centered around an *atrium*, a rectangular courtyard. In the ceiling of the atrium an open skylight let in light and rainwater, which fell into a basin for later use. Surrounding the atrium were a large dining room, for the dinner

and drinking parties that were an important part of the social life of the aristocracy, an interior garden, a kitchen, and, perhaps, a private bath. Bedrooms were on the upper level. The floors were decorated with pebble mosaics. The walls and ceilings were covered with frescoes (paintings done directly on wet plaster) representing mythological scenes or outdoor vistas, which gave a sense of openness in the absence of windows. The typical aristocrat also owned a number of villas in the Italian countryside, a retreat from the pressures of city life.

The poor of Rome lived in crowded slums in the low-lying parts of the city. Their wooden tenements were subject to frequent fires and must have been damp, dark, and smelly, with few furnishings. Fortunately, for much of the year they could spend the day outdoors.

The cities, towns, and even the ramshackle settlements that sprang up on the edge of frontier forts were miniature replicas of the capital city in political organization, physical layout, and appearance. A town council and two annually elected officials drawn from men of property were responsible for maintaining law and order and for collecting from both the urban center and the agricultural hinterland assigned to it the taxes due the state. In return for the privilege of running local affairs with considerable autonomy and in appreciation for how the Roman state protected their wealth and position, this municipal aristocracy loyally served the interests of Rome. In their drive to imitate the manners and values of Roman senators, they made lavish gifts to their communities. They endowed cities and towns, which had very little revenue of their own, with attractive elements of Roman urban life—a *forum* (an open plaza that served as a civic center), public office buildings, temples, gardens, baths, theaters, amphitheaters, and games and public entertainments of all sorts. Because of these amenities, the situation of the urban poor was superior to that of the rural poor. Poor people living in a city could pass time at the baths, seek refuge from the elements amid the colonnades, and attend the games.

Life in the countryside was much as it always had been. Hard work and drudgery were relieved by an occasional holiday or village festival and by the everyday pleasures of sex, family, and social exchange. Most of the time the rural population had to fend for itself in dealing with bandits, wild animals, and other hazards of country life. People living away from urban centers had little direct contact with the Roman government other than an occasional run-in with bullying soldiers and the dreaded arrival of the tax collector.

The process by which ownership of the land tended to become concentrated in ever fewer hands had been temporarily reversed during the civil wars that brought an end to the Roman Republic. In the era of the emperors it resumed. However, after the era of conquest ended in the early second century C.E., slaves were no longer plentiful or inexpensive, and landowners had to find a new source of labor. Over time the numbers of the independent farmers decreased, and they were replaced by *coloni*—tenant farmers— who had to give a portion of their crop to the landlord. In the early centuries C.E. the landowners still lived in the cities, operating their estates by means of foremen. Thus wealth was concen-

trated in the cities but was based on the productivity of rural agricultural laborers.

Another source of prosperity for some urban dwellers, was manufacture and trade. Commerce was greatly enhanced by the *pax romana* (Roman peace), the safety and stability guaranteed by Roman might. Grain, meat, vegetables, and other bulk foodstuffs usually could be exchanged only locally, because transporting them very far was not economical and many products spoiled quickly without refrigeration. The city of Rome depended on the import of massive quantities of grain from Sicily and Egypt to feed its huge population, and special naval squadrons were assigned this vital task.

Fine manufactured products, such as glass, metalwork and delicate pottery, were exported throughout the empire. Over time there was a tendency for the centers of production, which once had been located in Italy, to move outward into the provinces as knowledge of the necessary skills spread. The armies stationed on the frontiers were a large market of consumers, and their

Sign for a Roman shop   A woman behind the counter is selling fruit to one customer, while two other men are taking game hanging from a rack. The snail and two monkeys to the right of the shopkeeper may represent the name of the establishment. Towns served as markets where farmers brought their surplus products and exchanged them for crafted goods made by urban artisans. Local commerce in agricultural products must have been a major component of the economy of the Roman Empire but is hard to trace in the archaeological record. (Archivo Fotografico della Soprintendenza Archeologica di Ostia)

presence promoted the prosperity of border provinces. There also was a trade in luxury items coming from far beyond the boundaries of empire, especially silk from China and spices from India and Arabia.

Trade was of vital importance to the imperial system. Looking at the Roman Empire as a whole, we can see that the surplus revenues of rich interior provinces like Gaul (France) and Egypt were transferred in two directions: to Rome to support the emperor and the central government and to the frontier provinces to subsidize the armies. Two mechanisms made possible this transfer of wealth: the taxes demanded by the central government and the networks of trade that enabled armies on distant frontiers to buy much of what they needed on the spot.

One of the most enduring consequences of this empire, which encompassed such a wide diversity of ethnic and linguistic groups and forms of political and social organization, was *romanization*, the spread of the Latin language and the Roman way of life. This phenomenon was confined primarily to the western half of the empire, because the eastern Mediterranean already had Greek as a common idiom, a legacy of the Hellenistic kingdoms (see Chapter 5). Portuguese, Spanish, French, Italian, and Romanian all evolved from the Latin language, proving that the language of the conquerors eventually was taken over not just by elite groups in the provinces but also by the common people.

There is little evidence that the Roman government pursued a policy of forcibly Romanizing the provinces. The switch to Latin and adoption of the cultural habits that went with it were choices that the inhabitants of the provinces made for themselves. However, those who made this choice were responding to the very significant advantages available to individuals who spoke Latin and wore a toga (the traditional cloak of Roman citizens), just as today in developing nations there often are advantages to moving to the city, learning English, and putting on a suit and tie. The use of Latin facilitated dealings with the Roman administration, and a merchant who spoke Latin could get contracts to supply the military and be understood anywhere he went in the empire. Beyond these practical incen-

tives, many must have been drawn to the aura of success attached to the language and culture of a people who had conquered so vast an empire. The art, literature, and sophisticated lifestyle of the Romans had their own attractions.

As towns sprang up and acquired the characteristic features of Roman urban life, they served as magnets for ambitious members of the indigenous population. The Romans at first had been reluctant to grant Roman citizenship, with its attendant privileges, legal protections, and exemptions from certain types of taxation, to people living outside Italy. Nevertheless, a gradual extension of citizenship to individuals and communities did take place. Men who completed a twenty-six-year term of service in the native military units that backed up the Roman legions were granted citizenship and passed this coveted status on to their posterity. Emperors made grants of citizenship to individuals or entire communities as rewards for good service.

The culmination of this process occurred in 212 C.E., when the emperor Caracalla granted citizenship to all free, adult, male inhabitants of the empire. This gradual diffusion of citizenship epitomizes the process by which the empire was transformed from an Italian dominion over the Mediterranean lands into a commonwealth of peoples. Already in the first century C.E. some of the leading literary and intellectual figures came from the provinces, and by the second century even the emperors hailed from Spain, Gaul, and North Africa.

The Rise of Christianity

During this same period of general peace and prosperity, at the eastern end of the Mediterranean events were taking place that, though little noted at the moment, would prove to be of great historical significance. The Jewish homeland of Judaea (see Chapter 4), roughly equivalent to present-day Israel, was put under direct Roman rule in 6 C.E. Over the next half-century a series of Roman governors insensitive to the Jewish belief in one god managed to increase tensions. Among the Jews various kinds of opposition to Roman rule sprang up. Many waited for the arrival of the Messiah, the "Anointed One," who they thought would be a military leader who would liberate the Jewish people and drive the Romans out of the land.

It is in this context that we must see the career of Jesus, a young carpenter from the Galilee region in northern Israel. Offended by the materialism and lack of spirituality in the mainstream Jewish religion of his time, he prescribed a return to the fundamental spiritual tenets of an earlier age. Jesus eventually attracted the attention of the Jewish authorities in Jerusalem. They turned him over to the Roman governor, Pontius Pilate. Jesus was imprisoned, condemned, and executed by crucifixion, a punishment usually reserved for common criminals. His followers, the Apostles, carried on after his death and sought to spread the word of his mission and his resurrection (return from death to life) among their fellow Jews.

In the 40s C.E. Paul, a Jew from the Greek city of Tarsus in southeast Anatolia, became converted to the new creed and threw his enormous talent and energy into spreading the word. Traveling throughout Syria-Palestine, Anatolia, and Greece, he became increasingly frustrated with the refusal of most Jews to accept the revelation that he taught. Discovering a spiritual hunger among many non-Jews, he redirected his efforts toward this population (sometimes called "gentiles") and set up a string of Christian (from the Greek *Christ*, meaning "anointed one," given to Jesus by his followers) communities in the eastern Mediterranean.

The career of Paul exemplifies the cosmopolitan nature of the Roman Empire in this era. Speaking both Greek and Aramaic, he moved comfortably between the Greco-Roman and Jewish worlds. He used Roman roads, depended on the peace guaranteed by Roman arms, called on his Roman citizenship to protect him from the arbitrary action of local authorities, and moved from city to city in his quest for converts.

In 66 C.E. long-building tensions in Roman Judaea erupted into a full-scale revolt that lasted until 73. One of the casualties of the Roman reconquest of Judaea was the Jerusalem-based Christian community, which saw its primary

Important Events in Roman History

1000 B.C.E.	First settlement on site of Rome
507 B.C.E.	Establishment of Republic
290 B.C.E.	Defeat of Samnites gives Rome control of Italy
201 B.C.E.	Defeat of Hannibal and Carthage guarantees Roman control of western Mediterranean
200–146 B.C.E.	Wars against Hellenistic kingdoms lead to control of eastern Mediterranean
88–31 B.C.E.	Civil Wars and failure of the Republic
31 B.C.E.–14 C.E.	Augustus establishes the Principate
45–58 C.E.	Paul spreads Christianity in the eastern Mediterranean
235–284 C.E.	Third Century Crisis
324 C.E.	Constantine moves capital to Constantinople

mission among the Jews. This left the field clear for Paul's non-Jewish converts, and Christianity began to diverge more and more from its Jewish roots.

For more than two centuries, the sect grew slowly but steadily. Many of the first converts were from disenfranchised groups—women, slaves, the urban poor. They could hope to receive respect and obtain positions of responsibility not accorded to them in the larger society when the members of early Christian communities assembled to democratically elect their leaders. However, as the religious movement grew and prospered, it developed a hierarchy of priests and bishops and became subject to bitter doctrinal disputes (see Chapter 9).

Early Christians were vulnerable to persecution because Roman officials regarded their refusal to worship the emperor (as monotheists they were forbidden to worship other gods) as a sign of disloyalty. Nevertheless, despite occasional attempts at suppression, or perhaps because of them, the young Christian movement continued to gain strength and attract converts.

By the late third century C.E. adherents to Christianity were a sizable minority within the population of the Roman Empire, and membership in the sect had spread up the social ranks to include many educated and prosperous people who held posts in local and imperial government.

Technology and Transformation

We have seen how the early Christians took advantage of the relative ease and safety of travel brought by Roman arms and engineering to spread their faith. Remnants of roads, walls, aqueducts, and buildings still visible today testify to the engineering expertise of the ancient Romans. Some of the best engineers served with the army, building bridges, siege works, and ballistic weapons that hurled stones and shafts. In peacetime the soldiers were often put to work on construction projects. Aqueducts—long, elevated or underground conduits—carried water from its source to urban centers, using only the force of gravity. The Romans were pioneers in the use of the arch, which distributes great weights evenly without thick supporting walls. The invention of concrete—a mixture of lime powder, sand, and water that could be poured into molds set on scaffolding—allowed the Romans to create vast vaulted and domed interior spaces and to move away from the strictly rectilinear forms of the pillar-and-post construction methods employed by the Greeks.

One of the greatest challenges for the Roman administration was the defense of borders that stretched for thousands of miles. Augustus's posthumous recommendation to his successors had been that they not expand the empire further, because any subsequent acquisition would cost more to administer and defend than the revenues it brought in. Thus after Augustus's death the Roman army was reorganized and redeployed to reflect the shift from an offensive to a defensive strategy. The empire was protected at most points by natural features—mountains, deserts, and seas. The long Rhine/Danube river frontier in Germany and Central Europe, however, was a vulnerable point. This lengthy frontier was guarded by a string of forts whose relatively small garrisons were adequate for dealing with raiders. On particularly desolate frontiers, such as in Britain and North Africa, long walls were built to keep out the peoples who lived beyond.

Fortunately for Rome, its neighbors, with one exception, were less technologically advanced and more loosely organized peoples who did not pose a serious threat to the security of the empire as a whole. That one exception was on the eastern frontier, where the Parthian kingdom, heir to earlier Mesopotamian and Persian empires, controlled the lands that are today Iran and Iraq. For centuries Rome and Parthia engaged in a rivalry that, in the end, sapped both sides without leading to any significant territorial gain for either party.

The Roman state prospered for two-and-a-half centuries after Augustus stabilized the internal political situation and addressed the needs of the empire with an ambitious program of reforms. In the third century C.E. cracks in the edifice became visible. Historians use the expression "third-century crisis" to refer to the period from 235 to 284 C.E., in which the Roman Empire was beset and nearly destroyed by political, military, and economic problems.

The most visible symptom of the crisis was the frequent change of rulers. It has been estimated that some twenty or more men claimed the office of emperor during this period. Most of them reigned for a very short time before being overthrown by a rival or killed by their own troops. Germanic tribesmen on the Rhine/Danube frontier took advantage of the frequent civil wars and periods of anarchy to raid deep into the empire. For the first time in centuries, cities began to erect walls to protect themselves. Several regions, feeling that the central government was not adequately protecting them, turned power over to a man on the spot who promised to put their interests first.

These political and military emergencies had a devastating impact on the economy of the empire. The cost of rewarding troops and defending the increasingly permeable frontiers drained the state treasury, and the incessant demands of the central government for more tax revenues, as well as the interruption of commerce by fighting, eroded the prosperity of the towns. Shortsighted emperors, desperate for cash, secretly cut back the amount of precious metal in the coins and pocketed the excess. But the public quickly caught on, and the devalued coinage became less and less acceptable as a medium for exchange. Indeed, the empire reverted to a barter economy, a far less efficient system that further curtailed large-scale and long-distance commerce.

The municipal aristocracy, once the most vital and public-spirited class in the empire, was slowly crushed out of existence. As town councilors its members were personally liable to make up any shortfall in the tax revenues owed to the state. But the decline in trade eroded, as did their wealth, which usually was based on manufacture and commerce. Many began to evade their civic duties and even go into hiding.

There was an overall shift of population away from the cities and into the countryside. Many people sought employment and protection—from raiders and from government officials—on the estates of wealthy and powerful country landowners. In the shrinking of cities and the movement of the population to the country estates, we can see the roots of the social and economic structures of the European Middle

The Roman aqueduct near Tarragona, Spain   Provisions of an adequate water supply was a problem associated with the growth of towns and cities during the Roman Empire. An aqueduct brought water from a source, sometimes many miles away, to an urban complex, using only the force of gravity. Roman engineers skillfully designed structures that maintained a steady downhill slope all the way from source to destination, and Roman troops were often used in such large-scale construction. Scholars can sometimes roughly estimate the population of an ancient city by calculating the amount of water available. (Rapho/Photo Researchers, Inc.)

Ages—a roughly seven-hundred-year period in which wealthy rural lords dominated a peasant population tied to the land (see Chapter 9).

Just when things looked bleakest, a man arose who pulled the empire back from the brink of self-destruction. Like many of the rulers of that age, Diocletian was from one of the eastern European provinces most vulnerable to invasion. A commoner by birth, he had risen through the ranks of the army and gained power in 284. The measure of his success is indicated by the fact that he ruled for more than twenty years and died in bed.

Diocletian implemented a series of radical solutions that saved the Roman state by transforming it. To halt inflation, he issued an edict that specified the maximum prices that could be charged for various commodities and services. To ensure an adequate supply of workers in vital services, many people were frozen into their professions and were required to train their sons to succeed them. This kind of government regulation of prices and vocations was completely new in Roman history and had some unforeseen consequences. One was the creation of a black market among buyers and sellers who chose to ignore the government's price controls and establish their own prices for goods and services. Another was a growing tendency among the inhabitants of the empire to consider the government an oppressive entity that no longer deserved their loyalty.

When Diocletian resigned in 305, the old divisiveness reemerged as various claimants battled for the throne. The eventual winner was Constantine. By 324 he was able to reunite the entire empire under his sole rule.

In 312 Constantine had won a key battle at the Milvian Bridge over the Tiber River near Rome. He later claimed that before this battle he saw in the sky a cross (the sign of the Christian God) superimposed on the sun. Believing that the Christian God had helped him achieve victory, the new emperor converted to Christianity. Throughout his reign he supported the Christian church, although he tolerated other beliefs as well.

Historians disagree about whether Constantine was motivated by purely spiritual motives or whether he was seeking to unify the peoples of the empire under a single religion. In either case his conversion was of tremendous historical significance. Large numbers of people began to convert, because they saw that Christians seeking political office or favors from the government had clear advantages over non-Christians.

The other decisive step taken by Constantine was the transfer of the capital from Rome to Byzantium, an ancient Greek city on the Bosporus strait leading into the Black Sea. The city was renamed Constantinople, "City of Constantine." This move both reflected and accelerated changes already taking place. Constantinople was closer than Rome to the most threatened borders of the empire, in eastern Europe. The urban centers and prosperous middle class of the eastern half of the empire had better withstood the third-century crisis than had those of the western half. In addition, more educated people and more Christians were living in the eastern provinces (see Chapter 9).

The conversion of Constantine and the transfer of the imperial capital away from Rome often have been considered events marking the end of Roman history. This conventional view, however, is open to question for at least two reasons: (1) Many of the important changes that culminated during Constantine's reign had their roots in events of the previous two centuries. (2) The Roman Empire as a whole survived for at least another century, and the eastern, or Byzantine, portion of it (discussed in Chapter 9), survived Constantine by more than a thousand years. It is true that the Roman Empire of the fourth century was fundamentally different from what had existed before, and for that reason it is convenient to see in Constantine's reign the beginning of a new epoch in the West.

THE ORIGINS OF IMPERIAL CHINA, 221 B.C.E.–220 C.E.

The early history of China (described in Chapter 3) was marked by the fragmentation that geography seemed to dictate. The authority of the first dynasties, Shang (ca. 1750–1027 B.C.E.)

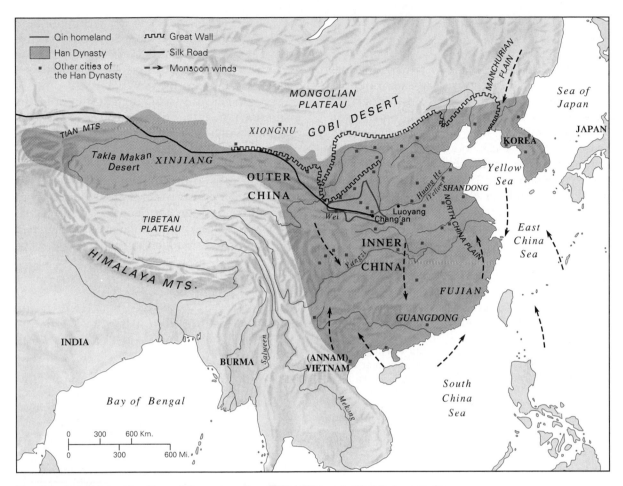

Map 6.2 Han China The Qin and Han rulers of northeast China extended their control over all of Inner China and much of Outer China. A series of walls in the north and northwest, built to check the incursions of nomadic peoples from the steppes, were joined together to form the ancestor of the present-day Great Wall of China. An extensive network of roads connecting towns, cities, and frontier forts, promoted rapid communication and facilitated trade. The Silk Road carried China's most treasured product to Central, Southern, and Western Asia and the Mediterranean lands.

and Zhou (1027–221 B.C.E.), was confined to a relatively compact zone in northeastern China. The last few centuries of nominal Zhou rule—the Warring States Period—was an age of rivalry and belligerence among a group of small states. They differed to some extent in language and culture and in many ways bring to mind the contemporary Greek city-states (see Chapter 5). As in Greece, so also in China: an era of competition and conflict saw the formation of many of the distinctive elements of a national culture.

In the second half of the third century B.C.E. one of the warring states—the Qin state of the Wei Valley—rapidly conquered its rivals and created China's first empire (221–206 B.C.E.). But the Qin Empire, itself built at a great cost in human lives and labor, barely survived the death of its founder, Shi Huangdi. Power soon passed over to a new dynasty, the Han, which ruled over China for the next four centuries (206 B.C.E.–220 C.E.) (see Map 6.2). Thus began the long history of imperial China—a tradition of political and cultural unity and continuity that lasted into the early twentieth century C.E. and still resonates in the very different China of our own time.

Resources and Population

This achievement is especially remarkable for a region that was not only vast in extent but also marked by extreme diversity in its topography, climate, plant and animal life, and human population. An imperial state controlling these lands faced greater obstacles to long-distance communications and to a uniform way of life than did the Roman Empire. The Roman state encompassed lands whose climates and agricultural potentials were similar. The Roman Empire also had the benefit of an internal sea—the Mediterranean—which facilitated relatively rapid and inexpensive travel and transport of commodities. What were the resources, technologies, institutions and values that made possible the creation and maintenance of a Chinese empire?

Agricultural production was the primary source of the wealth and taxes that supported the institutions of state. The main tax, a percentage of the annual yield of the fields, was used to support the government in its many manifestations, from the luxurious life-style enjoyed by members of the royal court to the many levels of officials and the military units stationed throughout the country and on the frontiers. The capital cities, first Chang'an and later Luoyang, had large populations that had to be fed. As intensive

A thick deposit of loess soil in the Shanxi region   For thousands of years winds from Central Asia have deposited layers of fine sand in the plains of the Yellow River and its tributaries in northeast China, and the periodic flooding of the rivers has left behind water-borne silt. The thick mantle of fine, soft soil which accumulated was very fertile and easily worked with digging sticks, while networks of irrigation channels from the rivers provided the necessary moisture. The efficient systems of agriculture developed in this region by the indigenous Han people supported a large population and were later carried by them to other parts of China, along with other elements of Chinese civilization. (Courtesy, Caroline Blunden)

agriculture spread in the Yangzi River Valley, transporting southern crops to the north became important, and the first steps were taken toward construction of canals to connect the two great river systems, the Yangzi and the Yellow. The government also exercised foresight in collecting and storing in prosperous times surplus grain that could be distributed at reasonable prices in times of shortage.

The other fundamental commodity was human labor. The government periodically carried out a census of inhabitants. The results for the years 2 C.E. and 140 C.E. are preserved in extant historical writings. The earlier survey indicates totals of approximately 12 million households and 60 million people; the later, not quite 10 million households and 49 million people. Thus the average household contained 5 persons. Then, as now, the vast majority of the population lived in the eastern portion of the country, the river-valley regions where intensive agriculture could support a dense population. Initially the largest concentration was in the Yellow River Valley and North China Plain, but by the early Han Empire the demographic center had begun to shift to the Yangzi River Valley.

How did the Qin and Han governments take advantage of an expanding population? In the intervals between seasonal agricultural tasks, every able-bodied male was expected to donate one month of labor a year to public works projects—work on the construction of palaces, temples, fortifications, and roads; transporting goods; excavating and maintaining canal channels; labor on imperial estates; or service in the mines. Another obligation was two years of military service. Young Chinese men were marched to the frontiers, where they built walls and forts, kept an eye on barbarian neighbors, fought when necessary, and grew crops to support themselves. Annually updated registers of land and households enabled imperial officials to keep track of money and services due (see Environment and Technology: Writing as an Imperial Technology). We again see strong parallels between the Roman and Chinese governments in their dependence on a large population of free peasants who contributed both taxes and services to the state.

Throughout the Han period there was a persistent, gradual expansion of Han Chinese at the expense of other ethnic groups. The growth of population in the core regions and a shortage of good, arable land spurred pioneers to push into new areas. Sometimes the government organized the opening up of new areas, as when it resettled people in colonies at militarily strategic sites and on the frontiers. Neighboring kingdoms also invited in Chinese settlers in order to exploit their skills and learn their technologies.

The pattern of expansion is significant. Han people tended to move into regions suitable for the kind of agriculture with which they were familiar from living in the eastern river valleys. They took over land on the northern frontier, pushing back nomadic populations. They also expanded into the tropical forests of southern China and settled in the western oases. In places not suitable for their preferred kind of agriculture, particularly the steppe and the desert, Han Chinese were not able to displace other groups.

Hierarchy, Obedience, and Belief

As the Han Chinese expanded into new regions, they brought with them their social organization, values, and other elements of their culture. The basic unit of Chinese society was the family. The Chinese family included not only the living generations but also all the previous generations—the ancestors. The Chinese believed their ancestors maintained an ongoing interest in the fortunes of living members of the family. Thus people were careful to consult, appease, and venerate their ancestors in order to maintain their favor. The family was viewed as a living, self-renewing organism, and it was absolutely necessary for each generation to have sons to perpetuate the family and ensure the immortality offered by ancestor cult.

Within the family absolute authority rested with the father. He served as an intermediary between the living members and the ancestors, presiding over the rituals of ancestor worship. Every member of the family saw himself or herself as part of an interdependent unit rather than as an individual agent. Each person had a place

Writing as an Imperial Technology

One of the most important technologies in China and Rome was writing. The Chinese word for writing—*wen*—is also the term for "civilization." The origins of Chinese writing may go back as far as the fifth millennium B.C.E., even before the development of cuneiform writing in Mesopotamia. The earliest *surviving* Chinese writing, however, is from the late third or early second millennium B.C.E. Originally developed as a medium for communication with ancestors and gods, writing was essential for the maintenance of the official records on which the imperial system of government depended.

The Chinese use of characters, originally pictures, to represent a concept or word is different from the principles underlying the Roman alphabet. Each letter of the alphabet stands for a sound. The Chinese system requires a person to learn thousands of characters but permits people who speak different languages to read the same text. As part of its program of political and cultural unification, the Qin government imposed a standard system of writing and introduced new characters to represent novel concepts. Paper was invented in China in the first century C.E.

The Roman alphabet is still used for English and many other languages in the modern world. Its ultimate source is the system of writing developed in Phoenicia in the late second millennium B.C.E. and refined by the Greeks after 800 B.C.E. (see Chapters 4 and 5). As in China, the effective functioning of the Roman imperial administration depended on keeping detailed records. In recent years scholars have tried to discover how common literacy was among the peoples of the Roman Empire. Roman emperors put slogans on coins to communicate news and propaganda throughout the empire. Surviving coins indicate that they changed the slogans frequently and suggest the power of the written word even in those times.

A wooden slip with Chinese writing, first century B.C.E. or first century C.E. It gives instructions for soldiers using fire signals to send messages along a chain of forts on the northwest frontier. (Courtesy of the Trustees of the British Museum)

A coin of the emperor Vespasian, 71 C.E. On the obverse (shown here) the ruler's portrait, titles, and offices. The reverse shows a Roman soldier and a weeping female figure under a palm tree representing the province of Judea after suppression of a revolt. (Courtesy of the Trustees of the British Museum)

and responsibilities within the domestic hierarchy, based on his or her gender, age, and relationship to other family members. The family inculcated the basic values of Chinese society: loyalty, obedience to authority, respect for elders and ancestors, and concern for honor and appropriate conduct. Because the hierarchy in the state mirrored the hierarchy in the family, these same attitudes carried over into the relationship between the individual and the state.

Another fundamental source of values was the doctrine of the philosopher Kong Zi (551–479 B.C.E.)—known in the West by the Latin form of his name: Confucius. Confucius came from one of the small states in Shandong during the late Zhou period. He was not particularly successful in obtaining administrative posts, but he developed a system of precepts for people in positions of power.

Confucius started with two assumptions: (1) hierarchy was innate in the order of the universe, and (2) the patterns of human society should echo and harmonize with the cycles of the natural world. From these assumptions, Confucius said, it followed that each person had a particular role to play, with prescribed rules of conduct and proper ceremonial behavior, in order to maintain the social order. Fortunately, people can be guided to the right path through education, imitation of proper role models, and self-improvement. Government exists to serve the people, and the administrator or ruler gains respect and authority by displaying fairness and integrity.

Confucian teachings emphasized benevolence, avoidance of violence, justice, rationalism, loyalty, and decorum. They aimed to affirm and maintain the political and social order by improving it.

The experiences of women in ancient Chinese society are hard to pinpoint because, as elsewhere, contemporary written sources are largely silent on the subject. Confucian ethics, deeply ingrained in the consciousness of the intellectual and administrative classes, stressed the impropriety of women participating in public life. Within the family, males monopolized formal authority. They alone could communicate with the all-important ancestors. Traditional wisdom about the conduct appropriate for women is preserved in an account of the life of the mother of Mengzi (ca. 371–ca. 289 B.C.E.), a major Confucian philosopher known in the West as Mencius. According to this account:

> A woman's duties are to cook the five grains, heat the wine, look after her parents-in-law, make clothes, and that is all! . . . [She] has no ambition to manage affairs outside the house. . . . She must follow the "three submissions." When she is young, she must submit to her parents. After her marriage, she must submit to her husband. When she is widowed, she must submit to her son.[1]

That is an ideal perpetuated by males of the upper classes, the social stratum about which we are best informed because it is the source of most of the written texts. Female members of this group probably were under considerable pressure to conform to those expectations. In contrast, women of the lower classes, less affected by Confucian ways of thinking, may have been less constrained than their more "privileged" counterparts.

Marriages were arranged by parents. A young bride left home to reside with her husband's family. To them she was a stranger who had to prove herself. In such circumstances ability and force of personality (as well as the capacity to produce sons) could make a difference. Dissension between the wife and her mother-in-law and sisters-in-law was frequent as they competed for influence with husbands, sons, and brothers and a larger share of the economic resources held in common by the family.

Like the early Romans, the ancient Chinese believed that divinity resided within nature rather than being outside and above it, and they worshiped and tried to appease the forces of nature. The state erected and maintained shrines to the lords of rain and winds as well as to certain great rivers and high mountains. Gathering at mounds or altars where the local spirit of the soil was felt to reside, people sacrificed sheep and pigs and beat drums loudly to promote the fertility of the earth. Strange or disastrous natural phenomena, such as eclipses or heavy rains, called for symbolic restraint of the deity by tying a red cord around the sacred spot.

The natural world was seen as a balance of forces: *yin*, embodying the female principle, dark and cold, and *yang*, representing the male, light and heat. Within this overarching dichotomy lay a series of fives: five elements (fire, water, metal, wood, and earth), five directions (north, south, east, west, and center), five colors, five senses, and so forth. Because it was believed that supernatural forces, bringing good and evil fortune, flowed through the landscape, experts in geomancy ("earth divination") were consulted to determine the most favorable location and orientation for buildings and graves. The faithful learned to adapt their lives to the complex rhythms they perceived in nature.

There was widespread interest in ways of cheating death, whether by making the body immortal with life-enhancing drugs or providing

Terracotta (baked clay) soldiers from the tomb of the First Emperor of China, third century B.C.E.   First discovered in 1974 in the tomb of the Qin emperor Shi Huangdi, thousands of these life-size figures of soldiers and horses continue to be unearthed by archaeologists. The ground plan of the tomb represents an imperial city, and the figures were arranged in military formation. The individual figures differ from one another in hair and facial features, garments, and weaponry, and were originally brightly painted. This may represent an adaptation of the Shang practice of sacrificing members of the royal retinue and burying them with the deceased ruler. (China Pictorial Service)

for a blessed afterlife. The rich built ostentatious tombs, flanked by towers or covered by mounds of earth, and filled them with the equipment they believed they would need to maintain the

quality of life they had enjoyed on earth. The objects in these tombs have provided archaeologists with a wealth of knowledge about Han society.

The First Chinese Empire

For centuries eastern China had been divided among the compact, rival states whose frequent hostilities gave rise to the label "Warring States Period." In the second half of the third century B.C.E. one of these states, that of the Qin, suddenly burst forth and took over the other states one by one. For the first time the northern plain and the Yangzi River Valley were unified under one rule, marking the creation of China and the inauguration of the imperial age. Many scholars maintain that the very name *China*, by which this land has been known in the Western world, is derived from *Qin*.

Several factors account for the meteoric rise of the Qin. The Qin ruler, who took the title *Shi Huangdi* ("First Emperor"), and his adviser and prime minister Li Si, were able and ruthless men who exploited the exhaustion resulting from the long centuries of interstate rivalry. The Qin homeland in the valley of the Wei, a tributary of the Yellow River, was less urbanized and commercialized than the kingdoms farther east, and the leadership could draw on a large pool of sturdy peasants to serve in the army. Moreover, long experience of mobilizing manpower for the construction of irrigation and flood-control works had strengthened the authority of the Qin king at the expense of the nobles and endowed his government with superior organizational skills.

Shi Huangdi and Li Si created a totalitarian structure in which the individual was subordinated to the needs of the state. They cracked down on Confucianism, regarding its demands for benevolent and non-violent conduct from rulers as a check on the absolute power that they claimed to hold. A new school of political thought—Legalism—emerged to justify the actions of the Qin government. According to this philosophy, whose major exponent was Li Si himself, the will of the ruler was supreme, and his subjects were to be trained in discipline and obedience through the rigid application of rewards and punishments.

The new regime was determined to eliminate any rival centers of authority. Its first target was the landowning aristocracy of the old kingdoms and the system on which aristocratic wealth and power had been based. The Qin government abolished *primogeniture*—the right of the eldest son to inherit all the landed property—because primogeniture allowed a small number of individuals to accumulate vast tracts of land. The Qin required estates to be broken up and passed on to several heirs.

The large estates of the aristocracy had been worked by slaves (see Voices and Visions: Slavery in Rome and China) and by a serf class of peasants who turned over to the landlord a substantial portion of what they grew. The Qin abolished slavery and took steps to bring into being a free peasantry. The members of this group were numerous small landholders who could not evade the government's demands for taxes and who would serve in the army and devote a portion of their labor each year to state projects.

The Qin government's commitment to standardization in many areas of life helped to create a unified Chinese civilization. During the Warring States Period (480 B.C.E.–221 B.C.E.), the small states had emphasized their independence through a wide array of symbolic practices. For example, each state had its own particular forms of music, with different scales, systems of notation, and instruments. The Qin imposed standard weights, measures, and coinage, a uniform law code, a common system of writing, and even regulations governing the axle length of carts so as to leave just one set of ruts on the roads.

Thousands of miles of roads were built—comparable in scale to the roads of the Roman Empire—to connect the parts of the empire and to facilitate the rapid movement of Qin armies. The various frontier walls of the old kingdoms began to be linked into a continuous barricade, the precursor of the Great Wall (see Chapter 11), to protect cultivated lands from incursions by nomadic invaders from the north. To build these walls and roads, large numbers of citizens were forced to donate their labor and often their lives. So op-

pressive were the financial exploitation and the demands for forced labor that when Shi Huangdi died, in 210 B.C.E., a series of rebellions broke out and brought down the Qin dynasty.

The Long Reign of the Han

When the dust cleared, Liu Bang, who may have been from a peasant background, had outlasted his rivals and established a new dynasty, the Han (206 B.C.E.–220 C.E.). The new emperor claimed to reject the excesses and mistakes of the Qin and to restore the institutions of a venerable past. In reality, the Han system of administration maintained much of the structure and Legalist ideology put in place by the Qin, though with less fanatical zeal. The Han system of administration became the standard for later ages, and the Chinese people refer to themselves ethnically as "Han."

The first eighty years of the new dynasty was a time of consolidation. Then, in the later second century B.C.E., Emperor Wu (r. 140–87 B.C.E.) launched a period of military expansion, south into Fujian, Guangdong, and present-day north Vietnam and north into Manchuria and present-day North Korea. Armies were also sent west, to inner Mongolia and Xinjiang, to secure the lucrative Silk Road (see Chapter 8). However, maintaining control of the newly acquired territories was expensive, and Wu's successors curtailed further expansion.

The Han Empire endured with a brief interruption between 9 and 23 C.E. for more than four hundred years. From 202 B.C.E. to 8 C.E.—the period of the Early, or Western, Han—the capital was at Chang'an, in the Wei Valley, an ancient seat of power from which the Zhou and Qin dynasties had emerged. From 23 to 220 C.E. the Later, or Eastern, Han established its base farther east, in the more centrally located Luoyang.

Chang'an, well protected by a ring of hills but having ready access to the fertile plain, was surrounded by a wall of pounded earth and brick 15 miles (24 kilometers) in circumference. We know from contemporary descriptions that it was a bustling place, filled with courtiers, officials, soldiers, merchants, craftsmen, and foreign visitors.

A population of 246,000 is recorded for 2 C.E. Part of the city was carefully planned. Broad thoroughfares running north and south intersected with those running east and west. High walls protected the palaces, administrative offices, barracks, and storehouses of the imperial compound, and access was restricted. Temples and marketplaces were scattered about the civic center. Chang'an became a model of urban planning, its main features imitated in the cities and towns that sprang up throughout the Han Empire.

The complaints of moralists provide glimpses of the private lives of well-to-do officials and merchants in the capital. Living in multistory houses, dressed in fine silks, traveling about the city in ornate horse-drawn carriages, they devoted their leisure time to art and literature, occult religious practices, elegant banquets, and diverse entertainments—music, dance, jugglers and acrobats, dog and horse races, cock and tiger fights. Far different were the lives of the common people of the capital. They inhabited a sprawling warren of alleys, living in dwellings packed "as closely as the teeth of a comb," as one poet put it.

As in the Zhou monarchy (see Chapter 3), the emperor was the "Son of Heaven," and he had the "Mandate of Heaven" to rule. The emperor stood at the center of government and society. As the father held authority in the family and was a link between the living generations and the ancestors, so the emperor was supreme in the state. He brought the support of powerful imperial ancestors and guaranteed the harmonious interaction of heaven and earth. To a much greater degree than his Roman counterpart, he was regarded as a virtual divinity on earth, and his word was law. If he failed to govern worthily, however, Heaven's mandate could be withdrawn. Since the Chinese believed there was a strong correspondence between events in heaven, in the natural world, and in human society, they viewed natural disasters such as floods, droughts, and earthquakes as both the consequence and the proof of the emperor's ethical failure and mismanagement. Successful revolutions were viewed as proof that Heaven's mandate had been withdrawn from an unworthy ruler.

The emperor lived in seclusion within the walled palace compound, surrounded by his many wives, eunuchs, courtiers, and officials. Life in the palace compound was an unceasing round of pomp and ritual emphasizing the worship of Heaven and imperial ancestors as well as the practical business of government. The royal compound was also a hive of intrigue, particularly when the emperor died. His chief widow had the prerogative of choosing the heir from among the male members of the ruling clan.

The central government was run by two top officials—a prime minister and a civil service director—by nine ministers with responsibility in areas such as recordkeeping, the treasury, court protocol, security, criminal punishment, and religious ceremonial, and by the army commanders. The empire was divided into commanderies and kingdoms under the direction of civil and military authorities and subordinate kings, usually members of the imperial family. These administrative regions were subdivided into prefectures, districts, and wards.

Like the imperial Roman government, the Han government depended on local officials to carry out the day-to-day business of administering the vast empire. Local people were responsible for collecting taxes and dispatching revenues to the central government, for regulating the system of conscription for the army and for labor projects, for protection of the area, and for settling disputes. The central government was a remote entity that rarely impinged on the lives of most citizens; their only experience of government was their contact with local officials. Who, then, made up the large bureaucracy of local officials in the Han Empire?

A significant development during the Han period was the rise of a class that scholars refer to as the "gentry." As part of their strategy to weaken the rural aristocrats and to exclude them from political posts, the Qin and Han emperors entered into an alliance with the class next in wealth below the aristocrats. The members of this class were moderately prosperous landowners and professionals. Like the Roman equites favored by Augustus and his successors, the gentry class was the source of the local officials that the central government required. These officials were a privileged and respected group within Chinese society, and they made the government more efficient and responsive than it had been in the past.

The Han period saw a revival of the code of ethics and conduct first advanced by Confucius in the fifth century B.C.E. The new gentry class of officials adopted a somewhat revised Confucianism. It provided them with a system of education for training generations of officials to be both intellectually capable and morally worthy of their role in administration, and it embodied a code of conduct against which to measure individual performance. An imperial university, located just outside of Chang'an and said to have as many as thirty thousand students, and provincial centers of learning were established. From these centers, students were chosen to enter various levels of government service.

As civil servants advanced in the bureaucracy, they received distinctive emblems and other privileges of rank, including preferential treatment at law and exemption from military service. In theory, young men from any class could rise in the state hierarchy. In practice, the sons of the gentry class had an advantage, because they were in the best position to receive the necessary training in the Confucian classics. Over time the gentry became a new aristocracy of sorts, banding together in cliques and family alliances that had considerable clout and worked to advance the careers of members of their group.

In the Han period Daoism took root. Based on the teachings of Lao Zi (whose date is unknown) and Zhuang Zi (369–286 B.C.E.), it soon attached to itself a mixture of popular beliefs, magic, and mysticism. Daoism was popular with the common people. Its religious and philosophical world-view in many respects was at odds with the Confucianism of the elite and provides a glimpse of the tensions within Chinese society.

Daoism emphasized the search for the *dao,* or "path," of nature and the value of harmonizing with the cycles and patterns of the natural world. But Daoists believed that the successful conclusion of the search was to be achieved not so much by education as by solitary contemplation, physical and mental discipline, and striving to reach that instant in which one suddenly, intu-

Important Events in Early Imperial China

221 B.C.E.	Qin emperor unites eastern China
206 B.C.E.	Han dynasty succeeds Qin
140–87 B.C.E.	Emperor Wu expands the Chinese empire
23 C.E.	Capital transferred from Chang'an to Luoyang
220 C.E.	Fall of Han empire

itively, grasps the nature of things. Daoism was skeptical, calling into question age-old beliefs and values and rejecting the hierarchy, rules, and rituals of Confucianism. In the end, it urged passive acceptance of the disorder of the world, denial of ambition, contentment with simple pleasures, and following one's instincts about what was right.

Technology and Trade

China was the home of many important inventions, and what the Chinese did not invent, they improved. Tradition seems to have recognized the importance of technology for the success and spread of Chinese civilization. The legendary first five emperors were all culture heroes whom the Chinese credited with the introduction of major new technologies.

The advent of bronze tools around 1500 B.C.E. had given a powerful impetus to the effort to clear the forests of the North China Plain in order to open up more land for agriculture. Almost a thousand years later, iron arrived. One possible explanation for the military superiority of the Qin is that they were among the first to take full advantage of the new iron technology. In later centuries, the crossbow and use of cavalry helped the Chinese military to beat off the attacks of nomads from the steppe regions. The watermill, which harnessed the power of running water to turn a grinding stone, was in use in China long before it appeared in Europe. The development of a horse collar that did not constrict the animal's breathing allowed horses in China to pull loads much heavier than the loads pulled by horses in Europe at the same time.

The Qin had undertaken an extensive program of road building, and the Han rulers continued this project. These roads connected an expanding network of urban centers. Growth in population and increasing trade resulted in the development of local market centers. The importance of these thriving towns grew as they became county seats from which imperial officials operated. Estimates of the proportion of the population living in towns and cities range from 10 to 30 percent.

Along with the growth of local and regional trade networks came the development of long-distance commerce. China's most important export commodity was silk. Silk cocoons are secreted onto the leaves of mulberry trees by silkworms. For a long time this simple fact was a closely guarded secret that gave the Chinese a monopoly on the manufacture of silk. Carried on a perilous journey westward through the Central Asian oases to the Middle East, India, and the Mediterranean, and passing through the hands of many middlemen, each of whom raised the price in order to make a profit, this beautiful textile may have increased in value a hundredfold by the time it reached its destination. The Chinese government sought to control the Silk Road and the profits that it carried by launching periodic campaigns into Central Asia. Garrisons were installed and colonies of Chinese settlers were sent out to occupy the oases.

Decline of the Han Empire

For the Han government, as for the Romans, maintaining the security of the frontiers—particularly the north and northwest frontiers—was a primary concern. Yet, in the end, the pressure of non-Chinese peoples raiding from across the frontier or moving into the prosperous lands of the Empire led to the decline of Han authority.

In general, the Han Empire had been able to consolidate its hold over lands occupied by sedentary farming peoples, but living in nearby regions were nomadic tribes whose livelihood depended on their horses and herds. The very different ways of life of farmers and herders gave rise to suspicions and insulting stereotypes on both sides. The settled Chinese tended to think of nomads as "barbarians"—rough, uncivilized peoples—much as the inhabitants of the Roman Empire looked down on the German tribes living beyond their frontier.

Along the boundary between settled agriculturalists and nomadic pastoralists there was frequent contact. Often the closeness of the two populations led to significant commercial activity. The nomads sought the food commodities and crafted goods produced by the farmers and townsfolk, and the settled peoples depended on the nomads for horses and other herd animals and products. Sometimes, however, contact took the form of raids on the settled lands by nomad bands, which seized what they needed or wanted. Tough and warlike because of the demands of their way of life, mounted nomads could strike swiftly and just as swiftly disappear.

Although nomadic groups tend to be relatively small and to fight often with each other, from time to time circumstances and a charismatic leader can create a large coalition of tribes. The major external threat to Chinese civilization in the Han period came from the Xiongnu, a great confederacy of Turkic peoples. For centuries Chinese policy had succeeded in containing the Xiongnu. The Chinese used a range of strategies: periodic campaigns onto the steppe, maintenance of military colonies and garrisons on the frontier, the settlement of compliant nomadic groups within the borders of the empire to serve as a buffer against warlike groups, bribes to promote dissension within the nomad leadership, and payment of protection money. One successful approach was the "tributary system," in which nomad rulers accepted Chinese supremacy and sent in payments of tribute in return for which they were rewarded with marriages to Chinese princesses, dazzling receptions at court, and gifts from the Han emperor which exceeded the value of the tribute.

In the first century C.E. the Xiongnu were defeated by the Chinese and pushed west. Several centuries later they arrived on the northern frontier of the Roman Empire and the Huns, as the Romans called them, plagued that other great empire and helped to bring about its downfall.

In the end, the cost of continuous military vigilance along the frontier imposed a crushing bur-

Han era (first century B.C.E.) stone rubbing of a horse-drawn carriage   The "trace harness," a Chinese invention which attached a strap across the chest, allowed horses to pull far heavier loads than was possible with the constricting throat harness used in Europe at that time. In the Han period, towns and cities sprang up across the Chinese landscape. They were primarily inhabited by a growing class of officials, professionals, and soldiers who served the regime. This class used its social position and prosperity to create a conspicuous lifestyle that included fine clothing, comfortable transportation, servants, and delightful pastimes, at the same time that it was guided by a Confucian emphasis on duty, honesty, and appropriate behavior. (From Wu family shrine, Jiaxiang, Shantung. From *Chin-shih-so* [Jinshisuo]. Photographer: Eileen Tweedy)

den on Han finances and worsened the economic troubles of later Han times. And, despite the earnest efforts of Qin and Early Han emperors to reduce the power and wealth of the aristocracy and to turn land over to a free peasantry, by the end of the first century B.C.E. nobles and successful merchants again were beginning to acquire control of huge tracts of land, and many peasants were seeking their protection against the exactions of the government. This trend became widespread in the next two centuries. Strongmen largely independent of state control emerged, and the central government was deprived of tax revenues and manpower. The system of military conscription broke down, forcing the government to hire more and more foreign soldiers and officers. These men were willing to serve for pay, but their loyalty to the Han state was weak.

Several factors combined to weaken and eventually bring down the Han dynasty in 220 C.E.: factional intrigues within the ruling Han clan, official corruption and inefficiency, uprisings of desperate and hungry peasants, the spread of banditry, unsuccessful reform movements, attacks by nomadic groups on the northwest frontier, and the ambitions of rural warlords. After 220, China entered a period of political fragmentation and economic and cultural regression that lasted until the rise of the Sui and Tang dynasties in the late sixth and early seventh centuries C.E., a story that we take up in Chapter 11.

CONCLUSION

The parallels between the Roman Empire and the Han Empire are quite striking. Both employed similar means to control vast territories and large populations over a long period of time. In both, subject peoples adopted the language and culture of the rulers. A marked rise in prosperity and in the general standard of living, the growth of cities, increased long-distance trade, more widespread education and literacy, and significant technological developments occurred against a backdrop of peace and stability. Even in the manner of their demise there were strong similarities.

However, there also are significant differences between Rome and Han China. These differences become clear from an examination of the long-term effects of the failure of central authority. In China, the imperial tradition and the class structure and value system that maintained it were eventually revived (see Chapters 11 and 14), and they survived with remarkable continuity into the twentieth century C.E. In Europe, North Africa, and the Middle East, in contrast, there never has been a restoration of the Roman Empire, and the subsequent history of these lands has been marked by great political changes and cultural diversity. Several interrelated factors help to account for the different outcomes.

First, these cultures had different attitudes toward the importance of the individual and the obligations of individuals to the state. In China the individual was deeply embedded in the larger social group. The Chinese family, with its emphasis on a precisely defined hierarchy, unquestioning obedience, and solemn rituals of deference to elders and ancestors, served as the model for society and the state. Thus in China respect for authority always has been a deep-seated habit. The architects of Qin Legalism largely got their way, and the emperor's word was regarded as law. Although the Roman family had its own hierarchy and traditions of obedience, the cult of ancestors was not as strong among the Romans as it was among the Chinese, and the family did not serve as the model for the organization of Roman society and the Roman state.

It is probably also fair to say that economic and social mobility, which make it possible for some people to rise dramatically in wealth and status, tends to enhance a society's sense of the significance of the individual. In ancient China opportunities for individuals to improve their economic status were more limited than they were in the Roman Empire, and the merchant class in China was frequently disparaged and constrained by government control. The more important role played by commerce in the Roman Empire, and the resulting economic mobility, heightened Roman awareness of the uniqueness and prerogatives of individuals. To a much greater extent than the Chinese emperor, the Roman emperor had to resort to persuasion, threats, and promises in order to forge a consensus for his initiatives.

Another factor differentiating the empires of Han China and Rome is political and religious ideology. Although Roman emperors tried to create an ideology to bolster their position, they were hampered by the persistence of Republican traditions and the ambiguities about the position of emperor deliberately cultivated by Augustus. As a result, Roman rulers were likely to be chosen either by the army or by the Senate, the dynastic principle never took deep root, and the cult of the emperor had little spiritual content. This stands in sharp contrast to the iron-clad Chinese ideology of the Mandate of Heaven, the belief in the emperor as the divine Son of Heaven, and the imperial monopoly of access to the beneficent power of the royal ancestors. Thus, in the West, there was no compelling basis for reviving the position of emperor and the territorial claims of empire in later ages.

Finally, weight also must be given to differences in the new belief systems that took root in each empire. Christianity, with its insistence on monotheism and one doctrine of truth, negated the Roman emperor's pretensions to divinity and was essentially unwilling to come to terms with pagan beliefs. Thus the triumphant spread of Christianity through the provinces of the late Roman Empire, and the decline of the western half of the empire in the fifth century C.E. (see Chapter 9), constituted an irreversible break with the past. However, Buddhism, which came to China in the early centuries C.E. and flourished in the post-Han era (see Chapter 11), was easily reconciled with traditional Chinese values and beliefs. In the next chapter we turn to the homeland of Buddhism and Hinduism in South Asia and trace the development of Indian civilization.

SUGGESTED READING

Tim Cornell and John Matthews, *Atlas of the Roman World* (1982), offers a general introduction, pictures, and maps to illustrate many aspects of Roman civilization. Michael Grant and Rachel Kitzinger, eds., *Civilization of the Ancient Mediterranean*, 3 vols. (1988), is an invaluable collection of essays with bibliographies by specialists on every major facet of life in the Greek and Roman worlds. Among the many good surveys of Roman history is Michael Grant, *History of Rome* (1978). Naphtali Lewis and Meyer Reinhold, eds., *Roman Civilization*, 2 vols. (1951), contains extensive ancient sources in translation.

For Roman political and legal institutions, attitudes, and values see J. A. Crook, *Law and Life of Rome: 90 B.C.–A.D. 212* (1967). Michael Crawford, *The Roman Republic*, 2nd ed. (1993), and Chester G. Starr, *The Roman Empire, 27 B.C.–A.D. 476: A Study in Survival* (1982), assess the evolution of the Roman state during the Republic and Principate. Fergus Millar, *The Emperor in the Roman World (31 B.C.–A.D. 337)* (1977), is a comprehensive study of the position of the princeps.

For the Roman military expansion and defense of the frontiers, see W. V. Harris, *War and Imperialism in Republican Rome* (1979); and Stephen L. Dyson, *The Creation of the Roman Frontier* (1985). David Macaulay, *City: A Story of Roman Planning and Construction* (1974), uses copious illustrations to reveal the wonders of Roman engineering.

Kevin Greene, *The Archaeology of the Roman Economy* (1986), showcases new approaches to social and economic history. U. E. Paoli, *Rome: Its People, Life and Customs* (1983) looks at everyday life. Jo-Ann Shelton, ed., *As the Romans Did: A Sourcebook in Roman Social History* (1988), offers a selection of translated ancient sources. Elaine Fantham, Helene, Peet Foley, Natalie Boymel Kampen, Sarah B. Pomeroy, and H. Alan Shapiro, *Women in the Classical World: Image and Text* (1994), provide an up-to-date discussion of women in the Roman world. Many of the ancient sources on Roman women can be found in Mary R. Lefkowitz and Maureen B. Fant, eds., *Women's Life in Greece and Rome: A Source Book in Translation* (1982). Thomas Wiedemann, ed., *Greek and Roman Slavery* (1981), contains the ancient sources in translation.

A number of the chapters in John Boardman, Jasper Griffin, and Oswyn Murray, eds., *The Roman World* (1988) surveys the intellectual and literary achievements of the Romans. R. M. Ogilvie, *The Romans and Their Gods in the Age of Augustus* (1969) is an introduction to religion in both its public and its private manifestations. R. A. Markus, *Christianity in the Roman World* (1974), investigates the rise of Christianity.

For the geography and demography of China see the well-illustrated *Cultural Atlas of China* (1983) by Caroline Blunden and Mark Elvin. Basic surveys of Chinese history include Jacques Gernet, *A History of Chinese Civilization* (1982); and John K. Fairbank, *China: A New History* (1992). In greater depth for the ancient period is Denis Twitchett and Michael Loewe, eds., *The Cambridge History of China*, vol. 1, *The Ch'in and Han Empires, 221 B.C.–A.D. 220* (1986), and Michele Pirazzoli-t'Serstevens, *The Han Dynasty* (1982). Kwang-chih Chang, *The Archaeology of Ancient China*, 4th ed. (1986), emphasizes the archaeological record. W. de Bary, W. Chan, and B. Watson, eds., have assembled sources in translation in *Sources of Chinese Tradition* (1960).

For social history see Michael Loewe, *Everyday Life in Early Imperial China During the Han Period, 202 B.C.–A.D. 220* (1988); and the chapter by Sharon L. Sievers in *Restoring Women to History*, ed. (1988). For economic history and foreign relations see Ying-shih Yu, *Trade and Expansion in Han China* (1967). For scientific and technological achievements see Robert Temple, *The Genius of China: 3,000 Years of Science, Discovery, and Invention* (1986).

Benjamin I. Schwartz addresses intellectual history in *The World of Thought in Ancient China* (1985). Spiritual matters are taken up by Laurence G. Thompson, *Chinese Religion: An Introduction*, 3d ed. (1979). For art see Michael Sullivan, *A Short History of Chinese Art*, rev. ed. (1970).

NOTE

1. Patricia Buckley Ebrey, ed., *Chinese Civilization and Society: A Sourcebook* (The Free Press, New York, 1981) 33–34.

CHAPTER SEVEN

India and Southeast Asia,

1500 B.C.E.–1100 C.E.

Foundations of Indian Civilization · Imperial Expansion and Collapse

Southeast Asia

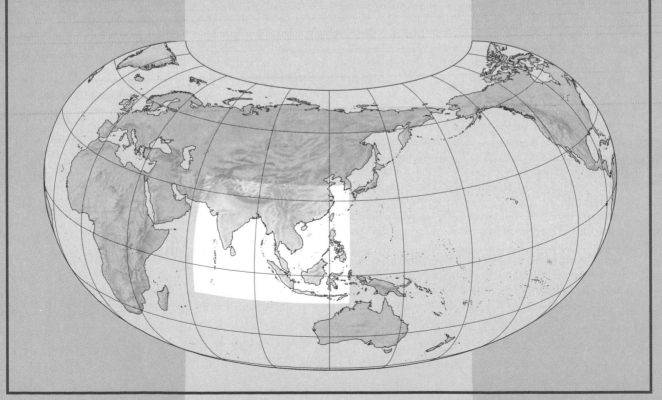

In the *Bhagavad-Gita,* the most renowned of all Indian sacred texts, Arjuna, the greatest warrior of Indian legend, rides out in his chariot between two armies preparing for battle. Torn between his social duty to fight for his family's claim to the throne and his conscience, which balks at the prospect of killing the relatives, friends, and former teachers who are in the enemy camp, Arjuna slumps down in his chariot and refuses to fight. But his chariot driver, the god Krishna in disguise, persuades him, in a carefully structured dialogue, both of the necessity to fulfill his duty as a warrior and of the proper frame of mind for performing these acts. In the climactic moment of the dialogue Krishna endows Arjuna with a "divine eye" and permits him to see the true appearance of god:

> It was a multiform, wondrous vision,
> with countless mouths and eyes
> and celestial ornaments,
> Everywhere was boundless divinity
> containing all astonishing things,
> wearing divine garlands and garments,
> anointed with divine perfume.
> If the light of a thousand suns
> were to rise in the sky at once,
> it would be like the light
> of that great spirit.
> Arjuna saw all the universe
> in its many ways and parts,
> standing as one in the body
> of the god of gods.[1]

In all of world literature, this is one of the most compelling attempts to depict the nature of deity. Graphic images emphasize the enormity, diversity, and multiplicity of the god, but in the end we learn that Krishna is the organizing principle behind all creation, that behind diversity and multiplicity lies a higher unity.

This is an apt metaphor for Indian civilization. If there is one word that might be used to characterize India in both ancient and modern times, it is *diversity*. The enormous variety of the Indian landscape is mirrored in the patchwork of ethnic and linguistic groups that occupy it, the political fragmentation that has marked most of Indian history, the elaborate hierarchy of social groups into which the Indian population is divided, and the thousands of deities who are worshiped at the innumerable holy places that dot the subcontinent. Yet, in the end, one can speak of an Indian civilization that is united by a set of shared views and values.

In this chapter we survey the history of South and Southeast Asia from approximately 1500 B.C.E. to 1100 C.E., focusing on the evolution of defining features of Indian civilization: economic activities, technologies, social divisions, and a religious tradition whose distinctive conceptions of space, time, gods, and the life cycle have shaped virtually every aspect of South Asian culture. Considerable attention is given to Indian religious conceptions. This is due, in part, to religion's profound role in shaping Indian society. It is also a consequence of the sources of information available to historians.

Lengthy epic poems, such as the *Mahabharata* and *Ramayana*, may preserve useful information about early Indian society, but most of the earliest texts are religious documents—such as the *Vedas, Upanishads,* and Buddhist stories—that were preserved and transmitted orally long before they were written down. In addition, Indian civilization held a conception of vast expanses of time during which creatures are repeatedly reincarnated and live many lives. This belief may account for why ancient Indians did not develop a historical consciousness like that of their Israelite and Greek contemporaries but instead took little interest in recording specific historical events: such events seemed relatively insignificant when set against the long cycles of time and lives.

Despite the limited evidence, the political history of early India is also our subject. In the face of powerful forces that tended to keep India politically fragmented, two great empires emerged:

the Mauryan Empire, which lasted from the fourth to the second century B.C.E., and the Gupta Empire, from the fourth to the sixth century C.E. The chapter concludes by looking at how a number of states in Southeast Asia became wealthy and powerful by exploiting their advantageous position on the international trade routes between India and China and by adapting Indian ideas and technologies to their needs.

FOUNDATIONS OF INDIAN CIVILIZATION

India is often called a *subcontinent* because it is a large—roughly 2,000 miles (3,200 kilometers) in both length and breadth—and physically isolated landmass within the continent of Asia. It is set off from the rest of Asia by the Himalayas, the highest mountains on the planet, to the north, and by the Indian Ocean on its eastern, southern, and western sides (see Map 7.1). The most permeable frontier, and the one used by a long series of invaders and migrating peoples, lies to the northwest. But people using even this corridor must cross over the mountain barrier of the Hindu Kush and the Thar Desert east of the Indus River.

The Indian Subcontinent

This region—which encompasses the modern nations of Pakistan, Nepal, Bhutan, Bangladesh, India, and the adjacent island of Sri Lanka—can be divided into three distinct topographical zones. The mountainous northern zone takes in the heavily forested foothills and high meadows on the edge of the Hindu Kush and Himalaya ranges. Next come the great basins of the Indus and Ganges Rivers. Originating in the ice of the Tibetan mountains to the north, through the millennia these rivers have repeatedly overflowed their banks and deposited layer on layer of silt,

creating large alluvial plains. Northern India is divided from the third zone, the peninsula proper, by the Vindhya range and the Deccan, an arid, rocky plateau that brings to mind parts of the American West. The tropical coastal strip of Kerala (Malabar) in the west, the Coromandel Coast in the east with its web of rivers descending from the central plateau, the flatlands of Tamil Nadu on the southern tip of the peninsula, and the island of Sri Lanka often have followed paths of political and cultural development separate from those of northern India.

The rim of mountains looming above India's northern frontier shelters the subcontinent from cold Arctic winds and gives it a subtropical climate. The most dramatic source of moisture is the monsoon (seasonal wind). The Indian Ocean is slow to warm or cool, and the vast landmass of Asia swings rapidly between seasonal extremes of heat and cold. The temperature difference between the water and the land acts like a bellows, producing a great wind in this and adjoining parts of the globe. The southwest monsoon begins in June. It carries huge amounts of moisture picked up from the Indian Ocean and deposits it over a swath of India that encompasses the rainforest belt on the western coast and the Ganges Basin. Three harvests a year are possible in some places. Rice is grown in the moist, flat Ganges Delta (the modern region of Bengal). Elsewhere the staples are wheat, barley, and millet.

The Indus Valley, by contrast, gets little precipitation (see Chapter 2). In this arid region the successful practice of agriculture depends on extensive irrigation. Moreover, the volume of water in the Indus is irregular, and the river has changed course from time to time.

Although invasions and migrations usually came by land through the northwest corridor, the ocean surrounding the peninsula has not been a barrier to travel and trade. Indian Ocean mariners learned to ride the monsoon winds across open waters from northeast to southwest in January and to reverse the process in July. Ships made their way west across the Arabian Sea to the Persian Gulf, the southern coast of Arabia, and East Africa, and east across the Bay of Bengal to Indochina and Indonesia (see Chapter 8).

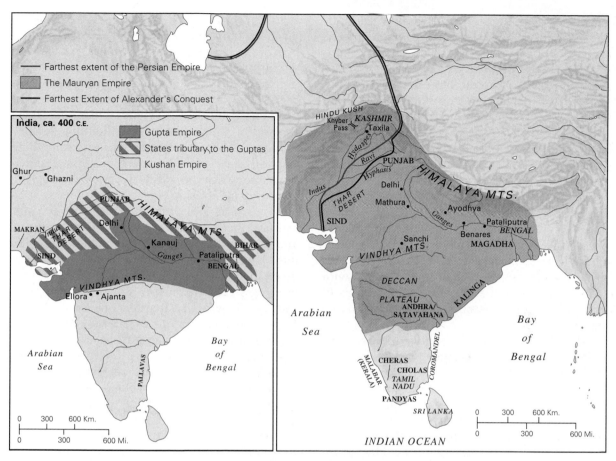

Map 7.1 Ancient India The Indian subcontinent is largely cut off from the mass of Asia by mountains and sea. Migrations and invasions usually came through the northwest corridor (Hindu Kush). Sea-borne commerce with western Asia, Southeast Asia, and East Asia often flourished. While peoples speaking Indo-European languages migrated into the broad valleys of the Indus and Ganges Rivers in the north, Dravidian-speaking peoples remained the dominant population in the south. The diversity of the Indian landscape, the multiplicity of ethnic groups, and the primary identification of people with their class and caste, lie behind the division into many small states which characterizes much of Indian political history.

The Vedic Age, 1500–500 B.C.E.

It is tempting to trace many of the characteristic features of later Indian civilization back to the Indus Valley civilization of the third and early second millennia B.C.E., but proof is hard to come by because the writing from that period has not yet been deciphered. That society, which responded to the challenge of an arid terrain by developing high levels of social organization and technology, seems to have succumbed around

1800 B.C.E. to some kind of environmental crisis (see Chapter 2).

Historians call the period from 1500 to 500 B.C.E. the "Vedic Age," after the Vedas, religious texts that are our main source of information about the period. The foundations for Indian civilization were laid in the Vedic Age. Most historians believe that new groups of people—nomadic warriors speaking Indo-European languages—migrated into northwest India around 1500 B.C.E. Some argue for a much earlier Indo-European presence in this region in conjunction with the spread of agriculture. In any case, in the mid-second millennium B.C.E. northern India entered a new historical period associated with the dominance of Indo-European groups.

In the arid northwest, large-scale agriculture depends on irrigation. After the collapse of the Indus Valley civilization there was no central authority to direct these efforts, and the region became home to kinship groups that depended mostly on their herds of cattle for sustenance, and perhaps also on some gardening to supplement their diet. Like other Indo-European peoples—Celts, Greeks, Iranians, Romans—these societies were patriarchal. The father dominated the family as the king ruled the tribe. Members of the warrior class boasted of their martial skill and courage, relished combat, celebrated with lavish feasts of beef and rounds of heavy drinking, and filled their leisure time with chariot racing and gambling.

After 1000 B.C.E. some of these groups began to push east into the Ganges Plain. New technologies made this advance possible. Iron tools—harder than bronze, more durable, and able to hold a sharper edge—allowed settlers to fell trees and to work the newly cleared land with plows pulled by oxen. The soil of the Ganges Plain was fertile, well watered by the annual monsoon, and able to sustain two or three crops a year. As in Greece at roughly the same time (see Chapter 5), in India the use of iron tools to open up new land for agriculture must have led to a significant increase in population.

Stories about this era, not written down until much later but long preserved by memorization and oral recitation, speak of bitter rivalry and warfare between two groups of people: the Aryas, relatively light-skinned speakers of Indo-European languages, and the Dasas, dark-skinned speakers of Dravidian languages. Some scholars argue that the real process by which Arya groups became dominant in the north was more complicated, involving the absorption of some Dasas into Arya populations and a merging of elites from both groups. For the most part, however, Aryas pushed the Dasas south into central and southern India, where their descendants still live. A sign of the ultimate success of the Aryas in the north is the languages spoken in northern India today: they are primarily members of the Indo-European language family. Dravidian speech prevails in the south.

Skin color has been a persistent concern of Indian society and is one of the bases for its historically sharp internal divisions. Over time there evolved a system of *varna*—literally "color," though the word came to indicate something akin to "class." There were four class designations into which individuals were born: *Brahmin*, the group comprising priests and scholars; *Kshatriya*, warriors and officials; *Vaishya*, merchants, artisans, and landowners; and *Shudra*, peasants and laborers. The designation *Shudra* originally may have been reserved for Dasas, who were given the menial jobs in society. Indeed, the very term *dasa* came to mean "slave." Eventually a fifth group was also marked off: the Untouchables. They were excluded from the class system, and members of the other groups literally avoided them because of the demeaning or polluting work to which they were relegated—such as leather tanning, which involved touching dead animals, or sweeping away ashes after cremations.

People at the top of the social pyramid in ancient India could explain why this hierarchy existed. According to one creation myth, a primordial creature named Purusha allowed himself to be sacrificed. From Purusha's mouth sprang the class of Brahmin priests, the embodiment of intellect and knowledge. From his arms came the Kshatriya warrior class, from his thighs the Vaishya landowners and merchants, and from his feet the Shudra workers.

The varna system was just one of the mechanisms that Indian society developed to regulate relations between different groups. Within the broad class divisions, the population was also further subdivided into numerous *jati*, or birth groups (sometimes called *castes* from a Portuguese term meaning "breed"). Each jati had its proper occupation, duties, and rituals. The individuals who belonged to a given jati lived with members of their group, married within the group, and ate only with members of the group. Elaborate rules governed their interactions with members of other groups. Members of higher-status groups feared pollution from contact with lower-caste individuals and had to undergo elaborate rituals of purification to remove the taint.

The class and caste systems came to be connected to a widespread belief in reincarnation. The Brahmin priests taught that every living creature had an immortal essence: the *atman*, or "breath." Separated from the body at death, at a later time the atman was reborn in another body. Whether the new body was that of an insect, an animal, or a human depended on the *karma*, or deeds, of the atman in its previous incarnations. People who lived exemplary lives would be reborn into the higher classes. Those who misbehaved would be punished in the next life by being relegated to a lower class or even a lower life form. The underlying message was: You are where you deserve to be, and the only way to improve your lot in the next cycle of existence is to accept your station and its attendant duties.

The dominant deities in Vedic religion were male and were associated with the heavens. To release the dawn, Indra, god of war and master of the thunderbolt, daily slew the demon encasing the universe. Varuna, lord of the sky, maintained universal order and dispensed justice. Agni, the force of fire, consumed the sacrifice and bridged the worlds of gods and humans.

Sacrifice was the essential ritual. People believed that the dedication to a god of a valued possession, often a living creature, created a relationship between themselves and the gods. These offerings were made to invigorate the gods and thereby sustain their creative powers and promote stability in the world. The person making the sacrifice also hoped that the deity would respond favorably to his or her request. An important ingredient of Vedic ritual was *soma*, the nectar of immortality, a hallucinogenic liquid of some kind. The chief religious event of the year was the soma sacrifice, held just before the arrival of the June monsoon and credited with the reappearance of the life-giving rains.

Brahmin priests controlled the technology of sacrifice, for only they knew the precise rituals and prayers. The *Rig Veda*, a collection of more than a thousand poetic hymns to various deities,

and the Brahmanas, detailed prose descriptions of procedures for ritual and sacrifice, were collections of priestly lore couched in the Sanskrit language of the Aryan upper classes. This information was handed down orally from one generation of priests to the next. Some scholars have hypothesized that the Brahmins opposed the introduction of writing. Their opposition would explain why this technology did not come into widespread use in India until the Gupta period (320–550 C.E.), long after it had begun to play a conspicuous role in other societies of equivalent complexity. The priests' "knowledge" (the term *veda* means just that) was the basis of their economic well-being. They were amply rewarded for officiating at sacrifices, and their knowledge provided them with social and political power because they were the indispensable intermediaries between gods and humans.

As in virtually all ancient societies, it is difficult to uncover the experiences of women in ancient India. Limited evidence indicates that in the Vedic period women studied sacred lore, composed religious hymns, and participated in the sacrificial ritual. They had the opportunity to own property and usually were not married until they reached their middle or late teens. A number of strong and resourceful women appear in the epic poem *Mahabharata*. One of them, the beautiful and educated Draupadi, married by her own choice the five royal Pandava brothers. This accomplishment probably should not be taken as evidence for the regular practice of polyandry (having more than one husband). In India, as in Greece, legendary figures could play by their own rules.

The rigid internal divisions of Indian society, the complex hierarchy of groups, and the claims of some to superior virtue and purity served important social functions in Indian culture. They provided each individual with a clear identity and role and offered the benefits of group solidarity and support. There is evidence that groups sometimes were able to upgrade their status. Thus the elaborate system of divisions was not static and provided a mechanism for working out social tensions. Many of these features persisted into modern times.

Challenges to the Old Order: Jainism and Buddhism

After 700 B.C.E. various forms of reaction against Brahmin power and privilege emerged. People who objected to the rigid hierarchy of classes and castes or the community's demands on the individual could always retreat to the forest. Despite the clearing of extensive tracts of land for agriculture, much of ancient India was covered with forest. These wild places which were never very far from the civilized areas, served as a refuge and symbolized freedom from societal constraints.

Certain individuals abandoned their town or village and moved to the forest. Sometimes these hermits attracted bands of followers. Calling into question the exclusive claims to wisdom of the priests and the necessity of Vedic chants and sacrifices, they offered, as an alternate path to salvation, the individual pursuit of insight into the nature of the self and the universe through physical and mental discipline (*yoga*), special dietary practices, and meditation. They taught that by distancing oneself from desire for the things of this world, one could achieve *moksha,* or "liberation," union with the divine force that animates the universe. This release from the cycle of reincarnations sometimes was likened to "a deep, dreamless sleep." The Upanishads—a collection of over one hundred mystical dialogues between teachers and disciples—reflect this questioning of the foundations of Vedic religion.

The most serious threat to Vedic religion and to the prerogatives of the Brahmin priestly class came from two new sects that emerged around this time: Jainism and Buddhism. Mahavira (540–468 B.C.E.) was known to his followers as *Jina,* "the Conqueror," from which is derived *Jainism,* the name of the belief system that he established. Emphasizing the holiness of the life force that animates all living creatures, Mahavira and his followers practiced strict nonviolence. They wore masks to prevent themselves from accidentally inhaling small insects, and before sitting down, they carefully brushed off the surface of the seat. Those who gave themselves over completely to Jainism practiced extreme asceticism and nudity, ate only what they were given by others, and eventually starved themselves to death. Less zealous Jainists, restricted from agricultural work by the injunction against killing, tended to be city dwellers engaged in commerce and banking.

Of far greater significance for Indian and world history was the rise of Buddhism. So many stories have been told about Siddhartha Gautama (563–483 B.C.E.), known as the *Buddha,* "the Enlightened One," that it is difficult to separate fact from legend. He came from a Kshatriya family of the Sakya tribe in the foothills of the Himalayas. As a young man he enjoyed the lifestyle to which he had been born, but at some point he experienced a change of heart and gave up family and privilege to become a wandering ascetic. After six years of self-deprivation, he came to regard asceticism as being no more likely to produce spiritual insights than the luxury of his previous life had been. He decided to adhere to a "Middle Path" of moderation. Sitting under a tree in a deer park near Benares on the Ganges River, he had a revelation of "Four Noble Truths": (1) life is suffering; (2) suffering arises from desire; (3) the solution to suffering lies in stemming desire; and (4) this can be achieved by following the "Eightfold Path" of right views, aspirations, speech, conduct, livelihood, effort, mindfulness, and meditation. Rising up, he preached his First Sermon, a central text of Buddhism, and set into motion the "Wheel of the Law." The Buddha soon attracted followers who took vows of celibacy, nonviolence, and poverty.

In its original form Buddhism centered on the individual. Although it did not quite reject the existence of gods, it denied their usefulness to a person seeking enlightenment. What mattered was living one's life in a manner that minimized desire and suffering and emphasized the search for spiritual truth. The ultimate reward was *nirvana,* literally "snuffing out the flame." With nirvana came release from the cycle of reincarnations and achievement of a state of eternal tranquillity. The Vedic tradition emphasized the survival beyond death of the atman, the "breath" or nonmaterial essence of the individ-

Stone relief of women adoring the Buddha, from the Great Stupa at Amaravati (central India), second century C.E. Many stories circulated concerning the life of the Buddha and his many previous lives. Such stories were represented in the rich carvings which decorated the gates and walls of *stupas*, mounds containing relics of the founder which became major pilgrimage sites. For centuries after his death, artists refrained from directly depicting the Buddha, instead using a repertoire of symbols: the tree under which he achieved enlightenment, his begging bowl, and, as here, his seat and footprints. The fact that he is not represented in human form emphasizes that he has achieved the state of *nirvana*, nonexistence. (Robert Fisher)

ual. In contrast, Buddhism regarded the individual as a composite without any soul-like component that survived death. Nirvana is an eternal state of nonexistence.

When the Buddha died, he left no rules or instructions, instead urging his disciples to "be their own lamp." As the Buddha's message spread throughout India and beyond into Central, Southeast, and East Asia, its very success began to subvert the individualistic and essentially atheistic tenets of the founder, however. Buddhist monasteries were established, and a hierarchy of Buddhist monks and nuns came into being. Worshipers erected *stupas* (large earthen mounds that symbolized the universe) over relics of the cremated founder and walked around them in a clockwise direction. Indeed, the Buddha himself began to be worshiped as a god. Buddhists also revered *bodhisattvas*, enlight-

ened men and women who had earned nirvana but chose to be reborn into mortal bodies to help others along the path to salvation.

The makers of early pictorial images had refused to show the Buddha as a living person and represented him only indirectly, through symbols such as his footprints, begging bowl, or the tree under which he achieved enlightenment, as if to emphasize his achievement of a state of nonexistence. From the second century C.E., however, statues of the Buddha and bodhisattvas began to proliferate, done in native sculptural styles and in a style that showed the influence of the Greek settlements established in Bactria (modern Afghanistan) by Alexander the Great (see Chapter 5). A deep schism emerged within Buddhism. Devotees of Mahayana, or "Great Vehicle," Buddhism embraced the popular new features. In contrast, practitioners of Theravada

Sculpture of the Buddha, second or third century C.E.   This depiction of the Buddha, showing the effects of a protracted fast, is from Gandhara in the northwest. It displays the influence of Greek artistic styles emanating from the settlements of Greeks which had been established in that region by Alexander the Great in the late fourth century B.C.E. This work illustrates how some of the Buddha's own precepts were superseded in the Mahayana form of Buddhism which gained popularity by the early centuries C.E. (Robert Fisher)

Buddhism, "The Way of the Elders" (also called Hinayana, or "Lesser Vehicle"), followed most of the original teachings of the founder.

The Rise of Hinduism

Challenged by new, spiritually satisfying, and egalitarian movements, Vedic religion made important adjustments, evolving into Hinduism,

the religion of hundreds of millions of people in South Asia today. (The term *Hinduism*, however, was imposed from outside. When Islamic invaders reached India in the eleventh century C.E., they labeled the diverse range of practices they saw there as Hinduism: "what the Indians do.")

The foundation of Hinduism is the Vedic religion of the Aryan tribes of northern India. But Hinduism also incorporated elements drawn from the Dravidian cultures of the south, such as an emphasis on intense devotion to the deity and the prominence of fertility rituals and symbolism, as well as elements of Buddhism. The process by which Vedic religion was transformed into Hinduism by the fourth century C.E. is largely hidden from us. The Brahmin priests emerged with their high social status and influence essentially intact. But sacrifice, though still part of traditional worship, was less central, and there was much more opportunity for direct contact between gods and individual worshipers.

The gods were altered, both in identity and in their relationships with humanity. Two formerly minor deities, Vishnu and Shiva, assumed a preeminent position in the Hindu pantheon. Hinduism emphasized the worshiper's personal devotion (*bhakti*) to a particular deity, usually Vishnu, Shiva, or Devi ("the Goddess"). These gods can appear in many guises. They are identified by various cult names and epithets and are represented by a complex symbolism of stories, companion animals, birds, and objects.

Vishnu, the preserver, is a benevolent deity who helps his devotees in time of need. Hindus believe that whenever demonic forces threaten the cosmic order, Vishu appears on earth in a series of *avataras*, or incarnations. Among his incarnations are the legendary hero Rama, the popular cowherd-god Krishna, and the Buddha (a blatant attempt to co-opt the rival religion's founder). Shiva, who lives in ascetic isolation on Mount Kailasa in the Himalayas, is a more ambivalent figure. He represents both creation and destruction, for both are part of a single, cyclical process. He often is represented performing dance steps that symbolize the acts of creation and destruction. Devi manifests herself in various ways—as a full-bodied mother-goddess who promotes fertility and procreation, as the docile and loving wife Parvati, and as the frightening deity who, under the name Kali or Durga, lets loose a torrent of violence and destruction.

Both Shiva and Devi appear to be derived from the Dravidian tradition, in which fertility cult and female deities played a prominent role. Their origin is a telling example of how Aryan and non-Aryan cultures fused to form classic Hindu civilization. It is interesting to note that Vishnu, who has a clear Aryan pedigree, remains more popular in northern India, while Shiva is dominant in the Dravidian south.

The multiplicity of gods (330 million according to one tradition), sects, and local practices within Hinduism is dazzling, reflecting the ethnic, linguistic, and cultural diversity of India. Yet within this variety there is unity. A worshiper's devotion to one god or goddess does not entail denial of the other main deities or the host of lesser divinities and spirits. Ultimately, all are seen as manifestations of a single divine force that pervades the universe. This sense of underlying unity is expressed in many ways: in texts such as the passage from the Bhagavad-Gita quoted at the beginning of this chapter; in the different potentials of women represented in the various manifestations of Devi; in composite statues that are split down the middle—half Shiva, half Vishnu—as if to say that they are complementary aspects of one cosmic principle.

Hinduism offers the worshiper a variety of ways to approach god and obtain divine favor, whether through special knowledge of sacred truths, mental and physical discipline, or extraordinary devotion to the deity. The activity of worship centers on the temples, which range from humble village shrines to magnificent, richly decorated stone edifices built under royal patronage. Beautifully proportioned statues beckon the deity to take up temporary residence within the image, where he or she can be reached and beseeched by eager worshipers. A common form of worship is *puja*, service to the deity, which can take the form of bathing, clothing, or feeding the statue. Potent blessings are conferred on the man or woman to whom *darsan*, a glimpse of the divine image, is given.

Pilgrimage to famous shrines and attendance at festivals offer additional opportunities to

Stone relief depicting Vishnu asleep and dreaming on the ocean floor, from a Vishnu temple at Deogarh (central India), fifth century C.E. Vishnu lies on the coiled body of a giant, multi-headed serpent which he had subdued. The beneficent god of preservation, Vishnu appears in a new *avatara* (incarnation) whenever the world is threatened by demonic forces. The Indian view of the vastness of time is embodied in this mythic image, which conceives of Vishnu as creating and destroying universes as he exhales and inhales. (John C. Huntington)

show devotion. The entire Indian subcontinent is dotted with sacred places where the worshiper can directly perceive and obtain benefit from the inherent power of divinity. Mountains, caves, and certain plants and rocks are enveloped in an aura of mystery and sanctity. The literal meaning of *tirthayatra*, the term for a pilgrimage site, is "journey to a river-crossing," pointing up the frequent association of Hindu sacred places with flowing water. Hindus consider the Ganges River to be especially sacred, and each year millions of devoted worshipers flock to its banks to bathe and receive the restorative and purifying power of its waters. The habit of pilgrimage to the major shrines promotes contact and the exchange of ideas among people from different parts of India and has helped to create a broad Hindu identity and the concept of India as a single civilization, despite enduring political fragmentation.

Religious duties may vary, depending not only on the worshiper's social standing and gender but also on his or her stage of life. A young man from one of the three highest classes (Brahmin, Kshatriya, or Vaishya) undergoes a ritual rebirth through the ceremony of the sacred thread, marking the attainment of manhood and access to religious knowledge. From this point, the ideal life cycle passes through four stages: (1) the young man becomes a student and studies the sacred texts; (2) he then becomes a householder, marries, has children, and acquires material wealth; (3) when his grandchildren are born, he gives up home and family and becomes a forest dweller, meditating on the nature and meaning of existence; (4) he abandons his personal identity altogether and becomes a wandering ascetic awaiting death. In the course of a virtuous life he has fulfilled first his duties to society and then his duties to himself, so that by the end of his life he is so disconnected from the world that he can achieve moksha (liberation).

The successful transformation of a religion based on Vedic antecedents and the ultimate victory of Hinduism over Buddhism—Buddhism was driven from the land of its birth, though it maintains deep roots in Central, East, and Southeast Asia (see Chapters 8 and 11)—is a remarkable phenomenon. Hinduism succeeded by responding to the needs of people for personal deities with whom they could establish direct connections. The austerity of Buddhism in its most authentic form, its denial of the importance of gods, and its expectation that individuals find their own path to enlightenment may have demanded too much of ordinary individuals. And the very features that made Mahayana Buddhism more accessible to the populace—gods, saints, and myths—also made it more easily absorbed into the vast social and cultural fabrics of Hinduism.

IMPERIAL EXPANSION AND COLLAPSE

Political unity, on those rare occasions when it has been achieved, has not lasted for long in India. A number of factors have contributed to India's habitual political fragmentation. The landscape of India—mountains, foothills, plains, forests, steppes, deserts—is extremely varied. Different terrains called forth different forms of organization and economic activity, and the peoples who occupied topographically diverse zones differed from one another in language and cultural practices. Perhaps the most significant barrier to political unity lay in the complex social hierarchy. Individuals identified themselves primarily in terms of their class and caste (birth group); allegiance to a higher political authority was of secondary concern.

Despite these divisive factors, two empires arose in the Ganges Plain: the Mauryan Empire of the fourth to second centuries B.C.E. and the Gupta Empire of the fourth to sixth centuries C.E. Each extended political control over a substantial portion of the subcontinent and expedited the formation of a common Indian civilization.

The Mauryan Empire, 324–184 B.C.E.

Around 600 B.C.E. the landscape of north India was dotted with many separate tribal groups and independent states. The kingdom of Magadha, in eastern India south of the Ganges (see Map 7.1), began to play an increasingly influential role, however, thanks to wealth based on agriculture, iron mines, and its strategic location astride the trade routes of the eastern Ganges Basin. In the late fourth century B.C.E. Chandragupta Maurya, a young man who may have belonged to the Vaishya or Shudra class, gained control of the kingdom of Magadha and expanded it into India's first centralized empire. He may have been inspired by the example of Alexander the Great, who had followed up his conquest of the Persian Empire with a foray into the Punjab (northern Pakistan) in 326 B.C.E. (see Chapter 5).

Indeed, Greek tradition claimed that Alexander met a young Indian native by the name of "Sandracottus," an apparent corruption of "Chandragupta."

The collapse of Greek rule in the Punjab after the death of Alexander created a power vacuum in the northwest. Chandragupta (r. 324–301 B.C.E.) and his successors Bindusara (r. 301–269 B.C.E.) and Ashoka (r. 269–232 B.C.E.) extended Mauryan control over the entire subcontinent except for the southern tip of the peninsula. Not until the height of the Mughal Empire of the seventeenth century C.E. or the advent of British rule in the nineteenth century would so much of India again be under the control of a single government.

Tradition holds that Kautilya, a crafty elderly Brahmin, guided Chandragupta in his conquests and consolidation of power. Kautilya is said to have written a surviving treatise on government, the *Arthashastra*. Although recent studies have shown that the *Arthashastra* in its present form is a product of the third century C.E., its core text may well go back to Kautilya. This coldly pragmatic guide to political success and survival advocates the so-called *mandala* (circle) theory of foreign policy: "My enemy's enemy is my friend." It also relates a long list of schemes for enforcing and increasing the collection of tax revenues, and it prescribes the use of spies to keep watch on everyone in the kingdom.

The Mauryan kings and government were supported by a tax equivalent to one-fourth of the value of the agricultural crop. Administrative districts, based on traditional tribal boundaries, were governed by close relatives and associates of the king. A large national army—with infantry, cavalry, chariot, and elephant divisions—and royal control of mines, shipbuilding, and the manufacture of armaments further secured the power of the central government. Standard coinage issued throughout the empire both fostered support for the government and military apparatus and promoted trade.

The Mauryan capital was at Pataliputra (modern Patna), where five tributaries join the Ganges. Several extant descriptions of the city composed by foreign visitors provide valuable information and testify to the international connections of the Indian monarchs. Surrounded by a timber wall and moat, the city extended along the river for 8 miles (13 kilometers). It was governed by six committees with responsibility for features of urban life such as manufacturing, trade, sales, taxes, the welfare of foreigners, and the registration of births and deaths.

Ashoka, Chandragupta's grandson, is a towering figure in Indian history. At the beginning of his reign he engaged in military campaigns that

A stone pillar inscribed with edicts of King Ashoka, ca. 240 B.C.E. Ashoka, the most powerful and charismatic of the Mauryan kings, became a convert to Buddhism early in his reign. He argued nonviolence, moderation, justice, and religious tolerance on his officials and subjects, and put up inscriptions on stone pillars and great rocks around his realm to broadcast his pronouncements. Many are preserved and constitute the first extant examples of writing in India. (Borromeo/Art Resource, NY)

extended the boundaries of the empire. During his conquest of Kalinga (modern Orissa, a coastal region southeast of Magadha), hundreds of thousands of people were killed, wounded, or deported. The brutality of this victory overwhelmed the young monarch. He became a convert to Buddhism and an exponent of nonviolence, morality, moderation, and religious tolerance both in government and in private life.

Ashoka publicized this program by inscribing edicts on great rocks and polished pillars of sandstone scattered throughout his enormous empire. Among the inscriptions that have survived and constitute the earliest decipherable Indian writing is the following:

> For a long time in the past, for many hundreds of years have increased the sacrificial slaughter of animals, violence toward creatures, unfilial conduct toward kinsmen, improper conduct toward Brahmans and ascetics. Now with the practice of morality by King Devanampiya Piyadasi [Ashoka], the sound of war drums has become the call to morality. . . . You [government officials] are appointed to rule over thousands of human beings in the expectation that you will win the affection of all men. All men are my children. Just as I desire that my children will fare well and be happy in this world and the next, I desire the same for all men. . . . King Devanampiya Piyadasi . . . desires that there should be the growth of the essential spirit of morality or holiness among all sects. . . . There should not be glorification of one's own sect and denunciation of the sect of others for little or no reason. For all the sects are worthy of reverence for one reason or another.[2]

Ashoka, however, was not naive. Despite his commitment to employ peaceful means where possible, he hastened to remind potential transgressors that "the king, remorseful as he is, has the strength to punish the wrongdoers who do not repent."

Commerce and Culture in an Era of Political Fragmentation

The Mauryan Empire prospered for a time after Ashoka's death in 232 B.C.E. Then, weakened by dynastic disputes, it collapsed from the pressure of attacks in the northwest in 184 B.C.E. Five hundred years would pass before another indigenous state was able to extend its control over northern India.

In the meantime, a series of foreign powers dominated the Indus Valley and extended their influence east and south. The first was the Greco-Bactrian kingdom (180–50 B.C.E.), descended from troops and settlers that Alexander the Great had left behind in Afghanistan. Domination by two nomadic peoples from Central Asia followed: the Shakas (known as Scythians in the Mediterranean world) from 50 B.C.E. to 50 C.E. and the Kushans from 50 to 240 C.E. Several foreign kings—most notably the Greco-Bactrian Milinda (Menander in Greek) and the Kushan Kanishka—were converts to Buddhism, a logical choice because Hinduism had no easy mechanism for working foreigners into its system of class and caste. The eastern Ganges region reverted to a patchwork of small principalities, as it had been before the Mauryan era.

This period of political fragmentation in the north also saw the rise of important states in central and southern India, particularly the Andhra, or Satavahana, dynasty in the Deccan (from the second century B.C.E. to the second century C.E.) and the three southern Tamil kingdoms of Cholas, Pandyas, and Cheras (see Map 7.1). Although there were frequent military conflicts among these societies, this was a period of great literary and artistic productivity that manifested itself in poetry, epic, and the performances of troupes of wandering actors and musicians (see Voices and Visions: Tamil Culture).

Indeed, despite the political fragmentation of India in the five centuries after the collapse of the Mauryan Empire, there were many signs of economic, cultural, and intellectual development. The network of roads and towns that had sprung up under the Mauryans fostered lively commerce within the subcontinent, and India was at the heart of international land and sea trade routes that linked China, Southeast Asia, Central Asia, the Middle East, East Africa, and the lands of the Mediterranean. In the absence of a strong central authority, guilds (shreni) of merchants and artisans in the Indian towns became politically powerful, regulating the lives of their members and

Tamil Culture

The majority of the population in southern India speak languages that belong to a non-Indo-European family of languages called Dravidian. The Tamil language of the inhabitants of the southern tip of the peninsula (as well as the northern part of the island of Sri Lanka) is one of these, and the Tamil people have an ancient conception of this region as Tamilakam, "the homeland of the Tamils." In their own traditions they have always lived in this region, but long ago it was much larger, before great floods and tidal waves swallowed up land that now lies beneath the ocean.

Historical evidence, while quite limited for southern India, does point to the existence of Tamil kingdoms from as early as the fifth century B.C.E. The three kingdoms of Pandyas, Cholas, and Cheras, which were in frequent conflict with one another, experienced periods of ascendancy and decline, but persisted in one form or another for two thousand years or more. The period from the third century B.C.E. to the third century C.E. is regarded as a "classical" period in which Tamil society, under the patronage of the Pandya kings and intellectual leadership of the sangham, an academy of 500 authors, produced works of literature on a wide range of topics, including grammatical treatises, collections of ethical proverbs, epics, and shorter poems about love, war, wealth, the beauty of nature, and the joys of music, dance, and drama.

The following passage, from an anthology called "The Ten Idylls," describes the port of Pukar at the mouth of Cauvery River:

At this great ancient and lovely port of Pukar, which has stood forever like a heaven of rare attainments, the fishermen bathe in the confluence to wash off their sin and bathe again in fresh water to wash off the salt. They dash into the waves, play with the crabs, make images in the sands and play throughout the day with never-abating enthusiasm.

In the well-lit storied mansions with high colonnades, young wives whose husbands have joined them, take off their silks and put on fine clothes of cotton. They enjoy the drinks poured out of the receptacles. . . . On the wide highways leading from the port lined with aloes of white blossoms and long leaves are the officials of the kings who collect the customs revenue of the land. They are famous for their honesty and untiring work. . . . The buildings in the bazaar streets rise up to the clouds with many floors and apartments, tall winding stairs of short steps, long corridors and wide and narrow doorways. . . . In the streets below, god-intoxicated girls sing and dance in honor of Muruga in tune to the call of the flute, the sound of the lute and the beat of the drums. . . . Flags fly over the decorated gates of temples, where gods of great repute are enshrined, before which many bow down. . . . Famous scholars, great authorities in knowledge and learning, have raised awe-inspiring flags as a sign of challenge for debates. Flags are seen on the top masts of ships lying at anchor in the beautiful open harbor of Pukar tossing in their moorings like restless elephants moving to and fro."

What physical features of an ancient Tamil city are evident in the passage above? What were the different elements of Tamil society? What kinds of work did they engage in, and what kinds of recreation were available to them?

In the religious sphere, in contrast to the primarily male orientation of Brahmin–dominated northern India, the Tamil south has had a pronounced female orientation. Worship of fertility goddesses in humble local temples has always been strong. The Tamils perceived a potent connection between female chastity and spiritual power, and in their stories they recollected how this power had protected the Tamil lands and culture from internal injustice and outside threats. The epic Silipathikaram tells the story of Kannagi, a heroine who resolutely sets out to prove the innocence of her husband, who had been executed for a crime he did not commit:

"She rose bewildered and fell down on earth
like the moon behind the pouring rain,
and with her eyes blood-shot, she cried and sighed,
'O husband mine, where have you sped'. . .
(She addresses the Sun)
'Thou knowest all in this wide sea-girt earth,
Say if my husband was a thief, O Sun!'
'No thief was he, O dame with jet-black eyes,
This town will be for fire a feast' said he. . .
(Kannagi speaks again)
'Where can I get this solved? This can't be truth.
Even so, unless my anger is appeased
I will not seek to join my husband dear.
The cruel king I will see and demand the right.'
So she said; she rose and stood and paused
Remembering her evil dream, and cried.
She stood and dried her blinding tears and went
And reached the gates of the palace of the king."

Kannagi's quest leads to the death of the unjust king who ordered the execution, the destruction by fire of his capital, and the transformation of Kannagi, who is transported to the skies in a chariot to become the goddess of chastity. What does this story tell us about the importance and influence of women in Tail society? What qualities are expected of them and admired in them? Why might Tamil society have valued these qualities?

Source: Translations from J. M. Somasundaram Pillai, *Two Thousand Years of Tamil Literature* (Madras, 1959), pp. 150–152, 205–211.

having an important say in local affairs. Their economic clout enabled them to serve as patrons of culture and to endow the religious sects to which they adhered—particularly Buddhism and Jainism—with richly decorated temples and monuments.

During the last centuries B.C.E. and first centuries C.E. the two greatest Indian epics, the *Ramayana* and the *Mahabharata*, based on oral predecessors dating back many centuries, achieved their final form. The events of both epics are said to have occurred several million years in the past, but the political forms, social organization, and other elements of cultural context—proud kings, beautiful queens, tribal wars, heroic conduct, and chivalric values—seem to reflect the conditions of the early Vedic period, when Aryan warrior societies were moving into the Ganges Plain.

The vast pageant of the *Mahabharata* (it is eight times the length of the Greek *Iliad* and *Odyssey* combined) tells the story of two sets of cousins, the Pandavas and Kauravas, whose quarrel over succession to the throne leads them to a cata-

Wall painting from the caves at Ajanta (central India), seventh century C.E. Kings and other wealthy patrons donated lavishly for the construction and decoration of Buddhist, Hindu, and Jain religious shrines, including elaborate complexes of caves. At Ajanta, twenty-nine caves are filled with paintings and relief sculpture illustrating religious and secular scenes. This segment represents a visit of envoys from Persia or Central Asia to the court of an Indian monarch. The ruler, seen at left on his pillow-covered throne, is surrounded by male and female members of court. The envoys, at bottom right, who have non-Indian facial features and wear long coats, are presenting gifts to the king. (Harvard College Library)

clysmic battle at the field of Kurukshetra. The battle is so destructive on all sides that the eventual winner, Yudhishthira, is reluctant to accept the fruits of so tragic a victory.

The Bhagavad-Gita, quoted at the beginning of this chapter, is a self-contained (and perhaps originally separate) episode set in the midst of those events. The great hero Arjuna, at first reluctant to fight his own kinsmen, is tutored by the god Krishna and learns the necessity of fulfilling his duty as a warrior. Death means nothing in a universe in which souls will be reborn again and again. The climactic moment comes when Krishna reveals his true appearance—awesome and overwhelmingly powerful—and his identity as time itself, the force behind all creation and destruction. The Bhagavad Gita offers an attractive resolution to the tension in Indian civilization between duty to society and duty to one's own soul. Disciplined action—that is, action taken without regard for any personal benefits that might derive from it—is a form of service to the gods and will be rewarded by release from the cycle of rebirths.

This era also saw significant advances in science and technology. Indian doctors had a wide knowledge of herbal remedies and were in demand in the courts of western and southern Asia. Indian scholars made impressive strides in the field of linguistics. Panini (late fourth century B.C.E.) undertook a remarkably detailed analysis of the word forms and grammar of the Sanskrit language. He and the commentators who built on his work contributed to a standardization of Sanskrit usage which arrested its natural development and turned it into a formal, literary language. Prakrits—popular dialects—emerged to become the ancestors of the modern Indo-European languages of northern and central India.

The Gupta Empire, 320–550 C.E.

In the early fourth century C.E. a new imperial entity coalesced in northern India. Like its Mauryan predecessor, the Gupta Empire grew out of the kingdom of Magadha on the Ganges Plain and had its capital at Pataliputra. There can be no clearer proof that the founder of this empire consciously modeled himself on the Mauryans

than the fact that he called himself Chandra Gupta (r. 320–335), borrowing the very name of the Mauryan founder. A claim to wide dominion was embodied in the title that the monarchs of this dynasty assumed—"Great King of Kings"— although they never controlled territories as extensive as those of the Mauryans. Nevertheless, over the fifteen-year reign of Chandra Gupta and the forty-year reigns of his three successors— Samudra Gupta, Chandra Gupta II, and Kumara Gupta—Gupta power and influence reached across northern and central India, west to Punjab and east to Bengal, north to Kashmir and south into the Deccan (see Map 7.1).

This new empire enjoyed the same strategic advantages as its Mauryan predecessor, sitting astride important trade routes, exploiting the agricultural productivity of the Ganges Plain, and controlling nearby iron deposits. It adopted similar methods for raising revenue and administering broad territories. The chief source of revenue was a tax on agriculture, requiring that one-fourth of the annual produce be paid to the state. Those who used the irrigation network also had to pay for the service, and there were special taxes on particular commodities. The state maintained monopolies in key areas, such as the mining of metals and salt, owned extensive tracts of farmland, and demanded a specified number of days of labor annually from the citizens for the construction and upkeep of roads, wells, and the irrigation network.

Gupta control, however, was never as effectively centralized as Mauryan authority. The Gupta administrative bureaucracy and intelligence network were smaller and less pervasive. A powerful army maintained tight control and taxation in the core of the empire, but outlying areas were left to their governors to organize. The position of governor offered tempting opportunities to exploit the populace. It often was hereditary, passed on to high-ranking members of the civil and military administration. Distant subordinate vassal kingdoms and tribal areas were expected to make annual donations of tribute, and certain key frontier points were garrisoned to keep open the lines of trade and expedite the collection of customs duties.

Historians often point to the Gupta Empire as a good example of a "theater-state." Limited in its ability to enforce its will on outlying areas, it instead found ways to "persuade" others to follow its lead. One medium of persuasion was the splendor, beauty, and order of life at the capital and royal court. A constant round of rituals, ceremonies, and cultural events were a potent advertisement for the benefits that derived from association with the empire.

The relationship of ruler and subjects in a theater-state also has an economic base. The center is a focal point for the collection and redistribution of luxury goods and profits from trade through the exchange of gifts and other means of sharing accumulated resources with dependents. Subordinate princes sought to emulate the Gupta center on whatever scale they could manage, and to maintain close ties through visits, gifts, and intermarriage.

Because the moist climate of the Ganges Plain does not favor the preservation of buildings and artifacts, there is for the Gupta era, as for earlier eras in Indian history, relatively little archaeological data. An eyewitness account, however, provides valuable information about the Gupta kingdom and Pataliputra, its capital city. A Chinese Buddhist monk named Faxian made a pilgrimage to the homeland of his faith around 400 C.E. and left a record of his journey:

> The royal palace and halls in the midst of the city, which exist now as of old, were all made by spirits which [King Ashoka] employed, and which piled up the stones, reared the walls and gates, and executed the elegant carving and inlaid sculpture-work—in a way which no human hands of this world could accomplish. . . . By the side of the stupa of Ashoka, there has been made a Mahayana [Buddhist] monastery, very grand and beautiful; there is also a Hinayana one; the two together containing six hundred or seven hundred monks. The rules of demeanor and the scholastic arrangements in them are worthy of observation. . . . The cities and towns of this country are the greatest of all in the Middle Kingdom. The inhabitants are rich and prosperous, and vie with one another in the practice of benevolence and righteousness. . . . The heads of the Vaishya families in them establish in the cities houses for dispensing charity and medicines. All the poor and destitute in the country, orphans, widowers, and childless men, maimed people and cripples, and all who are diseased, go to those houses, and are provided with every kind of help.[3]

The endeavors of astronomers, mathematicians, and other scientists received royal support. Indian mathematicians invented the concept of zero and developed a revolutionary system of place-value notation that is in use in most parts of the world today (see Environment and Technology: Indian Mathematics).

The Gupta kings were also patrons of the arts. A number of the works of drama of this age were love stories, providing us glimpses of the lifestyle and manners of high society. The greatest of all ancient Indian dramatists, Kalidasa, was active in the reign of Chandra Gupta II (r. 375–415). Seven of his plays survive, written in the elite Sanskrit and everyday Prakrit of the time. As the Athenian dramatists of the fifth century B.C.E. had drawn their plots from the legendary tradition preserved in Homer but altered details and reworked the characters to comment on the values and issues of their own times, so Kalidasa refashioned elements drawn from the great Indian epics. In Indian legend a female heroine named Shakuntala resolutely pursued a prince who had forgotten his promise that the child who resulted from their brief love affair in the forest would inherit his throne. In *Shakuntala or the Ring of Recollection*, Kalidasa turned Shakuntala into a largely docile figure animated more by forlorn love than by confident self-assertion. In this way he validated the prevailing conception of women, emphasizing the importance of female passivity, chastity, and devotion to the husband. This and other evidence seem to indicate that women's situations worsened after the Vedic period.

In all likelihood, this development was similar to developments in Mesopotamia from the second millennium B.C.E., Archaic and Classical Greece, and China from the first millennium B.C.E. In these civilizations, several factors—urbanization, the formation of increasingly complex political and social structures, and the emergence of a nonagricultural middle class that placed high value on the acquisition and inheritance of property—led to a loss of women's rights and increased male control over women's

Indian Mathematics

The so-called Arabic numerals used in most parts of the world today were developed in India. The Indian system of place-value notation was far more efficient than the unwieldy numerical systems of Egyptians, Greeks, and Romans, and the invention of zero was a profound intellectual achievement. Indeed, it has to be ranked as one of the most important and influential discoveries in human history. This system is used even more widely than the alphabet derived from the Phoenicians (see Chapter 4) and is, in one sense, the only truly universal language.

In its fully developed form the Indian method of arithmetic notation employed a base-ten system. It had separate columns for ones, tens, hundreds, and so forth, as well as a zero sign to indicate the absence of units in a given column. This system makes possible the economical expression of even very large numbers. And it allows for the performance of calculations that were not possible in a system like the numerals of the Romans, where any real calculation had to be done mentally or on some sort of counting board.

A series of early Indian inscriptions using the numerals from 1 to 9 are deeds of property given to religious institutions by kings or other wealthy individuals. They were incised in the Sanskrit language on copper plates. The earliest known example has a date equivalent to 595 C.E. A sign for zero is attested by the eighth century. Other textual evidence leads to the inference that a place-value system and the zero concept were already known in the fifth century.

This Indian system spread to the Middle East, Southeast Asia, and East Asia by the seventh century. Other peoples quickly recognized its capabilities and adopted it, sometimes using indigenous symbols. Europe received the new technology somewhat later. Gerbert of Aurillac, a French Christian monk, spent time in Spain between 967 and 970, where he was exposed to the mathematics of the Arabs. A great scholar and teacher who eventually became Pope Sylvester II (r. 999–1003), he spread word of the "Arabic" system in the Christian West.

Knowledge of the Indian system of mathematical notation seems to have spread throughout Europe primarily through the use of a mechanical calculating device, an improved version of the Roman counting board, with counters inscribed with variants of the Indian numeral forms. Because the counters could be turned sideways or upside down, at first there was considerable variation in the forms. But by the twelfth century they had become standardized into forms close to those in use today. As the capabilities of the place-value system for written calculations became clear, the counting board fell into disuse. The abandonment of this device led to the adoption of the zero sign—not necessary on the counting board, where a column could be left empty—by the twelfth century.

Why was this marvelous system of mathematical notation invented in ancient India? The answer may lie in the way in which the range and versatility of this number system corresponds to elements of Indian cosmology. The Indians conceived of immense spans of time—trillions of years (far exceeding current scientific estimates of the age of the universe as between 15 billion and 20 billion years old)—during which innumerable universes like our own were created, existed for a finite time, then were destroyed. In one popular creation myth Vishnu is slumbering on the coils of a giant serpent at the bottom of the ocean and worlds are being created and destroyed as he exhales and inhales. In Indian thought our world, like others, has existed for a series of epochs lasting more than 4 million years, yet the period of its existence is but a brief and insignificant moment in the vast sweep of time. The Indians developed a number system that allowed them to express concepts of this magnitude.

From another perspective, the goal of both Hindu and Buddhist devotees was to escape from the toilsome cycle of lives and to achieve a state akin to nonexistence. The philosophical/religious concepts of moksha and nirvana correspond to the numerical concept of zero.

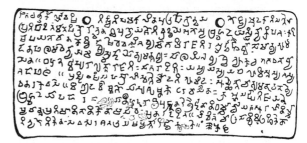

Copper plate from western India (Facsimile by Georges Ifrah. Reproduced by permission of Georges Ifrah)

behavior. Over time women in India lost the right to own or inherit property. They were barred from studying sacred texts and participating in the sacrificial ritual and in many respects were treated as equivalent to the lowest class, the Shudra. As in Confucian China, they were expected to obey first their father, then their husband, and finally their sons (see Chapter 6). Girls were married at an increasingly early age, sometimes as young as six or seven. This practice meant that the prospective husband could be sure of his wife's virginity and, by bringing her up in his own household, could train and shape her to suit his purposes.

Some women escaped these instruments of male control. One way to do so was by entering a Jainist or Buddhist religious community. Women who belonged to powerful families and courtesans trained in poetry and music as well as in ways of providing sexual pleasure had high social standing and sometimes gave money for the erection of Buddhist stupas and other shrines. In the emerging Hindu culture, however, a woman's primary *dharma*, or duty, was to be a mother and wife. The most extreme form of control of women's conduct took place in certain parts of India where a widow was expected to cremate herself on her husband's funeral pyre. This ritual, called *sati*, was seen as a way of keeping a woman "pure." Women who declined to make this ultimate gesture of devotion to a deceased husband were forbidden to remarry, shunned socially, and given little opportunity to earn a living.

The period of political fragmentation between the eclipse of the Mauryan Empire and the rise of the Guptas had seen the development of extensive networks of trade within India, as well as the creation of land and sea routes to foreign lands. This vibrant commerce continued into the Gupta period. Coined money served as the medium of exchange, and well-organized artisan guilds played an influential role in the economic, political, and religious life of the towns. The Guptas sought control of the ports on the Arabian Sea but saw a decline in trade with the weakened Roman Empire. In compensation, trade with Southeast and East Asia was on the rise. Adventurous merchants from the ports of eastern and southern India made the sea voyage to the Malay Peninsula and islands of Indonesia in order to exchange Indian cotton cloth, ivory, metalwork, and exotic animals for Chinese silk or Indonesian spices. The overland silk route from China also continued in operation but was vulnerable to disruption by Central Asian nomads.

The Mauryans had been Buddhists, but the Gupta monarchs were Hindus. They revived ancient Vedic practices to bring an aura of sanctity to their position, and this period also saw a reassertion of the importance of class and caste and the influence of Brahmin priests. Nevertheless, it was an era of religious tolerance. The Gupta kings were patrons for Hindu, Buddhist, and Jain endeavors. Buddhist monasteries with hundreds or even thousands of monks and nuns in residence flourished in the cities. Northern India was the destination of Buddhist pilgrims from Southeast and East Asia, traveling to visit the birthplace of their faith.

The classic form of the Hindu temple evolved during the Gupta era. Sitting atop a raised platform surmounted by high towers, the temple was patterned on the sacred mountain or palace in which the gods of mythology resided, and it represented the inherent order of the universe. From an exterior courtyard worshipers approached the central shrine, where the statue of the deity stood. In the best-endowed sanctuaries paintings or sculptured depictions of gods and mythical events covered the walls. Cave-temples carved out of rock were also richly adorned with frescoes or with sculpture.

By the later fifth century C.E. the Gupta Empire was coming under pressure from the Xiongnu. These nomadic invaders from the steppes of Central Asia poured into the northwest corridor. Defense of this distant frontier region eventually exhausted the imperial treasury, and the empire collapsed by 550.

The early seventh century saw a brief but glorious revival of imperial unity. Harsha Vardhana (r. 606–647), ruler of the region around Delhi, extended his power over the northern plain and moved his capital to Kanauj on the Ganges River. We have an account of the life and long reign of this fervent Buddhist, poet, patron of artists, and dynamic warrior, written by the courtier Bana. In addition, the Chinese Buddhist pilgrim Xuanzang (600–664) left an account of his travels in

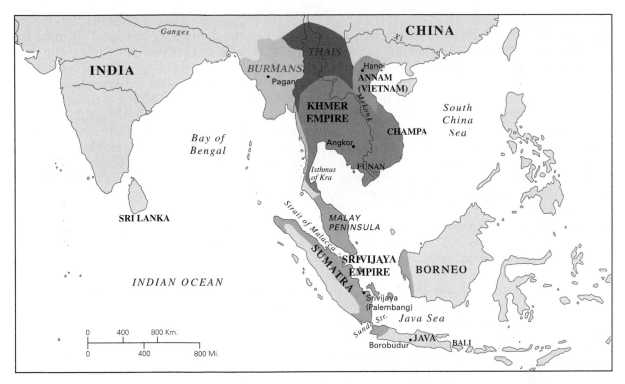

Map 7.2 Southeast Asia The position of Southeast Asia between the ancient centers of civilization in India and China had a major impact on its history. A series of powerful and wealthy states arose in the first millennium C.E. by gaining control of major trade routes: first Funan, based in southern Vietnam and the Malay peninsula, then Srivijaya on the island of Sumatra, followed by a number of states on the island of Java. Shifts in the trade route led to the demise of one and the rise of another.

India during Harsha's reign. After Harsha's death, northern India reverted to its customary state of political fragmentation and would remain divided until the Islamic invasions of the eleventh and twelfth centuries (see Chapter 15).

During the centuries of Gupta ascendancy and decline in the north, the Deccan Plateau in central India and the southern part of the peninsula had a separate existence. In this region the landscape was more segmented by mountains, rocky plateaus, tropical forests, and sharply cut river courses than in the broad northern plains, and there were multiple small centers of power. The village-based inhabitants of the lowland plains and river basins found themselves in conflict with tribal peoples from the uplands and forest.

From the seventh to twelfth centuries the Pallavas, Cholas, and other warrior dynasties collected tribute and plundered as far as their strength permitted, storing their wealth in urban fortresses. These rulers sought legitimacy and fame as patrons of religion and culture, and much of the distinguished art and architecture of the period was produced in the kingdoms of the south (see Voices and Visions: Tamil Culture). These kingdoms also served as the conduit through which Indian religion and culture reached Southeast Asia.

SOUTHEAST ASIA

Southeast Asia consists of three geographical zones: the Indochina mainland, the Malay Peninsula, and thousands of islands extending on an east-west axis far out into the Pacific Ocean (see Map 7.2). Encompassing a vast area of land and water, today this region is occupied by the countries of Myanmar (Burma), Thailand, Laos, Cambodia, Vietnam, Malaysia, Singapore, Indonesia, Brunei, and the Philippines. Poised between the ancient centers of China and India, Southeast Asia has been influenced by the cultures of both civilizations. The region first rose to prominence and prosperity because of its intermediate role in the trade exchanges between southern and eastern Asia.

The strategic importance of Southeast Asia is enhanced by the region's natural resources. This is a geologically active zone; the islands are the tops of a chain of volcanoes. Lying along the equator, Southeast Asia has a tropical climate. The temperature hovers around 80 degrees Fahrenheit (30 degrees Celsius), and the monsoon winds provide dependable rainfall throughout the year. There are several growing cycles each year, so the region is capable of supporting a large human population. The most fertile agricultural lands lie along the floodplains of the largest silt-bearing rivers or contain rich volcanic soil deposited by ancient eruptions.

Early Civilization

Rain forest covers much of Southeast Asia. Rain forest ecosystems are particularly fragile because of the great local variation of plant forms within them and because of the vulnerability of their soil to loss of fertility if the protection of the forest canopy is removed. As early as 2000 B.C.E. this circumstance led to the development of *slash-and-burn agriculture*, a system in which a patch of land is cleared for farming by cutting and burning the vegetation growing on it. The land, known as *swidden*, is farmed for several years, then abandoned and reclaimed by the forest.

A number of plant and animal species that first developed in Southeast Asia spread to other regions. These included wet rice (rice cultivated in deliberately flooded fields), soybeans, sugar cane, yams, bananas, coconuts, cocoyams, chickens, and pigs. Rice was the staple food product, for even though rice cultivation is labor-intensive (see Chapter 3), it can support a large population.

The indigenous population of this region consisted primarily of Malay peoples. Historians believe that rising population and disputes within communities prompted streams of people to leave the Southeast Asian mainland in the longest-lasting movement of colonization in human history. By the first millennium B.C.E. the inhabitants of Southeast Asia had developed impressive navigational skills. They knew how to ride the monsoon winds and to interpret the patterns of swells, winds, clouds, and bird and sea life. Over a period of several thousand years groups of Malays in large double outrigger canoes spread out across the Pacific and Indian Oceans—half of the circumference of the earth—to settle thousands of islands.

The inhabitants of Southeast Asia tended to cluster along the banks of rivers or in the fertile volcanic plains. Fields and villages were never far from the rain forest, with its wild animals and numerous plant species. Forest trees provided fruit, wood, and spices. The shallow waters surrounding the islands teemed with fish. This region was also an early center of metallurgy, particularly bronze. Metalsmiths heated bronze to the requisite temperature for shaping by using hollow bamboo tubes to funnel a stream of oxygen to the furnace.

Political units at first were small. The size of the fundamental unit reflected the number of people who drew water from the same source. Water resource "boards," whose members were representatives from the leading families of the different villages involved, met periodically to allocate and schedule the use of this critical resource.

The early centuries C.E. saw the emergence of larger states. This development was a response to two powerful forces: commerce and Hindu/Buddhist culture. First, Southeast Asia was strategically sited along what turned out to be a new international trade route carrying Chinese silk to India and the Mediterranean. The movements of nomadic peoples had disrupted the old land route across Central Asia. But in India there was increasing demand for silk—for domestic use and for transshipment to the Arabian Gulf and Red Sea to satisfy the fast-growing luxury market in the Roman Empire. At first a sea-land-sea route developed between India, the Isthmus of Kra on the Malay peninsula, and the South China Sea. Over time merchants extended this exchange network to encompass goods from Southeast Asia, including aromatic woods, resins, and spices such as cinnamon, pepper, cloves, and nutmeg. Southeast Asian centers rose to prominence by serving this trade network and controlling key points.

The second force leading to the rise of larger political entities was the influence of Hindu/Buddhist culture imported from India. Commerce brought Indian merchants and sailors into the ports of Southeast Asia. As Buddhism spread, Southeast Asia became a way station for Indian missionaries and East Asian pilgrims on their way to and from the birthplace of their faith. Indian cosmology, rituals, art, and statecraft constituted a rich treasury of knowledge and a source of prestige and legitimacy for local rulers who adopted them. The use of Sanskrit terms such as *maharaja* (great king), the adaptation of Indian ceremonial practices and forms of artistic representation, and the employment of scribes skilled in writing all proved invaluable to the most ambitious and capable Southeast Asian rulers.

The first major Southeast Asian center, called "Funan" by Chinese visitors, flourished between the first and sixth centuries C.E. Its capital was at the modern site of Oc-Eo in southern Vietnam (see Map 7.2). Funan occupied the delta of the Mekong River, a "rice bowl" capable of supporting a large population.

By extending its control over most of southern Indochina and the Malay Peninsula, Funan was able to dominate a key point on the trade route from India to China—the Isthmus of Kra. Seaborne merchants from the ports of northeast India found that offloading their goods from ships and carrying them across the narrow strip of land was both safer and quicker than making the thousand-mile (sixteen-hundred-kilometer) voyage around the Malay Peninsula—a dangerous trip marked by treacherous currents, rocky shoals, and pirates. Once the portage across the isthmus was finished, the merchants needed food and lodging while they waited for the monsoon winds to shift so that they could make the

A stone image of Durga, a fierce manifestation of the Goddess, slaying the buffalo demon, from Java, thirteenth century C.E. The Goddess, one of the three major Hindu divinities, appeared in a number of complementary manifestations. The most dramatic is Durga, a murderous warrior equipped with multiple divine weapons. That the same divine figure could, in its other manifestations, represent life-bringing fertility and docile wifely duties in the household, shows how attuned was Indian thought to the interconnections among different aspects of life. (Eliot Elisofon Collection, Harry Ransom Humanities Center, University of Texas, Austin)

last leg of the voyage to China by sea. Funan stockpiled food and provided security for those engaged in this trade—in return, most probably, for customs duties and other fees.

According to one legend (a sure indicator of the influence of Indian culture in this region), the kingdom of Funan arose out of the marriage of an Indian Brahmin and a local princess. Chinese observers have left reports of the prosperity and sophistication of Funan, emphasizing the presence of walled cities, palaces, archives, systems of taxation, and state-organized agriculture. Nevertheless, for reasons not yet clear to modern historians, Funan declined in the sixth century. The most likely explanation is that international trade routes changed, bypassing Funan.

The Srivijayan Kingdom

By the sixth century, a new, all-sea route had developed. Merchants and travelers from south India and Sri Lanka sailed through the Strait of Malacca (lying between the west side of the Malay Peninsula and the northeast coast of the large island of Sumatra) and into the South China Sea. This route presented both human and navigational hazards, but it significantly shortened the journey.

Another factor promoting the use of this route was a decline in the demand of the Eastern Roman (Byzantine) Empire for imported Chinese silk. Christian monks had hidden silkworms in bamboo stalks, smuggled them out of China, and brought them to Constantinople, thereby exposing the secret of silk production and breaking the Chinese monopoly.

A new center of power, Srivijaya—Sanskrit for "Great Conquest"—was dominating the new southerly route by the late seventh century C.E. The capital of the Srivijayan kingdom was at modern-day Palembang, 50 miles (80 kilometers) up the Musi River from the southeastern coast of Sumatra. Srivijaya had a good natural harbor on a broad and navigable river and a productive agricultural hinterland. The kingdom was well situated to control the southern part of the Malay Peninsula, Sumatra, parts of Java and Borneo, and the Malacca and Sunda straits—vital passageways for shipping (see Map 7.2).

The Srivijayan capital, one of several thriving Sumatran river ports, gained ascendancy over its rivals and assumed control of the international trade route by fusing four distinct ecological zones into an interdependent network. The core area was the productive agricultural plain along the Musi River. The king and administrative specialists—clerks, scribes, judges, and tax collectors—whom he employed controlled this zone directly. Less direct was the king's control of the second zone, the upland regions of Sumatra's interior that were the source of commercially valuable forest products. The local rulers of this area were bound to the center in a dependent relationship held together by oaths of loyalty, elaborate court ceremonies, and the sharing of profits from trade. The third zone consisted of river ports that had been Srivijaya's main rivals. They were conquered and controlled thanks to an alliance between Srivijaya and neighboring sea nomads, pirates who served as a Srivijayan navy as long as the king guaranteed them a steady income.

The fourth zone was the fertile "rice bowl" on the central plain of the nearby island of Java—a region so productive, because of its volcanic soil, that it houses and feeds the majority of the population of present-day Indonesia. Srivijayan monarchs maintained alliances with several ruling dynasties that controlled this region. The alliances were cemented by intermarriage, and the Srivijayan kings even claimed descent from the main Javanese dynasty. These arrangements gave Srivijaya easy access to the large quantities of foodstuffs needed by the people living in the capital and by the merchants and sailors visiting the various ports.

The kings of Srivijaya who constructed and maintained this complex network of social, political, and economic relationships were men of extraordinary energy and skill. Although their authority depended in part on force, it owed much more to diplomatic and even theatrical talents. Like the Gupta monarchy, Srivijaya should be seen as a theater-state, securing its position of prominence and binding dependents to it by its sheer splendor and its ability to attract labor resources, talent, and luxury products. According to one tradition, the Srivijayan monarch was so wealthy that he deposited bricks of gold in the river estuary to appease the local gods, and a hillside near town was said to be covered with silver and gold images of the Buddha to which devotees brought lotus-shaped vessels of gold. The gold originated in West Africa and came to

Southeast Asia through trade with the Muslim world (see Chapter 8).

The Srivijayan king was believed to have great magical powers. He mediated between the spiritually potent realms of the mountains and the sea, and he embodied powerful forces of fertility associated with the rivers in flood. His capital and court were the scene of ceremonies designed to dazzle observers and reinforce the image of wealth, power, and sanctity surrounding the king. Subjects and visitors recognized the king as a "winner" and wanted to be associated with his success. Subordinate rulers took oaths of loyalty that carried dire threats of punishment for violations, and in their own home locales they imitated the splendid ceremonials of the capital.

The kings built and patronized Buddhist monasteries and schools. In central Java local dynasties allied with Srivijaya built magnificent temple complexes to advertise their glory. Borobodur, the most famous of these, was the largest human construction in the Southern Hemisphere. The winding ascent through the ten tiers of this virtual mountain of volcanic stone is a Buddhist allegory for the progressive enlightenment of the soul. Numerous sculptured reliefs depicting Buddhist legends provide modern viewers with glimpses of daily life in early Java.

In all of this, the cultural influence of India was paramount. Shrewd Malay rulers looked to Indian traditions to supply conceptual rationales for kingship and social order. They utilized Indian models of bureaucracy and the Sanskrit system of writing to expedite government business. Their special connection to powerful gods and higher knowledge raised them above their rivals. Southeast Asia's central position on long-distance trade routes and pilgrimage routes guaranteed the presence of foreigners with useful skills to serve as priests, scribes, and administrators. Hindu beliefs and social structures have survived to this day on the island of Bali, east of Java. Even more influential was Buddhism because of the flow of Buddhist pilgrims and missionaries between East Asia and India.

The Southeast Asian kingdoms, however, were not just passive recipients of Indian culture. They took what was useful to them and synthesized it with indigenous beliefs, values, and in-

stitutions—for example, local concepts of chiefship, ancestor worship, and forms of oaths. Moreover, they trained their own people in the new ways, so that the bureaucracy contained

View of the Buddhist monument at Borobodur, Java The powerful dynasties which emerged in Sumatra (Srivijaya) and Java were influenced by Indian religion and statecraft. The great monument at Borobodur in central Java was begun around 780 C.E. by the Sailendra dynasty. It is the largest human construction in the southern hemisphere, more than 300 feet (90 meters) in length and over 100 feet (30 meters) high. Pilgrims made a three-mile-long winding ascent through ten levels which represents the ideal Buddhist journey from ignorance to enlightenment. (From N. J. Krom and T. Van Erp, *Beschrijving van Barabudur* (The Hague: Martinus Nijhoff, 1916) Reproduced with permission)

Important Events in India and Southeast Asia

1500 B.C.E.	Migration of Indo-European peoples into northwest India
1000	Indo-European groups move into the Ganges Plain
500	Siddhartha Gautama (the Buddha) and Mahavira found Buddhism and Jainism
324	Chandragupta Maurya becomes king of Magadha and lays foundation for Mauryan Empire
184	Fall of Mauryan Empire
First Century C.E.	Establishment of Funan, first major center in Southeast Asia
320	Chandra Gupta establishes Gupta Empire
550	Collapse of Gupta Empire
606–647	Reign of Harsha Vardhana
683	Rise of Srivijaya in Sumatra
1025	Collapse of Srivijaya

both foreign experts and native disciples. The whole process was a cultural dialogue between India and Southeast Asia, one in which both partners were active participants.

The kings of Srivijaya carried out this marvelous balancing act for centuries. However, the system they erected was vulnerable to various external forces, including shifts in the pattern of international trade. Some such dynamic must have contributed to the collapse of Srivijaya in the eleventh century, even though the immediate cause was a destructive raid on the Srivijayan capital by forces of the Chola kingdom of southeast India.

Despite the decline of Srivijaya, the maritime realm of Southeast Asia remained prosperous and connected to the international network of trade. The impetus passed to new, vigorous kingdoms on the eastern end of the island of Java.

At one end of these long-distance trade routes lay the lands of western Europe. Goods and occasional reports from South and Southeast Asia long continued to filter west, and some Europeans were aware of this region as a source of

spices and other luxury items. Some four centuries after the decline of Srivijaya, an Italian navigator serving under the flag of Spain—Christopher Columbus—would embark on a westward course across the Atlantic Ocean, seeking to establish a direct route to the fabled "Indies" from which the spices came.

CONCLUSION

This chapter traces the emergence of complex societies in South and Southeast Asia between the second millennium B.C.E. and the first millennium C.E. Because of the migrations of people, trade, and the spread of belief systems, an Indian style of civilization spread throughout the subcontinent and adjoining regions and eventually made its way to the mainland and island chains of Southeast Asia. In this period were laid cultural foundations that in large measure still characterize these regions.

The development and spread of belief systems—Vedism, Buddhism, Jainism, and Hinduism—has a central place in this chapter, because nearly all the sources from which scholars can reconstruct the story of antiquity in this part of the world come from the religious sphere. A visitor to a museum who examines the artifacts from ancient Mesopotamia, Egypt, the Greco-Roman Mediterranean, China, and India will find that objects originally located in a religious shrine or having a primarily cultic function compose a prominent part of the collection. Only in the Indian case, however, would the artifacts be almost exclusively drawn from the religious sphere.

The prolific use of writing came later to India than to other parts of the Eastern Hemisphere, for reasons particular to the Indian situation. As with artifacts, the vast majority of ancient Indian texts are of a religious nature. Ancient Indians did not generate historiographic texts of the kind written elsewhere in the ancient world, primarily because they held a strikingly different view of time. Mesopotamian scribes compiled lists of political and military events and the strange celestial and earthly phenomena that coincided with them. They were inspired by a cyclical conception of time and believed that the recurrence of an omen at some future date signaled a repetition of the historical event associated with it. Greek and Roman historians described and analyzed the progress of wars and the character of rulers. They believed that these accounts would prove useful because of the essential constancy of human nature and the value for future leaders and planners of understanding the past as a sequence of causally linked events. Chinese annalists set down the deeds and conduct of rulers as inspirational models of right conduct. In contrast, the distinctive Indian view of time—as vast epochs in which universes are created and destroyed again and again and the essential spirit of living creatures is reincarnated repeatedly—made the particulars of any brief moment appear to be relatively unilluminating.

The tension between divisive and unifying forces can be seen in many aspects of Indian life. Political and social division has been the norm throughout much of South Asian history. It is a consequence of the topographical and environmental diversity of the subcontinent and the complex mix of ethnic and linguistic groups inhabiting it. The elaborate structure of classes and castes was a response to this diversity—an attempt to organize the population and locate individuals within an accepted hierarchy, as well as to regulate group interactions. Strong central governments, like those of the Mauryan and Gupta kings, gained ascendancy for a time and promoted prosperity and development. However, as in Archaic Greece and Warring States China, the periods of fragmentation and multiple small centers of power seemed to be as economically and intellectually fertile and dynamic as the periods of unity.

India possessed many of the advanced technologies available elsewhere in the ancient world—agriculture, irrigation, metallurgy, textile manufacture, monumental construction, military technology, writing, and systems of administration. But of all the ancient societies, India made the most profound contribution to mathematics, devising the so-called Arabic numerals used al-most everywhere on the planet (see Environment and Technology: Indian Mathematics).

Many distinctive social and intellectual features of Indian civilization—the class and caste system, models of kingship and statecraft, and Vedic, Jainist, and Buddhist belief systems—originated in the great river valleys of the north, where descendants of Indo-European immigrants came to dominate. Hinduism, however, also contained elements drawn from the Dravidian cultures of the south and from Buddhism. Hindu beliefs and practices are less fixed and circumscribed than the beliefs and practices of Judaism, Christianity, and Islam, which rely on clearly defined textual and organizational sources of authority. The capacity of the Hindu tradition to absorb and assimilate a wide range of popular beliefs facilitated the gradual spread of a common Indian civilization across the subcontinent, although there was, and is, considerable variation from one region to another.

This same malleable quality also came into play as the pace of international commerce quickened in the first millennium C.E. and Indian merchants embarking by sea for East Asia passed through Funan, Srivijaya, and other commercial centers in Southeast Asia. Indigenous elites in Southeast Asia came into contact with Indian merchants, sailors, and pilgrims. They found elements of Indian civilization attractive and useful, and they fused it with their own traditions to create a culture unique to Southeast Asia. Chapter 8 describes how the networks of long-distance trade and communication established in the Eastern Hemisphere in antiquity continued to expand and foster technological and cultural development in the subsequent era.

SUGGESTED READING

A useful starting point for the Indian subcontinent is Karl J. Schmidt, *An Atlas and Survey of South Asian History* (1995), with maps and facing text illustrating geographic, environmental, cultural, and historical features of South Asian civilization. Concise discussions of the history of ancient India can be found in Stanley Wolpert, *A New History of India* (3rd edition, 1989), and Romila Thapar, *A History of India, volume I* (1966). D. D. Kosambi, *Ancient India: A History of Its Culture and Civilization* (1965) is a fuller presentation.

Ainslie T. Embree, *Sources of Indian Tradition, volume 1* (2nd edition, 1988), contains translations of primary texts, with the emphasis almost entirely on religion and few materials from southern India. Barbara Stoler Miller, *The Bhagavad-Gita: Krishna's Counsel in Time of War* (1986), is a readable translation of this ancient classic with a useful introduction and notes. An abbreviated version of the greatest Indian epic can be found in R. K. Narayan, *The Mahabharata: A Shortened Modern Prose Version of the Indian Epic* (1978). The filmed version of Peter Brook's stage production of *The Mahabharata* (3 videos—1989) generated much controversy because of its British director and multicultural cast, but is a painless introduction to the plot and main characters. For those who want to sample the fascinating document on state-building supposedly composed by the advisor to the founder of the Mauryan Empire, see T. N. Ramaswamy, *Essentials of Indian Statecraft: Kautilya's Arthasastra for Contemporary Readers* (1962). James Legge, *The Travels of Fa-hien: Fa-hien's Record of Buddhistic Kingdoms* (1971), and John W. McCrindle, *Ancient India as Described by Megasthenes and Arrian* (1877), provide translations of reports of foreign visitors to ancient India.

A number of works explore political institutions and ideas in ancient India: Charles Drekmeier, *Kingship and Community in Early India* (1962); John W. Spellman, *Political Theory of Ancient India: A Study of Kingship from the Earliest Times to Circa A.D. 300* (1964); and R. S. Sharma, *Aspects of Political Ideas and Institutions in Ancient India* (2nd edition, 1968). Romila Thapar, *Asoka and the Decline of the Mauryas* (1963), is a detailed study of the most interesting and important Maurya king.

For fundamental Indian social and religious conceptions, see David R. Kinsley, *Hinduism: A Cultural Perspective* (1982). See also David G. Mandelbaum, *Society in India, 2 volumes* (1970), who provides essential insights into the complex relationship of class and caste. Jacob Pandian, *The Making of India and Indian Tradition* (1995), contains much revealing historical material, with particular attention to often neglected regions such as southern India, in its effort to explain the diversity of contemporary India. Stella Kramrisch, *The Hindu Temple, 2 volumes* (1946), and Surinder M.

Bhardwaj, *Hindu Places of Pilgrimage in India: A Study in Cultural Geography* (1973), examine important elements of worship in the Hindu tradition.

Roy C. Craven, *Indian Art* (1976), is a clear, historically organized treatment of its subject. Mario Bussagli and Calembus Sivaramamurti, *5000 Years of the Art of India* (1971) is lavishly illustrated.

For the uniqueness and decisive historical impact of Indian mathematics, see Georges Ifrah, *From One to Zero: A Universal History of Numbers* (1985).

Jean W. Sedlar, *India and the Greek World: A Study in the Transmission of Culture* (1980), relates the interaction of Greek and Indian civilizations. Lionel Casson, *The Periplus Maris Erythraei: Text With Introduction, Translation and Commentary* (1989), explicates a fascinating mariner's guide to the ports, trade goods, and human and navigational hazards of Indian Ocean commerce in the Roman era.

Richard Ulack and Gyula Pauer, *Atlas of Southeast Asia* (1989), provides a very brief introduction and maps for the environment and early history of Southeast Asia. Nicholas Tarling (ed.), *The Cambridge History of Southeast Asia*, volume 1 (1992), and D. R. DeSai, *Southeast Asia: Past and Present* (3rd edition, 1994), provide general accounts of Southeast Asian history. Lynda Shaffer, *Maritime Southeast Asia to 1500* (1996), focuses on early Southeast Asian history in a world historical context. Also useful is Kenneth R. Hall, *Maritime Trade and State Development in Early Southeast Asia* (1985).

The art of Southeast Asia is taken up by M. C. S. Diskul, *The Art of Srivijaya* (1980), and B. P. Groslier, *The Art of Indochina, Including Thailand, Vietnam, Laos and Cambodia* (1962).

NOTES

1. Barbara Stoler Miller, *The Bhagavad-Gita: Krishna's Counsel in Time of War* (Bantam, N.Y., 1986) 98–99.

2. B. G. Gokhale, *Asoka Maurya* (Twayne, N.Y., 1966) 152–153, 156–157, 160.

3. James Legge, *The Travels of Fa-hien: Fa-hien's Record of Buddhistic Kingdoms* (Oriental Publishers, Delhi, 1971) 77–79.

PART THREE

Growth and Interaction of Cultural Communities, 300–1200

Technologies of food production and local religious and political systems long distinguished specific human societies from one another. The civilizations born in great river valleys differed markedly from one another in irrigation techniques, forms of worship, conceptions of government, and patterns of daily life despite similar environmental situations. The pastoral societies that came into existence in various regions similarly differed in types of animals herded, use of animal products, social organization, and relations with settled peoples. Around the world, even among peoples who were responding to parallel ecological challenges, or who had a linguistic kinship with neighboring peoples, diversity of all sorts was normal.

Over time, some groups prospered more than others, and a few expanded from localized states into extensive empires. As we have seen, the imperial armies of Assyria, Macedon, Rome, and Han China effectively united disparate societies under unified political rule for greater or lesser periods of time. But peaceful exchange along trade routes, folk migrations by people equipped with especially productive technologies, and missionary efforts to convert people to new religions regardless of their political allegiances had a more profound and long-lasting impact on the coming together of the world's peoples. The continent-spanning technological, social, and cultural exchange and interaction that marked the centuries from 300 to 1200 differed substantially from earlier instances of cultural expansion in both mechanisms of exchange and eventual historical impact. Some of these interactions relate to trade, some to migration, some to religion, and some to political purpose. They do not add up to an easily summarized story, but they are so different from earlier interactions arising primarily from conquest or the extension of political boundaries that they constitute a distinct era in world history.

In the realm of trading connections, three types of long-distance routes rose and flourished: the Silk Road across Central Asia from Mesopotamia to China, trans-Saharan caravan routes linking northern with sub-Saharan Africa, and a variety of maritime routes connecting the coastal lands of the Indian Ocean. By means of such routes, Mesopotamian farmers started to plant rice, cotton, citrus trees, and other Eastern crops; African farmers acquired bananas and yams from Southeast Asia; and Chinese farmers learned about wine grapes, alfalfa, and other crops of the Mediterranean region. The techniques of silk production and papermaking spread westward from China, musical instruments and styles reached China from Iran, and gold dust reached the Mediterranean from West Africa in exchange for cloth and metal manufactures. Each of these exchanges, and many more, had a significant impact on the receiving societies and economies.

In the realm of change brought on by movements of human groups, the spread of the Bantu peoples eastward and southward from West

Africa brought iron implements and new techniques of food production to sub-Saharan Africa and helped foster a distinctive African cultural pattern. Quite differently, the Arabs of the Arabian peninsula, under the inspiration of the Prophet Muhammad, in the seventh century C.E. conquered an empire that stretched from Spain to India; and they implanted in it their language, their faith, and their cultural values.

In the realm of religion, while Arab military prowess set the stage for a centuries-long process of converting non-Arabs to Islam, the division of the Roman Empire into east and west and the decline of its western portion in the fifth century C.E. provided the background for the slow conversion of Europe to Christianity. As in the case of Islam, Christian beliefs became wedded to political structures: the Byzantine Empire in the eastern Mediterranean and the Carolingian and, later, the Holy Roman Empires in western Europe, as well as Christian kingdoms in Ethiopia, Armenia, and Russia. Simultaneously, Buddhism drew on the energies of missionaries and pilgrims as it made its way by land and sea from northern India and Afghanistan to Sri Lanka, Tibet, Southeast Asia, China, Korea, and Japan.

Finally, in the realm of political purpose, the era of the Crusades in the eleventh century saw European Christian armies attack Muslim territories in the eastern Mediterranean and Spain, thereby contributing to a reopening of contacts between lands long separated. While military arts such as siegecraft and castle building made significant advances on both sides, the impact of the Crusades had far-ranging consequences in fields such as philosophy and medicine.

Meanwhile, at the other end of Eurasia, the demise, at the close of the ninth century C.E., of the Tang Empire, which was strongly oriented toward contacts with the pastoral peoples of Central Asia, led the leaders of smaller successor states in the north to encourage a steady and ongoing migration toward the south. This contributed, under the Song Empire, to a clearer distinction between the civilization of the pastoral and trading peoples of Central Asia and the comparatively unified civilization that had come to cover most of China. The consequences of these developments included great strides forward in science, technology, and size of population under the Song.

This era also witnessed the culminating stages

Technology

ca. 800 B.C.E.—Iron smelting south of the Sahara

ca. 250 B.C.E.—Silk Road opens from China to Mesopotamia

ca. 100 C.E.—Stirrup spreads from northern Afghanistan

ca. 750—Trans-Saharan trade routes become active

ca. 800—Efficient horse harnessing in northern Europe

800s—Woodblock printing in East Asia, to a lesser extent in Islamic lands

1000s—Song Empire develops compasses, large ships; extensive coal and iron production

Environment

ca. 5000–1000 B.C.E.—Spread of maize, potatoes, and manioc in America

ca. 2500 B.C.E.—Sahara reaches maximum aridity

ca. 100 C.E.—Bananas and yams from Southeast Asia spread to Africa

ca. 200–400—Introduction of rice cultivation into Japan from Korea

ca. 300—Chinese crops in Mesopotamia: rice, sugar, and citrus

ca. 700–1000—Cotton becomes dominant fabric in Islamic lands

ca. 1100–1200—European population growth and agricultural expansion

North America
ca. 70–1500 C.E.—Mississippian culture
ca. 100–400—Hopewell culture
ca. 450–1300—Anasazi culture

Central America
ca. 1200–400 B.C.E.—Olmec culture
ca. 100–750 C.E.—Teotihuacán
ca. 350–800—Classic Maya civilization
ca. 1200–1421—Aztec state

Andes
ca. 900–325 B.C.E.—Chavín culture
ca. 200–700 C.E.—Mochica state
ca. 250–1000—Tiahuanaco
ca. 1300–1432—Incan state

of technological, cultural, and civilizational development in the Western Hemisphere. The near absence of written records makes a detailed history impossible, but it is apparent that an early succession of urban, agricultural civilizations in the Andes, the Yucatán lowlands, and the central plateau of Mexico reached a climax in the Aztec and Incan Empires and the somewhat earlier flourishing of the Maya. All of the aspects of long-distance cultural exchange and interaction that mark this era in Eurasia and Africa have their counterparts in the Western Hemisphere. The spread of cultivated plants such as potatoes, manioc, and corn attests to long-distance exchanges of technology and to the impact of such exchanges on landscapes and lifestyles from the eastern woodlands of North America, through the Caribbean islands, to the far reaches of the Andes. Migrations of human groups were crucial to the peopling of the Caribbean islands and the formation of urban civilization in central Mexico. Similar religious ideas and ritual practices are found over broad areas. And the political policies of the Aztec and Incan rulers, in the only stage of this development that is well documented, testify abundantly to their interests in expansion and

their devising of economic and social means of advancing their aims.

In the long sweep of human history, civilizational expansion through increasing the size of political units could not remain the sole or dominant form of societal interaction. Empires lacked the technological means to communicate with or defend borders that were too distant from the imperial center. Thus, other mechanisms of interaction and exchange played stronger roles as distant peoples gradually became aware of one another. Trade, migration, travel for the purpose of telling people about new ideas or beliefs, and political determination to invade or make contact with peoples in distant lands did not begin in this era, but they characterize and dominated this era in an unprecedented fashion. And in so doing, they make the centuries from 300 to 1200 a critical link between an earlier world of societies living largely apart with only limited contact and, at the era's end, a world of pervasive interconnections among peoples and continent-spanning exchanges of technologies, products, and ideas.

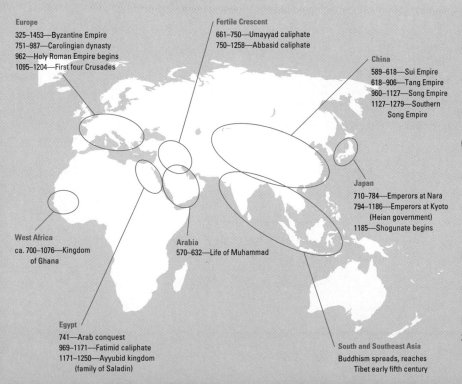

Europe
325–1453—Byzantine Empire
751–987—Carolingian dynasty
962—Holy Roman Empire begins
1095–1204—First four Crusades

Fertile Crescent
661–750—Umayyad caliphate
750–1258—Abbasid caliphate

China
589–618—Sui Empire
618–906—Tang Empire
960–1127—Song Empire
1127–1279—Southern Song Empire

Japan
710–784—Emperors at Nara
794–1186—Emperors at Kyoto (Heian government)
1185—Shogunate begins

West Africa
ca. 700–1076—Kingdom of Ghana

Arabia
570–632—Life of Muhammad

Egypt
741—Arab conquest
969–1171—Fatimid caliphate
1171–1250—Ayyubid kingdom (family of Saladin)

South and Southeast Asia
Buddhism spreads, reaches Tibet early fifth century

Society

ca. 2000 B.C.E.–1500 C.E.—Urban temple complexes in Central and South America

ca. 500 B.C.E.–1000 C.E.—Bantu migrations from West Africa

ca. 400–800 C.E.—Decline of urbanism and monetary economy in Europe

600s—Introduction of Chinese examination system

ca. 800–1000—Islamization leads to rapid urbanization in Iran

ca. 1000—Decline of Confucian elite in Japan, rise of warrior classes

Culture

ca. 4000–200 B.C.E.—Saharan rock art

From ca. 50 C.E.—Christianity spreads from Jerusalem

From ca. 100—Buddhism spreads eastward

325—Christianity becomes official Roman faith

ca. 600–840—Buddhist political and cultural influence in China

CHAPTER EIGHT

Expanding Networks of Communication and Exchange, 300 B.C.E.–1100 C.E.

The Silk Road • The Indian Ocean • Routes Across the Sahara

Sub-Saharan Africa • The Spread of Ideas

A round the year 800 C.E., a Chinese poet named Bo Zhuyi nostalgically wrote:

> Iranian whirling girl, Iranian whirling girl—
> Her heart answers to the strings,
> Her hands answer to the drums.
> At the sound of the strings and drums, she raises her arms,
> Like whirling snowflakes tossed about, she turns in her twirling dance.
>
> Iranian whirling girl,
> You came from Sogdiana.
> In vain did you labor to come east more than ten thousand tricents.
> For in the central plains there were already some who could do the Iranian whirl,
> And in a contest of wonderful abilities, you would not be their equal.[1]

An exotic foreign dancer would not seem particularly remarkable to us, accustomed as we are to a world closely interconnected through television and satellite communications. But the western part of Central Asia, the region around Samarkand and Bukhara known in the eighth century C.E. as Sogdiana, was 2,500 miles (4,000 kilometers) from the Chinese capital of Chang'an. The average caravan took more than four months to trek across the mostly unsettled deserts, mountains, and grasslands. How many Iranian dancing girls reached China by this route? Enough to make their style of dance legendary and the object of local imitation. Indeed, contemporary pottery figurines excavated from Chinese graves show troupes of Iranian performers.

The Silk Road connecting China and the Middle East across Central Asia was an important conduit for the exchange of agricultural goods, manufactured products, and ideas. But musicians and dancing girls traveled, too—as did camel pullers, merchants, monks, and pilgrims. The Silk Road, like any important trade route, was not just a means of bringing peoples and parts of the world into contact; it was a social system. However, it was a social system that neither lay within a state or empire nor gave rise to one. Consequently, this and other major trading networks that have had a deep impact on world history deserve special scrutiny.

As we have seen, political units in ancient times grew only slowly into kingdoms, and a few developed further into empires. With every expansion of territory, the accumulation of wealth by temple, leaders, kings, and emperors enticed traders to venture ever farther afield for cargoes of precious goods. For the most part, their customers were wealthy elites. But the knowledge of new products, agricultural and industrial processes, and foreign ideas and customs these long-distance traders brought with them sometimes affected an entire society.

Nevertheless, travelers and traders were not always admired or respected. They seldom owned much land, wielded political power, or achieved military glory. Moreover, they were often socially isolated (sometimes by law) and secretive since dissemination of knowledge about markets, products, routes, and travel conditions could give advantage to their competitors. On balance, however, their mostly anonymous efforts contributed more to drawing the world together than did the efforts of all but a few kings and emperors.

This chapter examines the social systems and historical impact of exchange networks that developed between 300 B.C.E. and 1100 C.E. in Europe, Asia, and Africa. The Silk Road, the Indian Ocean maritime system, and the trans-Saharan caravan routes in Africa illustrate the nature of long-distance trade in this era, when major parts of the globe began the slow process of getting to know one another.

Trading networks were not the only medium for the spread of new ideas, products, and customs over wide distances, however. Chapter 6 discussed the migration into the Roman Empire of peoples speaking Germanic languages and the

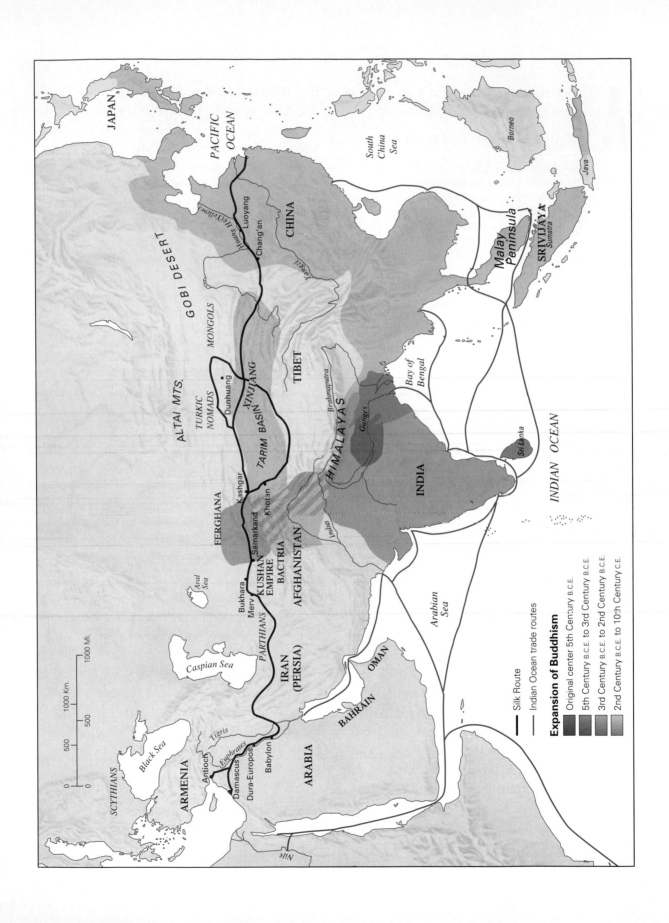

JAPAN

PACIFIC
OCEAN

Borneo

*South
China
Sea*

Luoyang

CHINA

Chang'an

Huang He (Yellow)

Yangzi

GOBI DESERT

MONGOLS

Malay
Peninsula

SRIVIJAYA

Sumatra

Java

TIBET

Dunhuang

*TURKIC
NOMADS*

XINJIANG

Brahmaputra

ALTAI MTS.

TARIM BASIN

HIMALAYAS

Ganges

*Bay of
Bengal*

Kashgar

Khotan

Sri Lanka

INDIA

INDIAN OCEAN

FERGHANA

Samarkand

Indus

*Aral
Sea*

KUSHAN
EMPIRE

BACTRIA

Bukhara

Merv

AFGHANISTAN

PARTHIANS

IRAN
(PERSIA)

*Arabian
Sea*

OMAN

Caspian Sea

BAHRAIN

1000 Mi.

ARABIA

1000 Km.

500

Tigris

500

SCYTHIANS

Black Sea

Antioch

Euphrates

0

0

ARMENIA

Damascus

Dura-Europos

Babylon

Nile

—— Silk Route

—— Indian Ocean trade routes

Expansion of Buddhism

Original center 5th Century B.C.E.

5th Century B.C.E. to 3rd Century B.C.E.

3rd Century B.C.E. to 2nd Century B.C.E.

2nd Century B.C.E. to 10th Century C.E.

beginning of Christian missionary activity in Europe. This chapter compares the development of the Saharan trading system of northern Africa with the simultaneous folk migrations of Bantu-speaking peoples within sub-Saharan Africa that laid the foundation for that region's special type of cultural unity. This chapter also discusses the spread of Buddhism in Asia and of Christianity in Africa that marked this period. The politically and militarily more consequential expansion of Islam is the subject of Chapter 10.

THE SILK ROAD

Archaeology and linguistic studies show that the peoples of Central Asia engaged in long-distance movement and exchange from at least the second millennium B.C.E. In Roman times the imagination of Europeans became captivated by the idea of the Silk Road. A trade route linking the lands of the Mediterranean with China by way of Mesopotamia, Iran, and Central Asia, the Silk Road experienced several periods of heavy use. The first extended from approximately 150 B.C.E. to 900 C.E., when the collapse of the Tang dynasty in China led to disruption at its eastern end (see Chapter 11). Another period of heavy use began in the thirteenth century C.E. and lasted until the 17th century. During that period, much of the Silk Road's traffic flowed north of Iran, skirted the northern shore of the Caspian Sea, and ended at ports on the Black Sea (see Map 8.1). The operation of that segment of the route is considered in Chapter 13. This chapter

Map 8.1 Asian Trade and Communication Routes The overland Silk Road was much shorter than the maritime route from the South China Sea to the Red Sea, and ships were more expensive than pack animals. Moreover, China's political centers were in the north. It was more vulnerable, however, to political disruption. Historians remain puzzled by the lack of Buddhist expansion westward from Afghanistan.

examines the origins of trade along the Silk Road and the importance of the Silk Road in drawing together different parts of the Eurasian landmass during its first centuries of use.

Origins and Operations

The Seleucid kings who succeeded to the eastern parts of Alexander the Great's empire in the third century B.C.E. focused their energies on Mesopotamia and Syria, allowing an Iranian nomadic leader to establish an independent kingdom in northeastern Iran. Historians disagree about the stages by which the Parthians, named after their homeland just east of the Caspian Sea, took over Iran and then Mesopotamia. The Parthians remained wedded to their nomadic origins. They left few written sources, and recurring wars between the Parthians and the Seleucids, and later between the Parthians and the Romans, prevented travelers from the Mediterranean region from gaining a firm knowledge of the Parthian kingdom. It seems most likely, however, that their place of origin on the threshold of Central Asia and the lifestyle they had in common with nomadic pastoral groups farther to the east were key to their encouragement of trade along what became known as the Silk Road.

In 128 B.C.E., a Chinese general named Chankien made his first exploratory journey westward across Central Asia on behalf of Emperor Wu of the Han dynasty. After crossing the broad and desolate Tarim Basin north of Tibet, he reached the fertile valley of Ferghana, nestled between the Pamir and Tian Mountains, and for the first time encountered westward-flowing rivers. There he found horse breeders whose animals far outclassed any other horses he had ever seen. In China these noble animals would be deemed descendants of a heavenly horse.

Later Chinese historians looked on General Zhang Qian as the originator of overland trade with the western lands, and they credited him with personally introducing into China a whole garden of new plants and trees. Zhang Qian's own account proves that the people of Ferghana were already receiving goods from China, though probably by way of India. Specifically, he saw them using canes

Felt funerary cloth from central Asia   Fourth Century B.C.E. burial mounds at Pazaryk in the Peltai Mountains contain some of the earliest indications of life and art among central Asian nomads. Felt, made by wetting wool and matting it under pressure, was a common central Asian fabric. Here a horseman wearing characteristic nomad clothing approaches a figure in an ornamented robe. Metal horse harness parts also feature in archaeological finds from nomadic culture. (Hermitage, Leningrad)

We need to distinguish between, first, trips made by occasional travelers or the movements of migrating pastoralists and, second, the deliberate fostering of trading connections. The keys to the opening of the Silk Road were, on the eastern end, Chinese eagerness for western products, especially horses, and on the western end, the organized Parthian state controlling the flourishing markets of Mesopotamia and culturally linked to the pastoralists of Central Asia. In between were caravan cities to support the traders and camel- and horse-breeding nomads to supply them with livestock.

Historians put great emphasis on the long distances traveled: once the route was fully functioning, around 150 B.C.E., for example, Greeks could buy Chinese silk from Parthian traders in Mesopotamian border entrepôts. Yet caravans bought and sold goods along the way in prosperous Central Asian trading cities like Kashgar, Khotan, Samarkand, Bukhara, and Marv. These cities grew and flourished, often under the rule of local princes who cultivated good relations with the nomads who provided the camels, guides, and animal handlers for the caravans.

One industry that developed along with the caravan trade was the specialized breeding of hybrid camels. Figurines, graffiti, and other pictorial sources show that the two-humped Bactrian camel (named for Bactria in northern Afghanistan) was initially the mainstay of the Central Asian caravan trade. Closely related to the one-humped camel, or dromedary, of torrid Arabia, the Bactrian camel has a heavy coat of hair and is built to withstand the frigid winters of Central Asia.

Hybrid camels began to appear early in the Silk Road's operations. The historian Diodorus of Siculus wrote in the first century B.C.E. about an area that seems to be Parthian-controlled southern Mesopotamia where Arabs bred different types of camels, including "both the hairless and the shaggy, and those which have two humps, one behind the other, along their spines." Diodorus's "shaggy" camel is the first evidence of the hybrid camel, which combined the merits of both Bactrian camel and dromedary: it was larger and stronger than either parent and had a

made from a square type of bamboo that only grows in western China. But this does not diminish the fact that Chankien, as leader of some eighteen imperial expeditions, was an important pioneer on the more northerly route that became the Silk Road.

Long-distance travel was much more familiar to the Central Asians than to the Chinese. Kin to the trouser-wearing, horse-riding Parthians in language and customs, the populations of Ferghana and neighboring regions included many nomads. For more than a thousand years they had lived by following their herds of horses, cattle, and sheep across the Asian deserts, steppes, and mountains from the Black Sea to the Chinese frontier. But their migrations had had little to do with trade, despite the occasional piece of silk or Chinese manufactured item that found its way into their animals' packs.

Caravan Cities

Archaeology reveals a lot about daily life in caravan cities, but travelers' descriptions give a better indication of the impact that such cities made at the time. Two geographer-historians from the first century B.C.E., Diodorus of Siculus and Strabo, provide valuable descriptions of the terminal cities of the Arabian caravan route that linked the incense-producing region of southern Arabia with Jordan and Syria. At the southern end was Sabae, in Yemen. At the northern end of the route was Petra, in Jordan.

SABAE

And a natural sweet odor pervades the entire land because practically all the things which excel in fragrance grow there unceasingly. Along the coast, for instance, grow balsam . . . and cassia. . . . And throughout the interior of the land there are thick forests, in which are great trees which yield frankincense and myrrh, as well as palms and reeds, cinnamon trees and every other kind which possesses a sweet odor such as these have. . . .

This people surpassed not only the neighboring Arabs but also all other men in wealth and in their several extravagancies besides. For in the exchange and sale of their wares they, of all men who carry on trade for the sake of the silver they receive in exchange, obtain the highest price in return for things of the smallest weight. Consequently, since they have never for ages suffered the ravages of war because of their secluded position, and since an abundance of both gold and silver abounds in the country, especially in Sabae, where the royal palace is situated, they have embossed goblets of every description, made of silver and gold, couches and tripods with silver feet, and every other furnishing of incredible costliness, and halls encircled by large columns, some of them gilded, and others having silver figures on the capitals. . . . For the fact is that these people have enjoyed their felicity unshaken since ages past because they have been entire strangers to those whose own covetousness leads them to feel that another man's wealth is their own godsend. . . . And there are prosperous islands nearby, containing unwalled cities. . . . These islands are visited by sailors from every part and especially from Potana, the city which Alexander founded on the Indus River.

Source: Diodorus Siculus, Book III, 46–47.

PETRA

The Nabataeans are a sensible people, and are so much inclined to acquire possessions that they publicly fine anyone who has diminished his possessions and also confer honors on anyone who has increased them. Since they have but few slaves, they are served by their kinsfolk for the most part, or by one another, or by themselves; so that the custom extends even to their kings. They prepare common meals together in groups of thirteen persons; and they have two girl-singers for each banquet. The king holds many drinking bouts in magnificent style, but no one drinks more than eleven cupfuls, each time using a different golden cup. The king is so democratic that, in addition to serving himself, he sometimes even serves the rest himself in his turn. He often renders an account of his kingship in the popular assembly; and sometimes his mode of life is examined. Their homes, through the use of stone, are costly; but, on account of peace, the cities are not walled. . . . The sheep are white-fleeced and the oxen are large, but the country produces no horses. Camels afford the service they require instead of horses. Some things are imported wholly from other countries, but others not altogether so, especially in the case of those that are native products, as, for example, gold and silver and most of the aromatics, whereas brass and iron, as also purple garb [for the kings], styrax, crocus, costaria, embossed works, paintings, and molded works are not produced in their country.

What role do imported goods play in the economy of these cities? To what degree is monarchy associated with trade?

Source: Strabo, Book 16, 4.26.

Caravan animals from either end of the Silk Road   Though the elongated two-humped camel from the sixth century C.E. Sui dynasty in China is more elegant than the broken two-humped Parthian camel, they carry what appear to be identical rounded loads, possibly silk cloth or thread. The similarity in loads proves that some commodities traveled the entire distance from China to Mesopotamia. Caravan camels carried approximately 500 pounds of cargo carefully balanced on either side of the animal. Most two-humped camels disappeared in Mesopotamia by the first century C.E., being replaced by the one-humped camels of Arabia as Arab nomads became increasingly involved in caravan trade. (Private collection)

heavy coat that suited it to the Central Asian climate. The hybrid was so perfectly adapted for work on the Silk Road that the eventual decline of the route after 1600 C.E. led to its almost total disappearance.

The breeding of hybrid camels called for careful herd management and is an example of how the caravan trade itself generated new economic activities. Of greater importance, however, was the exchange of products between East and West. Chinese sources abound in references to products imported across the Silk Road, sometimes specifically mentioning the Anxi (the Parthians) or Bose (the Persians).

General Zhang Qian seems to have brought back two plants during one of his many trips west: alfalfa and domestic grapes. The former provided the best fodder for the growing Chinese herds of Ferghana horses. The latter were integral to the famous trio of "wine, women, and song" that Chinese explorers noted as central to Central Asian life. Later images of Iranian musicians and whirling dancing girls confirm the allure of these western ways.

In addition, Chinese farmers adopted pistachios, walnuts, pomegranates, sesame, corian-

der, spinach, and many other new crops. Chinese artisans and physicians used other trade products, such as jasmine oil, oak galls (used in tanning animal hides, dyeing, and ink making), sal ammoniac (for medicines), copper oxides, zinc, and precious stones.

Caravan traders going from east to west brought back from China new fruits such as the peach and the apricot, which the Romans attributed to Persia and Armenia, respectively, demonstrating the route of dissemination farther westward. They also brought cinnamon, ginger, and other spices that could not be grown in the West. Above all, however, China was known for its manufactured goods—particularly silk, pottery, and paper—all of which were eventually adopted or imitated in western lands, starting with Iran.

Chinese pottery figurines of pack camels usually show them with almost hemispherical loads hanging on either side of the animal, as do figurines of the Parthian period found in Mesopotamia. If we assume that the potters depicted items of special distinction, these loads most likely contained silk. Thus, despite the great diversity of goods exchanged by caravan across Central Asia, the traditional name of the Silk Road seems well justified.

The Impact of Silk Road Trade

As trade became a more important part of Central Asian life, the Iranian-speaking peoples settled increasingly in trading cities and surrounding farm villages. This allowed nomads originally from the Altai Mountains farther east to spread west across the steppes and become the dominant pastoral group. These peoples spoke Turkic languages unrelated to the Iranian tongues and are well in evidence by the sixth century C.E. The prosperity that trade created affected not only the ethnic mix of the region but also cultural values. The nomads continued to live in the round, portable felt huts called yurts that can still be seen occasionally in Central Asia, but prosperous merchants and landholders built stately homes decorated with brightly colored wall paintings. The paintings show these merchants and landholders wearing Chinese silks and Iranian brocades and riding on richly outfitted horses and camels. They also give evidence of an avid interest in Buddhism, which competed with Christianity, Zoroastrianism, and—eventually—Islam in a lively and inquiring intellectual milieu.

Religion (discussed later in this chapter) exemplifies the impact of foreign customs and beliefs on the Central Asian peoples, but their culture also affected surrounding areas. For example, Central Asian military practices had a profound impact on both East and West. Chariot warfare, horse-harnessing techniques, and the use of mounted bowmen all originated in Central Asia and spread eastward and westward through military campaigns and folk migrations that began in the second millennium B.C.E. and recurred throughout the period of the Silk Road.

Evidence of the use of stirrups, one of the most important inventions, comes first from the Kushan people in northern Afghanistan in approximately the first century C.E. Ideas and styles from farther east and west along the Silk Road strongly influenced the culture of these people, and we may presume that their use of the stirrup

spread by means of the same route. At first a solid bar, then a loop of leather to support the rider's big toe, and finally a device of leather and metal or wood supporting the instep, the stirrup gave riders far greater stability in the saddle—which in all likelihood was an earlier central Asian invention.

Using stirrups, a mounted warrior could supplement his bow and arrow with a long lance, and, leaning forward, he could charge his enemy

Iranian musicians from Silk Road   This three-color glazed pottery figurine, 23 inches (58.4 centimeters) high, is one of hundreds of Silk Road camels and horses found in northern Chinese tombs from the sixth to ninth centuries C.E. The musicians playing Iranian instruments testify to the migration of Iranian culture across the Silk Road. At the same time dishes decorated by the Chinese three-color glaze technique were in vogue in northern Iran. (The National Museum of Chinese History)

Linkages between World Regions

ca. 1200 B.C.E.	Horse herders supplant cattle herders in central Sahara
500 B.C.E.–1000 C.E.	Bantu migrations from west Africa
ca. 250 B.C.E.–900 C.E.	Silk Road flourishes from China to Mesopotamia
From ca. 50 C.E.	Christianity spreads in all directions from Jerusalem
From ca. 100	Buddhism spreads eastward by land and sea
ca. 750–1076	Islam spreads in Ghana south of Sahara
ca. 900	Hindu and Arab merchants in Canton

at a gallop without fear that the impact of his attack would push him backward off his mount. Nevertheless, the bow and arrow remained the weapon of choice in Central Asia. The Parthians were famous for what the Romans called "the Parthian shot"—an arrow shot backward while the warrior was riding away from his enemy. Far to the west, however, the stirrup made possible the armored knights who dominated the battlefields of Europe (see Chapter 9), and it contributed to the superiority of the Tang cavalry in China (see Chapter 11).

The success of the Silk Road sowed the seeds of eventual change. From Parthian times until well after the Arab invasions of the 7th century C.E. (see Chapter 10), each Central Asian caravan city and mountain valley seems to have had its own ruling family. These many small states enjoyed various sorts of relations, presumably centered on their common interest in trade. Fear of disrupting the trade may be why none seems to have tried to conquer the others and establish an empire. Yet the Turkic-speaking pastoral nomads who initially provided traders with animals and animal handlers gradually came to grasp the potential for political activity on a larger scale. Although traffic along the Silk Road tapered off for awhile after 900 C.E., in large part because of the collapse of the Tang state in China, the following two centuries saw the emergence of larger territorial states based on the military force of the Turkic nomads (see Chapter 14).

THE INDIAN OCEAN

Some Chinese and western products were exchanged by sea rather than by land. Just as nomads and city traders in Central Asia played the major role in trade along the Silk Road, so a multilingual, multiethnic society of seafarers carried on most of the trade across the Indian Ocean and the South China Sea. These people left few records and seldom played a visible part in the rise and fall of kingdoms and empires, but they forged increasingly strong economic and social ties between the coastal lands of East Africa, southern Arabia, the Persian Gulf, India, Southeast Asia, and southern China.

This trade took place in three distinct regions: (1) In the South China Sea, Chinese and Malays (including Indonesians) dominated trade. (2) From the east coast of India to the islands of Southeast Asia, Indians and Malays were the main traders. (3) From the west coast of India to the Persian Gulf and the east coast of Africa, merchants and sailors were predominantly Persians and Arabs. These ethnic divisions were customary rather than politically formalized, however. Chinese and Malay sailors could and did voyage to East Africa, and Arab and Persian traders reached southern China.

In coastal areas, small groups of seafarers sometimes had a significant social impact despite their usual lack of political power. Women seldom accompanied their menfolk on long sea voyages, so sailors and merchants often married local women in port cities. The families thus established were bilingual and bicultural. As in many other situations in world history, women played a crucial, if not well-documented, role as mediators between cultures. Not only did they raise their children to be more cosmopolitan than children from inland regions, but they introduced their menfolk to customs and attitudes that they carried off when they returned to sea. As a consequence, the designation of specific seafarers as Persian, Arab, Indian, or Malay often conceals mixed heritages and a rich cultural diversity.

The Indian Ocean Maritime System

With their frequent reliance on written records, historians sometimes exaggerate the importance of chance literary references and overlook other types of historical evidence. From the time of Herodotus in the fifth century B.C.E., Greek writers regaled their readers with stories of marvelous voyages down the Red Sea into the Indian Ocean and around Africa from the east, or out of the Mediterranean Sea through the Pillars of Hercules and around Africa from the west. Most often, they attributed such trips to the Phoenicians, the most fearless of Mediterranean seafarers. But occasionally a Greek appears. One such was Hippalus, a Greek ship's pilot who was said to have discovered the seasonal monsoon winds that facilitate sailing across the Indian Ocean. Though this story is questionable, it highlights the importance of the monsoon.

In early spring, the warming of the East African landmass gives rise to a northward wind along the coast. Laden with ocean moisture, this wind brings rain to the highlands of Ethiopia (causing the Nile flood) and Yemen and then veers due east until it encounters the southern part of the Indian subcontinent, which it drenches with rains during the summer months before proceeding to the islands and mainland of Southeast Asia. Six months later, again impelled by temperature differentials between water and land, a reverse monsoon blows westward from Southeast Asia to the East African coast.

This regular rotation of steady winds could not have remained unnoticed for thousands of years, waiting for an alert Greek to happen along. Looked at more realistically, the great voyages and discoveries made before written records became common should surely be attributed to the peoples who lived around the Indian Ocean—Africans, Arabs, Persians, Indians, Malays—rather than to interlopers from the Mediterranean Sea. The story of Hippalus resembles the Chinese story of General Chankien, whose role in opening up trade with Central Asia so strongly overshadows the anonymous contributions made by the indigenous peoples.

The sailing traditions and techniques of the Indian Ocean differed markedly from those of the Mediterranean. Mediterranean sailors of the time of Alexander used square sails and long banks of oars to maneuver among the sea's many islands and small harbors. Indian Ocean vessels relied on triangular lateen sails and normally did without oars in running before the wind on long ocean stretches. The triangular sail made for greater stability, since the pressure of the wind was strongest on its lower portion; and it was somewhat more maneuverable than a square rig. Mediterranean shipbuilders nailed their vessels together. The planks of Indian Ocean ships were pierced, tied together with palm fiber, and caulked with bitumen. Mediterranean sailors rarely ventured out of sight of land. Indian Ocean sailors, thanks to the monsoon winds, could cover the long reaches between southern Arabia and India entirely at sea.

The world of the Indian Ocean developed differently from the world of the Mediterranean Sea. The Phoenicians and the Greeks fostered trade around the Mediterranean by establishing colonies that maintained contact with their home city, thus giving rise to the maritime empires of Carthage and Athens (see Chapters 4 and 5). The traders of the Indian Ocean, where distances were greater and contacts less frequent, seldom retained political affiliations with their homelands. The colonies they established were sometimes socially distinctive but rarely independent of the local political powers. The Mediterranean region was smaller than the Indian Ocean basin and more competitive with respect to a small number of exchangeable goods—copper, tin, wine, olive oil, pottery. These political and environmental factors contributed to the recurrent war and intense rivalry that marked the Mediterranean world, a political situation favoring rowed warships that retained great maneuverability even in windless conditions. By contrast, war seldom beset the Indian Ocean maritime system prior to the arrival of the European explorers at the end of the fifteenth century C.E. Its early history is primarily concerned with population movements and the exchange of goods and ideas.

Origins of Contact and Trade

As early as the third millennium B.C.E., Sumerian records spoke of regular trading contacts between Mesopotamia, the islands of the Persian Gulf, Oman, and the Indus Valley. However, this early trading contact eastward broke off, and later Mesopotamian trade references refer more often to East Africa than to India.

A similarly early chapter in Indian Ocean history concerns migrations from Southeast Asia to Madagascar, the world's fourth largest island, situated off the southeastern coast of Africa. Some two thousand years ago, people from one of the many islands of Southeast Asia established themselves in that forested, mountainous land some 6,000 miles (9,500 kilometers) from home. Since they could not possibly have carried enough supplies for a direct voyage across the Indian Ocean, their route must have touched the coasts of India and southern Arabia. No remains of their journeys have been discovered, however.

Apparently, their sailing canoes plied the seas along the increasingly familiar route for several hundred years. The settlers farmed the new land and entered into relations with Africans, who found their way across the 250-mile-wide (400 kilometers) Mozambique Channel around the 5th century C.E. The descendants of the seafarers preserved the language of their homeland and some of its culture, such as xylophone music and the cultivation of bananas, yams, and other native Southeast Asian plants. Both musical instruments and food crops spread to mainland Africa. But gradually the memory of their distant origins faded away, not to be recovered until modern times, when scholars established the linguistic link between the two lands.

These two examples illustrate the difficulty historians encounter in writing the history of the Indian Ocean trading system. Written sources are extremely rare, and archaeological finds are often hard to interpret. Yet the historical importance of communication across the Indian Ocean is unquestionable.

The Impact of Indian Ocean Trade

The only extensive written account of trade in the Indian Ocean before the rise of Islam in the seventh century C.E. is an anonymous work by a Greco-Egyptian of the first century C.E. *The Periplus of the Erythraean Sea* (that is the Red Sea) describes ports of call along the Red Sea and down the East African coast to somewhere south of the island of Zanzibar. Then it describes the ports of southern Arabia and the Persian Gulf before continuing eastward to India, mentioning ports all the way around the subcontinent to the mouth of the Ganges River. Though the geographer Ptolemy, who lived slightly later, had heard of ports as far away as Southeast Asia, the author of the *Periplus* had obviously voyaged to the places he mentions and was not merely an armchair traveler. What he describes is unquestionably a trading *system* and is clear evidence of a steady growth of interconnections in the region during the preceding centuries.

What inspired mariners to persist in their long ocean voyages was the demand for products from the coastal lands. Africa produced exotic animals, wood, and ivory. However, since ivory also came from India, Mesopotamia, and North Africa, the extent of African ivory export cannot be determined. The highlands of northern Somalia and southern Arabia grew the scrubby trees whose aromatic resins were valued as frankincense and myrrh. Trees on the island of Socotra near the entrance of the Red Sea produced "dragon's blood," a scarlet resin that Roman artists highly valued as a pigment. Pearls abounded in the Persian Gulf, and evidence of ancient copper mines has been found in Oman in Southeast Arabia. India shipped spices and manufactured goods, and more spices came from Southeast Asia, along with manufactured goods, particularly pottery, obtained in trade with China. In sum, the Indian Ocean trading region was one of enormous potential richness. Given the long distances and the comparative lack of islands, however, the volume of trade there was undoubtedly much lower than in the Mediterranean Sea.

The culture of the ports was often isolated from the hinterlands, particularly in the west. The coasts of the Arabian peninsula, the African side of the Red Sea, southern Iran, and northern India (today Pakistan) were mostly barren desert. Ports in all these areas tended to be small, and many suffered from meager supplies of fresh water. Farther south in India, the monsoon provided ample water, but steep mountains—the Western Ghats—cut the coastal plain off from the interior of the country. Thus few ports between Zanzibar and Sri Lanka had substantial inland populations within easy reach. The head of the Persian Gulf was one exception: shipborne trade was possible as far north as Babylon and, from the eighth century C.E., nearby Baghdad.

By contrast, eastern India, the Malay Peninsula, and Indonesia afforded more hospitable and densely populated shores with easier access to inland populations. Though the fishers, sailors, and traders of the western Indian Ocean system supplied a long series of kingdoms and empires with precious goods, none of these consumer societies became primarily maritime in orientation, as did the Greeks and Phoenicians in the Mediterranean. In the east, on the other hand, seaborne trade and influence seem to have been important even to the earliest states, such as that of Srivijaya (see Chapter 7). The inland forest dwellers of Malaysia were far less potent politically than the citizens of the port cities.

The pace of communication across the Indian Ocean increased over time. By the early Islamic era of the eighth century C.E., eastern products were well known in the Middle East, Javanese and Indian communities had been established in Mesopotamia, a partially seaborne Arab expedition had conquered the lower Indus Valley, and a large colony of Arab and Persian traders was growing up in southern China. Evidence of the worship of Hindu gods by Indian traders can be found in caves in southwestern Iran, and close relations exist to this day between Arab families long settled in Singapore and Jakarta and the land of their ancestors in southern Yemen.

ROUTES ACROSS THE SAHARA

The windswept Sahara, stretching from the Red Sea to the Atlantic Ocean and broken only by the Nile River, isolates sub-Saharan Africa from the Mediterranean world. The current dryness of the Sahara dates only to about 2500 B.C.E., however. The period of drying out that preceded that date was twenty-five centuries long and encompassed several cultural changes. During that time, travel between an only slowly shrinking number of grassy areas was comparatively easy. However, by 300 B.C.E., scarcity of water was restricting travel to a few difficult routes initially known only to desert nomads. Trans-Saharan trade over these routes was at first only a trickle, but it eventually expanded into a significant stream. By 1100 C.E., the riches in gold, slaves, and tropical goods flowing northward had begun to excite the envy of the Europeans, whose desire to find the source of the Saharan trading wealth helped trigger their farflung explorations after the year 1400 C.E.

Early Saharan Cultures

Sprawling sand dunes, flat sand plains, and vast expanses of exposed rock make up most of the great desert. Stark and rugged mountain and highland areas—Air, Ahaggar, Tassili, Tibesti, and others—separate its northern and southern portions. The cliffs and caves of these highlands, which were the last spots where water and grassland could be found as the climate changed, preserve a vast treasury of rock paintings and

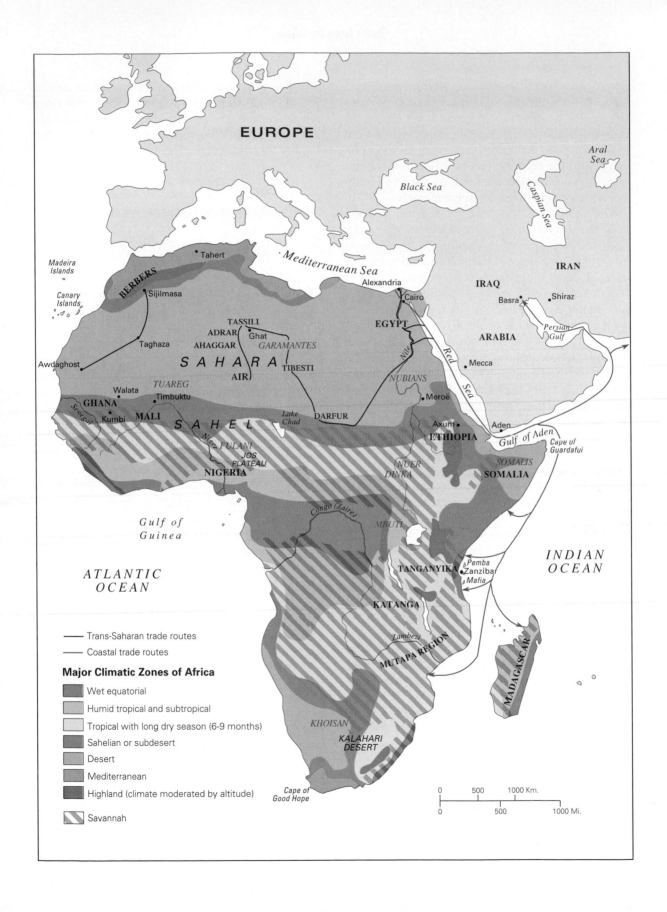

EUROPE

Aral Sea

Black Sea

Caspian Sea

Mediterranean Sea

Madeira Islands

Canary Islands

BERBERS

• Tahert

• Sijilmasa

Alexandria •
Cairo •

EGYPT

IRAN

IRAQ

Basra • • Shiraz

Persian Gulf

ARABIA

• Mecca

• Taghaza

TASSILI

ADRAR
AHAGGAR • Ghat
  GARAMANTES

S A H A R A

TIBESTI

AIR

NUBIANS

Nile

Red Sea

Awdaghost •

TUAREG

• Walata
  • Timbuktu

GHANA

• Kumbi

MALI

Senegal

S A H E L

Niger *FULANI*

JOS
PLATEAU

NIGERIA

Lake Chad

DARFUR

• Meroë

Axum •

ETHIOPIA

SOMALIS

Aden • *Gulf of Aden*

Cape of Guardafui

SOMALIA

*NUER
DINKA*

Gulf of Guinea

Congo (Zaire)

MBUTI

ATLANTIC
OCEAN

TANGANYIKA

KATANGA

Zambezi

MUTAPA REGION

Pemba
Zanzibar
Mafia

INDIAN
OCEAN

MADAGASCAR

KHOISAN

KALAHARI
DESERT

Cape of
Good Hope

—— Trans-Saharan trade routes

—— Coastal trade routes

Major Climatic Zones of Africa

Wet equatorial

Humid tropical and subtropical

Tropical with long dry season (6-9 months)

Sahelian or subdesert

Desert

Mediterranean

Highland (climate moderated by altitude)

Savannah

0   500   1000 Km.

0   500   1000 Mi.

Cattle herders in Saharan rock art   These paintings, the most artistically accomplished type of Saharan art, succeeded the depictions of hunters characteristic of the earliest art. Herding societies of modern times living in the Sahel region just south of the Sahara strongly resemble the society depicted here. This suggests that as the Sahara became completely arid, the cattle herders moved south and played a role in the formation of sub-Saharan African culture. (Henri Lhote)

engravings that constitute the primary evidence for early Saharan history.

Scholars have never discovered a method of dating these pictures. Some are darker than others because of longer exposure to the sun, which draws minerals to the surface of the rock to form

Map 8.2 Africa and the Saharan Trade Routes The Sahara desert and the surrounding oceans isolated most of Africa from foreign contact before 1000 C.E. The Nile valley, a few trading points on the east coast, and limited transdesert trade provided exceptions to this rule; but the dominant forms of sub-Saharan African culture originated fare to the west, north of the Gulf of Guinea.

a hard film. This difference in brightness, however, indicates only that one picture is older than another; it does not yield a fixed date. Since artists sometimes used the same flat surfaces again and again, relative dating can also be accomplished by seeing which paintings or engravings overlap others. Regrettably, no archaeological remains such as charcoal, which might be dated by means of carbon 14, or stone projectiles, which might be compared with datable materials from elsewhere, have ever been found in clear association with any of this rock art. Ashes from a prehistoric campfire at the foot of a rock painting, after all, could date from centuries earlier or later than the painting itself.

In what appear to be the earliest images, left by hunters in obviously much wetter times, elephants, giraffes, rhinoceroses, crocodiles, and other animals that have long been extinct in the region come vividly alive. Presumably these early hunting peoples followed their game animals southward or northward as the rivers and luxuriant grasslands disappeared because of climatic change. But whether they were more closely related to the later peoples of sub-Saharan Africa or to the Berber-speaking peoples who inhabited the mountains and plains of North Africa in Greco-Roman times cannot be determined.

Overlaps in the artwork indicate that the hunters were gradually replaced by new cultures based on cattle breeding and well adapted to the sparse grazing that remained. Cattle domestication probably originated in western Asia and reached Africa before the Sahara became completely dry. However, the beautiful paintings of cattle and detailed scenes of daily life found in the Sahara depict pastoral societies that bear little similarity to any in Asia. Rather, the people seem physically akin to today's West Africans, and the customs depicted, such as dancing and wearing masks, as well as the long-horned breeds of cattle, strongly suggest later sub-Saharan societies. These factors support the hypothesis that some sub-Saharan cultural patterns originated in the Sahara and migrated southward. In the Sahara itself, however, the cattle herders seem little related to the peoples who followed them.

Overlaps in artwork also clearly indicate that horse herders succeeded the cattle herders. The rock art changes dramatically in style. The superb realism of the cattle pictures is replaced by sketchier images that are often strongly geometric. Moreover, the horses are frequently shown drawing light chariots. This phase of Saharan rock art has provoked numerous theories. According to the most common theory, the charioteers were intrepid travelers from the Mediterranean shore who drove their flimsy vehicles across the desert and established societies in the few remaining green areas of the central Saharan highlands. The characteristic "flying gallop" posture of the horses—all four legs are extended in a dramatic though unrealistic fashion—has been compared with similar representations in early Greek art. Some scholars have suggested possible chariot routes that refugees from the collapse of the Mycenaean and Minoan civilizations of Greece and Crete might have followed deep into the desert around the twelfth century B.C.E.

However, no archaeological evidence of actual chariot use in the Sahara has ever been discovered, much less any convincing indication of extensive migration along chariot routes. Moreover, though rock art in the mountainous areas of North Africa is rare compared with the abundant images from the central Saharan highlands, images of chariots are strikingly absent. Given the extreme aridity of the Sahara by the twelfth century B.C.E. and the absence of indications that charioteers penetrated the more inviting lands north of the desert, it is difficult to imagine large numbers of refugees from the politically chaotic Mediterranean region trekking and driving their chariots into the trackless desert in search of a new homeland somewhere to the south.

As in the case of the cattle herders, therefore, the identity of the Saharan horse breeders, and the source of their passion for drawing chariots, remain a mystery. Only with the coming of the camel is it possible to make firm connections with the Saharan nomads of today through the depiction of objects and geometric patterns still used by the veiled, blue-robed Tuareg people of the highlands in Algeria, Niger, and Mali.

The Coming of the Camel

Taking note of two Roman military expeditions into central Libya in the first century B.C.E., some historians maintain that the Romans inaugurated an important trans-Saharan trade, but only scanty archaeological evidence supports this theory. More plausible is the idea that the Saharan trade and the spread of camel domestication developed together. Supporting evidence is visible in the highland rock art, where overlaps of paintings and engravings imply that camel riders in desert costume constitute the latest Saharan population. As in the transition from cattle to horses,

Chariot in Saharan rock art   Horse herding followed cattle herding as the Sahara became a desert in the second millennium B.C.E. Art became less naturalistic. The motif of spoked chariot wheels seen in profile with almost no place to stand appears in Indo-European cultures as far away as Sweden and central Asia. The "flying gallop" motif with the horses' legs unrealistically extended forward and backward resembles early Greek imagery. (Gerard Franceschi)

artistic styles again change. The camel-oriented images are decidedly the crudest and most elementary to be found in the region.

Latin texts from the first century B.C.E. first mention camels in North Africa. The camel is not native to Africa, so it must have reached the Sahara from Arabia. Scholars do not know exactly when, but scattered sources hint that camels probably came into use in Egypt in the first millennium B.C.E. and from there became known to the people who lived in the deserts bordering the Nile Valley. From the upper Nile region in the Sudan they could have been adopted by peoples farther and farther to the west, from one central Saharan highland to the next, only much later becoming disseminated northward and coming to the attention of the Romans.

Evidence for this south-to-north diffusion of camels comes not from written sources but from the design of camel saddles and patterns of camel use (see Environment and Technology: Camel Saddles). In North Africa, including the northern Sahara, pack saddles of obvious Middle Eastern design predominate, and Greco-Roman sources stress the fact that the camel-using Berber groups native to the region did not fight on camelback but dismounted and used their animals as shields. By contrast, the peoples in the central and southern Sahara used riding saddles of an entirely different design and are regularly depicted, both in art and in later historical texts, as fighting with sword and spear while on camelback.

The southern riding saddles undoubtedly developed in a warrior society rather than a commercial society. Indeed, the forms of camel use in the south fit much more closely the military image conveyed by the preceding chariot-riding

Camel Saddles

As seemingly simple a technology as saddle design can be an indicator of a society's economic structure. The South Arabian saddle was good for riding, and baggage could easily be tied to the wooden arches that attached it to the animal in the front. It was comparatively inefficient militarily, however, because the rider knelt on the cushion behind the camel's hump and was thus poorly positioned both to control his mount and to use his weapons.

The North Arabian saddle was a significant improvement that came into use in the first centuries B.C.E. Its wooden framework made tying on cargo easy, and its prominent front and back arches and placement over the camel's hump gave warriors a decent perch from which to wield their swords and spears. Arabs in northern Arabia took control of the caravan trade in that region by using these saddles.

The best riding saddles were developed by the peoples south of the Sahara. The saddles of the Tuareg seated the rider on the camel's shoulders, giving him complete freedom to use his sword and allowing him to control his mount by pressure from his toes on the animal's neck. These excellent war saddles could not be used for baggage, however, because they did not offer a convenient place to tie bundles.

Two styles of camel saddles The South Arabian saddle, featuring two closely spaced arches in front holding a pad that extends behind the camel's hump, is used for baggage purposes from Morocco to India, and for riding in southern and eastern Arabia. The saddle of the Tuaregs, with a pommel shaped like a cross, is a superior riding saddle but cannot be used for carrying baggage. (Private collection)

society than they fit the later image of long-distance caravan trade. Once camel herding was established in the south, it became easier for people to move away from the highlands and roam the deep desert. Through contacts made by the new society of far-ranging camel herders, the people north of the Sahara finally gained access to camels. Because they were within the economic sphere of the Roman Empire, however, they adopted the saddling technology of Rome's Middle Eastern provinces because it was better suited than the riding saddles of the south to carrying baggage. Ignoring the camel's military potential, they exploited it primarily as a work animal, even developing harnesses for attaching camels to plows and carts. These practices, entirely unknown in the southern Sahara, are still in evidence in Tunisia today.

Trade Across the Sahara

The coming of the camel did not automatically stimulate the beginning of trade across the Sahara. People on both sides of the desert used camels, but in different ways, and they seem to have had little influence on each other even though most of them spoke Berber languages. Trade between two different trading systems, one in the south, the other in the north, developed slowly.

The southern traders concentrated on supplying salt from large deposits in the southern desert to the peoples of sub-Saharan Africa. Salt is a physiological necessity in torrid climates, and natural deposits are rare outside the desert. Traders from the equatorial forest zone brought forest products, such as kola nuts or palm oil, to trading centers near the desert's southern fringe. Each received from the other, or from the farming peoples of the Sahel—literally "the coast" in Arabic, the southern borderlands of the Sahara—the products they needed in their homelands. Middlemen who were native to the Sahel played an important role in this trade, but precise historical details are lacking.

In the north, the main trade of Roman North Africa consisted of supplying Italy with agricultural products, primarily wheat and olives, and with wild animals from the Atlas Mountains for the arena. Cities near the coast, such as Carthage (rebuilt as a Roman city after its destruction in the Punic Wars), Hippo in Tunisia, and Leptis Magna in Libya, were centers of exchange. People living on the farms and in the towns of the interior consumed Roman manufactured goods and shared Roman styles, as is evident from abundant ruins with mosaic pavements depicting scenes from daily life.

This northern pattern began to change with the decline of the Roman Empire, which saw the abandonment of many Roman farms, the growth of nomadism, and a lessening of trade across the Mediterranean. After the Arabs invaded North Africa in the middle of the seventh century C.E., the direction of trade shifted to the Middle East, the center of Arab rule. Since the Arab conquests were inspired by the new religion of Islam (see Chapter 10), and the Christian lands of Europe constituted enemy territory, trans-Mediterranean trade diminished still further. Meanwhile, an east-west overland trade grew to compete with the coastal sea route, which was limited in effectiveness in Algeria and Morocco because high mountains separated most seaports from the interior. Since many of the Arabs belonged to camel-breeding tribes back in their Arabian homeland, they felt a cultural kinship with those Berbers who had taken up camel pastoralism during the preceding few centuries and thus related better to the peoples of the interior than any previous conquerors had done.

A series of Berber revolts against Arab rule from 740 onward led to the appearance of several small principalities in what are today Morocco and Algeria. The rulers of these city-states on the northern fringe of the Sahara held Islamic beliefs somewhat different from those of the Arab rulers in the east. Their religious differences may have interfered with their east-west overland trade and led them to look for new possibilities elsewhere. From the fragmentary records that survive, it appears that traders from these city-states, Sijilmasa and Tahert, were the first places to develop significant and regular trading contact with the south in the 9th century. Most of their populations were Berbers, so it is reasonable to assume that they already knew that nomads speaking closely related languages were roaming the central and southern reaches of the great desert. But prior to 740, they had little reason to explore the possibilities of trade with the south.

Once they did look south, however, they discovered that gold dust was one of the products the southern nomads received in exchange for salt. The gold came from deposits along the Niger and other West African rivers. The people who panned for the gold seem not to have used it extensively, and they did not value it nearly as highly as did the traders from Sijilmasa. For the latter, trading salt for gold was a dream come true. They were able to provide the nomads of the southern desert, who controlled the salt sources but had little use for gold, with products not available from the south, such as copper and certain manufactured goods. Thus everyone benefited from the creation of the new trade link. Sijilmasa and Tahert became wealthy cities, the former minting gold coins that circulated as far away as Egypt and Syria. The high value placed on gold in the Mediterranean lands greatly increased the profitability of the trade at every stage.

The Kingdom of Ghana

The earliest known sub-Saharan beneficiary of the new exchange system was the kingdom of Ghana. First mentioned in an Arabic text of the late eighth century as "the land of gold," Ghana inaugurates the documentable political history of West Africa. Yet until the mid-eleventh century, few details are available about this realm, established by the Soninke people and covering parts of Mali, Mauritania, and Senegal. Then the Arab geographer al-Bakri (d. 1094) described it as follows:

> The city of Ghana consists of two towns situated on a plain. One of these towns is inhabited by Muslims. It is large and possesses a dozen mosques, one being for the Friday prayer, and each having imams [prayer leaders], muezzins [people to make the call to prayer], and salaried reciters of the Quran. There are jurisconsults [legal specialists] and scholars. Around the town are sweet wells, which they use for drinking and for cultivating vegetables. The royal city, called al-Ghaba ["the grove"], is six miles away, and the area between the two towns is covered with habitations. Their houses are constructed of stone and acacia wood. The king has a palace with conical huts, surrounded by a fence like a wall. In the king's town, not far from the royal court, is a mosque for the use of Muslims who visit the king on missions. . . . The interpreters of the king are Muslims, as are his treasurer and the majority of his ministers.
>
> Their religion is paganism, and the worship of idols. . . . Around the royal town are domed dwellings, woods and copses where live their sorcerers, those in charge of their religious cults. There are also their idols and their kings' tombs.[2]

Typical of monarchs with imperial powers, the king of Ghana required the sons of vassal kings to attend his court. He meted out justice and controlled trade, collecting taxes on the salt

and copper coming from the north. His large army of bowmen and cavalry made Ghana the dominant power in the entire region. By the end of the tenth century, the king's sway extended even to Awdaghost, the trade entrepôt that had grown up in the desert at the southern end of the track to Sijilmasa. Awdaghost was populated by Arabs and Berbers.

After 1076, Ghana fell prey to a new state formed by desert nomads who had been drawn into the trade in the region of Awdaghost. These conquerors, the Muslim Almoravids, ruled both sides of the desert from their newly built capital city of Marrakesh in Morocco. After little more than a decade, during which later Muslim historians assert many people in Ghana converted to Islam, Almoravid strength in the south dwindled because of demands for military manpower in the north. Although Ghana thereby regained its independence, many of its former provinces had been permanently lost, and it never recovered its former greatness. Ghana's strength had clearly derived from its dominance of the new trading system. But with the Almoravids still powerful in Morocco, the old system could not easily be recreated.

Prior to the arrival of the religiously zealous Almoravids, the traders who had reached Ghana from the north had not been overly insistent on propagating Islam. Over the three centuries separating al-Bakri's account in the eleventh century from the earliest mention of Ghana, Muslims had come to hold high economic positions in Ghana, and the kings tolerated their religious practices. But, in general, the people of Ghana had not been stirred to convert to Islam. General adoption of the Islamic religion, with consequent impact on the way of life of the Sahel peoples, would only come under later kingdoms.

SUB-SAHARAN AFRICA

The Indian Ocean network and, somewhat later, trade across the Sahara provided the vast region of sub-Saharan Africa with a few external contacts. The most important African network of cultural exchange from 300 B.C.E. to 1100 C.E., however, was within sub-Saharan Africa, and it led to the formation of enduring characteristics of African culture.

That a significant degree of cultural unity developed in sub-Saharan Africa is especially remarkable because of the many geographic obstacles to movement. The Sahara, the Atlantic and Indian Oceans, and the Red Sea form the boundaries of the region. With the exception of the Nile, a ribbon of green traversing the Sahara from south to north, the major river systems empty either into the South Atlantic, in the case of the Senegal, Niger, and Zaire, or into the Mozambique Channel of the Indian Ocean, in the case of the Zambezi. Moreover, rapids limit the use of these rivers for navigation.

Stretching over 80 degrees of latitude, Africa encompasses a large number of dramatically different environments. A 4,000-mile (6,500 kilometers) trek from the southern edge of the Sahara to the Cape of Good Hope would take a traveler from the semiarid steppes of the Sahel region to tropical savanna covered by long grasses and scattered forest, next to tropical rain forest on the lower Niger and in the Zaire Basin. The rain forest then gives way to another broad expanse of savanna, followed by more steppe and desert, and finally a region of temperate highlands at the southern extremity, located as far south of the equator as Greece and Sicily are to its north. East-west travel is comparatively easy in the steppe and savanna regions but difficult in the equatorial rain-forest belt and across the mountains and deep rift valleys that abut the rain forest to the east and separate East from West Africa.

The Development of Cultural Unity

As we learned in Part II, by the first millennium C.E., distinctive cultural regions had come into existence from China to the Mediterranean as the result of political expansion and conquest. More enduring than the political units, however, were cultural heritages shared by the educated elites within each region—heritages that some anthropologists call "great traditions." They typically included a written language, common legal and belief systems, ethical codes, and other intellectual traditions. They loom large in surviving written records as traditions that rise above the diversity of local customs and beliefs commonly distinguished as "small traditions."

By the first millennium C.E., sub-Saharan Africa, too, had become a distinct cultural region, but one that was not shaped by imperial conquest and not characterized by a shared elite culture, a "great tradition." The cultural unity of sub-Saharan Africa was especially complex because it rested on similar characteristics shared to varying degrees by myriad popular cultures, or "small traditions." These popular cultures had developed during sub-Saharan Africa's long period of isolation from the rest of the world and had been refined, renewed, and interwoven by repeated episodes of migration and social interaction. Unfortunately, historians know very little about this complex prehistory. Thus, to a greater degree than in other regions, they call on anthropological descriptions, oral history, and comparatively late records of various "small traditions" to reconstruct the broad outlines of prehistoric cultural formation.

Sub-Saharan Africa's cultural unity is less immediately apparent than its diversity. Indeed, both students and scholars find the number and variety of the continent's social and cultural forms bewildering. By one estimate, for example, two thousand distinct languages are spoken on the continent, many of them corresponding to social and belief systems endowed with distinctive rituals and cosmologies. There are likewise numerous food production systems, ranging from hunting and gathering—very differently carried out by the Mbuti Pygmies of the equatorial rain forest and the Khoisan peoples of the southwestern deserts—to the cultivation of bananas, yams, and other root crops in forest clearings and of sorghum and other grains in the savanna lands. Pastoral societies display a similar diversity. Among cattle herders, the Dinka and Nuer of the upper Nile have customs quite unlike those of the Fulani in West Africa. Among camel herders, the practices of the Somalis living in the Horn of East Africa bear little resemblance to those of the Tuareg far to the west in the southern Sahara.

Such diversity is not surprising. Sub-Saharan Africa covers an area much larger than any of the other cultural regions of the first millennium C.E., and the diversity of its climate, terrain, and vegetation is more pronounced. Africans adapted to these many environments in distinctive ways. Moreover, the overall density of population was in most areas lower than in the temperate lands to the north. Thus societies and polities had abundant room to form and reform, and a substantial amount of space separated different groups. The contacts that did occur were neither so frequent nor so long lasting as to produce rigid cultural uniformity.

Another factor accounts for the persisting diversity of sub-Saharan Africa—the inability for centuries of external conquerors to penetrate the region's natural barriers and impose any sort of uniform culture. The Egyptians occupied Nubia for long periods but were blocked from going farther south by the Nile cataracts and the vast swampland in the Nile's upper reaches. The Romans sent expeditions against people living in the Libyan Sahara but could not incorporate them into the Roman world. Arabic sources tell of military expeditions reaching the southern parts of the Sahara in the seventh century C.E., but these accounts are tinged with legend and had little, if any, effect. Indeed, not until the nineteenth century would outsiders gain control of the continent and begin the process of establishing an elite culture, that of western Europe.

African Cultural Characteristics

Despite these great cultural variations, outside visitors who got to know the sub-Saharan region well in the nineteenth and twentieth centuries were always struck by the broad commonalities that underlay African life and culture. Though there were many varieties of African kingdoms, kingship displayed common features, most notably the ritual isolation of the King (see Voices & Visions: Personal Styles of Rule in India and Mali in Chapter 15). Even in societies too small to organize themselves into kingdoms, there was a strong concern for distinct and parallel social categories—age groupings, fixed kinship divisions, distinct gender roles and relations, and occupational groupings. Though not hierarchial, these filled a role similar to the prevalent divisions between noble, commoner, and slave where kings ruled.

Commonalities are also evident in music. Africans played many musical instruments, yet there were underlying traditions, particularly in rhythm, that made African music as a whole distinctive. Music played an important role in social rituals, as did dancing and wearing masks. In agriculture, the common technique was cultivation by hoe and digging stick instead of plowing with a team of animals.

These and other indications of underlying cultural unity have led modern observers to identify a common African quality throughout most of the region, even though most sub-Saharan Africans themselves did not perceive it—just as Greeks and Persians, though both part of a broad Indo-European linguistic and cultural grouping, did not recognize the shared features of their pantheons, social structures, and languages. An eminent Belgian anthropologist, Jacques Maquet, has called this quality "Africanity."

Some historians hypothesize that this cultural unity emanated originally from the peoples who once occupied the southern Sahara. In Paleolithic times, periods of dryness alternated with periods of wetness as the ice ages that locked up much of the world's fresh water in glaciers and icecaps came and went. As European glaciers receded with the waning of the last ice age, a storm belt brought increased wetness to the Saharan region. Deep canyons were scoured by rushing rivers. Now filled with fine sand, those canyons are easily visible on flights over the southern parts of the desert, which long ago were among the most habitable parts of the continent and perhaps the most densely populated. As the glaciers receded still farther, the storm belt moved northward to Europe, and a dry belt that had been farther south moved northward between 5000 and 2500 B.C.E. As a consequence, runs the hypothesis, the region's population migrated south, where it became increasingly concentrated in what is now the Sahel. That region may have been the initial incubation center for what were to become Pan-African cultural patterns.

Eventually, however, the dryness of the land and the pressures of population concentration drove some people out of this cultural core into more sparsely settled lands to the east, west, and south. A parallel process may have occurred in the northern Sahara, but the evidence there is much more limited. As for the Nile Valley, migration away from the desert was surely one of the triggers for the emergence of the Old Kingdom of Egypt at the start of the third millennium B.C.E.

The Advent of Iron and the Bantu Migrations

Although some aspects of this reconstruction are speculative, archaeological investigation has shown that sub-Saharan agriculture first became common north of the equator by the early second millennium B.C.E., and then spread southward, displacing hunting and gathering as a way of life. Moreover, there is botanical evidence that banana trees, probably introduced to southeastern Africa from Southeast Asia, made their way north and west, retracing the presumed migrations of the first agriculturalists.

A second dispersal involved metallurgy. Copper mining is in evidence in the Sahara from the early first millennium B.C.E., in the Niger Valley somewhat later, and in the Central African copper belt between 400 and 900 C.E. Gold mining is evident in Zimbabwe by the eighth and ninth centuries C.E. Most important of all, iron smelting is documented in northern sub-Saharan Africa in the early first millennium C.E., and from there it spread southward to the rest of the continent, becoming firmly established in southern Africa by the year 800.

Iron does not naturally occur in metallic form, except in meteorites, and a very high temperature is necessary to extract it from ores. Thus many historians believe that the secret of smelting iron was discovered only once, by the Hittites of Anatolia (modern Turkey) around 1500 B.C.E. (see Chapter 3). But while its spread from this presumed point of origin can generally be traced in Europe and Asia, how iron smelting

reached sub-Saharan Africa is not clear. By way of the Nile Valley is one possibility, but the earliest evidence of ironworking from the kingdom of Meroë, on the upper Nile, is no earlier than the evidence from West Africa (northern Nigeria). Even less plausible is the idea of a spread southward from Phoenician settlements in North Africa, since archaeological evidence has not substantiated vague Greek and Latin accounts of Phoenician contacts with the south by land.

Some historians, therefore, suggest that Africans may have discovered for themselves how to smelt iron. They might have done so while firing pottery in kilns. No firm evidence exists to prove or disprove this theory.

Linguistic analysis provides the strongest evidence of extensive contacts among sub-Saharan Africans in the first millennium C.E.—and offers suggestions about the spread of iron. Linguists recognize that most of the people of sub-Saharan Africa speak languages belonging to one giant family, often called the Niger-Kongo, that stretches from the Senegal River in West Africa to the southern tip of the continent. Virtually all of the more than three hundred languages spoken south of the equator are closely related, belonging to the branch of the Niger-Kongo family known as Bantu after the word meaning "people" in most of the languages.

The distribution of the Bantu languages both north and south of the equator is consistent with a divergence beginning in the first millennium B.C.E. By comparing core words common to most of the languages, linguists have drawn some conclusions about the original Bantu-speakers, whom they call "proto-Bantu." The proto-Bantu engaged in fishing, using canoes, nets, lines, and hooks. They lived in sedentary villages on the edge of the rain forest, where they grew yams and grains and harvested wild oil palms. They possessed domesticated goats, dogs, and perhaps other animals. They made pottery and cloth. From this and other evidence, linguists surmise that the proto-Bantu homeland was near the modern boundary of Nigeria and Cameroon, from which they trace western and eastern routes of linguistic dispersal into the equatorial rain forests to the south. Although dates for this long process are scarce, Bantu-speaking people are evident in East Africa by the eighth century C.E.

Because the presumed home of the proto-Bantu lies near the known sites of early iron smelting, migration by Bantu-speakers seems a likely mechanism for the southward spread of iron. Supplied with iron axes and iron hoes, the migrating Bantus are presumed to have hacked out forest clearings and planted crops. According to this scenario, they established an economic basis for new societies that were able to sustain much denser populations than could earlier societies dependent on hunting and gathering. Thus the period from 500 B.C.E. to 1000 C.E. saw a massive transfer of Bantu traditions and practices southward, eastward, and westward and their transformation into Pan-African traditions and practices.

THE SPREAD OF IDEAS

Ideas, like social customs, religious attitudes, and artistic styles, can spread along trade routes and through folk migrations. In either event, documenting the dissemination of ideas, particularly in preliterate societies, poses a difficult historical problem. Customs surrounding the eating of pork are a case in point. Scholars disagree about whether the idea to domesticate pigs occurred only once and spread or whether several different peoples hit on the same idea.

Southeast Asia was an important and possibly the earliest center of pig domestication. There the eating of pork became highly ritualized, sometimes being prohibited except on ceremonial occasions. On the other side of the Indian Ocean, in ancient Egypt, wild swine were common in the Nile swamps, pigs were considered sacred to the underworld god Set, and eating them was prohibited. The biblical prohibition on the Israelites' eating pork, echoed later by the Muslims, probably came from Egypt in the second millennium B.C.E.

In eastern Iran, an archaeological site dating from the third millennium B.C.E. provides strong

evidence of another religious taboo on eating pig. Although the area around the site was swampy and home to many wild pigs, not a single pig bone has been found there. Yet small pig figurines seem to have been used as symbolic religious offerings.

What accounts for the apparent connection between the domestication of pigs and religion in these widespread areas? There is no way of knowing. It has been hypothesized that pigs were first domesticated in Southeast Asia by people who had no herd animals—sheep, goat, cattle, horses—and who relied on fish for most of their animal protein. The pig was thus a special animal to them. From Southeast Asia, pig domestication and the religious beliefs and rituals associated with the consumption of pork could have spread along the maritime routes of the Indian Ocean, eventually reaching Iran and Egypt.

A more certain example of the spread of an idea is the practice of hammering a carved die onto a piece of precious metal and using the resulting coin as a medium of exchange. From its origin in Anatolia in the first millennium B.C.E., the idea of trading by means of struck coinage spread rapidly to Europe, North Africa, and India. Was the low-value copper coinage of China, made by pouring molten metal into a mold, also inspired by this practice from far away? It may have been, but it might also derive from indigenous Chinese metalworking. There is no way to be sure. Theoretically, all that is needed for an idea to spread is a single returning traveler telling about some wonder that he or she saw abroad.

The Spread of Buddhism

The spread of ideas in an organized way emerges as a new phenomenon in the first millennium B.C.E. From its original home in northern India in the fifth century B.C.E., Buddhism grew to become, with Christianity and Islam, one of the three most popular and widespread religions in the world (see Chapter 7). In all three cases, the religious ideas being spread were distinctive because of *not* being associated with specific ethnic or kinship groups.

King Ashoka, the Maurya ruler of India, and Kanishka, the greatest king of the Kushans of northern Afghanistan, were powerful royal advocates of Buddhism between the third century B.C.E. and the second century C.E. However, monks, missionaries, and pilgrims were the people who crisscrossed India, followed the Silk Road, or took ship in the Indian Ocean to bring the Buddha's teachings to Southeast Asia, China, Korea, and ultimately Japan.

The Chinese pilgrims Faxian (died between 418 and 423 C.E.) and Xuanzang (600–664 C.E.) left written accounts of their travels (see Chapter 7). Both followed the Silk Road, from which Buddhism had arrived in China, encountering along the way Buddhist communities and monasteries that previous generations of missionaries and pilgrims had established. Faxian began his trip in the company of a Chinese envoy to an unspecified ruler or people in Central Asia. After working his way from one Buddhist site to another across Afghanistan and India, he reached Sri Lanka, a Buddhist land where he lived for two years. Then he embarked for China on a merchant ship with two hundred men aboard. A storm drove the ship to Java, which he did not describe because its religion was Hindu rather than Buddhist (the presence of Hinduism is an indication of earlier seaborne influences from India on island Southeast Asia). After five months ashore, Faxian finally reached China on another ship. The narrative of Xuanzang's journey two centuries later is quite similar, though he returned to China the way he had come, along the Silk Road.

Less reliable accounts make reference to missionaries traveling to Syria, Egypt, and Macedonia, as well as to Southeast Asia. One of Ashoka's sons allegedly led a band of missionaries to Sri Lanka. Later his sister brought a company of nuns along with a branch of the sacred Bo tree under which the Buddha received enlightenment. According to Buddhist tradition, she accomplished her journey by air. At the same time, there are reports of other monks traveling to Burma, Thailand, and Sumatra. Ashoka's missionaries may also have reached Tibet by way of trade routes across the Himalayas. A firmer tradition maintains that in 622 C.E. a minister of the

Textile with Buddha image from northwest China Images of the Buddha, with or without various attendants, are central in the art of all Buddhist countries. The image of the Buddha first emerged in Gandhara in northwest Pakistan around the third century B.C.E. Originally influenced by Greek artistic styles introduced by Alexander the Great, it developed many variations as Buddhism spread across the Silk Road and Indian Ocean. (Courtesy of the Trustees of the British Museum)

Tibetan king traveled to India to study Buddhism and on his return introduced writing to his homeland.

The different lands that received the story and teachings of the Buddha preserved or adapted them in different ways. Theravada Buddhism, "Teachings of the Elders," centered in Sri Lanka. Holding closely to the Buddha's earliest teachings, it maintained that the goal of religion, available only to monks, is *nirvana*, the total absence of suffering and the end of the cycle of rebirth (see Chapter 7). This teaching contrasted with

Mahayana, or "The Greater Vehicle," Buddhism, which stressed becoming a *bodhisattva*, a "being striving for enlightenment," a status all Buddhists could aspire to. Compassion for others and helping to relieve their suffering were more important in this system than achieving nirvana.

An offshoot of Mahayana Buddhism stressing ritual prayer and personal guidance by "perfected ones" became dominant in Tibet after the 8th century C.E. In China, another offshoot, Chan (called Zen in its Japanese form), focused on meditation and sudden enlightenment. It and Pure Land Buddhism, also derived from Mahayana scriptures and devoted to repetition of the name of the Buddha Amitabha, became the dominant sects in China, Korea, and Japan (see Chapter 11).

The Spread of Christianity

The post-Roman development of Christianity in Europe is discussed in Chapter 9. The Christian faith spread earlier in northern Africa and Asia, however. Aksum, the first Christian kingdom of Ethiopia, provides an illuminating example of the role of trade routes. In the fourth century C.E., a Syrian philosopher, traveling with two youths, took ship for India to acquaint himself with distant lands. Returning, they put into a port on the Red Sea occupied by Ethiopians who had had a falling out with the Romans. The Ethiopians killed everyone aboard the ship except for the two boys, Aedesius—who later narrated this story—and Frumentius. They were taken before the king. He was strongly impressed with their learning and made the former his cupbearer and the latter his treasurer and secretary.

When the king died, his wife pleaded with Frumentius to take over the reins of government on behalf of her and her infant son, Ezana. Vested with such power, Frumentius sought out Roman Christians among the merchants who visited the country and urged them to establish Christian communities. It is not stated whether he converted Ezana before he reached his majority and became king. Once Ezana was in power, however, Aedesius and Frumentius were free to

return to Syria. From there, Frumentius traveled to Egypt to report to the patriarch of Alexandria on the progress of Christianity in Aksum. Though Frumentius had not previously been a clergyman, the patriarch elevated him to the rank of bishop and in approximately 330 sent him back to inaugurate that post at Aksum, thus beginning the still-continuing tradition of the patriarch of Alexandria appointing the head of the Ethiopian church.

As in Europe, where Christmas trees, Easter eggs, and many other customs preserve pre-Christian traditions, Ethiopian Christianity developed its own unique features. One popular belief, perhaps deriving from the Ethiopian Jewish community was that the Ark of the Covenant, the most sacred object of worship of the ancient Hebrews (see Chapter 4), had been transferred from Jerusalem to the Ethiopian church of Our Lady Mary of Zion. Another tradition maintains that Christ miraculously dried up a lake to serve as the site for this church, which became the place of coronation for Ethiopia's rulers.

Christianity, Buddhism, and Islam (as will be discussed in Chapter 10) all developed local customs and understandings as they spread, despite the overall doctrinal unity of each. As "great traditions," these religions linked priests, monks, nuns, and religious scholars across vast distances. The masses of believers, however, seldom considered their faith in such broad contexts. Missionary religions imported through long-distance trading networks merged with myriad "small traditions" to provide for the social and spiritual needs of peoples living in many lands under widely varying circumstances.

CONCLUSION

Exchange within early long-distance trading systems differed in many ways from the ebb and flow of culture, language, and custom that folk migrations brought about. New technologies and agricultural products worked great changes on the landscape and in people's lives, but nothing akin to the Africanity observed south of the Sahara can be attributed to the societies involved in the Silk Road, Indian Ocean, or trans-Saharan exchanges. The peoples directly involved in travel and trade were not very numerous in comparison with the agricultural populations their routes brought into contact, and their specialized lifestyles as pastoral nomads or seafarers isolated them still further. The Bantu, however, if current theories are correct, brought with them metallurgical skills and agricultural practices that permitted much denser habitation in the lands they spread to. Moreover, they themselves settled among and merged with the previous inhabitants, becoming not just the bearers of new technologies but their primary beneficiaries as well.

The most obvious exception to this generalization lies in the intangible area of ideas. Circumstantial evidence, reinforced by legendary accounts of missionary exploits, offer the persuasive argument that trade routes and networks of exchange played vital roles in the spread of religion. How people received, adapted, and utilized each religion as it spread from one country to the next is difficult to determine. But, as the next two chapters will show, the spread of religion plays as important a role as agricultural and technological innovation in shaping the patterns of cultural change and diversity in this first era of long-distance interchange among the peoples of the earth.

SUGGESTED READING

Broad and suggestive overviews on issues of cross-cultural exchange in this era may be found in Philip D. Curtin, *Cross-Cultural Trade in World History* (1985), and C. G. F. Simkin, *The Traditional Trade of Asia* (1968).

For readable overviews of the Silk Road see Luce Boulnois, *The Silk Road* (1966), and Irene M. Franck and David M. Brownstone, *The Silk Road: A History*

(1986). A more detailed examination of products traded across Central Asia in the eighth century based on a famous Japanese collection is provided by Ryoichi Hayashi, *The Silk Road and the Shoso-in* (1975). Owen Lattimore gives a superb first-person account of traveling by camel caravan in the region in *The Desert Road to Turkestan* (1928). More generally on peoples and historical developments in Central Asia see Denis Sinor, *Inner Asia, History-Civilization-Languages: A Syllabus* (1987), and Karl Jettmar, *Art of the Steppes*, rev. ed. (1967). The Middle Eastern trading entrepôts are treated by M. Rostovzeff, *Caravan Cities* (1975).

For a readable but rather sketchy historical overview of the history of connections across the Indian Ocean see August Toussaint, *History of the Indian Ocean* (1966). Alan Villiers provides a stimulating account of what it was like to sail dhows between East Africa and the Persian Gulf in *Sons of Sinbad* (1940).

On a more scholarly plane, K. N. Chaudhuri's *Trade and Civilization in the Indian Ocean: An Economic History from the Rise of Islam to 1750* (1985), stresses the economic aspect of trading relations. Pierre Vérin gives an archaeologist's perspective on the special problem of Madagascar in *The History of Civilisation in North Madagascar* (1986). The question of Roman contact with India is the topic of E. H. Warmington's *The Commerce Between the Roman Empire and India* (1974); J. Innes Miller's *The Spice Trade of the Roman Empire, 29 B.C. to A.D. 641* (1969); and Vimala Begley and Richard Daniel De Puma's edited collection of articles, *Rome and India: The Ancient Sea Trade* (1991). The indispensable primary source for early Indian Ocean history is Lionel Casson, ed. and trans., *The Periplus Maris Arythraei: Text with Introduction, Translation, and Commentary* (1989). Seafaring as revealed in Arabic texts is the topic of George F. Hourani's brief book *Arab Seafaring in the Indian Ocean in Ancient and Early Medieval Times* (1975).

Richard W. Bulliet's *The Camel and the Wheel* (1975) deals with the development of camel use in the Middle East, along the Silk Road, and in North Africa and the Sahara. For an entertaining and well-illustrated account of the discovery of Saharan rock art, see Henri Lhote, *The Search for the Tassili Frescoes: The Story of the Prehistoric Rock-Paintings of the Sahara* (1959). Additional views on the history and impact of Saharan trade may be found in E. Ann McDougall, "The Sahara Reconsidered: Pastoralism, Politics and Salt from the Ninth Through the Twelfth Centuries," *History in Africa* 12 (1983): 263–286, and Nehemia Levtzion, *Ancient Ghana and Mali*, 2d ed. (1980). The latter work is also essential to the broader topic of early West

African history. For translated texts relating to both the Sahara and West Africa see J. F. P. Hopkins and Nehemia Levtzion, eds., *Corpus of Early Arabic Sources for West African History* (1981).

Two general works on the early history of sub-Saharan Africa containing many articles by numerous authors are J. F. A. Ajayi and Michael Crowder, *A History of West Africa,* vol. 1 (1976), and G. Mokhtar, ed., *General History of Africa II: Ancient Civilizations of Africa* (1981). The latter work contains extensive treatments of the issues of ironworking and the Bantu migrations.

The spread of Christianity and the spread of Buddhism are enormous topics. To follow up the particular aspects treated in this chapter see Stuart Munro-Hay, *Aksum: An African Civilisation of Late Antiquity* (1991); Xinru Liu, *Ancient India and Ancient China: Trade and Religious Exchanges, A.D. 1–600* (1988); Rolf A. Stein, *Tibetan Civilization* (1972); Tilak Hettiarachchy, *History of Kingship in Ceylon up to the Fourth Century A.D.* (1972); and Yoneo Ishii, *Sangha, State, and*

Society: Thai Buddhism in History (1986). The Chinese travelers, accounts cited are Fa-hsien [Faxian], *The Travels of Fa-hsien (399–414 A.D.), or, Record of the Buddhistic Kingdoms,* trans. H. A. Giles (1923; reprint, 1981), and Hiuen Tsiang [Xuanzang], *Si-Yu-Ki: Buddhist Records of the Western World,* trans. Samuel Beal (1884; reprint, 1981).

NOTES

1. Victor H. Mair, ed. *The Columbia Anthology of Traditional Chinese Literature* (New York, 1994) p. 485. Translated by Victor H. Mair.

2. J. F. A. Ajayi and Michael Crowder, eds. *History of West Africa* (New York, 1976) vol. 1, pp. 120–121.

Christian Europe Emerges,

300–1200

The Post-Roman Transformation · The Western Church

The Byzantine Empire · Western Europe Revives

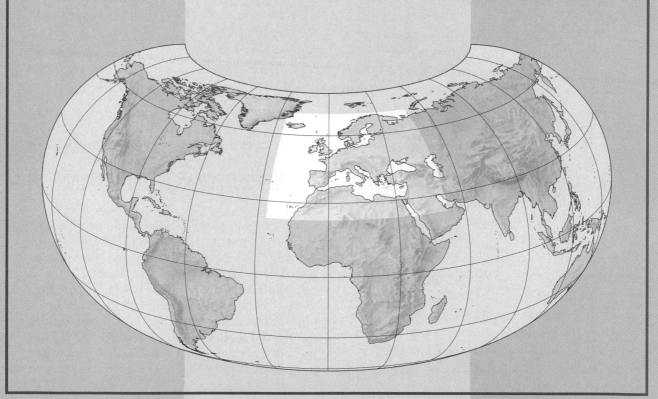

Christmas Day of the year 800 found Charles, the king of the Franks, in Rome instead of his palace in Aachen, in northeastern France. At six-foot-three, Charles was a foot taller than the average man of his time, and his royal career had been equally gargantuan. Crowned king in his mid-twenties in 768, he had spent three decades crisscrossing western Europe, waging war on Muslim invaders from Spain, Avar invaders from Hungary, and a myriad of German princes.

Charles subdued many enemies and established himself as the protector of the papacy. So it is hard to believe the eyewitness report of his secretary and biographer, the Saxon Einhard, that Charles was surprised when Pope Leo III stepped forward as the king rose from his prayers in the church of Saint Peter and placed a new crown on his head. "Life and victory to Charles the August, crowned by God the great and pacific Emperor of the Romans," proclaimed the pope.[1] Then, amid the cheers of the crowd, he humbly knelt before the new emperor.

Charlemagne (from the Latin *Carolus magnus*, "Charles the Great") was the first to bear the title *emperor* in western Europe since 476, when a Germanic commander had deposed the Roman emperor in the West. Rome's decline and Charlemagne's rise marked a shift of focus for Europe—away from the Mediterranean and toward the north and west. The world of Charlemagne, dominated by the Germanic peoples of the north, opened a new era in European history, in which German custom and Christian piety transformed a Roman heritage to create a new civilization. This civilization is commonly called medieval, literally "middle age," because it comes between the era of Greco-Roman civilization and the intellectual, artistic, and economic changes of the Renaissance in the fourteenth century. Irish monks replaced Greek philosophers as the leading intellectuals. Crimes were defined the German way, as offenses against family, not against society, as in Rome. The sumptuous villas of the Roman emperors gave way to cold, stone castles. One of Charlemagne's consisted of a simple stone building with three large rooms and eleven small ones, surrounded by a wooden stockade enclosing stables, kitchen, and bakery, and stocked with 355 pigs, 22 peacocks, one set of bedding, and one tablecloth.

The imperial title did not survive Charlemagne. The unity of his realm fell apart under less able successors; and even he had to acknowledge a rival emperor in the East, where the political and legal heritage of Rome continued in the Eastern Roman, or Byzantine Empire. Western Europeans lived amid the ruins of an empire that haunted their dreams but was never rebuilt. The Byzantines, in contrast, continued and reinterpreted Roman traditions for centuries. In the East, the authority of the Byzantine emperors blended with the influence of the Christian church to form a new and creative synthesis. The western area of the old Roman Empire, despite the respite of Charlemagne's reign, experienced generations of chaos among scores of competing regional powers; there the only unifying force was the growing authority of the church.

THE POST-ROMAN TRANSFORMATION

The migrations of the Germanic peoples, the disappearance of the legal framework of unity and order that persisted even in the final days of the Western Roman Empire, and the fragmentation of political allegiance among scores of kings, nobles, and chieftains dramatically changed the landscape in western Europe during the period 500–800 leading up to the reign of Charlemagne. In region after region, the traditional, family-based law of the Germanic peoples supplanted the imperial edicts of the emperors.

The Roman order broke down in other ways, as well. Fear and physical insecurity, particularly in areas subject to Viking raids, was one of several factors that induced many communities to adopt defensive attitudes and seek the protection of local strongmen. When looters and pillagers from the sea were likely to appear at any moment, a distant king was not nearly so important as a local lord with a fortified castle where peasants could take refuge. This sort of personal dependency became a hallmark of the post-Roman period in the Latin West.

From Roman Empire to Germanic Kingdoms

Rome's decline, beginning in the third century, marked not just the end of an empire but the end of a long era during which the eastern Mediterranean Sea was the geographic center of a group of interrelated societies and economies. Although Rome's political institutions and military prowess had united the Mediterranean Basin, (see Chapter 6), Rome always had been on its western fringe, far from the great Eastern cities such as Athens, Antioch, Damascus, Jerusalem, and Alexandria. Thus it is not surprising that when the empire weakened, the emperors Diocletian and Constantine concerned themselves most with preserving power in the East in what became known as the Byzantine Empire.

Left on its own, the Western Roman Empire fragmented in the fifth century into a handful of kingdoms under Germanic rulers: Frankish kings of the Merovingian family, who preceded the Carolingians (family of Charlemagne) in much of Gaul, Visigothic kings in Spain, Burgundians in eastern Gaul, Saxons on the eastern side of the Rhine, among others (see Map 9.1). Italy itself saw the establishment in the sixth century of a strong Lombard kingdom in its north and a Byzantine foothold around Ravenna along the northeast coast. Rome proper lost virtually all political importance even though it retained prominence as the seat of the papacy, which local noble families competed to control.

Visigothic crown of King Recceswinth from 7th century Spain Jewelry was one of the best developed Germanic arts. Set with 30 pearls and 30 sapphires, this gold crown featured pendant letters spelling "Reccesvinthus Rex Offerata"—"KING RECCESWINTH OFFERS IT." (Museo Archeologico, Madrid)

Local versions of Latin were understood only by speakers for whom they were a native language. The educated few, more and more to be found among Christian priests and monks, retained a somewhat simplified form of Latin. The speech of the uneducated masses rapidly evolved into Romance dialects—Portuguese, Spanish, Catalan, Provençal, French, Italian, Romanian—except in northern and northeastern Europe, where Latin was too poorly established to stand in the way of the Germanic and Scandinavian di-

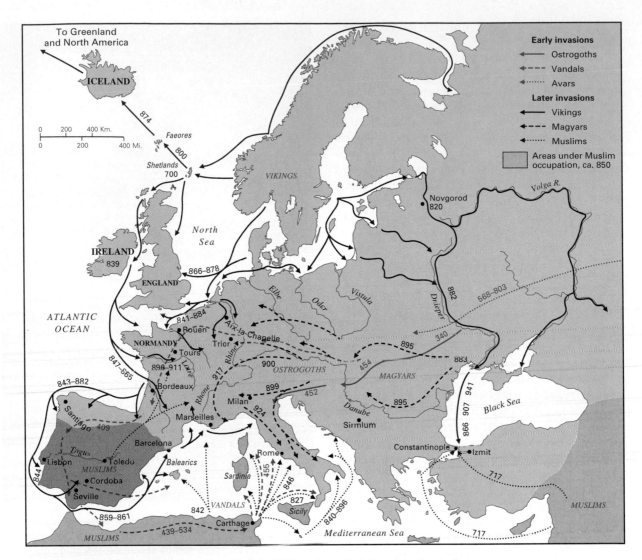

Map 9.1   Raids and Invasions in the Era of Political Disruption   Early invasions focused on the primary care centers of Roman imperial authority: Rome, Milan, Carthage, and Constantinople. Later invasions reflect the shift of power to northern Europe. In contrast to raids in the northwest, extensive Viking activity along the rivers of eastern Europe consisted partly of establishing authority over Slavic peoples and partly of opening up trade routes to Byzantium and Iran.

alects. Thus Europe came to be divided roughly into three linguistic zones: countries in the west and south speaking Romance tongues, countries in the north and center speaking Germanic and Scandinavian tongues, and countries in the east speaking the Slavic languages of peoples who moved westward on the heels of the Germanic folk migrations (see Voices and Visions: The Evolution of the Germanic Languages).

Despite the warlike behavior of the new rulers in the West, lack of unity impaired their military strength. In 711 a frontier raiding party of Arabs and Berbers, acting under the authority of the Muslim ruler in Damascus, in Syria, crossed the Strait of Gibraltar and overturned the kingdom of the Visigoths in Spain. The Europeans were too disunited to stop them from consolidating their hold on the Iberian Peninsula. After push-

The Evolution of the Germanic Languages

People in almost every country in Europe speak a distinctive language because of the consolidation of kingdoms between 1200 and 1500 and the rise of modern nation-states. In post-Roman Europe, however, language was in flux. Literacy was mostly confined to Latin, which changed only slowly because it was a written tongue. A great variety of spoken dialects that were seldom written evolved more rapidly from intermixtures of Italic, Celtic, Germanic, and Slavic tongues—all belonging to the Indo-European language family that extended as far as India and Central Asia.

The following quotations from the Gospel of Saint Luke indicate the variety and change over time in the Germanic dialects that eventually developed into modern English and German.

And shepherds were in that same land abiding and keeping watch by night over their flocks. But the angel of the lord approached them and the glory of the lord shone about them, and they feared greatly.

Gothic (fourth century)
Jah hairdjos wesun in thamma samin landa thairhwakandas jah witandans wahtwom nahts ufaro hairdai seinai. Ith aggilus fraujins anaqam ins jah wulthus fraujins biskain ins, jah ohtedun agisa mikilamma.

Old English (tenth/eleventh century)
& hydras waeron on tham ylcan rice waciende. & nihtwaeccan healdende ofer heora heorda. Tha stod dri-

htnes engel with hig & godes beorhtnes him ymbescean. & hi him mycelum ege adredon.

Middle English
And schepherdis weren in the same cuntre, wakinge and hepinge the watchis of the nyzt on her fick. And loo! The aungel of the Lord stood by sydis hem, and the clerenesse of God schynedet aboute hem; and thei dredden with greet drede.

Low German (fifteenth century)
Unde de herden weren in der suluen iegenode wakende. Unde helden de wake auer ere schape. Unde seet de engel des heren stunt by en unde de clarheit godes ummevench se unde se vruchteden sick myt groten vruchten.

High German (sixteenth century)
Und es woren Hirten in derselbigen Gegend auf dem Felde bei den Hurden, die huteten des Nachts ihrer Herde. Und siehe, des Herrn Engel trat zu ihnen, und die Klarheit des Herrn leuchtete um sie; und sie furchteten sich.

What do these quotations indicate about the similarities of English and German? How important is language as a social bond?

Source: J. P. Mallory, *The Search for the Indo-Europeans* (London: Thames and Hudson, 1989), p. 86.

ing the remaining Christian chieftains into the Pyrenees Mountains, the Muslims moved on to France. There they conquered much of the southern coast and penetrated as far north as Tours, less than 150 miles (240 kilometers) from the English Channel, before Charlemagne's grandfather, Charles Martel, stopped their most advanced raiding party in 732.

The Arabs never returned to northern Europe, but Viking sea raiders from Scandinavia perpetuated feelings of insecurity in coastal regions in the succeeding centuries. Local sources from France, the British Isles, and Muslim Spain attest

to widespread dread of Viking warriors descending from multi-oared dragon-prowed boats to pillage monasteries, villages, and towns. In the ninth century, raiders from Denmark and Norway harried the British and French coasts while the Swedes pursued raiding and trading interests along the rivers of eastern Europe. Although many Viking attacks were private pirate raids for booty and slaves, the eleventh century saw concerted efforts at colonization and political expansion with the settlement of Iceland, Greenland, and, for a brief time, Vinland on the eastern coast of Canada.

The most important and ambitious expeditions in terms of numbers of men and horses and long-lasting impact were by Vikings long settled in Normandy (in northeastern France). These Norman (from "North men") conquests of England in 1066 by the Duke of Normandy, William the Conqueror, and of Muslim Sicily from the 1060s to the 1090s resulted in permanent changes of government.

A Basic Economy

Archaeological investigations and analyses of records kept by Christian monasteries and nunneries reveal that a profound economic transformation was under way beneath the political jumble of the newly arising Germanic kingdoms. With the ascent of the Germanic peoples, the urban-based civilization of the Romans withered and shrank. Cities built according to Roman architectural and institutional models lost population, in some cases becoming villages. Roads the Romans had built to facilitate the march of their legions, and secondarily to foster commerce, fell into disuse and disrepair. Small thatched houses sprang up beside abandoned villas, and public buildings made of marble became dilapidated in the absence of the laborers, money, and civic leadership needed to maintain them. Purchases paid for in coin largely gave way to the bartering of goods and services.

Trade languished. The wheat that had once been shipped from Egypt to feed the multitudes of Rome now went to Constantinople. The wheat-growing lands of Tunisia, another of Rome's breadbaskets, were cut off in 439 by an invasion of Germanic Vandals from Spain, never to be effectively reintegrated with Europe. Although occasional shipments of goods from Egypt and Syria continued to reach Western ports, for the most part western Europe had to rely on its own resources. These meager resources, however, underwent a redistribution.

Roman centralization had long diverted the wealth and production of the empire toward the capital, from which Roman culture radiated outward to the provinces. As Germanic and other territorial lords replaced Roman governors, local self-sufficiency became ever more important, and the general disappearance of literacy and other aspects of Roman civilized life made room for new trends to flourish. These trends were based on local folk cultures, the "small traditions" of the various Germanic and Celtic peoples.

The diet in the northern countries was based on beer, lard or butter, and bread made of barley, rye, or wheat, all amply supplemented by pork from herds of swine fed with forest acorns and beechnuts, and by game from the same forests. The Roman diet based on wheat, wine, and olive oil persisted in the south. Nutritionally, the average western European of the ninth century probably did better than his or her descendants three hundred years later, when population was increasing and the forests were more and more reserved for the nobility.

In both north and south, self-sufficient farming estates, known as *manors* or *villas*, became the primary centers of agricultural production. Wealthy Romans had commonly owned country houses situated on their lands. From the fourth century onward, political insecurity prompted common farmers to give their lands to large landowners in return for political and physical protection. The warfare and instability of the post-Roman centuries made unprotected country houses even more vulnerable to pillaging and encouraged the fortification of manors. Isolated by poor communications and lack of organized government, landowners depended on their own resources for survival. Many became warriors or maintained a force of armed men. Others swore allegiance to landowners who had the armed force to protect them.

A well-appointed manor possessed fields, gardens, grazing lands, fish ponds, a mill, a church, workshops for making whatever implements or goods were needed, and a village for the farmers dependent on its lord. The degree of protection that a manor required, ranging from a ditch and wooden stockade to a stone wall surrounding a fortified keep (a stone building), varied with local conditions. The trend was toward ever greater fortification down to the twelfth century (see Environment and Technology: Castles and Fortifications).

Castles and Fortifications

The word *castle* most often brings to mind great stone fortresses like Krak des Chevalliers. These came as the climax of a long evolution, however. The Romans had built square army camps surrounded by stockades to protect their frontiers. Once those frontiers were breached, the new rulers of Europe, each with far fewer men than a Roman legion, turned to smaller fortifications: either a ringwork (a circular wooden stockade surrounding a group of wooden buildings) or, more often, a motte-and-bailey. The motte was an artificial mound with a trench around it and a wooden tower of some sort on top. The bailey was a courtyard or enclosed area with a wooden stockade at the foot of the mound. Archaeologists have identified the remains of over 200 ringworks and 1,050 mottes in Britain, Wales, and Scotland alone, but wood construction has caused most of their buildings to perish.

As security needs increased, some lords and rulers built a keep within the bailey or atop the motte. A keep was a fortified stone building. Castle Acre in England began as a country house surrounded by a fairly weak ringwork. In the mid-twelfth century the mound was raised and the house redesigned as a keep within a smaller, more imposing ringwork. The builders doubled the thickness of the house walls and buried much of the first floor to strengthen the house's foundation. The final twelfth-century version of the keep, looking more like today's image of a castle, was taller, smaller, and surrounded by a still more formidable wall.

Stone walls steadily replaced wooden stockades. Most interior buildings, except for the keep, were of wood, as were drawbridges, stairways, and other essential parts of the fortification. Further advances in castle design featured towers along the walls from which archers shooting through arrow slits could flank enemies attacking the walls; heavily fortified gateways; and a barbican, or fortified gateway, on the far side of the bridge over a moat.

Source: All illustrations are from John R. Kenyon, *Medieval Fortifications* (Leicester, England: Leicester University Press, 1990). Used with permission of Girando/Art Resource, NY.

Life on the manor depended on one's personal status. The lord and his family exercised almost unlimited power over their serfs—agricultural workers who belonged to the manor. Serfs were obligated to till their lord's fields and were subject to other dues and obligations. Moreover, they were prohibited from leaving the manor where they were born and attaching themselves to another lord. Particular conditions varied from region to region. The majority of peasants in England, France, and western Germany were unfree serfs in the tenth and eleventh centuries. In Bordeaux, Saxony, and a few other regions a tradition of free peasantry stemming from the egalitarian social structure of the Germanic peoples during their period of migration still survived. Outright slavery, the mainstay of the Roman economy (see Chapter 6), diminished as more and more peasants became serfs in return for a lord's protection.

Feudal Society

Although Europe's reversion to a basic economy limited the freedom and potential for personal achievement of most of the population, an emerging class of nobles reaped great personal benefits. During the period of Germanic migrations, and continuing much later among the Vikings of Scandinavia, men regularly answered the call to arms of the war chiefs to whom they swore allegiance. All warriors shared in the booty gained from raiding. But as settlement enhanced the importance of agricultural tasks as compared with swineherding and hunting, trading the plow for the sword at the chieftain's call became harder.

Those who, out of loyalty or desire for adventure, continued to join the war parties included a growing number of horsemen. The mounted warrior was the mainstay of the Carolingian army, but fighting from horseback did not make a person either a noble or a landowner. Women could be landowners and perform important administrative duties on their domains. By the tenth century, however, nearly constant warfare to protect rights to land or to support the claims

of a superior lord brought about the gradual transformation of the mounted warrior into the noble knight—a transformation that eventually led to landholding becoming inseparable from military service.

This process, culminated in what later historians labeled "feudal" society, was a specifically European response to conditions of weak central government, a lack of effective law, the need to defend one's land militarily, and respect for personal oaths of loyalty. It brought together the Roman practice of granting land in return for military service and the German custom of swearing allegiance to a war chief. Other parts of the world developed similar social and political structures to which some historians apply the term *feudalism*, but each instance has its own particular features as, indeed, does feudal society in different regions of Europe itself.

The German foes of the Roman legions had equipped themselves with a helmet, a shield, and a sword, spear, or throwing ax. They did not wear body armor. Some rode horses, but most fought on foot. The rise of the mounted warrior as the paramount force on the battlefield is associated with the use of stirrups. For hundreds of years horsemen had gripped their mounts with their legs and fought with bow and arrow, throwing javelin, stabbing spear, and sword. Stirrups allowed the rider to stand in the saddle, lean forward with a sturdy lance held under his arm, and thus absorb the impact of striking his enemy at full gallop.

This type of warfare required heavy, grain-fed horses rather than the small, grass-fed animals of the Central Asian pastoralists who seem to have invented the stirrup around the first century C.E. Thus it was in predominantly agricultural Europe rather than among the nomads of the steppe that charges of mounted knights came to dominate the battlefield.

By the eleventh century, the knight had emerged as the central figure in medieval warfare. He wore an open-faced helmet and a long linen shirt, or hauberk, studded with small metal disks. A century later, knightly equipment commonly included a visored helmet that covered the head and neck and a hauberk of chain mail.

Armor was made for the knight's horse, too. From these evolved, in the thirteenth century, metal plate protection for the knight's chest, thighs, and other vulnerable areas, and in the fifteenth century, completely enclosed iron plating.

Each increase in armor for knight and horse entailed a greater financial outlay. Since land was the basis of all wealth, it rapidly became impossible for anyone to serve as a knight who did not have financial support from land revenues. Accordingly, kings took to rewarding meritorious armed service with grants of land from their own property. Nobles with extensive properties did the same to build up their own military retinues.

A grant of land in return for a sworn oath to provide specified military service was called a *feudum*, or *fief*. At first, kings granted fiefs only on a temporary basis, but by the tenth century, most fiefs could be inherited—by sons from their fathers, for example—as long as the specified military service continued to be provided. Although feudalism varied greatly from one part of Europe to another, and generally was more developed in the north and west than in the Mediterranean region, it lent a distinctive cast to medieval European history.

In feudal societies kings tended to be weak and dependent on their *vassals*, noble followers whose services a king or some other noble might be able to command for only part of the year depending on the agreement between them. A lord granted land and owed protection to a vassal; the vassal swore an oath of loyalty and service to the lord. Vassals who held land from several different lords were likely to swear loyalty to each one. Moreover, the allegiance that a vassal owed to one lord was likely to entail military service to that lord's master in time of need.

A "typical" feudal realm—actual practices varied between and within realms—consisted of some lands directly owned by a king or a count and administered by his royal officers. Other lands, often the greater portion, were held and administered by the king's or count's major vassals in return for military service. These vassals, in turn, granted land to their own vassals. Instead of taxes, therefore, the lands of kings and other nobles yielded primarily military service.

The Rise of Christendom in Europe

313	Edict of Milan; Christianity tolerated in Roman Empire
325	Constantine convenes Council of Nicaea
476	End of Roman Empire in the west
ca. 547	Death of St. Benedict
800	Coronation of Charlemagne
910	Monastery of Cluny founded
936	Beginning of Holy Roman Empire
989	Ruler of Russia adopts Orthodox Christianity
1054	Final schism between Catholic and Orthodox churches
1007	Pope Gregory VII and Emperor Henry IV at Canossa
1095	Pope Urban II preaches First Crusade

A lord's manor was the effective source of governance and justice in most areas. Direct royal government was quite limited. The king had few financial resources at his disposal and seldom exercised legal jurisdiction at a local level. The fact that all members of the clergy, as well as the extensive agricultural lands owned by monasteries and nunneries, fell under the supervision and legal jurisdiction of the church further limited the reach and authority of the feudal monarch.

Noblewomen became enmeshed in the tangle of feudal obligations as heiresses and as candidates for marriage. A man who married the widow or daughter of a lord with no sons could gain for himself control of that lord's property. Entire kingdoms were put together or taken apart through marriage alliances. Noble daughters and sons had little say in marriage matters, for the important issues were land, power, and military service, not the feelings or preferences of individuals. Noblemen guarded the women in their families as closely as they guarded their other valuables.

Noblewoman directing construction of a church   This picture of Berthe, wife of Girat de Rouissillion, acting as mistress of the works is from a tenth-century manuscript but shows a scene from the ninth-century. Wheel-barrows rarely appear in medieval building scenes. (Copyright Bibliothèque royale Albert Ier, Bruxelles, Ms. 6, fol. 554 verso.)

This does not mean that all women lived powerless, sheltered lives. Some noblewomen exercised real power, administering their husband's lands when they were away at war. Women of the manor who were not of the noble class usually worked alongside their menfolk, performing agricultural tasks such as raking and stacking hay, shearing sheep, and picking vegetables. As artisans, women spun, wove, and sewed clothing. Indeed, one of the greatest works of craft and art surviving from medieval Europe is the Bayeux Tapestry, a piece of embroidery 230 feet (70 meters) long and 20 inches (51 centimeters) wide designed and executed entirely by women.

It depicts in cartoon form the story of the invasion of England in 1066 by William the Conqueror, duke of Normandy.

Dhuoda, a ninth-century Frankish noblewoman, reflected the social distinctions of an emerging feudal society in the counsel she gave her son on how to direct his prayers. She urged young William to pray for "kings and all those of the highest ranks" at the pinnacle of society, then, in descending order, for his lord, his father, his enemies, and a final group consisting of the wayfarer, the infirm, the poor and suffering, and "all sorts of others whom I have omitted here." Among the omitted are the serfs of the manor.

Notably, Dhouda placed one category above even the king. "Pray first," she writes, "for the bishops and all the priests, that they may pour forth to God pure and worthy prayers for you and for all the people."[2] Already by her time the Christian church was showing promise of being the one institution capable of combating the political fragmentation, social stratification, and warfare of post-Roman Europe.

THE WESTERN CHURCH

T he Christian church was the sole institution claiming jurisdiction over, and the loyalty of, large segments of Europe's population. The growing Christian populations in eastern Europe recognized the authority of the patriarch of Constantinople even in Slavic lands beyond the control of the Byzantine emperor (see Map 9.2). The pope commanded similar authority over church affairs in the Latin west. There, missionaries added territory to Christendom with forays into the British Isles and the lands of the Germans. Yet travels by Christian preachers did not necessarily mean significant conversions among those who heard their words, which must have been tiny minorities of the population. Lists of bishops and wonder-filled lives of missionaries are often historians' only sources for assessing the penetration of Christianity into new lands, and these say little about the actual pattern of adoption of the new religion or about the effectiveness of the pope's control of bishops far from Italy.

Regional disagreements over church regulations, shortages of educated and trained clergy, difficult communications, political disorder, and the general insecurity of the period were formidable obstacles to unifying church standards and practices. By the eleventh century, clerics in some parts of western Europe were still issuing prohibitions against the worship of rivers, trees, and mountains and other superstitions. In the face of residual paganism and lax enforcement of prohibitions against practices such as clergy marrying, nepotism (giving preferment to one's close kin), simony (selling ecclesiastical appointments, often to people who were not members of the clergy), and even the wearing of beards, the persistence of the papacy in asserting its legal jurisdiction over clergy, combating heretical beliefs, and calling on secular rulers to recognize its authority constituted a rare force for unity and order in a time of disunity and chaos.

Faith and Rule

From the fourth century onward, divisions on matters of doctrine endangered the Christian church. Jesus' disciples had established Christian communities in Jerusalem, Antioch, Alexandria, and Rome, and most Christians recognized the successors of these early authorities, called patriarchs or, in the Roman case, popes, as the paramount leaders of the church. The emperor Constantine made his capital city, Constantinople, a fifth patriarchate in the fourth century. The patriarchs and popes appointed bishops throughout the regions that recognized their authority, and the bishops consecrated priests in smaller localities. Church rules could be set by the patriarch or by councils of bishops.

Priests were expected to follow these rules in servicing the needs of the ordinary believers. These needs focused on major life events: baptism after birth; admission to participation in and personal performance of the ritual of communion, which consisted of consuming the body and blood of Jesus in the form of sacred wine and bread; performance of marriage ceremonies; and anointing the dead. These ceremonies and rituals, along with the ordination of priests, were considered sacred mysteries, or sacraments, that only priests—bishops and patriarchs were also priests—could perform.

The hierarchy of church ranks theoretically ensured a consistency in Christian ritual and belief throughout the Christian community. In fact, patriarchs, popes, and bishops sometimes disagreed on important religious issues. One area of

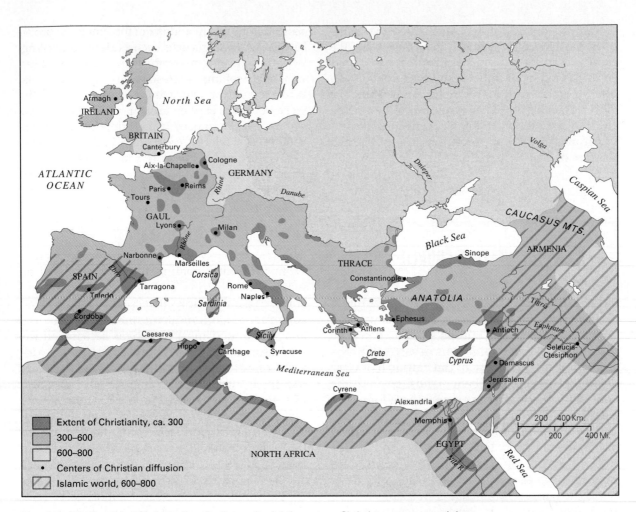

Map 9.2 The Spread of Christianity   By the early eighth century, Christian areas around the southern Mediterranean from northern Syria to northern Spain, accounting for most of the Christian population, had fallen under Muslim rule; and the slow process of conversion to Islam had begun. This accentuated the importance of the patriarchs of Constantinople, the popes in Rome, and the later converting regions of northern and eastern Europe.

confusion and disagreement centered on Jesus' relationship to God the Father and to the Holy Spirit. Christians generally agreed that these together formed a divine Trinity in which three aspects or manifestations of God were somehow united, but they did not all understand the Trinity in the same way. They also disagreed on such matters as whether Mary was the mother of God, or the mother of a man named Jesus; and on whether images of God or Jesus or Mary, called icons, were proper objects to pray toward because they stimulated pious thoughts, or whether praying toward them was too much like praying to pagan statues.

Disagreements like these could lead to charges and countercharges of heresy, defined as beliefs or practices that were so unacceptable as to be un-Christian. Charges of heresy were important to ordinary people, even when they involved hard-to-understand theological issues, because they brought into question the sacraments performed by the priests or bishops charged as heretics. They also threatened the unity of the Christian church at a time when political fragmentation was rapidly increasing.

The most severe challenges to ecclesiastical authority arose in North Africa and the lands of the eastern Mediterranean and resulted in schism—a formal division over differences in doctrine. Some doctrinal disagreements, such as Monophysite doctrine, which puts primacy on the divine character of Jesus Christ and minimizes his human characteristics, persist to this day. The Coptic Church of Egypt, the Ethiopian Church, and the Armenian Apostolic Church all accept Monophysitism. Other potential sources of schism were stamped out. One of these was the Donatist Church of North Africa, which denied the authority of the Roman pope because of disagreements over whether a sacrament like baptism was still valid if a person temporarily gave in to persecution and abandoned Christianity.

The common way of dealing with such challenges to Christian unity was for a council of bishops to deliberate and declare a particular doctrine true or false. In the East, the Byzantine emperor claimed the prerogative of calling such conferences. In the West, the pope took the lead. Schismatics could call conferences of their own. The bishops of particular regions often met in council to set rules, called *canons*, to regulate the priests and lay people (men and women who were not members of the clergy) under their jurisdiction. The doctrine that most endangered papal authority was Arianism, which was widespread among the Germanic peoples. Although the teaching of the Alexandrian bishop Arius that Jesus was a creation of God the father and a lesser sort of divinity was declared heretical in 325 at the Council of Nicaea called by the emperor Constantine (see Chapter 6), it did not quickly disappear.

Charges of heresy focused on matters of dogma but often reflected underlying social or political issues, such as the desire of Monophysite Egyptians to resist the authority of Con-

stantinople or the desire of North African Berbers to use Donatism as a means of standing up to Roman colonizers. In some cases, practices as ordinary as the wearing of beards—permitted in the Byzantine East but forbidden in the Latin West—or the way of shaving the priest's head stirred local desires for ecclesiastical independence. The overriding issue in such cases was *orthopraxy*, "correct practices," rather than *orthodoxy*, "correct beliefs." Ireland, in particular, challenged Rome in the eighth and ninth centuries by extolling its own church practices and exporting them to Scotland, Britain, France, and Switzerland by means of missionaries who established important monasteries like Iona, off the Scottish coast, and Saint Gall in Switzerland.

In politically fragmented western Europe, the pope needed allies. He found them in rulers like Charlemagne, who upheld papal rights in return for religious legitimation of his rule. Charlemagne's descendants did not maintain his empire intact, however, and it was not until 962, with the papal coronation of a Holy Roman Emperor (Charlemagne never held this title), that a secular political authority came into being that claimed to represent general Christian interests. Essentially a loose confederation of German princes who named one of their own to the highest office, the Holy Roman Empire held little sway west of the Rhine River.

Although the pope crowned the Holy Roman Emperors, the law of the church (known as *canon law*) and the various secular laws in effect in different regions were on a collision course. According to canon law, the pope had exclusive legal jurisdiction over all clergy and all church property wherever located. Kings and princes saw this claim as an intrusion on their territory, but one that they generally were fearful of objecting to because the pope could excommunicate them, that is, bar them from all church activities and sacraments. Complicating things, many bishops controlled lands that owed military support or other feudal services and dues to the kings and princes. The secular rulers argued that they should have the power to appoint those bishops because that was the only way to ensure that they would fulfill their duties as feudal vassals. The popes disagreed.

In the eleventh century, this conflict came to a head. Hildebrand, an Italian monk, capped a career of reforming and reorganizing church finances by being named Pope Gregory VII in 1073. His personal notion of the papacy (preserved among his letters) represents an extreme position, stating among other claims, that

§ The pope can be judged by no one;
§ The Roman church has never erred and never will err till the end of time;
§ The pope alone can depose and restore bishops;
§ He alone can call general councils and authorize canon law;
§ He can depose emperors;
§ He can absolve subjects from their allegiance;
§ All princes should kiss his feet.[3]

Such claims antagonized lords and monarchs, who had become accustomed to controlling the nomination, or *investiture*, of bishops and abbots in their domains. Historians use the term *investiture controversy* to refer specifically to the struggle to control ecclesiastical appointments; the term also refers to the broader conflict of popes versus emperors and kings. When Holy Roman Emperor Henry IV opposed Gregory's reforms, Gregory excommunicated him in 1076. Stung by the resulting decline in his influence, Henry stood barefoot in the snow for three days outside a castle in northern Italy waiting for Gregory, a guest there, to receive him. Henry's formal act of penance forced Gregory to forgive him and return him to the church, but the reconciliation, amounting to a defeat for the pope, did not last. In 1078, Gregory declared Henry deposed. The emperor forced the pope to flee from Rome to Salerno, where two years later, Gregory died, supported only by Sicily's Norman rulers.

However, the reforming legacy of Gregory VII survived. The struggle between the popes and emperors continued until 1122, when a compromise was reached at Worms, a town in Germany. In the Concordat of Worms, Emperor Henry V renounced his rights to choose bishops and abbots or confer them with spiritual symbols such as a staff and a ring. In return, Pope Calixtus II permitted the emperor to invest papal nominees for the position of bishop or abbot with any lay rights or obligations before their spiritual consecration. This was essentially a victory for the church, though not a complete one.

Conflicts between secular and ecclesiastical authority erupted in other areas as well. Though barely twenty when he became king of England in 1154 (see below), Henry II instituted reforms designed to strengthen the power of the Crown and weaken the feudal lords. He appointed traveling justices to enforce his laws. He made juries, a holdover from traditional Germanic law, into powerful legal instruments. He established the principle that criminal acts violated the "king's peace" and should be tried and punished in accordance with charges brought by the crown instead of in response to charges brought by victims.

Henry had a harder time controlling the church. His closest friend, the chancellor, or chief administrator, of England, was Thomas Becket (ca. 1118–1170). A supporter of the king, Becket was a typical courtier who lived in a grand and luxurious manner. In 1162 Henry persuaded Becket to become a priest in order to assume the position of archbishop of Canterbury, the highest church office in England. Becket agreed but warned Henry that if he became an official of the church, he would act solely in the interest of the church when it came into conflict with the Crown. Accordingly, when Henry sought to try clerics accused of crimes in royal instead of ecclesiastical courts, Archbishop Becket, now leading an austere and pious life away from court luxuries, resisted.

In 1170 four of Henry's knights, knowing that the king desired Becket's death, murdered the archbishop in Canterbury Cathedral. Their crime backfired, however. An outpouring of sympathy caused Canterbury to become a major pilgrimage center, and in 1173 the pope declared the martyred Becket to be a saint. Henry allowed himself twice to be publicly whipped in penance for the crime, but his authority had been badly damaged.

Although the Latin Church repeatedly and effectively defended its claim as the sole arbiter of doctrinal religious truth, the investiture controversy and Henry II's conflict with Thomas Becket yielded no clear victor. Western Europe was heir to three legal traditions: (1) feudal law, based in large part on Germanic custom; (2) canon law, based in large part on Roman law in its visualization of a single hierarchical legal institution covering all of Western Christendom; and (3) Roman law, which, after centuries of disregard, began to be studied anew at the fledgling University of Bologna, in Italy, around 1088. This pattern of church-state division became a noteworthy feature of western European civilization and one that set the region apart from both the

Byzantine Empire and the Muslim states that succeeded the Byzantines in Syria, Egypt, and Tunisia (see Chapter 10).

Monasticism

Another distinctive feature of Western Christendom rooted in the period from 300 to 1200 was monasticism. The origins of monasticism lay in the eastern lands of the Roman Empire. Practices such as celibacy, continual devotion to prayer, and living apart from society (alone or in small groups) were not new, but they came together in

Cloister of Benedictine Monastery   Interior courtyards with fountains and gardens, also a common feature of Muslim palaces in Spain, recall the architecture of Roman villas. The semicircular arches identify this architectural style as Romanesque. (Rheinisches Archiv)

Christian guise in Egypt. Athanasius (d. 373), the patriarch of Alexandria, portrays Anthony, perhaps the most important early hermit monk, as a pious desert dweller continually tempted by Satan. On one occasion, "when he was weaving palm leaves . . . that he might make baskets to give as gifts to people who were continually coming to visit him . . . he saw an animal which had the following form: from its head to its side it was like a man, and its legs and feet were those of an ass."[4] As was his custom, Anthony prayed to God upon seeing this sight, and Satan left him alone.

In western Europe holy hermits given to mystic visions were comparatively few. The most important form of monasticism involved groups of monks or nuns living together in a single community. Benedict of Nursia (ca. 480–547), in Italy, began his pious career as a hermit in a cave but eventually organized several monasteries, each headed by an abbot. The Rule he promulgated to govern the monks' behavior emphasizes celibacy, poverty, and obedience to the abbot; but it is moderate compared with some Eastern practices. The Rule of Benedict was the starting point for most forms of western European monastic life and remains in force today in Benedictine monasteries. It discusses both ritual activities and everyday life in passages like the following:

§ Since the spirit of silence is so important, permission to speak should rarely be granted even to perfect disciples, even though it be for good, holy, edifying conversation. . . . If anything has to be asked of the Superior, it should be asked with all the humility and submission inspired by reverence. But as for coarse jests and idle words or words that move to laughter, these we condemn everywhere with a perpetual ban. . . .

§ Let clothing be given to the brethren according to the nature of the place in which they dwell and its climate. . . . In ordinary places the following dress is sufficient for each monk: a tunic, a cowl (thick and woolly for winter, thin or worn for summer), a scapular [sleeveless cloak] for work, stockings and shoes to cover the feet. The monks should not complain about the color or the coarseness of any of these things, but be content with what can be found in the district where they live and can be purchased cheaply.[5]

Monastic life removed thousands of pious men and women from towns and villages and thus reinforced a tendency toward separation between religious affairs and secular politics and economics. Jesus' axiom that one should "render unto Caesar what is Caesar's and unto God what is God's" was taken seriously in the monastery despite the fact that many bishops who were based in towns came to control vast properties and numerous retainers and behave like secular lords. Monasteries were also the primary centers of literacy and learning in the centuries following the decline of the Western Empire. Many lay nobles were illiterate and interested in little other than warfare and hunting. Monks (but seldom nuns) saw copying manuscripts and even writing books as part of their religious calling. Were it not for monks of the ninth century, most ancient works in Latin would have disappeared.

Monasteries and nunneries served other functions as well. Although a few planted Christianity in new lands, as the Irish monks did in parts of Germany, most of them serviced the needs of travelers, organized agricultural production on their lands, and took in foundlings. Nunneries provided refuges for widows and other women who lacked male protection in a harsh world or who desired a spiritual life. All such religious houses, however, presented problems of oversight to the church. A bishop might have authority over an abbot or abbess (head of a nunnery), but there was no way to exercise constant vigilance over what transpired behind monastery walls.

An influential movement of reform and centralization of monastic authority is named for the Benedictine abbey of Cluny in eastern France. Cluny was founded in 910 by William the Pious, the first duke of Aquitaine, who freed it completely of lay authority. A century later Cluny gained similar freedom from the local bishop. Its abbots then embarked on a vigorous campaign, in alliance with reforming popes like Gregory VII, to improve the discipline and administration of European monasteries. A magnificent new abbey church, designed in the Romanesque style with small arched windows and heavy stone walls, symbolized Cluny's claims to eminence.

With later additions, it became the largest church in the world.

At the peak of Cluny's influence, nearly a thousand Benedictine abbeys and priories (lower-level monastic houses) in various countries accepted the authority of the abbot of Cluny. Where the original Benedictine Rule presumed that each monastery would be independent, the Cluniac reformers stipulated that every abbot and every prior (head of a priory) be appointed by the abbot of Cluny and have had personal experience of the religious life of Cluny. The Cluniac movement set the pattern for the organizations of monasteries, cathedral clergy, and preaching friars that would dominate ecclesiastical life in the thirteenth century.

Shaping European Society

The magnitude of the changes in the society of Western Europe that took place under the influence of Christianity is difficult to overestimate. Roman society in Jesus' time had felt comfortable with slavery, religious pluralism, and overt sexuality. Christian society demanded a celibate clergy and discouraged sexual activities outside marriage, advocated monogamy while deploring divorce and concubinage, frowned on slavery, and looked on non-Christians with suspicion and sometimes hatred.

The fragile legal status of the Jews led them into money-changing, goldsmithing, and other trades that they could practice anywhere. Rulers and popes protected or expelled Jews to suit their own political and economic ends and whims. When crusading enthusiasm overtook Europe in the early eleventh century (see below), some Christian zealots decided to murder and loot local Jewish communities rather than trek to the Holy Land. Muslims were even more unwelcome than Jews because Islam was seen as a political threat (see Chapter 10).

Where Roman society had been based on extended kinship lineages (see Chapter 6), Christian Europe conceived the family in a somewhat narrower sense. The lines of social division separating nobles from clergy or landowners from

serfs were quite different from those of the Roman era. Festivals and rituals, monumental building programs, artistic endeavor of all kinds—everything that conveyed a sense of civilization—manifested itself in Christian form rather than in the trappings of the secular empire of Rome. In the fourth and fifth centuries, Germanic customs and tastes were seen as overriding and destroying the more sophisticated traditions of Rome. However, by the year 1200, Christianity had forged in Western Europe a new civilization that preserved selected features of the Roman and German past while evolving its own distinctive features.

THE BYZANTINE EMPIRE

In the eastern region of the old Roman Empire, European Christian civilization was very different from its counterpart in the West. The Byzantine emperors represented the continuation of Roman imperial rule and tradition and brought to political, social, and religious life a continuity that was almost entirely absent in the West. Roman law, which the Eastern emperors inherited intact, lessened the impact of church proscriptions, and the Byzantine emperors, exercising an authority known as *caesaropapism*, combining both the imperial ("Caesar") and the papal, made a comfortable transition into the role of all-powerful Christian monarchs.

The Byzantine drama, however, played on a smaller and steadily shrinking stage. The loss of Syria, Egypt, and Tunisia to Muslim invaders in the seventh century, Slavic pressure on Byzantium's Balkan frontiers, and the eventual Byzantine failure to prevent the Muslims from overwhelming Anatolia (modern Turkey) in the late eleventh century deprived the empire of long-lasting periods of peace. Christianity progressively withered in lands that fell to the Muslims, despite occasional bursts of imperial military power, such as occurred in the tenth century, when Christian forces temporarily recaptured the city of Antioch. By the end of the twelfth century, at least two-thirds of the Christians in the former Byzantine territories had adopted the Muslim faith.

The peoples to the north, however, provided room for Christian missionary expansion. As the Slavs gradually adopted Christianity—except for the Poles, who were brought into Latin Christianity by German missionaries and knights—they also adopted a reverence for the customs, rituals, and imperial tradition of Byzantium. These factors were to have a profound impact on the later history of Russia.

The Fortunes of Empire

The Roman emperors who ruled in the East retained many imperial traditions and outlooks that disappeared in the West. In 324, in the nineteenth year of his reign, Constantine led a procession marking out the expanded limits of the city he had selected as his new capital: the millennium-old Greek city of Byzantium, located on a long, narrow inlet at the entrance to the Bosporus strait. In the forum of the new Constantinople, he erected a 120-foot-tall (36-meter) column topped with a statue of Apollo, and he retained the old Roman title *pontifex maximus* (chief priest). Nevertheless, he was a Christian, and he studded the city with churches.

The pope in Rome was chosen by ecclesiastical election and eventually claimed complete independence and authority over Western Christendom. In contrast, the Byzantine emperor appointed the patriarch of Constantinople and became closely involved in doctrinal disputes over which beliefs constituted heresy. In 325 Constantine called hundreds of bishops to a council at the city of Nicaea (modern Iznik in northwestern Turkey) and persuaded them to reject the Arian doctrine that Jesus was of lesser importance than God the Father. In doing this, he was applying the characteristically Eastern principle of caesaropapism. Nevertheless, the Byzantine Empire was torn for centuries by disputes over theology and by quarrels among the

patriarchs of Constantinople, Alexandria, and Antioch. Much of the surviving literature of the Byzantine period is devoted to religious affairs, and it is apparent that religious differences permeated society. As the fourth-century bishop Gregory of Nyssa reports: "Everything is full of those who are speaking of unintelligible things. . . . I wish to know the price of bread; one answers, 'The Father is greater than the Son.' I inquire whether my bath is ready; one says, 'The Son has been made out of nothing.'"[6]

In contrast with the West, polytheism died fairly quickly in the Byzantine world, surviving longest among the country folk. (Latin *pagani*, whence the word "pagan" for people who believe in strange gods). The emperor Julian (r. 361–363) tried in vain to restore the old polytheistic faith. When a blind Christian called Julian an apostate (a renegade from Christianity) he said, "You are blind, and your God will not cure you," to which the Christian replied, "I thank God for my blindness, since it prevents me from beholding your impiety." In 392 the emperor Theodosius banned all pagan ceremonies. The following year he terminated the Olympic games. He also removed the pagan altar of victory from the Senate in Rome.

Having a single ruler endowed with supreme legal and religious authority prevented the breakup of the Eastern Empire into a mosaic of petty feudal principalities, but it did not guarantee either peace or prosperity. In the fourth century the empire was threatened from the east, along its Euphrates River frontier, by a new Iranian empire ruled by the Sasanid family (see Chapter 10), and from the north by Germanic Goths and the nomadic Huns from Central Asia. Bribes, diplomacy, and occasional military victories persuaded the Goths and Huns either to settle peacefully or move on toward targets in western Europe. War with the Sasanids recurred for almost three hundred years, however, until a new enemy appeared from the Arabian peninsula in the form of marauding tribes led by followers of the Arab prophet Muhammad. During the first half of the seventh century, these Muslim invaders destroyed the Sasanid Empire and captured Egypt, Syria, and Tunisia.

The loss of some of its most populous and prosperous provinces permanently reduced the power of the Byzantine Empire, and its political trajectory was generally downward. Although it survived until 1453, its later emperors were continually threatened by the Muslims to their south and by newly arriving Slavic and Turkic peoples to their north. At the same time, relations with the popes and princes of western Europe steadily worsened. As early as the mid-ninth century the patriarchs of Constantinople had challenged the territorial jurisdiction of the popes of Rome and some of the established practices of the Latin Church. Rather than going away, these arguments worsened over time and in 1054 culminated in a formal schism between the Latin Church and the Orthodox Church—a break that has never been mended. This ill will did not prevent Eastern and Western Christians from cooperating in some measure during the crusading era of the twelfth century. But it contributed to the decision by the leaders of the Fourth Crusade (see below) to sack Constantinople in 1204, send the Byzantine emperor fleeing to an outlying province, and establish Latin principalities on Byzantine territory.

Society and Urban Life

The maintenance of imperial authority, and the accompanying urban prosperity, in the eastern provinces of the old Roman Empire buffered Byzantium against the population decline and severe economic regression suffered in the West from the third century on. Nevertheless, a similar though less pronounced transformation set in around the seventh century, possibly sparked by the loss of Egypt and Syria to the Muslims. Narrative histories give scant coverage to this period, but saints' lives show a transition from stories about educated saints hailing from cities to stories about saints originating as peasants. In many areas, barter replaced money transactions, and cities declined in population and prosperity, causing the virtual disappearance of the traditional class of local urban notables.

The disappearance of that class left a social gap between the high aristocracy centered on the imperial court and the rural landowners and peasants. By the end of the eleventh century, a family-based military aristocracy somewhat similar to the feudal nobility of western Europe had emerged, though without being institutionalized in feudal law codes. Of Byzantine emperor Alexius Comnenus (r. 1081–1118) it was said: "He considered himself not a ruler, but a lord, conceiving and calling the empire his own house."

The situation of women changed, too. Earlier Roman family structure had been loose, and women had been comparatively active in public life. Now the family became a more rigid unit, and women increasingly found themselves confined to the home by their husbands and by social custom. When they went out in public, they concealed their faces behind veils. The only males they socialized with were family members. Paradoxically, however, from 1028 to 1056 women ruled the Byzantine Empire with their husbands.

To what extent these changes are related to the social conditions that brought about a parallel seclusion of women in the neighboring Islamic countries has not yet been established. It is likely, however, that the two developments are linked despite the differences in religion. By comparison with Christianity in western Europe, Byzantine Christianity manifested less interest in, or felt less need for, the provision of refuge for women in nunneries. This, too, finds its parallel in the development of Islam.

Economically, the Byzantine emperors continued a late Roman inclination to set prices, control the provision of grain to the capital city, and monopolize trade in certain goods, like purple cloth. Whether government intervention contributed to the comparative lack of technological development and economic innovation in Byzantium is difficult to determine. As long as merchants and pilgrims hastened to the metropolis of Constantinople from all corners of the compass, rare and costly goods were readily available for aristocratic consumption. The decline of other Eastern cities, however, emphasized the basis of the economy in agriculture and animal husbandry.

There Byzantine farmers continued to use light scratch plows and creaky oxcarts long after farmers in western Europe had adopted heavy plows and efficiently harnessed horses. Despite this stagnation, the Byzantines continued for a time to outclass western Europe in the variety and quality of manufactured goods.

Because Byzantium's inheritance from the earlier Roman Empire was so much richer than western Europe's, there was little recognition that the slow deterioration that set in during the seventh century constituted a problem. Gradually, however, pilgrims and visitors from the West began to see the reality beyond the awe-inspiring, incense-filled domes of cathedrals like Constantinople's Hagia Sophia and beneath the glitter and silken garments of the royal court. An eleventh-century French visitor wrote:

> The city itself [Constantinople] is squalid and fetid and in many places harmed by permanent darkness, for the wealthy overshadow the streets with buildings and leave these dirty, dark places to the poor and to travelers; there murders and robberies and other crimes which love the darkness are committed. Moreover, since people live lawlessly in this city, which has as many lords as rich men and almost as many thieves as poor men, a criminal knows neither fear nor shame, because crime is not punished by law and never entirely comes to light. In every respect she exceeds moderation; for, just as she surpasses other cities in wealth, so too, does she surpass them in vice.[7]

The view from the other side was expressed by Anna Comnena, the brilliant daughter of Emperor Alexius Comnenus. She described the Western knights of the First Crusade (1096–1099) as uncouth barbarians, albeit sometimes gifted with an impressive manliness. She even turned her scorn on a prominent churchman and philosopher who happened to be from Italy: "Italos . . . was unable with his barbaric, stupid temperament to grasp the profound truths of philosophy; even in the act of learning he utterly rejected the teacher's guiding hand, and full of temerity and barbaric folly, [believed] even before study that he excelled all others."[8]

By the time of the Crusades, the Byzantines were being surpassed by the western Europeans. Their most valuable provinces had been lost. Their army played only a supporting role in the conquest of the Holy Land. And their maritime commerce was mostly carried in ships from Genoa, Venice, and Pisa. From the sack of Constantinople during the Fourth Crusade in 1204 to its fall to the Ottoman sultan Mehmed the Conqueror in 1453, vestiges of the legendary Byzantine imperial pomp and political intrigue remained, but this heir to the Roman Empire amounted to little more than a small, weak principality centered on a shrunken, looted, and dilapidated Constantinople and a few outlying cities.

Byzantine church as shown in twelfth century manuscript Upper portion shows church facade and domes—one over each arm of a Greek cross and one over the central crossing. Lower portion shows interior with picture or mosaic of Christ enthroned at the altar end. (Bibliothèque nationale de France)

Cathedral of St. Dmitry in Vladimir   Built between 1193 and 1197, this Russian Orthodox cathedral shows Byzantine influence. Three-arch facade, small dome, and symmetrical Greek-cross floor plan strongly resemble the painting on page 266. (Sovfoto)

Cultural Achievements

Just as the maintenance of imperial authority facilitated the emergence of the Byzantine emperor as the ultimate arbiter of religious disputes, so his power persisted in secular legal affairs. Several emperors had collections of laws and edicts made. The most famous and complete collection was the *Corpus Juris Civilis* (*Body of Civil Law*) compiled in Latin by seventeen legal scholars at the behest of the emperor Justinian (r. 527–565). In the late eleventh century, it began to be studied at the University of Bologna and became the

began to use teams of horses to pull plows through the moist, fertile river-valley soils that were too heavy for teams of oxen. Stronger and faster than oxen, horses increased the productivity of these and other lands by reducing the number of hours needed for plowing. This development undoubtedly contributed to a greater agricultural surplus, but the breeding of larger horses for knightly warfare may have been as important a factor as the new technology in starting the move away from oxen.

Accompanying improvements in tilling the soil was improved understanding of how to maximize its productivity. A three-field system of cultivation emerged. Two-thirds of the land of a manor or village was planted in grain or other foodstuffs each year; this land was plowed once and then sown with seed. The other third was left fallow but was plowed twice a year to turn under the weeds and thus return nitrogen to the soil. Some fallow (unplanted) land was also used for grazing. We will take a village with 300 acres (120 hectares) of farmland as an example. Under the earlier half-and-half system, 150 acres (60 hectares) would be plowed once and the other 150 acres twice for a total of 450 acres (180 hectares) of plowing. Under the three-field system, 200 acres (80 hectares) would be plowed once, and the remaining 100 acres (40 hectares) twice for a total of 400 acres (160 hectares) of plowing. The time and energy that farmers saved could go into other productive activities, including increasing the total area under cultivation.

Cities and the Rebirth of Trade

Associated with the growth of population was the appearance, first in Italy and Flanders and then elsewhere, of independent cities governed and defended by communes of leading citizens. Lacking the extensive farmlands that had been virtually the sole basis of wealth in western Europe since the decline of Rome, these cities turned to manufacturing and trade. Equally important, they won for themselves a legally independent position between the jurisdiction of the church and that of the feudal lord and therefore could frame their laws specifically to favor manufacturing and trade. These laws made serfs free, so these cities attracted many migrants from the countryside.

Cities in Italy that had shrunk within walls built by the Romans now filled those walls to overflowing, forcing the construction of new ones. Pisa built a new wall in 1000 and expanded it in 1156. Other twelfth-century cities that built new walls include Florence, Brescia, Piacenza, Pavia, Pistoia, and Siena. Bologna, Lucca, Mantua, and Parma followed in the thirteenth century.

Venice was a new city situated on a group of islands at the northern end of the Adriatic Sea that had been largely uninhabited in Roman times. In the eleventh century it rose to be the dominant seapower in the Adriatic. With its rivals Pisa and Genoa from the western side of Italy, Venice competed for leadership in the trade of goods from Muslim ports in North Africa and the eastern Mediterranean. A merchant's list from 1310 mentions some 300 "spices" (including dyestuffs, textile fibers, and raw materials) then traded, among them alum (for dyeing), 11 types; wax, 11 types; cotton, 8 types; indigo, 4 types; ginger, 5 types; paper, 4 types; and sugar, 15 types; along with cloves, caraway, tamarind, dragon's blood (a scarlet pigment), and fresh oranges.

Ghent, Bruges, and Ypres in Flanders were the only cities in western Europe—except Cordoba and Seville in Muslim Spain—that could rival the Italian cities in prosperity, trade, and industry. Enjoying comparable independence based on privileges gained by their communes from the counts of Flanders, these cities centralized the wool trade of the North Sea, transforming raw wool from Britain into woolen cloth that enjoyed a very wide market.

The Crusades

The Crusades dominated the politics of Europe from 1000 to 1200. Though touted as a series of religiously inspired military campaigns designed to recapture the Holy Land, on the Eastern shore

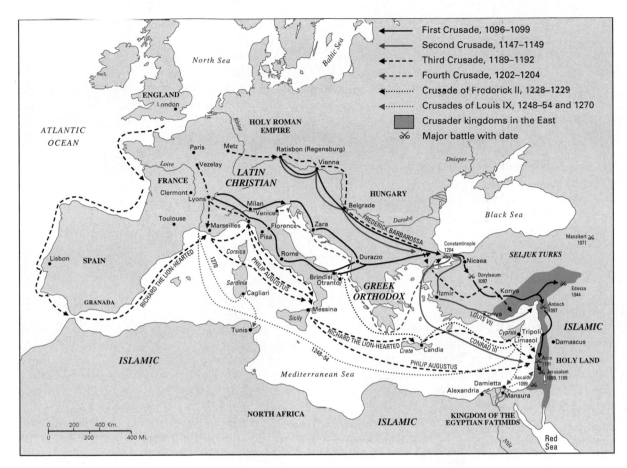

Map 9.3 The Crusades The first two crusades proceeded overland through Byzantine territory. The third crusade included contingents under the French and English kings, Philip Augustus and Richard the Lion-Hearted, that traveled by sea, and a contingent under the Holy
Roman Emperor Frederick Barbarossa that took the overland route. Frederick died in southern
Anatolia. Later crusades were mostly seaborne, with Sicily, Crete, and Cyprus playing important roles.

of the Mediterranean, from the Muslims, they actually were a manifestation of many of the social
and economic currents of the eleventh century.
Reforming leaders of the Latin Church interested
in softening the warlike tone of society worked
to popularize the Peace of God. This was a movement to limit fighting between feudal lords by
specifying times of truce, such as during Lent
(the 40 days before Easter) and on the Sunday
sabbath. Ambitious rulers were looking for new
lands to conquer, an objective best represented
by the Norman invasions of England and Sicily.
Feudal knights, particularly younger sons in

areas where the oldest son inherited everything,
were becoming increasingly anxious about
lacking the land they needed to maintain their
noble status. Italian merchants were eager to increase trade in the eastern Mediterranean and to
acquire trading posts in Muslim territory.

Several influences focused attention on the
Holy Land, which had been under Muslim rule
for four centuries. Pilgrimages were particularly important. Pilgrimage was an important
aspect of religious life in western Europe.
Pilgrims traveled in special costume under royal
protection. Some were actually tramps, thieves,

Battle of knights   Though the stirrups are not shown, the triumphant knight's posture indicates that the force of his blow has forced him back in his saddle and he is bracing himself in place by pushing his feet against stirrups and his body against the cantle (back) of his saddle. Without stirrups he would fall off over his horse's rump. (British Library)

beggars, peddlers, and merchants using pilgrimage as a safe way of traveling. Others were deeply affected by the old churches and sacred relics preserved in ecclesiastical centers like Rome, Constantinople, and Jerusalem. Genuinely pious pilgrims often journeyed to fulfill a vow or as a penance for sin.

Knights who followed the popular pilgrimage route across northern Spain to pray at the shrine of Santiago de Compostela at its northwest corner learned of the expanding campaigns of the Christian kings to dislodge the Muslims. Others heard of the war conducted by seafaring Normans against the Muslims in Sicily, whom they

finally defeated in the 1090s after thirty years of fighting.

The tales of pilgrims returning from the East further induced both churchmen and nobles to think of the Muslims as a proper target of Christian militancy. Muslim rulers, who had controlled Jerusalem, Antioch, and Alexandria ever since the seventh century, generally tolerated and protected Christian pilgrims. But after 1071 that changed when a Turkish army defeated the Byzantine emperor at the Battle of Manzikert and opened the way for Turkish tribal bands, generally associated with the rise of the Seljuk Empire in Iran and Iraq (see Chapter 10), to spread throughout Anatolia. Ancient centers of Christianity previously under Byzantine control were now threatened with absorption into a growing Muslim political realm, and this peril was duly reported back to western Europe.

From time to time the Byzantine emperor Alexius Comnenus suggested to the pope and western European rulers that they help him confront the Muslim threat. In 1095, at the Council of Clermont, Pope Urban II responded. He addressed a huge crowd of people gathered in a field and called on them, as Christians, to stop fighting one another and go to the Holy Land to fight Muslims.

"God wills it!" exclaimed voices in the crowd. People cut cloth into crosses and sewed them on their shirts to symbolize their willingness to march on Jerusalem. And thus began the holy war now known as the "First Crusade," a word taken from Latin *crux* for "cross." People at the time, however, spoke not of a "crusade" but of *peregrinatio*, a "pilgrimage." Indeed, the Crusades were basically armed pilgrimages. Urban promised that crusaders who had committed sins would be freed from the normal penance, the usual reward for peaceful pilgrims to Jerusalem.

The three crusades of the eleventh and twelfth centuries signaled the end of western Europe's centuries of isolation, not just political but also intellectual. Sicily, seized from the Muslims, yielded treasures in the form of Arabic translations of Greek philosophical and scientific works and equally important original works by Arabs and Iranians. Spain yielded an even greater bounty to translators who worked in both the Christian and the Muslim kingdoms. Later, Greece was ransacked for ancient Greek manuscripts after the Venetians persuaded the leaders of the Fourth Crusade in 1204 to satisfy their financial debts by capturing Constantinople and taking over, for a century, most of the shrunken Byzantine Empire. Generations passed before all these works were translated into Latin and studied, but they eventually transformed the thought of the western Europeans, who hitherto had had little familiarity with Greek writings except through Latin intermediaries.

The impact of the Crusades on the Islamic world was not nearly so great as on Europe, even though the invaders did establish four small principalities along the eastern Mediterranean at Jerusalem, Edessa, Antioch, and Tripoli, the last surviving until 1289. Knights of the higher nobility who became the rulers of these new principalities instituted feudal laws and granted Latin clergy ecclesiastical jurisdiction despite the fact that most local Christians owed allegiance to Constantinople. Later Crusades saw western Europe's most powerful kings embarking on lengthy campaigns to show their might and prove their piety, but they seldom stayed long in the Holy Land.

The Decline of Feudal Society

The interplay of manufacturing and commercial revival in the Italian and Flemish city-states, aggressive papal and monastic reform of the Latin Church, and mass military (and thus financial) mobilization to launch the Crusades tolled the death knell of feudal society though its actual demise extended over several centuries. Feudal society had emerged unevenly and haphazardly from the fifth century onward as a response to the collapse of a unified political order, widespread violence, and severe economic regression accompanied by a decline in interregional communication. Based on Germanic custom and on remnants and recollections of Roman practices, feudal society had protected populations and productive capacities in western Europe and had generated a distinctive culture centered on the court life of the nobility. Moreover, it had provided the political and social framework within which western Europe became a truly Christian land.

Born of disunity, chaos, and poverty, feudal society was ill suited to the economic, political, and ecclesiastical revival that began to stir Europe to new life in the twelfth century and ultimately gave birth to a robust and expansive Europe in the following centuries (see Chapter 16). Nobles and serfs subsisting on the agricultural and craft production of isolated manors and minimally connected to any broader monetary or market network gradually became obsolete in a time of urban-based manufacturing, large-scale imports from the East, and the need for cash to support a noble's long trip to the Holy Land. Steady improvements in fortifications and armaments added to the financial burden of nobility, enabling a few kings and great nobles to achieve an unprecedented degree of dominance and desire to enlarge, consolidate, and economically exploit their domains.

All of these tendencies had counterparts in the area of religion. Monasteries that had lived from the yield of their lands and from the work of their serfs had been little different from feudal manors. Their abbots had played the role of ecclesiastical lords. With monastic reform, whether under Cluny or later reforming movements, the independence of abbots dwindled along with the power of many petty nobles. In the growing cities, belatedly including royal capitals like Paris and London, cathedrals took on growing importance, both as symbols of civic pride and as ecclesiastical centers of a new, reviving Europe. Cathedral building brought together the political authority, financial resources, and technical skills of urban communities. The impact of a new cathedral was therefore much greater than that of a rural monastery.

The decline of feudal society, like its initial growth, was quite diverse in different parts of Europe. In Germany and eastern Europe monarchs actually became weaker in the twelfth century and great nobles stronger. In Spain, the objective of expelling the Muslims seemed achievable after the Muslim defeat at the Battle of Las Navas de Tolosa in 1212, and this objective provided in Spain a unifying focus for political action, and eventually for national unity, that was lacking elsewhere. In Italy and Flanders, the cities protected their new-found autonomy, thwarting the efforts of monarchs and popes to draw them into their own domains.

The struggle waged by King Henry II (r. 1154–1189) to gain control of the church in England (see above) was an extension of measures to centralize the realm that had begun under Henry I (r. 1100–1135). Under the first

Henry's predecessors, the king's *curia*, or court, had been made up of his noble companions of the moment. Henry I turned it into a more formal body possessed of specialized skills. More and better records were kept. Financial and judicial functions became more professional and developed into separate government departments (financial functions were called the "Exchequer" because of the practice of calculating accounts on a table marked off like a checkerboard).

These factors did not in themselves bring feudalism to an end. Noble society seemed to be flourishing, and most of the nobility of the twelfth century never imagined that their great-grandchildren would lose many of their privileges to increasingly powerful kings. Even as the seeds of feudal decline were germinating, long-lasting expressions of feudal culture such as ideas of chivalry and courtly love were receiving their highest expression in poetry and story.

The life of western Europe's leading female noble illustrates many of the changes taking place in the turbulent twelfth century. It is also representative of the degree to which people of that era saw the political order revolving around the lives and passions of the high nobility.

In 1137, a fifteen-year-old woman named Eleanor came into a vast inheritance upon the death of her father William, duke of Aquitaine and count of Poitou. Her lands in southwestern France were richer and more extensive than those of the French king, Louis the Fat. William had nevertheless been a vassal of Louis, and Louis feared that Eleanor of Aquitaine (as she is known to history) would marry one of his enemies. So he decided to marry her to his son, the future Louis VII. Five hundred of the king's most important vassals escorted the seventeen-year-old prince to Bordeaux, the capital of Aquitaine, for the wedding. During their return to Paris, the newlyweds learned that Louis the Fat was dead. Eleanor thus left Bordeaux a duchess and arrived in Paris a queen.

Louis and Eleanor ruled with little regard for the interests of the church until 1141, when a dispute broke out between Louis and Bernard, abbot of the monastery of Clairvaux, over the appointment of a bishop. As shrewd politically as he was influential as a theologian and mystic, Bernard easily won his contest with the young king and forced him to undertake a crusade to the Holy Land. Eleanor, who had given birth to a daughter in 1145, accompanied Louis along with her own band of women equipped as knights.

Once in Antioch, Eleanor became enamored of her attractive uncle, the poet Raymond of Toulouse, and decided to renounce her royal throne and remain in Antioch as duchess of Aquitaine and countess of Poitou. One of the many ballads later written about her imagines her saying to King Louis: "Why do I renounce you? Because of your weakness. You are not worth a rotten pear." Louis, however, seized her and carried her back to France because he did not want to lose control of her valuable properties.

After a second daughter was born in 1150, Louis began to worry about the lack of a son to succeed him as king. For her part, Eleanor became interested in Count Geoffrey of Anjou, called "Plantagenet" because he always wore on his helmet a sprig of yellow broom, the plant called *genista* in Latin. In 1152 Louis had their marriage annulled. Geoffrey had died in the meantime, so Eleanor married his son Henry, soon to become King Henry II of England.

While her new husband was reforming his monarchy, Queen Eleanor gave birth to three more daughters and five sons between 1153 and 1167. At about the time the last was born, Henry fell in love with Rosamond Clifford, the daughter of a Norman knight. Although Eleanor had overlooked earlier infidelities, she became enraged by the public nature of his dalliance with Rosamond and returned to Poitiers, the capital of Poitou. A majestic, commanding personality, she attracted knights, troubadours, and storytellers from all over France to her court. The idea of chivalry as an elaborate type of courtesy paid by knights to noble ladies reached a peak in Eleanor's court.

When a revolt against King Henry by his sons misfired, he captured Poitiers and took Eleanor back to England as a prisoner. Refusing to retire from the world as abbess of a nunnery, Eleanor remained under loose detention for fifteen years.

When Henry II died in 1189, their son Richard, known as "the Lion Hearted," became king and set his mother free.

While King Richard was on crusade in the Holy Land, Eleanor ruled England, using the title *queen*. On his way back, Richard was shipwrecked and captured by enemies in Europe. Queen Eleanor raised a ransom of 100,000 silver pieces to free him and then accompanied him back to England, where he easily suppressed the revolt of his usurping brother John Lackland. When Richard died in 1199 of a chance arrow shot while fighting against King Philip Augustus of France, he left no sons. So John succeeded legitimately to the throne. Eleanor died in 1204 at the age of eighty-two.

In 1215, King John was forced by a rebellion of his greatest vassals to put his seal to Magna Carta ("Great Charter"), a document that confirmed the rights of England's great barons with respect to the Crown (see Chapter 16). This was ostensibly a victory for the idea of feudalism, though it set a precedent for negotiating limitations on the king's power that later worked in favor of the common people and against the nobility. Its objective was not to dismantle the centralized administration that John's predecessors had established but to prevent future rulers from using it tyrannically.

In France, which witnessed parallel efforts at royal centralization under Philip Augustus (r. 1180–1223), the inevitable wave of feudal resistance to growing royal power came exactly a century later (1314–1315) and resulted in a series of provincial agreements that subsequent kings were able to whittle down one by one, ultimately giving rise to unlimited power for the French kings.

CONCLUSION

The collapse of imperial Rome was not a unique phenomenon in world history. China's Han dynasty (see Chapter 6) and the

Christian Europe Emerges, 300-1200

Abbassid caliphate (discussed in Chapter 10) both dissolved into a myriad of successor states, as had Alexander the Great's short-lived empire in the fourth century B.C.E. (see Chapter 5). Although the chaos, disunity, and economic regression experienced in post-Roman western Europe were particularly severe, the cultural vitality that eventually emerged from the centuries of disorder bears comparison with other instances. The Hellenistic Age, which followed the death of Alexander in 323 B.C.E., was a remarkable period of intellectual, religious, and scientific ferment and creativity. The Tang Empire, which emerged in China in the seventh century C.E. (see Chapter 11), was a powerful new state with a distinctive and lively culture, based only in part on survivals from the Han era. And in the Middle East the emergence of a mass society based on the Islamic religion was largely a phenomenon of the period following the collapse of the central Islamic state in the tenth century (see Chapter 10). The dynamic development of Islam after this political collapse is remarkably parallel to the overwhelming influence gained by Christianity in western Europe by the end of the twelfth century.

In contrast, the Byzantine Empire continued and built on Roman practices in an economic and political environment that was both more prosperous and more peaceful than that of western Europe. Furthermore, Byzantine society became deeply Christian well before a comparable degree of Christianization had been reached in western Europe. Yet despite their success in transmitting their own version both of Christianity and of the imperial tradition to Russia and to the peoples of the Balkans, the Byzantines largely failed to demonstrate the dynamism and ferment that characterized both the Europeans to their west and the Muslims to their south.

Although historians often have been limited by their sources to the investigation of imperial greatness and expansion, the intermediate periods between empires seem to be unusually creative and culturally dynamic times, as these examples show. Perhaps one reason for this is the opportunity that imperial dissolution affords different localities and peoples to follow their own particular lines of social, economic, and cultural

development. The history of the rise and development of Islam told in the next chapter will offer an opportunity to test this hypothesis.

SUGGESTED READING

Of the many general histories of Europe during this period, Roger Collins's *Early Medieval Europe, 300–1000* (1991) is the best survey stressing institutional and political developments. Georges Duby, *The Early Growth of the European Economy* (1974), provides an outstanding overview of economic and social history reflecting up-to-date historical methods. Jacques Le Goff, *Medieval Civilization, 400–1500* (1989), puts more stress on questions of social structure. Richard W. Southern, *Western Society and the Church in the Middle Ages* (1970), offers a survey concentrating on the all-important history of the church. The same author's *The Making of the Middle Ages* (1953) is a classic that gives a memorable impression of the period based on specific lives and events. Archibald R. Lewis, *Naval Power and Trade in the Mediterranean, A.D. 500–1100* (1951), offers an unusual focus on war and trade in the Mediterranean Sea and the ebb and flow of power between Christians and Muslims.

More specialized studies of economic and technological issues include Lynn White, Jr., *Medieval Technology and Social Change* (1962), a pathbreaking work on technological history; C. M. Cipolla, *Money, Prices and Civilization in the Mediterranean World, Fifth to Seventeenth Century* (1956), an insightful and easily understood explanation of important economic matters, and Cipolla's more general history, *Before the Industrial Revolution: European Society and Economy, 1000–1700* (1980); J. C. Russell, *The Control of Late Ancient and Medieval Population* (1985), a thorough analysis of demographic history and the problems of interpreting medieval European data; and Georges Duby, *Rural Economy and Country Life in the Medieval West* (1990), a detailed portrayal of rural life accompanied by translated documents.

Good works focusing on specific countries include, on France, Pierre Riché, *Daily Life in the World of Charlemagne* (1978), and Georges Duby, *The Chivalrous Society* (1977); on England, Dorothy Whitelock, *The Beginnings of English Society* (1952), and Doris Mary Stenton,

English Society in the Early Middle Ages (1066 1307) (1951); on Italy, Edward Burman, *Emperor to Emperor: Italy Before the Renaissance* (1991); on Germany and the Holy Roman Empire, Timothy Reuter, *Germany in the Early Middle Ages, c. 800–1056* (1991); and on Viking Scandinavia, Gwyn Jones, *A History of the Vikings* (1984).

Amy Kelly, *Eleanor of Aquitaine and the Four Kings* (1950), is an extraordinary biography of an extraordinary woman. Dhuoda, *Handbook for William: A Carolingian Woman's Counsel for Her Son*, trans. Carol Neel (1991), offers a firsthand look at the life of a noblewoman of the Carolingian era. More general works on women include Margaret Wade's classic popular history, *A Small Sound of the Trumpet: Women in Medieval Life* (1986), and Bonnie S. Anderson and Judith P. Zinsser's *A History of Their Own: Women in Europe from Prehistory to the Present* (1989). In the area of religion, Caroline Bynum's *Jesus as Mother: Studies in the Spirituality of the High Middle Ages* (1982) illustrates new trends in the study of women in this period.

Hans Eberhard Mayer's *The Crusades* (1988) is an excellent brief history of the crusading era. For a longer masterful account, stressing particularly the Byzantine standpoint, see Steven Runciman, *A History of the Crusades*, 3 vols. (1987). Benjamin Z. Kedar, *Crusade and Mission: European Approaches Toward the Muslims* (1988), explains the religious issues underlying the conflict.

The classic account of the revival of trade and urban life is Henri Pirenne's *Medieval Cities: Their Origins and the Revival of Trade* (1952). A similarly influential work is Robert S. Lopez, *The Commercial Revolution of the Middle Ages, 950–1350* (1971). Lopez and Irving W. Raymond have compiled and translated an excellent collection of primary documents dealing with trade and urban life: *Medieval Trade in the Mediterranean World: Illustrative Documents with Introductions and Notes* (1990).

The standard histories of the Byzantine Empire are Georgij A. Ostrogorsky, *History of the Byzantine State* (1969), and Alexander Aleksandrovich Vasiliev, *History of the Byzantine Empire*, 2 vols. (1952). Volume 1 of Vasiliev's work takes the history down to 1081. Cyril Mango's *Byzantium: The Empire of New Rome* (1980) provides a synthesis with a strong emphasis on cultural matters. Later Byzantine history, for which conventional narratives are scarce, is unusually well covered by A. P. Kazhdan and Ann Wharton Epstein in *Change in Byzantine Culture in the Eleventh and Twelfth Centuries* (1985). This book stresses social and economic issues instead of religion and politics and covers broader topics than its title indicates.

NOTES

1. Lewis G. M. Thorpe, *Two Lives of Charlemagne* (Harmondsworth: Penguin, 1969).

2. Dhuoda, *Handbook for William: A Carolingian Woman's Counsel for her Son* (Lincoln: University of Nebraska Press, 1991), pp. 83–89.

3. R. W. Southern, *Western Society and the Church in the Middle Ages* (Harmondsworth: Penguin, 1970), p. 102.

4. Anne Fremantle, *A Treasury of Early Christianity* (New York: New American Library of World Literature, 1960), pp. 400–401.

5. *St. Benedict's Rule for Monasteries*, tr. Leonard J. Doyle (Collegeville, Minn.: The Liturgical Press, 1948), pp. 20–21, 75–76.

6. A. A. Vasiliev, *History of the Byzantine Empire 324–1453* (Madison: University of Wisconsin Press, 1978), Vol. I, pp. 79–80.

7. A. P. Kazhdan and Ann Wharton Epstein, *Change in Byzantine Culture in the Eleventh and Twelfth Centuries* (Berkeley: University of California Press, 1985), p. 255.

8. *Ibid*. p. 248.

The Sasanid Empire and the Rise of Islam, 600 B.C.E.–1200

The Sasanid Empire   •   The Origins of Islam

The Caliphate in Power   •   Islamic Civilization

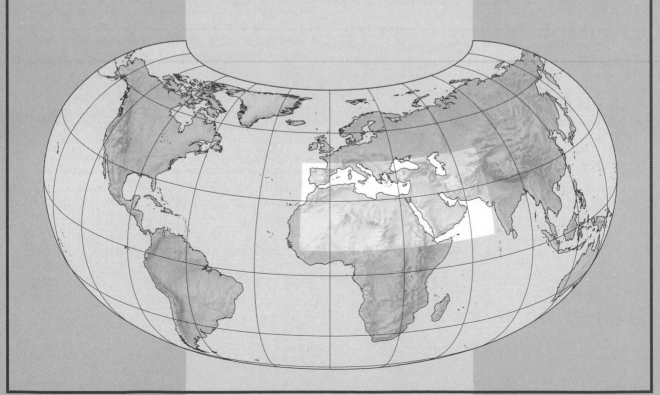

In 803 Harun al-Rashid, the ruler of the empire of Islam, abruptly dismissed and executed his long-time favorite, Ja'far, a member of the illustrious Barmakid family. He also threw Ja'far's father and brother into a dungeon, where they died. Arabic chronicles give conflicting reasons for the disgrace of the Barmakids, who had controlled the financial and administrative affairs of the empire for over twenty-five years. One report has Harun arranging a marriage of convenience between his beloved sister Abbasa and Ja'far and then becoming enraged when the pair actually engaged in marital relations. Harun's only purpose in arranging the marriage had been to facilitate social contact without violating the prohibition on Abbasa being with a man she was not related to.

The story is probably a fiction embodying a favorite theme in Islamic historical writing: the negative influence of women on government affairs. It had the zest of court gossip, however, and contributed significantly to the legendary stature of the Barmakids.

The most extraordinary part of the story was not the Barmakids' fall but their rise. Ja'far's great-grandfather had been the chief monk of a Buddhist monastery in northern Afghanistan. How did an Afghan Buddhist family acquire such power in an empire established by Arab armies, embodying Persian traditions of rule, and devoted to the religion of Islam? Although the story of Islam begins in Arabia with the Prophet Muhammad, the dramatic growth of Islam as a political, social, and cultural community involved many peoples and had roots in developments that long preceded him.

Arab conquerors in the seventh century established an empire that maintained its political cohesion for less than three centuries. But this was long enough to sustain a massive religious conversion that turned Islam from a religion of desert Arabs into a multiethnic universal faith. Islam fostered a vibrant and productive urban culture that contrasted dramatically with the urban decline of the Latin Christian West. Islamic society developed approaches to law, piety, and social relations that differed from those of the Christians, despite the Judaic roots that both religions shared.

THE SASANID EMPIRE

The rise in the third century of a new Iranian empire—the Sasanid Empire—as the foe of the Byzantine Empire seems superficially to continue the old rivalry between Rome's legions and the Parthians along the Euphrates frontier. However, behind this façade of continuity, a social and economic transformation was in the making in the Middle East. The outcome of this transformation was not a return to a simpler, more fragmented, and less urbanized pattern of life, as in western Europe. Rather, together the Sasanid Empire and the Byzantine Empire made possible a new and powerful religio-political movement: Islam.

Ardashir, a descendant of one Sasan, defeated the Parthians around 224 and established a new Iranian kingdom: the Sasanid. Unlike the Parthians, their nomadic predecessors from the northeast, the Sasanids hailed from Fars province (Persis in Greek) in southwestern Iran, the homeland of the Achaemenid dynasty, which had fallen to Alexander the Great (see Chapter 5). The Sasanids were urbane and sophisticated and established their capital on the Tigris River at Ctesiphon, near the later site of Baghdad. Thus Mesopotamia, a land populated mostly by speakers of Semitic rather than Iranian languages, was the capital province of the new Iranian dynasty.

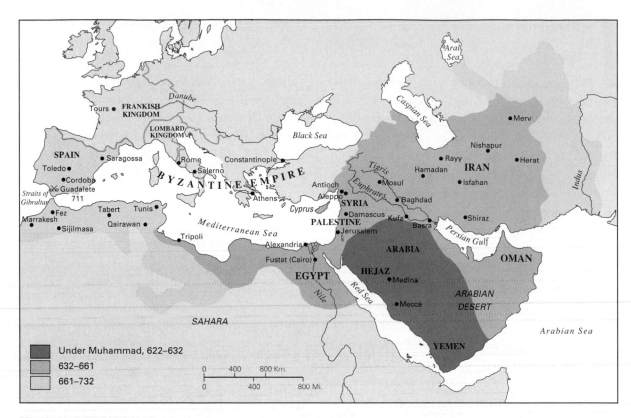

Map 10.1 Early Expansion of Muslim Rule   The territory brought under Muslim rule during the Arab conquests of the first Islamic century was vast. However, the expansion of Islam as the religion of the majority of the population was much slower. In most areas outside the Arabian peninsula, the only region where Arabic was then spoken, conversion was uncommon during the first century but accelerated during the second.

Politics and Society

To their west, the new rulers confronted first the Romans and then, after 330, the Byzantines. Along their desert frontier west of the Euphrates, the Sasanids subsidized the chieftains of nomadic Arab groups to protect their empire from invasion, just as the Byzantines did with Arabs on their Jordanian frontier. This practice served to bring some Arab pastoralists into the orbit of imperial politics and culture, though others farther to the south remained isolated and independent. Farther north, the international frontier ran down the upper Euphrates River in Mesopotamia, and the rival Sasanid and Byzantine Empires launched numerous attacks on each other across that frontier between the 340s and 628.

Nevertheless, in times of peace, exchange between the empires flourished, allowing goods transported over the Silk Road to enter the zone of Mediterranean trade. Cities like Antioch, Damascus, and Aleppo—all in Syria—were thriving cultural, commercial, and manufacturing centers and benefited greatly from contacts with the Sasanids to the east. Just as the Arabs who traversed the desert between Syria and Mesopotamia were drawn into imperial political affairs, so these pastoralists benefited from the trade between the empires. They not only supplied camels and guides but played a significant role as merchants and organizers of caravans, especially during the mid-third century flourishing of the Arab kingdom of Palmyra in the middle of the Syrian desert (see Map 10.1). Roman conquerors destroyed Palmyra's temples and colonnaded avenues in 273, but depictions of the Palmyrene caravan-god leading his camel are still visible in the ruins.

The mountains and plateaus of Iran proper formed the Sasanids' political hinterland, often ruled by the Shah's (King's) cousins or by powerful nobles. Cities there were small walled communities that served more as military strongpoints than as major centers of population and production. Society revolved around a minor, local aristocracy who lived on rural estates and cultivated the arts of hunting and war just like the noble warriors described in the sagas of ancient kings and heroes sung at their banquets. The small principalities of Central Asia that mostly lay beyond Sasanid control were home to a more developed urban culture imbued

Sasanid Shah Shapur II (309–379) The ruler hunting or banqueting is a common symbol of royalty in pre-Islamic Iran, seen here on a silver plate. Wild boar were dangerous prey. Later Muslim society considered them unclean and prohibited eating them. Aristocratic Sasanid society favored silver plates like these. After the Muslim Arabs conquered Iran in the seventh century, landed aristocracy gradually disappeared. Prosperous city dwellers made do with elegant, but cheaper, glazed pottery plates. (Smithsonian Institution, Courtesy of the Freer Gallery of Art, Washington, D.C. Neg. #34.23)

with Buddhism and buoyed by the prosperity of the Silk Road (see Chapter 8).

Sasanid political structure was unlike the feudal relationships of western Europe. Despite the dominance of powerful baronial families on the Iranian Plateau, long-lasting political fragmentation along feudal lines did not develop. Also, although Arabs and other nomadic or seminomadic peoples were numerous in mountain and desert regions, no folk migration arose comparable to that of the Germanic peoples of the late Roman empire. The Sasanid and Byzantine Empires successfully maintained central control of imperial finances and military power and found effective ways of integrating frontier peoples as mercenaries or caravaneers.

Nor did urban life and the money-based economy erode as it did in the West. The silver coins of the Sasanid rulers and the gold coins of the Byzantine emperors were plentiful, and trade with the East remained robust. The Silk Road brought new products to Mesopotamia, some of which became part of the agricultural landscape. Sasanid farmers pioneered in planting cotton, sugar cane, rice, citrus trees, eggplants, and other crops adopted from India and China. Although the acreage devoted to new crops spread slowly, these products were to become important consumption and trade items during the Islamic period following the fall of the Sasanid Empire.

Religion and Empire

The Sasanids were Zoroastrians (see Chapter 5) and established their faith, which the Parthians before them had never particularly stressed, as a state religion just as Constantine made Christianity the official religion of the Byzantine Empire in the 320s (see Chapter 6). The Zoroastrian equivalent of the patriarch of Constantinople was the *Mobadan-mobad*, "Priest of Priests," appointed by the Sasanid *Shahan-shah*, "King of Kings."

The Hellenistic kingdoms that arose from Alexander's empire and, after them, the early Roman Empire, had sponsored official cults focusing on the deified ruler, but they also had rec-

ognized the great variety of religious beliefs among their diverse populations. Moreover, the rulers and the urban upper class were often more interested in varieties of Greek philosophy than in a specific religious sect. But the proclamation of Christianity and Zoroastrianism as official faiths marked the emergence of religion as an instrument of politics both within and between the empires, thus setting a precedent for the subsequent rise of Islam as the focus of a political empire.

Both Zoroastrianism and Christianity embraced intolerance. A late-third-century inscription in Iran boasts of the persecutions of Christians, Jews, and Buddhists carried out by the Zoroastrian high priest Kartir, and the councils of Christian bishops declared many theological beliefs heretical from the fourth century onward. Yet sizable Christian and Jewish communities remained, especially in Mesopotamia, and the Christians became pawns in the political rivalry with the Byzantines, sometimes persecuted and sometimes patronized by the Sasanid kings.

Sasanid policy took advantage of the bitter schisms among the Christian sects of Byzantium. In 431 a council of bishops called by the Byzantine emperor declared the Nestorian Christians heretics for overemphasizing the human side of Christ's nature. The Nestorians believed that human and divine natures existed side by side in Jesus and that Mary was not the mother of God, as many other Christians maintained, but the mother of the human Jesus. After the ruling the Nestorians sought refuge under the Sasanid shah and eventually spread their missionary activities across Central Asia. Ten years earlier, in 421, war had broken out with Byzantium because of Sasanid persecution of Christians. Moreover, Armenia, whose Christian population had cultural links with Iran, was a bone of contention between the empires. The Armenian Apostolic Church used the Armenian language in its services and hewed to Monophysite doctrine, which was considered heretical by the Byzantine state (see Chapter 9).

In the third century a preacher named Mani founded a new religion in Mesopotamia known as Manichaeism. He preached a dualist faith—a struggle between good and evil—theologically derived from Zoroastrianism. Although he first enjoyed the favor of the shah, Mani was martyred in 276 with many of his followers. Yet his religion survived and spread widely. The Nestorian missionaries in Central Asia competed with Manichaean missionaries for converts.

The Arabs who guarded the desert frontiers of the two empires became enmeshed in this web of religious conflict. Those subsidized by the Byzantines adopted the Monophysite faith; the allies of the Sasanids, the Nestorian. Thus both Arab groups retained a measure of religious independence from their patrons; and through them, knowledge of Christianity penetrated deeper into the Arabian peninsula during the fifth and sixth centuries.

The politicizing of religion contrasts sharply with earlier periods of East-West rivalry along the Euphrates frontier during the time of the Greek city states (see Chapter 5) and the Roman-Parthian rivalry (see Chapter 8) when language, ethnic identity, or citizenship in a particular city-state defined political allegiances. Now, religion penetrated into all aspects of community life. Most subjects of the Byzantine emperors and Sasanid shahs identified themselves first and foremost as members of a religious community. Their schools and law courts were religious. They looked on priests, monks, rabbis, and mobads as moral guides in daily life. Most books were on religious subjects. And in some areas, religious leaders represented their flocks even in secular matters such as tax collection.

As we saw in Chapter 9, western Europe was experiencing a thoroughgoing reorientation toward Christianity during the centuries following the fall of the Western Roman empire. The Sasanid and Byzantine territories, however, were marked by much more religious diversity. They included many different Christian, Jewish, and Zoroastrian communities along with smaller groups adhering to other faiths. Relations between religious groups, fluctuating between tolerance and intolerance, were a major determinant of social order or conflict.

THE ORIGINS OF ISLAM

The activities of the Arabs who lived beyond the frontiers of the empire were seldom of interest to the Sasanid rulers. The Sasanids displayed some interest in the Arab side of the Persian Gulf and to Yemen, which were along their maritime trade routes. But as for the interior of the Arabian peninsula, the Sasanid view, evident in a phrase attributed in later centuries to Muhammad, was that the Arabs were "monkeys on the backs of camels."

Yet it was precisely in the interior of Arabia, far from the gaze and political reach of the Sasanid and Byzantine Empires, that the religion of Islam was to take form and inspire a movement that would humble the proud emperors. Both the socioreligious complexity of the Sasanid and Byzantine Empires and their inattention to events far from their borders are key to understanding the phenomenal rise and success of Islam.

The Arabian Peninsula Before Muhammad

Throughout history most of the people living on the Arabian peninsula have lived in settled communities rather than as pastoral nomads. The highlands of Yemen are fertile and abundantly watered by the spring monsoon blowing northward along the East African coast. The interior mountains farther east in southern Arabia are much more arid but in some places receive enough water to support farming and village life. And small inlets along the coast favored the rise of an occasional fishing and trading community. These regions are largely cut off from the Arabian interior by the enormous sea of sand known as the "Empty Quarter." In the seventh century, most people in southern Arabia knew more about Africa, India, and the Persian Gulf than about the forbidding interior of the great peninsula and the scattered camel- and sheep-herding nomads who lived there.

Exceptions to this pattern were mostly associated with caravan trading. Several kingdoms—Qataban, Himyar, Sabae (biblical Sheba)—rose and fell in Yemen, leaving stone ruins and enigmatic inscriptions to testify to their bygone prosperity. From these commercial entrepôts came frankincense and myrrh (crystallized resins harvested from low trees that grew in eastern Yemen). Nomads derived income from providing camels, guides, and safe passage to merchants wanting to transport incense northward, where the fragrant substances had long been burned in religious rituals. Return caravans brought manufactured products from Mesopotamia and the Mediterranean.

Just as the Silk Road enabled small towns in Central Asia to become major trading centers, so the trans-Arabian trade gave rise to desert caravan cities (see Voices and Visions: Caravan Cities, in Chapter 8). The earliest and most prosperous, Petra in southern Jordan and Palmyra in northern Syria, were swallowed up by Rome. This, coupled with early Christians' distaste for incense, which seemed too much a feature of pagan worship, contributed to a slackening of trade in high-value goods in Sasanid times and a period of political turbulence among the nomadic groups. Nevertheless, trade across the Arabian desert did not lapse altogether. Camels, leather, and gold and other minerals mined in the mountains of western Arabia, took the place of frankincense and myrrh as exports, and grain and manufactured goods were imported. This reduced trade kept alive the relations between the Arabs and the settled farming regions to the north forged in earlier centuries, and it familiarized the Arabs who accompanied the caravans with the cultures and lifestyles of the Sasanid and Byzantine empires.

In the desert, Semitic polytheism, with its worship of natural forces and celestial bodies, still thrived but was affected by other religions. Christianity, as practiced by the Arab tribes guarding the imperial frontiers in Jordan and southern Mesopotamia, and Judaism, possibly carried by refugees from the Roman expulsion of the Jews from their homeland in the first century C.E., made inroads on polytheism.

Mecca, a late-blooming caravan city, lies in a barren mountain valley halfway between Yemen and Syria along the Red Sea coast of Arabia (see Map 10.2). The torrid coastal plain was ill suited to caravan travel, giving Mecca a good position in the trade from Yemen to the north and east. A nomadic kin group known as the Quraysh settled in Mecca in the fifth century and assumed control of this trade. Mecca rapidly achieved a measure of prosperity, partly because it was too far from Byzantine Syria, Sasanid Iraq, and Ethiopian-controlled Yemen for them to attack. It came nowhere near to rivaling the earlier luxuries of Palmyra and Petra, but some subgroups of the Quraysh became wealthy.

Mecca was also a cult center. A cubical shrine called the Ka'ba, a holy well called Zamzam, and a sacred precinct surrounding the two wherein killing was prohibited contributed to the emergence of Mecca as a pilgrimage site. Some Meccans associated the shrine with stories known to Jews and Christians. They regarded Abraham (Ibrahim in Arabic) as the builder of the Ka'ba, and they identified a site outside Mecca as the location where God asked Abraham to sacrifice his son. The son was not Isaac (Ishaq in Arabic), the son of Sarah, but Ishmael (Isma'il in Arabic), the son of Hagar, cited in the Hebrew Old Testament as the forefather of the Arabs.

Muhammad in Mecca

Muhammad was born in Mecca in 570 and grew up an orphan in the house of his uncle, Abu Talib. He engaged in trade and married a widow named Khadija, also a member of the Quraysh, whose caravan interests he superintended. They had several children, but their one son died in childhood. Around the year 610, Muhammad adopted the practice of meditating at night in the mountainous terrain around Mecca. During one night vigil, known to later religious tradition as "The Night of Power and Excellence," a being whom Muhammad later understood to be the angel Gabriel (Jibra'il in Arabic) spoke to him:

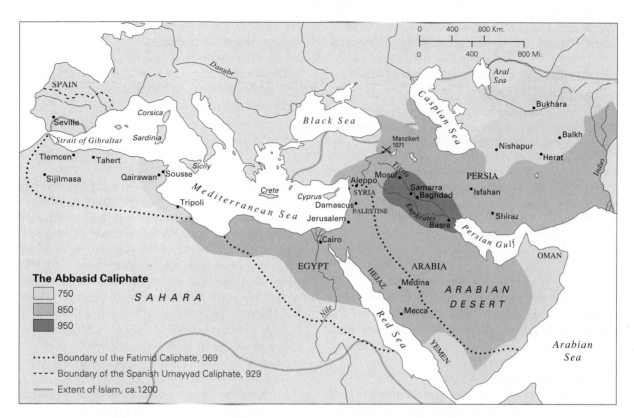

Map 10.2 Rise and Fall of the Abbasid Caliphate   Though Abbasid rulers occupied the caliphal seat in Iraq from 750 to 1258, when Mongol armies destroyed Baghdad, real political power waned sharply and steadily after 850. Nevertheless, the idea of the caliphate remained central to Sunni Muslim political theory. The rival caliphates of the Fatimids (909–1171) and Spanish Umayyads (929–976) were comparatively short-lived.

Proclaim! In the name of your Lord who created.
Created man from a clot of congealed blood.
Proclaim! And your Lord is the Most Bountiful.
He who has taught by the pen.
Taught man that which he knew not.[1]

Over the next three years he shared this and subsequent revelations only with his closest friends and family members. This period culminated in Muhammad's conviction that the words he was hearing were from God (Allah in Arabic). Khadija, his uncle Abu Talib's son Ali, his friend Abu Bakr, and others close to him shared this conviction. The revelations continued until Muhammad's death in 632.

Like most people in the ancient world, includ-

ing Christians and Jews, the Arabs believed in unseen spirits: gods, desert spirits called *jinns*, demons known as *shaitans*, and so forth. They further believed, just as most other ancient peoples did, that certain individuals had contact with the spirit world. Some were oracles or seers; others poets, who were thought to be possessed by a jinn. Therefore, when Muhammad began to recite his sonorous rhymed revelations in public, many people believed that he was inspired by an unseen spirit even as they questioned whether that spirit was, as Muhammad asserted, the one true god.

The content of Muhammad's earliest revelations called on people to witness that one god had created the universe and everything in it, including themselves. At the end of time, their souls would be judged, their sins balanced against their good deeds. The blameless would go to paradise; the sinful would taste hellfire:

> By the night as it conceals the light;
> By the day as it appears in glory;
> By the mystery of the creation of male and female;
> Verily, the ends ye strive for are diverse.
> So he who gives in charity and fears God,
> And in all sincerity testifies to the best,
> We will indeed make smooth for him the path to Bliss.
> But he who is a greedy miser and thinks himself self-sufficient,
> And gives the lie to the best,
> We will indeed make smooth for him the path to misery.[2]

All people were called to submit themselves to God and accept Muhammad as the last of his messengers. Those who did so were called *muslim*, meaning one who makes "submission," *islam*, to the will of God.

Because earlier messengers mentioned in the revelations included Noah, Moses, and Jesus, it was clear to Muhammad's hearers that what he was saying was in agreement with the Judaism and Christianity they were already somewhat familiar with. Yet his revelations were distinctly different. They charged the Jews and Christians with being negligent in preserving God's revealed word, just as other peoples, such as those of Sodom and Gomorrah, to whom God had sent the prophet Lot, had rejected it outright. Thus, even though the Ka'ba, which superseded Jerusalem as the focus of Muslim prayer in 624, was founded by Abraham/Ibrahim, whom Muslims consider the first Muslim, and even though many revelations narrated stories also found in the Bible, Muhammad's followers considered his revelation more perfect than that of the Bible.

Some non-Muslim scholars have maintained that Muhammad's revelations appealed especially to Meccans who were distressed that wealth was replacing kinship as the most important aspect of social relations. Verses criticizing taking pride in wealth and neglecting obligations to orphans and other powerless people are seen as conveying a message of social reform. Other

scholars, along with most Muslims, consider Muhammad's revelations an oral document of enormous power and beauty. The force of its rhetoric and poetic vision, coming in the Muslim view directly from God, thus goes far to explain Muhammad's early success.

The Formation of the Umma

Though conceding that Muhammad's eloquence might stem from possession by a jinn, most Meccan leaders felt that their power and prosperity would be threatened by acceptance of Muhammad as the sole agent of the one true God. They put pressure on his kin to disavow him, and they persecuted the weakest of his followers. Stymied by this hostility, Muhammad and his followers fled Mecca in 622 to take up residence in the agricultural community of Medina 215 miles (346 kilometers) to the north. This carefully planned flight, the *hijra*, marks the beginning of the Muslim calendar.

Prior to the hijra, representatives of the major kin groups of Medina had met with Muhammad and agreed to accept and protect him and his community of Muslims because they saw him as an inspired leader who could calm their perpetual feuding. Together, the Meccan migrants and major groups in Medina bound themselves into a single *umma*, a community defined solely by acceptance of Islam and of Muhammad as the "Messenger of God," his most common title. Three Jewish kin groups chose to retain their own faith. Their decision is one reason why Muslims changed the direction of their prayer away from Jerusalem and toward the Ka'ba in 624.

During the last decade of his life, Muhammad took active responsibility for his umma. The Meccan immigrants in the community were terribly vulnerable without the support of their Meccan kinsmen. Fresh revelations provided a framework for regulating social and legal affairs and stirred the Muslims to fight against the still-unbelieving city of Mecca. Sporadic war, much of it conducted by raiding and negotiation with desert nomads, sapped Mecca's strength and convinced many Meccans that God was on

Muhammad's side. In 630 Mecca surrendered, and Muhammad and his followers made the pilgrimage to the Ka'ba unhindered.

Muhammad did not return to Mecca again. Medina had grown into a bustling Muslim city-state. The Jews, whom he accused of disloyalty during the war, had been expelled or eliminated. Delegations from tribes all over Arabia came to meet the new leader, and Muhammad sent emissaries back with them to teach them about Islam and collect their alms. Whether he planned or desired it or not, Muhammad's mission to bring God's message to humanity had resulted in his unchallenged control of a state that was coming to dominate the Arabian peninsula. Yet unlike preceding short-lived nomadic kingdoms, the supremacy of the Medinan state was based not on kinship but on a common faith in a single god.

In 632, after a brief illness, Muhammad died. Within twenty-four hours a group of Medinan leaders, along with three of Muhammad's close friends, determined that Abu Bakr, one of the earliest believers and the father of Muhammad's favorite wife A'isha, should succeed him. They called him the *khalifa*, or "successor," the English version of which is *caliph*. But calling Abu Bakr a successor did not clarify the capacity in which he was succeeding the Prophet. Everyone knew that neither Abu Bakr nor anyone else could receive revelations, and they likewise knew that Muhammad's revelations had made no provision for succession, or for any government purpose beyond maintaining the Muslim community, the *umma*. Indeed, some people thought the world would soon end because God's last messenger was dead.

Abu Bakr's immediate task was to reestablish and expand Muslim authority over Arabia's many nomadic and settled communities. After Muhammad's death, some had abandoned their allegiance to Medina or even switched allegiance to would-be prophets of their own. Muslim armies fought hard to confirm the authority of the newborn caliphate. In the process, some fighting spilled over into non-Arab areas in Iraq.

Abu Bakr summoned those who had acted as secretaries for Muhammad and ordered them to organize the revelations into a book. Hitherto

Rise and Fall of the Caliphate

611	Muhammad's first revelations
632–634	Abu Bakr first caliph
661	Civil war ends; Umayyads rule from Damascus
750	Abbasids overthrow Umayyads, caliphate moves to Iraq
836–892	Capital at Samarra: Turkish troops dominate caliphate
909	Shi'ite Fatimid caliphate in Tunisia
945	Buyids occupy Baghdad, strip caliph of temporal power
976	Spanish Umayyad caliphate dissolves, successor states quarrel
1171	End of Fatimid caliphate; Saladin restores Sunni rule in Egypt
1258	Mongols sack Baghdad, kill Abbasid caliph
1517	Last Abbasid caliph dies; Ottomans take Cairo

written haphazardly on pieces of leather or bone, the verses of revelation were now written as a single document on parchment and gathered into chapters. The resulting book, which acquired its final form when Uthman, the third caliph, ordered a definitive fixing of its short vowels, which are not normally indicated in Arabic script, was called the Quran, or the Recitation. Muslims regard it not as the words of Muhammad but as the unalterable word of God. As such, it is comparable not so much to the Bible, a book written by many hands over a long period of time, as to the person of Jesus Christ, who, according to Christian belief, is a direct manifestation of God.

Though theoretically united in its acceptance of God's will, the umma soon fell prey to human disagreement over the succession to the caliphate. The first civil war in Islam followed the assassination of the third caliph, Uthman, in 656. His assassins, rebels from the army, nominated to succeed him Ali, Muhammad's first cousin and husband of his daughter Fatima. Ali had been passed over three times previously even though many people considered him to be the natural heir to the Prophet's mantle. Indeed, he and his supporters felt that Muhammad had indicated as much in public remarks, though other Muslims interpreted his words differently.

When Ali accepted the nomination to be caliph, two of Muhammad's close companions and his favorite wife A'isha challenged him. Ali defeated them in the Battle of the Camel (656), so called because the fighting raged around the camel on which A'isha was seated in an enclosed woman's saddle. But blood had been spilled within the umma. After the battle, the governor of Syria, Mu'awiya, a kinsman of Uthman from the Umayya subgroup of the Quraysh, renewed the challenge. Inconclusive battle gave way to arbitration. The arbitrators decided that Uthman had been killed unjustly and that Ali had been at fault in accepting the nomination. Ali rejected the arbitrators' findings, but before he could resume fighting, he was killed by one of his own supporters, who faulted him for agreeing to arbitration in the first place. Mu'awiya offered Ali's son Hasan a dignified retirement in the holy cities and thus emerged as caliph in 661.

Mu'awiya chose his own son, Yazid, to succeed him and thus instituted the Umayyad dynasty. Yazid aroused opposition in 680 when he ordered the interception and killing of Hasan's brother Husain, and his family, when Husain tried to reestablish the right of Ali's family to rule. Sympathy for Husain's martyrdom was pivotal in the transformation of a political movement, the Party of Ali—in Arabic, Shi'at Ali, or Shi'ites for short—into a religious sect.

Several variations in Shi'ite belief developed, but Shi'ites have always agreed that Ali was the rightful successor to Muhammad and that God's choice as *Imam*, or leader of the Muslim community, at any given time is one or another of Ali's descendants. Because the Shi'ites were seldom strong enough to establish their Imams in power, their religious feelings came to focus on outpourings of sympathy for Husain and other martyrs and on messianic dreams of one of their Imam's someday triumphing.

Those Muslims who thought the first three caliphs had been properly selected gradually came to be called the People of Tradition and Community—in Arabic, Ahl al-Sunna wa'l-Jama'a, or Sunnis for short. As for Ali's militant followers who had abhorred his acceptance of arbitration in a matter they regarded as already determined by God, they evolved into small and rebellious Kharijite sects (from *kharaja* meaning "to secede or rebel"). These three main divisions of Islam, the last one now quite minor, still survive. Today the umma has grown to over 800 million people.

THE CALIPHATE IN POWER

The Islamic caliphate was transformed into a mighty empire by the conquests carried out by the Arabs after Muhammad's death. It lasted until 1923, when the secular government of the newly established Republic of Turkey voted to abolish it. During the last thousand years or so of its existence, however, it only occasionally exerted real power. By the late 800s the caliphs already were losing control as one piece after another of their huge realm broke away. Yet they always retained the respect of the Sunni community, and the idea of a caliphate, however unrealistic it became, remained a touchstone of Sunni belief in the unity of the umma.

The residual religious authority of the declining caliphate cannot be compared with the authority of the popes in Rome or the patriarchs in Constantinople. Islam never recognized a single person as the absolute arbiter of true belief with the power to expel heretics and discipline clergy. Thus the caliphs had little theoretical basis for reestablishing their originally universal authority over the umma once they began to lose political and military power.

The Islamic Conquests

Arab conquests outside Arabia began under the second caliph, Umar (r. 634–644), possibly prompted by the first forays into Iraq. Within

Tomb of the Samanids in Bukhara   This early tenth century structure has the basic layout of a Zoroastrian fire temple: a dome on top of a cube. However, geometric ornamentation in baked brick marks it as an early masterpiece of Islamic architecture. The Samanid family achieved independence as rulers of northeastern Iran and western central Asia in the tenth century. (Private collection)

fifteen years Arab armies, organized according to kin groups, had wrenched Syria and Egypt— twenty years later Tunisia—away from the Byzantine Empire and defeated the Sasanid shah, Yazdigird III (r. 632–651) (see Map 10.1). After a decade-long lull, expansion began again. In 711, Spain fell to an Arab-led army mostly composed of Algerian and Moroccan Berbers, who, as nomads, had fallen in rather easily with Arab plans. In the same year, Sind, the southern Indus River valley and westernmost region of India, succumbed to partially seaborne invaders from Iraq.

Although a few pieces of territory were added later, such as Sicily in the ninth century, the extent of Muslim dominion remained roughly stable for the next three centuries. After that, conquest began anew in India, Anatolia, and Africa even as Islam was expanding peacefully by trade in these and other areas (see Chapter 15).

Muslim chroniclers portray the Arab conquests as manifestations of God's will. Non-Muslim historians have had a more difficult time explaining them. The speed and political cohesiveness of the campaigns of these warriors from Arabia set them apart from the piecemeal incursions of the Germanic peoples or the Vikings. Lust for booty, a frequently offered explanation, exaggerates the idea that pastoral Arab society was naturally war-like. A majority of the Arabs lived in settled communities, and many of the nomadic groups had long experience in servicing the caravan trade. Greed also fails to explain the persistence of the campaigns in regions where difficult terrain slowed the conquest and booty was scarce. Yet the alternative theory—fanatic religious fervor—ignores the fact that most of the warriors had no firsthand experience of life in Medina and knew comparatively little about Islam. Moreover, non-Arab converts to Islam were limited to a marginal role in the fighting, and certain Christian Arab kin groups were allowed to participate in the conquests without converting, as if Arab ethnicity rather than religion defined the movement.

Nor were the Arabs' adversaries powerless or fatally divided by religious quarrels as some historians have suggested. Although the Byzantine and Sasanid Empires had pummeled each other in a war that shortly preceded the Arab conquests, they still resisted the initial Muslim onslaught. Indeed, the Byzantines successfully defended their Anatolian heartland, despite recurrent Muslim attacks, for four centuries after their loss of Syria, Egypt, and Tunisia. Moreover, even though the Muslim rulers tolerated their non-Muslim subjects, most Christians, Zoroastrians, and Jews knew absolutely nothing about Muhammad or Islam while the conquests were under way and thus could not have acquiesced in Arab rule in anticipation of its leniency.

Historians have further been puzzled by the absence of a single great war leader like Alexander the Great. Three possible explanations present themselves. First, Muhammad himself died before the conquests began. Second, the caliphs rarely led an army. And third, the kin-group organization of the armies and the geographical sweep of the campaigns called for many commanders, whose abilities ranged from outstanding to mediocre.

The best explanation for this watershed in world history, the establishment of the caliphate through conquest as a great empire, is that the close Meccan companions of the Prophet were men of political and economic sophistication who were truly inspired by their experience of his charisma. They guided the conquests. The social structure and hardy nature of Arab society lent itself to flexible military operations, and the authority of Medina, reconfirmed during the caliphate of Abu Bakr, assured obedience.

More important than any specific military quality, however, was the decision taken during Umar's caliphate to prohibit the Arab pastoral groups from taking over conquered territory for their own use. Umar tied army service, with its regular pay and occasional windfalls of booty, to residence in large military camps—two in Iraq, one in Egypt, and one in Tunisia. The desert fringe areas of Syria seem to have been more open to dispersed Arab occupation. East of Iraq, Arabs were assigned to much smaller garrison towns at strategically crucial locations, though one large garrison was established at Marv in present-day Turkmenistan.

Down to the early eighth century, this policy not only kept the armies together and ready for action but preserved life in the countryside, where at least three-fourths of the population lived, virtually unchanged. Most people who became subjects of the caliphate by conquest probably never saw an Arab during their lifetimes, and only a tiny proportion, in Syria and Iraq, understood the Arabic language.

Spread over the largest territorial empire ever achieved, the million or so Arabs who participated in the conquests constituted a small, self-isolated ruling minority living on the taxes paid by a vastly larger non-Arab, non-Muslim subject population. Far from requiring their conquered subjects to convert, the Arabs had little material incentive to encourage conversion; and there is no evidence of a coherent missionary effort to spread Islam during the conquest period. All of these factors contradict the common assumption that the Arabs sought to force their faith on the peoples they conquered.

The Umayyad and Abbasid Caliphates

The Umayyad caliphs who came to power in 661 presided more over an ethnically defined Arab realm than over an Islamic empire. Ruling from Damascus, they stemmed from a wealthy Meccan family that initially had opposed Muhammad. Their military forces were composed almost entirely of Muslim Arab warriors. They adopted and adapted the administrative practices of their Sasanid and Byzantine predecessors, as had the four caliphs who preceded them. Only gradually did they replace non-Muslim secretaries and tax officials with Muslims and introduce Arabic as the language of government. A major symbolic step was the introduction of distinctively Muslim silver and gold coins early in the eighth century. From that time on, silver dirhams and gold dinars bearing Arabic religious phrases but devoid of images held pride of place in monetary exchanges from Morocco to the borders of China. Islamic coins were even imitated occasionally in England and France.

The Umayyad dynasty fell in 750 after a decade of growing unrest from many quarters. Converts to Islam by that date were no more than 10 percent of the indigenous population, but they were numerically significant because of the comparatively small number of Arab warriors, and they resented not achieving equal status with the Arabs. The Arabs of Iraq and elsewhere felt the Syrian Arabs were too powerful in caliphal affairs. Pious Muslims looked askance at the secular and even irreligious behavior of the caliphs. And Shi'ites and Kharijites attacked the Umayyad family's religious legiti-

Frescoes from the caliphal palace in the Syrian desert Painted early in the eighth century, these scenes show a stage of Islamic art before calligraphy and geometric ornament became standard. The bottom scene is strikingly similar to the royal hunt depicted on page 281, but the rider has been stripped of royal crown and fancy dress. The top scene reflects Sasanian banqueting and entertainment motifs. The lute and flute became popular instruments in Muslim society, but some religious authorities frown on music. (Syria Museum, Damascus)

macy as rulers, giving rise to a number of rebellions.

One rebellion, in the region of Khurasan in northeastern Iran, Afghanistan, and Central Asia, overthrew the last Umayyad caliph. Even with triumph at hand, however, it was uncertain on whose behalf the fight had been fought. Many supporters of the rebellion were Shi'ites who thought they were fighting for the family of Ali.

Dome of the Rock of Jerusalem   Begun in 687 with a Byzantine architectural layout, this shrine is a monument to the Muslim belief that Muhammad, riding a miraculous steed called al-Buraq, ascended to heaven on a night journey from this point. It is located on the great artificial mound where the Jewish temple was situated before its destruction by the Romans in 70 C.E. (Laurie Platt Winfrey, Inc.)

As it turned out, the secret organization that coordinated the revolt was loyal to the family of Abbas, one of Muhammad's uncles. Some of the Abbasid caliphs who ruled after 750 were lenient toward their relatives in Ali's family, and one even flirted with transferring the caliphate to them. The Abbasid family, however, held on to the caliphate until 1258, when Mongol invaders killed the last of them in Baghdad (see Chapter 13). A branch of the family resumed the title in Cairo a few years later, establishing a new caliphate that lasted until 1517, but the Cairo Abbasids were mere puppets of local warlords.

At the outset the Abbasid dynasty made a fine show of leadership and concern for Islam. Theology and religious law became preoccupations at court and among a growing community of scholars, along with interpretation of the Quran, collection of the sayings of the Prophet, and Arabic grammar. Some caliphs fought on the Byzantine frontier to expand Islam. Others sponsored ambitious projects to translate the great works of Greek, Persian, and Indian thought into Arabic such as the writings of Aristotle and the Sanskrit book of instructive animal fables, the *Panchatantra*.

At the same time, the new dynasty, with its roots among the semi-Persianized Arabs of Khurasan, gradually adopted many of the ceremonials and customs of the Sasanid shahs. Government grew increasingly complex in Baghdad, the newly built capital city. As more and more non-Arabs converted to Islam, the ruling elite became more cosmopolitan. Greek, Iranian, Central Asian, and African cultural currents met in the capital and gave rise to an abundance of literary products, a process greatly facilitated by the timely introduction of papermaking from China. Arab poets neglected the traditional odes extolling life in the desert and wrote instead to praise their patrons, the drinking of wine (despite its prohibition in Islam), or other features of the vibrant urban scene.

The translations of Aristotle into Arabic, the founding of the main currents of theology and law, and the splendor of the Abbasid court—reflected in stories of *The Arabian Nights* set in the time of Harun al-Rashid (r. 776–809)—in some respects warrant the designation of the early Abbasid period as a "golden age." Yet the refinement of Baghdad culture only slowly made its way into the provinces. Egypt was still predominantly Christian and Coptic-speaking in the early Abbasid period. Iran never did adopt the Arabic language as a spoken tongue. Spain (in Arabic al-Andalus), where an Umayyad fleeing the overthrow of his family in 750 had created an independent state, was affected by Berber, Visigothic, Jewish, and Roman traditions quite different from those in the East. And North Africa freed itself almost entirely of caliphal rule: Morocco and Algeria through Kharijite revolts in 740, Tunisia after 800 by agreeing to pay a regular tribute to Baghdad.

Moreover, the gradual conversion to Islam of the conquered population did not accelerate until the second quarter of the ninth century. But by that time most social discrimination against non-Arab converts had faded away, and the Arabs themselves—at least those living in cosmopolitan urban settings—had abandoned their previously strong attachment to kinship and ethnic identity. If the expression "golden age of Islam" implies a mass, multilingual, multiethnic society of Muslims with only minority non-Muslim elements, it existed around the end of the tenth century. By then, however, the Abbasid caliphate had lost most of its power.

Political Fragmentation

The decline of Abbasid power became evident in the second half of the ninth century when the pace of conversion to Islam was at its peak (see Map 10.2). The idea of a single government ruling an empire stretching almost a quarter of the way around the world would be hard to entertain even under modern conditions. But the Abbasids had to reckon with the fact that caravans traveled only 20 miles (32 kilometers) a day, and dispatches through the official post system usually did not exceed a hundred miles (160 kilometers) a day. News of revolts on the frontier took weeks to reach Baghdad. Military responses might take months. Economically, it was hard to centralize tax payments, which were often made in grain or other produce rather than in cash, and to ensure that provincial governors forwarded the proper amounts to Baghdad. Moreover, coins were minted in many locations, providing yet another opportunity for local strongmen to profit from seizing power.

When the first Arab garrisons with their surrounding communities of Muslims had been strung like beads along communication routes that crossed territory populated mostly by non-Muslims, revolts against Arab rule had always been feared. Hence, the Muslim community, the umma, had had every reason to cling together, despite the long distances. Nobody knew whether Islam would become a permanent feature of society or whether someday, somehow, foreign foes or a resurgence of non-Muslim strength within the caliphate would reverse the apparent tide of history.

With the massive conversion of the population to Islam, this perception fundamentally changed. The idea that Islam might pass away or be destroyed faded as Muslims became the overwhelming majority. At the same time, it became increasingly apparent that a highly centralized empire meant wealth and splendor for the capital but did not necessarily serve the interests of people in the provinces. Many eighth-century revolts had been directed against Arab or Muslim domination. By the middle of the ninth century, this type of rebellion gave way to movements within the Islamic community that concentrated on seizure of territory and formation of a principality. None of the states carved out of the Abbasid caliphate after 850 repudiated or even threatened Islam. What they did was prevent tax revenues from flowing to Baghdad, thereby increasing the prosperity of the locality. It is hardly surprising that the local Muslim communities either supported such rebels or remained neutral.

Increasingly starved for funds by breakaway provinces and by a fall in revenues from Iraq itself, the caliphate entered a period of crisis in the late ninth century. Distrusting the generals and troops from outlying areas, the caliphs purchased Turkic slaves (*Mamluks*) from Central Asia and established them as a standing army. Well trained and hardy, the Turks proved an effective military force. But they were also expensive. When the government could not pay them, the Mamluks took it on themselves to seat and unseat caliphs, a process made easier by the construction of a new capital at Samarra, north of Baghdad on the Tigris River. There the Turks dominated the court without interference from an unruly Baghdad population that regarded them as rude and highhanded. Samarra weakened the caliphate in another way as well. The money and effort that went into building the huge city, which was occupied only from 835 to 892, sapped the caliphs' financial strength and deflected labor from more productive pursuits.

In 945, after several attempts at finding a strongman who would reform government administration and restore military power, the Abbasid caliphate itself fell under the control of new rulers from the mountains of northern Iran, the remote and unsophisticated province of Daylam. Led by the Buyid family, they conquered western Iran as well as Iraq and divided their territory among leading family members, each of whom ruled his own principality. After almost two centuries of glory, the sun began to set on Baghdad. The Abbasid caliph remained, but he was subject to the control of a Buyid prince or his lieutenant. Being Shi'ites, the Buyids had no special reverence for the Sunni caliph. But, according to their particular Shi'ite sect, the twelfth and

last divinely appointed Imam had disappeared around 873 and would return as a messiah only at the end of the world. Thus they retained the caliph to help control their predominantly Sunni subjects, who regarded him as a rightful ruler, while the Buyids themselves disregarded his views.

Dynamic growth in outlying provinces paralleled the caliphate's gradual loss of temporal power. In the east, the dynasty of the Samanids, one of several Iranian families to achieve independent rule, presided over a glittering court in Bukhara, a major city on the Silk Road (see Map 10.1). The Samanid princes patronized literature and learning much as the early Abbasids had, but the language they favored was Persian written in Arabic letters. For the first time, a non-Arabic literature rose to challenge the eminence of Arabic within the Islamic world. The new Persian poetry and belles lettres foreshadowed the world of today, in which Iran sharply distinguishes itself from the Arab world.

In Egypt a Shi'ite ruler established himself as a rival caliph in 969 after the sixty-year struggle of his family, the Fatimids, to extend their power beyond an initial base in Tunisia. His governing complex outside Fustat was named Cairo, and for the first time Egypt became a major cultural, intellectual, and political center of Islam (see Map 10.2). The al-Azhar Mosque built at this time remains a paramount religious and educational center to this day. Although the Fatimid family was Shi'ite, their religious influence on Egypt was rather slight during their two centuries of rule. Most of the population remained Sunni. Nevertheless, the abundance of their gold coinage, derived from West African sources, made them an economic power in the Mediterranean.

Cut off from the rest of the Islamic world by the Strait of Gibraltar and, from 740 onward, by independent city-states in Morocco and Algeria, Spain developed a distinctive Islamic culture (see Map 10.1). Historians disagree on how rapidly and completely the Spanish population converted to Islam. If we assume that the process was similar to what took place in the eastern re-

The Fraternity of Beggars

Beggars, tricksters, and street performers were considered members of a single loose fraternity: Banu Susan, or Tribe of Sasan. Tales of their tricks and exploits amused staid, pious Muslims, who often encountered them in cities and on their scholarly travels. Beggars and scholars were among the most mobile elements of the population. These descriptive verses come from a tenth-century poet who studied beggars' jargon and way of life.

For we are the lads, the only lads who really matter, on land or on sea.

We exact a tax from all mankind, from China to Egypt,

And to Tangier; indeed, our steeds range over every land of the world.

When one region gets too hot for us, we simply leave it for another one.

The whole world is ours, and whatever is in it, the lands of Islam and the lands of unbelief alike.

Hence we spend the summers in snowy lands, whilst in winter we migrate to the lands where the dates grow.

We are the beggars' brotherhood, and no one can deny us our lofty pride . . .

And of our number if the feigned madman and mad woman, with metal charms strung from their [sic] necks.

And the ones with ornaments drooping from their ears, and with collars of leather or brass round their necks . . .

And the one who simulates a festering internal wound, and the people with false bandages round their heads and sickly, jaundiced faces.

And the one who slashes himself, alleging that he has been mutilated by assailants, or the one who darkens his skin artificially pretending that he has been beaten up and wounded . . .

And the one who practices as a manipulator and quack dentist, or who escapes from chains wound round his body, or the one who uses almost invisible silk thread mysteriously to draw off rings . . .

And of our number are those who claim to be refugees from the Byzantine frontier regions, those who go round begging on pretext of having left behind captive families . . .

And the one who feigns an internal discharge, or who showers the passers-by with his urine, or who farts in the mosque and makes a nuisance of himself, thus wheedling money out of people . . .

And of our number are the ones who purvey objects of veneration made from clay, and those who have their beards smeared with red dye.

And the one who brings up secret writing by immersing it in what looks like water, and the one who similarly brings up the writing by exposing it to burning embers.

Source: Clifford Edmund Bosworth, *The Mediaeval Islamic Underworld: The Banu Sasan in Arabic Society and Literature* (Leideu: E. I. Brill, 1976), 191-199.

gions, it seems likely that the most rapid surge in Islamization occurred in the mid-tenth century.

Just as in the east, governing cities were at the core of the Islamic presence in al-Andalus, as the Muslims called the regions they ruled in Spain. Cordoba, Seville, Toledo, and other cities grew substantially, becoming much larger than comparable cities in neighboring France. Converts to Islam and their descendants, unconverted Arabic-speaking Christians, and Jews joined with the comparatively few descendants of the Arab invaders to create new architectural and literary styles. In the countryside, where the Berbers preferred to settle, a fusion of preexisting agricultural technologies with new crops, notably citrus fruits, and irrigation techniques from the east gave Spain the most diverse and sophisticated agricultural economy in Europe.

The rulers of al-Andalus did not take the title *caliph* until 929, when Abd al-Rahman III

(r. 912–961) did so in response to a similar step taken by the newly established Fatimid ruler in Tunisia. Toward the end of the tenth century, this caliphate encountered challenges from breakaway movements that eventually splintered al-Andalus into a number of small states. But political decay did not stand in the way of cultural growth. Some of the greatest writers and thinkers in Jewish history—Judah Halevi, Solomon ibn Gabirol, Abraham ibn Ezra—worked in Muslim Spain in the eleventh and twelfth centuries, sometimes writing in Arabic. At the same time, Islamic thought in Spain was attaining its loftiest peaks in Ibn Hazm's treatises on love and other subjects, the philosophical writings of Ibn Rushd (known in Latin as Averroës) and Ibn Tufayl, and the mystic speculations of Ibn al-Arabi.

Several dozen principalities came and went between the tenth and the twelfth centuries while these states were flourishing. The Samanids, Fatimids, and Spanish Umayyads are representative of the political diversity and awakening of local awareness that characterized the period of Abbasid decline. Yet drawing and redrawing political boundaries did not result in a rigid division of the Islamic world into kingdoms as was then occurring in Europe. Religious and cultural developments, particularly the rise in cities throughout the Islamic world of a social group of religious scholars known as the *ulama*—Arabic for "people with (religious) knowledge"—worked against the permanent division of the Islamic umma.

Assault from Within and Without

Outside the urban milieu, political fragmentation enabled nomadic groups to assert themselves. In the west, trade across the Sahara had brought prosperity to northern city-states—Sijilmasa in Morocco and Tahert in Algeria—and to the kingdom of Ghana in Senegal and Mali (see Chapter 8). In the mid-eleventh century, however, recently converted Berber nomads from the western Sahara overpowered these trading centers and established a kingdom that stretched from Morocco to Mali (see Chapter 15) and even penetrated into Spain. These Almoravid rulers, established in their new capital of Marrakesh, wore blue veils over their faces and retained other traits from their Saharan past. A century later, such practices offended Ibn Tumart, a zealous Muslim preacher. He recruited a Berber army in the Atlas Mountains and launched a movement that, after his death in 1130, supplanted the Almoravids and established an Almohad empire that ruled from Tunisia to Spain from Fez, its capital, located in Morocco. In both instances, the rulers were sometimes sophisticated and urbane, but they depended on unruly rural warrior peoples and often resorted to harsh and intolerant measures.

More gradually, Arabs from southern Egypt slowly made their way across North Africa. Contemporary historians portray these invaders of the Bani Hilal and Bani Sulaim as locusts bent on destroying the agrarian-based prosperity of the region. Modern historians are still debating the actual impact of the so-called Hilali invasions. The question is the role they may have played in a significant economic change that took place in North Africa during this period. Prior to the eleventh century, Muslim rule in North Africa had been based on cities surrounded by agricultural hinterlands. Tahert, Sijilmasa, and, in Tunisia, Qairawan, were interior cities in contact with the desert. Coastal cities were less important, at least until the rise of the Fatimids. The farmers and the pastoralists of the mountains and deserts were largely Berber-speaking and little affected by Islam.

The Hilali tribal incursions coincided with a shift of the North African economy toward the Mediterranean Sea. Ports and cities situated between the mountains and the coast—Tunis and Sousse in Tunisia, Tlemcen in Algeria, Marrakesh and Fez in Morocco—flourished while cities connected with the desert dwindled. Trading contact across the Mediterranean grew, and Andalusian culture influenced urban styles throughout the region. Meanwhile, agriculture languished. The interior plains and habitable parts of the northern Sahara became mostly Arabic-speaking. Berber became the language of the mountains and of the Tuareg tribes in the southern Sahara. Trans-Saharan trade continued, but the new Muslim societies south of the desert developed in substantial isolation from the urban culture of the Mediterranean.

Syria and Iraq experienced nomadic upsurges as well. Political life along the eastern Mediterranean became increasingly fragmented. Nomad-based Arab kingdoms came and went, subjecting cities like Damascus, Aleppo, and Jerusalem to an ever-shifting array of political forces. Here, too, coastal cities like Acre and Tripoli began to grow as Mediterranean trade revived. In the Tigris and Euphrates valley Shi'ite Arabs from the desert and Sunni Kurds from the mountains competed in building small principalities.

But a powerful new Turkish presence overshadowed both Arabs and Kurds. Nomadic groups speaking one or another Turkic language had been known as allies or enemies ever since the Arab conquests. After 1000, these horse-breeding pastoralists from the steppes and deserts north and east of the Black, Caspian, and Aral Seas filtered into more central Islamic lands.

The role played by Turkish Mamluks in the decline of Abbasid power had established an enduring stereotype of the Turk as a trained and ferocious warrior little interested in religion or the sophistication of urban life. This image was reinforced in the 1030s when the Seljuk family established the first Turkish Muslim state based on nomadic power. Taking the Arabic title *Sultan*, meaning "power," and the revived Persian title *Shahan-shah*, the Seljuk ruler Tughril Beg created a kingdom that stretched from northern Afghanistan to Baghdad, which he occupied in 1055. After a century under the thumb of the Shi'ite Buyids, the Abbasid caliph breathed a bit easier under the slightly lighter thumb of the Sunni Turks. The Seljuks pressed on into Syria and Anatolia, administering a lethal blow to Byzantine power at the Battle of Manzikert in 1071. The Byzantine army fell back on Constantinople, leaving Anatolia open to the entry of the Turks.

Under Turkish rule, cities shrank as their agricultural hinterlands, already short on labor because of migration to the cities, were overrun by pastoralists. Irrigation works suffered from lack of maintenance in the unsettled countryside. Tax revenues fell. Cities were fought over as Seljuk princes contested for power in the twelfth century. But few Turks participated in urban cultural and religious life. Thus a gulf that had arisen between the religiously based urban society and the culture and personnel of the government deepened. When factional riots broke out between Sunnis and Shi'ites, or between rival schools of Sunni law, the government remained aloof, even when destruction and loss of life were extensive. Similarly, when princes fought for the title *sultan*, religious leaders advised citizens to remain neutral.

By the early twelfth century, unrepaired damage from floods, fires, and civil disorder had reduced old Baghdad on the west side of the Tigris to ruins. The caliphs took advantage of fighting among the Seljuks to regain some power locally and built a wall around the palace precinct on the east side of the river. Nevertheless, the heart of the city died, not to be restored to prosperity until the twentieth century. The withering of Baghdad, moreover, betrayed an even broader change in the environment: the collapse of the canal system that irrigated the Tigris and Euphrates valley. For millennia a world center of civilization, Mesopotamia suffered population losses that today still make Iraq an underpopulated country.

The Turks alone cannot be blamed for the demographic and economic misfortunes of Iran and Iraq. Their rise to power is as much symptom as cause. Too-robust urbanization that strained food resources, political fragmentation that resulted in reduced revenues, and the growing practice of using land grants (*iqta'*) to pay soldiers and courtiers also played a role. When absentee grant holders used agents to collect taxes, the inevitable result was a tendency to gouge the villagers and to take little interest in improving production, all of which weakened the agricultural base of the regime.

Just as the Seljuk Empire was beset by internal quarreling, the first crusading armies reached the Holy Land. Chapter 9 recounts the expeditions of Christian soldiers who trekked across the Balkans or sailed across the Mediterranean to fight for the cross. Though charged with the stuff of romance, the Crusades had little lasting impact on the Islamic lands. The four principalities of Edessa, Antioch, Tripoli, and Jerusalem simply became parts of the shifting pattern of politics already in place. Newly arrived knights were eager to attack the Muslim enemy, whom they called "Saracens." But those who had lived in the region longer, including the religious orders of the Knights of the Temple (Templars) and the Knights of the Hospital of St. John (Hospitallers), recognized that diplomacy and seeking partners of convenience among the rival Muslim princes was a sounder strategy.

The challenge to the Muslims, with their impotent caliph and endemic political fragmentation, was unification to face the European enemy. That unification finally came in the late twelfth century under Nur al-Din ibn Zangi and his military commander Salah al-Din, known in the West as Saladin (ca. 1137–1193). The former established a strong state based on Damascus and sent an army to terminate the Fatimid caliphate in Egypt. The latter, a nephew of the Kurdish commander of the expedition to Egypt, profited by Nur al-Din's timely death to unify Egypt and Syria and, in 1187, recapture Jerusalem from the Europeans.

Although the Christians of Spain would eventually succeed in destroying Islamic rule there, Saladin's descendants fought off all subsequent Crusades to the Holy Land. However, after one such battle, in 1250, their Turkish Mamluk troops seized control of the government, thus ending Saladin's dynasty. In 1260 these Mamluks rode east to confront a new invading force. At the Battle of Ain Jalut (Spring of Goliath), in Syria, they met and defeated an army of Mongols from Central Asia, thus stemming an invasion that had begun several decades before and legitimizing their claim to dominion over Egypt and Syria.

The Mongol invasions administered a great shock to the world of Islam. The full story of their conquests is told in Chapters 13 and 14, but the impact of their destruction of the Abbasid caliphate in Baghdad in 1258 and their imposi-

tion of non-Muslim rule from Iraq eastward for most of the thirteenth century bears mention here. Although the Mongols left few ethnic or linguistic traces in these lands, their initial destruction of cities, their subsequent promotion of trans-Asian trade along northerly routes instead of by way of the traditional Silk Road, and their casual disregard for urban and religious life, even after they themselves converted to Islam, hastened currents of change already under way.

ISLAMIC CIVILIZATION

Though complex and unsettled in its political dimension, life in the ever-expanding Islamic world underwent a creative, supportive, and fruitful evolution in the areas of law, social structure, and religious expression. From the interlocking phenomena of religious conversion and urbanization emerged a distinct Islamic civilization. Because of the immense geographical and human diversity of the Muslim lands, many "little traditions" coexisted with the developing "big tradition" of Islam—a "big tradition" that was more an urban than a rural phenomenon. Nevertheless, the adaptability of Islamic civilization to new situations was one of its most salient features.

Law and Dogma

The hallmark of Islamic civilization is the Shari'a, the law of Islam. Yet aside from certain parts of the Quran that conveyed specific divine ordinances—most pertaining to personal and family matters—no legal system was in place in the time of Muhammad. Only Arab custom and the Prophet's own authority offered guidance. After Muhammad died, the umma tried to conduct itself according to his *sunna*, or tradition. This became harder and harder to do, however, as those

who knew Muhammad best passed away and many Arabs found themselves living in far-off parts of the conquered territories. Living in accordance with the sunna was even harder for non-Arab converts to Islam, who at first were expected to follow Arab customs they had little familiarity with.

Islam slowly developed laws to shape social and religious life. Certain basic matters are likely to have been a part of Islam from the beginning—namely, the so-called Five Pillars, all referred to in the Quran: (1) avowal that there is only one god and Muhammad is his messenger, (2) prayer five times a day, (3) fasting during the lunar month of Ramadan, (4) paying alms, and (5) making the pilgrimage to Mecca at least once during one's lifetime. The full sense of Islamic civilization, however, goes well beyond these basics.

Some Muslim thinkers felt that the reasoned consideration of a mature and intelligent man—women were only rarely heard in religious matters—provided the best way of resolving issues not covered by Quranic revelation. Others argued that the best guide was the sunna of the Prophet and that the best way to understand that sunna was to collect and study the many reports in circulation purporting to describe the precise words or deeds of Muhammad. These reports were called *hadith*, and it gradually became customary to precede each hadith with a statement indicating whom the speaker had heard it from, whom that person had heard it from, and so on, back to the Prophet personally.

Some hadith dealt with ritual matters, such as how to perform ablutions before prayer; others were simply anecdotes. A significant number provided answers to legal questions not covered by Quranic revelation, or they suggested principles for resolving such matters. By the eleventh century, most specialists on Islamic legal thought had accepted the idea that Muhammad's personal behavior was the best model for society in general, and that the hadith were therefore the most authoritative basis for Islamic law after the Quran itself.

Yet the hadith themselves posed a problem. This body of lore, numbering tens of thousands of anecdotes, included not only genuine reports

Spanish Muslim textile of the twelfth century This fragment of woven silk, featuring confronted peacocks and Arabic writing, is one of the finest examples of Islamic weaving. While the cotton industry flourished in the early Islamic centuries, silk remained a highly valued product. Some fabrics were treasured in Christian Europe. (Victoria & Albert Museum)

about the Prophet but also invented ones, politically motivated ones, and stories derived from non-Muslim religious traditions. Only a specialist could separate a sound from a weak tradition. As the importance of hadith grew, so did the branch of learning devoted to their analysis. Thousands of hadith were deemed weak and were discarded. The most reliable ones were collected into books that gradually were accorded a canonical, or irrefutable, status. Sunnis placed six books in this category; Shi'ites, four.

The Shari'a was built up over centuries. It incorporated the ideas of many legal scholars as well as the implications of thousands of hadith, a body of material whose origin in the very mouth of the Prophet is sometimes disputed by modern scholars.

Nevertheless, the Shari'a embodies a vision of an umma in which all Muslims are brothers and sisters and subscribe to the same moral values. From this perspective, political or ethnic divisions are not important, for the Shari'a assumes that a Muslim ruler will abide by and enforce the religious law. In practice, this vision was often lost in the hurly-burly of political life. Even so, it was an important basis for an urban lifestyle that varied surprisingly little from Morocco to India.

Converts and Cities

The caliphs' determination that Arab warriors should live in garrisons at governing centers led to a significant change in the social and economic landscape of the conquered lands by encouraging urbanization. The early political history of Islam concentrates on Mecca and Medina; Damascus and Baghdad, which became capitals in 661 and 762 respectively; and a few military encampments that grew into major cities: Kufa and Basra in Iraq, Fustat in Egypt, and Qairawan in Tunisia.

A major cause of urbanization was conversion to Islam. Conversion was more an outcome of the gradual communication of knowledge about the new rulers' religion than it was a step that people took to escape the tax on non-Muslims, as some scholars have suggested. Conversion was fairly simple. No extensive knowledge of the faith was required. To become a Muslim, a person recited, in the presence of a Muslim, the profession of faith in Arabic: "There is no God but God, and Muhammad is the Messenger of God."

Few converts knew Arabic, and most people were illiterate and hence unable to read the Quran. Indeed, many converts knew no more of the Quran than the few verses necessary for their daily prayers. Moreover, Muhammad had established no priesthood to define and propagate the faith. Thus new converts, whether Arab or non-

Arab, faced the problem of finding out for themselves what Islam was about and how they should act as Muslims.

The best way to solve this problem was to congregate with other Muslims, learn their language, imitate their behavior, and gradually acquire a Muslim social identity. In many areas, the only way to do this was to migrate to an Arab governing center. The alternative, to convert to Islam but remain in one's home community, posed an additional problem. Even before the emergence of Islam, religion had become the main component of individuals' social identity in the Middle East. Converts to Islam thus encountered discrimination if they went on living within their Christian, Jewish, or Zoroastrian communities. Again, one solution was migration, an option made attractive by the fact that tax revenues from the conquered lands flowed into the Arab governing centers, providing many economic opportunities for converts.

Kufa and Basra in Iraq were the first new Arab settlements to blossom as cities. Both became important centers for Muslim cultural activities. But as conversion rapidly spread in the mid-ninth century, urbanization increased in other regions as well. It was particularly noticeable in Iran, where most cities previously had been quite small. Nishapur in the northeast grew from less than 10,000 at the time of conquest to between 100,000 and 200,000 by the year 1000. Other Iranian cities—Marv, Isfahan, Ray, Balkh, Herat, Shiraz, and Hamadan—experienced similar growth. In Iraq, Baghdad and Mosul joined Kufa and Basra as major cities. In Syria, Aleppo and Damascus flourished under Muslim rule. New districts were added to Fustat—the final one in 969 was named Cairo—to form one of the largest and greatest of the Islamic cities. The primarily Christian patriarchal cities of Jerusalem, Antioch, and Alexandria were not Muslim governing centers, did not benefit from this wave of migration, and consequently shrank and stagnated.

In Europe, the spread of Christianity by missionaries roaming the countryside coincided with a sharp decline of urban life. The spread of Islam was just the opposite. Cities were the centers of Islam; the countryside was slower to con-

Teacher and students   This is a typical scene from urban Muslim society of the eleventh century. Teachers or storytellers usually sat on a mat or stool, or rested against a pillar while their listeners sat before them. Hadith were either recited from memory or read from the teachers' notes while the students copied them down for their own use. Note the variety of headdress and robes. (Topkapi Saray Museum)

vert. Muhammad and his first followers had lived in a commercial city, and Islam acquired a peculiarly urban character very different from that of medieval European Christianity. Mosques in large cities were not just ritual centers but places for learning and all sorts of social activities.

Urban social life was colored by Islam. Without religious officials to instruct them, the new Muslims imitated Arab dress and customs and sought out for guidance individual Muslims whom they regarded as particularly pious. Inevitably, in the absence of a central religious authority comparable to a pope or patriarch, there was great local variation in the way people practiced Islam and in the collection of hadith attributed to the Prophet. That same absence of a

centralized organization gave to the rapidly growing religion a flexibility that accommodated many different social situations. The fundamental profession of Islamic faith called only for the acknowledgment of God's unity and Muhammad's prophethood and did not involve intrinsically difficult concepts such as the Trinity or divine incarnation in human form. So Islam escaped most of the severe conflicts over heresy that beset the Christians at a comparable stage of development.

By the tenth century, the growth of cities was also affecting the countryside by producing an expanding market of consumers. Citrus fruits, rice, and sugar cane increased in acreage and were introduced to new areas. Cotton became a major crop in Iran and elsewhere and gave rise to a diverse and profitable textile industry. Irrigation works, too, expanded in certain areas. Diet diversified. Abundant Islamic coinage made for a largely monetized economy. Intercity and long-distance trade flourished, providing regular links between isolated districts and integrating into the region's economy the pastoral nomads who provided the necessary animals. Manufacturing expanded as well, particularly the production of cloth, metal goods, and pottery. The market economy grew under the strong influence of Islamic ethics and law. Indeed, one of the few officials specified by the Shari'a was the market inspector.

Islam, Women, and Slaves

Women rarely traveled. Those living in rural areas worked in the fields and tended animals. Urban women, particularly members of the elite, lived in seclusion and did not leave their homes without covering themselves completely. The practice of secluding women in their houses and veiling them in public already existed in Byzantine and Sasanid urban society. With textual support from the Quran, these practices now became fixtures of Muslim social life. Although women sometimes studied and became literate, they did so in seclusion from the gaze of men who were not related to them. Although women played an influential role within the family, any public role had to be indirect, through their husbands. Slave women were an exception. They alone were permitted to perform before men as musicians and dancers, and a man could have sexual relations with as many slave concubines as he pleased, in addition to as many as four wives.

In some ways, however, Muslim women fared better legally under the developing practices of Islamic law than did Christian and Jewish women under the practices of Christianity and Judaism. Muslim women could own property and retain it in marriage. They could remarry if their husbands divorced them, and they were entitled to a cash payment upon divorce. Although a man could divorce his wife without stating a cause, a woman was able to initiate divorce

under specified conditions. Women could practice birth control. They could testify in court, although their testimony was weighed as half that of a man. And they could go on pilgrimage. Nevertheless, a mysogynistic tone is sometimes evident in Islamic writings. One saying attributed to the Prophet observed: "I was raised up to heaven and saw that most of its denizens were poor people; I was raised into the hellfire and saw that most of its denizens were women."[3]

Because writings by women about women are almost unknown from this period, the status of women must be deduced from the writings of men. The Prophet's wife A'isha, the daughter of Abu Bakr, provides an example of how Muslim men appraised the role of women in society. A'isha was only eighteen when Muhammad died. She lived for another fifty years. The earliest reports stress her status as Muhammad's favorite and the only virgin he married. She was the only wife to see the angel Gabriel. These reports emanate from A'isha herself, who was an abundant source of hadith.

A'isha was especially known, however, for two episodes. As a fourteen-year-old she became separated from a caravan and rejoined it only after traveling through the night with a man who found her alone in the desert. Gossips accused her of being untrue to the Prophet, and it took a revelation from God to prove her innocence. The other event was her participation in the Battle of the Camel, fought to prevent Ali from becoming the fourth caliph. These two episodes came to epitomize what Muslim men feared most about women: sexual infidelity and meddling in politics. As a result, even though the earliest literature dealing with A'isha stresses her position as Muhammad's favorite, his first wife, Khadija, and his daughter, Fatima, who was married to Ali, eventually surpass A'isha as ideal women. Both were portrayed as model wives and mothers, and neither aroused suspicions of sexual irregularity or political manipulation.

As the seclusion of women became commonplace in urban Muslim society, some writers recommended that men cultivate homosexual relations, partly because a male lover was presentable in public or on a journey. Although Islam frowned on homosexuality, one ruler

Slave girls from Samarra This early ninth century wall painting is from the harem quarters of the Abbasid palace in Samarra. Women were expected to be veiled outside the house and in the presence of unrelated men, but unveiled slave girls commonly sang, danced, and played instruments at parties. Islamic law prohibited wine but wine songs feature prominently in Arabic poetry in this period. (Bildarchiv Preussischer Kulturbesitz)

wrote a book in which he advised his son to follow moderation in all things and thus to share his affections equally between men and women. Another ruler and his slaveboy became models of perfect love extolled in the verses of mystic poets.

Islam sanctioned slavery, with the provision that Muslims could not enslave other Muslims or so-called People of the Book—Jews, Christians, and Zoroastrians, who revered holy books re-

spected by the Muslims—living under their protection, except when slavery resulted from being made a prisoner of war. In later centuries there was a constant flow of slaves into Islamic territory from lands conquered by the Arabs in Africa and Central Asia. A hereditary slave society, however, did not develop. Usually slaves converted to Islam, which caused many masters to free them as a pious deed; and the offspring of slave women and Muslim men were born free.

The Recentering of Islam

The caliphate had originally been the center of Islam, the concrete political expression of the unity of the umma. The process of conversion, however, was not directed by any formal organization or hierarchy. Thus there emerged a multitude of local Islamic communities that were so disconnected from each other that numerous competing interpretations of the developing religion arose. Inevitably, the centrality of the caliphate diminished (see Map 10.2). The appearance of rival caliphates in Tunisia and Cordoba accentuated the problem of decentralization just when the Abbasids were losing the last of their temporal power.

The rise of the ulama as the leaders of Muslim communities did not at first ameliorate the growing fragmentation because the leaders themselves were often divided into contentious factions. During the twelfth century, however, this factionalism began to abate, and a new set of socioreligious institutions emerged to provide the umma with a different sort of religious center.

These new developments stemmed in part from an exodus of religious scholars from Iran in response to the economic and political disintegration of the late eleventh and twelfth centuries. This flow of Iranians to the Arab countries and to newly conquered territories in India and Anatolia became a flood after the Mongol invasion. As scholars fully versed in Arabic as well as their native Persian, they were well received wherever they went, and they brought with them a view of religion developed in the urban centers of Iran. A new sort of higher religious college, a *madrasa*, thus gained sudden popularity outside Iran, where madrasas had been known since the tenth century. Scores of madrasas, many under the patronage of local rulers, were established throughout the Islamic world.

Also in the twelfth and thirteenth centuries, and with a strong input from Iranians, mystic fraternities known as *Sufi brotherhoods* developed. The spread of the doctrines and rituals of certain Sufis from city to city gave rise to the first geographically extensive Islamic religious organizations. The doctrines of various Sufis varied enormously, but the common denominator was the quest for a sense of union with God through rituals and training. This type of spiritual endeavor had begun in early Islamic times and had doubtless benefited from the ideas and beliefs of converts to Islam from other religions with mystic traditions.

The early Sufis had been saintly individuals given to ecstatic and poetic utterances and wonderworking. They attracted disciples but did not try to organize them. The growth of brotherhoods, an altogether less ecstatic form of Sufism, set a tone for society in general. It soon became common for most Muslim males to belong to at least one Sufi brotherhood, particularly in the cities.

A sense of the social climate that the Sufi brotherhoods fostered can be gained from a twelfth-century manual:

> Every limb has its own special ethics. . . . The ethics of the tongue. The tongue should always be busy in reciting God's names (*dhikr*) and in saying good things of the brethren, praying for them, and giving them counsel. . . . The ethics of hearing. One should not listen to indecencies and slander. . . . The ethics of sight. One should lower one's eyes in order not to see forbidden things. . . . The ethics of the hands: to give charity and serve the brethren and not use them in acts of disobedience.[4]

For people who merely wanted to emulate the Sufis and enjoy their company there were special dispensations that allowed them to follow less demanding rules:

> It is allowed by way of dispensation to possess an estate or to rely on a regular income. The Sufis' rule in this matter is that one should not use all of it for himself, but should dedicate this to public charities and should take from it only enough for one year for himself and his family. . . .
>
> There is a dispensation allowing one to be occupied in business; this dispensation is granted to him who has to support a family. But this should not keep him away from the regular performance of prayers. . . .
>
> There is a dispensation allowing one to watch all kinds of amusement. This is, however, limited by the rule: What you are forbidden from doing, you are also forbidden from watching.[5]

Some Sufi brotherhoods spread to the countryside, where there was a simultaneous proliferation of local shrines and pilgrimages to the

Automata

Muslim scientists made discoveries and advances in almost every field, from mathematics and astronomy to chemistry and optics. Many worked under the patronage of rulers who paid for translations from Greek and other languages into Arabic and built libraries and observatories to facilitate their work. In return, some engineers designed elaborate mechanical devices for the entertainment of the rulers.

In this example, a conventional-looking *saqiya* of a type in use from Morocco to Afghanistan to raise water appears to be powered by a wooden cow. A saqiya is a chain of buckets descending to a water source from a spoked drum attached to interlocking gears. An animal walks in a circle turning the first gear and setting the rest in motion. In this device the real power comes from a water wheel and gears hidden underground. These turn the platform the cow is mounted on, causing the gears above it to operate the chain of buckets lifting water to the outlet trough on the upper left.

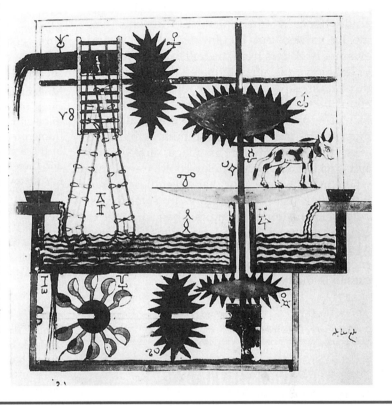

Saqiya (Widener Library Photographic Services)

tombs of Muhammad's descendants and saintly Sufis. The pilgrimage to Mecca, too, received new prominence as a religious duty. The end of the Abbasid caliphate enhanced the religious centrality of Mecca, which eventually became an important center of madrasa education.

Altogether, the twelfth and thirteenth centuries saw a transition from the politically volatile and socially and religiously effervescent earliest centuries of Islamic history to the later centuries, in which the weight of the fully developed Shari'a, of madrasa education, and of the Sufi brotherhoods would create a more regimented, though more organized and supportive, society. The Islamic civilization that spread into

Asia, Africa, and Europe after the period of the Mongols was of this later form.

CONCLUSION

The centuries surveyed in this chapter witnessed profound changes in the political, religious, social, and economic environment of the Middle East, North Africa, and Central Asia. Despite the renewal of trade with Europe in the twelfth century, the rise of Islam permanently severed long-standing links among the various Mediterranean lands. Islam was tolerant of Jews, Christians, and Zoroastrians but demanded that they remain subordinate and do nothing to threaten Muslim dominance. Christianity was even more intolerant of Muslims than it was of Jews. Few Muslims lived in Christian lands. Trade between Christians and Muslims was mostly carried out by Jews, Armenians, and eventually traders from the Italian city-states.

Religiously, Islam culminated the transition in the late ancient world from identity based on ethnicity and localism to identity based on religion. The concept of the umma united all Muslims in a universal community, embracing enormous diversity of language, appearance, and social custom. A scholar could travel anywhere in the Islamic world and blend easily into the local Muslim community. In some areas, however, Muslim communities had to adapt to equally powerful cultural traditions. This was particularly true in China and the lands influenced by Chinese civilization as will be discussed in the next chapter.

SUGGESTED READING

Two comprehensive surveys of Islamic history devote substantial space to the period covered in this chapter and set it in broader contexts. Ira M. Lapidus, *A History of Islamic Societies* (1990), focuses on social developments and includes the histories of Islam in India, Southeast Asia, sub-Saharan Africa, and other parts of the world. Marshall G. S. Hodgson, *The Venture of Islam*, 3 vols. (1974), presents a critique of traditional ways of studying the Islamic Middle East while offering an interpretation based on the contributions of major intellectual and religious figures.

For a much shorter but eminently readable survey see J. J. Saunders, *History of Medieval Islam* (1965; reprint, 1990). Richard W. Bulliet, *Islam: The View from the Edge* (1993), provides, in a fairly brief book, a different approach by minimizing discussion of major political events and concentrating on the lives of converts to Islam and of the local religious notables who guided their lives.

R. Stephen Humphreys, *Islamic History: A Framework for Inquiry*, rev. ed. (1991), provides the best introduction to issues of historiography and some of the major issues in current scholarship. Gerhard Endress, *An Introduction to Islam* (1988), is less insightful but contains an excellent bibliography and chronology and deals with many more subjects than Humphreys does. Bernard Lewis, ed. and trans., *Islam: From the Prophet Muhammad to the Capture of Constantinople*, 2 vols. (1974; reprint, 1987), is an excellent selection of brief, well-introduced translations from primary historical sources.

Muslims believe that the Quran is untranslatable because they consider the Arabic in which it is couched to be an inseparable part of God's message. There are numerous "interpretations" in English, however. Most of these adhere reasonably closely to the Arabic text, and there is no agreement on which is the best. Arthur J. Arberry, *The Koran Interpreted*, 2 vols. in 1 (1955; reprint, 1986), represents more than most an effort to capture the poetic quality of Quranic language.

Muslims and non-Muslims disagree strongly on the best way to narrate the life of the Prophet Muhammad. Muslims prefer biographies that accept the basic lines of the story as contained in the earliest Muslim sources. Non-Muslims display greater skepticism about those sources and often lean toward social and economic interpretations. Martin Lings, *Muhammad: His Life Based on the Earliest Sources*, rev. ed. (1991), is a readable biography incorporating the Muslim point of view. The standard Western treatments have long been W. Montgomery Watt's *Muhammad at Mecca* (1953) and *Muhammad at Medina* (1956; reprint, 1981); there is a one-volume abbreviated version of those two works: *Muhammad, Prophet and Statesman* (1974). Michael A. Cook, *Muhammad* (1983), is a brief, intelligent discussion of the historiographical problems and source difficulties inherent in the subject.

G. R. Hawting, *The First Dynasty of Islam: The Umayyad Caliphate, A.D. 661–750* (1987), offers a sophisticated but easily readable history of a crucial century.

Western historians have much debated the beginning of the Abbasid caliphate. Moshe Sharon, *Black Banners from the East: The Establishment of the 'Abbasid State— Incubation of a Revolt* (1983), gives a lively account based on recently discovered sources. For a broader history that puts the first three centuries of Abbasid rule into the context of the earlier periods see Hugh N. Kennedy, *The Prophet and the Age of the Caliphates: The Islamic Near East from the Sixth to the Eleventh Century* (1986). Harold Bowen, *The Life and Times of Ali ibn Isa "The Good Vizier"* (1928; reprint, 1975), supplements Kennedy's narrative superbly with a detailed study of corrupt caliphal politics in the tumultuous early tenth century.

With the fragmentation of the Abbasid caliphate beginning in the ninth century, studies of separate areas become more useful than general histories. Richard N. Frye, *The Golden Age of Persia: The Arabs in the East* (1975), skillfully evokes the complicated world of early Islamic Iran and the survival and revival of Iranian national identity. Thomas F. Glick, *Islamic and Christian Spain in the Early Middle Ages* (1979), gives a geographically and technologically oriented interpretation that provocatively questions standard ideas about Christians and Muslims in Spain. For North Africa, Charles-André Julien, *History of North Africa: Tunisia, Algeria, Morocco, From the Arab Conquest to 1830* (1970) summarizes the dominant ideas of a literature primarily written in French. This same French historiographical tradition is challenged and revised by Abdallah Laroui, *The History of the Maghrib: An Interpretive Essay* (1977).

Few medieval historical narratives are available in good, readable translations. An excellent one is Usamah ibn Munqidh, *An Arab-Syrian Gentleman and Warrior in the Period of the Crusades*, trans. Philip Hitti (1929; reprint, 1987).

Studies of particular aspects of Islamic history are useful for comparison with other regions. Roy P. Mottahedeh, *Loyalty and Leadership in an Early Islamic Society* (1980), deals with the ethos and organization of tenth-century Iranian politics and society. Ira Marvin Lapidus, *Muslim Cities in the Later Middle Ages* (1984), deals with similar questions in fourteenth-century Syria, particularly in cities. These books make for an interesting comparison with each other and with similar books on medieval Europe and China.

Ahmad Y. al-Hassan and Donald R. Hill, *Islamic Technology: An Illustrated History* (1986), is a well-illustrated introduction to this little-studied field. For a less theoretical and more crafts-oriented look at the same subject see Hans E. Wulff, *The Traditional Crafts of Persia: Their Development, Technology, and Influence on Eastern and Western Civilizations* (1966).

The study of women is difficult in Islamic contexts because of the lack of sources. Denise Spellberg, *Politics, Gender, and the Islamic Past: The Legacy of 'A'isha bint Abi Bakr* (1994), provides pathbreaking guidance. Basim Musallam, *Sex and Society in Islamic Civilization* (1983), is an excellent treatment of the social, medical, and legal history of birth control in medieval Islam.

Islamic prohibitions on the taking of interest have raised many questions about the economic ideology of the medieval Islamic world and its capacity for capitalistic expansion. Maxime Rodinson, *Islam and Capitalism* (1978), is a good introduction to this problem.

Among the numerous introductory books on Islam as a religion, a reliable starting point is Hamilton A. R. Gibb, *Mohammedanism: An Historical Survey*, 2d ed. (1969). For more advanced work, Fazlur Rahman, *Islam*, 2d ed. (1979), skillfully discusses some of the subject's difficulties.

Islamic law, one of the most important specialized fields of Islamic studies, is well covered in Noel J. Coulson, *A History of Islamic Law* (1979). For Sufism, the mystic tradition in Islam, see Annemarie Schimmel, *Mystical Dimensions of Islam* (1975).

Two particularly valuable religious texts available in translation are Abu Hamid al-Ghazali, *The Faith and Practice of al-Ghazali*, trans. W. Montgomery Watt (1967; reprint, 1982), and Abu al-Najib al-Suhrawardi, *A Sufi Rule for Novices*, trans. Menahem Milson (1975). Both date from the twelfth- and thirteenth-century transition period of Islamic history and show the variety of religious perspectives then common. Al-Ghazali's view is that of a scholar and teacher, al-Suhrawardi's that of a Sufi who is concerned about everyday behavior.

Jere L. Bacharach, *A Middle East Studies Handbook*, 2d rev. ed. (1984), contains many useful reference features designed for students: outline maps, dynasty charts, a chronology, a glossary of common terms, and a table giving equivalents between dates A.H. (*anno Hegirae*, "in the year of the hijra") and dates A.D. (*anno Domini*, "in the year of the Lord"). For more detailed maps see William C. Brice, ed., *An Historical Atlas of Islam* (1981). The most complete reference work for people working in Islamic studies is *The Encyclopedia of Islam*, new ed. (1960–).

NOTES

1. Quran. Sura 96, verses 1–5.
2. Quran. Sura 92, verses 1–10.
3. Richard W. Bulliet. *Islam: The View from the Edge* (1994), p. 87.
4. Abu Najib al-Suhrawardi. *A Sufi Rule for Novices*, tr. Menahem Milson (1975), pp. 45–58.
5. Ibid., pp. 73–82.

CHAPTER ELEVEN

Central and Eastern Asia, 400–1200

The Tang Empire and the Power of Transmission

Localism and Specialization After the Tang

In the fourth century C.E., the multiply talented scholar Ge Hong (281–361 C.E.) provided a vivid description of epidemics that had afflicted populations in north China. In detail the diseases strongly resembled measles or smallpox. Ge described several partial remedies and then commented sharply on the circumstances under which the diseases had been introduced in his time: "Because the epidemic was introduced . . . when Chinese armies attacked the barbarians . . . it was given the name of `Barbarian pox.'"[1] This was a profound comment on the times. After the fall of the Han Empire in 220 C.E., the Chinese territories were divided among smaller states which frequently were at war with one another. Certain diseases could be transmitted between warring armies and spread rapidly from the soldiers to noncombatant populations. Refugees from war were continually driven from north of the Yellow River toward the south. They carried with them waves of infectious disease, earlier arriving in northern China from Central Asia.

But Ge Hong was more than a medical commentator, and the diversity of his achievements is a reminder that the turmoil of these times produced not only social dislocation and disease but remarkable discovery and innovation. Ge himself was a Daoist with strong interests in both medicine and alchemy. He combined these interests in his search for the elixir of life, the formula for immortality. He passed to later ages his knowledge on such diverse topics as hallucinogenic drugs, the prevention of rabies, and magnetism. His contemporaries knew how to refine and use the stimulant ephedrine, and they understood the basic functioning of the digestive and circulatory systems. Drawing on the ideas of Daoism, these groups of scholars also made and recorded significant advances in metallurgy and pharmacology (thanks to their interest in alchemy) and in mathematics.

When China was reunified in the late sixth century, skills and theoretical knowledge gained in the period of disunity could be collected and disseminated. The knowledge discovered in China during the third to sixth centuries would later produce advances in such dissimilar fields as iron and steel smelting, the production of more durable and more reliable compasses, and the development of variolation (an early form of vaccination). The Sui Empire, which reunited China in 589, and the Tang Empire, which followed it (618–906 C.E.), were the greatest disseminators of knowledge and cultural influence in medieval Asia.

After the Tang Empire ended in the early tenth century, East Asia comprised a number of local kingdoms, including the Liao and Jin in northern China and Mongolia, the Song in southern China, the Tangguts to the west of China, and the countries of Tibet, Japan, Korea, Annam (the ancestor of modern Vietnam), Champa (in what is now southern Vietnam), and the Turkic khanates of Central Asia. In many of these societies, the cultural and political heritage of the Tang Empire persisted. These small, often highly centralized regimes were able to take the cultural traditions and technological methods introduced under the Tang and develop them in local, specialized, and often advanced ways. Song China, in particular, became famous for its achievements in science, mathematics, and engineering. This specialization and diversification of knowledge in turn created rich new sciences and technologies that could be disseminated again once East Asia was reunified—which happened when the Mongols invaded after the year 1200 (see Chapters 13 and 14).

THE TANG EMPIRE AND THE POWER OF TRANSMISSION

Some of the kingdoms that sprang up from the ruins of the Han Empire were run in the Chinese style, with an emperor, a bureaucracy using the Chinese language exclusively, and a Confucian state philosophy. Others were affected by the Xiongnu, Tibetan, Turkic, and other regional cultures that predominated in some parts of the former Han domain. These kingdoms often used the emperorship to support unorthodox cultural influences, primarily Buddhism. When China was later reunified under the Sui Empire at the end of the sixth century, Buddhism became a profoundly important political and cultural influence.

Reunification Under the Sui and Tang

In less than forty years the Sui Empire (among other achievements) reunified China, Korea, and parts of Southeast Asia under its rule; designed a new imperial capital near Chang'an, the old capital of the Han Empire; and built the Grand Canal, a waterway linking the Yellow and Yangzi Rivers. Although traditional histories have explained the brevity of the Sui Empire (it lasted less than forty years) in terms of its "good first emperor" Wendi and its "bad last emperor" Yangdi, the empire probably was exhausted by its extraordinary pace of expansion and its overcentralization.

In 618 the militarily powerful Li family ended the Sui and created a new empire of their own, the Tang (Map 11.1). They maintained the eastern borders established by the Sui and expanded primarily westward into Central Asia, under the brilliant emperor Li Shimin (r. 627–649). The Tang avoided the problem of overcentralization by allowing significant power to local nobles, gentry, officials, and religious establishments. And they relied on a variety of political ideologies—not only Confucianism but also Buddhism and the central Asian respect for the title khan (leader)—to legitimate their power and increase their appeal.

The Tang emperors were descendants of the Turkic elites of small kingdoms existing in northern China after the Han, and of Chinese officials and settlers who had intermarried with them. Consequently the Tang nobility were heavily influenced by central Asian culture but were also knowledgeable about Chinese political traditions. In warfare, for instance, the Tang were ready to combine Chinese weapons—the crossbow and armored infantrymen—with central Asian expertise in horsemanship and the use of iron stirrups. As a result, from about 650 to 750, the Tang armies were the most formidable on earth. Among Li Shimin's political allies were powerful Turkic and Sogdian (a people of eastern Iran) generals, and the first king of Tibet married into Li's family. The Tang drive westward across Central Asia was stopped only in the middle 700s by a combined force from Central and western Asia. Thereafter the Tang Empire was stable until it began to decline in the ninth century.

Chang'an at the Eastern Terminus of the Silk Road

The hub of Tang communications was at its primary capital, Chang'an (modern-day Xi'an in Shaanxi province, China). This was near the site of old Chang'an, the Han capital, in the Wei Valley (see Chapter 6), but it was a newly designed city. Tang Chang'an was a terminus of the overland trade with Central Asia, the Middle East, Tibet, and India. It was connected by well-maintained road and water transport to the rudimentary coastal towns of south China, of which Canton (Guangzhou) was most important. Chang'an was also the center for the ambassadors and students sent to the Tang capital as part of the *tributary system*. This was a practice, begun in Han times, in which countries not conquered by the empire acknowledged the empire's supremacy by sending regular embassies to the capital to pay tribute. Thus Chang'an was regarded as the cultural and economic capital of eastern Asia.

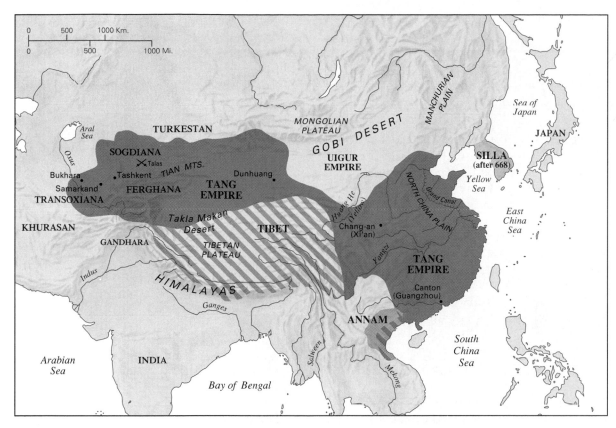

Map 11.1 Eastern Asia in the Tang Era The Tang Empire controlled not only China but also a very large part of Central Asia. Tibet was closely associated with the Tang by political and marital ties, while Japan, the Korean kingdom of Silla, and Annam were leading tributary states.

The Wei Valley had been heavily populated since the time of the Han Empire. During the Tang period, Chang'an was the most populous city in the world, with possibly as many as 2 million inhabitants. Its original ground plan, completed under the Sui, called for construction on 30 square miles (78 kilometers²); under the Tang, the city grew to occupy a much larger area. Only a minority of the population lived in the central city. Most people lived in the suburbs that extended out from each of the main gates. Many dwelt in specialized towns in the countryside—such as those responsible for maintaining the imperial tombs in the Wei Valley or those operating the imperial resort at Huaqing Pool at the foot of Mount Li, where the aristocracy relaxed in

sunken tile tubs while the steamy waters of the springs swirled around them.

The market networks of Chang'an, both within the city and in its suburbs, kept the city's economy vibrating. A system of roads connected the central city and the suburbs to the smaller cities, towns, and villages that extended south and east along the Yellow River. Special compounds, including living accommodations and general stores, were established for foreign merchants, students, and ambassadors drawn from all over Asia by the tributary system and by trade. Along the main streets were restaurants, inns, temples, mosques, and street stalls that kept the population entertained every evening. At curfew, generally between eight and ten o'clock, commoners

Iron stirrups   This bas-relief from the tomb of Li Shimin depicts in detail the type of horse on which the Tang emperor's armies conquered China and Central Asia. The horses were equipped with saddles having high supports in front and back, breastplate and crupper, all indicating the importance of high speeds and quick maneuvering on the field of battle. Most significant, perhaps, were the iron stirrups, which were generally used in Central Asia from the time of the Huns (fifth century). The stirrups could support the weight of fully shielded and well-armed soldiers who rose in the saddle to shoot arrows, use lances, or simply urge the horse to greater speeds. (University of Pennsylvania Museum, neg. #S8-62844)

had to return to their neighborhoods, which were surrounded by brick walls and wooden gates that guards locked until dawn to control crime.

Market roads, major long-distance roads, caravan routes (the Silk Road), sea routes, and canals all brought people and commerce toward Chang'an. Under the Sui and Tang, for the first time the 1,100-mile (1,771 kilometers) distance between the Yellow and the Yangzi Rivers was spanned by construction of the Grand Canal (see Map 11.1). Special armies patrolled the canal, special boats were designed for travel on it, spe-

cial towns appeared along its route, and a special budget for its maintenance was established. The Grand Canal allowed the integration of the Yangzi Valley with north China and contributed to the development of an economic and cultural center in the eastern part of China. After the fall of the Tang Empire, rulers of China made their capitals in the eastern part of the country, largely because of the economic and political effects of the Grand Canal.

The Grand Canal was the eastward extension and enhancement of overland routes reaching Chang'an from Central Asia and other westerly points over the Silk Road (see Chapter 8). Into the markets of Chang'an came caravans of camels originating in Iran or north India, led by bearded Arab and Iranian camel drivers and bringing a variety of passengers—including Indian monks, Turkic soldiers, Arab merchants, and enslaved female musicians and dancers. They brought tea from India, and horses, cotton, grape wine in soft leather sacks, fruits and vegetables, musical instruments, beaten gold and silver jewelry, and glassware. From Chang'an, ceramics, paper, ink, and silk went westward with the caravans toward the Middle East.

Chang'an was also the terminus of the Persian Gulf trade route that began by sea in the Strait of Hormuz, landed at Canton in the south, then continued north overland. By this circuit, Chang'an was linked with the Mediterranean, East Africa, India, and Southeast Asia. These regions benefited from Chinese skills in compass design and shipbuilding in the late Tang period, and China drew much from them as well. The overland route to India by way of Central Asia and Tibet was not the only access that East Asia had to Indian culture. During the Tang, Chinese control of what is now coastal southern China was consolidated, and this, together with geographical information of the sort provided in earlier times by Faxian (see Chapter 8) and other religious travelers, increased Chinese access to the Indian Ocean. These sea routes also were a factor in the spread of Islam to East Asia. Indeed an uncle of Muhammad is credited with having erected the small, pagoda-like "red mosque" at Canton in the middle seventh century.

The sea route between the Middle East and Canton was also the means of transmission of bubonic plague to East Asia. In the fifth century, bubonic plague had moved from North Africa into the Middle East. From there, the sea trade brought it to East Asia. Evidence of plague is found in references to Canton and south China in the early 600s. The plague found a hospitable environment in parts of southwestern China and lingered there after the virtual eradication of the disease in the Middle East and Europe. The trade and embassy routes of the Tang Empire quickly became channels for transmission of plague to Korea, Japan, and Tibet, all of which experienced their first outbreaks after the establishment of diplomatic ties with Chang'an in the seventh century. Plague was soon controlled in urban East Asia but remained active in some isolated rural pockets until the Mongol invasions in the thirteenth century, when a new outbreak occurred.

Buddhism and Society

Along the trade routes of East Asia came Buddhism, which had been influential in Central Asia and northern China for centuries before the Tang Empire (see Map 8.1). Buddhism set forth a religious function for kings and emperors: to bring humankind into the Buddhist realm. Buddhists believed that protective spirits would aid the king in the governing of the state and prevent harm from coming to the people living under him. State cults based on this idea were important in the kingdoms of Central Asia and north China during the period of disunity after the fall of the Han Empire. China's next unifying empires, the Sui and the Tang, inherited the cults from those kingdoms. From there, they spread quickly to Korea, Japan, and Tibet.

The most important Buddhist school of teaching in Central and eastern Asia was Mahayana, or "Great Vehicle," Buddhism. Like all Buddhist sects, Mahayana Buddhism considered belief in the reality of the material world to be the root of suffering. But Mahayana specifically fostered a faith in enlightened beings—*bodhisattvas*—who have postponed achieving *nirvana* (eternal bliss) in order to help others achieve enlightenment. Faith in bodhisattvas led to the acceptance of many local gods and goddesses into Buddhist sainthood. In contrast to some other schools of Buddhism, Mahayana encouraged the translation of Buddhist scripture into local languages, and it accepted forms of religious practice that had little or no connection with written texts. These qualities allowed Mahayana Buddhism to assert its influence over many diverse societies and over many classes of people within those societies. The tremendous reach of Mahayana invigorated travel, language learning, and cultural exchange throughout northern India, Central Asia, and East Asia.

Precisely because of its social, cultural, and political influence, Buddhism was first an important ally of the Tang emperors and later their enemy. In 840 the state moved to crush the economic power and the influence of the Buddhist monasteries, and the Tang elites strongly reasserted Confucian ideology. The repression reflected the wish of the state to decrease Buddhist interference in court politics and to increase tax revenues by repealing exemptions granted to the monasteries. The repression also reflected the elites' anxiety that Buddhism was encouraging both the dissolution of the family (as idealized by Confucians) and the empowerment of women.

The family estates of the Tang period were a fundamental component of the economic and political structure of the empire. Thus the government and the elites regarded with suspicion anything that endangered the stability of these estates or endangered the values of family cohesiveness on which they rested.

Because of Buddhism's disapproval of earthly ties, a man or woman had to sever relations with the secular world in order to begin the journey to salvation. Monasteries, where monks continually prayed for the preservation of the state and the salvation of souls, were exempt from taxes. This economic edge allowed them to employ large numbers of serfs and to purchase large tracts of land as well as precious objects. Many poor people flocked to the monasteries and nunneries as artisans, fieldworkers, cooks, housekeepers, and guards. Some eventually converted to Buddhism and took up the monastic life. Others came as beggars and then began to study the religion. Among the gentry and nobility were some who turned away from their families for the peace and spirituality of the religious life. Wealthy believers often gave large tracts of land to the monasteries.

By the ninth century, hundreds of thousands of people had entered monasteries and nunneries. Those people were exempt from taxes and military service. They deprived their families of the advantages that might have resulted from their marriages. And they denied descendants to their ancestors, which was strictly contrary to Confucian teaching, an element of the religion that eventually aroused the suspicion of the gentry.

Equally obvious to the Tang court was the subversive influence of Buddhism on politics: Buddhism could be used as a legitimating philosophy opposed to the Confucian idea of the family as the model for the state. A woman who had married into the imperial family, Wu Zhao, seized control of the government in 690, declared herself a female emperor, and reigned until 705. She legitimated herself by claiming she was a bodhisattva, and she favored Buddhists and Daoists over Confucianists. In the later Tang era, Emperor Wu and other powerful women such as the concubine Yang Guifei were despised by Confucian critics such as the poet Bo Zhuyi. In his poem "Everlasting Remorse" Bo lamented women's influence at the Tang court—influence that had caused "the hearts of fathers and mothers everywhere not to value the birth of boys, but the birth of girls."[2]

When the Tang forced dissolution of the monasteries, the loss in cultural artifacts was incalculable, and many of the great sculptures and grottoes that survived were permanently defaced. Most of the temples and the façades built to shelter the great stone carvings from the weather were made of wood and disappeared in the fires that accompanied the suppression of Buddhism. The suppression also created the population of wandering, impoverished monks who became a common theme in Tang and Song art, and were also transmitters of information they picked up on their travels (see Voices & Visions: Ennin in China). In later times monasteries would be legalized again, but Buddhism in China was never afterward the profound social, political, and cultural force it had been in early Tang times.

Central Asia as the Crossroads of Trade

Since prehistoric times, exchanges of technology between Central Asia and the peripheries of Eurasia had resulted in major advances in methods of transport, modes of warfare, differentiation of languages and development of written literatures, and the spread of religious ideas. The religious influences in Central Asia might be

Ennin in China

Since the spread of Buddhism to eastern Asia in Han times, monks making pilgrimages to China and India had been a major source of new knowledge about geography, travel routes, languages, and economic conditions. The notes of these monks remain from as early as the third century C.E., when pilgrims from the Korean kingdoms recorded part of their travels through China. In the 400s Faxian and in the 600s Xuanzang brought to China new knowledge of India, Southeast Asia, and Tibet. Perhaps the most famous traveler of the period 400–1200, however, was the Japanese monk Ennin (794–864).

By the 800s Japan was recognized throughout East Asia as a center of Buddhist worship and study. Ennin intended in 838 to follow in the steps of many other Japanese monks who had made pilgrimages to sacred sites in China and to return promptly to Japan. His plans were disrupted when he was shipwrecked on the coast of Shandong, the peninsula stretching into the Sea of Bohai, through which the increasing traffic of Japanese and Korean monks regularly passed. He spent the next nine years wandering eastern China during the height of the suppression of Buddhism, and he learned the esoteric folk doctrines that were the predecessors of Zen Buddhism.

Ennin's diary provides many details of the everyday life of the people he encountered and often had to depend on. His petition to a local monastery reveals something of the life in this poor and isolated region:

There have been plagues of locusts for the past three or four years which have eaten up the five grains so that the officials and commoners alike have gone hungry. In the [Shandong] region they have been using only acorns for food. It is difficult for travelling monks passing through this rugged area to obtain provisions. Millet costs eighty cash per dou and non-glutinous rice one hundred cash per dou. We are without provisions to eat . . . .

The said Ennin and others left their homeland far away in order to search for Buddhist teachings, but, because he is asking for official credentials, he has not yet moved on. He makes his home anywhere and finds his hunger beyond endurance, but, because he speaks a different tongue, he is unable to beg for food himself. He humbly hopes that in your compassion you will give the surplus of your food to the poor monk from abroad. You have already given him a certain amount, and he is extremely embarrassed to be troubling you again. He humbly sends his disciple Isho to inform you. Respectfully stated . . . .

What does Ennin's presence in China and the pattern of his travels tell you about the international Buddhist world of his time? What was the status of Buddhism and Buddhist priests in China at the time? How did this compare to the situation in Japan and Korea?

Source: "Ennin's Diary of His Pilgrimage to China," in David John Lu, *Sources of Japanese History*, Volume I (New York: McGraw-Hill, 1974), .58–59.

seen as streams flowing from the Mediterranean toward eastern Asia. Earliest was Iranian culture and religion, which left a lasting impression on the royal traditions, city architecture, and the religious character of Central Asia.

Another early influence, and one well remembered in the Tang Empire, was the campaigns of Alexander the Great (see Chapter 5). In the third century B.C.E. he had conquered the lands between Iran, India, and Central Asia. In the "Alexandrias"—cities established by Alexander, including Samarkand and Gandhara—a partial Greek heritage persisted. The stone bas-reliefs and full-figure statuary that would become characteristic of Indian Buddhist art and later be transmitted to East Asia, for instance, were Greek in inspiration. Hellenic knowledge of mathematics, astronomy, and physiology had been transmitted from these centers to northern India, and had also gone eastward into Central Asia and Tibet. These regions were also familiar with the *Romance of Alexander*, which was first

Tang Developments

581	Reunification of China under the Sui empire
618	Founding of the Tang empire
627–649	Reign of Li Shimin
645–710	Taika era of state formation in Japan
668	Silla state unifies Korea
690–705	Reign of Empress Wu
751	End of Tang expansion in Central Asia at Battle of Talas
752	"Eye opening" ceremony makes Nara Japan prominent in Buddhist world
755–757	An Lushan rebellion
880	Outbreak of Huang Chao rebellion
906	Last Tang emperor deposed

written in Egypt, in Greek, to celebrate Alexander's adventures. Literate men of Central Asia who read Greek in the third and fourth centuries C.E. translated, illustrated, and elaborated on the Alexander stories. By the time of the Mongols, all the peoples of Central Asia and Tibet were acquainted with the *Romance*, and a Mongolian version of the epic later reached China and Korea by the 1300s.

The fortunes of the Tang Empire were related to the development of Turkic power in the region extending from Siberia to the eastern borders of Iran. The original homeland of the Turks was north and east of China, in the vicinity of modern Mongolia. After the fall of the Han Empire in 220 C.E., Turkic populations began moving westward, through Mongolia, then on to Central Asia. This long migration eventually would take them to Anatolia and the region we now call Turkey. During the period of disunion in East Asia between the Han and the Tang Empires, Central Asia was united under the rule of the Turks. But as East Asia was reunited around 600 C.E., internal warfare weakened the Turks' control of Central Asia. In the mid-seventh century

the Turkic Empire was split in two. It was partly this fracturing of the Turks' power that allowed the Tang Empire to establish control over Central Asia. Within about fifty years, however, a new Turkic order arose, and by the early 700s much of Central Asia was under the control of a new Turkic group, the Uigurs (see Map 11.1).

As part of the Uigur Empire, Central Asia's great cities of Bukhara, Samarkand, and Tashkent—all critical to the caravan trade—had a literate culture with strong ties to both the Middle East and to China. The Uigurs were famous as merchants and as professional scribes who were specially skilled to deal with the many languages of the region. In the time of the earlier Turkic empires a simple script had been used, and on occasion it was employed in Central Asia by the Tang Empire as well. But from the borders of Iran, the Sogdians introduced a running syllabic script, related to the Semitic Syriac script of the Middle East. The spread of Nestorian Christianity in Central Asia made the running syllabic script widely familiar. The Uigurs adopted it and refined it for the writing of their language (see Environment & Technology: Writing in East Asia). The new script made possible several innovations in Uigur government, including the change from a tax paid in kind (with products or services) to a money tax and, subsequently, the minting of coins.

An urban culture embracing the Buddhist classics, religious art based on the styles of northern India, and clothing, tools, and architecture revealing the mixture of East Asian and Middle Eastern styles flourished. By the mid-ninth century Uigur power in Central Asia was in eclipse, but Uigur culture continued to influence urban life in the region for centuries.

In the 1000s many of the intellectual and artistic treasures of Central Asia were sealed in the caves at Dunhuang, a settlement in modern-day Gansu province, China, that lay on the caravan route to Tibet and India. These paintings and manuscripts lay undisturbed until the nineteenth century, when intense competition among European explorers and collectors brought them to light. The treasures give us a vivid picture of the religious and material life of Central Asia before

Writing in East Asia, 600–1200

Chinese ideographic writing—script based on the depiction of ideas rather than the representation of sounds (syllabic or phonetic script)—was widespread throughout East Asia by the reunification of China in the late sixth century under the Sui Empire. Many of the peoples of East Asia attempted to adapt the characters to the writing of their own languages, which were not related to Chinese in grammar or in sound.

In Korea and in Japan, Chinese characters were often simplified and associated with the sounds of the Korean or Japanese languages. For instance, the Chinese character *an,* meaning peace (figure 1), was pronounced *an* in Japanese and was familiar as a Chinese character to Confucian scholars in the Heian period. But others besides scholars simplified the character and began to use it to write the Japanese sound *a* (figure 2). With a set of more than thirty of these syllabic symbols adapted from Chinese characters, any Japanese word could be written, complete with all its grammatical inflections. It was with a syllabic system of this sort that Murasaki Shikibu wrote the *Tale of Genji* around 1000 C.E.

A more complex change occurred in northern Asia. The Kitans, who spoke a language related to early Mongolian, developed an ideographic system of their own, inspired by Chinese characters. For instance, the Chinese character *wang* (figure 3), meaning "king, prince, ruler," was changed slightly to represent the Kitan word for an emperor (figure 4) by adding an upward stroke, representing a "superior" ruler. Because the system was ideographic, we do not now know exactly how this Kitan word was pronounced. But following the same ideographic logic, a further innovation was the Kitan character for "God" or "Heaven" (figure 5)—the symbol for ruler, but with a top stroke added, meaning the "ultimate" ruler or power. Though inspired by Chinese characters, the Kitan characters could not be read by any who were not specially educated in them.

Like the Koreans and Japanese, the Kitans developed a second method of writing, that was intended to represent the sounds and the grammar of the language. They used small, simplified elements arranged together within a frame, to indicate the several sounds in any word. This practice might have been inspired by Kitan knowledge of the phonetic script used by the Uigur Turks. In this example (figure 6), we see three words from a Kitan inscription. Only the second one

("horse") has been deciphered. This method of fitting sound elements within a frame also occurred later in *han'gul,* the Korean phonetic system introduced in the 1400s. Here (figure 7), we see the two words of the city name "Pyong-yang."

Though the Chinese ideographic writing system was powerful and has served well the needs of the Chinese elite to nearly the present day, peoples speaking unrelated languages were continually experimenting with the Chinese invention to produce new ways of expressing their own cultures. The result was the emergence of several sound-based writing systems in East Asia, some of them still being deciphered today.

Figure 1

Figure 2

Figure 3

Figure 4

Figure 5

Figure 6

Figure 7

the dominance of Islam. The culture they recall was predominantly Buddhist, but strong Greek and Iranian influences are apparent in textile designs, sculpture, painting, and architecture.

After the Tang empire reunited Central Asia with China in the early seventh century, the material culture of China was vividly affected by influences from Central Asia and the Middle East of the sort depicted by the Dunhuang artifacts. Lively new animal motifs and colors from Iran and Central Asia brightened the ceramics, painting, and silk designs of the Tang period, and life-size sculpture became common. In north China, the mode of dress changed. Working people no longer wore robes but adopted pants, which horse-riding Turks from Central Asia had introduced. Cotton, which the Central Asian trade imported in large and affordable quantities, gradually replaced hemp in the clothes worn by commoners. Pastimes now included polo, also

Tang women playing polo   The Tang empire, like the Sui, was strongly influenced by Central Asian as well as Chinese traditions. As in many Central Asian cultures, women were likely to exercise greater influence in the management of property, in the arts, and in politics than women in Chinese society of later times. They were not excluded from public view, and noble-women could even compete at polo. The game, which was widely known in various forms in Central Asia from a very early date, combined the Tang love of riding, military arts, and festive spectacles. (The Nelson-Atkins Museum of Art)

introduced from Central Asia and strongly promoted by the Tang court (which, in accord with Central Asian tradition, allowed noblewomen to compete). Music changed as a host of stringed instruments were imported by means of the Silk Road, along with the folk melodies of the Central Asian peoples. Food changed, too, particularly with the introduction of grape wine and tea.

China also influenced the Middle East across the central Asian connection—not only through trade but also through warfare. Chinese technicians captured by the Muslim armies in the middle 700s, for instance, took to the Middle East their knowledge of papermaking, woodblock printing, ironworking, and ceramics. In ensuing centuries, knowledge of the crossbow and of gunpowder also filtered from East Asia westward. These technologies profoundly changed the societies of the Middle East and Europe.

Renewed Migrations and Fragmentation of the Tang

The Tang order was destroyed by the very forces that were essential to its creation and maintenance. The campaigns of expansion in the seventh century had left the empire large and powerful but dependent on local military commanders and on a complex system of tax collection. A series of ruinous westward campaigns ended in 751 at the Battle of the Talas River, near Samarkand. There, a combined army of Arabs, Turks, and Tibetans defeated the Tang forces. The reverses contributed to the demoralization and underfunding of the Tang armies. In 755 the rebellion of An Lushan, a Sogdian general close to the Tang imperial family and supported by the influential concubine Yang Guifei, broke out. In a few years it was suppressed, but at the price of the establishment of independent military governors whose power grew steadily to the end of the Tang period. These governors virtually assumed control of the empire when it was engulfed by the great Huang Chao peasant rebellion of 880. Residents of north China were uprooted and

driven toward the frontier regions of southern China as renewed migrations of Central Asians moved into northern China.

In the later eighth and ninth centuries, Turkic populations moving in from the east buffeted both the Uigur and the Tang Empires—as well as their western contemporary, the Abbasid caliphate (see Map 10.2). After the final decline of the Uigur and Tang Empires, control of Central Asia passed from Turks to Arabs in the west and to the Kitans and Tangguts in the east. The politically weakened Turkic populations continued the westward migrations that would eventually transform portions of the Middle East.

When the Tang empire ended in 906, a set of smaller states succeeded it. Each of them controlled considerable territory, and some of them had lasting historical influence. But none could match the capacity of the Tang for integrating the economic and cultural interests of vastly disparate territories or for transmitting knowledge across huge distances. In the ensuing three centuries East Asia was fragmented, and its communication with Europe and the Middle East was crippled. Important artistic styles, technical advances, and philosophical developments emerged in East Asia, but the particular brilliance that had resulted from the cosmopolitanism of the Tang was not seen again for centuries. Instead, regional states refined and implemented much of the cultural influence and technological knowledge introduced during the Tang.

LOCALISM AND SPECIALIZATION AFTER THE TANG

Just as in the aftermath of the Han, so in the aftermath of the Tang new states emerged and competed to inherit the legacy of the dissolved empire. Earliest and in some ways most distinctive was the Liao Empire of the Kitan people (related to the Mongols), who est

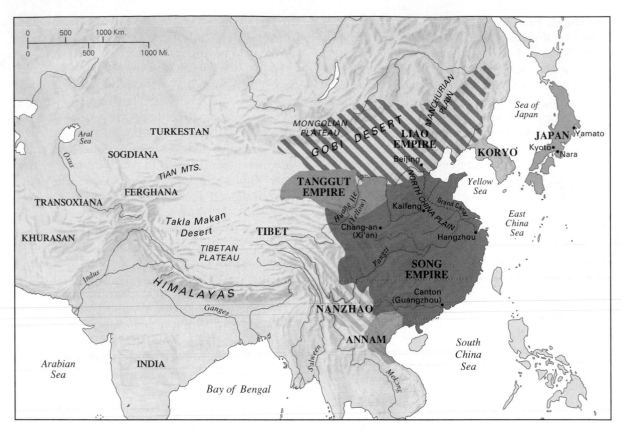

Map 11.2 Liao and Song Empires   The hostile states of Liao in the north and Song in the south generally ceased open hostilities after a treaty in 1005 stabilized the border and imposed an annual tribute upon Song.

ablished their rule in 906 at what is now Beijing immediately following the overthrow of the last Tang emperor. Not long after, the Minyak people (closely related to the Tibetans) established a large empire in what is now western China and called themselves "Tangguts" to show their own connection with the former empire (see Map 11.2).

By the end of the tenth century, an empire adopting the name Song was established in central China. In the early 1100s the Jurchens (distantly related to the Koreans and closely related to the hunting peoples of northeastern Asia) destroyed the Liao Empire and eventually took northern China from the Song (see Map 11.3). There ensued years of continuous warfare among the Jin, Song, and Tangguts, until in the

1200s the Mongols subjugated or destroyed them all.

The period in which East Asia was dominated by the smaller empires that emerged after disintegration of the Tang was a complex time. The continuous relations between Eastern and Central Asia that had existed in earlier times ended. Sea connections among East Asia, the Middle East, and Southeast Asia continued, and the Song in particular distinguished themselves in seafaring technologies. But the intensity of the demands on Song resources fundamentally changed the relationships of the east Asian perimeter with the rest of Asia.

The Song state struggled under enormous military demands, and Song elite society rejected what it considered "barbaric" or "foreign" influ-

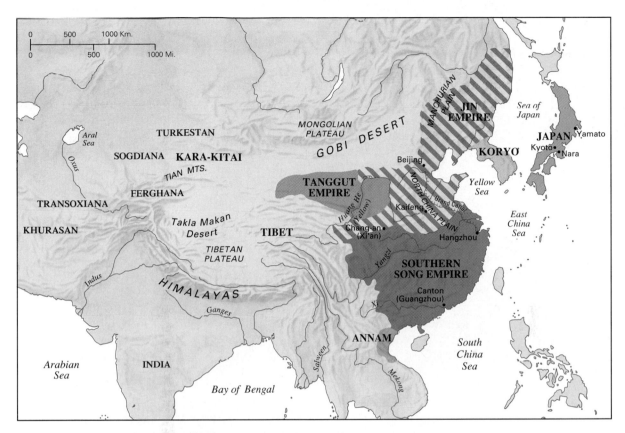

Map 11.3 Jin and Southern Song Empires   The Jin and Song engaged in frequent warfare, which resulted in the loss of Song control over the region between the Yellow and the Yangzi Rivers. The diminished Song domain is generally referred to as the "Southern Song."

ences from Central and southern Asia. Korea and Japan forged strong political and cultural ties with Song China, and some states of Southeast Asia, relieved that they were no longer threatened by the military power of the Tang, entered into new, friendly relations with the Song court. The allied societies of East and Southeast Asia formed a Confucian milieu in which goods, resources, and knowledge were vigorously traded.

The Northern and Central Asian Empires: Nomadism and Buddhism

In the Liao, Jin, and Tanggut Empires, the state ideology differed dramatically from that used in

Song China, in Korea, Japan, and Annam. In each of these northern empires, a significant portion of the population was nomadic or relocated seasonally. The rulers of these empires had to accommodate economies and the social structures of these parts of the population within the empire as a whole. This meant that the languages, religions, and political ideologies of the nomadic peoples were recognized and preserved alongside those of the agriculturalist.

In these multinational empires, no attempt was made to consolidate a single elite culture. Chinese elites within these empires were encouraged by the emperors to use their own language, study their own classics, and see the emperor through Confucian eyes. Other peoples were instructed to use their own languages and see the

Hunters with falcons   The Liao period was distinguished for its achievements in the arts, particularly porcelain, architecture, and water colors. In this painting, a small group of Kitan hunters have paused to rest their horses and hounds. The artist details the distinctive soft riding boots, leggings, and robes of the Kitans, much like those later used by the Mongols. Their hairstyle, with part of the scalp shaved and part of the hair worn long, was a shared tradition in central and northern Asia (including Japan) by which men used patterned hairstyles to show their political allegiance. The custom was documented in the 400s (and is certainly much older) and continued up to the famous queue (pigtail) worn by the Manchus, who conquered China in 1644 and governed it till the twentieth century. (National Palace Museum, Taiwan, Republic of China)

emperor as a champion of Buddhism or as a nomadic leader. As a consequence, Buddhism was far more powerful than Confucianism in these states, where emperors depended on their roles as bodhisattvas or as Buddhist kings to legitimate their power.

The earliest of the states to emerge from the ruins of the Tang was the Liao Empire of the Kitan people, who ruled a tremendous expanse from Siberia to Central Asia (see Map 11.2). They were the intermediaries between the Chinese territories and all other regions to the north and west. As a result, variations on the name of the Kitans became the name for China in these regions of the world: "Kitai" for the Mongols, "Khitai" for the Russians, and "Cathay" for those, like the contemporaries of Marco Polo, reaching China from the medieval West. In all, the Liao Empire of the Kitans was one of the largest and most long-lived in medieval history, lasting from 906 to 1121. It was also the first empire to make the city we now know as Beijing one of its capitals; relics of the Liao period can still be seen there. In ceramics, painting, horsemanship, religion, and some forms of architecture, Liao made a lasting contribution to Asian civilization and constructed much of the foundation on which the Mongols would build their great empire.

The Liao had a fascinating postscript. After losing their primary capital in Mongolia to the Jurchens in 1121, the imperial family went westward into Central Asia. There they established a new empire, the "black Kitans," or Kara-Kitai, which mixed Confucian bureaucratic philosophy with a culture that was part Buddhist and part Islamic with traces of Christianity and other religious influences. Among its distinctive features was the fact that several of the Kara-Kitai rulers were women. This multinational and multicultural empire survived for almost a century, until the Mongols destroyed it, as they destroyed the other states in its region. But the Kara-Kitai made a unique impression on Europe: their ruling family was probably the inspiration for the legends of Prester John, a mysterious Asiatic Christian king whom Europeans hoped would help them conquer religious sites in Palestine, Lebanon, and Syria.

The Minyaks, like the Liao, also believed themselves to be the rightful heirs of the Tang Empire, although they were not Chinese. Their culture was Tibetan, and their Tanggut Empire was in a sense the last empire sustained by a Tibetan people (see Map 11.3).

In earlier centuries, Tibet itself had been a large empire. At roughly the same time that Tang power was consolidated under Li Shimin in the early 600s, Tibet's first king centralized political power in Tibet. The Tang and Tibetan Empires declared their friendship when a Tang princess,

Tang Successor States

907	Liao Empire establishes "southern" capital at Beijing
935	Koryo state succeeds Silla in Korea
939	Annam wins independence from Tang Empire
960	Song Empire establishes its capital at Kaifeng
990	Tanggut Empire created
1000	Murasaki depicts life of Fujiwara Japan in *Tale of Genji*
1005	Peace treaty between Liao and Song
1125	Jin Empire destroys Liao
1185	Creation of Kamakura shogunate in Japan

whom the Tibetans called Kongjo, was sent to Tibet as the king's wife in 634. The arrival of Kongjo was also the arrival in Tibet of Mahayana Buddhism, which combined there with the native shamanic religion, Bon, to create a distinctive local religious style. Kongjo's entourage introduced to Tibet the technologies for which China was famous at the time: the manufacture of millstones, paper, ink, and rice wine. Tibetans thereafter joined Koreans, Japanese, and other nationalities as students in the imperial capital at Chang'an.

Because of Tibet's location between Central, East, South, and Southeast Asia, the variety of cultural influences in Tibet was extraordinary. In the seventh century, Chinese Buddhists began to route their pilgrimages to India through Tibet, so contacts between India and Tibet flourished. It was from India that Tibetans took their alphabet, and from India also came various artistic and architectural influences. From both India and China the Tibetans learned of mathematics, astronomy, and divination. From Central Asia and the Middle East came knowledge of Islam and of the monarchical traditions of Iran and Rome. From Iran came knowledge of the medical science of the Greeks, which in medieval Tibet the royal family favored over all other forms of healing.

The Tibetan Empire also excelled in military arts. Horses and armor, both of which were introduced through contacts with the Turks, were used and improved by the Tibetans, to a level that startled even the Tang. In the later 600s and the 700s Tibet and the Tang fought each other frequently. Tibet was extending its influence over what are now Qinghai, Sichuan, and Xinjiang provinces in China.

By the end of the 700s relations between Tang and Tibet had improved, probably because of the influence of Buddhism in Tibet. Like the early emperors of the Tang, the Tibetan kings encouraged the growth of Buddhist religious establishments and prided themselves on their role as intermediaries between India and China. At about the time of the persecutions of Buddhism in China in the 800s, a new king in Tibet decided to follow the Tang lead and eradicate the political and social influence of the monasteries.

The result in Tibet was very different from the outcome in China. Monks assassinated the king, and control of the Tibetan royal family passed into the hands of religious leaders. In later years the system of monastic domination, which continued into modern times, isolated Tibet from neighboring territories and drew around Tibet the veil of timeless mysticism for which modern Tibet is still known.

While the Tibetans secluded themselves, their cultural relatives, the Tangguts, continued an expansive, militaristic (though intensely Buddhist) government. The Tangguts successfully fended off both the Jurchens of the Jin Empire and the Chinese of the Song, falling only to the Mongols (see Chapter 14).

The Emergence of East Asia: Rice and Confucianism

With these alien and often hostile regions to the north and west, it is not surprising that the Song looked east and south for their closest allies, and during the tenth and eleventh centuries the eastern perimeter of Asia—East Asia—became a distinctive region. In Korea, Japan, and Annam,

Song China found societies that, like itself, were overwhelmingly agricultural. Throughout East Asia, many crops were important, but rice was being widely disseminated. Rice fit well with Confucianism as a social ideology, because tending the young rice plants, irrigating the rice paddies, and managing the harvest required the coordination of considerable numbers of village and kin groups.

In East Asian societies, the Confucian emphasis on hierarchy, obedience, and self-sacrifice was increasingly important, and these values were instilled into the minds of ordinary people through popular education and indoctrination by members of the elite. Since Han times, the spread of Confucianism through East Asia had been strongly associated with the spread of the Chinese system of writing. In all these countries, the elite learned to read Chinese and the Confucian classics. Literate Koreans used Chinese characters to write the Korean language even before China was reunited under the Tang Empire. This method was later adopted in Japan, and a similar technique was developed independently in Annam (see Environment & Technology: Writing in East Asia).

Political ideologies in Korea, Japan, and Annam varied somewhat from the ideology of the Song, which asserted the predominance of Confucianism over all other philosophies, particularly Buddhism. These three East Asian neighbors of the Song had first centralized power under a ruling house in the early Tang period, and their state ideologies continued to resemble the ideology of the early Tang period, when Buddhism and Confucianism were compatible political philosophies. The states of East Asia nevertheless had far more in common with the Song than did their rivals—the Liao, Jin, and Tangguts—to the north and west and were able to agree that the Song Empire was the rightful successor of the Tang.

Chinese bureaucrats of the third century B.C.E. first documented Korean history when the Qin Empire established its first colony in Korea. During the Han Empire, the small kingdoms of Korea were distinguished for their knowledge of the horse, their strong hereditary elites, and their shamanism. But they quickly absorbed Confucianism and Buddhism, both of which they transmitted to Japan. Examinations in Korea (unlike those in China) never were able to influence the social structure. The hereditary elites remained strong and in the early 500s made the system of inherited status—the "bone ranks"—permanent in the leading state of Shilla. Professional training was limited to the ranks of scribes, translators, bookkeepers, and some artisans.

The same hereditary specialization applied to woodblock printing in Korea, which was introduced during the Tang period. The oldest surviving example of Chinese characters printed from wood blocks comes from Korea and is dated to the middle 700s. Korean printers rapidly made their own advances in printing techniques, and by Song times China was benefiting from Korean experiments with movable type.

Immediately after the fall of the Tang in the early 900s, a coup in the leading Korean kingdom led to establishment of a new dynasty, the Koryo, from which the modern name "Korea" is taken (see Map 11.2). The Koryo governed the peninsula, as a state friendly to China, until the fourteenth century (see Chapter 14). The Koryo kings were great patrons of Buddhism, and among their outstanding achievements are superb printed editions of Buddhist texts.

Japan's earliest history, like Korea's, is first known from Chinese records. The first description, dating from the fourth century C.E., tells of an island at the eastern edge of the world, divided into hundreds of small countries and ruled over by a shamaness named Himiko or Pimiko. Japan is mountainous and has small pockets and stretches of land suitable for agriculture (see Map 11.2). So this early account hints at the ways in which Japan's terrain influenced the social and political structures of the period.

The unification of central Japan appears to have occurred in the fourth or fifth century C.E. There is evidence that unification may have involved a significant immigration from Korea—possibly warriors on horseback who brought the small countries of Japan under the control of a new central government at Yamato, on the central plain of Honshu Island. It is also possible that Korean immigrants made a fundamental contribution to early Japanese agriculture (particularly the importation and cultivation of rice), writing, and knowledge of ceramics and metallurgy, and it is certain that in the early period of recorded Japanese history Korea was a fundamental conduit to Japan of major elements of continental Asian civilization.

By the middle of the seventh century the Taika Reforms were implemented by the rulers based at Yamato, allowing the Yamato regime in Japan to assume many of the features of the Chinese government, with which it was now in direct contact through embassies to Chang'an. There was a legal code, an official variety of Confucianism, a strong state interest in Buddhism, and within a century a complex system of state documentation, including the production of a massive history in the Confucian style. The Japanese mastered Chinese architectural science and styles so well that Japan's ancient cities of Nara and Kyoto have been invaluable for the study of Chinese wooden buildings that have vanished. During the eighth century Japan in some ways surpassed China as a center of Buddhist study. In 752 the enormous statue of the Buddha Vairocana (Roshana) was unveiled in its "eye-opening" ceremony (at which priests painted in the great statue's eyes), and dignitaries from all over Buddhist Asia gathered at the great Todaiji temple, near the capital at Nara, to celebrate the event.

There were also significant departures from Chinese practice. Chinese buildings and some street plans were reproduced in Japan, but Chinese city walls were not. Unlike central China, central Japan of the seventh and eighth centuries was not a site of constant warfare, so Japanese cities were built without fortifications. Chinese Confucianism emphasized the importance of the Mandate of Heaven for legitimating the government; but there was no need for the Mandate of Heaven in Japan. The *tenno*, or hereditary head of state—often called "emperor" in English—was a member of the line that had ruled Japan continuously since the beginning of its known history. And by the seventh century the Japanese regarded him as a direct descendant of the sun-goddess Amaterasu, who they believed created Japan and the Japanese people. Because there

The Great Buddha Hall   The central hall in the enormous Todaiji temple complex is the largest wooden building in the world. It housed the gigantic statue of the Buddha of light, the object of the "eye-opening" ceremony in 752, when a priest from India painted the eyes onto the statue and completed it. The Todaiji complex was ruined in the civil war that led to establishment of the Kamakura shogunate in the late 1100s, but reconstruction began soon afterward. Today, the Todaiji is a monument to Nara civilization, and to the Chinese influence which shaped its architecture. (Werner Forman/Art Resource, NY)

had been no dynastic changes in Japan, there was no need of the Mandate of Heaven to justify such a change.

The primary reason for the continuation of the royal line in Japan was that only in exceptional cases did the emperors wield any real political power. Control was in the hands of a prime minister and of the leaders of the native religion, which in later times would be called *Shinto*, the "way of the gods." This distinct outlook was also preserved in historical writing that, unlike the Confucian style, emphasized the authority of myths and religious ideas. The *Kojiki*, completed in 712, exemplified this approach and existed alongside the more Confucian histories also produced under court sponsorship.

At the time of the Tang Empire, members of an ancient family, the Fujiwara, were the leading priests, bureaucrats, and warriors in Japan. They controlled power in the country and assumed responsibility for protecting the emperor from harm. The Fujiwara elevated men of Confucian learning over the warriors, who generally were illiterate. Japanese noblemen spent their time reading the Chinese classics, appreciating painting and poetry, and refining their sense of wardrobe and interior decoration. But to sustain their highly aesthetic life, the nobles of the Fujiwara period had to entrust responsibility for local government, policing, and tax collection to the warriors in their employ. Although many of these warrior clans had humble beginnings, by the late 1000s a small number of them had become wealthy, cultivated, and very powerful. The nobility's control over these ambitious and violent men began to weaken. By the middle 1100s the capital was engulfed in a civil war.

A literary epic, the *Tale of the Heike,* later commemorated the heroic losers in this first clash of warrior clans and celebrated the rise of a new elite culture based on military values. The standing of the Fujiwara family at court was destroyed, as nobles hurried to accommodate the new warlords. The emperor, too, had to acknowledge them as his protectors. Though the new warrior class (in later times called *samurai*) would in coming years absorb some of the values of the Fujiwara aristocracy, the age of the civil elite in Japan was ending.

In 1185 the Kamakura shogunate, the first of three decentralized military regimes, was established in eastern Honshu, far from the old religious and political center at Kyoto. Until the nineteenth century, Japan would remain under the control of hereditary warrior elites.

Annam, like Korea, had been under Chinese influence since the Qin Empires (see Map 11.2). The rice-based agriculture of this area made it well suited to integration with southern China. Wet climate and hilly terrain called for expertise in irrigation. The early Annamese were perhaps ahead of the Chinese in their use of draft animals in farming, in their metalworking, and in their mastery of certain forms of ceramics. With the collapse

of Han military control in Southeast Asia in the third century C.E., Annam became vulnerable to aggression from the south. Not until the eighth century did the Tang Empire restabilize Annam as an outpost of Chinese elite culture. Confucian bureaucratic training revived, and Mahayana Buddhism was given pride of place among the varied religious influences of the region. When the Tang Empire was destroyed at the beginning of the tenth century, Annamese elites decided to continue a government resembling the early Tang. Annam maintained good relations with Song China but as an independent country.

Champa was the greatest challenger to Annam for influence in continental Southeast Asia (see Map 13.1). Cultural affinity and commercial activities made Champa part of the networks of trade and cultural influence that linked the Indian Ocean, the Malay Peninsula, Sumatra, Java, Indonesia, the Philippines, and the Pacific Ocean. The impact on Champa of the cultures of India and Malaya was particularly strong. During the period of Tang domination of Annam, the posture of Champa toward its northern neighbor was hostile. But during the Song period, when Annam was independent, Champa voluntarily became a tributary state of Song China. Indeed "Champa rice," a fast-maturing rice of the region, was sent to the Song by Champa as a tribute gift and became critical in the advancement and specialization of Song agriculture.

Elite Life in East Asia Under the Song

Perhaps because of the incessant military troubles of the Song period, Song elite culture idealized civil pursuits. In the social hierarchy the civilian man outranked the military man, and a classical revival marked the Song period. Private academies, designed to train men for the official examinations and to develop their intellectual interests, became influential in culture and politics. In the aftermath of the rejection of Buddhism in China, speculative philosophy flourished, and the rationalist school of neo-Confucianism predominated. In its theorizing about the sources of material experience, energy, and morality, this type of philosophy would have a later impact on Korea and Japan also.

But popular sects of Buddhism remained vigorous in the Song period, and elites adopted some folk practices. Most remarkable of these was Chan Buddhism (in Japan known as *Zen* and in Korea as *Sŏn*). It was inspired by varieties of Buddhist belief introduced under the Tang dynasty, and it asserted that salvation was possible through mental discipline alone.

Under the Song, the examination system for officials assumed the form it would retain for nearly a thousand years. Introduced during the Tang period, it was a dramatic departure from the tradition of the Han Empire, when officials were hired and promoted on the basis of recommendations. In theory the written examinations were intended to recruit the most talented men for government service, whether their backgrounds were prestigious or humble. In practice, however, it was generally men from wealthy families who did well in the examinations. They excelled because the tests were based on the Confucian classics, which, along with commentaries written over the centuries, had to have been memorized by anyone who hoped to pass the examinations. Preparation for the examinations was so time consuming that peasant boys, who had to spend their days working the fields with their families, could rarely compete.

The examination system is another case of a Tang institution taking on complexity and refinement under the Song, who made it more specialized and practical. A large bureaucracy oversaw the design and administration of the examinations, in which candidates competed for degrees at the county, provincial, and national levels. Test questions often related to fiscal management or foreign policy.

In the new context, the social implications of the examinations were stronger, for Song society was less bound by hereditary class distinctions than Tang society had been. Many men from the gentry and merchant classes who hoped to enter government service spent much of their adult lives studying for and taking the examinations. Through study and testing, men established lifelong bonds that they could use to advantage. Success in the examinations brought good marriage prospects, hope of a high salary, and enormous prestige. Failure, however, could bankrupt a family and ruin a man both socially and psychologically. These were not comforting thoughts for degree candidates who had to endure days at a time in tiny, airless, almost lightless examination cells, attempting to produce in beautiful calligraphy their answers to that year's examination questions.

The gentry—powerful landholding classes below the aristocracy—had emerged in Han times and remained prominent in the ensuing centuries. In the Song period many men from gentry families chose not to compete in the examinations even if they were well educated. They saw that agriculture and commerce could be extremely rewarding. Patterns of landholding in central and south China promoted the concentration of ownership in the hands of comparatively few, very wealthy, people. This was partly a consequence of the fact that in Tang times what is now south China was still a frontier for Chinese settlers, who claimed extensive tracts of land for themselves before later colonists arrived on the scene. During the period of settlement, the indigenous inhabitants of the region, who were related to modern-day populations of Malaysia, Thailand, and Laos, were driven into the mountains and southward toward Annam.

The concentration of landownership in southern China reflected the type of agriculture practiced in the region. Northern China is dry, and the soil is sandy. Millet, beans, and wheat grew well there and could be cultivated by individual families. In the south of China, there are more rivers and the land is more adaptable to the cultivation of rice. Productive rice growing demands large concentrations of land and labor and generally involves village or family cooperatives working together. In the south, small landowners lost out and had to sell their land to larger ones.

Under these conditions, well-off farmers tended not to divide their property among multiple sons, a practice also widespread in Korea, Japan, and Annam. Brothers lived together and worked the fields, and the family remained cohesive as long as its lands and yields grew. Family members could pool their resources to avoid debts to outsiders and could command high interest rates when lending money. A family with large holdings could afford to set aside some land for specialized crops such as mulberry trees for feeding silkworms. One or two brothers could take charge of managing the land. Other brothers could become merchants, selling the family's rice or raw silk in nearby towns. In China, still other brothers might prepare for the official examinations and increase the family's influence through government service.

Women, Commerce, and Private Wealth

Song China is renowned for its brilliant achievements in speculative philosophy, in technology, in the arts, and in the creation of a highly urbanized commercial economy. But not everyone's lot in life improved during the period, and for women the Song era marked the beginning of a long period of cultural subordination, legal disenfranchisement, and social restriction. This outcome was consistent with the backlash against Buddhism and elevation of Confucianism that began under the Tang and intensified under the Song. It also was closely tied to the economic and status concerns of the gentry and rising merchant classes.

Merchants needed to be away from their homes for long periods of time, and many maintained more than one household. Frequently these men depended on their wives (a wealthy man would have more than one wife and perhaps numerous concubines) to manage their homes and even their businesses. As women were obliged to assume some responsibility for the management of their husbands' property, they were systematically deprived of the right to have and control property of their own. Laws relating to dowries were changed in the Song period, so that a woman's property automatically passed to her husband, and women were forbidden to remarry if their husbands divorced them or died.

Confucianism could be interpreted to require the absolute subordination of women to men, so it became fashionable to educate girls in gentry or noble families just enough to read simple versions of Confucian philosophy, edited to emphasize the lowly role of women. Modest education increased the value of these young women in the eyes of gentry or noble families and made them more desirable as wives and mothers. The poet Li Qingzhao (1083–1141) was one of the very few women of extremely high station and unusual personal determination who were permitted extensive education and freedom to pursue literary arts.

The most dramatic change in the status of Chinese women resulted from footbinding. When the foot is bound, the toes are forced under and toward the heel, the bones eventually break, and the woman cannot walk on her own. This practice first appeared among dancing slave women of the Tang court and was not widespread in China before the Song period.

In families of the gentry and nobles, footbinding typically began when a girl was between five and seven years old. In many less wealthy families girls had to work until they were older, so footbinding began later, perhaps even as late as their teen years. Protests, most strongly voiced by many literate men, condemned this maiming of innocent girls and the general uselessness of the practice. Nevertheless, bound feet became a powerful status symbol in rapidly changing Song society, and by the year 1200 footbinding was firmly entrenched among elites. Almost without exception, families that were members of the elite or that aspired to elite status bound the feet of their girls. Mothers generally oversaw the binding of their daughters' feet. They knew that girls without bound feet would be rejected by society, by prospective husbands, and ultimately by their own families.

Among working women in general and among the native peoples of what is now southern China, footbinding was unknown. Women in these classes and cultures enjoyed considerably more independence than did elite women.

Despite the importance of Confucian influence in East Asian societies, footbinding did not spread beyond China. In medieval Korea, strong lineage alliances that functioned like political and economic organizations allowed women to retain a role in the negotiation and disposition of property. In Annam, before the arrival of Confucianism from China, it appears that women enjoyed higher status than women in China, perhaps because of the need for the whole community—both women and men—to participate in wet-rice cultivation. This suggests that the women of south and southeastern China may also have enjoyed relatively high status prior to the growth of influence from northern China. The Trung sisters of Annam, who lived in the second century C.E. and led local farmers in resistance against the invading forces of the Han Empire, have been revered for almost two thousand years as national symbols in Vietnam and as

The players Women—often enslaved—were used as entertainers at the courts of China from very early times. These Song singers, however, show some significant differences from their predecessors of Tang times. While Tang art often depicts women with slender figures, there was clearly also great tolerance for, even admiration of, more robust physiques. By Song times, pale women with willowy figures were favored. In a more dramatic change, these women clearly have bound feet. Though foot-binding appears to have first been practiced in Tang times, it was not a widespread custom until the Song. Then, foot-binding was nearly universal among the gentry, and became increasingly common in merchant families and those who hoped to move upward on the social ladder. The image of weak, housebound women who were unable to work became a powerful status symbol, and pushed aside the earlier enthusiasm for healthy women who participated in the business of their families. (The Palace Museum, Beijing)

Going up the river Song cities hummed with commercial and industrial activity, much of it concentrated on the rivers and canals linking the capital of Kaifeng to the provinces. This detail from the famous painting *Going Upriver at the Qingming [Spring] Festival*, shows only a tiny portion of the panorama that the great scroll represents. Zhang Zeduan, who completed the painting sometime before 1125, was a master at the depiction of daily life, and this scroll is one of the most important sources of information on the activities of working people. Here, the open shop fronts and tea houses are clearly displayed, a camel caravan departs, goods are offloaded from donkey carts, a scholar rides loftily (if gingerly) on horseback above the crowd, and sedan chair carriers transport shaded women of wealth. (The Palace Museum, Beijing)

local heroes in southern China. They represented a memory of when women were visible and active in community and political life.

Japan, like China, valued a limited amount of education for elite women. The hero of the novel *The Tale of Genji*, written around the year 1000, remarks, "Women should have a general knowledge of several subjects, but it gives a bad impression if they show themselves to be attached to a particular branch of learning."[3] The author of the novels, the noblewoman Murasaki Shikibu, was both accurate and ironic in her observation.

Fujiwara noblewomen were expected to live in virtual isolation. Generally they spent their leisure time studying Buddhism. To communicate with their families or among themselves, they depended on writing. The simplified syllabic script that they used permitted them to write the Japanese language in its fully inflected form (Fujiwara men using the Chinese classical script that they had been taught could not do so). The combination of loneliness, free time, and a ready instrument for expression produced an outpouring of poetry, diaries, and storytelling by women of the Fujiwara era. Their best-known achievement, however, remains Murasaki's stunning portrait of Fujiwara court culture.

During the twelfth century the total population of the Chinese territories rose above 100 million for the first time. Increasing numbers of people were living in large towns and cities. The Northern Song capital at Kaifeng and the Southern Song capital at Hangzhou probably did not exceed a million people by very much, but they were the largest cities in the world at the time, as Chang'an had been earlier, and they dwarfed all other cities in East Asia (see Map 11.3).

In the Song cities, multistory wooden apartment houses were common, and the narrow streets—sometimes little more than 4 or 5 feet wide (1.2 or 1.5 m)—were often impassable. The crush of people made expertise in the management of waste and the water supply and expertise in firefighting necessities. Song cities were also adept at controlling rodent and insect infestations and thus kept the bubonic plague isolated in certain rural pockets for most of the period.

Hangzhou, in particular, was engineered in such a way that the currents of the nearby Qiantang River generated a steady movement of water and air through the city, flushing away waste and disease. Turkic, Arab, and European travelers of the 1200s—sensitive to the urban crowding that troubled their own societies—recorded their amazement at Hangzhou's effective management of the dangers stemming from tremendous population density and the presence in the Southern Song capital of restaurants, parks, bookstores, wine shops, tea houses, and theaters that gave beauty and pleasure to the inhabitants.

To handle the growth of regional and national trade, Song merchants and traders developed institutions of credit. "Flying money"—paper money that could be redeemed for silver or gold in another city—made possible the transportation of goods without cumbersome guarantees and allowed the rise of a new industry based on banking and usury. The idea of credit had been introduced during the Tang but, like many other innovations, was not widely applied until the Song.

Economic growth under the Song was so rapid that the government could not maintain the huge monopolies and strict regulation that had been traditional in China before the Song period. As a consequence the government was hard pressed to gain the revenue it needed to maintain the army, the canals, the roads, the waterworks, and other state functions. Some government processes, including tax collection, were sold off to privateers. The result was exorbitant rates for services and much heavier tax burdens on the common people.

But the privatization of the economy created new opportunities for those with capital to enter businesses which had previously been monopolized by the state. Now merchants and artisans as well as gentry and officials could make fortunes, and urban life, in particular, was transformed by the elite's growing taste for fine cloth, porcelain, exotic foods, larger houses, and exquisite paintings and books.

Printing and Society

In Song China, the influence of Korean printing with movable type was felt, and improvements in printing technology profoundly changed the social impact of the official examinations. Woodblock printing, in common use during the Tang period, required time-consuming work by skilled artisans who had to carve hundreds of characters on a single piece of wood before a single printed page could be produced. In Song China, page molds and individual Chinese characters were cast in metal or porcelain. Movable pieces of type set in reusable page molds made possible the accurate printing of texts. Thanks to these new techniques, printers could quickly publish study materials for young men hoping to sit for the examinations.

The government recognized the potential of the new printing technology and by the year 1000 was mass-producing official preparation books for the examinations. In this way, the government was able to influence the ideological development of students, and more students gained a hope of competing in the examinations. Though the examination system did not become egalitarian in this way (a man had to be literate to buy even the cheap preparation books, and basic education was still not common), the opportunities for men of humbler background to take the examinations increased, and a moderate number of men without a noble, gentry, or elite background entered government service. The new printing technology also brought changes to the practical arts and sciences. Increasing numbers of illustrated books transmitted knowledge of ceramics, loom building, carpentry, iron and steel smelting, and medicine.

Landlords frequently gathered their tenants and workers together to show them the illustrated texts and explain what they meant. Printed materials provided information about planting and irrigation, harvesting, tree cultivation, threshing, and weaving. In combination with other technological advances, the dissemination of knowledge by means of texts printed from movable type contributed to the colonization of what is now southern China. Plows, rakes, and other iron agricultural implements, that had been introduced during the Tang dynasty were modified during the Song for use in wet-rice cultivation as the population moved south. Landowners and village leaders gained information about the control of malaria, which bedeviled the southern regions. With malaria under control, more and more northerners moved south, and there was a sharp increase in the local population.

The Song Technological Explosion

Technological innovations in farming introduced in Tang times were widely applied in the Song period. Iron plows facilitated the planting of seeds, prevented the loss of seeds to birds and deer, and improved the efficiency of land use. Such implements were not common in Europe until the beginning of the nineteenth century. New crops, such as cotton (brought to northern China from Central Asia) and quick-ripening rice (brought into southern China from Champa), were planted soon after they were introduced. Information about these and other agricultural advances—in seed selection, double cropping, soil preparation, and mechanization—was widely accessible because of the new printing technology. In some instances, the in-

formation had been available in China since Han times but never had been distributed.

Like Indian, Uigur, and Middle Eastern scholars of the time, Song scholars were absorbed in the arts of measurement and observation. Song specialization in these areas was a consequence of the migration of Indian and West Asian mathematicians and astronomers to China during the Tang period. Song mathematicians are the first known to have used fractions, which they originally employed to describe the phases of the moon. On the basis of their lunar observations, Song astronomers constructed a very precise calendar. They were extremely persistent and methodical. As an outgrowth of their work in astronomy and mathematics, Chinese scholars made significant contributions to timekeeping and development of the compass.

The most spectacular Song achievement in timekeeping was a gigantic mechanical celestial clock constructed by Su Song in 1088. Escapement mechanisms for the control of the revolving wheels in water-powered clocks had been developed under the Tang, as had the application of water wheels to weaving and threshing machines. But this knowledge had not been generalized and widely applied. Su Song adapted the escapement and water wheel to his chain-driven clock, the earliest known chain-drive mechanism in history. The clock told not only the time of day but the day of the month, and it indicated the movement of the moon and certain stars and planets across the night sky. The 80-foot (24-meter) structure was topped by an observation deck and a mechanically rotated armillary sphere (a globe with moving markers indicating the positions of stars and planets). The celestial clock was a monument to the Song ability to integrate observational astronomy, applied mathematics, and engineering.

Familiarity with celestial coordinates, particularly the Pole Star, refined the production of compasses in the Song era. Long known in China, in Song times the magnetic compass was reduced in size and attached to a fixed stem and in some instances was put into a small protective case that had a glass covering for the needle. These changes made the compass suitable for seafaring; the first attested naval application was in

Su Song's astronomical clock   Song expertise in observational astronomy later made great contributions to integrated Eurasian knowledge of mathematics, astronomy, and calendar-making. The gigantic clock built at Kaifeng 1088–1092, however, joined these skills with an equally dramatic aspect of Song achievement: engineering. The team overseen by Su Song combined an observation platform with an armillary sphere. The sphere was automatic, powered by chains attached to the water-driven central mechanism shown here. Also motored from the central wheel were rotating Buddhas in a small pagoda, and devices to display the daily, monthly, and annual time. All the technologies of Su Song's clocktower had been known in China for some time, but had not before been combined into a public display. The clocktower was the inspiration for the large mechanical clocks in churches and towers that appeared in medieval Europe a few centuries later. (Courtesy, Joseph Needham, *Science and Civilization in China*)

1090. The Chinese compass and the Greek astrolabe, introduced later, would improve navigation throughout Southeast Asia and the Indian Ocean in ensuing centuries.

Development of a seaworthy compass coincided with the improvement of techniques in the building of junks. A stern-mounted rudder improved the steering of these large ships in rough seas, and watertight bulkheads helped keep them afloat in emergencies. Mariners on the Persian Gulf quickly adopted these features. Chinese traders in gigantic junks were able to reach the Middle East, the Philippines, and possibly more-distant points by sea. China's Grand Canal was fitted with a series of locks, which allowed large vessels to travel far inland.

The Song technological explosion that gave rise to these and other advances was stimulated not only by a vibrant and expanding economy but also by military pressure. East Asia in general, and Song China in particular, were under constant military pressure from the northern empires. Liao, Tanggut, and Jin societies were fundamentally nomadic and excelled in the use of cavalry in warfare. The Song defended the empire with an infantry-based army, which made up for its strategic disadvantages with its enormous size. Although the Song Empire was less than half the size of the Tang Empire, it maintained an army four times as large, about 1.25 million men. For military leadership, the Song employed men educated specially for the task, examined on military subjects, and paid regular salaries.

In addition to meeting the cost of the military, Song rulers made annual, large tribute payments to the Liao to prevent warfare. In some years, military expenditures consumed as much as 80 percent of the Song government budget—a burden that threatened to crush the state. Thanks to the advances in printing, the government attempted to alleviate some of its financial troubles by distributing paper money, the first of its kind. But the result was inflation so severe that by the beginning of the 1100s Song paper money traded for 1 percent of its face value. Eventually it was withdrawn, and the government attempted to meet its expenses with new taxes, monopolies,

and financial incentives to merchants. The only real solution to Song financial problems would have been peace, which was not achieved until after the Mongol conquest in the thirteenth century.

Because of the importance of iron and steel to warfare, the ore- and coal-producing regions of north China were constantly a site of military confrontation between the Song and their northern rivals. The volume of Song mining and iron production (which once again became a government monopoly in the eleventh century) was huge. By the end of the eleventh century, Song production of cast iron was 125,000 tons (113,700 metric tons), which in absolute terms would have rivaled the output of eighteenth-century Britain. Song engineers became skilled at high-temperature metallurgy. They produced steel weapons of unprecedented strength through the use of enormous bellows, often driven by water wheels, to superheat the molten ore. Casting and assembly were made more efficient by the refinement of mass-production techniques that had been used in China with bronze and ceramics for nearly two thousand years.

Song defensive works also incorporated iron, which was impervious to fire or concussion. Bridges and small buildings were made of iron, and so was mass-produced body armor for soldiers in small, medium, and large sizes. To counter the devastating cavalry assaults made by the Liao and Jin, the Song experimented with projectiles that could destroy groups of men and horses. The explosive properties of gunpowder were well known in China, but a formula that could produce an intense charge had not yet been developed (see Chapter 14). At this time, gunpowder was used to propel flaming arrows into oncoming cavalry. Not until the wars against the Jin in the 1100s did the Song introduce a new and terrifying weapon. Shells launched from Song fortifications exploded in the midst of the enemy, sending out shards of iron. The Jin were horrified by the resulting carnage—wholesale dismemberment of men and animals. But the small range of the shells limited them to defensive uses, and they made no major impact on the overall conduct of war.

CONCLUSION

The fragmentation of Asia that followed the end of the Tang Empire in 906 allowed the emergence of regional cultures that experimented with and in many cases improved the cultural, military, architectural, and scientific technologies whose transmission had been facilitated by Tang rule. In northern and Central Asia, these refinements included state ideologies based on Buddhism, bureaucratic practices based on Chinese traditions, and military techniques combining nomadic horsemanship and strategies with Chinese armaments and weapons. In Song China, the application of technological knowledge introduced during the Tang years transformed society. The results were privatization of commerce; production of larger ships and exploitation of long-distance sea trade; rapid advancement in the iron, steel, and porcelain industries; increased productivity in agriculture; the colonization of new regions; and deeper exploration of ideas about time, cosmology, and mathematics. China, however, was not self-reliant. Like its East Asian neighbors—Korea, Japan, and Annam—China was enriched by the mutual sharing of improvements in agriculture, ceramics, and printing.

At the same time, the relatively small scale of political organization and attendant inability to amass military resources left most of East Asia vulnerable to attack from a large and well-organized force. The test of the local systems arising in Asia from the tenth century on would arrive in the early thirteenth century. Some of the states would survive, most would be swept away in the persisting, systematic conquests of the Mongols. As they united the Eurasian world that had been so strongly linked in the time of the Tang and Abbasid empires, the Mongols and their subordinates would decide whether to nurture, exploit, suppress, or ignore the technological and cultural legacies of the independent Asian kingdoms that had thrived in the tenth to twelfth centuries.

These large patterns of contact and change would appear to their participants to literally affect the whole world. In fact, they omitted vast lands and peoples in the Americas, which a few Eurasian societies knew only as legend, and most could not have imagined in any form.

SUGGESTED READING

Moss Roberts's *Three Kingdoms* (1991) is an excellent abridged translation of Luo Guanzhong's *Romance of the Three Kingdoms*. There are many good books on the history and cultures of Central Asia. Rene Grousset's *The Empire of the Steppes: A History of Central Asia* (1988) is a classic text. It can be very profitably supplemented by selected chapters from Denis Sinor, ed., *The Cambridge History of Early Inner Asia* (1990). On the transport technologies of early Central Asia see Richard Bulliet, *The Camel and the Wheel* (1975). On the Uigur Empire, see Colin MacKerras, *The Uighur Empire* (1968).

Arthur Wright's *The Sui Dynasty* (1978) is a readable narrative about the reunification of China in the sixth century. The Tang Empire is the topic of a huge literature, but for a variety of enduring essays see Arthur F. Wright and David Twitchett, eds., *Perspectives on the T'ang* (1973). On the contacts of the Tang Empire with the cultures of Central, South, and Southeast Asia see Edward Schafer, *The Golden Peaches of Samarkand* (1963), *The Vermilion Bird* (1967), and *Pacing the Void* (1977). For an introduction to medieval Tibet see Christopher I. Beckwith, *The Tibetan Empire in Central Asia* (1987), and Rolf Stein, *Tibetan Civilization* (1972).

There is comparatively little literature on the Central and northern Asian empires that succeeded the Tang. But for a classic text see Karl Wittfogel and Chia-sheng Feng, *History of Chinese Society: Liao* (1949). On the Jurchen Jin see Jin-sheng Tao, *The Jurchens in Twelfth Century China* (1976); and on the Tangguts see Ruth Dunnell, *Buddhism and the State in Eleventh-Century Xia* (1996).

On the Song, there is a large volume of material, particularly relating to technological achievements. For an introduction to the monumental work of Joseph Needham see his *Science in Traditional China* (1981). For a large and now classic thesis on Song advancement (and Ming backwardness) see Mark Elvin, *The Pattern of the Chinese Past* (1973), particularly Part II. Joel

Mokyr, *The Lever of Riches* (1990), is a more recent, comparative treatment. On Li Qingzhao, see Hu Pinch'ing, *Li Ch'ing-chao* (1966). See also W. T. de Bary, W.-T Chan, and B. Watson, compilers, *Sources of Chinese Tradition, Volume 1* (1964); Miyazaki Ichisada, *China's Examination Hell* (1976); Richard von Glahn, *The Country of Streams and Grottoes* (1987); and Patricia Ebrey, *The Inner Quarters: Marriage and the Lives of Chinese Women in the Sung Period* (1993).

On the history of Korea see Andrew C. Nahm, *Introduction to Korean History and Culture* (1993), and Ki-Baik Kim, *A New History of Korea* (1984). An excellent introduction to Japanese history is Paul H. Varley, *Japanese Culture*, 3d ed. (1984). Relevant documents are reprinted in David John Lu, *Sources of Japanese History, Volume One* (1974), and R. Tsunoda, W. T. de Bary, and D. Keene, compilers, *Sources of Japanese Tradition, Volume I* (1964). Ivan Morris's *The World of the Shining Prince: Court Life in Ancient Japan* (1979), is a classic introduction to the literature and culture of Fujiwara Japan at the time of the writing of Murasaki Shikibu's novel *The Tale of Genji*. For Annam see Keith Weller Taylor, *The Birth of Vietnam* (1983).

NOTES

1. Edited quotation from William H. McNeill, *Plagues and Peoples* (Garden City: Anchor Press, 1976), 118. McNeill, following his translator, has mistaken Ge Hong as "Ho Kung" (pinyin romanization "He Gong").

2. Quoted in David Lattimore, "Allusion in T'ang Poetry," in A. Wright and D. Twitchett, eds., *Perspectives on the T'ang* (New Haven: Yale University Press, 1973), 436.

3. Quoted in Ivan Morris, *The World of the Shining Prince: Court Life in Ancient Japan* (New York: Penguin Books, 1979), 221–222.

CHAPTER TWELVE

Peoples and Civilizations of the Americas, to 1500

First Peoples • Mesoamerica, 2000 B.C.E.–800 C.E.

The Postclassic Period in Mesoamerica, 800–1500 • Northern Peoples

Andean Civilizations

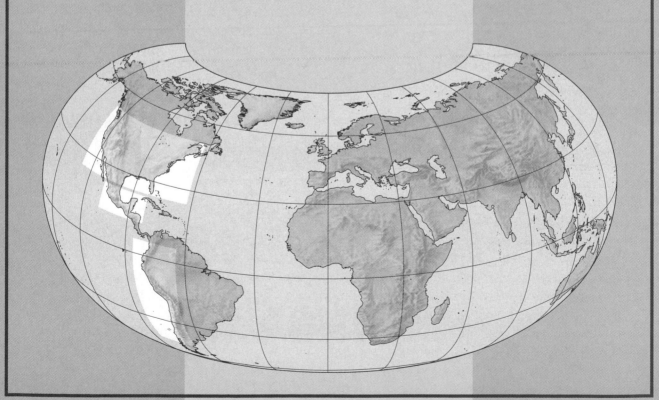

The Maya kingdoms of Tikal and Uaxactún were located less than 12 miles (19 kilometers) apart. Led by their kings and great nobles, the armies of the two kingdoms had met often in battle to secure captives for the gods. War and sacrifice held a central place in the Maya social order, but war seldom threatened the survival of dynasties or territorial boundaries. These limits were overturned on January 16, 378 C.E., when the forces of Uaxactún were decisively defeated by Great-Jaguar-Paw, king of Tikal.

The battle began in the traditional way: the opposing armies shouted challenges and insults at each other across the grassy plain that separated them. Filled with anger by these taunts, individual warriors broke ranks and rushed to engage their tormentors. As individuals and small groups struggled with clubs and stabbing spears, subdued warriors were dragged away from the battle for later sacrifice.

After hours of hand-to-hand combat, many warriors on both sides had been wounded, but only a few had been killed or taken captive. It was then that Smoking-Frog, war leader of Tikal's forces and kinsman of the king, ordered a reserve force hidden in the nearby forest to attack. These warriors were armed with atlatls, a device for throwing obsidian-tipped spears long distances (obsidian is a hard, glassy volcanic rock). Used before by the Maya only for hunting large game, the atlatl was an efficient killing weapon that transformed the battlefield. Uaxactún's forces had no response. When a massed counterattack collapsed under repeated volleys of spears, the king of Uaxactún and the remnants of his army fled the battlefield.

Customary preparations for war had failed the royal house of Uaxactún. Days of fasting, prayers, and rituals had not won for Uaxactún the support of the gods. Elaborate war regalia and carefully

painted faces had not protected the king and his nobles. Their courage and skill were no match for the weapons and tactics of Tikal. In the aftermath of defeat, the ancient lineage of Uaxactún was extinguished by ritual sacrifice. Tikal's war leader, Smoking-Frog, and his heirs would reign in their place. New technology had altered warfare and geopolitics in the Maya world. War for the first time in the Americas was associated with the conquest and subordination of a rival dynasty.[1]

For more than ten thousand years peoples in the Western Hemisphere lived in virtual isolation from the rest of the world. Although some scholars suggest that limited contacts with the Old World may have occurred, most experts believe that the Americas developed without significant cultural influence from elsewhere. The duration and comprehensiveness of this isolation distinguishes the history of the Americas from the world's other major cultural regions. While technological innovations passed back and forth among the civilizations of Asia, Africa, and Europe, the peoples of the Americas faced the challenges of the natural environment on their own.

As suggested by the story of Smoking-Frog's victory over Uaxactún, the indigenous peoples of the Americas were in constant competition for resources. Although political and technological innovations helped to determine events, no single set of political institutions or technologies worked in every environment, and enormous cultural diversity existed in the ancient Americas. In Mesoamerica (Mexico and northern Central America) and in the Andes, indigenous peoples developed some of the world's most productive and diversified agriculture. They also built great cities that rivaled in size and beauty the capitals of the Chinese and Roman Empires. In the rest of the hemisphere, indigenous peoples adapted combinations of hunting and agriculture to maintain a wide variety of settlement patterns, political forms, and cultural traditions. These cultural traditions, as well as the civilizations of Mesoamerica and the Andes, experienced cycles of expansion and vitality followed by contraction and reorganization as they were challenged by environmental changes, population growth, class conflict, and warfare.

FIRST PEOPLES

The Western Hemisphere became inhabited as the result of migrations from the Asian mainland (see Chapter 1). The lower sea levels of the late Ice Age linked Siberia and Alaska and made it possible for groups of hunters to cross to the Americas on foot. Given that Australia had been peopled by seaborne migrants as early as 50,000 B.C.E., it is possible that some migrants arrived in small boats as well. Some scholars believe the first migrations occurred as early as the period 35,000-25,000 B.C.E. Others, relying on physical evidence from archaeological excavations, insist on a later date, between 20,000 and 13,000 B.C.E.

Great variation in the Western Hemisphere's environments and climates contributed to the development of enduring cultural differences among these first peoples.[2] Unique strategies were needed to adapt to environments as different as the frozen regions of the polar extremes, the tropical rain forest of the Amazon and Orinoco Basins, the deserts of coastal Peru and the southwest of the present-day United States, the high altitudes of the Andes and Rocky mountain ranges, and the woodlands and prairies of both North and South America. Within each of these regions human communities produced new technologies and uncovered useful natural resources.

Early Cultures

The early residents of the Americas first lived in small hunting bands made up of related adults and children. Because these bands moved often to follow game and collect edible plants, they had no fixed settlements. These early peoples depended on hunting, but seeds, nuts, and berries gained a larger place in their diet with the passage of centuries. Men were the primary hunters of large game. Women supplemented the unreliable results of their hunts with small game and edible plants. Because women found and harvested edible plants, they probably played a central role in the development of plant domestication.

Like the peoples of the Stone Age cultures of the Old World, these peoples had a rich religious life that gave meaning to their collective experience and provided motifs for the decoration of both utilitarian and ritual objects. They also had a sophisticated knowledge of the natural environment, allowing them to identify a remarkable number of medicinal and hallucinogenic plants. Technological innovations, like improved projectile points, the spear thrower (atlatl) and, later, the bow and arrow, increased their efficiency as hunters. The success of hunters was also increased by tactics such as stampeding herds of bison over cliffs. This maneuver resulted in the deaths of many more animals than could be killed by individual hunters. These advances in hunting technology were accompanied by the development of grinding devices, baskets, and pottery that eased the processing and storage of seeds and nuts.

The Beginnings of Agriculture

Between 5000 and 3000 B.C.E. advances in plant domestication and agricultural technology permitted growth in the number and size of settlements in the Americas. Although domesticated plant varieties and related technologies were commonly disseminated over vast distances, four distinct regional agricultural complexes based on different staple crops eventually appeared. Between approximately 4000 and 3000 B.C.E. inhabitants of the central Mexican plateau domesticated maize. Maize eventually became the most important staple in the Americas. As climatically suitable varieties were developed, maize cultivation soon spread south to South America and then north and east through North America, reaching Canada and the northeast of what is now the United States after 1000 C.E.

The great civilizations of the Andean region relied in similar ways on the potato. Varieties of potato became the most important staple crop at higher elevations of the Andean region after 1000 B.C.E. It was supplemented where possible by maize cultivation after 2500 B.C.E. and, at high elevations, by quinoa, an indigenous grain.

The third region was also in South America. In the Amazonian and Orinocan regions of South America, manioc (a tuber) became the staple after 1500 B.C.E. It then spread to the Caribbean. Though little known in temperate regions even today, manioc is a hearty plant that produces more calories per acre than any other staple crop. Located between the maize and manioc regions, societies of the Caribbean cultivated both crops.

Between 2000 and 1000 B.C.E. eastern North America became the fourth center of independent plant domestication. By 100 C.E. a complex agriculture based on varieties of squash and locally domesticated seed crops sustained the first permanent North American agricultural societies along the Ohio and Mississippi river valleys. Unlike the maize, potato, and manioc agricultures, this seed-based agricultural economy did not survive into the modern era. It was abandoned soon after 100 C.E. in favor of growing a frost-resistant maize.

In addition to the development of improved plant varieties, the progress of agriculture depended on increasingly sophisticated and costly technological solutions to environmental challenges. Long before the appearance of Europeans, the first peoples of the Americas had dramatically altered the landscape as they met these challenges. In sparsely populated regions

with limited agriculture, like the northeast of North America and the Amazon region, periodic burning and the introduction of new plant species altered the natural landscape. In Mesoamerica and in the southern Andes, expanding agricultural productivity and growing population had an even more profound environmental impact beginning about 1000 B.C.E. In both regions powerful states with populous and prosperous cities appeared at about the time that the Hittite kingdom of the Middle East was destroyed and the Shang period ended in China. The cultural legacies of the two most important of these early civilizations, the Olmec of Mesoamerica and Chavín of the Andean region, persisted for more than a thousand years.

MESOAMERICA, 2000 B.C.E.–800 C.E.

Mesoamerica is a region of great geographic and climatic diversity located between the large landmasses of North and South America. It includes central and southern Mexico and most of Central America north of the isthmus of Panama. In the centuries before 1000 C.E., it sustained a coherent and dynamic regional culture that produced the most highly urbanized civilizations of the Americas. Mesoamerica has three distinct ecological zones, each hosting a great variety of plant and animal life. The hot and humid plains of the Gulf coast are bordered to the west by the temperate areas of the coastal foothills and fertile basin of the central mesa (tableland). These regions are surrounded by semi-arid high mountains. Differences in rainfall, temperature, and soil create micro environments where early agriculturalists produced both staples and specialized products for trade with neighbors. Within these ecological niches, Mesoamerican societies developed specialized agricultural technologies and exploited useful minerals like obsidian and chert (flintlike quartz) to make sharp tools and weapons.

The Development of Cultural Unity

Although large areas of Mesoamerica were sometimes controlled by powerful imperial states, the region was never united politically. Instead, Mesoamerica was unified by cultural traditions. Important regional differences were always present, but in agriculture, religion, political organization, art, architecture, and sport shared characteristics were found throughout the region. Scholars have created broad historical categories to represent changes in levels of urbanization, increased class distinctions, the growing power of state authority, and an escalation in levels of military conflict.

The economic basis for Mesoamerican culture was a highly diverse and productive agriculture. Maize, squash, and beans became dietary staples by 2500 B.C.E. Supplementing them were such foods as avocado, tomato, cacao (chocolate beans), chilies, and amaranth (an edible flowering plant). As populations grew and political institutions gained the power to mobilize labor for collective tasks, the environment was transformed. In the lowlands of the Gulf coast and along lake shores of the central mesa labor was organized to construct raised fields and drainage canals to reduce the threat of flooding during the rainy season. Similar efforts terraced the coastal foothills and mountains of the interior to slow erosion and increase available land for planting. In semiarid regions massive irrigation works, reservoirs, and aqueducts allowed farmers to grow food on marginal lands. Even in heavily forested regions the use of fire and seed selection altered the distribution of plant varieties to favor those most useful to nearby populations.

There was great variation in the names and personas of the gods that inhabited the pantheons of Mesoamerica's peoples, but nearly all the region's cultures accepted that the gods had dual (male/female) natures. A form of kingship that melded religious and secular powers and roles was also common. Kings, priests, and shamans were assumed to have the power to transform themselves into powerful supernatural actors through bloodletting rituals and the use of hallucinogens. Images of men transformed into jaguars were common decorative motifs. Warfare and the sacrifice of prisoners were tied to ritual needs and a general belief that bloodletting was central to the survival and well-being of human society.

Other shared characteristics included monumental sculpture, a number system based on 20, the development of both ritual and solar calendars, and writing. There were also similarities in urban planning. Cities were architecturally dominated by high temple pyramids, the residences of elite families, and ball courts. The ball game was played with a solid rubber ball on steep-sided courts. In some cases elite captives were forced to play this game before being sacrificed.

These cultural attributes were shared by linguistically distinct local cultures organized in most cases as independent political states. In Mesoamerica cultural exchange depended more on long distance trade and well-developed markets than on political integration or military expansion. Technologies, beliefs, and ritual practices were exchanged along with subsistence goods and the valuable products of skilled artisans who worked with jade, shell, and feathers.

The Preclassic Olmecs

The preclassic period witnessed increased levels of urbanization, growth in the power of hereditary aristocracies and kings, and expanded long-distance trade. The Olmecs were the most influential Mesoamerican preclassic civilization (see Figure 12.1, p. 354). They flourished between 1200 and 400 B.C.E., roughly the period of the golden age of Athens. The major Olmec centers were located along the tropical coast of Vera Cruz and Tabasco in Mexico. San Lorenzo (1200–900 B.C.E.) was the largest early Olmec center. La Venta inherited cultural primacy when San Lorenzo was abandoned or destroyed. Tres Zapotes became the principal center when La Venta underwent a similar collapse around 600 B.C.E. (see Map 12.1). In each case monuments were defaced and buried before the abandonment of a center. Archaeologists have recently excavated other important

Olmec head   Giant heads sculpted from basalt are one of the most widely recognized legacies of the Olmec culture of Mesoamerica (1200 to 400 B.C.E.). Sixteen heads have been found, the largest approximately 11 feet tall. Each head has a unique personality and highly individualized appearance. Experts in Olmec archaeology believe the heads are portraits of individual rulers, warriors, or ballplayers. (Georg Gerster/Comstock)

Olmec sites along the Pacific coast of southern Mexico and in Central America.

The Olmecs made extensive use of raised fields. They dug drainage canals and used the excavated mud to build up planting areas. This technology enabled them to farm more intensively and produce the surpluses needed to sustain large-scale construction and craft specialization of their urban centers. Little is known about the political structure of Olmec civilization, but it is clear that there was no Olmec empire. Olmec influence depended more on the control of rare and desirable commodities, like jade and colored clays, and on the apparent appeal of their religious practices than on political control. The Olmecs' jaguar-god, some have suggested, was the precursor to the important rain deity found in all the later cultures of Mesoamerica. Jaguars and men being transformed into jaguars were common decorative motifs throughout the Olmec region.

The architectural and artistic accomplishments of the Olmecs were extraordinary given the absence of the wheel and draft animals (oxen, horses, burros). Their greatest artistic achievements were in jade carving. Figurines, necklaces, and ceremonial knives of jade were common in elite burials. All the major centers included large artificial platforms and mounds of packed earth and smaller temples with stone veneers. The best-known monuments of Olmec culture, however, were colossal carved stone heads as big as 11 feet (3.4 meters) high. Since each head is

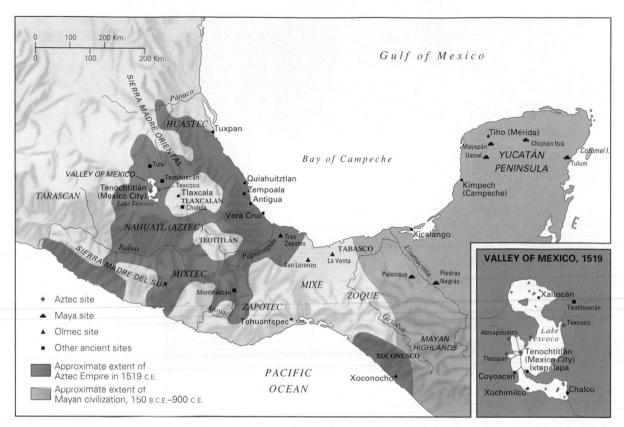

Map 12.1 Major Mesoamerican Civilizations, 1000 B.C.E.–1519 C.E.   From their island capital of Tenochtitlán, the Aztecs militarily and commercially dominated a large region. Aztec achievements were built on the legacy of earlier civilizations such as the Olmecs and Maya.

unique, most archaeologists believe that they represent individual rulers.

Both skilled artisans and large amounts of less skilled labor were needed to construct the urban centers. Only a powerful political class that commanded thousands of laborers could manage the quarrying and transportation of heavy stones. Other skilled craftsmen worked in stone, clay, and jade. Olmec society also had an important class of priests or shamans. Long-distance trade in luxury and ritual goods was probably carried on by a merchant class.

The Olmec played a crucial role in the early development of writing and astronomy, and they devised a calendar. It is likely that the ritual ball game eventually played widely throughout

Mesoamerica also originated with the Olmecs. The legacy of the Olmecs is most visible in the Maya lands to the south.

Two Classic Civilizations: Teotihuacán and the Maya

Located about 30 miles (48 kilometers) northeast of modern Mexico City, Teotihuacán (100 B.C.E.–750 C.E.) was one of Mesoamerica's most important classic-period civilizations (see Map 12.1). At the height of its power, from 450 to 600 C.E., Teotihuacán was the largest city in the Americas. With between 125,000 and 200,000 inhabitants, it was larger than all but a small number of contemporary European and Asian cities.

Religious architecture dominated the city center. Enormous pyramids dedicated to the Sun and Moon and more than twenty smaller temples devoted to other gods were arranged along a central avenue. The people recognized and worshiped many gods and lesser spirits. Among the gods were the Sun, the Moon, a storm-god, and Quetzalcóatl, the feathered serpent. Quetzalcóatl was a culture-god believed to be the originator of agriculture and the arts. Like the earlier Olmecs, people living at Teotihuacán practiced human sacrifice. More than sixty sacrificial victims were found during the excavation of the temple of Quetzalcóatl at Teotihuacán. Sacrifice was viewed as a sacred duty toward the gods and as essential to the well being of human society.

The rapid growth in urban population was the result of the forced relocation of farm families from smaller villages in the region. More than two-thirds of the city's residents continued to work in agriculture, walking out from urban residences to their fields. The elite of Teotihuacán used the city's growing labor resources to bring marginal lands into production. Swamps were drained, irrigation works were constructed, terraces were built into hillsides, and the use of chinampas was expanded. *Chinampas*, sometimes called "floating gardens," were narrow artificial islands anchored by trees and created by heaping lake muck and waste material on beds of reeds. Chinampas permitted year-round agriculture—because of subsurface irrigation and resistance to frost—and thus played a crucial role in sustaining the region's growing population. The productivity of the city's agriculture made possible its accomplishments in art, architecture, and trade.

As population grew, the housing of commoners underwent dramatic change. Apartment-like stone buildings were constructed for the first time. Among the residents of these early apartment blocks were the craftsmen who produced the pottery and obsidian tools that were the most important articles of long-distance trade. Teotihuacán pottery has been found throughout central Mexico and even in the Maya region of Guatemala. More than 2 percent of the urban population was engaged in making obsidian tools and weapons.

The city's role as a religious center and commercial power provided both divine sanction and a material basis for the elite's increased wealth and status. This elite controlled the state bureaucracy, tax collection, and commerce. The prestige and wealth of the elite were reflected in growing class distinctions in dress and diet and in the construction of separate residence compounds for the families of the aristocracy. The central position and great prestige of the priestly class are made clear in temple and palace murals. Teotihuacán's religious influence drew pilgrims from as far away as Oaxaca and Vera Cruz. Some of them became permanent residents.

Historians debate the role of the military in the development of Teotihuacán. The city's location in a valley and the absence of defensive structures before 500 c.e. suggest that Teotihuacán enjoyed relative peace during its early development. Archaeological evidence, however, reveals that the city's powerful military protected long-distance trade and enforced the elite's effort to compel peasant agriculturalists to transfer their surplus production to the city. The discovery of representations of soldiers in typical Teotihuacán dress in the Maya region of Guatemala suggests to some that Teotihuacán used its military to expand trade relations. But unlike later postclassic civilizations, Teotihuacán was not an imperial state controlled by a military elite.

It is unclear what forces brought about the collapse of Teotihuacán about 650 c.e. Weakness was evident as early as 500 c.e., when the urban population declined to about 40,000 and the city built defensive walls. These fortifications and pictorial evidence from murals suggest that the city's final decades were violent. Early scholars suggested that the city was overwhelmed militarily by Cholula, a rival city-state located in the Valley of Puebla, or by nomadic warrior peoples from the northern frontier. More recently, investigators have uncovered evidence of conflict within the ruling elite and the mismanagement of resources. This, they argue, led to class conflict and the breakdown of public order. As a result, most important temples in the city center were pulled down and religious images defaced. Elite palaces were also systematically burned and many of the residents killed. Regardless of the causes, the eclipse of Teotihuacán was felt throughout Mexico and into Central America.

During Teotihuacán's ascendancy in the north, the Maya developed an impressive civilization in the region that today includes Guatemala, Honduras, Belize, and southern Mexico (see Map 12.1). Given the difficulties imposed by a tropical climate and fragile soils, the cultural and architectural achievements of the Maya were remarkable. Although they shared a single culture, they were never unified politically. Instead, rival kingdoms led by hereditary rulers struggled with each other for regional dominance, much like the Mycenaean-era Greeks (see Chapter 3).

Modern Maya farmers prepare their fields by cutting down small trees and brush and then burning the dead vegetation. This *swidden agriculture* can produce high yields for a few years, but it uses up the soil's nutrients, eventually forcing people to move to more fertile land. The high population levels of the classic period (250–800 C.E.) required more intensive forms of agriculture. Maya living near the major urban centers achieved high agricultural yields by draining swamps and building elevated fields. They used irrigation in areas with long dry seasons, and they terraced hillsides in the cooler highlands. Nearly every household planted a garden to provide condiments and fruits to supplement dietary staples. Maya agriculturalists also managed nearby forests, favoring the growth of the trees and shrubs that were most useful to them, as well as promoting the conservation of deer and other semitame animals.

During the classic period, Maya city-states proliferated. Each city concentrated religious and political functions and controlled groups of smaller dependent cities and a broad agricultural zone. Classic-era cities, unlike earlier sites, had dense central precincts visually dominated by monumental architecture. These political and ceremonial centers were commonly positioned to reflect the movement of the Sun and Venus.

Open plazas were surrounded by high pyramids and by elaborately decorated palaces often built on high ground or on constructed mounds. The effect was to awe the masses drawn to these centers for religious and political rituals.

The Maya loved decoration. Nearly all of their public buildings were covered with bas-relief and painted in bright colors. Religious allegories, the genealogies of rulers, and important historical events were the most common motifs. Beautifully carved altars and stone monoliths were erected near major temples. This rich legacy of monumental architecture was constructed without the aid wheels—no pulleys, wheelbarrows, or carts—or metal tools. Masses of men and women aided only by levers and stone tools cut, carried, and put construction materials in place.

The Maya cosmos was divided into three layers connected along a vertical axis that traced the course of the Sun. The earthly arena of human existence held an intermediate position between the heavens, conceptualized by the Maya as a sky-monster, and a dark underworld. A sacred tree rose through the three layers; its roots were in the underworld, and its branches reached into the heavens. The temple precincts of Maya cities physically represented essential elements of this religious cosmology. The pyramids were sacred mountains reaching to the heavens. The doorways of the pyramids were portals to the underworld.

Rulers and other members of the elite served both priestly and political functions. They decorated their bodies with paint and tattoos and wore elaborate costumes of textiles, animal skins, and feathers to project both secular power and divine sanction. Kings communicated directly with the supernatural residents of the other worlds and with deified royal ancestors through bloodletting rituals and hallucinogenic trances. Scenes of rulers drawing blood from lips, ears, and penises are common in surviving frescoes and on painted pottery.

Even warfare, like the battle between Tikal and Uaxactún described at the beginning of the chapter, was infused with religious meaning and elaborate ritual. Battle scenes and the depiction of the torture and sacrifice of captives were fre-

The Great Plaza at Tikal   The ruins of Tikal, in modern Guatemala, demonstrate the impressive architectural and artistic achievements of the Classic Era Maya. The arrangement and construction of Maya centers provided a dramatic setting for the numerous rituals that dominated public life. This is one of a number of complexes dominated by one or more temples at Tikal. Early construction of this complex began before 150 B.C.E. The site was abandoned about 900 C.E. Temple I is on the right and Temple II on the left. In the background is an elevated platform with additional temples. The plaza also included elite residences and a ballcourt. (William Ferguson)

quent decorative themes. Typically, Maya military forces fought to secure captives rather than territory. Days of fasting, sacred ritual, and rites of purification preceded battle. The king, his kinsmen, and other ranking nobles actively participated in war. Elite captives were nearly always sacrificed; captured commoners were more likely to be enslaved.

Only two women are known to have ruled Maya kingdoms. At Palenque, Kan'anal-Ik'al ruled from 583 to 604 C.E., and Sak-K'uk ruled from 612 to 615 C.E. Maya women of the ruling

lineages did play important political and religious roles, however. The consorts of male rulers participated in bloodletting rituals and in other important public ceremonies, and their noble blood helped legitimate the rule of their husbands. Although Maya society was patrilineal (tracing descent in the male line), there is evidence that some male rulers traced their lineages bilaterally (in both the male and the female lines) and emphasized the female line if it held higher status. Much less is known about the lives of the women of the lower classes, but scholars believe that they played a central role in the household economy, maintaining essential garden plots and weaving, and in the management of family life.

Building on what the Olmecs had done, the Maya made important contributions to the development of the Mesoamerican calendar and to mathematics and writing. Their interest in time and in the cosmos was reflected in the complexity of their calendric system. Each day was identified by three separate dating systems. Like other peoples throughout Mesoamerica, the Maya had a calendar that tracked the ritual cycle (260 days divided into 13 months of 20 days) and a solar calendar (365 days divided into 18 months of 20 days, plus 5 unfavorable days at the end of the year). The concurrence of these two calendars every 52 years was believed to be especially ominous. The Maya, alone among Mesoamerican peoples, also maintained a continuous "long count" calendar, which began at a fixed date in the past that modern scholars identify as 3114 B.C.E., a date that was likely associated with creation.

These accurate calendric systems and the astronomical observations on which they were based depended on Maya contributions to mathematics and writing. Their system of mathematics incorporated the concept of the zero and place value but had limited notational signs. Maya writing was a form of hieroglyphic inscription that signified whole words or concepts as well as phonetic cues or syllables (see Environment & Technology: The Maya Writing System). Aspects of public life, religious belief, and the biographies of rulers and their ancestors were recorded in deerskin and bark-paper books, on pottery, and on the stone columns and monumental buildings of the urban centers. In this sense every Maya city was a sacred text.

Between 800 and 900 C.E. many of the major urban centers of the Maya were abandoned or

The Mesoamerican ball game   Archaeologists have found evidence from Guatemala to Arizona of an ancient ball game played with a solid rubber ball on slope-sided courts shaped like the capital letter T. Among the Maya the game was mythologically associated with creation, and thus had deep religious meaning. There is evidence that some players were sacrificed. In this scene found on a ceramic jar, players in elaborate ritual clothing which includes heavy, protective pads around the chest and waist play with a ball much larger than that actually used in games. In some representations, balls were drawn so as to suggest a human head. (Dallas Art Museum/Justin Kerr)

The Maya Writing System

Of all the cultures of precolombian America, only the Maya produced a written literature that has survived to the modern era. The literary legacy of the Maya is inscribed on stone monuments, ceramics, jade, shell, and bone. Books of bark paper were the original and most common medium of Maya scribes, but only four of these books exist today.

The historical and literary importance of the written record of the Maya has been recognized only recently. In the early nineteenth century, visitors to southern Mexico and Guatemala began to record and decipher the symbols they found on stone monuments. By the end of the nineteenth century, the Maya system of numbers and the Maya calendar were decoded.

Not until the 1960s did scholars recognize that Maya writing reflects spoken language by having a set word order. We now know that Maya writing was capable of capturing the rich meaning of spoken language.

Maya scribes could use signs that represented sounds or signs that represented whole words. *Jaguar* (*balam* in Maya) could be written by using the head of this big cat in symbolic form. Because there were other large cats in the Maya region, scribes commonly added a pronunciation cue like a prefix or suffix to the front or back of the symbol to clarify meaning. In this case they might affix the syllable sign *ba* to the front of the jaguar head or the syllable sign *ma* to the end. Because the Maya word for no other feline began with *ba* or ended with *ma*, the reader knew to pronounce the word as *balam* for "jaguar." Alternatively, because the last vowel was not sounded, *balam* could be written with three syllable signs: *ba la ma*.

These signs were expressed in a rich and varied array of stylized forms, much like illustrated European medieval texts, that make translation difficult. But these stylistic devices helped convey meaning. Readers detected meaning not only in what the text "said" but also in how and where the text was written.

The work of Maya scribes was not intended as mass communication, since few Maya could read these texts. Instead, as two of the most respected experts in this field explain, "Writing was a sacred proposition that had the capacity to capture the order of the cosmos, to inform history, to give form to ritual, and to transform the profane material of everyday life into the supernatural."

Source: Adapted from Linda Schele and David Freidel, *A Forest of Kings: The Untold Story of the Ancient Maya*, 1990 with figure of *balaam*. Copyright © 1990 by Linda Schele and David Freidel. Reprinted by permission of William Morrow & Co., Inc.

balam   ba - balam   balam - ma   ba - balam - ma   ba - la - m(a)

destroyed, although a small number of classic-period centers survived for centuries. This collapse was preceded in some areas by decades of urban population decline and increased warfare. Some experts have argued that the destruction of Teotihuacán about 750 C.E. disrupted trade, thus undermining the legitimacy of Maya rulers. Other scholars suggest that growing population pressure led to environmental degradation and falling agricultural productivity. This environmental crisis, in turn, might have led to class conflict and increased levels of warfare as desperate elites sought to acquire additional agricultural land through conquest. Although little evidence has been found, some scholars have proposed that epidemic disease and pestilence were the prime causes of the catastrophe. Most probably, a combination of factors caused the end of the classic period.

THE POSTCLASSIC PERIOD IN MESOAMERICA, 800–1500

The division between classic and postclassic periods is somewhat arbitrary. Not only is there no single explanation for the collapse of Teotihuacán and many of the major Maya centers, but these events occurred over more than a century and a half. In fact, some important classic-period civilizations, like Cholula in the Valley of Puebla, survived unscathed. Moreover, the essential cultural characteristics of the classic period were carried over to the postclassic. Similarities in religious belief and practice, in architecture and urban planning, and in social organization all link the two periods.

There were, however, some important differences between these periods. There is evidence that the population of Mesoamerica expanded during the postclassic period. Resulting pressures led to an intensification of agricultural practices and to increased warfare. The governing elites of the major postclassic states—the Toltecs and the Aztecs—responded to these harsh realities by increasing the size of their armies and by developing political institutions that facilitated their control of large and culturally diverse territories acquired through conquest.

The Toltecs

Little is known about the Toltecs prior to their arrival in central Mexico. Some scholars speculate that they were originally a satellite population that Teotihuacán placed on the northern frontier to protect against the incursions of nomads. After their migration south, the Toltecs borrowed from the cultural legacy of Teotihuacán and created an important postclassic civilization. Memories of their military achievements and the violent imagery of their political and religious rituals dominated the Mesoamerican imagination in the late postclassic period. In the fourteenth century, the Aztecs and their contemporaries erroneously believed that the Toltecs were the authors of nearly all the great cultural achievements of the Mesoamerican world. The actual accomplishments of the Toltecs, however, were primarily political and military.

The Toltecs created a powerful conquest state and extended their influence from the area north of modern Mexico City to Central America. Established about 968 C.E., Tula, the Toltec capital, was constructed in a grand style (see Map 12.1). Its public architecture featured colonnaded patios and numerous temples. Although the population of Tula never reached the levels of classic-period Teotihuacán, the Toltec capital dominated central Mexico. Toltec decoration had a more warlike and violent character than the decoration of earlier Mesoamerican cultures. Nearly all Toltec public buildings and temples were decorated with representations of warriors or with scenes suggesting human sacrifice.

The Toltec state apparently was ruled by two chieftains or kings at the same time. Evidence suggests that this division of responsibility eventually weakened Toltec power and led to the destruction of Tula. Sometime after 1000 C.E., a struggle between elite groups identified with rival religious cults undermined the Toltec state. According to legends that survived among the Aztecs, Topiltzin—one of the rulers and a priest of the cult of Quetzalcóatl—and his followers bitterly accepted exile in the east, "the land of the rising sun." These legendary events coincided with a growing Toltec influence among the Maya of the Yucatán Peninsula. One of the ancient texts relates these events in the following manner:

> Thereupon he [Topiltzin] looked toward Tula, and then wept. . . . And when he had done these things . . . he went to reach the seacoast. Then he fashioned a raft of serpents. When he had arranged the

raft, he placed himself as if it were his boat. Then he set off across the sea.[3]

The Toltec state began to decline after the exile of Topiltzin, and around 1168 C.E. Tula was overcome by northern invaders. After its destruction, a centuries-long process of cultural and political assimilation produced a new Mesoamerican political order based on the urbanized culture and statecraft of the Toltecs. Like Semitic peoples of the third millennium B.C.E. interacting with Sumerian culture, the new Mesoamerican elites were drawn in part from the invading cultures. The Aztecs of the Valley of Mexico would become the most important of these late postclassic peoples.

The Aztecs

The Mexica, more commonly known as Aztecs, were among the northern peoples who pushed into central Mexico in the wake of the collapse of

Costumes of Aztec warriors   In Mesoamerican warfare individual warriors sought to gain prestige and improve their status by taking captives. This illustration from the sixteenth-century Codex Mendoza was drawn by a Amerindian artist. It shows how the Aztecs used distinctive costumes to acknowledge the prowess of warriors. These costumes indicate the taking of two (top left) to six captives (bottom center). The individual on the bottom right shown without a weapon was a military leader. As was common in Mesoamerican illustrations of military conflict, the captives, held by their hair, are shown kneeling before the victors. (The Bodlelan Library, Oxford, Ma. Arch. Selder. A.I. fol. 64r.)

Tula. Once settled, they grafted onto their clan-based social organization elements of the political and social practices that they found among the urbanized agriculturalists of the valley. At first, the Aztecs served their more powerful neighbors as serfs and mercenaries. As their strength grew, they relocated to small uninhabited islands near the shore of Lake Texcoco and began the construction of their twin capitals, Tenochtitlán and Tlateloco, around 1325 C.E.

From this strong point, they became valued mercenaries of the region's dominant political power, Azcapotzalco. Military successes allowed the Aztecs to seize control of additional agricultural land along the lake shore. With the increased economic independence and greater political security that resulted from this expansion, the Aztecs transformed their political organization by introducing a monarchical system similar to that found in more powerful neighboring states. Clans survived to the era of Spanish conquest but increasingly lost influence to monarchs and hereditary aristocrats.

As the power of the nobility grew and the authority of kinship-based clans declined, class distinctions became more important. These alterations in social structure and political life were made possible by Aztec military expansion. Territorial conquest allowed the warrior elite of Aztec society to seize land and peasant labor as spoils of war (see Map 12.1). In time, the royal family and high aristocracy possessed extensive estates that were cultivated by slaves and landless peasants. Although commoners received some material rewards from imperial expansion, their ability to influence or control decisions was largely lost. Some commoners were able to achieve some social mobility through success on the battlefield or by entering the priesthood, but the highest social ranks were always reserved for hereditary nobles.

Nevertheless, the urban plan of Tenochtitlán and Tlateloco continued to be organized around the clans, whose members maintained a common ritual life and accepted civic responsibilities such as caring for the sick and elderly. Clan members also fought together as military units. However, the clans' historical control over common agricultural land and other scarce resources, such as fishing and hunting rights, was diminished. By 1500 C.E., Aztec society was characterized by great inequalities in wealth and privilege.

The kings and aristocracy legitimated their new ascendancy by creating elaborate rituals and ceremonies that separated them from the commoners. One of the Spaniards who participated in the conquest of the Aztec Empire remembered his first meeting with the Aztec ruler Moctezuma II (r. 1502–1520): "many great lords walked before the great Montezuma [Moctezuma II], sweeping the ground on which he was to tread and laying down cloaks so that his feet should not touch the earth. Not one of these chieftains dared look him in the face."[4] Commoners lived in small dwellings and ate a limited diet of staples, but members of the nobility lived in large, well-constructed two-story houses and consumed a diet rich in animal protein and flavored by condiments and expensive imports like chocolate. The elite were also set apart by their rich dress and jewelry. Even marriage customs in the two groups were different. Commoners were monogamous; nobles, polygamous.

The Aztec state met the challenge of feeding an urban population of approximately 150,000 by efficiently organizing the labor of the clans and additional laborers sent as tribute by defeated peoples to expand agricultural land. The construction of a dike more than 5½ miles (9 kilometers) long by 23 feet (7 meters) wide to separate the fresh and saltwater parts of Lake Texcoco was the Aztecs' most impressive land reclamation project. Once constructed, the dike allowed a significant extension of irrigated fields and the construction of additional chinampas. One expert has estimated that the project consumed 4 million person-days to complete. Aztec chinampas contributed maize, fruits, and vegetables to the markets of Tenochtitlán. The imposition of tribute obligations on conquered peoples also helped relieve some of the pressure of Tenochtitlán's growing population. Approximately one quarter of the Aztec capital's food requirements were satisfied by tribute payments of maize, beans, and other foods from nearby dependencies. The Aztecs also demanded cotton cloth, military equipment, luxury goods like jade and feathers, and sacrificial victims as tribute. They acquired other goods by trade.

A specialized class of merchants controlled long-distance trade. Given the absence of draft animals and wheeled vehicles, this commerce was dominated by lightweight and valuable products like gold, jewels, feathered garments, cacao, and animal skins. Merchants also provided essential political and military intelligence for the Aztec elite. Operating outside the protection of Aztec military power, merchant expeditions were armed and often had to defend themselves. Although merchants became wealthy and powerful as the Aztecs expanded their empire, they were denied the privileges of the high nobility and feared to publicly display their affluence.

As was true throughout the Mesoamerican world, Aztec commerce was carried on without money and credit. Barter was facilitated by the use of cacao, quills filled with gold, and cotton cloth as standard units of value to compensate for differences in the value of bartered goods. Aztec expansion facilitated the integration of producers and consumers in the central Mexican economy. As a result, the markets of Tenochtitlán and Tlateloco offered a rich array of goods produced from as far away as Central America and what is now the southwestern border of the United States. Hernán Cortés (1485–1547), the Spanish explorer who eventually conquered the Aztecs, expressed his admiration for the abundance of the Aztec marketplace:

> One square in particular is twice as big as that of Salamanca and completely surrounded by arcades where there are daily more than sixty thousand folk buying and selling. Every kind of merchandise such as may be met with in every land is for sale. . . . There is nothing to be found in all the land which is not sold in these markets, for over and above what I have mentioned there are so many and such various things that on account of their very number . . . I cannot detail them.[5]

The Aztecs succeeded in developing a remarkable urban landscape. The combined population of Tenochtitlán and Tlateloco and the nearby cities and hamlets of the surrounding lake shore was approximately 500,000 by 1500 C.E. The is-

land capital was designed so that canals and streets intersected at right angles. Three causeways connected the city to the lake shore. Startled by the size and orderliness of Tenochtitlán, the Spaniards compared it favorably to the largest cities in Spain.

Religious rituals dominated public life in Tenochtitlán. Like the other cultures of the Mesoamerican world, the Aztecs believed in and worshiped a large number of gods. Most of these gods had a dual nature—both male and female personas. The major contribution of the Aztecs to the religious life of Mesoamerica was the cult of Huitzilopochtli, the southern hummingbird. As the Aztec state grew in power and wealth, the importance of this cult grew as well. Eventually, Huitzilopochtli became associated with the Sun. It was believed that he required a diet of human hearts to sustain him in his daily struggle to bring the Sun's warmth to the world. Tenochtitlán was architecturally dominated by a great twin temple devoted to Huitzilopochtli and Tlaloc, the rain god, symbolizing the two bases of the Aztec economy: war and agriculture.

War captives were preferred as sacrificial victims, but criminals, slaves, and people provided as tribute by dependent regions were also sacrificed in large numbers. Although human sacrifice had been practiced since early times in Mesoamerica, the Aztecs and other societies of the late postclassic period transformed this religious ritual by dramatically increasing its scale. There are no reliable estimates for the total number of sacrifices, but the numbers clearly reached into the thousands each year, some say as high as 20,000 per year. In 1487, the rededication of the temple of Huitzilopochtli alone was celebrated by the sacrifice of more than 10,000 victims. Clearly this form of violent public ritual had political consequences and was not simply the celebration of religious belief. Some scholars have emphasized the political nature of this rising tide of sacrifice. Since sacrifices were carried out in front of large crowds that included leaders from enemy and subject states as well as the masses of Aztec society, a political subtext must have been clear: rebellion, deviancy, and opposition were extremely dangerous.

NORTHERN PEOPLES

By the end of the classic period in Mesoamerica, around 800 C.E., important cultural centers had appeared in the southwestern desert region and along the Ohio and Mississippi river valleys of what is now the United States (see Figure 12.1). In both regions improved agricultural productivity and population growth led to increased urbanization and more complex social and political structures. The introduction of maize, beans, and squash played an important role in these developments, but in the Ohio Valley large villages with monumental earthworks were sustained at first by locally domesticated seed crops combined with traditional hunting and gathering practices.

In both the southwestern desert cultures and the eastern river-valley cultures, large-scale irrigation projects were associated with growing dependence on maize. This development, in turn, indicates more centralized political power and greater social stratification. The two regions, however, evolved different political traditions. The Anasazi and their neighbors in the southwest maintained a more egalitarian social structure and retained collective forms of political organization based on kinship and age. The mound builders of the eastern river valleys evolved more hierarchical political institutions. Groups of smaller towns were subordinate to a political center ruled by a

Figure 12.1 Mesoamerican, North American, and Andean Civilizations, to 1500

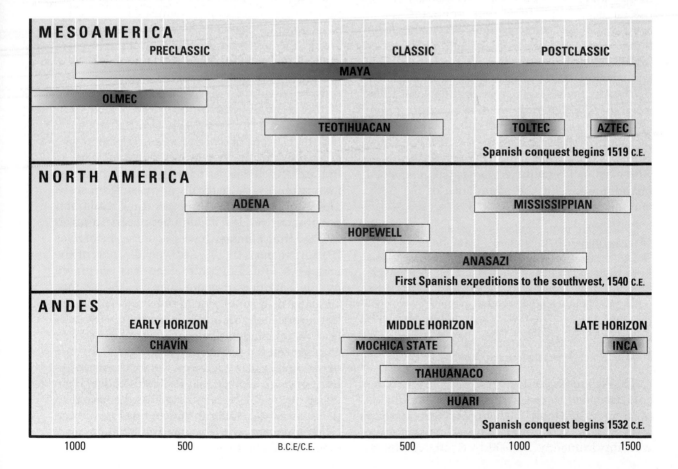

Pueblo Bonito   Located in Chaco Canyon in modern New Mexico, Pueblo Bonito was the largest Anasazi settlement. At the height of its power around 1100 C.E., Pueblo Bonito was the center of an extensive religious and commercial network. This multistory structure included small apartments for individual families, storage chambers, and many subterranean rooms called kivas. The Anasazi believed that humans had emerged from within the earth. By locating much of their religious life in the kiva, they reconnected themselves to this mystical origin. (CGI/Pathway Productions)

hereditary chief who wielded both secular and religious authority.

The Southwestern Desert Cultures

Immigrants from Mexico introduced agriculture based on irrigation to present-day Arizona around 300 B.C.E. Because irrigation allowed the planting of two crops per year, the population grew, and settled village life soon appeared. Of all the southwestern cultures, the Hohokam of the Salt and Gila river valleys show the strongest Mexican influence. Hohokam sites have platform mounds and ball courts similar to those of Mesoamerica. Their pottery, clay figurines, cast copper bells, and turquoise mosaics also show southern influence. By 1000 C.E., the Hohokam

had constructed an elaborate irrigation system that included one canal more than 18 miles (30 kilometers) in length. Hohokam agriculture and ceramic technology spread over the centuries to neighboring peoples, but it was the Anasazi of the north who left the most vivid legacy of these desert cultures.

Archaeologists used *Anasazi*, a Navajo word meaning "ancient ones," to identify a number of dispersed, though similar, desert cultures located in what is now called the Four Corners region of Arizona, New Mexico, Colorado, and Utah. Between 450 and 750 C.E. the Anasazi embraced maize, beans, and squash. Their successful adaptation of these crops permitted the formation of larger villages and led to an enriched cultural life centered on underground ritual buildings called *kivas*. Evidence suggests that the Anasazi may also have used kivas for weaving and pottery making. They produced pottery decorated in geometric patterns, learned to weave cotton cloth, and, after 900 C.E., began to construct large multistory residential and ritual centers.

One of the largest Anasazi communities was located in Chaco Canyon in what is now northwestern New Mexico. Eight large communities were built in the canyon and four more on surrounding mesas, suggesting a regional population of approximately 15,000. Smaller villages were also located in the region. Each town contained hundreds of contiguous rooms arranged in tiers around a central plaza. At Pueblo Bonito, the largest town, more than 650 rooms were arranged in a four-story block of residences and storage rooms. Pueblo Bonito had 38 kivas, including a great kiva more than 65 feet (19 meters) in diameter. Social life and craft activities were concentrated in small open plazas or common rooms. Men were often drawn away from the village by hunting, by trade, and by the need to maintain irrigation works. Women shared in agricultural tasks and were specialists in many crafts. They were also responsible for food preparation and child care. If the practice of modern Pueblos, cultural descendants of the Anasazi, is a guide, houses and furnishings may have belonged to the women who formed extended families with their mothers and sisters.

The high quality construction at Chaco Canyon, the size and number of kivas, and the discovery of a system of roads linking the canyon to outlying towns suggest that Pueblo Bonito and its nearest neighbors exerted some kind of political or religious preeminence over a large region. Some archaeologists have suggested that the Chaco Canyon culture originated as a colonial appendage of Mesoamerica, but there is little evidence for this theory in the archaeological record. Merchants from Chaco provided Toltec-period peoples of northern Mexico with turquoise in exchange for shell jewelry, copper bells, macaws, and trumpets. But these exchanges occurred late in Chaco's development, and more important signs of Mesoamerican influence like pyramid-shaped mounds and ball courts are not found at Chaco. Nor is there evidence from the excavation of burials and residences of clear class distinctions, which were so prominent in Mesoamerica. Instead, it appears that the Chaco Canyon culture developed from earlier societies in the region.

The abandonment of the major sites in Chaco Canyon in the twelfth century most likely resulted from a long drought that undermined the culture's fragile agricultural economy. Nevertheless, Anasazi continued in the Four Corners region for more than a century after the abandonment of Chaco Canyon. There were major centers at Mesa Verde in present-day Colorado and Canyon de Chelly and Kiet Siel in Arizona (see Map 12.2). The Anasazi settlements on the Colorado Plateau and in Arizona were constructed in large natural caves located above valley floors. This hard-to-reach location suggests increased levels of warfare, probably provoked by population pressure on limited arable land. Although the Anasazi disappeared before the arrival of Europeans, the Pueblo peoples of the Rio Grande Valley and Arizona live in multistory villages and worship in kivas today.

The Mound Builders: Hopewell and Mississippian Cultures

The Adena culture of the Ohio Valley constructed large villages with monumental earthworks from about 500 B.C.E. This early mound-building culture was based on traditional hunting and gathering supplemented by limited agriculture of locally domesticated seed crops. Most, but not all, of the Adena mounds contained burials. Items found in these graves indicate a hierarchical society with an elite distinguished by its access to rare and valuable goods like mica from North Carolina and copper from the Great Lakes region.

Map 12.2 Culture Areas of North America In each of the large ecological regions of North America, native peoples evolved distinctive cultures and technologies. Here the Anasazi of the arid southwest and the mound-building cultures of the Ohio and Mississippi River valleys are highlighted.

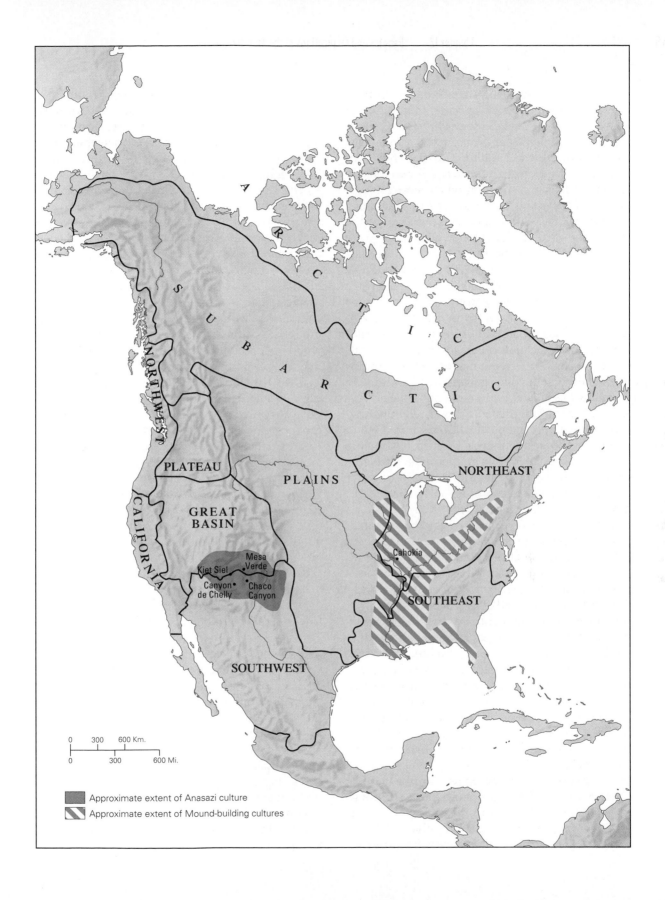

ARCTIC

SUBARCTIC

NORTHWEST

PLATEAU

CALIFORNIA

GREAT
BASIN

PLAINS

NORTHEAST

Mesa
Verde

Kiet Siel

Canyon
de Chelly

Chaco
Canyon

Cahokia

SOUTHEAST

SOUTHWEST

| 0 | 300 | 600 Km. |

| 0 | 300 | 600 Mi. |

Approximate extent of Anasazi culture

Approximate extent of Mound-building cultures

Around 100 C.E. the Adena culture blended into a successor culture, also centered in the Ohio River Valley, called Hopewell. The largest Hopewell centers appeared in Ohio, but Hopewell influence, either in the form of colonies or trade dependencies, spread west to Illinois, Michigan, and Wisconsin, east to New York and Ontario, and south to Alabama, Louisiana, Mississippi, and even Florida. For the necessities of daily life Hopewell people were dependent on hunting and gathering and on a limited agriculture inherited from the Adena.

Hopewell is an early example of a North American chiefdom. Chiefdoms had populations of up to ten thousand and were ruled by hereditary leaders who had both religious and secular responsibilities. Chiefs organized periodic rituals of feasting and gift giving that established bonds among diverse kinship groups and guaranteed access to specialized crops and craft goods. They also managed long-distance trade relations that provided luxury goods and additional food supplies. The large mounds built to house elite burials and as platforms for temples and elite residences dominated Hopewell centers.

Hopewell sites were ordered hierarchically. The largest towns in the Ohio Valley served as ceremonial and political centers and had populations that reached several thousand inhabitants. Smaller villages had populations of a few hundred. Modern excavations of Hopewell mounds have found strong evidence of social stratification as well. Chiefs and other elite members were buried in vaults surrounded by valuable goods such as river pearls, copper jewelry, and, in some cases, women and retainers who apparently were sacrificed to accompany a dead chief into the afterlife. As was true with the earlier Olmec culture of Mexico, the abandonment of major Hopewell sites around 400 C.E. has no clear environmental or political explanation.

Hopewell technology and mound building continued in smaller centers that were linked to the development of the Mississippian culture (700–1500 C.E.). Although some experts have suggested that contacts with Mesoamerica influenced Mississippian culture, there is no convincing evidence for this theory. It is true that

maize, beans, and squash, all first domesticated in Mesoamerica, were closely associated with the development of the urbanized Mississippian culture. But these plants and related technologies were probably passed along through numerous intervening cultures.

The development of these urbanized chiefdoms resulted instead from the accumulated effects of small increases in agricultural productivity, the adoption of the bow and arrow, and the expansion of trade networks. An improved economy led to population growth, the building of cities, and social stratification. The larger towns shared a common urban plan based on a central plaza surrounded by large platform mounds. Major towns were also trade centers where people bartered essential commodities, like flint used for weapons and tools.

The Mississippian culture reached its highest stage of evolution with the development of the great urban center of Cahokia, located near the modern city of East St. Louis, Illinois (see Map 12.2). At the center of this site was the largest mound constructed in North America, a terraced structure 100 feet (30 meters) high and 1,037 by 790 feet (316 by 241 meters) at the base. The center area of elite housing and temples was ringed by areas where commoners lived. At its height in about 1200 C.E., Cahokia had a population of about 30,000—about the same population as the great Maya city Tikal.

Like Tikal, Cahokia controlled surrounding agricultural lands and a number of secondary towns ruled by subchiefs. Burial evidence suggests that the rulers of Cahokia enjoyed an exalted position. In one burial more than fifty young women and retainers were apparently sacrificed to accompany a ruler on his travels after death. As with Hopewell, there is no evidence that links the decline and eventual abandonment of Cahokia (which occurred after 1250 C.E.) with military defeat or civil war. Experts argue that climatic changes and population pressures undermined its vitality. After the decline of Cahokia, smaller Mississippian centers continued to flourish in the southeast of the present-day United States until the arrival of Europeans.

ANDEAN CIVILIZATIONS

Geography played a greater role in directing the development of human society in the Andes than in any other area of the Americas. Much of the region's mountainous core is at altitudes that at first glance might seem too high for agriculture and human habitation. The arid coastal plain also posed difficult challenges to human populations. Yet Amerindian peoples in this area produced some of the most socially complex and politically advanced societies of the Americas. Perhaps the very harshness of the environment compelled the development of the administrative structures and supporting social and economic relationships that were central features of Andean civilization.

Cultural Response to Environmental Challenge

People living in the high mountain valleys and on the dry coastal plain were able to overcome the challenges posed by their environment through the effective organization of human labor. The remarkable collective achievements of Andean peoples were organized without writing, although a system of knotted colored cords, *quipus*, were used to aid administration. Large-scale drainage and irrigation works and the terracing of hillsides to control erosion and provide additional farmland led to an increase in agricultural production. Andean people also undertook road building, urban construction, and even textile production collectively.

The sharing of responsibilities began at the household level. But it was the clan, or *ayllu*, that provided the foundation for Andean achievement. Members of an ayllu held land communally. All members claimed descent from a common ancestor, but all members were not necessarily related. Ayllu members thought of each other as brothers and sisters and were obligated to aid each other in tasks that required more labor than a single household could provide. These reciprocal obligations provided the model for the organization of labor and the distribution of goods at every level of Andean society. Just as individuals and families were expected to provide labor to kinsmen, members of an ayllu were expected to provide labor and goods to their hereditary chief.

With the development of territorial states ruled by hereditary aristocracies and kings after 1000 B.C.E., these obligations were organized on a larger scale. The *mit'a*, or rotational labor obligation, required members of ayllus to work the fields and care for the herds of llamas and alpacas owned by religious establishments, the royal court, and the aristocracy. Mit'a laborers also built and maintained roads, bridges, temples, palaces, and large irrigation and drainage projects. Mit'a workers produced textiles and goods essential to ritual life such as beer made from maize and coca (dried leaves chewed as a stimulant and now also a source of cocaine). Once developed, the mit'a system remained an essential part of the Andean world for more than a thousand years.

Work was divided along gender lines, but the work of men and women was interdependent. Hunting, military tasks, and government were reserved largely for men. Women had numerous responsibilities in agriculture and the home. One early Spanish commentator described the responsibilities of Andean women in terms that sound very modern:

> [T]hey did not just perform domestic tasks, but also [labored] in the fields, in the cultivation of their lands, in building houses, and carrying burdens. . . . [A]nd more than once I heard that while women were carrying these burdens, they would feel labor pains, and giving birth, they would go to a place where there was water and wash the baby and themselves. Putting the baby on top of the load they were carrying, they would then continue walking as before they gave birth. In sum, there was nothing their husbands did where their wives did not help.[6]

The ayllu was intimately tied to a uniquely Andean system of production and exchange.

Because the region's mountain ranges created a multitude of small ecological areas with specialized resources, each community sought to control a mix of environments so as to guarantee access to essential goods. Coastal regions produced maize, fish, and cotton. Mountain valleys contributed quinoa (the local grain), plus potatoes and other tubers. Higher elevations contributed the wool and meat of llamas and alpacas, and the Amazonian region provided coca and fruits. Ayllus sent out colonies to exploit the resources of these ecological niches. Colonists remained linked to their original region and kin group by marriage custom and ritual. Historians commonly refer to this system of controlled exchange across ecological boundaries as *vertical integration,* or *verticality.*

The historical periodization of Andean history is similar to that of Mesoamerica (see Figure 12.1). Both regions developed highly integrated political and economic systems long before 1500. The pace of agricultural development, urbanization, and state formation in the Andes also approximated that in Mesoamerica. However, in the Andean region unique environmental challenges led to distinctive highland and coastal cultures with separate periodizations. Here, more than in Mesoamerica, geography influenced the process of regional cultural integration and state formation.

Chavín and Moche

Chavín was the first major urban civilization in South America. Its capital, Chavín de Huántar, was located at 10,300 feet (3,139 meters) in the eastern range of the Andes north of the modern city of Lima (see Map 12.3). Between 900 and 250 B.C.E., a period that roughly coincides with the Olmec culture of Mesoamerica, Chavín became politically and economically dominant in a densely populated region that included large areas of the coastal plain. Chavín de Huántar's location at the intersection of trade routes connecting the coast with populous mountain valleys provided an initial advantage. Military force may have spread its influence. The enormous scale of the capital and the dispersal of Chavín pottery styles, religious motifs, and architectural forms over a wide area suggest that Chavín imposed some form of political integration and trade dependency on its neighbors.

Chavín's development as a commercial center was probably associated with the spread of llamas to the coastal lowlands. Domesticated earlier in the mountainous region, their diffusion was crucial to regional development. The importance of llamas to Andean developments was similar to that of camels in the development of trans-Saharan trade (see Chapter 8). Llamas provided meat as well as wool. More important, they multiplied the scale of commercial exchange by decreasing the labor needed to transport goods, since a single driver could control from 10 to 30 animals, each carrying up to 70 pounds (32 kilograms).

At Chavín the essential characteristics found in later Andean civilizations were all present. The architectural signature for these civilizations was a large complex of multilevel platforms, usually packed earth or rubble faced with cut stone or adobe (sun-dried brick made of clay and straw). Although the construction was superior to that of the Ohio Valley mound builders, these platforms (like those in the Ohio Valley) held small buildings used for ritual purposes and residences for the elite. There is strong evidence of class differences and the growing authority of a chief or king. Platforms were decorated with relief carvings of serpents, condors, jaguars, and human forms. The largest of these constructions at Chavín de Huántar, the Castillo, measured 250 feet (76 meters) on each side and rose to a height of 50 feet (15 meters). About one third of its interior is hollow, containing narrow galleries and small rooms that may have housed the remains of important royal ancestors.

Archaeological investigations of Chavín de Huántar have revealed gold ornaments produced by means of revolutionary techniques that permitted artisans to forge three-dimensional objects. Chavín's artisans also introduced improvements in textile production. The most common decorative motif in sculpture and pottery was a jaguar-man similar in conception to the Olmec symbol of supernatural transformation.

Recent investigations suggest that increased warfare disrupted trade and eventually caused the collapse of Chavín around 200 B.C.E. Nevertheless, the material culture, statecraft, architecture, and urban planning associated with Chavín continued to influence the Andean region for centuries.

Some four centuries later, around 200 C.E., the next major Andean civilization appeared. The Mochica dominated the north coastal region of Peru between 200 and 700 C.E. from a capital, Moche, located near the modern Peruvian city of Trujillo (see Map 12.3). Archaeological evidence indicates that the Mochica cultivated maize, quinoa, beans, and potatoes with the aid of massive irrigation works. Since Moche itself was seriously damaged by a massive flood, the most important excavations have been carried out at secondary cities. A network of canals and aqueducts connected Moche's fields with water sources as far away as 75 miles (121 kilometers). These hydraulic works were maintained by mit'a labor imposed on commoners and subject peoples. Textile production, long-distance trade, and subsistence were all supported by large herds of llamas used for transporting goods as well as for wool and food.

Evidence from murals and decorated ceramics suggests that Moche was a highly stratified theocratic society controlled by priests and war leaders. The organizational requirements of the Mochica irrigation system promoted class division and ultimately gave political control to a small group. Hierarchy was then reinforced by military conquests of neighboring regions. The social elevation of the elite was architecturally represented by the placing of their residences on the top of platforms erected at ceremonial centers. Social distinctions were also evident in burial practices. A recent excavation in the Lambeyeque Valley discovered the tomb of a warrior-priest who was buried with a rich treasure that included gold, silver, and copper jewelry, textiles, feather ornaments, and shells. Also buried with this powerful man were two women and three men who accompanied him in his journey to the afterlife. The retainers had each had a foot amputated

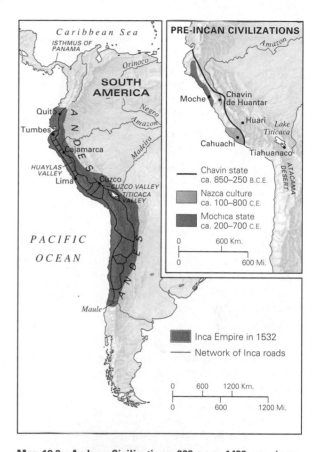

Map 12.3 Andean Civilizations, 900 B.C.E.–1432 C.E. In response to the environmental challenges posed by an arid coastal plain and high interior mountain ranges, Andean peoples made complex social and technological adaptations. Irrigation systems, the domestication of the llama, metallurgy, and shared labor obligations helped provide an abundant economic foundation for powerful, centralized states. In 1532, the Inca empire's vast territory stretched from modern Chile in the south to Colombia in the north.

to ensure their continued subservience and dependence.

Commoners devoted most of their time to subsistence farming and to the payment of labor dues owed to their ayllu and to the elite. They lived in one-room buildings clustered in the outlying areas of cities and in the surrounding agricultural zone. The high quality of Mochica metallurgy, textiles, and ceramics indicates the presence of a skilled artisan class involved full-time in their crafts. Both men and women were

A Moche portrait vase The Mochica of ancient Peru (100–800 C.E.) were among the most accomplished ceramic artists of the Americas. Mochica potters produced representations of gods and spirits, scenes of daily life, and portrait vases of important people. Both men and women were captured in stirrup jars such as the one shown here. This man wears a headdress adorned by two birds and sea shells. The stains next to the eyes of the birds represent tears. (Museo de Arqueologica y Antropologia, Lima/Lee Bolton Picture Library)

involved in agriculture and the household economy. Women had a special role in the production of textiles.

Mochica culture developed a brilliant representational art. Portrait vases produced by Mochica craftsmen adorn museum collections in nearly every city of the world. Among the most original products of these ceramic artisans were pottery vessels decorated with explicit sexual acts. In addition, the Mochica were accomplished weavers and metalsmiths. Their metallurgy was largely devoted to religious and decorative functions, but they also produced heavy copper and copper alloy tools for agricultural and military purposes. There is some evidence that the Mochica originated the quipu, a coded form of numeric recordkeeping that later became common throughout the Andes.

A detailed history of the Mochica will never be written, but it is clear that the culture was conquered by the Huari in the ninth or tenth century. The Mochica had been weakened some centuries earlier when the course of the Moche River was altered by earthquakes around 450 C.E. and the river flooded the capital of Moche. Although a new capital was constructed at Pampa Grande in the north after Moche was abandoned, the Mochica never fully recovered from this flood.

Tiahuanaco and Huari

After 500 C.E. two powerful civilizations developed in the Andean highlands. At nearly 13,000 feet (3,962 meters) on the high treeless plain near Lake Titicaca in modern Bolivia stand the ruins of Tiahuanaco (see Map 12.3). Initial occupation may have occurred as early as 400 B.C.E., but significant urbanization began only after 200 C.E. Tiahuanaco's expansion depended on the adoption of technologies that increased agricultural productivity. Modern excavations provide the outline of vast drainage projects that reclaimed nearly 200,000 acres (8,000 hectares) of rich lakeside marshes for agriculture. This system of raised fields and ditches permitted intensive cultivation similar to that achieved by use of chinampas in Mesoamerica. Fish from the nearby lake and llamas added protein to a diet largely dependent on potatoes and grains. Llamas were also crucial for the maintenance of long-distance trade relationships that brought in corn, coca, tropical fruits, and medicinal plants.

The urban center of Tiahuanaco was distinguished by the scale of its construction and by the high quality of its stone masonry. Large stones and quarried blocks were moved many miles to construct a large terraced pyramid, walled enclosures, and a reservoir—projects that probably required the mobilization of thousands of laborers over a period of years. Despite a limited metallurgy that only produced tools of copper alloy, Tiahuanaco's artisans built large structures of finely cut stone that required little mortar to fit the blocks. They also produced gigantic human statuary. The largest example, a stern figure with a military bearing, is cut from a single block of stone 24 feet (7 meters) high.

Little is known of the social structure or daily life of this civilization. Neither surviving murals nor other decorative arts offer the suggestive guidance found in the burial goods of the Mochica. Nevertheless, it is clear that Tiahuanaco was a highly stratified society ruled by a hereditary elite. Most women and men devoted their time to agriculture and the care of llama herds. However, the presence of specialized artisans is demonstrated by the high quality construction in public buildings and in locally produced ceramics. The distribution of these ceramics to distant places suggests the presence of a specialized merchant class as well.

Many scholars portray Tiahuanaco as the capital of a vast empire, a clear precursor to the later Inca state. It is clear that the elite controlled a large disciplined labor force in the surrounding region. Military conquests and the establishment of colonial populations linked the highland capital to dependable supplies of products produced in ecologically distinct zones. Despite this cultural influence eastward to the jungles and southward to the coastal regions and oases of the Atacama Desert in Chile, archaeological evidence suggests that Tiahuanaco had, in comparison with contemporary Teotihuacán in central Mexico, a relatively small full-time population of around 30,000. It was a ceremonial and political center for a large regional population, but not a metropolis like the largest Mesoamerican cities.

The contemporary site of Huari was located about 450 miles (751 kilometers) to the northwest of Tiahuanaco near the modern Peruvian city of Ayacucho. The site was larger than Tiahuanaco, measuring nearly 4 square miles (10 square kilometers). The city center was surrounded by a massive wall and included a large temple. The center had numerous multifamily housing blocks. Less-concentrated housing for commoners was located in a sprawling suburban zone. Unlike most other major urban centers in the Andes, Huari's development appears to have occurred without central planning.

The culture and technology of Huari were clearly tied to Tiahuanaco, but the exact nature of this relationship remains unclear. Some scholars argue that Huari began as a dependency of Tiahuanaco. Others suggest that they were joint capitals of a single empire. However, there is little evidence for either position. Clearly there were sustained cultural contacts between the two societies, but each had a unique cultural signature.

Huari was distinguished by the small scale of its monumental architecture and the near absence of cut stone masonry in the construction of both public and private buildings. It is not clear that these characteristics resulted from the relative weakness of the elite or the absence of specialized construction crafts. Huari ceramic style was also different from that of Tiahuanaco. This difference has allowed experts to trace Huari's expanding power to the coastal area earlier controlled by the Mochica and to the northern highlands. Huari's military expansion occurred at a time of increasing warfare throughout the Andes. As a result, roads were built to maintain communication with remote fortified dependencies. Perhaps as a consequence of military conflict, both Tiahuanaco and Huari declined to insignificance by about 1000 C.E. Their political legacy was inherited by the Inca.

The Incas

In little more than one hundred years, the Inca developed a vast imperial state, which they called Tawantinsuyu, "the Land of Four Corners." By 1525 the empire had a population of more than 6 million inhabitants and stretched from the Maule River in Chile to northern

Ecuador and from the Pacific coast across the Andes to the hot country of the upper Amazon and, in the south, into Argentina (see Map 12.3). In the early fifteenth century the Inca were one of many competing military powers in the southern highlands, an area of limited political significance since the collapse of Huari. Centered in the valley of Cuzco, the Inca were initially organized as a chiefdom based on reciprocal gift giving and the redistribution of food and textiles. Strong and resourceful leaders consolidated political authority in the early fifteenth century and undertook an ambitious campaign of military expansion.

The Inca state, like earlier highland powers, was built on traditional Andean social customs and economic practices. Tiahuanaco had extended the traditional use of colonists to incorporate distant resources. The Inca built on this legacy by adding more distant territories through military conquest and by increasing the scale of forced exchanges. Crucial to this process was the development of a larger and more professional military. Unlike the peoples of Mesoamerica, who distributed specialized goods by developing markets and tribute relationships, Andean peoples used state power to broaden and expand the vertical exchange system that had permitted ayllus to exploit a range of ecological niches.

Like earlier highland civilizations, the Inca were pastoralists. Inca prosperity and military strength depended on vast herds of llamas and alpacas, which provided food and clothing as well as transport for goods. Both men and women were involved in the care of these herds. Women were primarily responsible for weaving; men were drivers in long-distance trade. This pastoral tradition provided the Inca with powerful metaphors that helped to shape their political and religious beliefs. They believed that both the gods and their ruler shared the obligations of the shepherd to his flock—an idea akin to the Old Testament references to "The Lord is my Shepherd."

The collective efforts of mit'a laborers made the empire possible. Cuzco, the imperial capital, and the provincial cities, the royal court, the imperial armies, and the state's religious cults all rested on this foundation. This system also creat-

ed the material surplus that provided the bare necessities for the old, weak, and ill of Inca society. Each ayllu contributed approximately one-seventh of its adult male population to meet these collective obligations. These draft laborers served as soldiers, construction workers, runners to carry messages along post roads, and craftsmen. They also drained swamps, terraced mountainsides, filled in valley floors, built and maintained irrigation works, and built storage facilities and roads. The scale of their achievements is illustrated by the construction of nearly 13,000 miles (20,930 kilometers) of road that facilitated military troop movements, administration, and trade.

Imperial administration was similarly superimposed on existing political structures and established elite groups. Hereditary chiefs at the level of the ayllu carried out administrative and judicial functions. As the Inca expanded, they generally left local rulers in place. By leaving in place the rulers of defeated societies, the Inca risked rebellion, but they controlled these risks by means of a thinly veiled system of hostage taking and the use of military garrisons. The rulers of defeated regions were required to send their heirs to live at the Inca royal court in Cuzco. Even representations of important local gods were brought to Cuzco and made a part of the imperial pantheon. These measures promoted imperial integration while at the same time providing hostages to ensure the good behavior of subject peoples.

Conquests magnified the authority of the Inca ruler and led to the creation of an imperial bureaucracy drawn from among his kinsmen. The royal family claimed descent from the Sun, the primary god in the Inca pantheon. Members of the royal family lived in palaces maintained by armies of servants. The lives of the ruler and members of the royal family were dominated by political and religious rituals that helped to legitimate their authority. Among the many obligations associated with kingship was the requirement to extend imperial boundaries by warfare. Thus each new ruler began his reign with conquest.

The Aztec capital of Tenochtitlán had a population of about 150,000 in 1520, but Cuzco at the height of Inca power in 1530 had a population of under 30,000. Nevertheless, Cuzco was a remarkable place. The Inca were highly skilled stone craftsmen: their most impressive buildings were constructed of carefully cut stones fitted together without mortar. The city was laid out in the shape of a giant puma (a mountain lion). At the center were palaces that each ruler built when he ascended to the throne, as well as the major temples. The richest was the Temple of the Sun. Its interior was lined with sheets of gold, and its patio was decorated with golden representations of llamas and corn. The ruler made every effort to awe and intimidate visitors and residents alike with a nearly continuous series of rituals, feasts, and sacrifices. Sacrifices of textiles, animals, and other goods sent as tribute dominated the city's calendar. The destruction of these valuable commodities, and a small number of human sacrifices, helped give the impression of splendor and sumptuous abundance that legitimated the ruler's claimed descent from the Sun.

Inca cultural achievement was built on the strong foundation of earlier Andean civilizations. We know that astronomical observation was a central concern of the priestly class, as in Mesoamerica; the Inca calendar, however, is lost to us. All communication other than oral was transmitted by the quipus borrowed from earlier Andean civilizations. In weaving and metallurgy, Inca technology, building on earlier regional developments, was more advanced than Mesoamerican. Inca craftsmen produced utilitarian tools and weapons of copper and bronze as well as decorative objects of gold and silver. Inca women produced textiles of extraordinary beauty from cotton and the wool of llamas and alpacas.

Although the Inca did not introduce new technologies, they did increase economic output and added to the region's prosperity. The conquest of large populations in environmentally distinct regions permitted the Inca to multiply the productive potential of traditional forms of production and exchange. But the growth of imperial economic and political power was purchased at the cost of reduced equality and local autonomy. The imperial elite was almost cut off from the masses of society, living in richly decorated palaces in

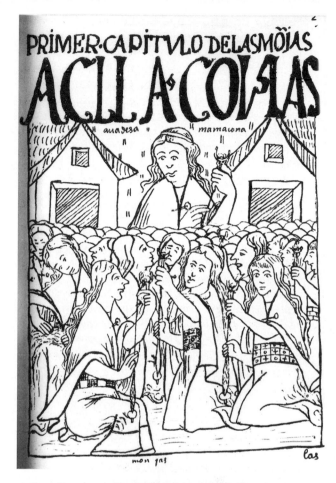

Acllas Representatives of the Inca ruler selected young virgins to serve the official religious cult devoted to Sun worship. Selection was generally seen as a sign of favor by the women's parents. Some of the women were given as wives or concubines to the Inca ruler and other favored nobles, but most lived celibate lives devoted to religious rituals and the production of beautiful textiles. This illustration drawn in the sixteenth century by Guaman Poma de Ayala, a member of the native aristocracy, shows acllas spinning thread. (Courtesy, Institut d'Ethnologie, Musee de l'Hommel)

Cuzco or other urban centers. Even members of the provincial nobility were held at arm's length by the royal court, subject to execution if they dared to look directly at the ruler's face.

The Inca Empire was in crisis on the eve of the Spanish conquest. In 1525 Huayna Capac, the Inca ruler, died, and two of his sons began a

Acllas

Acllas were young virgins selected by representatives of the Inca ruler to serve the cult of the Sun or be given as marriage partners and concubines to the Inca himself or to Inca nobles and favored nobles from dependencies. These young women were commonly chosen for their beauty from among the daughters of local rulers.

Eventually, selection came to be seen as a special sign of favor that strengthened the legitimacy and political authority of the woman's family. Yet close association with imperial power, while enhancing a family's social prestige, also weakened its traditional cultural position in the defeated community. With the passage of time, the interests of imperial and conquered elites melded. Assigning women from conquered regions as wives and concubines was essential to this process.

Our understanding of the acllas' lives and their place in Inca society is based primarily on Spanish-era sources. We know these women lived within the closely guarded walls of convent-like buildings located in the large towns of the empire and that their days were dedicated to religious observances and the production of fine textiles.

The following account was written in the early seventeenth century by Felipe Guaman Poma de Ayala. Although not a descendent of the Inca royal line, the author was proud of his high-ranking noble family. After long neglect, Guaman Poma's illustrated history of Inca and early Spanish colonial society study has become a fundamental source for Andean history. In this text, the word Inca is used to refer to both the people and to their ruler. Although obviously proud of the indigenous past, Guaman Poma's description of ancient images of gods as "idols" suggests the depth of cultural change among Amerindian people following the conquest.

During the time of the Incas certain women, who were called *acllas* or "the Chosen," were destined for lifelong virginity. Mostly they were confined in houses and they belonged to one of two main categories, namely sacred virgins and common virgins.

The so-called "virgins with red cheeks" entered upon their duties at the age of twenty and were dedicated to the service of the Sun, the Moon, and the Day-Star. In their whole life they were never allowed to speak to a man.

The virgins of the Inca's own shrine of Huanacauri were known for their beauty as well as their chastity. The other principal shrines had similar girls in attendance. At the less important shrines there were older virgins who occupied themselves with spinning and weaving the silk-like clothes worn by their idols. There was a still lower class of virgins, over 40 years of age and no longer very beautiful, who performed unimportant religious duties and worked in the fields or as ordinary seamstresses.

There was yet another class of aclla or "chosen," only some of whom kept their virginity and others not. These were the Inca's (the ruler of the Inca people) beautiful attendants and concubines, who were drawn from noble families and lived in his palaces. They made clothing for him out of material finer than taffeta or silk. They also prepared a maize spirit of extraordinary richness, which was matured for an entire month, and they cooked delicious dishes for the Inca. They also lay with him, but never with any other man.

Thus chastity was greatly prized in our country. It was the Inca who received our girls from the Sun and who allotted them, always as virgins, to his subjects. Until that time the man did not know the woman nor the woman the man. The man might be in Quito or Chile and might be assigned a woman from quite a different region but a contract of marriage was made with the help of the woman's brother.

What special qualities were most valued in the selection of acllas? What categories of acllas are described? What were their lives like? What do we know about how the Inca ruler was viewed from this description of his relationship with the acllas?

Source: From Felipe Guaman Poma de Ayala, *Letter to a King, A Peruvian Chief's Account of Life Under the Incas and Under Spanish Rule.* edited and translated by Christopher Dilke. New York: E.P. Dutton (1978), pp. 84–86.

bloody struggle for the throne. The ambitions and rivalries that divided professional military leaders from the elite of Cuzco, the resentments of conquered peoples, and the problems associated with governing a vast territorial state spread over more than 3,000 miles (4,830 kilometers) of mountainous terrain magnified the destructive consequences of the succession struggle. The scale and violence of this conflict suggest that its resolution would have imposed political and social changes as great as those associated with the collapse of earlier civilizations.

were challenged by powerful neighbors or by internal revolts. Similar challenges had contributed to the decline of earlier powers in both Mesoamerica and the Andean region. Previously, the collapse of a civilization was followed by a long period of adjustment and the creation of new indigenous institutions. With the arrival of Europeans, this cycle of crisis and adjustment would be transformed, and the future of Amerindian peoples would become linked to the cultures of the Old World.

CONCLUSION

The indigenous societies of the Western Hemisphere developed unique technologies and cultural forms in mountainous regions, tropical rain forests, deserts, woodlands, and arctic regions. In Mesoamerica, North America, and the Andean region, societies of hunters and gatherers as well as urbanized agricultural societies produced rich religious and aesthetic traditions as well as useful technologies and effective social institutions. Once established, these cultural traditions proved very durable.

The Aztec and Inca Empires represented the culmination of a long developmental process that had begun before the Olmec and Chavín civilizations. Each imperial state controlled extensive and diverse territories with populations that numbered in the millions. The capital cities of Tenochtitlán and Cuzco were great cultural and political centers that displayed some of the finest achievements of Amerindian technology, art, and architecture. Both states were based on conquests and were ruled by powerful hereditary elites who depended on the tribute of subject peoples.

The Aztec and Inca Empires were created militarily, their survival depending as much on the power of their armies as on the productivity of their economies or the wisdom of their rulers. As the Western Hemisphere's long isolation drew to a close in the late fifteenth century, these empires

SUGGESTED READING

In *Prehistory of the Americas* (1987) Stuart Fiedel provides an excellent summary of the early history of the Western Hemisphere. Alvin M. Josephy, Jr., in *The Indian Heritage of America* (1968), also provides a thorough introduction to the topic. *Canada's First Nations* (1992) by Olive Patricia Dickason is a well-written survey that traces the history of Canada's Amerindian peoples to the modern era.

Early Man in the New World, ed. Richard Shutler, Jr. (1983), provides a helpful addition to these works. *Atlas of Ancient America* (1986) by Michael Coe, Elizabeth P. Benson, and Dean R. Snow is a useful compendium of maps and information. George Kubler, *The Art and Architecture of Ancient America* (1962), is a valuable resource, though now dated.

Eric Wolf provides an enduring synthesis of Mesoamerican history in *Sons of the Shaking Earth* (1959). Linda Schele and David Freidel summarize the most recent research on the classic-period Maya in their excellent *A Forest of Kings* (1990). The best summary of Aztec history is Nigel Davies, *The Aztec Empire: The Toltec Resurgence* (1987). Jacques Soustelle, *Daily Life of the Aztecs,* trans. Patrick O'Brian (1961), is a good introduction. Though controversial in some of its analysis, Inga Clendinnen's *Aztecs* (1991) is also an important contribution.

Chaco and Hohokam (1991), ed. Patricia L. Crown and W. James Judge, is a good summary of research issues. Robert Silverberg, *Mound Builders of Ancient America* (1968), supplies a good introduction to this topic.

A helpful introduction to the scholarship on early Andean societies is provided by Richard W. Keatinge, ed., *Peruvian Prehistory* (1988). *The History of the Incas* (1970) by Alfred Metraux is dated but offers a useful summary. John Murra, *The Economic Organization of the Inca State* (1980), and Irene Silverblatt, *Moon, Sun, and Witches: Gender Ideologies and Class in Inca and Colonial Peru* (1987), are challenging, important works on Peru before the arrival of Columbus in the Western Hemisphere. Frederich Katz, *The Ancient Civilizations of the Americas* (1972), offers a useful comparative perspective on ancient American developments.

NOTES

1. This summary follows closely the narrative offered by Linda Schele and David Freidel in *A Forest of Kings: The Untold Story of the Ancient Maya* (New York: Morrow, 1990), 145–153.

2. Before 1492 the inhabitants of the Western Hemisphere had no single name for themselves. They had neither a racial consciousness nor a racial identity. Identity was derived from kin groups, language, cultural practices, and political structures. There was no sense that physical similarities created a shared identity. Racial consciousness and racial identity were imposed on America's original inhabitants by conquest and by the occupation of their lands by Europeans after 1492. All of the collective terms for these first American peoples are tainted by this history. *Indians, Native Americans, Amerindians, First Peoples,* and *Indigenous Peoples* are among the words in common usage. In this book the names of individual cultures and states are used wherever possible. *Amerindian* and other terms that suggest transcultural identity and experience are used most commonly for the period after 1492.

3. Quoted in Nigel Davies, *The Toltec Heritage: From the Fall of Tula to the Rise of Tenochtitlán* (Norman: University of Oklahoma Press (1980), 3.

4. Bernal Díazl del Castillo, *The Conquest of New Spain*, translated with an introduction by J. M. Cohen (London: Penguin Books, 1963), 217.

5. Hernando Cortés, *Five Letters, 1519–1526*, translated with an introduction by J. Bayard Morris (New York: W. W. Norton & Company, 1991), 87.

6. Quoted in Irene Silverblatt, *Moon, Sun, and Witches: Gender Ideologies and Class in Inca and Colonial Peru* (Princeton, NJ: Princeton University Press, 1987), 10.

PART FOUR

Interregional Patterns of Culture and Contact, 1200–1500

Between 1200 and 1500, dynamic events intensified cultural and commercial contacts across wide expanses of Eurasia, Africa, and the Indian Ocean. The Mongols established vast empires in Eurasia, greatly stimulating trade and cultural interaction. Muslim influence grew as well—through religious conversion, through the founding of new empires in West Africa, India, and the Balkans, and through the extension of trading networks among the Indian Ocean states and across the Sahara. In the Latin West, strong European kingdoms began maritime expansion in the Atlantic, creating direct ties with sub-Saharan Africa.

Interregional contact depended on the massive networks of trade—on both land and sea—that by the 1200s had come into existence in several parts of Eurasia and Africa. Trade on the Silk Road became even more vigorous under the Mongol empires, and men and women of many classes and occupations traveled it. From 1200 to 1500, the Mediterranean continuously served as a focus of commercial exchange for the peoples of Europe, Africa, and the Middle East. At the other end of Eurasia, both China and Japan sent regular trade missions to Southeast Asia, Indonesia, and the Philippines. Underlying the greatest maritime network, however, was the Indian Ocean, where Hindu, Muslim, Jewish, Malay, Chinese, and other merchants engaged in a vigorous and profitable trade. Indeed, Chinese fleets occasionally ranged as far as the Middle East and eastern Africa.

Between 1200 and 1500, new and more complex links developed between the cultural regions. The earliest of these were achieved by the empires of the Mongols, who arose in central Asia in the very late 1100s. Using their extraordinary command of the horse and refinements in traditional forms of military and social organization, Mongols and allied groups united under Genghis Khan in the early thirteenth century. By the later part of the century, a Mongol empire spread over Eurasia from Poland to Korea. It was segmented into four separate regimes: one based in Russia, one in Iran, one in central Asia, and one in China. Along with intensified commercial and cultural exchanges, the Mongols brought changes to the peoples and the environments of many parts of Eurasia.

Some of those changes affected local cultures, creating an early nationalist effect. Mongol rulers, who were not usually familiar with the agricultural systems or governments of the peoples they conquered, tended to seek native helpers. At the same time, the Mongols often became interested in local customs and pastimes. Consequently, they sponsored the vernacular languages and often the folk customs of the local peoples, laying a foundation for the later literatures of these countries. The political influence of the capitals the Mongols established in China, Iran, and Russia lingered after them, creating bases for the formation of new national regimes. Also long lasting was hatred of the Mongols, which unified the peoples of these regions both during and after the period of Mongol rule. Perhaps the most distinctive Mongol legacy to later centuries was the memory of a Eurasian commercial prosperity that had tied together the cities of Mediterranean Europe, the Middle East, and East Asia.

Population change stimulated use of new land and sea contacts arising in the Mongol period. After a long period of stagnation, or very slow growth, the population of the world shot up from about 200 million in 600 C.E. to over 350 million between 1200 and 1500. Scholars do not fully understand the reasons for this phenomenon but believe it may reflect climatic changes as well as improved political stability before about 1250 in China and Europe, where the greatest increases took place. The factors that halted this population growth are better known. At the end of the 1200s, the Chinese population, for instance, stood at about 100 million. In the following century that population declined by a third or more as a result of warfare, disease, and the disruption of agriculture during Mongol conquest and rule. In Europe, rapid population growth peaked at about 80 million around 1300. This produced a heavy strain on the environment before the bubonic plague—also a result of the contacts created by the Mongol campaigns—swept away millions of malnourished people. By 1500, however, the populations of both China and Europe were back to their former peaks. Chinese seeking to escape the crowding of the coastal regions migrated along the trade routes to Southeast Asia. Europeans in crowded Mediterranean cities looked outward for new sources of occupation and wealth.

The rise and fall of the Mongol empires interacted with the rise of political powers elsewhere in Eurasia. Especially worth noting are rising powers dominated by Turkic Muslims. First, Turkic war leaders from what is now Afghanistan created an imperial capital at Delhi, overwhelming the many small states that had dotted north and central India before the 1200s. Second, during the 1300s the Ottoman Turks took advantage of the weakness of the Christian Byzantine Empire to establish their rule over western Anatolia and the southern Balkans. In the late 1300s, the invasions of India and Iran by the central Asian conqueror Timur (Tamerlane) shattered the Delhi

Technology

Wind and water mills and iron and copper mining spread in China, Middle East, Europe

Sailors use dhows to ply monsoon winds of Indian Ocean

1100s–1200s—Mathematics and astronomy spread from Islamic world to Europe

1300–1450—Invention of cannon spreads from East Asia to Middle East and Europe

1300–1500—Use of movable type spreads in East Asia and Europe

1400s—Improved firearms and rise of infantry in Europe

1403–1433—Chinese imperial voyages through Southeast Asia and Indian Ocean

1454—Gutenberg Bible printed in Europe

1498—Portuguese complete sea route to India

Environment

West Africans clear fields in rain forest

1200–1500—Between 1200 and 1350, Chinese population falls from above 100 million to 60 million or 70 million; rises above 100 million by 1500

1340–1450—Bubonic plague spreads from southwest China westward across Eurasia; urban populations in Europe fall as much as 30 percent

Sultanate and stopped the growth of Ottoman power. Only after the decline of Timur's empire in the 1400s could the Ottomans reconstitute their dominion. Exploiting their knowledge of both cavalry and artillery, the Ottomans extended their sway deeper into Europe (taking the last of the Byzantine Empire in 1453) and southward into the Middle East, establishing an empire that endured into the twentieth century.

At the very end of the fifteenth century a new commercial and political force entered the Indian Ocean from politically decentralized western Europe. The stories recounted by many travelers—including Marco Polo—about the Mongol courts of Asia inspired merchants to seek greater riches in the lands bordering the Indian Ocean and in China. When European merchants found their access to the usual routes through the Mediterranean or the Persian Gulf disrupted by the expansion of Ottoman power, they sought new routes. Building on decades of explorations down the Atlantic coast of Africa, a Portuguese fleet rounded the southern tip of the continent and continued on to India in 1498. This sea route between western Europe and Asia proved more durable and adaptable than the ancient overland routes of central Asia.

Mongol, Muslim, and European expansions all amplified the transmission of technologies. Printing, compasses, crossbows, gunpowder, and firearms had all originated in Asia, and the Mongol conquests had hastened their spread westward. The recipients of these technologies significantly improved them and explored new applications. Both the Ottomans and the regional powers of Europe based their expansions on gunpowder. The Portuguese, for instance, mounted cannon on ships designed to bear the weight and withstand the recoil shock of such weapons. In circumnavigating Africa, they also employed navigational and sailing devices that put them at the forefront of maritime technology. By 1500, the Eurasian overland links that had been central to the Mongol empires were in eclipse. The armed, trade-oriented, resource-hungry empires emerging in Europe would use the seas to forge new global patterns, presenting unprecedented technological and economic challenges to the peoples of Africa, Asia, and America.

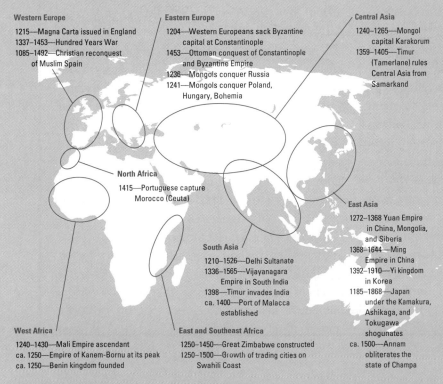

Western Europe
1215—Magna Carta issued in England
1337–1453—Hundred Years War
1085–1492—Christian reconquest of Muslim Spain

Eastern Europe
1204—Western Europeans sack Byzantine capital at Constantinople
1453—Ottoman conquest of Constantinople and Byzantine Empire
1236—Mongols conquer Russia
1241—Mongols conquer Poland, Hungary, Bohemia

Central Asia
1240–1265—Mongol capital Karakorum
1359–1405—Timur (Tamerlane) rules Central Asia from Samarkand

North Africa
1415—Portuguese capture Morocco (Ceuta)

South Asia
1210–1526—Delhi Sultanate
1336–1565—Vijayanagara Empire in South India
1398—Timur invades India
ca. 1400—Port of Malacca established

East Asia
1272–1368 Yuan Empire in China, Mongolia, and Siberia
1368–1644—Ming Empire in China
1392–1910—Yi kingdom in Korea
1185–1868—Japan under the Kamakura, Ashikaga, and Tokugawa shogunates
ca. 1500—Annam obliterates the state of Champa

West Africa
1240–1430—Mali Empire ascendant
ca. 1250—Empire of Kanem-Bornu at its peak
ca. 1250—Benin kingdom founded

East and Southeast Africa
1250–1450—Great Zimbabwe constructed
1250–1500—Growth of trading cities on Swahili Coast

Society

1220s–1260—Mongol conquests of northern China, Russia, and Iran
1295—Beginning of Il-khan conversion to Islam
1450–1500—Peasant rebellions and decline of serfdom in western Europe
1470s—Civil war in Japan results in rise of new class of warrior-commanders

Culture

1100–1300—Universities founded in Europe
After 1140—Gothic architecture in Europe
Bronze art at Ife and Benin in Nigeria
Islam spreads in Anatolia, sub-Saharan Africa, China, India, and Southeast Asia
1298—Publication of Marco Polo's Travels
1325–1354—Travels of Ibn Battuta
1368—Ming Empire reestablishes the examination system and state Confucianism in China
1378–1415—Great Schism in Western Christianity
1450–1500—Reunification of Mongolia with dominance of Tibetan Buddhism

change in the values and practices of government. In the Middle East, Russia, and East Asia generally, resentment of the Mongol occupation gave rise to aggressive nationalist feelings, which in subsequent centuries would bring grief to cultural minorities and to many neighboring states.

CENTRAL ASIA IN THE THIRTEENTH CENTURY

Large federations of nomads had dominated the steppes and deserts of Central Asia many times since the beginnings of recorded history. The Scythians, the Xiongnu (the nomadic rivals of the Han Empire), Turks, and Kitans all preceded the Mongols. The environment, economic life, cultural institutions, and political traditions of the steppes and deserts all contributed to the rise and contraction of empires. Similarly, the rise of the Mongols can be attributed at least as much to the long-term trends and particular pressures of Central Asia as to any special abilities of Genghis Khan and his followers.

Nomadism's Effects on Political and Social Organization

Nomadism is a way of life forced by a scarcity of resources. Nomadic groups have by far the lowest rates of population density. To find pastures and water for their livestock, they are continually on the move. In the course of their migrations they frequently come into contact with other nomadic groups seeking the same resources, and the outcomes of these encounters are commonly warfare, alliance, or both. In times of ecological stress such as drought, conflicts increase. The result is the extermination of small groups, the growth of alliances, and frequent outmigration from groups that have grown too large. It is believed that such a period of environmental stress afflicted northern Eurasia around 1000 C.E. and

contributed to the dislocations and conflicts out of which the Mongols eventually emerged.

Because nomads are constantly moving but also always under pressure to make their movements efficient and accurate, centralized decision making is a necessary part of their life. Nomadic groups in Central Asia frequently engaged in violence, and so every man was a full-time herdsman, full-time hunter, and full-time warrior. From childhood Mongols developed skills that were useful in wartime, such as riding and shooting arrows (see Environment & Technology: Horses). But mobility had a political effect as well, since the independence of Mongol individuals and their families forced decision making to be public, with many people voicing their views. Even at the height of a military campaign nomad warriors moved with their families and their possessions and sometimes struck off on their own if they disagreed with a decision. The political structures of the Central Asian empires all were designed to accommodate the conflicting centralizing and decentralizing forces of traditional nomadic life. Mongol groups had strong hierarchies, but the leader—the *khan*—was always required to have his decisions ratified by a council of the leaders of powerful families.

Competition for resources reinforced slavery and tribute in Central Asia. Many of the men and women captured during warfare or raids became slaves and were forced to do menial work in nomadic camps. Some individuals evidently entered into slavery willingly, to avoid starvation. Slaves were valuable not only for their labor but also as currency. Weak groups secured land rights and protection from strong groups by providing them with slaves, livestock, weapons, silk, or cash. Many powerful groups (such as the one to which Genghis Khan's father belonged) found that they could live almost entirely off tribute, so they spent less time and resources on herding and more on the warlike activities that would secure greater tribute. As each group grew in numbers and in wealth, its political institutions became more complex. Federations arose based on an increasing number of alliances among groups, almost always expressed in arranged marriages between the leading families. Children readily became pawns of diplomacy: their marriages were arranged for them in

Horses

Prior to the rise of the Mongols, the many breeds of horses in Eurasia had been improved and specialized by interbreeding with the large, quick, graceful horses of the Caucasus and the Middle East. In Mongolia, however, the early form of domesticated horse was preserved. The mounts on which the Mongols assaulted Europe looked not very different from the prehistoric horses that very early Europeans had painted on cave walls.

These ponies were an excellent example of the adaptation of traditional technologies (in this case horsebreeding) to environment. They were uniquely able to survive the very cold, very dry climate of Mongolia. Mongols never fed or sheltered their horses, so by natural selection the breed was able to survive on a minimal diet, to forage in the snow that covers some parts of Mongolia for most of the year, and to brave the plunging night temperatures of the region. The breeding technique required that the ponies be kept in a semiwild state. During the Tang Empire, the Central Asian ponies had been crossbred with specialized strains from the Middle East to produce larger, stronger, more beautiful horses. On occasion such horses were brought to Mongolia by the Turks and bred with the local horses. But only after the time of Genghis did the numbers of the Mongolian pony decline dramatically. The breed, or a near version of it, now survives only in game preserves.

Central Asian riding radically altered the conduct of war in Eurasia. The charioteers who had dominated warfare in ancient Middle East and East Asia were no match for well-coordinated and well-armed light horsemen, and chariot driving disappeared as a war art wherever extensive campaigns against Central Asian riders occurred. The Parthians of eastern Iran, whose riding skills astonished the empires of the Middle East, were legendary for their ability to shoot arrows at the enemy while retreating from them. In China, the Xiongnu drove out the chariot and forced Chinese soldiers to fight on horseback. The Huns were, for similar reasons, a revelation to Europe, which adopted the use of the iron stirrup from them.

Not only as a technology but also as a social institution, Central Asian horsemanship fundamentally altered the meaning of the horse. In the ancient Middle East, the use of horse teams and chariots in warfare was extremely expensive and demanded a select group of warriors wealthy enough to maintain their equipment and powerful enough to control grazing land for their animals. Horses had to be carefully bred to be large enough to pull the chariots and carefully trained to manage their loads with rather inefficient harnessing. In Central Asia, riding was an ability that all men and women in good health possessed. It required only a rudimentary saddle and experience. The deployment of riders in warfare blurred the distinction between a riding herdsman (or hunter) and a riding soldier, and there was no specialization of function along class lines. Because Central Asians did not enclose their herds but left them to forage, no question of individual landownership arose.

Like all their predecessors on the steppe, the Mongols were superb riders, both in agility and in endurance. They continued a tradition that Herodotus had noted among the Scythians—putting infants on goats in order to accustom them to riding. And like all Central Asian warriors the Mongols were adept at the special skill (for which there is a specialized word in all Central Asian languages) of shooting arrows from a moving horse. In Russia, the Middle East, and East Asia, the skills necessary for the use of the horse, including breeding, tacking, and military riding, were all adapted from the nomads. Under the Abbasids in western Asia and the Tang in eastern Asia, trousers became part of male dress through the influence of riding, and the sport of polo became popular, all, again, through nomadic influence.

Mongol ponies The stocky body and coarse mane of the Mongol pony are reminders of its descent from the northern ponies familiar to Paleolithic peoples of Europe. By the laws of Genghis Khan, the Mongols could not lead their ponies on the bit, but had to change to a gentle head-collar, as shown here. (National Palace Museum, Taipei, Taiwan)

childhood—in Temüjin's own case, at the age of eight. Because of the relationship between marriage and politics, women from prestigious families were often tremendously powerful in negotiation and management. And, when things became violent, they were just as likely as men to suffer assassination or execution.

Nomadic groups achieved a high degree of independence by attempting to restrict their diet to the products—primarily meat and milk—that they could provide for themselves and by wearing clothes produced from pastoral animals—felt (from wool), leather, and furs. Women generally oversaw the breeding and birthing of livestock and the preparation of furs, both of which were fundamental to the nomadic economy. But it was impossible for a large nomadic group to be completely independent forever. Trade with sedentary cultures—the agricultural societies such as

Animal husbandry In nomadic societies, it was common for men and boys to tend to the herds in the pastures. But the more technical tasks associated with animal husbandry—breeding, birthing, shearing, milking, and the processing of pelts—were usually performed by women who worked together in teams and passed the knowledge from older to younger members of the community. Their various activities are depicted in this contemporary painting. (Ulan Bator Fine Arts Museum)

Iran and China—was necessary for the acquisition of iron, wood, cotton and cotton seed, silk (the favored dress of the Central Asian elites), vegetables, and grains. Many nomads learned the value of having permanent settlements for the farming of grains and cotton, as well as for the working of iron, and they established their own villages—often with the help of migrants from the agricultural regions—at strategic points.

The result was extensive frontier regions, particularly east of the Caspian Sea and in northern China, where nomadic peoples and agricultural peoples created pluralistic civilizations in which farming, animal husbandry, ironworking, and long-distance trade were all important activities. Nevertheless, contact with the central agricultural zones, particularly in the Middle East and China, could not cease. When policy changes or economic difficulties within the sedentary societies obstructed trade, nomads frequently resorted to raiding or even to large-scale invasion to obtain what they needed.

Trade and Technology

The trade with sedentary societies that Central Asian nomads came to depend on normally benefited both groups. Because of their specialized way of life, nomads were important contributors to the industries of the cultural cores. Cotton, wool, leather, and many breeds of horses are among the products that nomadic peoples introduced to eastern Eurasia.

Iron was also important in nomadic Central Asia. It was used in bridles and stirrups, in wagons, and in weapons. Nomads did not develop large mining enterprises, but they eagerly acquired iron implements in trade and then reworked them to suit their own purposes. The Turks, for instance, had been famous for their large ironworking stations south of Mount Altai even before the rise of the Abbasid and Tang empires in the 600s. Agricultural empires in East Asia and the Middle East attempted to restrict the export of iron in any form to Central Asia. These attempts were never successful.

Central Asians not only continued to work in iron but improved many of the sedentary technologies and then exported them back to the sedentary regions. The effects of this exchange were strikingly illustrated in the seventh century, when the nearly invincible Tang imperial cavalry spread use of the Turkic iron stirrup throughout Eurasia (see Chapter 11). The Mongols retained the traditional Central Asian reverence for the qualities of iron and the secrets of ironworking. Temüjin, Genghis Khan's personal name, meant "blacksmith," and several of his prominent followers were sons of blacksmiths. The name of a later conqueror, Timur, meant "iron" in Turkish.

Movement and Cultural Diversity

The nomads of Central Asia were transmitters of cultural influences across Eurasia. Many of these influences were religious. As we have seen, Central Asian nomads aided in the spread of Manichaeism, Judaism, Christianity, and Buddhism across the continent. By the end of the Abbasid and Tang eras, Turkic nomads of Central Asia were increasingly active in the transmission of Islam, which quickly eroded the dominance of Buddhism, particularly in the cities of Central Asia. On the steppe, however, a mix of religious affiliations remained. There it was not unique to find within a single family individual believers in Buddhism, Manichaenism, Islam, Christianity, and Judaism, in combination with traditional shamanism (the ancient practices by which special individuals visited and influenced the supernatural world).

This plurality of religious practice reflected the fact that Central Asian nomads did not always associate ideas about rulership with ideas about religion. Since very early times, Central Asian societies had been permeated by the idea of world rulership by a khan, who, with the aid of his shamans, would speak to and for an ultimate god, represented in Central Asia as Sky, or Heaven. It was believed that this universal ruler, by virtue of his role as the speaker for Heaven, would transcend particular cultures and dominate them all. This idea may have derived from Iranian influences. It was evident in the government of the Xiongnu and was explicitly stated on numerous occasions in the Turkic empires. This idea was extremely important in the rise of the Mongols. It permitted them to appeal to any and all religions to legitimate their rule. And it authorized the Great Khan to claim superiority over all religious leaders.

Genghis Khan at first patronized only the Mongol shamans. Soon, however, he seemed to listen to the arguments of Buddhists, Daoists, Christians, and Muslims, all of whom believed they were about to convert the Great Khan and his family to their beliefs.

Unification of Eurasia and Overland Exchange

Religious zeal, hopes for power and wealth, and curiosity drew learned men, religious leaders, and merchants over long distances to the Mongol courts. These journeys produced travel literature that gives us vivid insights into the Eurasian world of the thirteenth century. The accounts were intriguing to their contemporary readers. Chinese and Westerners alike regarded the diet and hygiene of the Mongols as shocking and their powers of endurance as nearly superhuman. Some narratives, such as that of the Venetian traveler, Marco Polo (1254–1324), freely mixed the fantastic with the factual, to the delight of the audience. Most important, these books left an image of the inexhaustible wealth of the Mongols, and of Asia generally, that created in Europe a persisting ambition to find easier routes to Asia for trade and conquest.

Though the accounts of these travelers mesmerized readers for centuries, their unembellished experiences were not rare for their time. In the towns they visited in Central Asia or China, they regularly encountered other Europeans, sometimes from their own home regions. Some were travelers and some were captives, but all were part of the steady flow of people across Eurasia in these times. The economic, political, and cultural benefits of this traffic were great. Technical knowledge, whether of pharmacology, engineering, mathematics, or financial management, flowed between China and Iran.

At the same time, the steady stream of knowledge between Europe and the Middle East was widened by Mongol policy and occasionally by Mongol competition. For instance, the wish of the Mongols in the Middle East to drive the

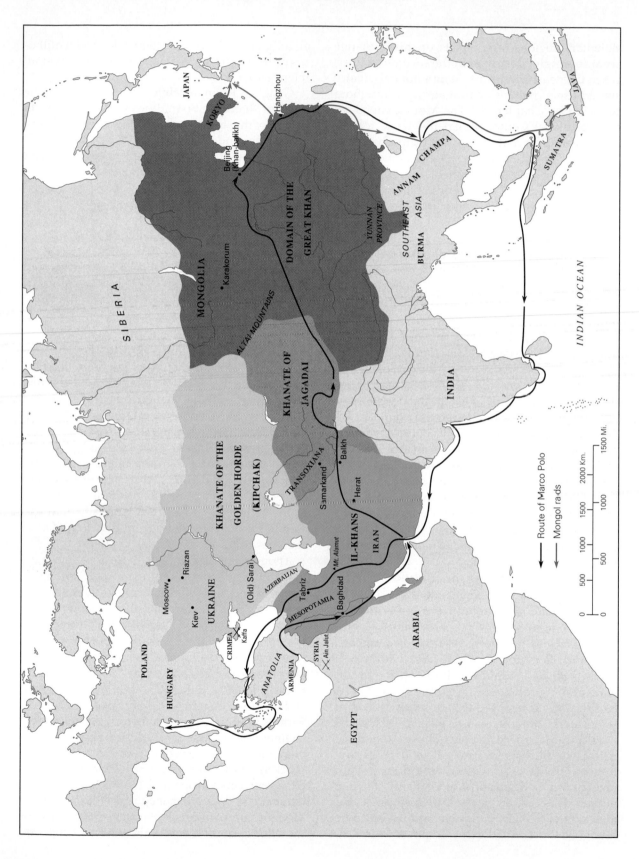

SIBERIA

JAPAN

KORYO

Hangzhou

Beijing (Khan-balikh)

MONGOLIA

Karakorum

ALTAI MOUNTAINS

DOMAIN OF THE GREAT KHAN

YUNNAN PROVINCE

ANNAM

CHAMPA

SOUTHEAST BURMA ASIA

INDIA

INDIAN OCEAN

SUMATRA

JAVA

KHANATE OF JAGADAI

KHANATE OF THE GOLDEN HORDE (KIPCHAK)

TRANSOXIANA

Balkh

Samarkand   Herat

IL-KHANS   IRAN

Moscow   Riazan

Kiev   UKRAINE

(Old) Sarai

AZERBAIJAN   Mt. Alamut

Tabriz

Baghdad

MESOPOTAMIA

POLAND

HUNGARY   CRIMEA   Kaffa

ANATOLIA

ARMENIA   SYRIA   Ain Jalut

EGYPT   ARABIA

→ Route of Marco Polo

⇒ Mongol raids

1500 Mi.

2000 Km.

1500

1000

1000

500

500

0   0

Mongols of Russia out of the Caucasus in the 1260s helped create a half-century of complex diplomacy in which Muslims often allied themselves with the European sponsors of the Crusader states—sometimes against Christians, sometimes against the Mongols. When the Mongols in Russia granted a special trade charter to merchants from Genoa, the Mongols in the Middle East granted a similar privilege to traders from Venice. It was this policy that brought Marco Polo, his uncles, and many others across Eurasia (Map 13.1). And it was probably also by this route that the cosmological ideas and technical knowledge of scholars working under Mongol patrons were communicated to Europe and helped to profoundly change its intellectual life.

There were also great dangers to the exchange. Europe had been free of bubonic plague —the Black Death (see Chapter 16)—since about 700. The Middle East had seen no plague since about the year 1200. In southwestern China, however, the plague had festered continuously in Yunnan province since the early Tang period. In the mid-thirteenth century, Mongol troops arrived in Yunnan and established a garrison. From that point, the military and supply traffic into and out of Yunnan provided the means for flea-infested rats carrying bubonic plague to be ferried from Yunnan to central China, to northwestern China, and across Central Asia. Along the routes, marmots and other desert rodents were massively infected and passed the disease on to dogs and to people. The caravan traffic across Central Asia infected the oasis towns, where the rats and fleas could disembark from overloaded camels, covered wagons, and the wagon-mounted felt tents (*yurts*) of the nomads. Finally, the Mongols themselves were incapacitated by the plague during their assault on Kaffa in Crimea in 1346. They withdrew, but Crimea was infiltrated by plague. From there, both Europe and Egypt would be repeatedly in-

Map 13.1 The Mongol Domains in Eurasia about 1300
Following the death of Genghis Khan in 1227, the empire was broken up into four large parts for his descendants: The Il-khans (founded by Hulegu) in the Middle East, the Golden Horde (founded by Batu) in southern Russia, the Jagadai khanate (founded by Genghis' son) in Central Asia, and the Yuan empire (founded by Khubilai) in eastern Asia.

Paisa The Mongol empire that united Eurasia in the middle 1200s provided good roads and protection for the movement of products, merchants, and diplomats. Under this system, individuals often traveled from one culture area to another via many intermediate zones, constantly encountering new languages, laws, and customs. The *paisa* (from a Chinese word for "card" or "sign"), with its inscription in Mongolian, proclaimed to all that the traveler had received the permission of the Khan to travel through the region. Europeans learned the practice and later applied it to travel through their small and diverse countries. The *paisa* was thus the ancestor of our modern passports. (The Metropolitan Museum of Art, neg. #257002)

fected by fleas from rats seeking the comfort of ships bound across the Mediterranean.

Bubonic plague was only one of the diseases at work, weakening the resistance of urban populations in particular and unleashing new waves of latent illness. Typhus, influenza, and smallpox traveled with the plague. The combination of these and other diseases created what is often called the "great pandemic" of 1347–1352. The human and cultural damage that resulted was far greater than any of the direct consequences of the Mongol military conquests. It is tempting to associate the social disorder of conquest and the plague as twin illnesses, but it was not the Mongol invaders who brought the disease westward. Rather, trade made possible by the Mongols assured the safety and order of the Eurasian trade routes. Peace and profit, in this case, were the channels by which pandemic illness terrorized Eurasia in the mid-fourteenth century.

THE FALL AND RISE OF ISLAM

Shortly after being acclaimed the Great Khan in 1206, Genghis began to carry out his plan to convince the kingdoms of Eurasia to surrender tribute to him. The ensuing two decades saw the bursting forth of Mongol aggression in nearly all directions. The earliest sustained action was westward, against Central Asia, the Middle East, and Russia. Genghis Khan died in 1227, possibly of the effects of alcoholism, but the campaigns continued. The Tanggut and then the Jin empires were destroyed, and their territories were put under Mongol governors (see Chapter 14). In 1236 a major offensive in the Russian territories gained the Mongols control of all the towns along the Volga River (see Map 13.1). Under siege by the Mongols in the 1230s, Europe would have suffered grave damage in 1241 had the Mongol forces not lifted their attack because of the death of the Great Khan Ogodei, and the necessity to head east for the election of a new Great Khan. After the installation of the new Great Khan Guyuk in 1246, Mongol pressure on the Middle East intensified and climaxed in 1258 in the capture and sacking of Baghdad and the murder of the last Abbasid caliph (see Chapter 10).

Mongols and Muslims

By 1260 the Mongols under Genghis' son Hulegu (ca. 1217–1265) controlled parts of Armenia and all of Azerbaijan, Anatolia, Mesopotamia, and Iran. The rulers of this regime became known as Il-khans, or "secondary" khans, subordinate only to the Great Khans in Mongolia. The role of

Muslims in the Mongol conquest of the region known as Transoxiana was critical. There is evidence that some members of the Mongol imperial family were believers in Islam before the Mongol assault on the Middle East, and Mongols frequently relied upon Muslims as advance men and intermediaries. In addition, certain of the Il-khans showed favoritism toward some Muslim groups. Hulegu, for instance, was a Buddhist but was inclined to give privileges to the Shi'ite sect to which his most trusted adviser belonged. As a whole, however, the Mongols under the command of Hulegu were slow to become exposed to the Muslim religion.

In the same way that the Mongols had utilized Muslim resentment against nonbelievers in their conquest of cities in Central Asia, they utilized Christian resentment of Muslim rule in their seizure of some cities in Syria (where Christians were a large group), forcing the conversion of mosques to churches. When Baghdad, which had been the capital both of the Abbasid caliphs and of the Seljuk sultans, was captured by the Mongols in 1258, Hulegu agreed to the requests of his Christian wife that Christians be sought out and put in prominent posts. More shocking to the Muslim world was the murder of the last Abbasid caliph. In accordance with Mongol customs for the execution of high-born persons, he was rolled in a rug and trampled to death by horses, to prevent his blood from spilling on the ground.

Until the end of the thirteenth century, the Il-khans were officially adherents of Buddhism, and they championed that religion in Iran and Iraq. One reason was conflicts between the doctrines of Islam and the Mongol way of life. A most stubborn problem was the contradiction between the traditional shamanic method of animal slaughter among the Mongols, which required that no blood be spilled, and the Islamic code of cleanliness, *halal*, which required the draining of blood from the carcass. Litigation on this and closely related matters flooded the law courts of the Il-khans. For their part, Muslims were repelled by the Mongol worship of idols that is fundamental to shamanism, and were unwilling to forgive the apparently wanton murder of the caliph in 1258.

Islam posed other dangers to the Mongol mission in the Middle East. At the time that Hulegu was leading the Mongol armies into Iran and Iraq, Mongols were also conquering southern Russia, north of the Caspian Sea. By the 1260s the Mongol leader in Russia had declared himself a Muslim, announced his intention to avenge the last caliph, and claimed the Caucasus, between the Black and Caspian Seas. By this route, the Mongols of Russia could gain direct access to the Il-khan territories, and particularly to the capital at Tabriz in Azerbaijan. The conflict was the first between the Mongol domains, and the fact that one of the parties was avowedly Muslim led the leaders of Europe to believe that they could enlist the other party, the Il-khans, to drive Muslims out of the contested religious sites in Syria, Lebanon, and Palestine. The result was a brief diplomatic correspondence between the Il-khan court and Pope Nicholas IV (r. 1288–1292) and an exchange of ambassadors that sent two Christian Turks—Markuz and Rabban Sauma—on a remarkable tour of western Europe as Il-khan ambassadors in the late 1200s.

The Il-khans, who were still Buddhists, attempted to enlist the aid of European countries to eject the Golden Horde—the Mongols based in southern Russia—from the Caucasus. Many Crusaders individually enlisted in the Il-khan effort, and some were later excommunicated by the pope for doing so. For their part, the Mongols in Russia attempted to forge a Muslim alliance with the Mamluks in Egypt, to oppose the Crusaders and the Il-khans. The net result was prolongation of the life of the Crusader kingdoms in Palestine and Syria and of European influence there; the Mamluks did not succeed in completely ejecting them until the fifteenth century.

Before the Europeans could realize their plan of allying with the Mongols, the new Il-khan, Ghazan (1271–1304), declared himself a Muslim in 1295. Ghazan had been convinced to convert by his prime minister and confidant, Rashid al-Din Fadl Allah, who was a convert from Judaism to Islam.

It was years before the Il-khans made the crucial decision to support Sunna and not Shi'a Islam, but they were not completely consistent. Some of the Il-khans were baptized Christians as children, and at least one Il-khan reversed dynastic policy and supported Shi'ism instead of Sunnism. Nevertheless, the public stance of the Il-khans as Muslims radically changed the relationship of state and religion in the Middle East. The Il-khans, like all the large Middle Eastern states before them since the time of Muhammad, were the declared protectors and advocates of Islam, and all Mongols under the Il-khans were ordered to convert to Islam. The Il-khan legal code was ordered brought into agreement with the principles of Islam.

Technologies of Conquest

The Mongols were particularly creative in the use of cavalry, and they exploited the special properties of the Mongol bow. These bows could shoot one-third farther (and were significantly more difficult to pull) than Middle Eastern or European bows of the same period. Their accuracy was improved not only by the composite structure of the bows but also by the use of a jade thumbring to allow the archer's hands to withstand the tremendous tension of the drawn bowstring.

Mounted Mongol archers rarely exhausted the five-dozen or more arrows they carried in their quivers. At the opening of battle, they used these arrows from a distance to destroy the ranks of enemy marksmen, then rode their swift horses virtually without challenge into sword, lance, javelin, and mace combat against enemy infantry. The Mongol cavalry met its match only at the Battle of Ain Jalut (Spring of Goliath) near Jerusalem in 1260, where it confronted the forces of the Mamluks, who had also based their war techniques on the riding traditions of Central Asia. Thus it was Central Asian knowledge that prevented the westward advance of the Mongols toward the Mediterranean seaboard.

The Mongols besieged walled cities with flaming arrows, then with enormous projectiles—frequently also on fire—hurled from catapults. The first Mongol catapults were taken from the Chinese and, though easy to transport, had short ranges and poor accuracy. From the defeated Khwarazmshahs in Central Asia the Mongols adapted a catapult design that was half again as powerful as the Chinese catapult, and with this improved weapon they set upon the cities of Iran and Iraq.

Mongol warfare The Mongols were in a long line of Central Asian conquerors who had mastered the art of shooting arrows from a galloping horse. They were renowned not only for their mobility, but the unusual distance and accuracy their archers could attain. This was largely due to the distinctive compound bow of the Mongols, which was more difficult to pull but much deadlier than the bows of Chinese or European archers. In combination with the advantage of using this deadly weapon from a speeding horse, the bow allowed the Mongols to overcome conventional infantry. (Courtesy, Edinburgh University Library)

Populations within the cities faced the prospect of immediate slaughter by the Mongols if they opened their gates to fight, or slow starvation followed by slaughter if they did not. On the other hand, the invaders offered their prospective victims food, shelter, and protection if they surrendered without a fight. The terrible bloodletting that the Mongols inflicted on cities such as Balkh in their early conquests gave staggering force to these appeals, and throughout the Middle East the Mongols found populations willing to acknowledge their overlordship in return for life. With each captured city the "Mongol" armies swelled in number, so that by its middle stage the conquest was accomplished by a small Mongol elite overseeing armies of recently recruited Turks, Iranians, and Arabs.

Muslims and the State

The original strategy of the Il-khans was to extract wealth from the country by peaceful means whenever possible but in any case to extract the maximum. This goal was most efficiently achieved through taxation, and the Mongols in many of their domains became masters of extraction. The method they used is generally called *tax farming*, a practice well developed in the Middle East before the coming of the Mongols. The government sold contracts for the collection of taxes to small corporations, most of which were owned by merchants who might work together to finance the caravan trade, small industries, or military expeditions. Those who bid to produce the highest revenues won the contracts and then proceeded by their own methods to collect the tax. The corporation kept anything over the contracted amount.

The short-term results for the government were good, for with a minimum of bureaucratic overhead the state collected large amounts of grain, cash, and silk. But the long-term results were different. The exorbitant rates to which the countryside was subjected drove many landowners into debt and servitude and prevented the reinvestment necessary to maintain productivity. Because many taxes were collected in kind, the price of grain rose so much that the government had difficulty in procuring supplies for the soldiers' granaries. As a consequence the state was forced to appropriate land to grow its own grain. These estates joined religious land grants, *auqaf*, in being tax exempt, and the tax base shrank further even though the demands of the army and the Mongol nobility for revenue continued to grow.

Economic troubles had become acute by the time Ghazan became Il-khan in 1295 and converted to Islam. To address the economic crisis, Ghazan appealed to the humane values of Islam and announced his intention to lessen the government's tax demands. At the same time, he used the international contacts of the Mongol empire to seek new methods of economic management. He believed he found one in the Chinese practice of using paper money, and at the time of his accession to the throne he ordered that paper money be used. But because the peoples of the Middle East had no previous exposure to paper money and no confidence in its value, the economy quickly sank into a depression from which it did not recover until after the end of the Il-khan period in the middle 1300s.

After Ghazan, the Il-khans experienced a slow decline that was like the decline of Mongol regimes elsewhere. The extraction of revenues from the population for the support of the Mongol military elite caused widespread popular unrest and elite resentment. The Mongol nobles themselves competed fiercely for the decreasing revenues, and fighting among Mongol factions destabilized the government. As the power of the Il-khans fragmented, the expansive ambitions of Mongols north of the Caspian were aroused again. In the mid-fourteenth century, the Mongols of the Golden Horde came down through the Caucasus into the western regions of the Il-khan empire and soon into the Il-khan's central territory, Azerbaijan. The Golden Horde aided in the dismemberment of the Il-khan empire and briefly occupied its major cities.

As the power of the Il-khans in the Middle East and of the Mongols in Russia weakened in the fourteenth century, a new power emerged in

Islamic conversion   The Il-khan ruler Ghazan (r. 1295–1304) was the first Mongol lord of Iran to convert to Islam. When a majority of Mongols in Iran followed his example, the Middle East became once again an overwhelmingly Muslim region, which altered balances of power in Europe, Russia, and Egypt. Il-khan law was altered to accommodate Islamic principles, and economic reforms were begun to alleviate the distress of farmers. But in many ways Ghazan remained Mongol. In this painting he is shown side by side with his primary wife, a standard practice in depicting Mongol leaders. She retains her distinctive Mongol hairstyle, while Ghazan is dressed in traditional Mongol robes and boots. (Bibliotheque Nationale de France)

Central Asia, where the Mongol rulers were descendants of Genghis's son Jagadai (d. 1242). Under the leader Timur (1336–1405), the Jagadai khanate drew on the political traditions of the Mongols and on Islam. The campaigns of Timur in western Eurasia were even more brutal than earlier Mongol campaigns had been, and by the late fourteenth century much of the Middle East was once again united under a single ruler. The Timurids (descendants of Timur) held the Middle East together long enough to deepen and consolidate Islamic influence, and they laid the groundwork for the later establishment in India of a Muslim Mongol regime, the Moguls, in the sixteenth century. But Timur was the last great Central Asian conqueror. After his time Central Asia was no longer the crossroads of Eurasia, as it had been since the earliest times.

Art and Science in Islamic Eurasia

Thanks partly to the wide-ranging cultural exchange fostered by the Mongols, the Il-khans and Timurids presided over a brilliant period in Islamic civilization. Many of the intellectual developments of the era had a strong direct effect on Europe. Others had an indirect but equally important influence. The sharing of artistic influences and political ideas between Iran and China created the illusion in European eyes that east of the Mediterranean there existed an "Orient" that was uniform in its tastes and its political cultures. In fact, the intimacy of Iran and China was a product of the millennia of Silk Road trade and only more recently of the Mongol Empire. It was not evidence of any fundamental "Oriental" character. Timur was not successful in his wish to reunite Iran and China under Mongol rule, but he made possible the advancement of some specific arts because of his practice, followed by his descendants, of forcibly concentrating scholars, artists, and craftsmen in his capital.

The historian Juvaini, who noted Genghis Khan's deathbed speech, was a central figure in literary development. His family came from the city of Balkh, which the Mongols devastated in 1221. At that time the family switched allegiance to the Mongols, and both Juvaini and his older

brother assumed high government posts. Juvaini had among his interests the composition of historical works. Il-khan Hulegu, seeing an opportunity to both immortalize and justify the Mongol conquest of the Middle East, enthusiastically supported Juvaini's projects. The result was the first comprehensive narrative describing the rise of the Mongols under Genghis Khan.

Juvaini's work and his methods—he often was critical of his subjects—were the inspiration for even more profound work by Rashid al-Din, the prime minister of the later Il-khan, Ghazan. Rashid al-Din completed the first attempt at a history of the world. It contains the earliest known general history of Europe, based on information from European monks. Editions of Rashid al-Din's world history were often richly illustrated with pictures adapted from European paintings to depict European persons or events and from Chinese paintings to depict Chinese people or events. In this way, the principles of watercolor composition and portraiture in China—where watercolor painting was extremely well developed—were introduced into Iran, where they exercised a lasting influence. Reproduction and distribution of Rashid al-Din's work spread throughout Eurasia knowledge of the arts and histories of the lands under Mongol rule.

The cosmopolitan influence of Rashid al-Din's world history was personified by Rashid himself. As a Jew converted to Islam, serving the Mongols and traveling very widely in their service, he was aware of many cultures and many points of view. He was in constant touch with the officials of Central Asia and China. When he could not see them in person, he often wrote letters to them explaining his ideas on economic management. It was partly as a result of these lines of communication that similar financial and monetary reforms occurred at roughly the same time in Iran, Russia, and China. Rashid was above all practical. It was he who advocated conducting government in accord with the moral principles of a majority of the population, and it was he who convinced Ghazan to convert to Islam.

Under the Timurids, the magnificent achievement of the Il-khan historians was augmented. Timur himself was acquainted with the greatest historian and geographer of the age, Ibn Khaldun (1332–1406), a Moroccan. Like his Mongol predecessors, Timur was an enthusiastic supporter of historical narratives in which he himself acted as the primary informant. In a scene reminiscent of the times when Ghazan had sat patiently answering Rashid al-Din's questions on the history of the Mongols, Timur and Ibn Khaldun sat in Damascus, exchanging historical, philosophical, and geographical viewpoints. Like Genghis, Timur saw himself as a world conqueror, so the story of his conquests was necessarily the story of the world. At their capitals of Samarkand and Herat (in modern-day Afghanistan), later Timurid rulers sponsored historical writing both in Iranian and in Turkish. Under them, the art of illustrating historical and fictional works, employed so strikingly in Rashid al-Din's history, reached a very high point of development.

Juvaini had accompanied Hulegu in 1256 in the campaigns against the Assassins, a radical religious sect, at Mount Alamut, and he worked to preserve the enormous historical archives that

Jonah and the whale Rashid al-Din was Ghazan's closest advisor. Rashid was a Jew who converted to Islam, and was influential in Ghazan's decision to become a Muslim. In addition to his roles as bureaucrat and political advisor, Rashid was one of the most important historians who ever lived. With the encouragement of Ghazan and of Ghazan's successor as Il-khan, Rashid completed the first comprehensive world history, drawing upon sources from Latin, Greek, Arabic, Persian, Mongolian, and Chinese. The work was illustrated with distinctive art from the regions he discussed, relating their folklore and artistic styles. In this panel, the story of Jonah and the whale is depicted. (Courtesy, Edinburgh University Library)

the Assassins maintained there. It was possibly the archives and libraries of the Assassins that had drawn the multi-talented Shi'ite believer Nasir al-Din Tusi to Mount Alamut, where Mongol forces took him into custody. Hülegü was quickly charmed by Nasir al-Din and used him in ensuing years as one of his most trusted advisers.

Nasir al-Din was interested in history, poetry, ethics, and religion, but his outstanding contributions were in mathematics and cosmology. He drew on the work of the great poet and mathematician of the Seljuk period, Omar Khayyam (1038?–1131), to lay the foundations for complex algebra and trigonometry. The impact of Nasir al-Din's work on later thinkers was considerable. A group of his followers, working at their Maraga observatory and academy near the Il-khan capital of Tabriz in Azerbaijan, were able to solve a fundamental problem in classical cosmology.

In astronomy and in mathematics, Islamic scholars had preserved and elaborated on the insights of the Greeks. They adopted the cosmological model of Ptolemy, which assumed a universe with the Earth at its center and the Sun and planets rotating around it in circular orbits. Astronomers knew Ptolemy's model was flawed, because the motions of the five visible planets were not in agreement with its predictions. Since Ptolemy's time, astronomers and mathematicians of the Middle East had been searching for mathematically consistent explanations that would account for the movement of the planets and reconcile them with Ptolemy's model.

Nasir al-Din proposed such a model. His approach was based on a concept of small circles rotating within a large circle, changing vectors in such a way as to account for their movement when viewed from the Earth. A student of Nasir al-Din reconciled the model with the ancient Greek idea of epicycles (small circles rotating around a larger circle) to explain the movement of the moon around the earth, and here occurred the breakthrough that changed cosmological thought. The mathematical tables and geometric models of this student were later transferred in their entirety to Europe and became known to the Polish astronomer Nicholas Copernicus (1473–1543). The means of transmission is still one of the tantalizing unknowns in world his-

tory. Copernicus adopted the lunar model as his own, virtually without revision. He then proposed that the model of lunar movement developed under the Il-khans was the proper model for planetary movement also—with the planets moving around the Sun.

Europe was indebted to the Il-khans not just for cosmological insights. Perhaps because of the Central Asian nomads' traditional dependence on the stars to guide their movement, or because of the suitability of high, dry, Central Asia for astronomical observation, Central Asian empires —particularly the Uigurs and the Seljuks—had excelled in their sponsorship of observational astronomy and the making of calendars. Under the Il-khans, Maraga became a sort of world center for the prediction of lunar and solar eclipses. Astrolabes, armillary spheres, three-dimensional quadrants, and other instruments in use there were much more precise than those used earlier.

The Il-khans made a deliberate attempt to amass at their observatory astronomical data from all parts of the Islamic world, as well as from China. In this way they achieved unprecedented accuracy in the prediction of eclipses. The predictions of the Il-khan astronomers were translated into Arabic for use in the hostile Mamluk territories. Byzantine monks took them to Constantinople and translated them into Greek. They were taken to Muslim Spain and translated into Latin. They were taken to India, where the Sultan of Delhi ordered them translated into Sanskrit. The Great Khan Khubilai was so impressed that he demanded a team of Iranians to come to Beijing to build an observatory for him. The Timurids continued to sponsor large observatories. Indeed, the Timurid ruler Ulugh Beg (1394–1449) was an astronomer and actively participated in the construction of the great observatory at Samarkand.

Such work required a system for writing numbers that would give mathematical calculations a precision that was not possible with the numerical systems inherited—both in the Middle East and in Europe—from the Greeks. By the 700s, Middle Eastern scholars had adapted the Indian numerical system, including the symbol for zero, to their own script. This advance made possible work on the level of the Nasir al-Din group. Until Leonardo of Pisa (also called Fibonacci, the discoverer of Fibonacci's Numbers) studied Iranian texts and used them to introduce Europeans to the abacus in the 1200s, Europeans were still using the clumsy Roman numerals to do their calculations. In his text, Leonardo adapted the "Arabic" numerals of the Middle East and in this way introduced columnar calculation and the zero. With this technology, Europeans were finally able to participate again in the study of complex mathematics, astronomy and astrology, music theory, and logic—scholarship that had begun in the ancient Greek world and had been advanced in Islamic and Indian civilizations.

The Timurids continued the Seljuk and Il-khan policies of sponsoring advanced work in astronomy and mathematics that integrated the traditions of Eurasia, and they underwrote another major advance in mathematics. Ghiyas al-Din Jamshid al-Kashi, in his studies of Chinese calendars, noted that Chinese astronomers had long used a unit for the measurement of new moons that was calculated as 1/10,000th of a day. It appears that this was the inspiration for al-Kashi's use of the decimal fraction, by which quantities less than 1 may be represented by the manipulation of a marker to show place value (a technology to which the zero was also crucial). With this means for representing decimal fractions, al-Kashi went on to propose a far more precise calculation for *pi* (π) than had been achieved since the value was established in classical times. This innovation, too, was transmitted to Europe by way of Constantinople, where al-Kashi's famous work on mathematics was translated into Greek in the fifteenth century.

NATIONAL DEFINITION IN RESPONSE TO THE MONGOLS

Major features of Iran and Iraq under the Il-khans were characteristic of many regions that the Mongols occupied. One was a marked disparity between the fortunes of the cities and the countryside. After the conquest, the volume of safe, reliable overland trade

Ulugh Beg's observatory The Timurid ruler Ulugh Beg (1394–1449) continued the reunification of Central Asia and the Middle East under Islamic rule that had begun under his grandfather Timur (Tamerlane). Even before the rise of the Mongols, empires of Central Asia had been distinguished for their achievements in observational astronomy and in calendar making. The foundations of Ulugh Beg's observatory near Samarkand are still standing, though the instruments have all been removed and the most distinctive feature is the gigantic groove in the floor that once guided the canopy around the enclosure. (Novosti)

throughout Eurasia economically stimulated many of the commercial cities of Iran and Iraq. But the countryside, subjected to extensive damage in the conquest, sporadically continuing violence, and crushing taxes, suffered terribly. Although from the time of Ghazan the Il-khan policy changed from maximum extraction from the rural sector to a policy that was more constructive and protective, the change came too late to stop the decline in population and further deterioration of agriculture.

There were also distinctive cultural changes under the Il-khans and Timurids. Both empires were inclined to promote the use of the written Iranian language, often in connection with popular or secular forms of writing such as poetry, epic writing, and songs. Similarly, both showed a strong interest in popular religious practices, especially the mystical form of Islam known as *Sufism*. This was somewhat in tension with the official stance of the later Il-khan and the Timurid courts as adherents of Sunna orthodoxy.

After 1500 a new regime was established in Iran, the Safavids. They were not Iranian—they were part of the ongoing westward migration of Turkic peoples that began before the Mongols and continued after them. Nevertheless, they were able to position themselves against the Mongols and Timurids, using nationalist sentiments to unite the population. In contrast to the Il-khans and Timurids, for instance, the Safavids were not Sunnites but Shi'ites. Yet the tools they used to create a nationalist consciousness—the Iranian language, popular religion, the geographical unity of Iran itself—were products of the Il-khan and Timurid periods. Thus, both by direct and indirect influence, the Mongol period shaped Iran as an early modern "nation."

Similar dynamics can be observed in Russia. In the Middle East the Mongols ended the long period of the political and cultural dominance of Baghdad and encouraged the emergence of new centers of power and commerce. In Russia the Mongols ended the dominance of Kiev and encouraged the rise of Moscow. As when they first occupied Iran, the Mongols in Russia had little interest in the dominant religious system. But in Russia, as we shall see, the distance between the Mongols and the local people never moved the Mongols to become patrons of the local religion.

The result was not only survival of the religious hierarchy but also the strong association of the Russian Orthodox Church with native identity and aspirations to independence. In connection with these religious influences, the Russian language for the first time became the dominant written language of Russia. Finally, in Russia as elsewhere, the Mongols were an impetus to centralization. In the aftermath of the Mongol period, Russia's strongest leaders and its most centralized political system emerged.

Russia and Rule from Afar

The first conflict between the Kievan state and the Mongols occurred in 1223, when the Mongols defeated a combined Russian and Kipchak (a Turkic people) army in southeastern Russia. The great onslaught did not come until the late 1230s, when a series of defeats for the Russians climaxed in the capture and spectacular pillage of the town of Riazan. Unlike others who invaded Russia before and after, the Mongols were capable of successful winter campaigning and found that only the springtime mud of Russia hindered their cavalry. The Russian princes failed to unite to oppose the invaders, and in 1240 the central town of Kiev fell. The princes of Hungary acknowledged the superiority of Genghis's grandson Batu (d. 1255) shortly afterward, and the entire region came under Mongol domination. Batu and his descendants established their own regime and were known as the "Golden Horde" (see Map 13.1). This was really a collection of small khanates, many of which survived when others died out at the end of the 1300s. The White Horde, for instance, ruled much of southeastern Russia until the 1480s, and the khan of Crimea was not overthrown until 1783.

The Mongols placed their capitals at the ends of the overland caravan routes, which were the infrastructure of their empires. But in Russia only the region at the mouth of the Volga could be connected to the steppe networks. Therefore the Mongols of the Golden Horde settled well to the south and west of their Russian domains, at Sarai just north of the Caspian Sea. As part of their rule-from-afar, the Mongols allowed great privileges to the Orthodox Church, which aided in reconciling the Russian population to their distant masters. Old Church Slavonic was revived, Russian chronicle-writing remained vigorous, and Greek was shunned by Russian scholars even though the khans of the Golden Horde gave their blessing to renewed contacts with Constantinople. The Golden Horde also enlisted Russian princes to act as their agents (primarily their tax collectors and census takers) and frequently as their ambassadors to the court of the Great Khans in Mongolia.

As in their other domains, the Mongols' primary concern in Russia was the extraction of wealth. The flow of silver and gold into the hands of the Mongols starved the local economy for currency. Like the Il-khans, the Khans of the Golden Horde attempted to introduce paper money. So vivid was the impression left by this Mongol innovation that the word in Russian for money (*denga*) comes from the Mongolian word for stamp (*tamga*).

Mongol domination strongly affected urban development and population movement in Russia, in part because of the role played by Alexander Nevskii (ca. 1220–1263), the prince of Novgorod. Alexander aided in the Mongol conquest by persuading many of the Russian princes that it would be better to submit to the Mongols than to resist them. In recognition of Alexander's service, the Mongols favored both Novgorod (under the rule of Alexander) and the emerging town of Moscow (under the rule of Alexander's brother Daniel). These towns eclipsed devastated Kiev as political, cultural, and economic centers during the period of Mongol domination. This, in turn, encouraged people to move northward, away from the Mongol pasture lands in the southwest, and it led to the opening of new agricultural land far north of the Caspian Sea. During the 1300s, Moscow emerged as the new center of Russia, and control of Moscow was equivalent to control of the entire country (see Map 13.2).

Russia preserved reminders of the Mongol presence for many years. Some regions of southern Russia, particularly Crimea, remained breeding grounds for the bubonic plague long after the caravans that were encouraged and protected by the Mongols had introduced the disease. In the late Kievan period, the Ukraine had been a fertile

and well-populated region. But under the Mongols, the Ukraine underwent a severe loss of population. The Mongols crossed the region repeatedly in their campaigns against eastern Europe and raided it continually to discipline villages that were slow to hand over their tax payments.

Historians debate the effect of the Mongol period of domination on the shaping of Russia. The destructiveness of the Mongol capture of Riazan, like the capture of Balkh in the Middle East,

Transformation of the Kremlin Like many peoples of northern medieval Europe, the Russians of the Kievan period had preferred to build in wood, which was easy to handle and comfortable to live in. But the fortification of the important political centers, which were vulnerable to assault, had to be constructed of stone. In the 1300s, the city of Moscow emerged as a leading political center, and its old palace, the Kremlin, was gradually transformed from a wooden to a stone structure. (Novosti)

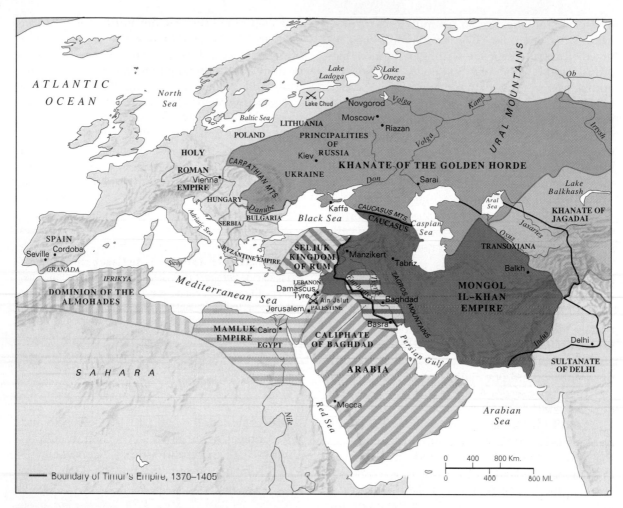

Map 13.2 Western Eurasia, 1258–1405 This map of the Mongol domains in the Middle East demonstrates the delicate balance of power that was upset by Ghazan's conversion to Islam in 1295. The Golden Horde became Muslim first, and began the first war between the Mongol domains in the 1260s when they combatted the Il-khans for control of the Caucasus, between the Black Sea and the Caspian Sea. Europeans hoped to exploit the conflict by enlisting the Il-khans against the Mamluks, but realized the cause was lost after Ghazan became Muslim. The Mamluks and the Golden Horde remained allies against the Il-khans, which aided Europeans in retaining their lands in Palestine and Syria.

seems to many to be typical of the Mongol conquests. In the opinion of many historians—as well as the eighteenth-century Russian poet Alexander Pushkin—the Mongol conquest of Russia and parts of eastern Europe isolated Russia from the great currents of development in early modern Europe, including the secularizing, neoclassical movements often called the *Renaissance* (see Chapter 16). These historians refer to

"the Mongol yoke" and hypothesize a sluggish economy and a dormant culture under the Mongols.

Other historians offer a different interpretation. They point out that the Kievan economy was in decline well before the coming of the Mongols and that the Kievan princes had already ceased to mint money. In addition, even though the Mongols' demands were high and their internationally oriented monetary measures sometimes inappropriate, the Russian territories regularly managed to pay their taxes in silver. These tax payments in silver suggest regular surpluses in income and an economy sufficiently well developed to make the conversion of goods to cash convenient. It is also clear that the tax burden was significantly increased not by the Mongols directly but by their tax collectors, Russian princes who often exempted their own lands from the tax and shifted the additional burden to the peasants. When the princes requested and received a lowering of the tax rate from the Mongols, the outcome was not necessarily more money in the hands of the common people.

More problematic is the cultural argument. Before the Mongol invasion, Russia was under the domination of the Byzantine Empire, which was not greatly affected by the Renaissance in western Europe. Prior to the time of the Russian ruler Peter the Great (r. 1682–1725), who did in fact establish strong relations with western Europe in the late 1600s, it is hard to see how Russian elites would have circumvented the influence of the Orthodox Church, with or without the influence of the Mongols.

The Mongols in Russia, as elsewhere, tended to undermine the local elites or to alter the status of individuals within the elite in order to enhance their ability to control the country. In the specific case of Russia, the question is whether the Mongols destroyed the traditional forms of elite participation in government. It does not appear that they did. There is good evidence that the structure of local government in Russia did not change significantly in this period. On the regional level, the princely families continued to battle among themselves for dominance as they had in the past. The Mongols were merely an additional factor in those struggles. It was Ivan III, the prince of Moscow (r. 1462–1505), who established himself as an autocratic ruler in the late 1400s. Before Ivan, the title *tsar* (from "caesar"), by which the rulers of Russia after the Mongols were known, had previously been used only for foreign rulers (whether the emperors of Byzantium or the Turkic khans of the steppe) who had dominated the disunited principalities of Russia. After being free of Mongol dominion, Russian leaders adopted the title *tsar* to show that Russia should be ruled by Russians and not from afar. This nationalistic response was not unlike others that occurred in the regions that for a time came under Mongol rule.

At the peripheries of Eurasia were countries that encountered the Mongols but remained independent. In many cases, these regions experienced the same upwellings of nationalist sentiment that arose in countries under Mongol domination. Yet those societies that were challenged but not conquered also tended to experience a centralization and strengthening of their institutions of command. It is probable that the long life of many of these regimes is partly due to the challenge of the Mongols, and the same is true for those regions where new, centralized, well-defined nations arose.

Social Change and Centralization in Europe and Anatolia

Communications between the Il-khans and Constantinople gave Europe a second doorway (Spain provided the first) to the scientific and philosophical achievements of Islamic culture. However, there were more direct consequences of the Mongol Empire for Europe. One was a shift in the power balances in the Middle East. Another was the invasion of Europe by Mongol forces in the very late 1230s and the 1240s.

The division of the western part of the Mongol Empire between the Golden Horde and the Il-khans had a parallel in the division of Europe at the same time between the political forces of the papacy and those of the Holy Roman Emperor and hereditary ruler of the German territories, Frederick II (r. 1212–1250) of the Hohenstaufen family (see Chapter 16). Frederick had been raised in Sicily and was sympathetic to Muslim culture. When the pope threatened Frederick with excommunication unless he participated in the Crusades waged by Europeans to capture religious sites in Palestine and Syria, Frederick conspired with the Mamluks to present the illusion of having captured Jerusalem.

Attempts by European leaders—including the popes—and the Il-khans to forge a diplomatic alliance against the Golden Horde alarmed the

Mamluks. They suspected that the Roman Catholic Church would use the alliance to destroy Frederick's power and then would turn its full force on the Mamluk territories in Syria and Egypt. In defense, the Mamluks created their long-lasting alliance with the Golden Horde. Frederick and his son Manfred became magnets for the hopes of some Islamic groups. The Assassins, who had been banished by the Seljuks to their stronghold on Mount Alamut and lived in fear of the Mongol onslaught, sent their ambassadors to Frederick in Sicily. The pieces for a medieval world war were in place.

With Europe divided between the pope and the Holy Roman Emperor, the kingdoms of eastern Europe—particularly Hungary, Poland, and Transylvania—were left on their own to deal with the onslaught of the Golden Horde. Many of the eastern princes decided to capitulate and went to Sarai to declare themselves slaves of Batu. One of the minority of the eastern groups unwilling to capitulate was the Teutonic Knights.

Like the Knights Templar in the Middle East, the Teutonic Knights had been sent on a crusade to Christianize the Slavic and Kipchak populations of northern Europe. Also like the Knights Templar, the Teutonic Knights were licensed to colonize their conquered territories, and they imported many thousands of German farmers, artisans, and clerics to populate their kingdoms. Alexander Nevskii, the prince of Novgorod, led the Mongol campaigns against the Knights and their Finnish allies, who lost so many of their number through the ice at Lake Chud that their power was broken and the northern crusades virtually ceased.

The role of Alexander Nevskii in the defeat of the Teutonic Knights is a reminder that the "Mongol" armies whom the Europeans encountered were barely Mongol at all. Commanders, of course, were Mongols. Sübüdei, who oversaw the campaigns in western Eurasia, has been ranked by historians as one of the world's great military geniuses. The Mongol policies of recruitment and conscription had created an international force in which combatants and support forces were composed of Mongols, Turks, Chinese, Iranians, and many Europeans, including at least one Englishman who went to the Middle East as a crusading knight and through capture or capitulation joined the Mongol forces, turning up in the Hungarian campaigns.

Eastern Europe came under direct assault from these forces in the winter of 1241, when the Danube River froze. Sübüdei's troops rode over it and inflicted a series of dazzling defeats on the eastern European kingdoms. Mongol forces appeared at the foot of the Alps, apparently menacing northern Italy and possibly Venice. They were also on the outskirts of Vienna. While Poles, Hungarians, Austrians, and Bohemians struggled frantically to safeguard themselves and mount some resistance, the rest of Europe was panicked by the sudden, terrifying onslaught by the unknown invaders.

Rumors and some written accounts described the Mongols as having bodies that were part dog. They were theorized to have come from Hell or from the caves where the monsters of ancient times had been banished by Alexander the Great. They were asserted to be cannibals. In Germany it was claimed that the Mongols were the lost tribes of Israel, returned, and in the eastern German territories there were instances of the lynching of Jews who were believed to be in secret alliance with the invaders. In Hungary, the recently Christianized Kipchaks were accused of aiding the Mongols; some were imprisoned, and some were killed. The king of France resigned himself to the destruction of his country, welcoming it as the will of God. The pope, despite his wish to keep pressure on Frederick II, authorized a crusade against the Mongols, and the liturgies for daily worship were altered to include a line begging God for deliverance from them.

It seemed that the prayers were answered. Before the Europeans could mount a united force to repel the Mongols, Sübüdei's forces turned and left in December 1241. The Great Khan Ögödei had died, and the Mongol princes wished to return to Mongolia to participate in the intense struggle that would elect the new Great Khan.

After the sudden retreat of Sübüdei's troops from Europe in 1241, several European leaders attempted to open peaceful channels of communication with the Il-khans, hoping through them to reach the Great Khans in Mongolia. Some

Dueling Pieties

Much of the written communication between Europe and the Mongols survives, but only as a result of an extraordinarily complex process. Europeans wrote to the Mongols in Latin, which was normally translated into Persian when the parties reached the Il-khan territories. On the route to the Mongol capital, a means had to be found to translate the Persian into Mongolian, although this translating could be done orally if the ambassadors received an audience with the Great Khan or his representatives. For messages going from east to west, the opposite process was applied.

Fortunately, the messages were not complicated, though each side found the other's ideas so bizarre that mistakes in translation were very often suspected. This passage in a letter from Pope Innocent IV to the Great Khan in 1245 is typical (Innocent did not know that there was no one to receive the letter, for Ögödei had died in 1241, and Güyük had not yet been installed as the next Great Khan):

It is not without cause that we are driven to express in strong terms our amazement that you, according to what we have heard, have invaded many countries belonging both to Christians and to others and are laying them waste in a horrible desolation, and with a fury still unabated you do not cease from breaking the bond of natural ties, sparing neither sex nor age, you rage against all indiscriminately with the sword of chastisement.

Like other popes before and after him, Innocent proceeded to explain that he was sending monks to convert the Great Khan to Christianity, to baptize him, and to make him not a waster of the Christian lands but their protector (an echo of the Prester John dream). Group after group of missionaries came from the church to convert the Mongols, and all were disappointed.

When Güyük was proclaimed Great Khan in 1246, he answered Innocent's letter. He expressed befuddlement at the idea that he should be chastised for invading Christian lands and at the suggestion that he himself should be baptized. Güyük satirized Innocent's arrogance in presuming to know God's intentions:

Though you also say that I should become a trembling Christian, worship God, and be an ascetic, how do you know whom God absolves, or in truth to whom He shows mercy? How do you know that such words as you speak are with God's approval? From the rising of the sun to its setting, all the lands have been made subject to me. Who could do this contrary to the command of God?

The Mongol Great Khans were consistent with traditional Central Asian religion in their belief that Heaven shows its will in the unfolding of history, that victors are necessarily the messengers of Heaven's will, and that the supreme victor is the supreme messenger. As often as the Popes warned the Great Khans to be baptized and submit to the guidance of the Vatican, the Great Khans responded with the simple message that they were not about to submit to the church and that all Europe had best submit to the Great Khans—or suffer the consequences.

Güyük sternly closed his letter to Innocent:

If you do not observe God's command, and if you ignore my command, I shall know you as my enemy. Likewise I shall make you understand. If you do otherwise, God knows what I know.

In 1254, the Great Khan Mongke—the last to rule the united Mongol Empire in Eurasia—used similarly ringing rhetoric on Louis IX of France:

If, when you hear and understand the decree of the eternal God, you are still unwilling to pay attention and believe it, saying "Our country is far away, our mountains are mighty, our sea is vast," and in this confidence you bring an army against us—we know what we can do: He who made what was difficult easy and what was far away near, the eternal God, He knows.

What did the Popes regard as the primary evidence that the Mongols were evil? What did the Mongols see as the basic test of their supreme righteousness?

Source: Adapted from Christopher Dawson, ed., *Mission to Asia*, Medieval Academy Reprints for Teaching Series (Toronto: University of Toronto Press, 1981), 75, 85–86, 204. Archaic language has been amended to make the quotations more readable.

kings of Europe, trade federations, and the popes sent repeated embassies to Iran, and many passed eastward toward the Mongol capital. The Mongol rulers often received merchants and craftsmen favorably, but they welcomed ambassadors from kings or from the Vatican only if they brought messages of submission from their lords (see Voices & Visions: Dueling Pieties).

European embassies to the Golden Horde and to the Great Khans in Mongolia increased in number through the thirteenth century. As Europeans learned to utilize the Mongol trade routes, and to exploit Mongol divisions in the Middle East, their terror of the Mongols was replaced by their awe of, and eventual idealization of, the wealth and power of the Mongol empires. From their contacts with the Mongols the Europeans gained their first systematic knowledge of Eurasian geography, cultural configuration, natural resources, and commerce. They learned about the use of diplomatic passports, the mining and uses of coal, movable type, high-temperature metallurgy, efficient enumeration and higher mathematics, gunpowder, and, in the fourteenth century, the casting and use of bronze cannon.

Nevertheless, Europe suffered greatly from the effects of Mongol domination of eastern Europe and Russia. The terror created by the Mongol invasion combined with other factors to ignite a storm of religious questioning and anxiety, most intense in regions of eastern and central Europe that had been virtually under the hooves of the Mongol horses. More devastating than the religious anxiety was an outbreak of bubonic plague in the 1340s (see Chapter 16). Europeans thought it was not a product of the trade encouraged by the Mongols but a disaster independently visited upon them by God.

Because in its later stages the plague can be passed from person to person by airborne particles, the crowded cities of Europe were mercilessly gutted. Overall Europe lost perhaps a third of its population in a decade, and many cities lost the vast majority of their residents. Eventually, changes in building practices, and new methods of controlling the rat population, eradicated the plague again from western Europe. However, whole strata of society, particularly those classes and occupations based in the cities, were undermined by disease.

One of the effects was the lessening of the influence of the professions and of those educated in Latin, resulting in the rise of popular culture and vernacular literatures. Thus the indirect effects on Europe of the Mongol invasion parallel the direct effects of Mongol policy throughout Eurasia: traditional elites and their languages were displaced in favor of new professional elites and literatures in local languages.

When, in the fourteenth century, the Mongol grip on eastern Europe was weakened, several regions emerged considerably centralized from the century of Mongol pressure. Lithuania was one of the European regions energized by the Mongol threat (see Map 13.2). Just as Russia fell to the Mongols and eastern Europe was first invaded, Lithuania was undergoing an unprecedented degree of centralization and military strengthening. Like Alexander Nevskii, the Lithuanian leaders struck a deal with the Mongols and maintained much independence for the country. In the late 1300s, when Mongol power in Russia was waning, Lithuania capitalized on its privileged position to dominate its neighbors, particularly Poland. Lithuania ended all hopes of a revival of the power of the Teutonic Knights in eastern Europe. In the Balkans, too, independent and well-organized kingdoms separated themselves from the chaos of the Byzantine Empire and thrived until the Turkic Ottomans conquered them in the 1500s and 1600s.

The Ottomans arose from the region of Anatolia formerly dominated by the Seljuks of Rum. In the time of the Il-khan Ghazan, the Ottomans began to struggle for autonomy on this western perimeter. As the Il-khans weakened, the emerging Ottomans gained local dominance, but Timur and his successors checked their power. Not until the disintegration of the Timurid Empire did the Ottomans gain free rein in Anatolia and parts of the Middle East. By the end of the 1400s they had delivered a fatal blow to the Byzantine navy and taken the Byzantine capital at Constantinople for their own, renaming it Istanbul. Like other empires arising in the wake of the Mongols, the Ottomans defined themselves by their opposition to the Il-khans and later to the Timurids. But in their institutions the Ottomans evinced both the Central Asian origins they shared with the Mongols and the direct adaptation of many Mongol techniques of government.

Stabilization of Mamluk Rule in Egypt

In the Middle East, the Mamluks were the outstanding example of a government that was strengthened, was centralized, and even gained some international support for its resistance to the Mongol advance. (In Abbasid times, mamluk was a term used for military slaves; later, the mamluks who established an empire in Egypt and Syria used the name Mamluk for their regime and its ruling class.) They retained control of their base in Egypt and their separated lands in Syria. During the campaigns against the Il-khans in the 1250s and 1260s, the Crusaders allowed the Mamluks to cross Palestine to maintain lines of supply and command. The Mamluks were brilliantly successful in their campaigns against the Il-khans, and this same strength was evident in the later defeat and destruction of the Crusader kingdoms. It was also demonstrated in the Mamluks' ruthless suppression of the well-organized and violent Assassins, which made the Mamluks one of the pillars (far more reliable than the Il-khans) of Sunni orthodoxy in the Middle East.

Mamluk society, particularly in Egypt, became very diverse. In the Abbasid and Seljuk eras the Mamluks had been Turkic immigrants from Central Asia, but by the thirteenth century the military servants who gave their name to the regime were drawn from sub-Saharan Africa, from parts of Europe, and from throughout the Middle East. Under the Mamluks, Egypt remained a military dictatorship until the forces of the Ottoman Empire conquered it in the 1500s. Even then, the Mamluks persisted as the dominant elites in Egypt until Napoleonic times at the end of the eighteenth century.

The Mamluks were cosmopolitan and practical in outlook. They continued their friendship

Western Eurasia, 1200–1500

1206	Temujin chosen as Genghis Khan of the Mongols
1221–1223	Mongol attacks on Iran, Russia
1227	Death of Genghis Khan
1241	Death of Ogodei, withdrawal of Mongol forces from Eastern Europe
1242	Alexander Nevskii defeats the Teutonic Knights
1258	Mongols take Baghdad, kill last Abbasid caliph
1260	First war between Il-khans and Golden Horde
1295–1304	Reign of Ghazan Khan in Iran
1346	Plague outbreak at Kaffa
1370–1405	Rule of Timur in Central Asia
1462–1505	Ivan III unites Russia under rule of Moscow

with the Hohenstaufen family and sent the Syrian diarist and judge Jamal al-Din Muhammad ibn Salim as ambassador to Frederick's son Manfred in Italy. Mamluk links with the Golden Horde, established during the conflict with the Il-khans, kept a steady stream of people and goods moving by ship between Cairo and Russia, particularly the port of Kaffa in Crimea. Historians now know that Kaffa was the primary point of embarkation for carriers of the plague to points on the Mediterranean, and it was by this route that Egypt suffered a continuing tragedy.

From the late 1300s to the very end of the 1700s, the Mamluks and their successors continued to import soldiers from Crimea. At the height of the fourteenth-century pandemic, Egypt may have lost as much as a third of its population. Lebanon, Palestine, and Syria all had many towns receiving caravan traffic from the east and ship traffic from the Mediterranean, and although plague spread swiftly through the urban populations, the epidemic was brief. Egypt, however, was continually reinfected by the traffic from Crimea, where plague lingered into the modern period.

CONCLUSION

Despite the official enmity and disdain that later national governments expressed against the Mongols, the effects of the Mongol occupation in the Middle East were profound. In Iran under the late Abbasid and Seljuk orders, the decentralization of control had effectively divided the country into northern and southern halves. The Il-khans destroyed those regimes and united Iran under their control. They also fostered the elevation, wider application, and standardization of the written Iranian language. The Timurids, by their patronage of Sunni doctrine, inspired their opponents to identify with Shi'ism and often with ecstatic sects such as Sufism. Thus, both positively and negatively, the period of Il-khan and Timurid domination established the terms of nationalism that became very important under the succeeding Safavid state.

Similarly, it was both by positive and negative influences that the Mongols helped to establish the terms of national identity in Russia. To efficiently control the Russian territories, the Mongols stabilized the rule of the Russian princes and solidified the control of powerful families over certain towns and cities. In this way, native control was unbroken during Mongol domination of Russia and parts of eastern Europe. In Russia, the Mongols showed the same favoritism toward the native language that they had shown in Iran. And as in Iran, the Mongols not only tolerated but strengthened the identification of the established religion with regional identity. Under the Russian leaders who succeeded the Mongols, the Orthodox Church would become a symbol of Russian nationhood.

Finally, in the same way that the Mongols ended the domination of the city of Baghdad in the Middle East, they ended the domination of Kiev in Russia. By establishing new centers, the Mongols redefined the elites, reshuffled the hierarchy of elite families, and shifted patterns of population. Moscow was largely a creation of the Mongols, and its continuing centrality in Russian life is a mark of the cultural and structural impact of the period of Mongol domination. Indeed, centralized government in Russia was an inspiration of the Mongols. Iran, which had a long history of unity and centralization, had been disunited during the late Abbasid centuries and was reunited under the Mongols.

It is important to compare the experiences of the Mongol domains to the Mongol peripheries. The domains frequently gained national definition and cultural coherence under the Mongols, and many sectors of the economy benefited economically from their participation in the Eurasian trade system. But in general their century or so of subjugation left them drained of wealth, sometimes demographically depressed, and—ironically—deprived of the technological stimulation they might have gained had the Mongols not imposed on them nearly a century of peace.

The peripheries, in contrast, frequently integrated themselves with the Mongol trade networks and enjoyed a flow of information, experience, and often wealth (as in the cases of Genoa and Venice) that aided in their growth. Under military pressure from the Mongols they tightened and strengthened their leadership (as in the cases of Lithuania and the Mamluks), or they explored new working alliances (as between the Mamluks and the Holy Roman Emperor). It was at the peripheries of the Mongol realm that Mongol influence over Eurasia was completed, and, as we shall see, the effects in eastern Eurasia were as marked as they were farther west.

SUGGESTED READING

An enormous amount has been written on the history of the Mongol Empire. An accessible recent introduction, now available in paperback, is David Morgan's *The Mongols* (1986). A more specialized study is Thomas T. Allsen, *Mongol Imperialism: The Policies of the Grand Qan Möngke in China, Russia, and the Islamic Lands, 1251–1259* (1987). Also in paperback is Rene

Grousset's classic *The Empire of the Steppes: A History of Central Asia* (1970; reprint, 1988). Two accessible but scholarly texts link early and modern Mongol history and culture: Sechin Jagchid and Paul Hyer, *Mongolia's Culture and Society* (1979), and Larry Moses and Stephen A. Halkovic, Jr., *Introduction to Mongolian History and Culture* (1985). Tim Severin's *In Search of Chinggis Khan* (1992) is a fascinating revisit by a modern writer to the paths of Genghis's conquest. The demographic effects of the Mongol conquests are outlined by William H. McNeill in *Plagues and Peoples* (1976), and Joel Mokyr discusses the technological effects in *The Lever of Riches: Technological Creativity and Economic Progress* (1990). For a thesis of global development that discusses the thirteenth century in depth, see Janet L. Abu-Lughod, *Before European Hegemony: The World System A.D. 1250–1350* (1989).

The history of Central Asia during the Mongol period, when it first came under the rule of the Jagadai khanate, is important but difficult. The best overview is S. A. M. Adshead, *Central Asia in World History* (1993). The most recent scholarly study of Timur is Beatrice Manz, *The Rise and Rule of Tamerlane* (1989).

The only "primary" document relating to Genghis Khan, *Secret History of the Mongols*, has been reconstructed in Mongolian from Chinese script and has been variously produced in scholarly editions by Igor de Rachewilz and Francis Woodman Cleaves, among others. Paul Kahn produced a readable prose English paraphrase of the work in 1984. Also of interest is the only version of the *Secret History* by a modern Mongol author: *The History and the Life of Chinggis Khan: The Secret History of the Mongols, Translated and Annotated by Urgunge Onon* (1990). Outstanding among recent biographies of Genghis Khan are Leo de Hartog, *Genghis Khan, Conqueror of the World* (1989); Michel Hoang, *Genghis Khan,* trans. Ingrid Canfield (1991); and Paul Ratchnevsky, *Genghis Khan: His Life and Legacy,* trans. and ed. Thomas Nivison Haining (1992), which is most detailed on Genghis's childhood and youth.

The best single volume in English on the Mongols in Russia is Charles Halperin, *Russia and the Golden Horde: The Mongol Impact on Medieval Russian History* (1987). A more detailed study is John Lister Illingworth Fennell, *The Crisis of Medieval Russia, 1200–1304* (1983) and those with a special interest might consult Devin DeWeese, *Islamization and Native Religion in the Golden Horde* (1994).

No single volume in English has yet been devoted to a history of the Il-khans. David Morgan, cited above, is a Persianist, and his chapters on the Il-khans in *The*

Mongols (1986) are presently the best general introduction to the history of the Il-khans in Azerbaijan and Iran. Interestingly, the great historians of the Il-khan period have been translated into several European languages. Available in English are Juvaini's history of the Mongols, Joveyni, 'Ala al-Din 'Ata Malek, *The History of the World-Conqueror, translated from the text of Mirza Muhammad Qazvini* by John Andrew Boyle (1958); a small portion of Rashid al-Din's work translated by: David Talbot Rice, *The Illustrations to the World History of Rashid al-Din,* ed. Basil Gray (1976); and *The Successors of Genghis Khan,* trans. John Andrew Boyle (1971). Equally important as illustrative reading are works related to Ibn Battuta. See C. Defremery and B. R. Sanguinetti, eds., *The Travels of Ibn Battuta, A.D. 1325–1354,* translated with revisions and notes from the Arabic text by H. A. R. Gibb (1994), and Ross E. Dunn, *The Adventures of Ibn Battuta, a Muslim Traveler of the 14th Century* (1986).

For Europe, a lively and well-known narrative is James Chambers, *The Devil's Horsemen: The Mongol Invasion of Europe* (1979). Many of the individuals who traveled from Europe to the Mongol courts—not only Marco Polo but also the Franciscan friars John of Plano Carpini and William of Rubruck—have had their accounts translated and annotated in modern editions. Christopher Dawson, ed., *Mission to Asia* (1955; reprint, 1981), is a compilation of some of the best known. But see also Frances Wood, *Did Marco Polo Really Go to China?* (1995). There is also some published material on the travels of Rabban Sauma, a Christian Turk, to Europe; the most recent and most comprehensive is Morris Rossabi, *Visitor from Xanadu* (1992). Some of the possible effects of the exposure of medieval Europe to Central Asian influence is suggested in Jacques Le Goff, *The Birth of Purgatory,* trans. Arthur Goldhammer (1984), and Carlo Ginzburg, *Ecstasies: Deciphering the Witch's Sabbath* (1991).

NOTES

1. Quotation adapted from Desmond Martin, *Chingis Khan and His Conquest of North China*:303.

CHAPTER FOURTEEN

Eastern Eurasia, 1200–1500

The Shaping of Eastern Eurasia

Social Change and National Definition in East Asia

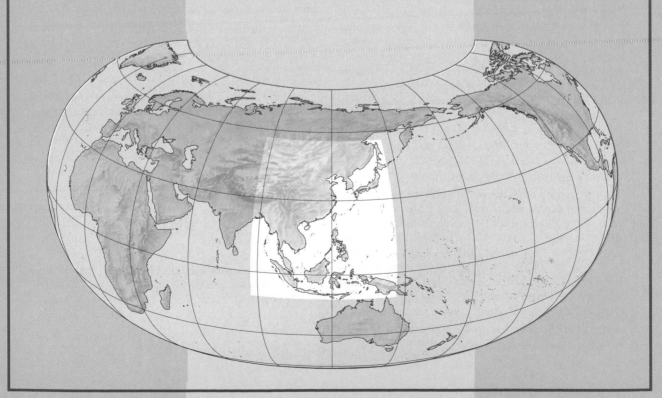

When Ogodei, Genghis's third son and successor as Great Khan, achieved stable Mongol control of northern China in the 1230s, he told his newly recruited Confucian adviser, Yelu Chucai, that he planned to turn the heavily populated North China Plain into a grazing pasture for the Mongols' livestock. Yelu was able to convince Ogodei that he could extract more wealth through taxation than by razing the cities to the ground. Ogodei quickly grasped the advantages of taxation as a means of redistributing wealth from Chinese to Mongol hands. What this oft-told story does not emphasize, however, is that the tax system Ogodei instituted was not the fixed-rate method traditional to China but the oppressive tax farming already in use in the Mongol empires of western Eurasia.

The Chinese in the early years of the Mongol occupation suffered under this system, but they also learned new sciences and technologies, thanks to the Mongols, and eventually turned them to their own ends. In eastern Eurasia as in western Eurasia, the enormous expanse of the Mongol empires and the Mongol emphasis on trade led to the spread of knowledge and skills. In western Eurasia, European countries and many Muslim cultures were able to exploit for their own military advancement or economic enrichment knowledge gained under the Mongols. Likewise in eastern Eurasia, knowledge first introduced under the Yuan Empire of the Mongols (1272–1368) enabled the societies of China, Korea, Southeast Asia, and Japan to experience unprecedented power and wealth. The economic and political practices of the Mongols, however, often created conditions that made the application and further development of these skills difficult.

Song China and Korea were able to resist the Mongols for decades, and Japan was invaded by the Mongols twice in the late 1200s but not conquered. This resistance prolonged the warfare in eastern Asia through virtually the entire thirteenth century. Technological developments of this century, particularly in warfare, were rapidly appropriated by the Mongols and disseminated westward. As a consequence, the Mongol period of Eurasian unity was a watershed in the refinement and dissemination of the technologies—both martial and peaceful—associated with gunpowder, metal casting, and the building of wagons and bridges. It also initiated the period in which large-scale trade in iron ore, sulfur, coal, and copper created new economies in eastern Eurasia. The Ming empire (1368–1644) in China and Yi kingdom (1392–1910) in Korea were beneficiaries of the technological developments that arose during the century of warfare in the 1200s.

THE SHAPING OF EASTERN EURASIA

The substitution of taxation for warfare is also a reminder of the changing effects of conflict in eastern Asia over the three centuries of the Yuan and early Ming empires. The Mongol conquest of southern China in the late 1200s marked the end of the prolonged struggle of the Song against northern invaders that had produced a centralization of government and many technological advances (see Chapter 11). After the fall of the Song, the Yuan empire absorbed much of the technology and disseminated it westward toward the Middle East and Europe. But in eastern Asia after the fall of the Yuan to the Ming in 1368 the intense need for technological advances in warfare waned, while an increase in population decreased the need to mechanize in agriculture and some manufacturing. Though, as will be discussed below, eastern Asia was a wealthy and culturally brilliant region after the fall of the Mongols, the long-term consequences for China of having no technologically innovative, ambitious rivals on the northern frontier led to a marked slowdown in technological change.

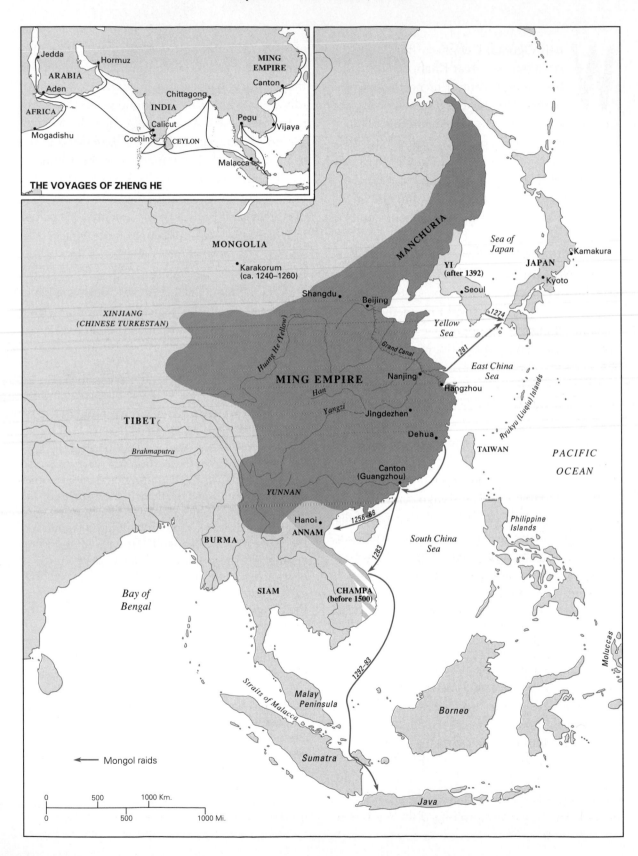

THE VOYAGES OF ZHENG HE

Jedda

Hormuz

ARABIA

Aden

AFRICA

Mogadishu

INDIA

Chittagong

Calicut

Cochin

CEYLON

MING
EMPIRE

Canton

Pegu

Vijaya

Malacca

MONGOLIA

Karakorum
(ca. 1240–1260)

MANCHURIA

Sea of
Japan

JAPAN

Kamakura

YI
(after 1392)

Kyoto

XINJIANG
(CHINESE TURKESTAN)

Shangdu

Beijing

Seoul

1274

Yellow
Sea

1281

Huang He (Yellow)

Grand Canal

East China
Sea

MING EMPIRE

Nanjing

Hangzhou

TIBET

Han

Yangzi

Jingdezhen

Ryukyu (Liuqiu) Islands

Brahmaputra

Dehua

TAIWAN

PACIFIC
OCEAN

YUNNAN

Canton
(Guangzhou)

Hanoi

ANNAM

1258–88

South China
Sea

Philippine
Islands

BURMA

1283

Bay of
Bengal

SIAM

CHAMPA
(before 1500)

Moluccas

1292–93

Malay
Peninsula

Borneo

Straits of Malacca

Sumatra

Mongol raids

Java

0   500   1000 Km.

0   500   1000 Mi.

The Impact of Trade and War

The Mongol assaults of the 1220s on the Jin Empire in northern Asia and on the Tangguts in northwestern China happened about the same time as the first Mongol invasions of Russia and the Middle East (see Chapter 13). Although the purpose of these campaigns was to convince the Jin and the Tanggut rulers to render tribute, Genghis Khan was also interested in establishing communications with the ruling elites and institutions. Buddhists, Daoists, and Confucianists from China visited the Great Khan and, like the Muslims and Christians from western Eurasia, believed that they had all but convinced him to convert to their religions or accept their philosophies. But only the religious leaders of Tibet seem to have exercised real influence over the Mongol rulers. The Tibetan idea of a militant universal ruler, bringing the whole world under control of the Buddha and thus bringing it nearer to salvation, was in agreement with the ancient idea of universal rulership in Central Asia.

Thus the Tibetan religious elite established a special place for itself in the Mongol order. In addition, Mongol leaders considered Tibet strategically important to their power in western Mongolia and Central Asia. When necessary, they supported their interests with military invasions. The Mongol Great Khans personally oversaw the governance of Tibet during the imperial period, and reinforced the dominance of the Tibetan variant of Buddhism, often called "Lamaism." A *lama* in Tibet was a teacher of special techniques for contacting the spirits, and Tibetan Buddhism was increasingly popular among Mongols after the time of Genghis Khan. After the fall of the Mongol Empire, Mongol leaders still tried to use Lamaism to legitimate themselves and to keep some portion of the Mongols united. This attempt ultimately led to invention of the title *Dalai* (a Mongolian word for "universal") *Lama* by Mongol khans in the 1500s.

Central Asia remained under the control of the descendants of Genghis's second son, Jagadai (d. 1242). In their attempts to hold on to their pastoral life, the Jagadai Mongols often came into conflict with the Yuan Empire in China, founded in 1272 by Genghis's grandson Khubilai (1215–1294) (see Map 14.1). The political prestige of the Jagadai domains and the ability of the Jagadai Mongols to defend themselves prevented the absorption of Central Asia by the Yuan. Moreover, the independence of the Jagadai Mongols contributed to the tendency of Central Asian Mongols to continue to strengthen their ties to Islam and to Turkic language and culture. Both the Islamic and the Turkic links were important to the rise of Timur in the later fourteenth century (Timur's empire is described in Chapter 13). The long-standing enmity between the Jagadai ruling family and the Yuan Empire may also have inspired Timur's wish to conquer China.

Mongolia itself had been subdued by Genghis Khan. While the Mongol Empire was united, the Mongol khans of the Golden Horde, the Jagadai domains in Central Asia, and the Il-khans in the Middle East were subordinate to the Great Khans in Mongolia. These Great Khans were chosen in the *khuriltai* gatherings of Mongol aristocrats, which took years to come to a conclusion. In the interim, the widow of the deceased Khan sometimes acted as head of the government. Genghis's son and successor as Great Khan, Ögödei (1185–1241), created the Mongol capital at Karakorum. Between 1240 and 1260 it functioned as the supreme center of the Eurasian empire. When the European missionary Giovanni di Piano Carpini (John of Plano Carpini) visited it in 1246, he found it isolated but very well populated and extremely cosmopolitan, with residents and visitors from all over Eurasia.

Karakorum disappeared virtually without a trace. The city was destroyed between 1260 and 1265 in a civil war between Khubilai and his younger brother, contesting the Great Khanship. Khubilai won, transferred his capital to China, and later declared himself the founder of a new

Map 14.1 Eastern Eurasia The Ming empire controlled China, but otherwise had a hostile relationship to peoples in Mongolia and Central Asia who had been under the rule of the Mongol emperors of the Yuan. The Mongol attempts at conquest by sea, which are marked on this map, were continued by the Ming mariner Zheng He, who between 1405 and 1433 sailed to Southeast Asia and then beyond, to India, the Persian Gulf, and East Africa.

empire, called by the Chinese name *Yuan*, meaning "origin." Some of the Mongols refused to accept Khubilai as Great Khan and withdrew further into Mongolia, where, like the Jagadai Mongols, they remained enemies of the Yuan.

To the north and east of Mongolia lived various peoples who depended on hunting, gathering, and fishing for their living. These peoples, some of whom were reindeer-riding nomads, were frequently seen in the trading villages of the region and were loosely under the control of the Great Khans. They paid the demanded tax on their trade and sometimes joined the Mongol armies. Their languages and their dress were slightly affected by the Mongols, but in general these peoples were too scattered and mobile to be effectively subjugated. In extreme northeastern Asia, these groups continued their ancient way of life and, by means of the Aleutian islands, maintained contact with the peoples of Alaska, who were their cultural and linguistic relatives.

Manchuria (see Map. 14.1) was more thickly populated and in addition to the traditional trades had a good number of farmers. Since the 600s there had been a steady influx of Chinese and Korean settlers, all of whom helped develop the agriculture and the towns of the region. Manchuria was more directly controlled by the Mongols and became their steppingstone to Korea. Using Mongolian terms and Mongol organizational institutions, the dominant indigenous people—the Jurchens, who had once ruled the area under the Jin empire—gained greater economic and military power. By the late 1400s they were a challenge to the Ming empire in China, which uneasily suppressed Jurchen power until the late 1500s.

War among these groups was frequent after decline of the Yuan empire in the middle 1300s. Overland Eurasian trade was hindered by the growing disorder but remained an important economic resource for the western and Jagadai Mongols in particular. There was also new trouble for Ming China, which hoped to bring all the Mongols under its domination and to convince them to participate in the tributary system (see Chapter 11). The Mongols did participate, but only to the extent that doing so made it easy for them to trade with the Chinese. They were other-

wise hostile, and Ming attempts to suppress a resurgence of Mongol power led to the disastrous war of the middle 1400s in which the Mongols captured the Ming emperor and briefly attacked the Chinese capital at Beijing.

The Yuan Empire

Khubilai Khan, a grandson of Genghis Khan, was the ruler among the Mongols who best understood the advantages of the Chinese traditions of imperial rule. He transferred the capital to Beijing in northern China in 1265 and reunified the Chinese territories for the first time since the Tang (see Map 14.1). The capital of Khubilai's empire, like the capitals of the regional Mongol empires, was placed at a critical spot on the overland trade routes that were the infrastructure of the Mongol world. Beijing was the easternmost terminus of the caravan routes of the Silk Road that began near Tabriz and Sarai.

Khubilai created the spirit, if not all the features that remain today, of Beijing, naming it his Great Capital (Dadu) or, as it was also called, City of the Khan (*khan-balikh*, Marco Polo's "Cambaluc"). Khubilai ordered massive mud walls built around Beijing (a tiny portion of them can still be seen) and designed the main streets to be broad and wide (Mongols needed good clear stretches for their horse runs). He also developed the linked lakes and artificial islands at the city's northwest edge as a closed imperial complex. As a summer retreat, Khubilai maintained the palace and parks at Shangdu, now in Inner Mongolia. This was the "Xanadu" celebrated by the English romantic poet Samuel Taylor Coleridge, and its "stately pleasure dome" was the hunting preserve where Khubilai and his courtiers practiced the traditional skills of riding and shooting.

When the Mongols came to Chinese territory in the 1220s, there was no "China" as we think of it today. Northern China was under the control of the Jin empire of the Jurchens, who a hundred years before had wrested it from the Liao empire of the Kitans (see Chapter 11). China south of the Yellow River was ruled by the Song. Western China was controlled by the Tangguts. Yunnan and its surrounding mountainous terrain were governed by the small Nanzhao kingdom of a people related to the Thais. These states had separate languages, separate writing systems, and variant forms of imperial government, and each had a distinctive elite culture. The Mongols had the power to subjugate or obliterate such states, co-opt or decimate their aristocracies, and impose Mongol control on them, reconstituting "China" as a base on which the Ming and later governments would stand.

In their creation of civil government in China, the Mongols did not merely copy and perpetuate the style of government that had developed under the Song. On the contrary, they introduced a radical restructuring of government. As they had in the Middle East, they put primary emphasis on counting the population and collecting taxes. In the early period, direct taxation was replaced by taxfarming in the Middle Eastern style. For this purpose the Yuan government brought to China a large number of Persian, Arab, Uigur, and Turkic administrators, who virtually controlled the offices of taxation and finance. Muslim scholars were also relied on to lead the offices of calendar making and astronomy.

By law, the status of individuals within the regime was dictated by where they or their ancestors had originated. Mongols were highest on the ladder, then came Central Asians and Middle Easterners, then came northern Chinese, and finally southern Chinese. This apparent racial ranking, it should be noted, was also a hierarchy of professions. The Mongols were the conquering caste, the warriors of the empire. The Central Asians and the Middle Easterners contributed the highly valued political functions of census taking, tax collection, and managing the calendar. The northern Chinese had come under Mongol control almost two generations before the southern Chinese and thus outranked them. The southern Chinese, the last to be conquered, were strongest in their attachment to the principles of Confucian thought.

Many Confucians were permanently alienated from the Yuan government because of their comparatively low status and their philosophical disagreements with the Yuan. The Confucians, for instance, were opposed to any elevation in status of merchants. But in the Yuan Empire, merchants were a privileged group, and most were of central Asian or Middle Eastern origin or were northern Chinese. Similarly, the Confucians regarded doctors as at best technicians and at worst heretical practitioners of Daoist mysticism. The Yuan, however, encouraged the theory and practice of medicine, and under the Yuan began the very long process of integrating the medical and herbal knowledge of China and the rest of Eurasia.

In China as in the Middle East, the Mongols found it convenient to redistrict the country for purposes of census taking and administration. China had previously been organized along the lines of the commandaries established in Qin and Han times (see Chapter 6). But the Mongols reorganized China's political administration into provinces, each one much larger than the previous units had been. Governors, tax collectors, and garrison commanders were also organized along provincial lines. The creation of the provinces was a strong assertion of Mongol ownership of the country. It marked a radical change in the regional configuration of China while increasing central control over selected matters.

Our understanding of the economy in the Yuan Empire, as in the other Mongol domains, is obscured by the vast difference between the experiences of the cities and of the countryside. The Yuan economic situation is also difficult to assess because of the scarcity of contemporary records and the influence of the later Chinese view of this period. In general, however, many cities in China seem to have prospered under the Mongols—not only the cities of north China that were on the caravan routes but also the cities of the interior that were on the Grand Canal and the well-developed cities along the coast. One outcome of the reunification of the country was the revitalization of trade between north and south China, the original purpose of the Grand Canal. Early in the Yuan period, Khubilai discovered that it was more economical to move grain from south China to Beijing by sea than by land, so the ports of eastern China also were invigorated. The urban economies were further stimulated by the reintegration of East Asia (though not Japan) with the overland Eurasian trade.

Mongol and wife (tomb painting)   Mongols who settled in China adopted many of the country's practices, including the use of tombs and of portraits on tomb walls, of the sort depicted here. But the couple are portrayed side by side according to the Mongol custom, which for a time became influential among northern Chinese. (From *Wenwu*, 1986 #4, pp. 40–46)

The isolation of Japan during the Mongol period actually helped to keep the Chinese economy stable. During the Song period, China and Japan had enjoyed a strong trade relationship (see Chapter 11). One of the Chinese exports to Japan had been copper coinage. The result of this trade had been a shortage of copper coins in China, which elevated the value of copper coins and destructively distorted the price ratio of copper to silver. There is evidence that Song trade and taxation were affected by the copper drain. But after the Mongol conquest of China, trade with Japan—which continued to resist the Mongol conquest—ceased. The stabilization in copper coinage helped encourage trade and credit in China and other regions of the Yuan Empire.

In addition to fostering long-distance transport and monetary stabilization, the privileges given merchants and the prestige they enjoyed under the Mongols changed urban life and the economy of China. The official examinations prevalent in Tang and Song times to select government personnel were suspended, and Chinese elites were eligible for only a limited number of posts in the government, many of which were hereditary. The great families who in the Song period had spent their fortunes on the education of their sons for competition in the examinations and entry into government service had to find other uses for their money. Many gentry families used their money to enter the mercantile professions, even though according to traditional Chinese values, merchants were a despised class.

Most commercial activities, from the financing of caravans to tax farming to lending money to the Mongol aristocracy, were managed through corporations. These corporations had evolved from the caravan-financing groups in the cities of Central Asia and the Middle East and were based on mutual risk sharing. In the early Yuan Empire, these corporations were mostly made up of Central Asians and Middle Easterners, but the Chinese quickly began to purchase an interest in them. Soon most of the corporations were mixed in membership, and many were entirely Chinese.

The financial and commercial life of Yuan China encouraged the gentry to live in the cities rather than in the countryside, a change from earlier times. The cities themselves began to cater to the tastes of merchants rather than to the tastes of the traditional scholars. Special shops dedicated to the sale of clothing, grape wine, furniture, and properly butchered meats (reflecting customers' religious convictions) were common. Teahouses—particularly those featuring sing-song girls, drum singers, operas, and other arts previously considered coarse— thrived. One result was a lasting cultural change: the rise of literature written in a popular style and the increasing influence of the northern, Mongolian-influenced Chinese language that in the West is often called *Mandarin.*

The countryside, where more than 90 percent of the population lived, presents a much darker picture. Cottage industries linked to the urban economies and agricultural engineering continued to advance. The cultivation of mulberry trees and cotton fields and the construction of new irrigation systems (encouraged by the Mongols, who favored the irrigation systems of the Middle East), dams, and water wheels were all common features of village technology. The production and dissemination of literature describing techniques for farming, harvesting, threshing, and butchering continued under the Mongols, and some of the most famous treatises were first published in this period. Villagers also continued to worship technological innovators as local gods. One of the most interesting of these cults began in the Yuan period: the worship of Huang

Dao Po, who brought her special knowledge of cotton growing, spinning, and weaving from her native Hainan Island to the fertile Yangzi Delta.

But the vast majority of farmers were less involved in producing cotton and other cash crops and more involved in producing rice and other staples. For them the Yuan period appears to have been one of persistent, often intense, hardship. Their troubles began with the conquests. After the fighting subsided, the Mongol princes summarily evicted many farmers from their land. Those who retained land rights were subjected to the exactions and the brutality of the tax farmers, their agents, and their enforcers. There is evidence that by the end of the 1200s the Mongol government in China had, as in Iran, begun to change its policies toward the farmers from exploitation to protection and encouragement. But, as in Iran, by this time serious damage had already been done. Many farmers had been driven into servitude or homelessness, and dams and dikes had been neglected to the point where flooding, particularly of the Yellow River, was recurring and disastrous.

In the 1340s, power contests among the Mongol princes shredded the political fabric of the Yuan Empire, and the countryside was in increasing turmoil. During this crisis, Zhu Yuanzhang, who previously had been a monk, a soldier, and a bandit, vanquished his own rivals in rebellion and established the Ming Empire in 1368.

Ming China on a Mongol Foundation

In many ways the change from Yuan to Ming was more ideological than structural. The Ming were strong in their nationalist passions, and partly to symbolize their rejection of the Mongols, they established their imperial capital at Nanjing ("southern capital") on the Yangzi River, rather than at Beijing ("northern capital") (see Map 14.1). The Ming were also aggressive in their attempts to intimidate the remaining Mongols and the other peoples of Central Asia and Southeast Asia. In these wars, Confucianism was used to depict the Ming emperor as the champion of civilization and virtue, justified in making war on uncivilized "barbarians."

But in its basic outlines the Ming government resembled that of the Yuan. In their new capital at Nanjing, the Ming built a replica of the observatory at Beijing and attached to it their own Muslim academy of astronomy and mathematics. They kept the academy that had been established for Mongol princes, and they employed Mongols who could handle the translation of communications between the Ming court and the Mongol powers of Central Asia and Mongolia. They retained the provincial style of administration, including the military garrison system introduced under the Yuan. In a continuation of Mongol social legislation, the Ming maintained hereditary professional categories. And though the reinstitution of the examinations allowed a return of the Confucian majority to the bureaucracy, the Ming also retained Muslims in the special tasks for which they had been imported by the Yuan. These tasks included the making of calendars, and the Ming continued to use the calendar promulgated by the Mongols.

In the early 1400s, the Yongle emperor (r. 1403–1421) of the Ming returned the capital to Beijing and set about improving on and enlarging the imperial complex that the Yuan had built there. Though the central part of this complex—the "Forbidden City" now visited by millions of people from all over the world each year—was elaborated in the centuries afterward, it was primarily during the 1400s that the enormous structure took on its present character, with moats, outer vermilion walls, enormous gates arranged in accordance with Chinese geomantic beliefs (see Chapter 6), golden roofs, paved interior courtyards, artificial streams, alabaster bridges, and dozens of palaces. This combination fortress, religious site, bureaucratic center, and imperial residential park was intended by the Yongle emperor to overshadow the imperial architecture at Nanjing, and in fact it is the most imposing traditional architectural complex still extant in any country. A significant portion of it is still reserved for China's rulers, closed to either foreign or native observers.

It appears that in their first half century the Ming also intended to pursue the Mongol program of aggression against Southeast Asia. This goal was partly inspired by the wish of the early Ming emperors—and the Yongle emperor in particular—to act out the role of universal ruler, which the Mongol Great Khans had embodied. Economic revitalization was also a consideration, and the Ming attempted, after an initial policy of isolation was reversed under the Yongle emperor, to restore commercial links with the Middle East. Because the hostile western Mongols controlled much of the territory through which the Eurasian land routes passed, the Ming attempted to establish their own imperial connection by sea. This was one reason for the expeditions of Zheng He from 1405 to 1433.

Historians have long been intrigued by the extraordinary adventure in Chinese seafaring that took place under the command of Zheng He in 1403 and continued sporadically until the 1430s, after Zheng He's death. The feat itself was remarkable, but to many it has appeared even more remarkable that the voyages were not continued and led to no sea-based colonialism by the Ming Empire. On the contrary, Chinese interest in the sea seemed to evaporate, and the country was set upon in the following centuries by nations that had acquired and exploited the skills that the Chinese had had earlier and then abandoned. The more closely the Zheng He episode is examined, however, the less mysterious it appears (see Voices & Visions: Pursuit and Renunciation of Universal Rule).

The Chinese and many of the peoples of Southeast Asia had been exchanging seafaring knowledge for many centuries. By the time Zheng He's fleet was outfitted, many thousands of ancestral Chinese had settled throughout Southeast Asia, in the regions ringing the Indian Ocean, almost certainly in some parts of coastal Australia, and quite possibly in some sites in eastern Africa. The hypothesis that Chinese also reached the Americas in this early period is technologically possible but unproven. From one point of view, Zheng He was merely attempting to trace the routes that the Chinese had been exploring for centuries but was doing so in a public, organized, and very dramatic way. In any event, he was a superb sea captain who believed that his exploits were measurably increasing the glory of the Yongle emperor, whom he served unflinchingly.

Pursuit and Renunciation of Universal Rule

Zheng He and his fellow eunuchs were not dispatched by the Yongle emperor to explore or to colonize. Their intention was to, in the words of the emperor, ". . . announce our Mandate to foreign nations." They had detailed maps of the regions they expected to visit and ample technical manuals for navigation. They were to attempt to open trade contacts that had been shunned in the beginning of the Ming, to seek out exotic products and medicines that would have a market in China (and be exempt from the taxes normally levied on trade), and to carry out such tasks as might seem necessary to demonstrate the universal jurisdiction of the Yongle emperor. Some of these tasks were pressing. The densely populated regions of southern China were experiencing repeated epidemics in the first years of the fifteenth century, and the herbs believed to be effective in controlling them had become impossible to attain because of the earlier ban on foreign trade. And revenue expected from the taxation of overseas Chinese populations who had lost contact with the court would be helpful in the Yongle emperor's plans for building his new capital at Beijing, sponsoring his grandiose cultural projects, and conquering the unruly Mongol groups to China's north and west.

Not all the business conducted by Zheng He and his crews focused on the pleasantries of making new friends and transporting exotic creatures. On many occasions, the troops accompanying the "Treasure Ships" got rough. In 1407 a Chinese community refused to acknowledge or pay tribute to the emperor, and it was devastated by the armada. In 1409, Zheng He decided to abduct the residents of a hostile village in Sri Lanka: "Straight away, their dens and hideouts we ravaged, and made captive that entire country, bringing back to our august capital their women, children, families, and retainers, leaving not one . . ." The next year, Zheng He gained the good will of a petty ruler in Sumatra (and demonstrated the omnipotence of the Yongle emperor) by capturing a rebel leader and bringing him to Beijing, where his execution was summarily ordered by the Yongle emperor.

The empire had enormous possibilities of expansion over land by the 1430s, and pressing responsibilities on its Mongol frontiers. Contacts had indeed been reopened with Southeast Asia, India, and the Middle East, and private traders followed in Zheng He's wake—their trade, unlike his, all to be taxed by the Ming state. When the Yongle emperor died in 1424, the greatest force behind the expeditions was gone. Government moneys were desperately needed to maintain public works and strengthen defenses in many areas. The new Xuande emperor waited long enough to show respect for the grand designs of his late father, and then ordered that

voyages should cease. He sent one of the last expeditions out with this message, a graceful fairwell to the universal ambitions that his dynasty had previously claimed:

The new reign has commenced, and everything has begun anew. But distant lands beyond the seas have not yet been informed. I send eunuchs Zheng He and Wang Jinghong with this imperial order to instruct these countries to follow the way of Heaven with reverence and to watch over their people so that all might enjoy the good fortune of lasting peace.

Moreover, after the death of the Yongle emperor, many high-ranking bureaucrats felt increasingly free to condemn Zheng He and anything he might have achieved: As a Muslim and a eunuch he was doubly repugnant to them, and there may well have been jealousy over the glamorous reputation he had procured. Not only were the voyages to cease, but all record of them—including the private accounts of at least three of the crew members— was to be suppressed.

The expeditions wasted uncountable money and grain, and moreover the people who met their deaths on these expeditions may be counted by the tens of thousands. Although he returned with wonderful precious things, what benefit was it to the state? This was merely an action of bad government of which ministers should severely disapprove. Even if the old archives were still preserved they should be destroyed in order to suppress a repetition of these things at the root.

The expeditions may indeed have been a less than efficient way to secure the goals of the Yongle emperor, but the fact is that they did succeed—which is the most important explanation for their cessation. China remained securely linked by sea as well as by land to a large number of markets, and for the remainder of the Ming period it was never again closed to foreign trade.

How did Zheng He see his mission in relation to the emperor? Why were later officials so anxious to bury the record of the Zheng He expeditions?

Source: The first three quotations are adapted from Louise Levathes, *When China Ruled the Seas* (New York: Simon & Schuster, 1993), 113, 115, 169. The fourth quotation is adapted from Joseph Levenson, *European Expansion* (Englewood, N.J.: Prentice-Hall, 1967), 88.

Because Zheng He had been castrated and entered the service of the imperial family, he was trusted to carry out a special mission from the ambitious Yongle emperor. He was also a eunuch. Thanks to Islam, he had knowledge of the Middle East. His paternal ancestors had come from the Strait of Hormuz, and both his father and his grandfather had made the pilgrimage to Mecca. Zheng He's religion also made him a good ambassador to the states of the Indian subcontinent, which was the destination of his first three voyages. On subsequent voyages similar ships reached Hormuz, sailed along the entire southern coast of the Arabian peninsula and the northeast coast of Africa, and reached as far south, perhaps, as the Strait of Madagascar (see Map 14.1).

An important objective of Zheng He's early voyages was to visit Chinese merchant communities in Southeast Asia, affirm their allegiance to the Ming empire, and demand taxes from them. If they resisted, as did a community on Sumatra, they were subject to severe military punishment from Zheng He's marines (who in Sumatra slaughtered the men of the community in question). The Ming court also hoped to establish lucrative trade relationships with the Middle East and possibly with Africa but was not successful in this. The primary achievement was to introduce the Ming empire to new countries and to sign them on as tributary states.

Zheng He's expeditions added as many as fifty new tributaries. The result was sporadic embassies to Beijing from rulers in India, the Middle East, Africa, and Southeast Asia. An early ruler of Brunei died in Beijing during such a visit and was buried at the Chinese capital with great fanfare and praise from the emperor.

The cessation of the voyages has raised many questions. Having accomplished long-distance navigation far in advance of the Europeans, why did the Chinese not develop seafaring for commercial and military gain? It might first be pointed out that the voyages of the Zheng He group were not based on developing technology. The design of the enormous junks and of the compasses that Zheng He used were not new, and neither were his navigation techniques. Most dated from the Song period (see Chapter 11). Any empire based in China since the eleventh

century that might have wanted to spread its reputation through the sponsorship of such voyages could have done so, but neither the Song nor the Yuan had considered it worth the trouble.

The expectation that the voyages would create new commercial opportunities, or awe overseas Chinese and foreign nations into immediate submission to the Ming, also was not realized. In the meantime, Japanese piracy along the coast had intensified, and the Mongol threat in the north and west had grown. The human and financial demands of fortifying the north, remodeling and strengthening Beijing, and outfitting new military expeditions against the Mongols were more than enough for a government that had outgrown its initial enthusiasm for world dominion.

Perhaps the Zheng He voyages are best seen as what people at the time understood them to be: the personal project of the Yongle emperor. This ruler had wrested control from a branch of the imperial family in 1403 and felt he was constantly being forced to prove his worthiness. In Beijing he accomplished most of the intense building that now represents the Forbidden City. He sponsored gigantic encyclopedia projects designed to collect and organize all known knowledge and literature. And he prosecuted effective campaigns against the nomadic and seminomadic peoples of Mongolia and northeastern Asia. His nearest model for what he wished to achieve in the voyages west may well have been Khubilai Khan, who also hoped to use enormous fleets of ships to demand the submission of Japan and Southeast Asia. Indeed, the self-image of the Yongle emperor was so like that of the Great Khans that he was rumored to be a Mongol.

It is important to remember that the cessation of the voyages did not represent a Chinese turning away from the sea. Zheng He's phenomenal fleet was only one episode in the saga of Chinese seafaring, which continued to be wide-ranging and vigorous after Zheng He's voyages had ceased. The question to be answered is not about Chinese involvement with the sea but about the Ming emperors' lack of interest in centralizing the organization of such voyages and turning them to military and mercantilist uses. The Ming empire was a large, complex, and constantly challenged land-based empire, and the Ming em-

Aerial of the Forbidden City   The general shape of the imperial complex at Beijing and the set of artificial lakes at its northwest corner were planned under the Mongol ruler Khubilai Khan in the late 1200s. It was during the Ming period (1368–1644), however, that the now-famous architecture was built. In addition to the gold-tiled roofs and the vermilion walls, the Forbidden City is noted for its marble-paved courtyards and three large central palaces, all set on a north-south axis that was part of a spatial pattern that the Forbidden City's planners believed would give it supernatural protection. (Reproduced by permission of the Commercial Press [Hong Kong] Limited, from *The Forbidden City*)

perors saw little reason to attempt to impose and sustain rule over distant and far-flung sea-based colonies. It was more than a century after the death of the Yongle emperor before the small, resource-starved kingdoms of Europe were forced to devise such strategies (see Chapter 16).

Technology and Population

It is tempting to link the cessation of Zheng He's long-distance voyages to the general slowdown in technological growth in Ming China, but they are two separate problems. The slowing of technological development took many forms and perhaps occurred first in mining and metallurgy. Following prodigious accomplishments during the Song period, the slowdown may have begun under the Yuan. One reason for it was the peace brought to the region by the Mongol conquest: peace removed the pressure to constantly manufacture weapons.

More surprising than the fall in the amount of mining and metal manufacture is the evaporation from China of the technical knowledge that had made possible the production of extremely high-quality bronze and steel. When instruments were cast for Khubilai's observatory at Beijing, for instance, the work was done not by Chinese technicians but by Central Asian and Middle Eastern technicians. The failure in China to preserve Song knowledge of high-temperature metallurgy has not been fully explained.

During the Ming period, Japan quickly surpassed China in the production of swords demanding extremely high-quality steel. It appears that at this time copper (which was once again draining away to Japan in the form of coins), iron, and steel had become very expensive commodities in China, so expensive that farm implements and well-caps made of these materials became prohibitive to manufacture. Shipbuilding

declined sharply, particularly after the death of the Yongle emperor in 1424. There were few advances in printing, timekeeping, or agricultural technology. Through the fifteenth century, it appears that some innovations in the mechanization of weaving occurred, but after the year 1500 such advances also became rare. Agricultural productivity peaked and remained stagnant for centuries.

The slowing of technological development might be at least partly due to the significant shift in the career patterns of educated men at this time. During the Yuan periods the examinations had been suspended, and comparatively few Chinese entered state service. Some went into the arts. But most men were not artistically inclined, and it must have been the case that commerce and agriculture in China were also

Observatory at Beijing   The Jurchens of the Jin empire were the first to build an observatory at Beijing in the 1200s. Later, the Mongols built a new observatory, expanded to include instruments designed and built by Islamic astronomers from the Middle East. In 1442 the Ming built a third observatory, at this site on Beijing's main street, with sighting tubes and armillary spheres, depicted here, built and maintained by Chinese Muslims. It was restored and enlarged by the Qing, and now is a major tourist and museum site in the capital. (Museum of History of Science, Oxford)

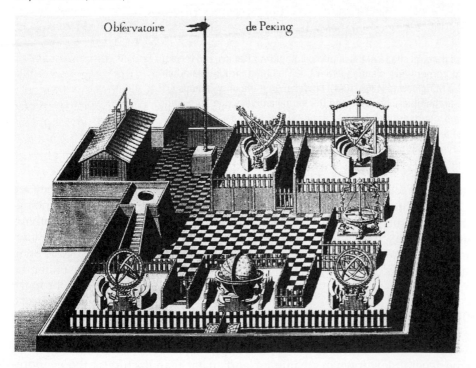

Observatoire   de Peking

stimulated in this period by China's educated, entrepreneurial elite. After the overthrow of the Mongols, the new Ming government reinstituted the examinations and began to employ large numbers of educated men in government again. The economy may have been deprived of the participation of some of its best educated, most ambitious leadership.

Another factor behind the economic and technological decline was the very rapid population growth of the early Ming period, following a steep drop in population under the Yuan. If the Song records of population levels before the Mongol conquest and the Ming census taken after the overthrow of the Mongols are reliable (each may be exaggerated in one direction or another), it appears that China may have lost as much as 40 percent of its population in the eighty years of Mongol rule. Many localities in northern China lost as much as five-sixths of their populations during the 1200s and early 1300s.

The reasons were complex. One was the continuous warfare of the 1220s due to effective resistance by the Southern Song to the Mongol invasion. Another was the massive, continuous, southward movements of population attempting to flee the Mongols. This might explain why population losses in northern China were greater than in southern China, though it is clear that the fall of the Southern Song also sparked large and panicked migrations to Southeast Asia. Among those who left was the last Song emperor, who drowned in 1279 with his entourage while trying to escape southward from Hangzhou. Those who stayed behind, particularly in the countryside, were subjected not only to crushing taxes and floods but also to the sporadic violence of the Mongol princes, Tibetan monks, and bandits.

Perhaps more important was the effect of bubonic plague and its attendant diseases, the spread of which was increased by the constant population movements of the period. The Mongol opening of Yunnan reexposed inland China to plague. The cities may have been better equipped to lessen or avoid outbreaks than the countryside. Rural portions of northern China were extensively affected by plague in the 1300s, and it is probable that the south was exposed before then. Privations in the countryside may

have been extreme enough to depress the rate of population growth, particularly if the traditional practice of female infanticide was employed.

From perhaps as low as 60 million at the end of the Yuan period in 1368, the population seems to have neared 100 million again by the year 1400. This growth is dwarfed by the population explosion of later centuries, but at the time it constituted a boom to which the economy may have adjusted very awkwardly.

The rapid growth shifted relative economic importance away from the commercial sectors, where innovation had been rewarded in the Song period, to the production of agricultural staples—primarily grain in the north and rice in the south. Staple crops, though necessary to sustain farming families and feed the rest of the population, did not have the profit margins of more specialized commercial crops and did not provide farmers with money to pay for capital improvements. Moreover, planting and harvesting were not easy to mechanize, and cheap labor caused by the growth of population may have lessened the incentives for mechanization.

Finally, remember that the materials necessary for the building of machines had become scarce. Iron was difficult to obtain, and wood was becoming expensive because of the progressive deforestation of southern and central China during the Ming period as trees were cut to provide houses and coffins for the expanding population.

The Mongols with whom the Ming were often at war were not, as the earlier imperial Mongols had been, avid students of the technological advances of the sedentary societies. They fought as their early Mongol ancestors had fought, and the Ming fought back with technology that was roughly as ancient: arrows, scattershot mortars, and explosive canisters. The Ming used a small number of cannon, but used them selectively. Thus they were not under pressure to innovate and advance in the technologies of warfare, as the Song had been (see Environment and Technology: Explosive Power).

Fear of technology transfer—whether from the state to the people or from China to foreign nations—seems evident in much of the behavior of the Ming government. Encyclopedias of practical knowledge, for instance, were produced in

Explosive Power

China is often credited with the invention of gunpowder. But anecdotal evidence in Chinese records gives credit for its introduction to a Sogdian Buddhist monk of the 500s and thus suggests that gunpowder was a Central Asian invention. The monk described the wondrous alchemical transformation of elements produced by a combination of charcoal and saltpeter. In this connection he also mentioned sulfur. Naphtha distillation, too, seems to have been a skill first developed in Central Asia, for some of the earliest devices for distilling naphtha have been found in the Gandhara region (in modern Pakistan).

By the eleventh century, the Chinese had made and used flamethrowers based on the slow igniting of naphtha, sulfur, or gunpowder in a long tube. They used these weapons not only to intimidate and injure foot soldiers and horses but also to set fire to thatched roofs in hostile villages and, occasionally, the rigging of enemy ships.

During their war against the Mongols, the Song learned to enrich saltpeter to increase the amount of nitrate in gunpowder and thereby produce forceful explosions that could cause destruction. Launched from catapults, canisters filled with the explosive material could rupture fortifications and inflict mass casualties. Ships could be set afire or sunk by an explosive hurled from a distance.

The Song also seem to have been the first to experiment with the construction of metal gun barrels from which to fire projectiles propelled by the explosion of gunpowder. The earliest of these gun barrels were broad and squat and were carried on special wagons to their emplacements. From the mouths of the barrels projected saltpeter mixed with scatter-shot minerals that were ignited by the firing of the gun. The Chinese and then the Koreans also learned to use gunpowder to shoot masses of arrows, as well as flaming arrows, at enemy fortifications. But it was the Mongols who used Song expertise to devise cannon.

In 1280, in the aftermath of the conquest of the Southern Song, the Yuan Empire produced a device featuring a projectile that completely filled the mouth of the cannon and thus concentrated the explosive force. They used cast bronze for the barrel and iron for the cannonball. The new weapon could be aimed better and shot farther than the earlier devices of the Song. Its ability to smash through brick, wood, and flesh without suffering destruction itself was unprecedented.

Knowledge of the cannon and cannonball moved westward across Eurasia. By the end of the thirteenth century, more accurate, more mobile cannon were being produced in the Middle East. By 1327, small, squat cannon called "bombards" were being produced and used in Europe (see Chapter 16, Environment and Technology: Cannon).

The development and improvement of guns and cannon by the Mongols is only one example of the application of knowledge about gunpowder. Gunpowder was used in China and Korea to do the excavation necessary for mining, canal building, and irrigation. Alchemists in China used formulas related to gunpowder to construct noxious gas pellets that they believed would not only paralyze enemies but also expel evil spirits and reduce the populations of disease-carrying insects—an aid to the colonization of malarial regions in China and Southeast Asia. And gunpowder was used in the Mongol Empire for fireworks displays on ceremonial occasions, delighting European visitors to Karakorum who saw them for the first time.

Gunpowder Though the formula for explosive gunpowder was known in China since the sixth century, it was only in the Southern Song period, as the last of China was being conquered by the Mongols in the late 1200s, that the Song devised cannon to allow gunpowder to propel large projectiles. The Mongols immediately adopted the technology, and it quickly spread to the Middle East and Europe. (British Library)

the early Ming as much as in the Song. But in the Ming case, the chapters on gunpowder and guns were censored. Ming shipyards and ports were closed to avoid contact with Japanese pirates and to prevent more Chinese from migrating to Southeast Asia. The Ming state, unlike the Song before it, did not encourage the rapid dissemination and application of technology. New crops, such as sweet potatoes, that were available were not adopted. Guns and cannon, known from contacts with the Middle East and later with Europeans, were not manufactured or used on any significant scale. Advanced printing techniques were not developed. When rapidly printed editions of rare books of the Tang or Song periods were desired, they were purchased from Korea. When superior steel was needed, it was purchased from Japan.

The Ming Achievement in Fine Arts

Despite those problems in the Ming period, the late 1300s and the 1400s were a time of cultural brilliance, particularly in literature. The interest in vernacular style that had been encouraged under the Yuan came to fruition in the early Ming in some of the world's earliest novels. One of the most famous, *Water Margin*, is based on the raucous drum-song performances famous during the Yuan (and loosely related to another famous entertainment, the Chinese opera). Its subject is the adventures of a group of dashing Chinese bandits opposed to Mongol rule (as Robin Hood and his merry men had been opposed to Norman rule). The fictional work distorts many of the original stories on which it is based, and it is clear that many authors were involved in its final commission to paper and print.

Luo Guanzhong (1330–1400), one of the authors of *Water Margin*, is the reputed author of *Romance of the Three Kingdoms*. Based on a much older series of story cycles, the saga resembles in some ways the Arthurian stories. It deals with the attempts of an upright but doomed war leader and his variously talented followers to restore the Han Empire (see Chapter 6) and resist the growing power of the cynical but brilliant villain, Cao Cao. *Romance of the Three Kingdoms* and *Water Margin* expressed much of the militant

but joyous nationalistic sentiment of the early Ming and have remained among the best appreciated fictional works in China.

The early Ming also elevated the arts and technology of porcelain, which had already been very accomplished in the Song and Yuan periods. The great imperial ceramic works at Jingdezhen, for instance, was a constant site not only of technological improvement but also of the organization and rationalization of labor (see Map 14.1). Ming patterns—most famous is the blue on white that is widely recognized as Ming "ware"—were stimulated in the 1400s by motifs from India, Central Asia, and the Middle East. In the later Ming, the foundations of a vigorous global trade in Chinese porcelain would be built on these achievements of the fifteenth century.

Nevertheless, the technological disparity between China and Europe that would have dramatic consequences in later centuries had its roots in the Ming period. It was unprecedented, for instance, for Korea to move ahead of China in the design and production of firearms and ships and in the sciences of weather prediction and calendar making. It was also unprecedented for Japan to surpass China in mining and metallurgy and in the manufacture of novel household goods. During the Ming period, China began to be afflicted with an underdevelopment complex—relative to its own past, relative to its immediate neighbors, and ultimately relative to its more distant rivals.

Continued Dissemination of Eurasian Knowledge

Despite the lack of relative material advance in China in the Ming, there was considerable growth in theoretical knowledge. During the Mongol period, technological, medical, mathematical, and astronomical knowledge was freely shared from one end of Asia to the other. Khubilai in China and Hülegü in Iran were brothers, and their primary advisers were constantly in touch. The economic and financial policies of the Yuan Empire and the Il-khans were similar, and so was their devotion to the sponsorship of engineering, astronomical study, and mathematics.

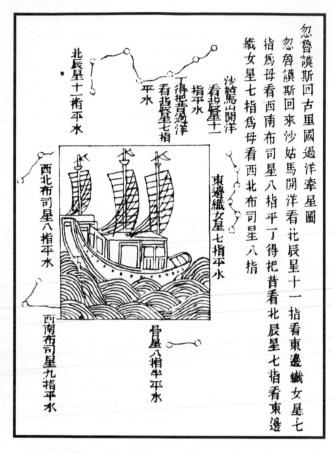

忽魯謨斯回古里國過洋牽星圖
忽魯謨斯回來沙姑馬開洋看北辰星十一指看東邊織女星七
指爲母看西南布司星八指平丁得把昔看北辰星七指看東邊
織女星七指爲母看西北布司星八指

北辰星十一指平水
看北斗辰星七指
丁得把昔星過洋
看北辰星十一指
沙鎖馬出開洋

西北布司星八指平水

西南布司星九指平水

骨星八指半水

東邊織女星七指平水

Zheng He's navigational manual The navigational techniques used by Zheng He and his crew were well established and precise, as his manual shows. Ships were guided by reference to the Pole Star, and the routes to India, the Middle East, and East Africa were well known. The manual underscores that Zheng He's mission was not to explore, but to carry out political and, if possible, economic mandates. (From the *Wubei zhi* [records of military preparations], 1621.)

as Chinese knowledge was integrated with other Eurasian knowledge at the Il-khan observatory and academy, so Il-khan science was reimported to China and Korea under Khubilai. He commissioned the Iranian philosopher Jamal al-Din to come to Beijing to construct an observatory and an institute for astronomical studies based on the Il-khans' facility at Maraga. For the remainder of the imperial period in China, maintaining and staffing the observatory continued to be regarded as an imperial responsibility. It was rebuilt in the Ming period and recently was rebuilt again, now standing on its original grounds on the main street in Beijing.

In mathematics as in astronomy, the Yuan Empire promoted an integration of Chinese skills with new ideas from the Middle East. The Chinese had contributed the concept of fractions to Middle Eastern mathematics, and Middle Easterners coming to China brought along their developments—algebra and trigonometry. In the Yuan period, brilliant Chinese mathematicians were encouraged to develop and publish their treatises. Two in particular, Guo Shoujing and Zhu Shijie, wrote and published advanced theses on mathematics, astronomy, calendrical science, and agronomy. Into the late Ming period, mathematics continued to be an obsession with some groups of scholars. Li Zhi, a descendant of Muslims who was himself a Confucian who converted to Buddhism, believed that moral realities were clearly revealed only in mathematics and dimly suggested by all other phenomena.

Islamic scholars from the Middle East were also important in the development of medicine and pharmacology in China. Before the Mongols, medicine had been a lowly profession in China, but the Yuan emperors—particularly Khubilai, who had alcoholism, gout, and many other health complaints—gave doctors an influential position. Chinese scholarship on herbs, drugs, and potions had been well developed before the Mongol period, but the introduction during the Yuan of new seeds, plants, and formulas from the Middle East stimulated an explosion of experimentation and publication. Again, it was a Ming scholar, Li Shizhen (living about the same time as Li Zhi), who brought the knowledge of previous centuries together into a encyclopedia of pharmacology.

During the Ming period in China, knowledge continued to be developed in both the government and the private spheres.

Muslims from the Middle East had overseen most of the weapons manufacture and engineering projects for Khubilai's armies. From China, the Il-khans imported the scholars and the texts that made possible their understanding of the use of many technological advances, including sighting tubes on equatorial mounts, mechanically driven armillary spheres, and techniques for measuring the movement of the moon. Just

When the Ming Empire succeeded the Yuan, the new emperors continued to employ Muslims as astronomers and calendar makers, and a few Muslim officials remained in charge of international relations with the Muslim countries. After 1368 the Ming continued the overland Eurasian trade, so Muslim livelihoods, apart from government work, were little affected by the transition from Yuan to Ming. For their overseas explorations, too, the Ming turned to Muslims and Chinese descended from Muslims (such as Zheng He), hoping to exploit the community's knowledge of outfitting, sustaining, and navigating fleets across the Indian Ocean to the Middle East and Africa.

SOCIAL CHANGE AND NATIONAL DEFINITION IN EAST ASIA

During the 1200s, the forty-five-year battle against the Southern Song led the Mongols to seek greater control of the coasts of East Asia. They hoped to find new launching sites for naval expeditions against the south and for strategic points to choke off Song sea trade. Once Korea was conquered in the mid-thirteenth century, Japan was the likely next stop. Japan was easily accessible by sea from Korea's southern tip, and from Japan's islands the coast of southern China might be controlled. But, as the Mongols were stopped in the west by the Mamluks (see Chapter 13), so they were stopped in the east by the Japanese. In both instances, there was an element of luck: the Mamluks benefited from the fact that the Mongol forces were diminished and their leaders were distracted by the need to elect a new Great Khan, and the Japanese benefited from unruly summer weather in the Strait of Tsushima and along the coast of Japan. But in both cases overextended Mongol forces were confronting strong regimes that, under pressure from the Mongols, had successfully pursued centralization and militarization.

Map 14.2 Korea and Japan before 1500 The proximity of Korea and of northern China to Japan gave the Mongols the opportunity for launching their enormous fleets. They were defeated by the warriors of the Kamakura shogunate which controlled most of the three islands (Honshu, Shikoku, and Kyushu) of central Japan. The northernmost island, Hokkaido, was not yet under colonization by Japanese settlers. It was the home of the Ainu and other Northeast Asian peoples who lived by fishing, hunting, and gathering.

Transmission and Specialization: The Case of Korea

In contrast to Ming China, other parts of East Asia after the fall of the Mongols managed to develop and use on a large scale the knowledge they had gained. A dramatic example is Korea (see Map 14.2). Formally, Korea was not a part of the Mongol Empire or the Yuan Empire, because the royal house of Koryŏ continued to govern. But in experience Korea resembles a Mongol domain. The Korean royal house became an extension of the Mongol imperial family, and Korea was subjected to the heavy tax burdens and military obligations of a Mongol domain. After the fall of the Mongols, however, a new royal family used its military knowledge to make Korea independent of China and to generate new wealth.

When the Mongols attacked in 1231, the leader of a prominent Korean family assumed the role of military commander and protector of the king (not unlike the shoguns of Japan or the hegemons of ancient China). Under this leader, Korean forces waged defensive warfare against the Mongol invaders for over twenty years, until the countryside and the Korean armies were exhausted. The cultural as well as the material losses that Korea experienced in the war were heavy. One of the most important wooden buildings in East Asia, the nine-story pagoda at Hwangnyong-sa, was destroyed, and the wooden printing blocks of the *Tripitaka*—the ninth-century masterpiece of printing art under the Koryŏ dynasty—were burned. In 1258 (the year the Abbasid caliph was executed in Baghdad) the Korean military commander was killed by his own underlings. Soon afterward, the Koryŏ king surrendered to the Mongols, and his family was joined by marriage to the family of the Great Khans.

By the middle 1300s the Koryŏ kings were mostly Mongol by descent and were comfortable with the Mongolian language, dress, and customs. Many resided at Khubilai's capital, Beijing, and the travel of the kings, princes, their families, and their entourages between China and Korea was steady. In this way, the Mongols opened Korea to direct influence from the most recent philosophical and artistic styles of China, including neo-Confucianism, Chan Buddhism (in Korea, called *Sŏn*), and celadon ceramics (see Chapter 11). Koryŏ attachment to the Mongol imperial family was so strong that when the Yuan Empire fell, Koryŏ decided to remain loyal to the Mongols and had to be forced to recognize the new Ming Empire in China. But soon afterward Koryŏ collapsed and was succeeded by the Yi kingdom in 1392.

The capacity of the Mongol Empire to facilitate the sharing of information among distant cultures strongly influenced medieval Korea.

Since the tenth century Korea had been somewhat isolated. Under the Mongols, the growing of cotton (introduced to northern China from Central Asia in Song times) was begun in southern Korea. Gunpowder, created in China but not used in artillery and firearms until the time of the Mongols, arrived in Korea for the first time. The arts of astronomical observation, at which the Chinese excelled, were combined with cosmological theories and mathematical skills from Central Asia and the Middle East, and all were introduced at once to Korea as a unified science of calendar making, eclipse prediction, and vector calculation. The direct influence of Central Asia is evident in the Korean celestial clocks built for the royal observatory at Seoul. A superficial resemblance to the Chinese celestial clock built by Su Song (see Chapter 11) is apparent in a machine that in its mechanics and its astronomical orientation is Islamic in inspiration.

The Mongols' conquest of Korea opened new avenues of advancement to Korean scholars who were willing to learn and translate Mongolian, to Korean landowners who were willing to open their lands to falconry and to grazing, to Korean merchants who capitalized on the new royal traffic to Beijing. In this and other ways, the Mongols encouraged the rise of a new, landed, educated class in Korea.

After the fall of the Mongol empires and of the Koryŏ kingdom, Korea's rulers were anxious to reestablish a national identity. Like Safavid Iran, Muscovite Russia, and Ming China, the Yi regime in Korea publicly rejected the period of Mongol domination but also adopted Mongol government practices and institutions. Mongol-style land surveys, techniques in the administration of military garrisons, and taxation in kind were all continued.

Like the Ming Empire, the Yi kingdom revived study of the Confucian classics. This scholarly activity required the Korean elites to retain their literacy in Chinese, and it also showed the dedication of the state to the promotion of reading and study. The revival of interest in the Confucian classics may have been the primary factor leading to a technological breakthrough.

Since the 700s, Koreans had been using Chinese woodblock printing, and Koryŏ later adopt-

Korean printing   Movable type was being experimented with by several peoples of eastern Asia before the Mongol period, but the Koreans were the first to create a reliable and efficient method using cast metal elements in a stable frame. Historical records first refer to the use of this method in 1234 in Korea. In combination with the phonetic system later used to write Korean in the 1400s, the country gained an unprecedented level of literacy and access to printed documents in this period. (Courtesy, Yushin Yoo)

ed the Song practice of printing from cast metal plates. These technologies were well suited to China, where a comparatively large number of literate men demanded many copies of a comparatively small number of texts. In Korea, however, the readership was comparatively small, and the range of reading demanded was comparatively great. Movable type had been used in Korea since the early thirteenth century and may have been invented there. But texts printed from movable type were frequently inaccurate and mostly difficult to read. Yi printers, working directly with the king in the 1400s, developed a reliable device to anchor the pieces of type to the printing plate. They replaced the old beeswax adhesive with solid copper frames. As a result, the legibility of the printed page improved, and high-volume, accurate reproduction of many pages in rapid succession became possible. In combination with the creation in Korea of the phonetic *han'gul* writing system (see the Environment & Technology feature in Chapter 11), this printing technology laid the foundation for a very high rate of literacy in early modern Korea.

Displaying their willingness to adapt and shape Eurasian knowledge imported by the Mongols, the Yi Koreans used the astronomical arts of the Koryŏ period to develop a meteorological science of their own. The astronomical clock and armillary spheres of the royal observatory at Seoul were augmented by redesigned and newly invented instruments to measure wind speed and rainfall, the first of their kind. Keen interest in agricultural specialization inspired the development of a local calendar based on minute comparisons with the calendrical systems of China and of the Islamic world. Interest in agriculture also sparked improvements in the production and use of fertilizer, the transplanting of seedlings in rice paddies, and the engineering of reservoirs (of which there were thousands in Yi times), all disseminated through the powerful new publishing abilities of the Yi government.

Yi agriculture was so well developed that the growing of cash crops became common. Cotton, introduced under the Mongols, was the primary cash crop. It was so highly valued by the state that it was accepted as payment for taxes. Demand was stimulated by the need of the large and frequently mobilized Yi army for cotton uniforms. Cotton also displaced traditional fabrics in the clothing worn by the Korean civil elite. Artisans built cotton gins and spinning wheels, often powered by water, to produce this profitable cloth. In mechanizing the processing of cotton, Korea advanced more rapidly than China. Soon, Korea was exporting considerable amounts of cotton both to China and to Japan.

The Yi also succeeded in reclaiming their coastlines from Japanese pirates who had previously operated at will and driven harassed farmers inland. In the 1400s, Koreans were innovators in military technology. Although both the Yuan and the Ming withheld the formula for destructive gunpowder from the Korean government, Korean officials acquired the information by subterfuge. By the later 1300s the Koreans had mounted cannon on their patrol ships and used gunpowder-driven arrow launchers against enemy personnel and to propel flaming arrows into the rigging of enemy ships. In combination with Koreans' skill in armoring ships, these techniques made the Yi navy, though small, a formidable defense force.

Power Imbalances and Political Transformation in Japan

The Mongols launched their first naval invasion against Japan in 1274. The invading force was diverse and formidable. It included not only the horses and riders of the Mongols, but also light catapults and incendiary and explosive projectiles manufactured by the Chinese. Some captains of the fleet were Koreans. Additional warriors were drawn from the Jurchens and other peoples from northeastern Asia, many of whom were both excellent archers and experienced sailors. They were joined by Korean foot soldiers and archers. In numbers—perhaps thirty thousand combatants—and in technical outfitting, the expedition presented a clear threat to the independence of Japan. But it was not equal to the weather of Hakata Bay on the north side of Kyushu Island (see Map 14.2). The Mongol forces were able to land and inflict stunning damage on mounted Japanese warriors, but a storm prevented them from establishing a base on the beach. The Mongol invaders returned to their ships and sailed back to the mainland for refitting.

The appearance of the Mongols, their large invasion force, and their superior military technology made a deep impression on the leaders of Japan and hastened social and political changes already under way. At the time Japan was organized under the Kamakura shogunate (see Chapter 11), although another powerful family had actually assumed control. The shogun distributed land and privileges to his followers, who paid him tribute and supplied him with soldiers. Based on the balancing of power among warlords, this system was comparatively stable, but it was also decentralized. Lords in the north and east of Japan were remote from those in the south and west, and beyond their declared devotion to the emperor and to the shogun, little united them. The Mongol threat served to pull them together, because it was alien, terrifying, and prolonged.

After the initial shocking foray in 1274, Khubilai sent envoys to Japan insisting on Japanese submission. Japanese leaders executed the ambassadors, but they knew the Mongols would return eventually.

Mongol sea invasion of Japan   The two unsuccessful Mongol attempts to invade Japan were the largest sea mobilizations of the medieval period. The ships, built and outfitted in northern China and in Korea, were designed to transport the war machines, horses, and armor of the invading force—as well as the tens of thousands of Turkic, Mongol, Korean, and Chinese warriors. The Japanese resisted the invaders both on the water and on land, but may well have owed thanks for failure of the Mongol campaigns to heavy seas and erratic weather—the *kamikaze,* or "wind of the gods," that destroyed the second and last Mongol fleet in 1281. (© Museum of Imperial Collections [Kunaityo Sannomal Shozokan])

The preparations to defend against a new attack included strengthening the position of middle-level military officials throughout Japan. Local military commanders hoping to increase their own power frequently had ignored the civil code that had been created under the Kamakura shoguns. In response to the Mongol attack, the shogun took steps to centralize his military government and his methods of communication. Warlords from the south and west of Honshu (Japan's main island) and from the island of Kyushu, which was closest to the expected point of attack, rose in influence.

Preparations also included an attempt by the Japanese military planners to imitate what they had observed of Mongol war tactics. Efforts were made to retrain Japanese warriors and to outfit the Japanese for defense against the advanced weaponry of the attackers. The entire realm was involved in attempts to construct fortifications for defense at Hakata and other points along the Honshu and Kyushu shores. This effort demanded, for the first time, a national system to move resources from elsewhere in Japan to western points.

The Mongols attacked again in 1281. They came in a sea force greater than any ever before amassed anywhere. They brought 140,000 warriors, including Mongols, Chinese, Koreans, and Jurchens, in hundreds of ships. Since the first Mongol attack, however, the Japanese had built a wall cutting off Hakata Bay from the mainland and depriving the Mongol forces of a reliable landing point. After a standoff lasting months, a typhoon struck and sent perhaps half of the Mongol ships to the bottom of the sea. The remainder of the fleet returned to the mainland, never again to harass Japan. The Japanese gave thanks to the "wind of the Gods"—*kamikaze*—for driving away the Mongols.

The belief that the Mongols still posed a threat continued to influence Japanese development. On his deathbed in 1294 Khubilai was planning a third expedition to Japan. His successors did not carry through with it, but the shoguns did not know that the Mongols had given up the idea of conquering Japan. They continued to make plans for coastal defense well into the fourteenth century. This planning helped to consolidate the social position of Japan's warrior elite. It also

Painting by Sesshu Sesshu Toyo (1420–1506) is renowned as the creator of a distinctive style in ink painting that contrasted with the Chinese styles that predominated earlier in Japan. He owed much of his training to the development of Japanese commerce in the period of the Ashikaga shogunate, because as a youth he was patronized by a great commercial family of southern Japan who financed his travel to China, where he first learned his techniques. As he developed a new style, a market for his art and those following in his footsteps developed among the merchant communities of the great castle towns of the Ashikaga periods, and spread to other urban elites. (Collection of the Tokyo National Museum)

stimulated the development of a national infrastructure for trade and communication. On the downside, it hastened the bankruptcy of the failing Kamakura regime.

In the 1330s a civil war ignited by the wish of the emperor Go-Daigo to reclaim power for himself from the shoguns and from rivals within his own family destroyed the shogunate, the power of its military overseers, and the political ambitions of the imperial family itself. In 1338 a new shogunate, the Ashikaga, was established.

The Ashikaga shogunate, not threatened by Mongols, was based at the imperial center of Kyoto. Government authority was more decentralized in the Ashikaga shogunate than in the Kamakura. The provincial warlords enjoyed greater independence. Around their imposing castles, these men sponsored the development of thriving market towns, religious institutions, and occasionally schools. The application of technologies imported in earlier periods, including the water wheel, improved plows, and Champa rice, increased the productivity of the land. The growing wealth and relative peace of the period stimulated artistic creativity, most of which reflected the Zen Buddhist beliefs of the warrior elite. In the simple elegance of the architecture and gardens, in the contemplative landscapes of such artists as Sesshu, and in the eerie, ritualized performances of the No theater, the unified aesthetic code of Zen became established in the Ashikaga era.

Despite the technological advancement, artistic productivity, and rapid urbanization of this period, the progressive aggrandizement of the warlords and their followers led to regional military conflicts. By the later 1400s these conflicts were so severe that they resulted in the virtual destruction of the warlords. In the aftermath of the great Onin War in 1477 Kyoto was devastated, and the Ashikaga shogunate remained a central government only in name. Ambitious but low-ranking warriors began to scramble for control of the provinces, eager to exploit political and economic resources in order to increase their power. They were aided by the revival of trade with continental Asia.

After the fall of the Yuan Empire, the sea trade among China, Korea, and the islands of Japan and Okinawa resumed. Although Japan, unlike

Korea, did not take the lead in the adaptation and application of gun and gunpowder technology, it benefited from the development of firearms on the Asian continent and exported to Korea and China copper, sulfur, and other raw resources. The folding fan, invented in Japan during the period of isolation, quickly became a desired item in Korea and China. The same was true of swords, for which Japan quickly became famous. From China, Japan imported books, porcelain, and copper coins, which it had absorbed in great quantity before the Mongol invasion. In the late Ashikaga period, this trade combined with the volatile political environment in Japan to produce energetic partnerships between warlords and their local merchants. All of them worked to strengthen their own towns and treasuries through exploitation of the overseas trade and, sometimes, through piracy.

Eastern Eurasia, 1200–1500

1206	Temujin chosen as Genghis Khan of the Mongols
1223	Deaths of last ruling emperors of the Tangguts and of the Jin Jurchens
1227	Death of Genghis Khan
1234	Mongol conquest of north China
1279	Mongol conquest of south China; end of southern Song
1333–1336	End of Kamakara shogunate in Japan; beginning of Ashikaga Shogunate
1368	Founding of Ming empire in China
1392	Founding of Yi kingdom in Korea
1403–1424	Yongle emperor's reign in China
1471–1500	Conquest of Champa by Annam

The Rise of Annam as a Conquest State

With the Southern Song destroyed in 1279, Khubilai was determined to subdue the independent state of Annam next. His troops crossed south of the Red River and attacked Hanoi three times. On each occasion the Mongol troops occupied the city, attained an agreement for the paying of tribute, and then withdrew. Later, the Mongols moved farther south, invading Champa in 1283 and making it a tribute nation as well. In 1293 a combined Mongol, Uigur, and Chinese force, numbering perhaps 40,000, set out from the southeast China coast for Java (see Map 14.1). The campaign was ruined by internal dissension among the commanders. There they became embroiled in an internal dispute and wasted their resources without conquering the island. In the case of Southeast Asia, as in the case of Eastern Europe, the ultimate extension of Mongol effort and the limits of Mongol war techniques were reached.

The Ming Empire adopted the Mongol program in Southeast Asia, but with greater success. In 1400, when Annam was distracted by a war with Champa (see Chapter 11), Ming troops occupied Hanoi and installed a puppet government. The new regime lasted until 1428, when it was destroyed in a war for Annamese independence. Ming troops withdrew, and Annam returned to the tributary status it had assumed with Song China. But like Lithuania, the Ottomans, and Korea, Annam was forged into a conquest state by its struggle against a greater empire. In a series of ruthless campaigns, Annamese armies moved southward and systematically annexed the territories of Champa. By 1500 the process was complete. Champa disappeared, and the ancestor of the modern state of Vietnam was born.

The new state reinforced its centralization with Confucian bureaucratic government and an examination system. But it differed from the Ming state in two important ways. The Vietnamese legal code preserved the tradition of group land-owning and decision making within the villages. It also preserved women's property rights. Both developments were probably related to the rural culture based on the growing of rice in wet paddies, but by this time they also were regarded by Annamese as distinctive features of a national culture.

CONCLUSION

The period of Mongol domination of Eurasia had different consequences for peoples of different regions and different classes. Partly because of the decentralized hierarchy that held Mongol regimes together, state expenditures, especially on the military, were always high. Mongol governments were primarily machines of extraction, and the collection of taxes kept intense pressure on farmers and on their rapidly exhausted farmlands. Later Mongol rulers in China and in Iran tried to lessen this burden, but the farming and laboring populations remained in distress. In the 1300s, when the Mongols' political control was weakened throughout their domains, the combination of rebellions and civil wars among the Mongol leaders brought to an end most of the Mongol khanates.

Peasants everywhere suffered under Mongol domination, but new vistas of experience and opportunities for advancement opened to merchants, artists, scholars, high-ranking soldiers, and many religious leaders. The Mongols were actively interested in developing the overland trade among Europe, the Middle East, and East Asia. A great variety of goods and knowledge crisscrossed Eurasia under their rule. Middle Eastern financial administrators immigrated to China to serve the Mongols. As a consequence, thousands of large Muslim communities and several long-lived Jewish communities were established in the Asian interior. They brought with them advanced knowledge of astronomy and mathematics, and Chinese scholars rapidly assimilated their expertise. In exchange, Chinese financial innovations, including paper money and a rudimentary form of banking, were brought to Iran.

Religious influences too were very mobile in the Mongol domains. The Mongol Great Khans patronized Buddhist, Confucianist, and Daoist leaders. The Il-khans reconciled themselves to Islam, and after them the Timurids elevated Sunni Islam to the dominant religious system of Central Asia as well as the Middle East. In Russia, the Mongols tolerated and in a few instances encour-

aged the continued domination of the Orthodox Church over local affairs.

Although the Mongol invasion of Europe in the mid-thirteenth century had excited terror (partly because the Mongols brought with them the bubonic plague, which had first afflicted them during their conquest of China), the Mongol Empire attracted European merchants and adventurers. Some Christian leaders hoped that the Mongols would play a role in the capture of religious sites in the Middle East from Muslim control. These hopes proved to be ill founded, for a large and growing portion of the Mongols who settled in the Middle East became Muslim. Nevertheless, the expectations of some European rulers led to diplomatic exchanges with the Mongols and to the appearance at European courts of emissaries from Asia. The European dream of harnessing Asian power and wealth that helped to inspire Marco Polo and others who, eager to discover the riches of the "East," would be followed centuries later by Christopher Columbus.

The legacy of the Mongols did not cease when their control over major cultural and political centers ended. Throughout Eurasia, succeeding regimes showed the marks of Mongol influence. Some were direct—for example, changes in modes of dress in the Middle East and the institutionalization of some aspects of Mongol rule in China and in Russia. More profound were the direct and indirect effects of the Mongol empires on the formation of nations in the post-Mongol period.

The Mongols brought unity to China, Iran, and Russia by destroying the small states within each region and gathering each region under the control of a single khanate. The Mongols established new capitals, and each of them remained a center of regional unity for centuries after the end of Mongol rule. The Mongol khans encouraged the use of vernacular languages, and in later times those languages became the vehicles for the creation of the literature of China, Iran, and Russia. Perhaps most important, Ming China, Safavid Iran, and Muscovite Russia all benefited from a state ideology that clearly defined each of them in contrast to the late, hated Mongol overlords.

Areas not actually invaded or dominated by

the Mongols nevertheless felt their impact. Lands as widely separated as Armenia and Thailand were regularly harassed by Mongol forces and received waves of refugees from the areas of warfare. Lithuania, Egypt, Japan, and Annam underwent surges of military centralization in anticipation of Mongol attacks.

The period of Mongol rule was a dynamic period for Eurasia and in many ways an unhappy one for the majority populations. It nevertheless changed the world. Heightened regional definition and centralization were critical to the major nations that emerged from the decaying Mongol empires. After the period of Mongol dominance, the land connections that the Mongols had established between Europe and Asia declined, permanently eclipsed by new sea routes. The age of exploration was the primary heir of the age of Mongol rule, and the early modern empires were its stepchildren. The quest for trade, new resources, exploration, conquest, and colonization that China had undertaken in the 1400s continued to draw Europeans toward Asia and, on the way, to East Africa. By the early sixteenth century, Portuguese and Spanish traders were familiar with the shorelines of the whole African continent and Southeast Asia, and they would be followed by the Dutch, the British, and ultimately traders from most of the major nations of Europe.

SUGGESTED READING

See Chapter 13 for works on the general history of the Mongols. For China under the Mongols see Morris Rossabi's *Khubilai Khan: His Life and Times* (1988). On the effects of the Mongol period on economy and technology in Yuan and Ming China see Mark Elvin, *The Pattern of the Chinese Past* (1973); Joel Mokyr, *The Lever of Riches: Technological Creativity and Economic Progress* (1990); and Joseph Needham, *Science in Traditional China* (1981).

Scholarly studies in English on the early Ming period are not so well developed as studies on some other periods of Chinese history. But see Albert Chan, *The Glory and Fall of the Ming Dynasty* (1982), and Edward L. Farmer, *Early Ming Government: The Evolution of Dual Capitals* (1976).

On early Ming literature see Lo Kuan-chung, *Three Kingdoms: A Historical Novel Attributed to Luo Guanzhong,* translated and annotated by Moss Roberts (1991); Pearl Buck's translation of *Water Margin,* entitled *All Men Are Brothers,* 2 vols. (1933), and a later translation by J. H. Jackson, *Water Margin, Written by Shih Nai-an* (1937); Richard Gregg Irwin, *The Evolution of a Chinese Novel: Shui-hu-chuan* (1953); Ellen Widmer, *The Margins of Utopia: Shui-hu hou-chuan and the Literature of Ming Loyalism* (1987); and Shelley Hsüeh-lun Chang, *History and Legend: Ideas and Images in the Ming Historical Novels* (1990).

On Ming painting see James Cahill, *Parting at the Shore: Chinese Painting of the Early and Middle Ming Dynasty* (1978). See also selected essays in Paul S. Ropp, ed. *Heritage of China* (1990).

The Zheng He expeditions are extensively discussed in secondary works. A classic interpretation is Joseph R. Levenson, ed., *European Expansion and the Counter-Example of Asia, 1300–1600* (1967). More recent scholarship is available in Philip Snow, *The Star Raft* (1988), and a full and lively account is Louise Levathes, *When China Ruled the Seas* (1993).

For a general history of Korea in this period see Andrew C. Nahm, *Introduction to Korean History and Culture* (1993); Ki-Baik Lee, *A New History of Korea* (1984); and William E. Henthorn, *Korea: the Mongol Invasions* (1963). On a more specialized topic, see Joseph Needham et al., *The Hall of Heavenly Records: Korean Astronomical Instruments and Clocks, 1380–1780* (1986).

Narrative histories of Japan are cited in Chapter 11, but see also John W. Hall and Toyoda Takeshi, eds., *Japan in the Muromachi Age* (1977), and H. Paul Varley, trans., *The Onin War: History of Its Origins and Background with a Selective Translation of the Chronicle of Onin* (1967). On the Mongol invasion see Yamada Nakaba, *Ghenko, the Mongol Invasion of Japan, with an Introduction by Lord Armstrong* (1916), and the novel *Fûtô* by Inoue Yasushi, translated by James T. Araki as *Wind and Waves* (1989). On the Nō theater and Zen aesthetics there is a great deal of writing. Perhaps most direct and charming are Donald Keene, *No: The Classical Theatre of Japan* (1966), and Ueda Makoto, trans., *The Old Pine Tree and Other Noh Plays* (1962).

Tropical Africa and Asia, 1200–1500

Tropical Lands and Peoples · New Islamic Empires · Indian Ocean Trade

Social and Cultural Change

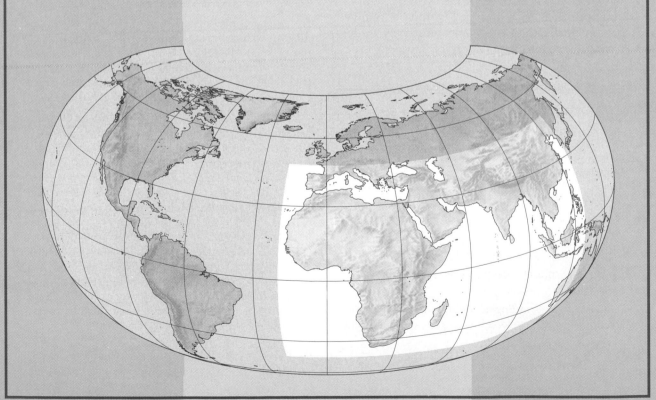

Sultan Abu Bakr customarily offered his personal hospitality to all distinguished visitors arriving at his city of Mogadishu, an Indian Ocean port on the northeast coast of Africa. In 1331 he provided food and lodging for Muhammad ibn Abdullah ibn Battuta (1304–1369), a young Muslim scholar from Morocco, who had set out to explore the Islamic world. Having already completed a pilgrimage to Mecca and traveled throughout the Middle East, Ibn Battuta was touring the trading cities of the Red Sea and East Africa. Subsequent travels took him to Central Asia and India, China and Southeast Asia, Muslim Spain, and sub-Saharan West Africa. Logging some 75,000 miles (120,000 kilometers) in the course of his twenty-nine years of travel, Ibn Battuta became the most widely traveled man of his times. For this reason his journal, which describes where he went and what he saw, is a valuable historical source for these lands.

Other Muslim princes and merchants welcomed Ibn Battuta as graciously as did the ruler of Mogadishu. Hospitality was a highly respected Muslim virtue, which ignored individuals' physical and cultural differences. Although the Moroccan traveler noted that Sultan Abu Bakr had skin darker than his own and spoke a different native language (Somali), that made little difference. They were brothers in faith when they prayed together at Friday services in the Mogadishu mosque, where the sultan greeted his foreign guest in Arabic, the common language of the Islamic world: "You are heartily welcome, and you have honored our land and given us pleasure." When Sultan Abu Bakr and his jurists heard and decided cases after the mosque service, they used the law code familiar in all the lands of Islam.

Islam was not the only tie that bound the peoples of Africa and southern Asia together. A network of land and sea trade routes joined their lands. These routes were older than Islam and an important means for the spread of beliefs and technologies as well as goods. Ibn Battuta made his way down the coast of East Africa in merchants' ships and joined their camel caravans to cross the Sahara to West Africa. He reached India by overland trade routes and sailed for China on another merchant ship.

An even more fundamental link among the diverse peoples of Africa and southern Asia was the tropical environment itself. Environmental differences had helped shape the region's cultural differences. Cultural and ecological differences, in turn, helped generate the trade in specialized products from one place to another. And the twice-a-year shift in the Indian Ocean winds made the ocean voyages possible.

During the period 1200 to 1500, commercial and cultural exchange among tropical peoples reached a much greater level of intensity than ever before. Human interaction was catching up with its geographical potential.

TROPICAL LANDS AND PEOPLES

The people who inhabited the tropical regions of Africa and Asia were profoundly affected by their natural setting. Members of each community obtained food by using methods that generations of experimentation had proved most successful in dealing with their particular environment, whether desert edge, grasslands, or tropical rain forest. Much of their success lay in learning how to blend human activities with the natural order, but their ability to modify the environment to suit their needs was also evident in their irrigation works and mining.

The Tropical Environment

Because of the angle of earth's axis, the tropics are warmed by the sun's rays year-round, instead of having alternating hot and cold seasons as in the temperate zones. The equator marks the

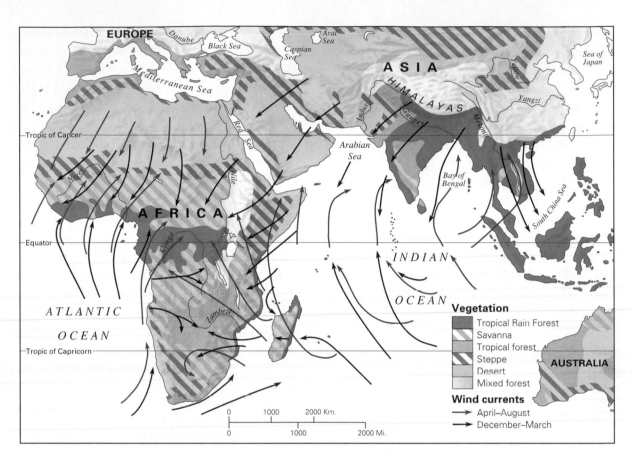

Map 15.1 Africa and the Indian Ocean Basin: Physical Characteristics   Seasonal wind patterns controlled the rainfall in the tropics and produced the different tropical vegetation zones to which human societies adapted over thousands of years. The wind patterns also dominated sea travel in the Indian Ocean.

center of the tropical zone, and the Tropic of Cancer and Tropic of Capricorn mark its outer limits. As Map 15.1 shows, Africa lies almost entirely within the tropics, and southern Arabia, most of India, and all of mainland Southeast Asia and the East Indies also fall within the tropics.

Lacking the hot and cold seasons of temperate lands, the Afro-Asian tropics have their own cycle of rainy and dry seasons caused by changes in wind patterns across the surrounding oceans. Winds from a permanent high-pressure air mass over the South Atlantic deliver heavy rainfall to the western coast of Africa during much of the year. However, in December and January large high-pressure zones over northern Africa and Arabia produce a southward movement of dry

air that limits the inland penetration of the moist ocean winds.

In the lands around the Indian Ocean the rainy and dry seasons reflect the influence of similar alternating wind patterns. A gigantic high-pressure zone over the Himalayas that is at its peak from December to March produces a strong southward air movement (the northeast monsoon) in the western Indian Ocean. This is southern Asia's dry season. Between April and August a low-pressure zone over India creates a northward movement of air from across the ocean (the southwest monsoon) that brings southern Asia its heaviest rains. This is the wet season.

Along with geographical features, these wind and rain patterns are responsible for the variations in tropical lands, from desert to rain forest. Where rainfall is exceptionally abundant, as in the broad belt along the equator in coastal West Africa and west-central Africa, the natural vegetation is dense tropical rain forest. Rain forests also characterize Southeast Asia and parts of coastal India. Somewhat lighter rains produce other tropical forests. The English word *jungle* comes from a Hindi word for the tangled undergrowth in the tropical forests that once covered most of India.

Although heavy rainfall is common in some of the tropics, other parts rarely see rain at all. Stretching clear across the width of northern Africa is the world's largest desert, the Sahara. This arid zone continues eastward, to include the Arabian Desert and the Thar Desert of northwest India. Another desert zone in southwestern Africa includes the Namib and Kalahari Deserts. In between the deserts and the rain forests are lands that receive moderate amounts of moisture during the rainy seasons. These are the majority of lands in tropical India and Africa and range from fairly wet woodlands to the much drier grasslands characteristic of much of East Africa and the desert edges.

Other variations in tropical climate result from the topography of the landmasses. Thin atmospheres at high altitudes can hold less of the tropical heat than can atmospheres at lower elevations. The volcanic mountains of eastern Africa rise to such heights that some are covered with snow all or part of the year. The Himalayas that form the northern frontier of India are also snow capped and so high that they block the movement of cold air into the northern India plains, giving this region a milder climate than its latitude would suggest. The many plateaus of inland Africa and the Deccan Plateau of central India also make these regions somewhat cooler than the coastal plains.

The mighty rivers that descend to the oceans from these mountains and plateaus carry water far from where it falls. The heavy rains falling in the highlands of Central Africa and Ethiopia supply the Nile's annual floods that make Egypt bloom in the desert. On its long route to the Atlantic, the Niger River of West Africa flows northward to the Sahara's edge, creating a rich floodplain (the inland Niger Delta) and providing waters to the trading cities that clustered along its great bend. In like fashion, the Indus River provides nourishing waters from the Himalayas to arid northwest India. The Ganges and its tributaries provide valuable moisture to northeastern India during the dry season. Mainland Southeast Asia's great rivers, such as the Mekong, are similarly valuable.

Human Ecosystems

Thinkers in temperate lands once imagined that, because of the absence of a harsh winter season, surviving in the tropics was as easy as picking wild fruit off a tree. In fact, mastering the tropics' many different environments had been a long and difficult struggle. A careful observer touring the tropics in 1200 would have noticed how much the differences in societies could be attributed to their particular ecosystems—that is, to how they made use of the plants, animals, and other resources of their physical environments. Tropical peoples' success in adapting to their natural worlds was fundamental to all their other achievements.

Centuries before 1200, most tropical Africans and Asians had taken up raising domesticated plants and animals as the best way to feed themselves. But in some environments people found it preferable to rely primarily on wild food that they obtained by hunting, fishing, and gathering. This was true of the dense forests of Central Africa where the small size of the Pygmy hunters was itself a physical adaptation that permitted them to pursue their prey through the dense undergrowth. Hunting was also a way of life in the upper altitudes of the Himalayas and in some desert environments. A Portuguese expedition led by Vasco da Gama visited the arid coast of southwestern Africa in 1497 and recorded the presence there of a healthy group of people who lived off both land and sea creatures, feeding themselves on "the flesh of seals, whales, and gazelles, and the roots of wild plants." Fishing was a highly skilled and successful form of food gathering everywhere in the region along all the major lakes and rivers as well as in the oceans, though it might be combined with farming. The ocean fishermen of the East African coast and the East Indies were particularly distinguished, as were those of coastal India. The boating skills of fishermen often led to their playing an important role in ocean trade.

In areas too arid for agriculture, tending herds of domesticated animals was common. Unencumbered by bulky personal possessions and elaborate dwellings, pastoralists' knowledge of the local waterholes and observation of the scattered rains enabled them to find adequate grazing for their animals in all but the severest droughts. They fed themselves with milk from their herds and with grain and vegetables obtained from farmers in exchange for hides and meat. The world's largest concentration of pastoralists was in the arid and semiarid lands of northeastern Africa and Arabia. Like Ibn Battuta's host at Mogadishu, some Somali were urban dwellers, but most grazed their herds of goats and camels in the desert hinterland of the Horn of Africa. The western Sahara sustained herds of sheep and camels belonging to the Tuareg, whose intimate knowledge of the desert also made them invaluable as guides to caravans, such as the one Ibn Battuta joined on the two-month-long journey across the desert. Along the Sahara's southern edge the cattle-herding Fulani people gradually extended their range during this period, so that by 1500 they were found throughout the western and central Sudan. A few weeks after its encounter with the hunter-gatherers of southern Africa, Vasco da Gama's expedition bartered for meat with a pastoral people possessing fat cattle and sheep.

Although food gathering and animal husbandry continued, farming was the dominant way of life for most tropical peoples between 1200 and 1500. The density of agricultural populations was closely tied to the adequacy of rainfall and soils. South and Southeast Asia were generally much better watered than tropical Africa and so could support much greater populations. In 1200 there were probably over 100 million people living in South and Southeast Asia, more than four-fifths of them on the fertile Indian mainland. This was three times the number of people living in all of Africa at that time and nearly twice as many as

in Europe, though still a little less than the population of China.

Because of India's lush vegetation, one Middle Eastern writer of the time identified it as "the most agreeable abode on earth . . . its delightful plains resemble the garden of Paradise."[1] Rice cultivation was particularly important in places such as the fertile Gangeatic plain of northeast India, mainland Southeast Asia, and southern China. In drier areas tropical farmers grew grains (such as wheat, sorghum, millet, and ensete) and legumes (such as peas and beans), whose ripening cycle matched the pattern of the rainy and dry seasons. A variety of tubers and tree crops were characteristic of farming in rain forest clearings.

By the year 1200 human migrations had spread many useful domesticated plants and animals around the tropics. Bantu-speaking farmers (see Chapter 8) had introduced grains and tubers from West Africa throughout the southern half of the continent. Bananas, brought to southern Africa centuries earlier by mariners from Southeast Asia, had become the stable food for people farming the rich soils around the Great Lakes of East Africa. Yams and cocoyams of Asian origin had spread clear across equatorial Africa. Asian cattle breeds grazed contentedly in pastures throughout Africa, while coffee of Ethiopian origin would shortly become common drink in the Middle East.

The spread of farming did not always create permanent changes in the natural environment. In most parts of sub-Saharan Africa and many parts of the East Indies until quite recent times, the basic form of cultivation was extensive rather than intensive. Instead of enriching fields with manure and vegetable compost so they could be cultivated year after year, farmers abandoned fields every few years when the natural fertility of the soil was exhausted and cleared new fields. Ashes from the brush, grasses, and tree limbs that were cut down and burned gave the new fields a significant boost in fertility. Even though a great deal of work was needed to clear the fields initially, modern research suggests that such shifting cultivation was an efficient use of labor in areas where soils were not naturally rich in nutrients.

Water Systems and Irrigation

In other parts of the tropics environmental necessity and population pressure led to the adoption of more intensive forms of agriculture. A rare area of intensive cultivation in sub-Saharan Africa was the inland delta of the Niger River, where large crops of rice were grown using the river's naturally fertilizing annual floods. The rice was probably sold to the trading cities along the Niger bend.

One of the great challenges of the tropical environment in parts of Asia was the uneven distribution of rainfall during the year. Unlike pastoralists who could move their herds to the water, farmers had to find ways of moving the water to their crops. Farmers met the challenge by conserving some of the monsoon rainfall for use during the drier parts of the year. Farming communities in Vietnam, Java, Malaya, and Burma constructed terraced hillsides with special water-control systems for growing rice. Water-storage dams and irrigation canals were also becoming common in both north and south India. For example, during these centuries Tamil villagers in southeast India built a series of stone and earthen dams across rivers to store water for gradual release through elaborate irrigation canals. Over many generations these canals were extended to irrigate more and more land. Although these dams and channels covered large areas, they were relatively simple structures that local people could keep working by routine maintenance.

As had been true since the days of the first river-valley civilizations (see Chapter 2), the largest irrigation systems in the tropics were government public works projects. Under the government of the Delhi Sultanate (1206–1526) northern India acquired extensive new water-control systems. Ibn Battuta commented appreciatively on a large reservoir, constructed under one ruler in the first quarter of the thirteenth century, that supplied the city of Delhi with water. Enterprising farmers planted sugar cane, cucumbers, and melons along the reservoir's shore as the water level fell during the dry season. In the fourteenth century the Delhi Sultanate built in the Gangeatic plain a large network of irrigation canals that would not be surpassed in size until the nineteenth century. These irrigation systems made it possible to grow crops throughout the year.

Since the tenth century the Indian Ocean island of Ceylon (modern Sri Lanka) had been home to the greatest concentration of irrigation reservoirs and canals in the world. These facilities enabled the powerful Sinhalese kingdom in arid northern Ceylon to support a large population. There was another impressive waterworks in Southeast Asia, where a system of reservoirs and canals served Cambodia's capital city Angkor.

Yet such complex systems were vulnerable to disruption. Between 1250 and 1400 the irrigation complex in Ceylon fell into ruin when invading Tamils from South India disrupted the Sinhalese government. The population of Ceylon then suffered from the effects of malaria, a tropical disease spread by mosquitoes breeding in the irrigation canals. The great Cambodian system fell into ruin in the fifteenth century when the government that maintained it collapsed. Neither system was ever rebuilt.

The vulnerability of complex irrigation systems built by powerful governments suggests an instructive contrast. Although village-based irrigation systems could be damaged by invasion and natural calamity, except in the most extreme cases they usually bounded back because they were the product of local initiatives, not centralized direction, and they depended on simpler technologies.

Mineral Resources

Metalworking was another way in which people made use of their environment's resources. Skilled metalworkers furnished their customers with tools, weapons, and decorative objects. The mining and processing of metals was also important for long-distance trade.

Iron was the most abundant of the metals worked in the tropics. People in most parts of the tropical world produced sufficient quantities of iron tools and implements to satisfy their own needs. The iron hoes, axes, and knives that enabled farmers to clear and cultivate their fields

Ife bronze head, thirteenth century   This sensuously beautiful head and some companion pieces unearthed at Ife in southwestern Nigeria in 1912 changed the world's image of African art and artistry. Such discoveries showed that sub-Saharan African artists were casting naturalistic images in copper with great skill in the thirteenth century. The crowned head represents a woman or a young man associated with the ancient rulers of the kingdom of Ife. (Werner Forman/Art Resource NY)

seem to have been used between 1200 and 1500 to open up the rain forests of coastal West Africa and Southeast Asia for farming. Iron-tipped spears and arrows improved hunting success. Needles were used in sewing clothes, nails in building. The skill of Indian metalsmiths was renowned, especially in making strong and beautiful swords. So great was the skill of

African iron smelters and blacksmiths that they were believed to possess magical powers.

Copper was of special importance in Africa, where copper and its alloys were used for jewelry and artistic casting. In the Copperbelt of southeastern Africa, copper mining was in full production in the fourteenth and fifteenth centuries. The refined metal was cast into large X-shaped ingots (metal castings). Local coppersmiths made these ingots into wire and decorative objects. Copper mining was also important in the western Sudan, where Ibn Battuta described a mining town that produced two sizes of copper bars that were used as a currency of exchange in place of coins. The skill of coppersmiths in West Africa reached a high level during these centuries, enabling them to cast copper and brass (an alloy of copper and zinc) statues and heads that are considered among the masterpieces of world art. These works were made by the lost-wax method, in which a thin layer of wax sandwiched between clay forms is replaced by molten metal that hardens and assumes the shape of the wax.

During this period, Africans also acquired an international reputation for their production of gold, which was exported in quantity across the Sahara and into the Indian Ocean and Red Sea trades. Gold was mined and collected from stream beds along the upper Niger River and further south in modern Ghana. In the hills south of the Zambezi River (in modern Zimbabwe) archaeologists have discovered thousands of mine shafts, dating from this period, that were sunk up to a 100 feet (30 meters) into the ground to get at gold ores. The gold and silver mines in India seem to have been exhausted by this period, although panning for gold remained important in the streams descending from the mountains of northern India. For that reason, Indians imported from Southeast Asia and Africa considerable quantities of gold for jewelry and temple decoration.

Metalworking and food-producing systems were important to tropical peoples for two reasons. First, most people made a successful livelihood through such skilled exploitation of their environment. Second, the labors and skills of such ordinary people made possible the rise of powerful states and profitable commercial systems. When considering the better documented lives of rulers and merchants described elsewhere in this chapter, ask yourself: Could the caravans have crossed the Sahara without the skilled guidance of desert pastoralists? Could the trade of the Indian Ocean have reached its full importance were it not for the seafaring skills of the coastal fishermen? Could the city-based empires of Delhi and Mali have endured without the food taxed from rural farmers? Could the long-distance trade routes have prospered without the precious metals, the spices, and the grains produced by such ordinary folks?

NEW ISLAMIC EMPIRES

The empires of Mali in West Africa and Delhi in northern India were the two largest and richest tropical states of the period between 1200 and 1500. Both utilized Islamic administrative and military systems introduced from the Islamic heartland, but in other ways these two Muslim sultanates were very different. Mali was founded by an indigenous African dynasty, which had earlier adopted Islam through the peaceful influence of Muslim merchants and scholars. In contrast, the Delhi Sultanate of northern India was founded and ruled by invading Turkish and Afghan Muslims. Mali depended heavily for its wealth on its participation in the trans-Saharan trade, but long-distance trade played only a minor role in Delhi's wealth.

Mali in the Western Sudan

The consolidation of the Middle East and North Africa under Muslim rule during the seventh and eighth centuries (see Chapter 10) greatly increased the volume of trade along the routes that crossed the Sahara. In the centuries that followed, the faith of Muhammad gradually spread to the lands south of the desert, which the Arabs called the *bilad al-sudan*, the "land of the blacks." The rulers of Ghana, the empire that preceded Mali in the western Sudan (see Chapter 8), had

employed foreign Muslims in government posts but were not Muslims themselves.

The role of force in spreading Islam south of the Sahara was limited. Muslim Berbers invading out of the desert in 1076 captured Ghana's capital and caused the collapse of that empire, but their conquest did little to spread Islam. To the east, the Muslim attacks that destroyed the Christian Nubian kingdoms on the upper Nile in the late thirteenth century opened that area to Muslim influences, but Christian Ethiopia successfully withstood Muslim advances. Instead, the usual pattern for the spread of Islam south of the Sahara was through gradual and peaceful conversion. The expansion of commercial contacts in the western Sudan and on the East African coast greatly promoted the process of conversion.

Africans adopted Islam because they believed in its teachings and found it suited their interests. The first sub-Saharan African state to adopt the new faith was Takrur in the far western Sudan, whose rulers accepted Islam about 1030. Shortly after the year 1200 Takrur expanded in importance under King Sumanguru. Then in about 1240 Sundiata, the upstart leader of the Malinke people, handed Sumanguru a major defeat. Even though both leaders were Muslims, Malinke legends recall their battles as the clash of two powerful magicians. Sumanguru is said to have been able to appear and disappear at will, assume dozens of shapes, and catch arrows in midflight. Sundiata defeated Sumanguru's much larger forces through superior military maneuvers and by successfully wounding his adversary with a special arrow that robbed him of his magical powers. This victory was followed by others that created Sundiata's Empire of Mali (see Map 15.2).

Mali's strength, like that of Ghana before it, rested on a well-developed agricultural base combined with control over lucrative regional and trans-Saharan trade routes. But Mali differed from Ghana in two ways. First, it was much larger in size. Mali controlled not only the core trading area of the upper Niger but the gold fields of the Niger headwaters to the southwest as well. Second, its rulers were Muslims, who fostered the spread of Islam among the political and trading elites of the empire. Control of the

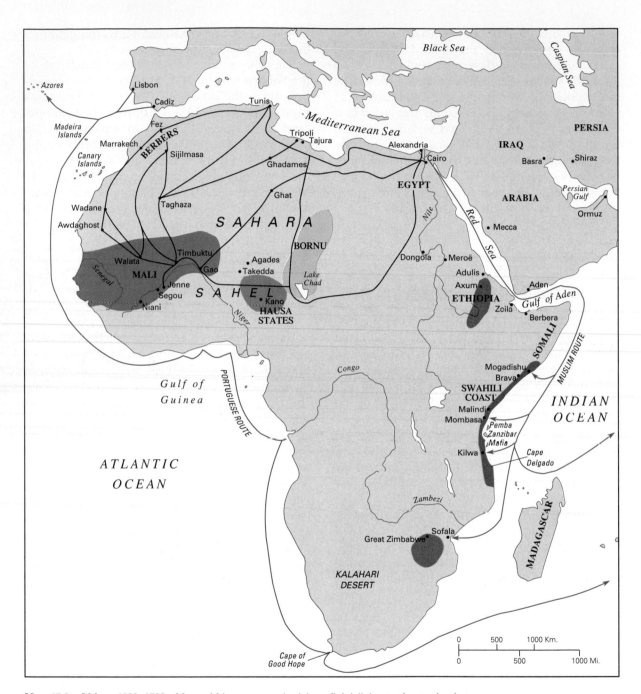

Map 15.2 Africa, 1200–1500 Many African states had beneficial links to the trade that crossed the Sahara and the Indian Ocean. Before 1500, sub-Saharan Africa's external ties were primarily with the Islamic world.

The Western Sudan (1375)   A Jewish geographer on the Mediterranean island of Majorca drew this lavish map in 1375, incorporating all that was known in Europe of the rest of the world. This portion of the Catalan Atlas shows a North African trader approaching the king of Mali, who holds a gold nugget in one hand and a golden scepter in the other. A caption identifies the black ruler as Mansa Musa, "the richest and noblest king in all the land." (Bibliotheque nationale de France)

important gold and copper trades and contacts with North African Muslim traders gave Mali and its rulers unprecedented prosperity.

Under the Mali ruler Mansa Kankan Musa (r. 1312–1337), the empire's reputation for wealth spread far and wide. Mansa Musa's pilgrimage to Mecca in 1324–1325, in fulfillment of his personal duty as a Muslim, also became an occasion for him to display the exceptional wealth of his empire. As befitted a powerful ruler, he traveled with a large entourage. Besides his senior wife and 500 of her ladies in waiting and their slaves, one account says there were also 60,000 porters and a vast caravan of camels carrying supplies and provisions. Even more lavish was the gold that Mansa Musa is reported to have taken along. For purchases and gifts he took 80 packages of gold each weighing 122 ounces (3.8 kilo-

grams). In addition, 500 slaves each carried a golden staff. When the entourage passed through Cairo, Mansa Musa gave away and spent so much gold that its value was depressed for years.

Mansa Musa returned from his pilgrimage eager to promote the religious and cultural influence of Islam in his empire. He built new mosques and opened Quranic schools in the cities along the Niger bend. When Ibn Battuta visited Mali from 1352 to 1354, during the reign of Mansa Musa's successor Mansa Suleiman (r. 1341–1360), the practice of Islam in the empire met with his approval. He lauded Malians for their faithful recitation of prayers and for their zeal in teaching children the Quran.

Ibn Battuta also had high praise for Mali's government. He reported that "complete and general safety" prevailed in the vast territories ruled by Suleiman and that foreign travelers had no reason to fear being robbed by thieves or having their goods confiscated if they died. (For Ibn Battuta's account of the sultan's court and his subjects' respect see Voices & Visions: Personal Styles of Rule in India and Mali.)

Two centuries after Sundiata founded the empire, Mali began to disintegrate. When Mansa Suleiman's successors proved to be less able rulers, rebellions broke out among the diverse peoples who had been subjected to Malinke rule. Avid for Mali's wealth, other groups attacked from without. The desert Tuareg retook their city of Timbuktu in 1433. By 1500 the rulers of Mali had dominion over little more than the Malinke heartland.

The cities of the upper Niger survived Mali's collapse, but some of the western Sudan's former trade and intellectual life moved east to other African states in the central Sudan. Shortly after 1450 the rulers of several of the Hausa city-states adopted Islam as their official religion. The Hausa states were also able to increase their importance as manufacturing and trading centers, becoming famous for their cotton textiles and leatherworking. Also expanding in the late fifteenth century was the central Sudanic state of Kanen-Bornu. It was descended from the ancient kingdom of Kanem, whose rulers had accepted

Sankore Mosque, Timbuktu   The wall and tower at the left and center represent traditional styles of construction in clay in a region where building stone is rare. At its peak in the fourteenth through the sixteenth centuries, Timbuktu was a major emporium for trade at the southern edge of the Sahara and a center of Islamic religion and education. (Aldona Sabalis/Photo Researchers, Inc.)

Personal Styles of Rule in India and Mali

Ibn Battuta wrote vividly of the powerful men who ruled the Muslim states he visited. His account of Sultan Muhammad ibn Tughluq of Delhi reflects a familiarity he acquired during a long stay in India in the 1340s.

Muhammad is a man who, above all others, is fond of making presents and shedding blood. There may always be seen at his gate some poor person becoming rich, or some living one condemned to death. His generous and brave actions, and his cruel and violent deeds, have obtained notoriety among the people. In spite of this, he is the most humble of men, and the one who exhibits the greatest equity. The ceremonies of religion are dear to his ears, and he is very severe in respect of prayer and the punishment which follows its neglect . . . . When drought prevailed . . . the Sultan gave orders that provisions for six months should be supplied to all the inhabitants of Delhi from the royal granaries . . . .

One of the most serious charges against this Sultan is that he forced all the inhabitants of Delhi to leave their homes. [After] the people of Delhi wrote letters full of insults and invectives against [him,] the Sultan . . . decided to ruin Delhi, so he purchased all the houses and inns from the inhabitants, paid them the price, and then ordered them to remove to Daulatabad . . . .

The greater part of the inhabitants departed, but [h]is slaves found two men in the streets: one was paralyzed, the other blind. They were brought before the sovereign, who ordered the paralytic to be shot away from a *manjanik* [catapult], and the blind man to be dragged from Delhi to Daulatabad, a journey of forty days' distance. The poor wretch fell to pieces during the journey, and only one of his legs reached Daulatabad.

In contrast, Ibn Battuta's description of 1353 Mansa Suleiman of Mali is remote and impersonal, which accords with African political traditions.

On certain days the sultan holds audiences in the palace yard, where there is a platform under a tree . . . . carpeted with silk, [over which] is raised the umbrella, . . . surmounted by a bird in gold, about the size of a falcon. The sultan comes out of a door in a corner of the palace, carrying a bow in his hand and a quiver on his back. On his head he has a golden skullcap, bound with a gold band which has narrow ends shaped like knives, more than a span in length. His usual dress is a velvety red tunic, made of the European fabrics called *mutanfas*. The sultan is preceded by his musicians, who carry gold and silver [two stringed guitars], and behind him come three hundred armed slaves. He walks in a leisurely fashion, affecting a very slow movement, and even stops and looks round the assembly, then ascends [the platform] in the sedate manner of a preacher ascending a mosque-pulpit. As he takes his seat, the drums, trumpets, and bugles are sounded. Three slaves go at a run to summon the sovereign's deputy and the military commanders, who enter and sit down . . . .

The blacks are of all people the most submissive to their king and the most abject in their behavior before him. They swear by his name, saying *Mansa Suleiman ki* [by Mansa Suleiman's law]. If he summons any of them while he is holding an audience in his pavilion, the person summoned takes off his clothes and puts on worn garments, removes his turban and dons a dirty skullcap and enters with his garments and trousers raised knee-high. He goes forward in an attitude of humility and dejection, and knocks the ground hard with his elbows, then stands with bowed head and bent back listening to what he says. If anyone addresses the king and receives a reply from him, he uncovers his back and throws dust over his head and back, for all the world like a bather splashing himself with water. I used to wonder how it was that they did not blind themselves.

How can the kind and cruel sides of Sultan Muhammad be reconciled? What role would Islam have played in his generosity? Could cruelty have brought any benefits to the ruler of a conquest state?

How did Mansa Suleiman's ritual appearances serve to enhance his majesty? What attitudes toward the ruler do his subjects' actions suggest? How different were the ruling styles of Muhammad and Suleiman?

Source: The first excerpt is from Henry M. Elliot, *The History of India as Told by Its Own Historians* (London: Trübner and Co., 1869-1871) 3: 609–614. The second excerpt is adapted from H. A. R. Gibb, ed., *Selections from the Travels of Ibn Battuta in Asia and Africa* (London: Cambridge University Press, 1929), pp. 326–327.

Islam in about 1085. At its peak about 1250, Kanem had absorbed the state of Bornu south and west of Lake Chad and gained control of important trade routes crossing the Sahara. As Kanem-Bornu's armies conquered new territories in the late fifteenth century, they also spread the rule of Islam.

The Delhi Sultanate in India

The arrival of Islam in India was in violent contrast to its peaceful penetration of West Africa. Having long ago lost the defensive unity of the Gupta Empire (see Chapter 7), the divided states of northwest India were subject to raids by Afghan warlords from the early eleventh century. Motivated jointly by a wish to spread their Islamic faith and by a desire for plunder, the raiders looted Hindu temples of their gold and jewels, kidnapped women for their harems, and slew Hindu defenders by the thousands. In the last decades of the twelfth century a new Turkish dynasty armed with powerful crossbows, which warriors could fire from the backs of their galloping horses thanks to the use of iron stirrups, mounted a furious assault that succeeded in capturing the important northern Indian cities of Lahore and Delhi. One partisan Muslim chronicler recorded, "The city [Delhi] and its vicinity was freed from idols and idol-worship, and in the sanctuaries of the images of the [Hindu] Gods, mosques were raised by the worshippers of one God."[2] The invaders' strength was bolstered by a ready supply of Turkish adventurers from Central Asia eager to follow individual leaders and by the unifying force of their common religious faith. Although the Indians fought back bravely, centuries of security from outside invasion and a lack of interest in the rising military aggressiveness of the peoples around them had left them unprepared to present an effective united front.

Between 1206 and 1236 the Muslim invaders extended their rule over the Hindu princes and chiefs in much of northern India. Sultan Iltutmish (r. 1211–1236) consolidated the conquest of northern India in a series of military expeditions that made his empire the largest state in India (see Map 15.3). He also secured official recogni-

tion of the Delhi Sultanate as a Muslim state by the caliph of Baghdad. Although the looting and destruction of temples, enslavement, and massacres continued, especially on the frontiers of the empire, the incorporation of north India into the Islamic world marked the beginning of the Muslim invaders' transformation from brutal conquerors to somewhat more benign rulers. Hindus, whose land came under the control of foreign Muslim military officials, were accorded special measures of protection, which freed them from persecution in return for the payment of a special tax. Yet Hindus never forgot the intolerance and destruction of their first contacts with the invaders.

To the astonishment of his ministers, Iltutmish passed over his weak and pleasure-seeking sons and designated as his heir his beloved and talented daughter Raziya. When they questioned the unprecedented idea of a woman ruling a Muslim state, he said, "My sons are devoted to the pleasures of youth: no one of them is qualified to be king. . . . there is no one more competent to guide the State than my daughter." In fact, his wish was not immediately carried out after his death, but after seven months of rule by the generous but inept Firoz—whose great delight was riding his elephant through the bazaar, showering the crowds with coins—the ministers relented and put Raziya on the throne. A chronicler of the time, who knew her, explained why the reign of this able ruler lasted less than four years (r. 1236–1240):

> Sultan Raziya was a great monarch. She was wise, just, and generous, a benefactor to her kingdom, a dispenser of justice, the protector of her subjects, and the leader of her armies. She was endowed with all the qualities befitting a king, but that she was not born of the right sex, and so in the estimation of men all these virtues were worthless. May God have mercy upon her![3]

Doing her best to prove herself a proper king, Raziya dressed like a man and rode at the head of her troops atop an elephant. Nothing, however, could overcome the prejudices of the Turkish chiefs against a woman ruler. In the end, she was imprisoned and later killed by a robber while trying to escape.

After a half-century of stagnation and rebel-

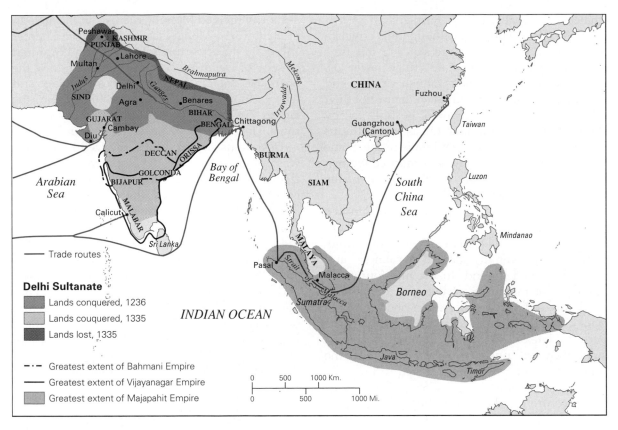

Map 15.3   South and Southeast Asia, 1200–1500   The rise of new empires and the expansion of maritime trade reshaped the lives of many tropical Asians.

lion, the ruthless but efficient policies of Sultan Ala-ud-din Khalji (r. 1296–1316) increased his control over the empire's outlying provinces. Successful frontier raids and high taxes kept his treasury full, wage and price controls in Delhi kept down the cost of maintaining a large army, and a network of spies stifled intrigue. When a Mongol threat from the northeast eased, Ala-ud-din's forces extended the sultanate's southern flank, seizing the rich trading state of Gujarat in 1298. Then troops drove into South India and briefly held the southern tip of the Indian peninsula.

At the time of Ibn Battuta's visit, Delhi's ruler was Sultan Muhammad ibn Tughluq (1325–1351), who received his visitor at his palace's celebrated Hall of a Thousand Pillars. The world traveler praised the sultan's piety and generosity—traditional Muslim virtues—but also recounted his cruelties (see Voices & Visions: Personal Styles of

Rule in India and Mali). In keeping with these complexities, the sultan resumed a policy of aggressive expansion against independent Indian states that enlarged the sultanate to its greatest extent. He balanced that policy with one of religious toleration intended to win the loyalty of Hindus and other non-Muslims. He even attended Hindu religious festivals. However, his successor Firuz Shah (r. 1351–1388) alienated powerful Hindus by taxing the Brahmins, preferring to cultivate good relations with the Muslim elite. Muslim chroniclers praised him for constructing forty mosques, thirty colleges, and a hundred hospitals.

A small minority in a giant land, the Turkish rulers relied on terror to keep their subjects submissive, on harsh military reprisals to put down rebellion, and on pillage and high taxes to sustain the ruling elite in luxury and power. Even under its most enlightened rulers, the Delhi Sultanate was probably more a burden than a bene-fit to most of its subjects. Although this criticism could be made of most large states of this time (including Mali), the sultanate's rulers never lost the disadvantage of their foreign origins and their membership in a faith alien to most of their subjects. Over time their initial hostility to any Hindu participation moderated as some Hindus were incorporated into the administration. Some members of the ruling elite also married women from prominent Hindu families, though the brides had to become Muslims.

Personal and religious rivalries within the Muslim elite, as well as the discontent of the Hindus, threatened the Delhi Sultanate with disinte-gration whenever it showed weakness and finally hastened its end. In the mid-fourteenth century Muslim nobles challenged the sultan's dominion and successfully established the Bah-mani kingdom (1347–1482), which controlled the Deccan Plateau. To defend themselves against the southward push of Bahmani armies, the Hindu states of South India united to form the Vijayanagar Empire (1336–1565), which at its height controlled the rich trading ports on both coasts of south India and held Ceylon as a tribu-tary state.

The conflict between Vijayanagar and the Bah-mani was as much a struggle among different elites as it was a conflict between Muslims and Hindus, since both states pursued policies that turned a blind eye to religious differences when doing so favored their interests. Bahmani rulers sought to balance devotion to Muslim domina-tion and the practical importance of incorporat-ing the leaders of the majority Hindu population into the government, marrying Hindu wives and appointing Brahmins to high offices. Vijayanagar rulers hired Muslim cavalry specialists and archers to strengthen their military forces and formed an alliance with the Muslim-ruled state of Gujarat.

By 1351, when all of South India was indepen-dent, much of north India was also in rebellion. In the northeast, Bengal successfully broke away from Delhi's rule in 1338, becoming a center of the mystical Sufi tradition of Islam (see Chapter 10). In the west Gujarat regained its indepen-dence by 1390. The weakening of Delhi's central authority revived Mongol interests in the area. In 1398 the Turko-Mongol leader Timur (see Chapter 13) seized the opportunity to invade and captured the city of Delhi. When his armies withdrew the next year, dragging vast quantities of pillage and tens of thousands of captives behind them, the largest city in southern Asia lay empty and in ruins. The Delhi Sultanate never recovered.

Despite its shortcomings, the Delhi Sultanate was important in the development of central-ized political authority in India. It established a bureaucracy headed by the sultan, who was aided by the prime minister (*wazir*) and provin-cial governors. There were efforts to improve food production, promote trade and economic growth, and establish a common currency. De-spite the many conflicts that Muslim conquest and rule provoked, Islam gradually acquired a permanent place in South Asia. Yet the mixture of indigenous political traditions with these Islamic practices served to distinguish the Delhi Sultanate, like Mali, from the states in the Mid-dle East, where Islam had first flourished.

INDIAN OCEAN TRADE

Food producers sustained the region's life; sul-tans and kings directed its political affairs. Merchants were a third force uniting the trop-ics. Their maritime network stretched across the Indian Ocean from the Islamic heartlands of Iran and Arabia to Southeast Asia and the East Indies. Connecting routes extended to Europe, Africa, and China. The world's richest maritime trading network at this time, the Indian Ocean routes also facilitated the spread of Islam.

Monsoon Mariners

Between 1200 and 1500 the volume of trade in the Indian Ocean increased, stimulated by the prosperity of Islamic and Mongol empires in Asia, of Latin Europe, as well as of Africa and the East Indies. There was greater demand for luxuries for the wealthy: precious metals and jewels, rare spices, fine textiles, and other manufactures. The construction of much larger ships in these centuries also made it profitable to ship bulk cargoes of ordinary cotton textiles, pepper, food grains (rice, wheat, barley), timber, horses, and other goods. When the collapse of the Mongol Empire in the fourteenth century disrupted the overland trade routes across Central Asia, the Indian Ocean routes assumed greater strategic importance in tying the peoples of Eurasia and Africa together.

Although some goods were transported from one end of this trading network to the other, few ships or crews made a complete circuit. Instead the trade was divided between the two sections of the Indian Ocean (the Arabian Sea in the west and the Bay of Bengal in the east) and among the three mainlands that bordered them (the Middle East, India, and the East Indies). This division was also true of the sailing vessels used in these two seas.

The characteristic cargo and passenger ship of the Arabian Sea was the *dhow* (see Environment & Technology: The Indian Ocean Dhow). Large numbers of these ships, which grew from an average capacity of 100 tons in 1200 to 400 tons in 1500, were constructed in Malabar coastal ports of southwestern India in this period. On a typical expedition a dhow might sail west from India to Arabia and Africa on the northeast monsoon winds (December to March) and return on the southwest monsoons (April to August). Small dhows kept the coast in sight. Relying on the stars to guide them, skilled pilots steered large vessels by the quicker route straight across the water. A large dhow could sail from the Red Sea to mainland Southeast Asia in from two to four months with stopovers in south India, Ceylon, and Sumatra. From 1200 onward, however, cargoes and passengers from dhows arriving on the Malabar Coast were more likely to be transferred to *junks*, which dominated the eastern half of the Indian Ocean and the South China Sea.

The largest, most technologically advanced, and most seaworthy vessels of this time, junks had been developed in China and spread with Chinese influence. They were built from heavy spruce or fir planks held together with enormous

nails. The space below the deck was divided into watertight compartments to minimize flooding in case of damage to the hull of the ship. According to Ibn Battuta, the largest junks had twelve sails made of bamboo and carried a crew of a thousand men, of whom 400 were soldiers. A large junk might have up to a hundred passenger cabins and could carry a cargo of over 1,000 tons. Chinese junks dominated China's foreign shipping to the East Indies and India, but not all of the junks that plied these waters were under Chinese control. During the fifteenth century, vessels of this type were built in Bengal and Malacca and were sailed by crews from South and Southeast Asia.

The trade of the Indian Ocean was decentralized and cooperative. Commercial interests, not political authorities, united the several distinct regions that participated in it (see Map 15.4). The Swahili Coast supplied gold from inland areas of eastern Africa. Ports around the Arabian Peninsula supplied horses and goods from the northern parts of the Middle East, the Mediterranean, and eastern Europe. In the center of the Indian Ocean trade, merchants in the cities of coastal India received goods from east and west, sold some locally, passed others along, and added vast quantities of Indian goods to the trade. The Strait of Malacca, between the eastern end of the Indian Ocean and the South China Sea, was the meeting point of trade from the East Indies, mainland Southeast Asia, China, and the Indian Ocean. In each region certain ports functioned as giant emporia for the trade, consolidating goods from smaller ports and inland areas for transport across the seas. The operation of this complex trading system can best be understood by looking at some of these regions and their emporia in greater detail.

Africa: The Swahili Coast and Zimbabwe

Trade expanded steadily along the East African coast from about 1250, giving rise to between thirty and forty separate city-states by 1500. Archaeological excavations reveal that after 1200 many mud and thatch African fishing villages were rebuilt with new masonry buildings, some-

The Indian Ocean Dhow

The sailing vessels that crossed the Indian Ocean shared the diversity of that trading area. The name by which we know them, *dhow*, comes from the Swahili language of the East African coast. The planks of teak from which their hulls were constructed were hewn from the tropical forests of south India and Southeast Asia. Their pilots, who navigated by stars at night, used an ancient technique that Arabs had used to find their way across the desert. Some pilots used a magnetic compass, which had originated in China.

Dhows came in various sizes and designs, but they all had two distinctive features in common. The first was the construction of their hulls. They consisted of planks that were sewn together, not nailed. Cord made of fiber from the husk of coconuts or other materials was passed through rows of holes drilled in the planks. Because cord is weaker than nails, outsiders considered this shipbuilding technique strange. Marco Polo fancifully suggested that it indicated sailors' fear that large ocean magnets would pull any nails out of their ships. The most likely explanations are that pliant sewn hulls were less likely than rigid nailed hulls to be damaged by groundings on coral reefs and were cheaper to build.

The second distinctive feature of dhows was their triangular (lateen) sails made of palm leaves or cotton. The sails were suspended from tall masts and could be turned to catch the wind.

The sewn hull and lateen sails were technologies developed centuries earlier, but there were two innovations in this period. First, a rudder positioned at the stern (rear end) of the ship replaced the large side oar that had formerly controlled steering. Second, shipbuilders increased the size of dhows to accommodate bulkier cargoes.

Modern reconstruction of a dhow (National Maritime Museum, London)

times three or four stories high. Archaeology also reveals the growing presence of imported glass beads, Chinese porcelain, and other exotic goods. This narrow strip of coast and islands, some 1,500 miles (2,400 kilometers) long, shared a common culture and language, African in grammar and vocabulary but enriched with many Arabic terms. In time it became known as *Swahili*, from the Arabic name *sawahil al-sudan*, meaning "the shores of the blacks."

Until shortly before Ibn Battuta's visit in 1331 the northern city of Mogadishu had been the Swahili Coast's most important commercial center, but in the fourteenth century the southern city of Kilwa surpassed it in importance. After visiting Kilwa, Ibn Battuta declared it "one of the most beautiful and well-constructed towns in the world." He noted that its dark-skinned inhabi-

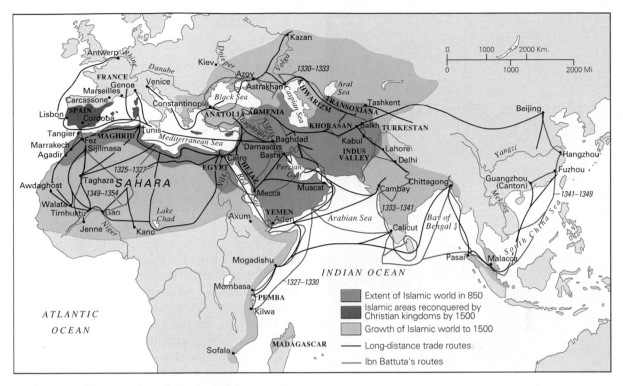

Map 15.4 Arteries of Trade and Travel in the Islamic World to 1500 Ibn Battuta's journeys across the vast expanse of Africa and Asia made use of land and sea routes, along which Muslim traders and the Islamic faith had long traveled.

tants were devout and pious Muslims, and he took special pains to praise their ruler as a man rich in the traditional Muslim virtues of humility and generosity.

Oral traditions associate the Swahili Coast's commercial expansion with the arrival of Arab and Iranian merchants, but what had attracted them? In Kilwa's case the answer is gold. By the late fifteenth century the city was exporting a ton of gold a year. It is also clear that the gold came from mines worked by Africans much farther south and inland from the coast. Much of it came from or passed through a powerful state on the plateau south of the Zambezi River, whose capital city is known as Great Zimbabwe. At its peak in about 1400, the city, which occupied 193 acres (78 hectares) may have had 18,000 inhabitants, the wealthiest of whom lived in dwellings made

of stone.

The stone ruins of Great Zimbabwe are one of the most famous historical sites in sub-Saharan Africa. The largest structure is a walled enclosure the size and shape of a large football stadium, carefully constructed of drystone masonry up to 17 feet (5 meters) thick and 32 feet (10 meters) high. Inside it were many buildings, including a large conical stone tower. Local African craftsmen built these stone structures between about 1250 and 1450 to serve as their king's court.

Like Mali, the Great Zimbabwe state rested on a mixed farming and cattle-herding economy, but its wealth depended on its role in long-distance trade. It first prospered in a regional trade based on copper ingots from the upper Zambezi Valley, salt, and local manufactures. The great expansion in the export of gold into the

Conical tower, Great Zimbabwe This graceful stone structure, situated inside the high-walled royal enclosure at Great Zimbabwe, was not used as a look out tower. Archaeologists believe the tower was a symbol of the African ruler's power, perhaps representing on a grand scale the clay granaries in which local chiefs stored the grain they received in tribute from their people. (Robert Aberman/Barbara Heller/Art Resource NY)

Indian Ocean in the fourteenth and fifteenth centuries brought Zimbabwe to the peak of its political and economic power. However, historians suspect that the city's residents depleted nearby forests for firewood while their cattle overgrazed surrounding grasslands. The result was an ecological crisis that hastened the empire's decline in the fifteenth century.

Arabia: Aden and the Red Sea

The city of Aden brought a double benefit to the Indian Ocean trade. Most of Arabia is desert, but monsoon winds brought Aden enough rainfall to supply drinking water to a large population and to grow grain for export. In addition, Aden's location (see Map 15.2) made it a convenient stopover for trade with India, the Persian Gulf, East Africa, and Egypt. Aden's merchants sorted out the goods from one place and sent them on to another: cotton cloths and beads from India, spices from the East Indies, horses from Arabia and Ethiopia, pearls from the Red Sea, luxurious manufactures from Cairo, slaves, gold, and ivory from Ethiopia. There were also grain, opium, and dyes from Aden's own hinterland.

After leaving Mecca, Ibn Battuta sailed to Aden in 1331 on his journey through the Red Sea, probably wedged in among bales of trade goods. He commented at length on the great wealth of Aden's leading merchants, telling a story about the slave of one merchant who paid the fabulous sum of 400 dinars for a ram in order to keep the slave of another merchant from buying it. Instead of punishing him for this extravagance, the master freed his slave as a reward for outdoing his rival. Ninety years later a Chinese Muslim visitor, Ma Huan, found "the country . . . rich, and the people numerous," with stone residences several stories high.

Common commercial interests generally promoted good relations among the different religions and cultures of this region. For example, in the mid-thirteenth century a wealthy Jew from Aden named Yosef settled in Christian Ethiopia, where he acted as an adviser. South Arabia had been trading with neighboring parts of Africa since before the times of King Solomon of Israel. The dynasty that ruled Ethiopia after 1270 claimed descent from Solomon and from the South Arabian princess Sheba. Solomonic Ethiopia's consolidation was associated with a great increase in trade through the Red Sea port of Zeila, including slaves, amber, and animal pelts, which went to Aden and on to other destinations.

Nevertheless, some religious and political conflict occurred. In the fourteenth century the

Sunni Muslim king of Yemen sent materials for the building of a large mosque in Zeila, but the local Somalis (who were Shiite Muslims) threw the stones into the sea. The result was a year-long embargo of Zeila ships in Aden. In the late fifteenth century Ethiopia's territorial expansion and efforts to increase control over the trade provoked conflicts with Muslims who ruled the coastal states of the Red Sea.

India: Gujarat and the Malabar Coast

The state of Gujarat in western India prospered as its ports shared in the expanding trade of the Arabian Sea and the rise of the Delhi Sultanate. Blessed with a rich agricultural hinterland and a long coastline, Gujarat attracted new trade after the Mongol capture of Baghdad in 1258 disrupted the northern land routes. Gujarat's forcible incorporation into the Delhi Sultanate in 1298 had mixed results. The state suffered from the violence of the initial conquest and from subsequent military crackdowns, but it also prospered from increased trade with Delhi's wealthy ruling class. Independent again after 1390, the Muslim rulers of Gujarat extended their control over neighboring Hindu states and regained their preeminent position in the Indian Ocean trade.

Much of the wealth of the state derived from its export of cotton textiles and indigo to the Middle East and Europe, largely in return for gold and silver. Gujaratis also dominated the trade from India to the Swahili Coast, selling cottons, carnelian beads, and foodstuffs in exchange for ebony, slaves, ivory, and gold. During the fifteenth century traders expanded their trade from Gujarat eastward to the Strait of Malacca. These Gujarati merchants helped spread the Islamic faith among East Indian traders, some of whom even imported specially carved gravestones from Gujarat.

Unlike Kilwa and Aden, Gujarat was important for its manufactures as well as its commerce. According to the thirteenth-century Venetian traveler Marco Polo, Gujarat's leatherworkers dressed enough skins in a year to fill several ships to Arabia and other places and also made beautiful sleeping mats for export to the Middle East "in red and blue leather, exquisitely inlaid with figures of birds and beasts, and skilfully embroidered with gold and silver wire," as well as leather cushions embroidered in gold. Later observers considered the Gujarati city of Cambay the equal of cities in Flanders and northern Italy (see Chapter 16) in the size, skill, and diversity of its textile industries. Gujarat's cotton, linen, and silk cloths, as well as its carpets and quilts, found a large market in Europe, Africa, the Middle East, and the East Indies. Cambay was also famous for its polished gemstones, gold jewelry, carved ivory, stone beads, and both natural and artificial pearls. At the height of its prosperity in the fifteenth century, this substantial city's well-laid-out streets and open places were lined with fine stone houses with tiled roofs. Although most of Gujarat's overseas trade was in the hands of its Muslim residents, its Hindu merchant caste profited so much from related commercial activities that their wealth and luxurious lives were the envy of other Indians.

Gujarat's importance in trade and manufacturing was duplicated farther south in the cities of the Malabar Coast. Calicut and other coastal cities prospered from their commerce in locally made cotton textiles and locally grown grains and spices, and as clearing-houses for the long-distance trade of the Indian Ocean. The Malabar Coast was united under a loose federation of its Hindu rulers, presided over by the Zamorin (ruler) of Calicut. As in eastern Africa and Arabia, rulers were generally tolerant of other religious and ethnic groups who were important to commercial profits. Most trading activity lay in the hands of Muslims, many originally from Iran and Arabia, who intermarried with local Indian Muslims. Jewish merchants also operated from Malabar's trading cities.

Southeast Asia: The Rise of Malacca

At the eastern end of the Indian Ocean, the principal passage into the South China Sea was through the Strait of Malacca between the Malay Peninsula and the island of Sumatra. As trade increased in the fourteenth and fifteenth centuries, this commercial choke point became the object of considerable political activity. The mainland kingdom of Siam gained control of most of the upper Malay Peninsula, while the Java-based kingdom of Majapahit extended its dominion over the lower Malay Peninsula and much of Sumatra. Majapahit, however, was not strong enough to suppress a nest of Chinese pirates who had gained control of the Sumatran city of Palembang and preyed on ships sailing through the strait. In 1407 a fleet sent by the Chinese government smashed the pirates' power and took their chief back to China for trial.

Weakened by internal struggles, Majapahit was unable to take advantage of China's intervention. The chief beneficiary of the safer commerce was the newer port of Malacca (or Melaka), which dominated the narrowest part of the strait. Under the leadership of a prince from Palembang, Malacca had quickly grown from an obscure fishing village into an important port by means of a series of astute alliances. Nominally subject to the king of Siam, Malacca also secured a tributary relationship with China that was officially conferred by the visit of the imperial fleet in 1407. The conversion of an early ruler from Hinduism to Islam helped promote trade with the Gujarati and other Muslim merchants who dominated so much of the Indian Ocean commerce. Merchants also appreciated Malacca's ability to offer them security and its absence of port duties except for presents to the ruler.

Besides serving as the meeting point for traders from India and China, Malacca also served as an emporium for Southeast Asian trade: rubies and musk from Burma, tin from Malaya, gold from Sumatra, as well as cloves and nutmeg from the Moluccas (or Spice Islands) to the east. Shortly after 1500, when Malacca was at its height, one resident counted eighty-four languages spoken among the merchants gathered there, who came from as far away as Turkey, Ethiopia, and the Swahili Coast. Four officials administered the large foreign merchant communities: one official for the very numerous Gujaratis, one for other Indians and Burmese, one for Southeast Asians, and one for the Chinese and Japanese. Malacca's wealth and its cosmopolitan residents set the standard for luxury in Malaya for centuries to come.

SOCIAL AND CULTURAL CHANGE

State growth, commercial expansion, and the spread of Islam between 1200 and 1500 led to many changes in the social and cultural life of tropical peoples. The political and commercial elites at the top of society grew in size and power. To serve their needs, the number of slaves increased considerably. There were also changes in lives of women in different social classes. The spread of Islamic practices and beliefs in many parts of the African and Asian tropics was a major aspect of social and cultural change, evident from the fact that the words *Sahara, Sudan, Swahili,* and *monsoon* are all Arabic in origin. Even so, traditional religious and social customs remained important.

Architecture, Learning, and Religion

As in other periods of history, social and cultural changes were more obvious in the cities than in rural areas. Some urban change was physical. As Ibn Battuta and other travelers observed, the merchants and ruling elites spent some of their wealth building new mansions, palaces, and places of worship. In architecture, as well as in education and religious practice, the spread of Islam was a major force for change in many tropical societies.

Most of the buildings that survive from this period are places of worship that exhibit fascinating blends of older traditions and new influences. Muslims in the western Sudan produced striking renditions of Middle Eastern mosque designs in local building materials of sun-baked clay and wood; Swahili cities built mosques of local coral stone. In India mosques were often influenced by the styles of existing temple architecture and even incorporated elements of older structures. Gujarati architecture of this period exhibited the finest blend of Hindu and Muslim styles. The congregational mosque at Cambay, built in 1325 with courtyard, cloisters, and porches typical of Islamic mosques, was assembled primarily out of pillars, porches, and arches taken from sacked Hindu and Jain temples of earlier generations. The congregational mosque erected at the Gujarati capital of Ahmadabad in 1423 was the culmination of a mature Hindu-Muslim architecture. It had an open courtyard typical of mosques everywhere, but the surrounding verandahs incorporated many typical Gujarati details and architectural conventions.

In some ways even more striking than these Islamic architectural amalgams were the Christian churches of King Lalibela of Ethiopia, constructed during the first third of the thirteenth century. As part of his new capital, Lalibela directed Ethiopian sculptors to carve eleven churches out of solid rock, each commemorating a sacred Christian site in Jerusalem. These unique structures carried on an old Ethiopian tradition of rock sculpture, though on a far grander scale.

Mosques were centers of education as well as of prayer. Muslims promoted literacy among their sons (and sometimes their daughters) so that they could read the religion's classic texts. Ibn Battuta reported seeing several boys in Mali who had been placed in chains until they completed memorizing passages of the Quran. In sub-Saharan Africa the spread of Islam was associated with the spread of literacy, which had previously been confined largely to Christian

Church of Saint George, Ethiopia   King Lalibela, who ruled the Christian kingdom of Ethiopia between about 1180 and 1220, had a series of churches carved out of solid volcanic rock to adorn his kingdom's new capital (also named Lalibela). The church of Saint George, excavated to a depth of 40 feet (13 meters) and hollowed out inside, has the shape of a Greek cross. (Robert Harding Picture Library)

tion of written texts in India, even though they still had to be copied by hand.

Although most of the education was concerned with basic literacy and the recitation of the Quran, advanced Muslim scholars studied Islamic law, theology, and administration, as well as classical Greek works of mathematics, medicine, and science. By the sixteenth century the West African city of Timbuktu had over 150 Quranic schools, and advanced classes were held in the mosques and homes of the leading clerics. So great was the demand that books were the most profitable item to bring from North Africa to Timbuktu. At his death in 1536 one West African scholar, al-Hajj Ahmed of Timbuktu, possessed some 700 volumes, an unusually large library for that time. In the East Indies, Malacca became a center of Islamic learning from where scholars spread Islam throughout the region. Other important centers of learning developed in Muslim India, particularly in Delhi, the capital.

As the changes in architecture and education suggest, the spread of Islam as a religion was a major theme of the period. Even where Islam entered as the result of conquest, as in India, conversions were rarely forced. Example and persuasion seem to have been far more important to the spread of Islam. The communities of Muslim merchants throughout the region, along with the large number of Muslim warriors and administrators who moved into India during these centuries, attracted interest in their religion. Many Muslims were active missionaries for their faith and worked hard to persuade others of its superiority.

Muslim domination of long-distance trade and markets was particularly important in fostering the adoption of Islam. Many commercial transactions took place between people of different religions, but trust was easier among individuals who shared the common code of morality and law that Islam provided. For this reason many local merchants were attracted to Islam. From the major trading centers along the Swahili Coast, in the Sudan, in coastal India, and in the East Indies, Islam's influence spread along regional trade routes.

Another important way in which Islam spread was through marriage. Most of the foreign Muslims who settled in tropical Africa and Asia were

Qutb Minar, India   A ruler of the Delhi Sultanate built this unusually tall minaret and mosque near Delhi in the early thirteenth century to display the power of Islam. Five times a day the muezzin climbed the 240-foot (73-meter) tower of red sandstone and white marble to call Muslims to prayer. (Jean Nou)

Ethiopia. Initially literacy was in Arabic, but in time Arabic characters were used to write local languages.

India already had a long literate heritage, so the impact of Islam on literacy there was less dramatic. Arabic spread among Indian scholars along with Persian (the language of Iran), which was considered more refined. Many new works of prose and poetry were written in Urdu, a Persian-influenced literary form of Hindi written in Arabic characters. Muslims also introduced papermaking in India, a second-century Chinese invention that had spread through the Indian Ocean trade routes. Paper facilitated the distribu-

single men. They often married local women, whom they required to be (or become) Muslims and to raise their children in the Islamic faith. Since Islam permitted a man to have up to four legal wives, as well as concubines, some wealthy men had dozens of children. In such large Muslim households the many servants, both free and enslaved, were also required by large elite Muslim households to be Muslims. Although such conversions were not fully voluntary, individuals could still find personal fulfillment in the Islamic faith.

In parts of southern Asia the upheavals of this period also promoted the spread of Islam. In India, Islamic invasions virtually destroyed the last strongholds of a long declining Buddhism. In 1196 the great Buddhist center of study at Nalanda in Bihar was overrun, its manuscripts were burned, and thousands of its monks were killed or driven into exile in Nepal and Tibet. Buddhism became a minor faith in the land of its birth (see Chapter 8), while Islam, swelled by substantial immigration, emerged as India's second most important religion. Hinduism remained India's dominant faith in 1500, but in most of maritime Southeast Asia the combined impact of Mongol invasion and the peaceful expansion of Muslim merchants led to the displacement of Hinduism by Islam.

Outside the cities, some peoples were attracted to Islam in this period. The seed of Islamic belief was planted among the pastoral Fulani of West Africa and Somali of northeastern Africa, as well as among pastoralists in northwest India. Low-caste rural Bengalis also began to adopt Islam, perhaps because they saw more hope in the universalism of Islam than in the fixed inequalities of the Hindu hierarchy. Yet the spread of Islam was not a simple process by which one set of beliefs was replaced by new ones. Islam too was changed by the cultures of the regions it penetrated, developing African, Indian, and Indonesian varieties.

Social and Gender Distinctions

The political, commercial, and religious changes of these centuries significantly affected the class structure and the status of at least some women. The gap widened between the elites and the masses. It is not clear that the poor became poorer —the 50 percent of the harvest that peasants in India paid in tax to the Delhi Sultanate may have been no more than what they formerly had paid to local lords—but the rich surely became richer and more numerous as a result of conquests and commerce.

The rising prosperity of the elites was accompanied by a growth in slavery. Many slaves were the product of wars of expansion by the powerful new states. The campaigns of conquest and pillage in India, according to Islamic sources, reduced Hindu "infidels" to slavery by the hundreds of thousands. The courts of the ruling elites of Delhi overflowed with slaves. Sultan Ala ud-Din owned 50,000; Sultan Firuz Shah had 180,000, including 12,000 skilled artisans. Sultan Tughluq sent 100 male slaves and 100 female slaves as a gift to the emperor of China in return for a similar gift. His successor prohibited any more exports of slaves, perhaps because of reduced supplies in the smaller empire.

In Africa, the growth of powerful states had also led to an increase in domestic slavery, as well as to a rising export trade in slaves. As Ibn Battuta reported, Mali and Bornu sent slaves across the Sahara to North Africa, including beautiful maidens and eunuchs (castrated males). The expanding Ethiopian Empire regularly sent captives for sale to Aden traders at Zeila. According to modern estimates, about 2.5 million enslaved Africans were sent across the Sahara and the Red Sea between 1200 and 1500. Some slaves were also shipped from the Swahili Coast to India, where Africans played conspicuous roles in the navies, armies, and administrations of some Indian states, especially in the fifteenth century. A few African slaves even found their way to China, where a Chinese source dating from about 1225 says rich families preferred gatekeepers whose bodies were "black as lacquer."

The status of slaves varied enormously, depending on their skill and sex. Relatively few in this period were used as field hands since "free" labor was so abundant and cheap. Most slaves were trained for special purposes. In some places, skilled trades and military service were dominated by hereditary castes of slaves, some of whom were rich and powerful. Indeed, the earliest rulers of the Delhi Sultanate were military slaves, though their status had long ceased to be a disadvantage. A slave general in the western Sudan named Askia Muhammad seized control of the Songhai Empire (Mali's successor) in 1493. Less fortunate were slaves who did hard menial work, such as those men and women who mined copper in Mali.

In all wealthy households there was a tremendous demand for slaves to be employed as servants. Ibn Battuta observed large numbers at the sultan of Mali's palace. Some servants were males, including the eunuchs who guarded the harems of wealthy Muslims, but most household slaves were female. Female slaves were also in great demand as entertainers and concubines. Having a concubine from every part of the world was a rich man's ambition in some Muslim circles. One of Firuz's nobles was said to have two thousand harem slaves, including women from Turkey and China.

Sultan Ala ud-Din's campaigns against Gujarat at the end of the thirteenth century yielded a booty of twenty thousand maidens in addition to innumerable younger children of both sexes. The supply of captives became so great that the lowest grade of horse sold for five times as much as an ordinary female destined for service, although beautiful young virgins destined for the harems of powerful nobles commanded far higher prices. Some decades later when Ibn Battuta was given ten girls captured from among the "infidels," he commented: "Female captives [in Delhi] are very cheap because they are dirty and do not know civilized ways. Even the educated ones are cheap." It would seem fairer to say that such slaves were cheap because the large numbers offered for sale had made them so.

How much the status of tropical women—whether slave or free—changed during this period is a subject needing more study. No one has yet offered a general opinion about Africa. Based on a reading of contemporary Hindu legal digests and commentaries (Smiriti), some authors speculate that the position of Hindu women may have improved somewhat compared to earlier periods, but in the absence of detailed information it is impossible to be sure. Hindu women continued to suffer from social and religious disabilities, but some restrictions on their lives may

have been relaxed—or, at the very least, not expanded—during these centuries. For example, the ancient practice of sati—that is, of an upper-caste widow throwing herself on her husband's funeral pyre—remained a meritorious act strongly approved by social custom. But Ibn Battuta leaves no doubt that, in his observation at least, sati was strictly optional. Since the Smiriti devote considerable attention to the rights of widows without sons to inherit their husbands' estates, one may conclude that sati was exceptional.

It remained the custom for Indian girls to be given in marriage before the age of puberty, although the consummation of the marriage was not to take place until the young woman was ready. Wives were expected to observe far stricter rules of fidelity and chastity than were their husbands and could be abandoned for many serious breaches. But women often were punished by lighter penalties than men for offenses against law and custom.

A female's status was largely determined by the status of her male master—father, husband, or owner. Women usually were not permitted to play the kind of active roles in commerce, administration, or religion that would have given them scope for personal achievements. Even so, women possessed considerable skills within those areas of activity that social norms allotted to them.

Besides child rearing, one of the most widespread female skills was food preparation. So far historians have paid little attention to the development of culinary skills, but preparing meals that were healthful and tasty required much training and practice, especially given the limited range of foods available in most places. One kitchen skill that has received greater attention is brewing, perhaps because it was the men who were the principal consumers. In many parts of Africa women commonly made beer from grains or bananas. These mildly alcoholic beverages, taken in moderation, were a nutritious source of vitamins and minerals. Socially they were an important part of male rituals of hospitality and relaxation that promoted social harmony.

Women's activities were not confined to the hearth, however. Throughout tropical Africa and Asia women did much of the farm work. They

Indian woman spinning, ca. 1500 This drawing of a Muslim woman by an Indian artist shows the influence of Persian styles. The female task of spinning cotton fiber into thread was made much easier by the spinning wheel, which the Muslim invaders introduced. The threads were woven into the cotton textiles for which India was celebrated. (British Library)

also toted home heavy loads of food, firewood, and water for cooking balanced on their heads. Other common female activities included making clay pots for cooking and storage and making clothing. In India the spinning wheel, introduced by the Muslim invaders, greatly reduced the cost of making yarn for weaving. Spinning was a woman's activity done in the home; the weavers were generally men. Marketing was a common activity among women, especially in West Africa, where they sold their agricultural surplus, pottery, and other craftwork.

It is difficult to judge how the spread of Islam affected the status of women. Women of some social classes found their status improved by becoming part of a Muslim household. The rare exception, such as Sultan Raziya, might even command supreme authority. Of course, many other women were incorporated into Muslim households as servants, concubines, and slaves.

Yet not all places that adopted Islam accepted all the social customs of the Arab world. In Mali's capital Ibn Battuta was appalled that Muslim women both free and slave did not completely cover their bodies and veil their faces when appearing in public. He considered their nakedness an offense to women's (and men's) modesty. In another part of Mali he berated a Muslim merchant from Morocco for permitting his wife to sit on a couch and chat with a male friend of hers. The husband replied, "The association of women with men is agreeable to us and part of good manners, to which no suspicion attaches." Ibn Battuta's shock at this "laxity" and his refusal to

ever visit the merchant again reveal the patriarchal precepts that were dear to most elite Muslims. So does the fate of Sultan Raziya of Delhi.

many ways more profound and disruptive. The
changes there would have great implications for
tropical peoples after 1500.

CONCLUSION

With nearly 40 percent of the world's population and over a quarter of its habitable
land, tropical Africa and Asia was a large
and diverse place. In the centuries between 1200
and 1500 commercial, political, and cultural expansion drew the region's peoples closer together. The Indian Ocean became the world's most
important and richest trading area. The Delhi
Sultanate brought the greatest political unity to
India since the decline of the Guptas. Mali extended the political and trading role pioneered
by Ghana in the western Sudan. The growth of
trade and empires was closely connected with
the enlargement of Islam's presence in the tropical world along with the introduction of greater
diversity into Islamic practice.

But if change was an important theme of this
period, so too was social and cultural stability.
Most tropical Africans and Asians never ventured far outside the rural communities where
their families had lived for generations. Their
lives followed the familiar pattern of the seasons,
the cycle of religious rituals and festivals, and the
stages from childhood to elder status. Occupations were defined by custom and necessity.
Most people engaged in food production by
farming, herding, and fishing; some specialized
in crafts or religious leadership. Based on the accumulated wisdom of how best to deal with their
environment, such village communities were remarkably hardy. They might be ravaged by natural disaster or pillaged by advancing armies,
but over time most recovered. Empires and kingdoms rose and fell in these centuries, but the villages endured.

In comparison, the social, political, and environmental changes taking place in the Latin
West, described in the next chapter, were in

SUGGESTED READING

The trading links among the lands around the Indian
Ocean have attracted the attention of recent scholars,
who include many details of the ecological underpin-
nings of that trade. Most ambitious, broadest (touching on all the regions), and perhaps most inclined to
overreach the evidence is Janet Abu-Lughod, *Before
European Hegemony: The World System A.D. 1250–1350*
(1989), which may usefully be read with K. N. Chaudhuri, *Asia Before Europe: Economy and Civilization of the
Indian Ocean from the Rise of Islam to 1750* (1991). Students will find clear summaries of Islam's influences
in tropical Asia and Africa in Ira Lapidus, *A History of
Islamic Societies* (1988), part II, and of commercial relations in Philip D. Curtin, *Cross-Cultural Trade in World
History* (1984).

Greater detail about tropical lands is found in regional
studies. For Southeast Asia see Nicholas Tarling, ed.,
The Cambridge History of Southeast Asia, vol. 1 (1992);
John F. Cady, *Southeast Asia: Its Historical Development*
(1964); and G. Coedes, *The Indianized States of Southeast
Asia*, ed. Walter F. Vella (1968). India is covered com-
prehensively by R. C. Majumdar, ed., *The History and
Culture of the Indian People*, vol. 4, *The Delhi Sultanate*,
2d ed. (1967); with brevity by Stanley Wolpert, *A New
History of India*, 4th ed. (1993); and from an intriguing
perspective by David Ludden, *A Peasant History of
South India* (1985). For advanced topics see Tapan Ray-
chaudhuri and Irfan Habib, eds., *The Cambridge Economic History of India*, vol. 1, *c. 1200–c. 1750* (1982).

Africa in this period is well served by the later parts of
Graham Connah's *African Civilizations: Precolonial
Cities and States in Tropical Africa: An Archaeological Perspective* (1987) and in greater depth by the relevant
chapters in D. T. Niane, ed., *UNESCO General History
of Africa*, vol. 4, *Africa from the Twelfth to the Sixteenth
Century* (1984), and in Roland Oliver, ed., *The Cambridge History of Africa*, vol. 3, *c. 1050 to c. 1600* (1977).

For accounts of slavery and the slave trade see Salim
Kidwai, "Sultans, Eunuchs and Domestics: New
Forms of Bondage in Medieval India," in *Chains of*

Servitude: Bondage and Slavery in India, eds. Utsa Patnaik and Manjari Dingwaney (1985), and the first two chapters of Paul E. Lovejoy, *Transformations in Slavery: A History of Slavery in Africa* (1983).

Three volumes of Ibn Battuta's writings have been translated by H. A. R. Gibb, *The Travels of Ibn Battuta A.D. 1325–1354* (1958–1971); the fourth volume is in preparation. Ross E. Dunn, *The Adventures of Ibn Battuta: A Muslim of the 14th Century* (1986), provides a modern retelling of his travels with commentary. For annotated selections see Said Hamdun and Noël King, *Ibn Battuta in Black Africa* (1995).

The most accessible survey of Indian Ocean sea travel is George F. Hourani, *Arab Seafaring,* expanded ed. (1995). For a Muslim Chinese traveler's observations see Ma Huan, *Ying-yai Sheng-lan, "The Overall Survey of the Ocean's Shore" [1433],* trans. and ed. J. V. G. Mills (1970). Another valuable contemporary account of trade and navigation in the Indian Ocean is G. R. Tibbetts, *Arab Navigation in the Indian Ocean before the Coming of the Portuguese, Being a Translation of the Kitab al-Fawa'id . . . of Ahmad b. Majidal-Najdi* (1981).

NOTES

1. *Tarikh-i-Wassaf,* in Henry M. Elliot, *The History of India as Told by Its Own Historians,* ed. John Dowson (London: Trübner and Co., 1869–1871), 2:28.

2. Hasan Nizami, *Taju-l Ma-asir,* ibid., 2:219.

3. Minhaju-s Siraj, *Tabakat-i Nasiri,* ibid., 2:332–333.

The Latin West, 1200–1500

Rural Growth and Crisis • Urban Revival • Cultural Advances and the Renaissance

The Rise of the New Monarchies

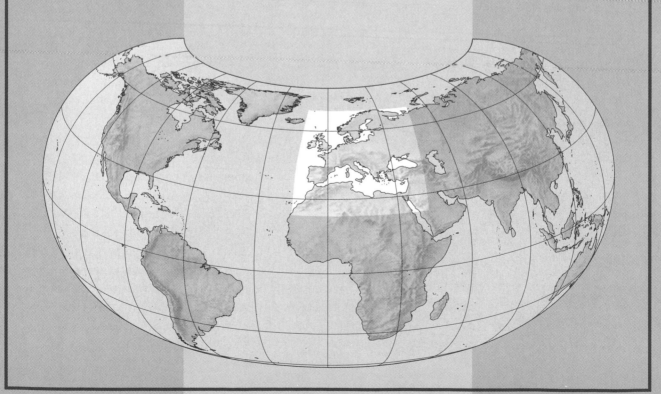

In the summer of 1454, Aeneas Sylvius Piccolomini was pessimistic about western Europe's future. A year earlier the Ottoman Turks, already in control of much of the Middle East and the Balkans, had captured the historic city of Constantinople, the last Christian stronghold in the eastern Mediterranean. As the pope's chief delegate in Germany, Aeneas Sylvius was charged with generating support for a crusade to halt further Muslim advances, but he doubted he would succeed. "How can you persuade the many rulers of the Christian world to take up arms under a single standard?" asked the man who in four years would be pope himself; "Christendom has no head whom all will obey—neither the pope nor the emperor receives his due."

Aeneas Sylvius reflected that, although French forces had recently won a decisive victory over the English in a series of conflicts that had begun in 1337 (now known as the Hundred Years War), the peace might easily be broken. The German emperor presided over dozens of states that were virtually independent of his control. The Spanish and Italians were divided into numerous kingdoms and principalities that often turned to war. With only slight exaggeration he lamented, "Every city has its own king, and there are as many princes as there are households," most more willing to fight with each other than to join a common front against the Turks.

This lack of unity, he believed, was due to Europeans' growing preoccupation with personal welfare and material gain:

> behold the huge and yawning maw of avarice, see how much inertia and how much greed there are. No one is devoted to letters or to the studies of the good arts. And do you think that an army of Turks could be destroyed by men of such morals?[1]

Such pessimism and materialism had increased during the previous century, partly in reaction to a devastating plague known in Europe as the Black Death. By 1351 it had carried off a third of western Europe's population.

Yet despite all these divisions, disasters, and wars, historians now see the period from 1200 to 1500 (Europe's later Middle Ages) as a time of unusual progress. The avarice and greed Aeneas Sylvius lamented were the dark side of the material prosperity that was most evident in the cities with their splendid architecture, institutions of higher learning, and cultural achievements. Frequent wars caused havoc and destruction, but in the long run they promoted the development of more powerful weapons and more unified monarchies.

Clearly the period looks rosier when one knows that the Turks did not overrun Europe, that the Hundred Years War had really ended, and that by 1500 explorers sent by Portugal and a newly united Spain would extend Europe's reach to other continents. Aeneas Sylvius knew only what had been, and the conflicts and calamities of the past made him shudder.

Although their contemporary Muslim and Byzantine neighbors commonly called western Europeans "Franks," they ordinarily referred to themselves as "Latins." That term underscored their allegiance to the Latin rite of Christianity (and to its patriarch, the pope) as well as the use by their literate members of the Latin language. The Latin West deserves special attention because its achievements during this period had profound implications for the future of the world. It was emerging from the economic and cultural shadow of its Islamic neighbors and, despite grave disruptions caused by plague and warfare, boldly setting out to extend its dominance into new regions. Some common elements promoted the Latin West's remarkable resurgence: competition, the pursuit of success, and the effective use of borrowed technology and learning.

Competition may be too mild a term to describe the often violent political, economic, and social conflicts of these centuries. Yet in the course of battles among themselves the people of the Latin West acquired the skills, tools, and determination that enabled them to challenge other parts of the world. Prolonged competition naturally promoted excellence, since besting one's rivals—whether in war, business, learning, or architecture—meant coming up with superior methods or tools. Technological and cultural borrowings in fields as different as milling and manufacturing, universities and printing, and weapons and navigation were vital to the pace of change. Although the Latin West's achievements ultimately depended on the activities of its own people, the ability to borrow from Muslim and Byzantine neighbors sped the region's rise, just as the Latin West's expansion overseas would accelerate new global exchanges.

RURAL GROWTH AND CRISIS

B etween 1200 and 1500 the Latin West brought more land under cultivation, introduced new farming techniques, and made greater use of machinery and mechanical forms of energy. Yet for most rural Europeans—and more than nine out of ten people were rural—the period from 1200 to 1500 was a time of calamity and struggle. Most rural men and women worked hard for their meager returns and suffered mightily from the effects of famine, epidemics, warfare, and social exploitation. From the low point caused by the Black Death in 1347–1351, peasant revolts sped social changes that released many persons from the bondage of serfdom and made some improvements in rural welfare.

Peasants, Population, and Plague

In 1200 most western Europeans were serfs, obliged to till the soil on large estates owned by the feudal nobility and the church (see Chapter 9). In return for using a portion of their lord's land, serfs had to provide their Lord with a share of their harvests, perform numerous labor services, and meet other obligations. Such rigid social relations slowed improvements in agricultural production.

As a consequence of the inefficiency of farming practices and of the obligations they owed to landowners, peasants worked hard for very meager returns. Despite the existence of numerous religious holidays, peasant cultivators probably devoted an average of 54 hours of hard labor a week in their fields. More than half of that labor went to support the local nobility. Each noble household typically rested on the labors of from fifteen to thirty peasant families. The standard of life in the lord's stone castle or manor house stood in sharp contrast to the peasant's one-room thatched cottage with little furniture and no luxuries.

Scenes of rural life show both men and women at work in the fields, although there is no reason to believe that equality of labor meant equality of decision making at home. In the peasant's hut as elsewhere in medieval Europe, women were subordinate to men. The influential theologian Thomas Aquinas (1225–1274) spoke for his age when he argued that, although men and women were both created in God's image, there was a sense in which "the image of God is found in man, and not in woman: for man is the beginning and end of woman; as God is the beginning and end of every creature."[2]

Rural poverty was not simply the product of inefficient farming methods and an unequal social system. It also resulted from the rapid growth of Europe's population. In 1200 Chinese may have outnumbered Europeans by two to one; by 1300 each population was about 80 million. China's population fell because of the Mongol conquest (see Chapter 14), but why Europe's population rose is not so clear. Some historians believe that the reviving economy may have stimulated population increase. Others argue that warmer-than-usual temperatures reduced the number of deaths from starvation and exposure while the absence of severe epidemics lessened deaths from disease.

Whatever the cause, more people required more productive ways of farming new agricultural settlements. One change gaining widespread acceptance in the region around Paris in the thirteenth century was to reduce the amount of farmland left fallow (uncultivated). Instead of following the custom of leaving half of the land fallow for a year to regain its fertility, more and more farmers tried a new three-field system in which they grew crops on two-thirds of the land each year. Many farmers using this system grew one field in oats to feed horses, which they could use to pull plows. In most of western Europe, however, farmers still let half of their land lie fallow and used oxen (less efficient but cheaper than horses) to pull their plows.

Population growth also led to the foundation of new agricultural settlements. In the twelfth and thirteenth centuries large numbers of German immigrants migrated into the fertile lands east of the Elbe River and in the eastern Baltic. Knights belonging to Latin Christian religious orders slaughtered or drove away the native inhabitants, who had not yet adopted Christianity. For example, during the century after its founding in 1231, the Order of Teutonic Knights conquered and resettled a vast area along the eastern Baltic that became Prussia (see Map 16.3). Latin Christians also founded new settlements on lands conquered from the Muslims and Byzantines in southern Europe and on Celtic lands in the British Isles.

By draining swamps and clearing forests, people also brought new land under cultivation within the existing boundaries of the Latin West. But as population continued to rise, people had to farm marginal lands that had poor soils or were vulnerable to flooding, frost, or drought. Because of the growing dependence on such marginal lands, average crop yields began to decline after 1250. More and more people lived at the edge of starvation, vulnerable to even slight changes in the food supply resulting from bad weather or the disruptions of war. According to one knowledgeable historian, "By 1300, almost every child born in western Europe faced the probability of extreme hunger at least once or twice during his expected 30 to 35 years of life."[3] One unusually cold spell led to the Great Famine of 1315–1317, during which there was widespread starvation in Europe. Other famines were more localized.

In time the cumulative effect of such crises might have reduced the population to a size that existing agricultural methods could more readily support. However, what actually eased population pressure was not famine but the *Black Death*. This terrible plague seems to have originated in India and then struck Mongol armies attacking the city of Caffa on the Black Sea in 1346 (see Chapter 13). A year later Genoese traders in Caffa carried the disease back to Italy and southern France. During the next two years the Black Death spread throughout western Europe, in some places carrying off two-thirds of the population. Overall the epidemic may have killed one of every three western Europeans by the time it subsided in 1351.

The plague's symptoms were ghastly to behold. Victims developed boils the size of eggs in their groins and armpits, black blotches on their skin, foul body odors, and severe pain. In most cases, death came within a few days. To prevent the plague from spreading, town officials closed their gates to people from infected areas and burned the victims' possessions. Such measures helped to spare some communities, but they could not halt the advance of the disease across Europe (see Map 16.1). It is now known that the Black Death was the bubonic plague, a disease that was spread not just from person to person but also by the bites of fleas that infested the fur of a certain black rat. But even if medieval Europeans had been aware of that route of infection, they could have done little to eliminate the rats, which thrived on urban refuse.

The plague left its mark not only physically but psychologically, bringing home to people how sudden and unexpected death could be. In response to the plague some people became more religious, giving money to the church or

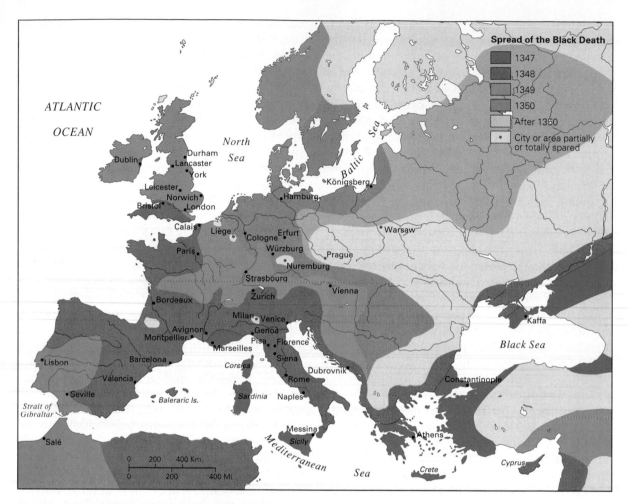

Map 16.1   The Black Death in Fourteenth-Century Europe   Spreading out of southwestern China along the routes opened by Mongol expansion, the bubonic plague reached the Black Sea port of Caffa in 1346. This map documents its deadly progress year by year from there into the Mediterranean and north and east across the face of Europe.

hitting themselves with iron-tipped whips to atone for their sins. Others chose to enjoy life while they still had it, spending their money on fancy clothes, feasts, and drinking. Whatever their mood, most people soon resumed their daily routines. Life went on.

Although population gradually rebounded from the low point of 1351, recovery was slow and uneven because of periodic returns of plague. By 1400 Europe's population had re-gained only the levels of 1200; not until after 1500 did it rise above its preplague levels. Meanwhile, China was recovering from its thirteenth-century losses (see Chapter 14).

Social Rebellion

Besides its demographic and psychological effects, the Black Death also set off social changes in western Europe. Skilled and manual laborers who survived demanded higher pay for their services. At first authorities tried to freeze wages at the old levels. Seeing such repressive measures as a plot by the rich, peasants rose up against wealthy nobles and churchmen. During a widespread revolt in France in 1358, known as the *Jacquerie*, peasants looted dozens of castles, killing dozens of persons. In another large revolt led by Wat Tyler in 1381, English peasants invaded London, calling for an end to all forms of serfdom and to most kinds of manorial dues. Some angry demonstrators murdered the archbishop of Canterbury and many royal officials. Authorities put down these rebellions with even greater bloodshed and cruelty, but they could not stave off the higher wages and other social changes the rebels demanded.

Serfdom practically disappeared in western Europe as peasants bought their freedom or just ran away. Many free persons who got higher wages from the landowners saved their money and bought their own land in depopulated areas. Unable to afford hiring enough fieldworkers to farm their lands, many large English landowners turned to pasturing sheep for their wool or to less labor-intensive crops and made greater use of draft animals and labor-saving tools. Because the plague had not killed wild and domesticated animals, more meat was available for each survivor and more leather for shoes. Thus the welfare of the rural masses generally improved after the Black Death, though the gap between rich and poor remained wide.

In urban areas employers had to raise wages to attract enough workers to replace those killed by the plague. Merchant guilds (see below) found it necessary to reduce the period of apprenticeship. Competition within crafts also became more common. Although the overall economy shrank with the decline in population, per capita production actually rose.

Mills and Mines

Despite calamities and conflicts, the use of mechanical energy, mining, and metallurgy grew so much in the centuries before 1500 that some historians have spoken of an "industrial revolution" in medieval Europe. That may be too strong a term, but the landscape fairly bristled with mechanical devices. England's many rivers had some 5,600 functioning watermills in 1086. After 1200 such mills spread rapidly across the western European mainland. By the early fourteenth century, for example, entrepreneurs had crammed 68 watermills into a one-mile section of the Seine River in Paris.

The lower part of a water wheel could be turned by a river, or water could be directed to flow over the top of the wheel. Some medieval designs made use of varying water flows, but for maximum efficiency dams were built to ensure the water wheels had a steady flow of water throughout the year. Ingenious machinery even enabled some watermills in France and England to harness the power of ocean tides.

Windmills were also common, especially in dry lands like Spain, where the flow of rivers was too irregular for efficient watermills, and in northern Europe, where the power of the wind could be tapped even in winter when ice made water wheels useless. Neither type of mill was a new invention nor unique to Europe. Water wheels and windmills had long been common in the Islamic world, but the medieval Latin West used such devices to harness the power of nature on a much larger scale than in any other part of the world.[4]

Mills were expensive to build, but they cost little to operate because free natural energy powered them. Thus, over time, they returned great profits to their owners. It was these profits that led to the proliferation of mills in medieval Europe. This also was the cause of conflicts among investors to secure prime sites and local monopolies. Some mills were built by individuals or by monasteries. Many more mills were built by groups of investors. The ability of mill owners to grow rich by grinding grain with wind or water power often aroused the jealousy of their neighbors. The English poet Geoffrey Chaucer (c. 1340–1400) captured many a miller's unsavory reputation (not always deserved) in this portrait in his *Canterbury Tales*:

Water mill, Paris Sacks of grain were brought to these mills under the Grand Pont to be ground into flour. These "undershot" water wheels were turned by the River Seine flowing under them. Gears translated the vertical motion of the wheel into the horizontal motion of the millstone. (Bibliotheque nationale de France)

He was a master-hand at stealing grain.
He felt it with his thumb and thus he knew
Its quality and took three times his due—
A thumb of gold, by God, to gauge an oat![5]

Water power also made possible such a great expansion of iron making that some historians say Europe's true Iron Age was in the later Middle Ages. Water powered the stamping mills that broke up the iron, the trip hammers that pounded it, and the bellows (first documented in 1323) that raised temperatures to the point where the iron was liquid enough to be poured into molds. Blast furnaces capable of producing high-quality iron are documented from 1380. The finished products included everything from armor to nails, from horseshoes to agricultural tools.

The demand for iron stimulated iron mining in many parts of Europe. There were also important new silver, lead, and copper mines in Austria and Hungary that supplied metals for coins and church bells, cannon and statues. Techniques of deep mining developed in central Europe were introduced farther west in the latter part of the fifteenth century. A building boom also led to more stone quarrying in France during the eleventh, twelfth, and thirteenth centuries than during all of the millennia of ancient Egypt.

The rapid growth of industry produced significant changes in the Latin West's landscape. Forests were cleared for farming, towns grew outward and new ones were founded, dams and canals changed the flow of rivers, and the countryside was marked by quarry pits and mines tunneled into hillsides. Pollution sometimes became a serious problem. Urban tanneries (factories that cured and processed leather) dumped large quantities of acidified waste water back into streams, where it mixed with human waste and the runoff of slaughterhouses. The first recorded antipollution law was passed by the British Parliament in 1388, although enforcement was difficult.

One of the most dramatic environmental changes during these centuries was deforestation. Trees were cut to provide timbers for buildings and for ships. Tanneries stripped bark to make acid for tanning leather. Many forests were cleared to make room for farming. The use of wood for fuel, especially by the glass and iron industries, was also a great consumer of forests. Charcoal was made by controlled burning of oak or other hardwood; then the charcoal was used to produce the high temperatures these industries required. It is estimated that a single iron furnace could consume all the trees within five-eighths of a mile (1 kilometer) in just 40 days. As a consequence of all these demands, many once dense forests in western Europe were greatly depleted in the later Middle Ages, except for those that powerful landowners protected as hunting preserves.

URBAN REVIVAL

In the tenth century not a single town in the Latin West could compare in wealth and comfort—still less in size—with the cities in the Byzantine Empire and the Islamic caliphates. Yet by the later Middle Ages wealthy commercial centers stood all along the Mediterranean, the Baltic, and the Atlantic, as well as on major rivers draining into these bodies of water (see Map 16.2). The greatest cities in the East were still larger, but those in the West were undergoing greater commercial, cultural, and administrative changes. Their prosperity was visible in impressive new churches, guild halls, and residences. This urban revival is a measure of the Latin West's recovery from the economic decline that had followed the collapse of the Roman Empire

(see Chapter 9) as well as an illustration of how the West's rise was aided by its ties to other parts of the world.

Trading Cities

Most urban growth in the Latin West after 1200 stemmed from the revival of trade and manufacturing. The greatest part of the trade was between cities and their hinterlands, but long-distance trade also stimulated urban revival. Cities in northern Italy in particular benefited from maritime trade with the bustling port cities of the eastern Mediterranean and, through them, with the great markets of the Indian Ocean and East Asia. In northern Europe commercial cities in the County of Flanders (roughly today's Belgium) and around the Baltic Sea profited from growing regional networks and from overland and sea routes to the Mediterranean.

Two events in the thirteenth century strengthened Italian trade with the eastern Mediterranean. One was the Venetian-inspired assault in 1204 against the city of Constantinople, which dominated the passage between the Mediterranean and Black Seas. Misleadingly named the "Fourth Crusade," this assault by Latin Christians on Greek Christians had little to do with the religious differences between them and much to do with Venice's desire to gain better access to the rich trade of the East. By crippling Byzantine power, Venetians were able to seize the strategic island of Crete in the eastern Mediterranean and expand their trading colonies around the Black Sea. The other boon to Italian trade was the westward expansion of the Mongol Empire, which opened up trade routes from the Mediterranean to China (see Chapter 13).

To take advantage of that trade the young Marco Polo set out from Venice in 1271 on the long trek across inner Asia. After reaching the Mongol court, the talented Marco spent many years serving the emperor Khubilai Khan as an ambassador and as the governor of a Chinese province. Marco later authored an immensely popular account of these adventures and of the

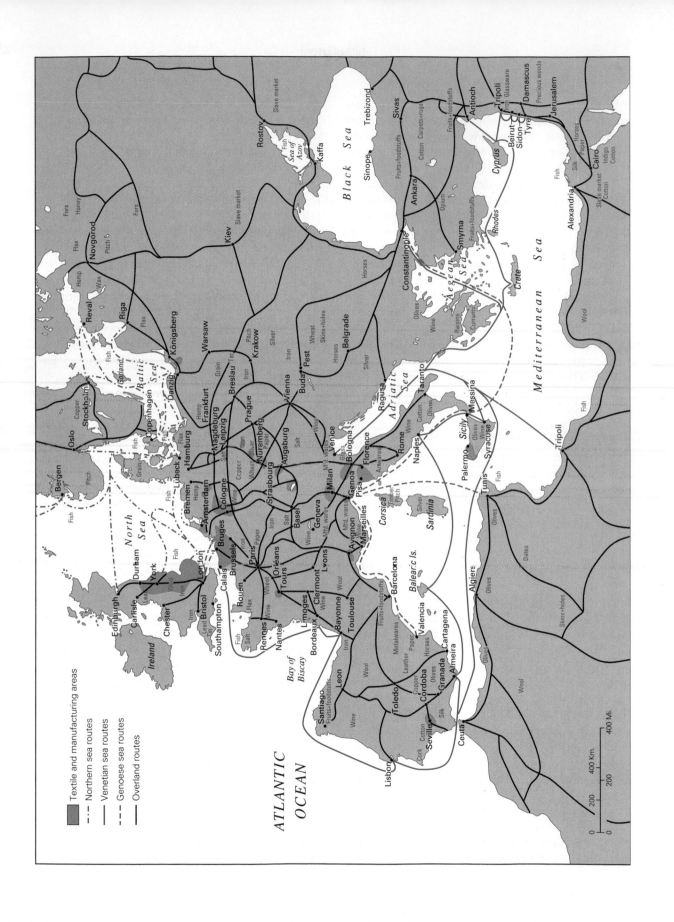

Legend:

Textile and manufacturing areas

--··-- Northern sea routes

──── Venetian sea routes

----- Genoese sea routes

──── Overland routes

ATLANTIC OCEAN

North Sea

Baltic Sea

Black Sea

Sea of Azov

Aegean Sea

Adriatic Sea

Mediterranean Sea

Bay of Biscay

Ireland

Corsica

Sardinia

Sicily

Crete

Rhodes

Cyprus

Balearic Is.

Scale: 0   200   400 Mi.
0   200   400 Km.

treacherous return voyage through the Indian Ocean that finally brought him back to Venice in 1295 after an absence of twenty-four years. Yet even in relatively prosperous Venice, few who had not seen for themselves could believe the stories of fabulous wealth of eastern lands.

While the disintegration of the Mongol Empire in the fourteenth century halted direct European contact with distant Asian cities, Venetian merchants continued to purchase eastern silks and spices brought by other middlemen to Constantinople, Beirut, and Alexandria. Three times a year galleys (ships powered by some sixty oarsmen each) sailed in convoys of two or three from Venice, bringing back some 2,000 tons of goods. Other merchants began to explore new overland or sea routes.

Venice was not the only Latin city whose trade expanded in the thirteenth century. The sea trade of Genoa on the west coast of northern Italy probably equaled that of Venice. Genoese merchants built up colonies on the shores of the eastern Mediterranean and around the Black Sea as well as in the western Mediterranean. In northern Europe an association of trading cities known as the *Hanseatic League* conducted extensive trade in the Baltic, including the newly conquered coasts of Prussia, and as far east as Novgorod in Russia and westward across the North Sea to London.

By the late thirteenth century, Genoese galleys from the Mediterranean and Hanseatic ships from the Baltic were converging on a third area, the trading and manufacturing cities in Flanders. In the Flemish towns of Bruges, Ghent, and Ypres skilled artisans turned raw wool from English sheep into a fine cloth that was softer and smoother than the coarse "homespuns" from simple village looms. Dyed in vivid hues, these

Map 16.2 Trade and Manufacturing in Later Medieval Europe The economic revival of European cities was associated with great expansion of commerce. Notice the concentrations of wool and linen textile manufacturing in northern Italy, the Netherlands, and England; the importance of trade in various kinds of foodstuffs; and the slave-exporting markets in Cairo, Kiev, and Rostov.

Flemish textiles appealed to wealthy Europeans who formerly had imported their fine textiles from Asia.

Along the overland route connecting Flanders and northern Italy important trading fairs developed in the Champagne region of Burgundy. These trading fairs began as regional markets, meeting once or twice a year, where manufactured goods, livestock, and farm produce were exchanged. When Champagne came under the control of the king of France at the end of the twelfth century, royal guarantees of safe conduct to all merchants turned the regional markets into international fairs. A century later fifteen Italian cities had permanent consulates in Champagne to represent the interests of their citizens who brought goods from Italy and eastern ports across the Alpine passes to exchange for Flemish cloths. The fairs were also important for exchanging currencies and conducting other financial transactions. During the fourteenth century the volume of trade grew so large that it became cheaper to send Flemish woolens to Italy by sea rather than overland on pack animals. As a consequence the fairs of Champagne lost some of their international trade but remained important regional markets.

Textile manufacturing also spread beyond Flanders. To increase revenue, in the late thirteenth century the English monarchy raised taxes on the export of raw wool, and it became more profitable to turn wool into cloth in England rather than in Flanders. Flemish textile specialists crossed the English Channel and introduced the spinning wheel and other devices to England. As a consequence the number of sacks of raw wool exported annually from England fell from 35,000 at the beginning of the fourteenth century to 8,000 in the mid-fifteenth, while exports of English wool cloth rose from 4,000 pieces in about 1350 to 54,000 a century later.

Florence was also developing as a wool-making center. Local banking families financed the profitable production of much of the high-quality cloth that in the past Florence had bought from the Flemish cities. In 1338, for example, Florence manufactured 80,000 lengths of cloth, while importing only 10,000. These changes in the textile industry

Flemish weavers, Ypres The spread of textile weaving gave employment to many people in the Netherlands. The city of Ypres in Flanders (now northern Belgium) was an important textile center in the thirteenth century. This drawing from a fourteenth-century manuscript shows a man and a woman weaving cloth on a horizontal loom, while a child makes thread on a spinning wheel. The cloth diaper takes it name from Ypres. (Stedelijke Openbare Bibliotheek, Ieper (Ypres))

show how competition promoted the spread of manufacturing and encouraged new specialties.

These growing industries made extensive use of windmills and water wheels. The power of wind and water was channeled through gears, pulleys, and belts to drive all sorts of machinery. The thriving textile industry in Flanders, for example, used mills to clean and thicken woven cloth by beating it in water, a process known as *fulling*. Another application of mill power was in papermaking. Although papermaking had been common in China and the Muslim world for centuries before it spread to southern Europe in the thirteenth century, Westerners were the first to

use machines to do the heavy work in its manufacturing.

Fifteenth-century Venice surpassed all of its European rivals in the volume of its trade in the Mediterranean as well as across the Alps into Central Europe. Its skilled craftspeople also manufactured luxury goods once obtainable only from eastern sources. Notable in this regard were its silk and cotton weaving, its glass and mirror industries, its jewelry, and its papermaking. At the same time exports of Italian and northern European woolens to the eastern Mediterranean were also on the rise. In the space of a few centuries western European cities used the eastern trade to increase their prosperity and then reduced their dependence on eastern goods.

Civic Life

As in the Indian Ocean basin (see Chapter 15), trading cities in Europe generally had more social mobility and religious diversity than rural places. Most northern Italian and German cities were independent states, sometimes controlling considerable land outside their gates. Cities in the larger European kingdoms commonly held special royal charters that exempted them from the authority of local nobles. Because of their autonomy, they were able to adapt to changing market conditions more quickly than cities in China and the Islamic world, which were controlled by imperial authorities. Social mobility was also easier in the Latin West because anyone who lived in a chartered city for over a year became free of all claims on his or her person. This made these cities a refuge for all sorts of ambitious individuals, whose labor and talent added to their wealth.

Cities were also home to most of Europe's Jews. The largest Jewish population was in Spain, where earlier Arab rulers had made them welcome. Before their expulsion in 1492, Jews numbered 3 percent of Spain's population. Other commercial cities had small Jewish communities, but nowhere else in the West were Jews more than 1 percent of the population. City officials welcomed Jews for their manufacturing and business skills, especially as moneylenders, because Latin Christians generally considered charging interest (usury) sinful. Despite their official protection, Jews were periodically subject to violent religious persecutions or expulsions (see Voices & Visions: Blaming the Black Death on the Jews). In all of the medieval West only the papal city of Rome left its Jews undisturbed throughout the centuries before 1500.

Along with opportunities, there were many restrictions on individual enterprise in European cities. Within most towns and cities powerful associations known as *guilds* dominated civic life. A guild was an association of persons, such as silversmiths or merchants, who worked in a particular trade. Each guild regulated the business practices of its members and the prices that they charged, trained apprentices, and promoted the interests of its members with the city government. By denying membership to newcomers and all Jews, guilds perpetuated the interests of the families that already belonged.

Guilds also perpetuated male dominance of most skilled jobs. Despite serious restrictions, some women were able to join guilds either on their own or as the wives, widows, or daughters of male guild members. Large numbers of poor women also toiled in non-guild jobs in urban textile industries and in the food and beverage trades, generally receiving lower wages than their male counterparts.

For many women marriage was an important means of social advancement. In *The Canterbury Tales* Chaucer includes a woman from the city of Bath in southern England, who had become wealthy by marrying a succession of old men for their money (and then two other husbands for love), "aside from other company in youth." She was also a skilled weaver, Chaucer says: "In making cloth she showed so great a bent,/She bettered those of Ypres and of Ghent."[6]

By the fifteenth century, growing commerce gave rise to a new class of merchant-bankers who had the wealth to operate on a vast scale and who often specialized in money changing, loans, and investments on behalf of other parties. Merchants great and small used their services, but the merchant-bankers also handled the financial transactions of ecclesiastical and secular officials. For example, they arranged for the transmission to the pope of the funds known as *Peter's pence*, a collection taken up annually in every church in the Latin West. Merchant-bankers also advanced large sums of money to the princes and kings of Europe to support their wars and lavish courts. Some merchant-bankers even developed their own news services, amassing information on every topic that could affect their businesses.

Florence had special importance in banking services. Its financiers invented checking accounts, organized private shareholding companies (the

Blaming the Black Death on the Jews, Strasbourg, 1349

Prejudice against Jews was common in the Latin West, as one can see in this selection from the official Chronicles of the Upper-Rhineland Towns.

In the year 1349 there occurred the greatest epidemic that ever happened. Death went from one end of the earth to the other, on that side and this side of the [Mediterranean] sea . . . . This epidemic also came to Strasbourg in the summer of [that] year, and . . . about sixteen thousand people died.

In the matter of this plague the Jews throughout the world were reviled and accused in all lands of having caused it through the poison which they are said to have put into the water and the wells—that is what they were accused of—and for this reason the Jews were burnt all the way from the Mediterranean into Germany, but not in Avignon, for the pope protected them there.

. . . The deputies of the city of Strasbourg were asked what they were going to do with their Jews. They answered and said that they knew no evil of them. [The town-council was deposed. A new council gave in to the mob and arrested the Jews.]

On Saturday—that was St. Valentine's Day—they burnt the Jews on a wooden platform in their cemetery. There were about two thousand people of them. Those who wanted to baptize themselves were spared. Many small children were taken out of the fire and baptized against the will of their fathers and mothers. And everything that was owed to the Jews was cancelled, and the Jews had to surrender all pledges and notes that they had taken for debts. The council, however, took the cash that the Jews possessed and divided it among the working-men proportionately. The money was indeed the thing that killed the Jews. If they had been poor and if the feudal lords had not been in debt to them, they would not have been burnt.

To what extent was the massacre of the Strasbourg Jews due to fear of the plague, to prejudice, and to greed? Why did some officials try to protect them?

Source: Jacob R. Marcus, ed., *The Jew in the Medieval World: A Source Book,* 315–1791, 1938, pp. 45–47. Reprinted with permission of the Hebrew Union College Press, Cincinnati.

Massacre of the Strasbourg Jews (From the Chronicarum Mundi, Nurnberg, 1493)

forerunners of modern corporations), and improved bookkeeping techniques. In the fifteenth century, the Medici family of Florence operated banks in Italy, Flanders, and London. They also controlled the government of Florence and were important patrons of the arts. By 1500 the greatest banking family in western Europe was the Fuggers of Augsburg, who had ten times the Medici bank's lending capital. Starting out as cloth merchants under Jacob "the Rich" (1459–1525), the family branched into many other activities, including the trade in Hungarian copper that was essential for casting cannon.

Bankers had to devise ways to profit from loans indirectly in order to get around the Latin Church's condemnation of usury. Some borrowers agreed to repay a loan in another currency at a rate of exchange favorable to the lender. Others added to the borrowed sum a "gift" in thanks to the lender. For example, in 1501 church officials agreed to repay a loan of 6,000 gold ducats in five months to the Fuggers along with a "gift" of 400 ducats, amounting to an effective interest rate of 16 percent a year. In fact, the return was much smaller since the church failed to repay the loan on time.

Gothic Cathedrals

Among the skilled people in greatest demand in the thriving cities of later medieval Europe were master builders and associated craftsmen. These craftsmen designed and erected buildings in a new style, later called *Gothic*, that were the wonders of the later Middle Ages. Cities competed with one another in the magnificence of their guild halls, town halls, and episcopal palaces, but especially in the size and beauty of their cathedrals, which symbolized their religious faith.

One distinctive feature of the new cathedrals that made their appearance about 1140 in France was the pointed, or Gothic, arch, which replaced the older round, or Roman, arch. Another was their incredible height. The arches stood atop high, thin stone columns stabilized by external

Portrait of a bourgeois marriage, 1434   In this picture, the Flemish artist Jan van Eyck, one of the masters of the new Renaissance oil paints, recorded the marriage of Giovanni Arnolfini and Giovanna Cenami, members of Italian merchant families that were resident in the cities of what is now Belgium. Fifteenth-century Europeans would have understood that the dog symbolized fidelity and the mirror reflected purity. (Reproduced by courtesy of the Trustees, The National Gallery, London)

buttresses. This method of construction permitted the outside walls to be filled with giant windows depicting religious scenes in brilliantly colored stained glass. During the next four centuries, interior heights soared heavenward, towers went ever higher, and walls became dazzling curtains of stained glass. The cathedral spire in Strasbourg reached 466 feet (142 meters) into the air—the height of a 40-story building. The record heights achieved by such thirteenth-century

Strasbourg cathedral Only one of the two spires that were originally planned for this Gothic cathedral was completed when work ceased in 1439. But the Strasbourg Cathedral was still the tallest masonry structure of medieval Europe. This engraving is from 1630. (Courtesy of the Trustees of the British Museum)

teacher, and as they constantly invented novel solutions to the problems they encountered, success rose from the rubble of their mistakes.

For most residents of western European cities, however, the wonders of new cathedrals provided only temporary distractions from the poverty and squalor of their lives. Even for the wealthy, European cities generally lacked the civic amenities, such as public baths and water supply systems, that had existed in the cities of Western antiquity and still survived in cities of the Islamic Middle East. Though thriving, the cities of the Latin West were still smaller than those of the eastern Mediterranean. On the eve of the Black Death, the largest, Venice, had nearly 200,000 inhabitants and Florence about half as many. To the north, Paris had some 80,000 inhabitants, but London (between 35,000 and 40,000) was no larger than the Flemish cities of Ghent (56,000) and Bruges (35,000). In comparison, Constantinople may have had a million inhabitants and Cairo even more.

structures would not be surpassed until the twentieth century.

These cathedrals were designed and built by men with little or no formal education and limited understanding of the mathematical principles of modern civil engineering. Master masons sometimes miscalculated, and parts of some overly ambitious cathedrals collapsed. The record-high choir vault of Beauvais Cathedral—154 feet (47 meters) high—for instance, came tumbling down in 1284. But practical experience was their greatest

CULTURAL ADVANCES AND THE RENAISSANCE

Urban revival involved more than markets and buildings. These cities were also centers of intellectual and artistic life. In part they rediscovered the cultural achievements of antiquity, and in some ways they surpassed them.

Throughout the Middle Ages people in the Latin West lived amid reminders of the achievements of the Roman Empire. They wrote and worshiped in its language, traveled its roads, and obeyed its laws. Even the vestments and robes of medieval popes, kings, and emperors were modeled on the regalia of Roman officials. Yet early medieval Europeans lost touch with much of the learning of classical antiquity. More vivid was the biblical world they heard about in the Hebrew and Christian scriptures.

Some fifteenth-century Italian authors proclaimed that their era had rediscovered the intellectual and artistic values of classical antiquity, ending a millennium of medieval superstition and ignorance. The Italian Renaissance ("rebirth") and its northern European extension were indeed a time of great intellectual and artistic achievement, but modern historians see the "Renaissance" less as a sudden break with the medieval past than as the culmination of a process of cultural enrichment that had been under way for several centuries. They also stress the importance of the Byzantine and Muslim worlds, where classical culture had never died out, in transmitting the learning of antiquity to their neighbors in the Latin West.

Though indebted to borrowings from its neighbors, Europe's cultural revival rested solidly on the prodigious talents of its own scholars and artists. The Latin West's cultural achievements were also fostered by new institutions of higher learning and by the perfection of mechanical printing as a means of disseminating knowledge. Moreover, it was not a coincidence that cultural revival was concentrated in Europe's thriving commercial centers. By itself the patronage of merchants and church prelates could not create great art, but it did give individuals the means to express their talents.

Universities

Before 1100 Byzantine and Islamic scholarship generally surpassed scholarship in Latin Europe. When southern Italy was wrested from the Byzantines and Sicily and Toledo from the Muslims in the eleventh century, many manuscripts of Greek and Arabic works came into Western hands and were translated into Latin for readers eager for new ideas. The manuscripts included previously unknown works of ancient philosophy by Plato and Aristotle and Greek treatises on medicine, mathematics, and geography. In addition there were scientific and philosophical writings by medieval Muslims. The works of the Iranian philosopher Ibn Sina (980–1037), known to the West as "Avicenna," were particularly in-

fluential. The Jewish scholarly community contributed significantly to the translation and explication of Arabic and other manuscripts.

The spread of these new classical manuscripts was intimately associated with new institutions of higher learning in the Latin West. Joining the older monastic schools were new independent colleges, endowed by contributions to provide subsidized housing for poor students and to pay the salaries of their teachers. The colleges first established in Paris and Oxford in the late twelfth and thirteenth centuries may have been modeled after similar places of study (madrasa) long known in the Islamic world.

However, the Latin West was the first part of the world to establish modern "universities," degree-granting corporations specializing in multidisciplinary research and advanced teaching. Some of the first universities were started by students; others were founded as guilds to which all the professors of a city belonged. These teaching guilds, like the guilds overseeing manufacturing and commerce, set the standards for membership in their profession, trained apprentices and masters, and defended their professional interests. The new universities set the curriculum of study for each discipline and instituted comprehensive final examinations for degrees. After passing exams at the end of their apprenticeship, students received a first diploma known as a "license" to teach. More advanced students, who completed longer training and defended a masterwork of scholarship, became "masters" and "doctors." In Paris the colleges were gradually absorbed into the city's university, but at Oxford and Cambridge the colleges remained independent, self-governing organizations.

Universally recognized degrees, well-trained professors, and exciting new texts promoted the rapid spread of universities in late medieval Europe. Between 1300 and 1500 the twenty oldest universities in Italy, France, England, and Iberia were joined by some sixty others throughout the Latin West. Because university courses were taught in Latin, students and masters could move freely across political and linguistic lines, seeking out the university that offered the courses they wanted and had the most interesting professors.

Universities offered a variety of programs of study but generally were identified with a particular specialty. Bologna was famous for the study of law; Montpellier and Salerno specialized in medicine; Paris and Oxford were best known for theology.

The importance of theology partly reflected the fact that many students were destined for ecclesiastical careers, but theology was also seen as the "queen of the sciences," the central discipline that encompassed all knowledge. For this reason thirteenth-century theologians sought to synthesize the newly rediscovered philosophical works of Aristotle, as well as the commentaries by Avicenna, with the revealed truth of the Bible. Their daring efforts were often controversial. The most notable case was the *Summa Theologica* issued between 1267 and 1273 by Thomas Aquinas, a doctor of theology at the University of Paris. Although his exposition of Christian belief organized on Aristotelian principles was eventually accepted as a brilliant demonstration of the reasonableness of Christianity, it upset many traditional thinkers. Some church authorities even tried to ban Aristotle from the curriculum. However, the considerable freedom of medieval universities from both secular and religious authorities enabled the new ideas of accredited scholars to prevail over the fears of church administrators.

Not all who studied theology followed careers in church administration. Chaucer's threadbare Oxford cleric, who "found no preferment [salaried post] in the church and . . . was too unworldly to make search for secular employment," became an independent scholar, repaying his benefactors with his prayers and spending their gifts on more books. "The thought of moral virtue filled his speech/And he would gladly learn, and gladly teach."[7] Many masters of theology preferred the freedom of the university over the cares of parish work or the discipline of monastic life.

In their quest for deeper understanding some fifteenth-century scholars studied classical texts in their original languages instead of in Latin translations. By comparing many different manuscripts, they produced critical editions of important works, correcting the errors introduced by generations of copyists. To aid in this task, Pope Nicholas V (r. 1447–1455) created the Vatican Library, buying scrolls of classical writings and paying to have expert copies and translations made. Working independently, the respected Dutch scholar Erasmus of Rotterdam (ca. 1466–1536) produced a critical edition of the Greek text of the New Testament. Erasmus was able to correct many errors in the Latin text that had been in general use throughout the Middle Ages, and he was able to issue hundreds of identical copies by means of the new technology of printing.

Printing

The Chinese were the first to use carved wood blocks for printing. During the tenth and eleventh centuries Chinese government presses had printed comprehensive editions of Confucian, Buddhist, and Taoist scriptures, but it seems that the direct inspiration for printing in Europe may have come from Chinese playing cards, which first appeared in Germany and Spain in 1377. Whatever the model, the high-quality books and pamphlets printed in the Latin West from the middle of the fifteenth century onward were a significant advance on Chinese printing techniques.

The man who did most to perfect the process was Johann Gutenberg (ca. 1394–1468) of Mainz, a goldsmith by training, who used his metalworking skills to cast individual letters of uniform style and size. He also developed a mechanical printing press and devised an ink suitable for printing. The Gutenberg Bible of 1454 was not only the first book in the West printed from moveable type but also an extremely beautiful and finely crafted work that bore witness to the printer's years of diligent experimentation. In addition to Gutenberg's Latin Bible, printers published critical editions of classical Latin writers. As interest in the past was stirred, the great Italian scholar-printer Aldo Manuzio (1449–1515) published classical Greek texts as well.

Printing spread with extraordinary speed. Paris alone had 75 printing presses in 1500; Venice had twice that number. By that date at least 10 million books had issued forth from presses in 238 towns in western Europe. Many of these presses were privately owned and printed whatever would sell, not just literary and religious texts.

Books were a boon to universities because students could buy a text rather than rent one or laboriously copy it by hand. Printing encouraged the spread of literacy and fostered the standardization of European languages. It also increased the circulation of works voicing unorthodox political and religious views. Not surprisingly, both church and state officials responded with efforts at censorship. The Catholic Church issued its first Index of Prohibited Books in 1564, but stopping the flow of works printed secretly in cellars and smuggled across political boundaries was difficult.

Renaissance Artists

The fourteenth and fifteenth centuries were as distinguished for their masterpieces of painting, sculpture, architecture, and literature as they were for their scholarship. Although artists continued to depict biblical subjects, the dissemination of classical knowledge led many artists especially in Italy to portray the deities and mythical tales of antiquity. Italy, where the Gothic style had never put down very deep roots, also pioneered the revival of Roman architectural motifs, including rounded arches, domes, and columned entrances.

This era abounded with artists of extraordinary talent. In Italy it was the age of Leonardo da Vinci (1452–1519), whose diverse works included the fresco (painting in wet plaster) *The Last Supper*, the oil painting *Mona Lisa*, and bronze sculptures, as well as imaginative designs for airplanes, submarines, and tanks. His younger contemporary Michelangelo (1472–1564) executed celebrated biblical frescoes on the ceiling of the Sistine Chapel in the Vatican, sculpted stat-

A French printshop, 1537 A workman operates the "press," quite literally a screw device that presses the paper to the inked type. Other employees examine the printed sheets, each of which holds four pages. When folded the sheets make a book. (Giraudon/Art Resource NY)

ues of David and Moses, and designed the dome for Saint Peter's Basilica. North of the Alps, the Flemish painter Jan van Eyck (ca. 1390–1441) created masterful realistic paintings on religious and domestic themes, and Hieronymus Bosch (ca. 1450–1516) produced complex allegorical fantasies.

The patronage of wealthy and educated merchants and prelates did much to foster this artistic blossoming in the cities of northern Italy and Flanders. The Florentine banker Cosimo de' Medici (1389–1464), for example, spent immense sums on paintings, sculpture, and public

buildings. His grandson Lorenzo (1449–1492), known as "the Magnificent," was even more lavish. The church also remained an important source of artistic commissions. In particular, the papacy launched an immense building program to restore Rome as the capital of the Latin church, culminating in the construction of the giant new Saint Peter's Basilica and a residence for the pope.

The achievements of Renaissance artists included several new techniques. Better understanding of perspective enabled painters to depict scenes of greater reality and depth on flat surfaces. The Flemish invention of oil paints in the fifteenth century provided artists with a medium that was easier to work in than the fast-drying frescoes, and the linseed-oil base of oil paints gave scenes an enduring luster. Da Vinci's ability to cast large statues in bronze owed much to techniques perfected in the casting of cannon.

Renaissance art, like Renaissance scholarship, owed a major debt not only to the contributions of individual artists but also to earlier generations. In Florentine painting, for example, the key precursor of the Renaissance was Giotto (ca. 1267–1337), of whom an influential modern art historian has said, "There are few men in the entire history of art to equal the stature of Giotto as a radical reformer."[8] In his religious scenes Giotto replaced the staring, otherworldly figures of the Byzantine style, which were intended to overawe viewers, with more natural and human portraits with whose emotions viewers could easily identify. Rather than floating on backgrounds of gold leaf, the saints of his Gothic style inhabit earthly landscapes. Renaissance artists

Africans in Renaissance Europe Fifteenth-century Renaissance artists regularly portrayed black Africans, often as regal princes as in this nativity scene of about 1500 by the Dutch artist Hieronymus Bosch. Portuguese explorers brought several delegations of African rulers and ambassadors to Europe in the fifteenth century. African servants are also shown in many artworks, reflecting the growing population of African slaves in Iberia and Italy. (Museo del Prado)

credited Giotto with singlehandedly reviving "the lost art of painting." In Leonardo da Vinci's view, Giotto set standards of artistic perfection so high that it was only in his own century that Italian painting regained Giotto's level.

Italian Renaissance literature similarly depended greatly on earlier achievements. Giotto's Florentine contemporary Dante Alighieri (1265–1321) completed his long, elegant poem, the *Divine Comedy*, just before his death. Written in the Italian dialect of Tuscany, this supreme expression of medieval preoccupations tells the allegorical story of Dante's journey through the nine circles of hell and the seven terraces of purgatory, guided by the Roman poet Virgil, and then his entry into Paradise guided by Beatrice, a woman whom he had loved from afar since childhood. In the view of some scholars the *Divine Comedy* may have been influenced by Islamic literary conventions from India and Persia. Dante's lead in writing in the spoken vernacular was followed by the Italian writers Francesco Petrarch (1304–1374) and Giovanni Boccaccio (1313–1375).

These scholarly and artistic achievements exemplify the innovation and striving for excellence of the later medieval centuries. The new literary themes and artistic styles of this period had lasting influence on Western culture, but the innovations in the organization of universities, in printing, and in oil painting had wider implications, for they were later adopted by cultures all over the world.

THE RISE OF THE NEW MONARCHIES

A consolidation and expansion of royal power paralleled the economic and cultural revivals under way in western Europe. The emergence of these "new monarchies" was due to three closely related transformations: monarchs' success in struggles with their vassals, the development of new weapons of war, and a clos-er relationship of rulers with commercial elites and with the church. The process unfolded somewhat differently in each state (see Map 16.3). In France and England, the events of the Hundred Years War played a critical role. In the Iberian kingdoms that became Spain and Portugal, the process depended heavily on territorial expansion against Muslim states.

Dynastic Conflict

In some of the Italian and Flemish city-states merchant elites displaced older ruling classes after 1200, but in most of the Latin West feudal aristocrats retained their political and economic power. Noble families controlled vast estates—even entire provinces—because of royal grants to their ancestors as rewards for loyal service and battlefield bravery. In theory the nobles were vassals of the reigning monarchs, obliged to furnish knights for their service whenever the monarch called them to do so. In practice vassals sought to protect their entrenched rights and increase their independence. Monarchs, in turn, fought hard to increase their political power at the expense of the feudal nobility. By 1500 the rulers of England, France, Spain, and Portugal had gained the upper hand in this struggle.

By conquering England in 1066 and subduing or replacing its nobility with his own men, the duke of Normandy greatly strengthened the power of the dynasty he founded. The Anglo-Norman kings also extended their realm by assaults on their Celtic neighbors. Between 1200 and 1400 they effectively incorporated Wales and reasserted control over most of Ireland. Persistent rebellion, however, frustrated their efforts to subdue Scotland.

Nevertheless, English royal power was not absolute. For example, in the span of just three years the ambitions of King John (r. 1199–1216) were severely set back. First he was compelled to acknowledge the pope as his overlord (1213). Then he lost his bid to reassert claims to Aquitaine in southern France (1214). Finally he was forced to sign the Magna Carta ("Great

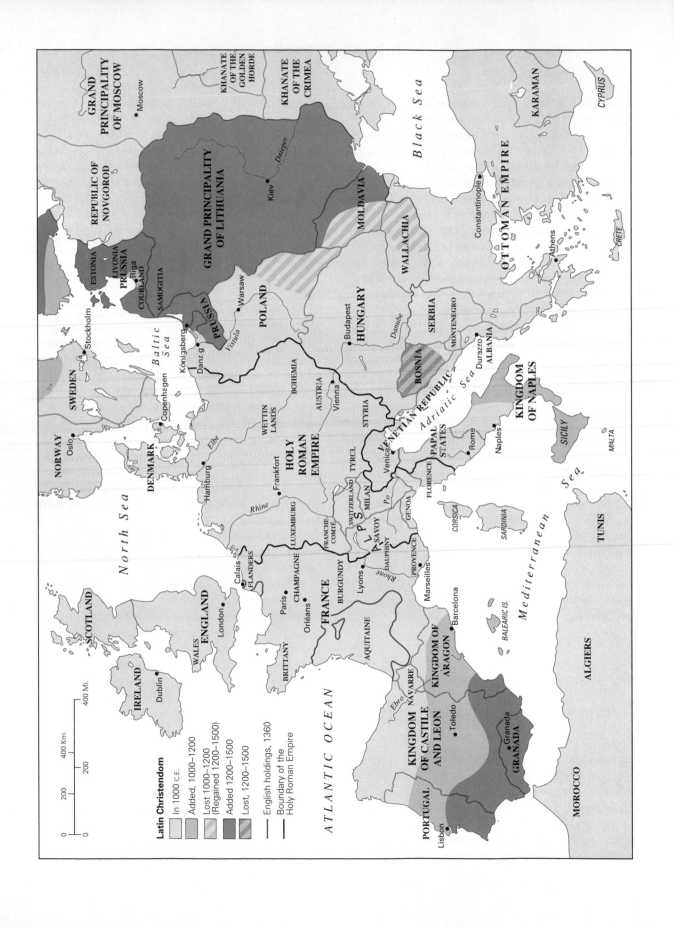

Latin Christendom

In 1000 C.E.

Added, 1000–1200

Lost 1000–1200
(Regained 1200–1500)

Added 1200–1500

Lost, 1200–1500

English holdings, 1360

Boundary of the
Holy Roman Empire

400 Mi.

400 Km.

200

200

0

0

GRAND
PRINCIPALITY
OF MOSCOW

Moscow

KHANATE
OF THE
GOLDEN
HORDE

KHANATE
OF THE
CRIMEA

Black Sea

KARAMAN

CYPRUS

REPUBLIC OF
NOVGOROD

GRAND PRINCIPALITY
OF LITHUANIA

Kiev

Dnieper

MOLDAVIA

WALLACHIA

OTTOMAN EMPIRE

Constantinople

Athens

CRETE

ESTONIA
LIVONIA
PRUSSIA
COURLAND
SAMOGITIA
Riga

PRUSSIA

POLAND

Warsaw

Vistula

Danzig

Königsberg

SERBIA

MONTENEGRO

BOSNIA

ALBANIA

Durazzo

KINGDOM OF
NAPLES

Stockholm

Baltic
Sea

HUNGARY

Budapest

Danube

VENETIAN REPUBLIC

Adriatic Sea

SWEDEN

Copenhagen

DENMARK

BOHEMIA

WETTIN
LANDS

AUSTRIA

Vienna

STYRIA

PAPAL
STATES

Rome

SICILY

MALTA

NORWAY

Oslo

North Sea

Elbe

HOLY
ROMAN
EMPIRE

Frankfort

Hamburg

TYROL

Venice

Naples

Milan

Po

GENOA

Rhine

SWITZERLAND

FRANCHE-
COMTÉ

ALPS

SAVOY

DAUPHINÉ

PROVENCE

FLORENCE

CORSICA

SARDINIA

Mediterranean Sea

TUNIS

SCOTLAND

IRELAND

Dublin

WALES

ENGLAND

London

LUXEMBURG

FLANDERS

Calais

BURGUNDY

CHAMPAGNE

Paris

Orléans

FRANCE

BRITTANY

AQUITAINE

Lyons

Rhône

Marseilles

BALEARIC IS.

Barcelona

ALGIERS

ATLANTIC OCEAN

NAVARRE

KINGDOM OF
ARAGON

KINGDOM
OF CASTILE
AND LEON

Toledo

Ebro

GRANADA

Granada

PORTUGAL

Lisbon

MOROCCO

Charter," 1215), which affirmed that monarchs were subject to established law, confirmed the independence of the church and the city of London, and guaranteed nobles' hereditary rights.

The kings of France began this period ruling a much larger and more populous kingdom than did the English monarchs but having less control of their noble vassals. By adroitly using the support of the towns, the saintly King Louis IX (r. 1226–1270) was able to issue ordinances that applied throughout his kingdom without first obtaining the nobles' consent. But there was prolonged resistance by the most powerful vassals to later kings' efforts to extend royal authority. These vassals included the kings of England (for lands that belonged to their Norman ancestors), the counts of prosperous and independent-minded Flanders in the north, the dukes of Brittany, and, later in the struggle, the dukes of Burgundy. For more than a century royal power in France rose and fell on the outcome of the battles that made up the Hundred Years War (1337–1453).

One of the factors central to these struggles was the hereditary nature of political authority. Both monarchs and vassals entered into strategic marriages with a view to strengthening their power and increasing their lands. Dynastic marriages sometimes produced unexpected results. For example, the marriage of Princess Isabella of France to King Edward II (r. 1307–1327) of England was meant to ensure that this powerful vassal remained loyal to the French monarchy. However, when Isabella's three brothers served in turn as kings of France without leaving a male heir, this gave her son, King Edward III (r. 1327–1377) of England, a possible claim to the French throne. When French courts instead awarded the throne to a more distant (and more

French) cousin, Edward decided to fight for his rights, beginning the Hundred Years War.

As this case shows, French rules of succession excluded women like Isabella both from inheriting the throne themselves and from passing on royal claims to their children. Elsewhere in the Latin West rules permitting royal women to rule in their own right when no male heir was available made marriage alliances even more important. An unmarried woman ruler was a most attractive bride, since such a union might join the spouses' territories as well as their persons. In 1386 the marriage of the queen of Poland to the grand duke of Lithuania created the largest state in Europe and also expanded the boundaries of Latin Christianity, for the duke agreed to accept that religion for himself and all his subjects as a condition of the marriage. (The Lithuanians were one of the last European peoples to adopt Christianity.) In 1469 the marriage of Ferdinand of Aragon (r. 1479–1516) and Isabella of Castile (r. 1474–1504) completed the amalgamation of several medieval Iberian kingdoms into Spain, sixteenth-century Europe's most powerful state.

Not all dynastic marriages benefited the female spouse. Despite her strategic marriage to an Austrian prince, Mary of Burgundy (1457–1482) was forced to surrender most of Burgundy to the king of France. In 1491 Anne of Brittany was compelled to marry the king of France, a step that led to the eventual incorporation of her duchy into France.

As these examples show, dynastic politics was in part a struggle among powerful families to retain control over ancestral lands and enlarge them by conquest, marriage, and inheritance. In this process both royal and noble families showed scant regard for "national" interests, regularly marrying across ethnic and linguistic lines and fighting to defend their claims to the diverse territories that resulted from such dynastic alliances. The resulting conflicts and boundary shifts make the political history of these centuries appear chaotic and unstable. Yet other parts of the tug of war between monarchs and vassals favored the strengthening of central authority and the creation of more stable (but not entirely fixed) state boundaries within which

Map 16.3 Europe in 1453 This year marked the end of the Hundred Years War between France and England and the fall of the Byzantine capital city of Constantinople to the Ottoman Turks. Muslim advances into southeastern Europe were offset by the Latin Christian reconquests of Islamic holdings in southern Italy and the Iberian Peninsula and by the conversion of Lithuania.

the nations of western Europe would in time develop. New technologies of war and the growing economy helped turn family dynasties into national monarchies.

New Weapons of War

Royal power rose as its dependence on feudal cavalry declined. The privileged economic and social position of the feudal nobility rested on the large estates that had been granted to their ancestors as fiefs so that they could support and train knights in armor to serve in a royal army. In the year 1200 the feudal knights were still the backbone of western European fighting forces, but by 1500 knights in armor were relics of the past. Two changes in weaponry did them in.

The first involved the humble arrow. Improved crossbows could shoot metal-tipped arrows with such force that they could pierce helmets and light body armor. Professional crossbowmen became more common and much feared. Indeed, a church council in 1139 outlawed the weapon as being too deadly for use against other Christians. The ban was largely ignored.

Early in the Hundred Years War French cavalry was reinforced by hired Italian crossbowmen, but arrows from another late medieval innovation, the English longbow, nearly annihilated the French force. Adopted from the Welsh, the six-foot longbow could shoot farther and more rapidly than the crossbow. Although arrows from longbows could not pierce armor, in concentrated showers they often found gaps in the knights' defenses or struck their less-well-protected horses. To defend against these weapons, armor became heavier and more encompassing, making it harder for a knight to move. If pulled off his steed by a foot soldier armed with a pike (hooked pole), a knight was usually unable to get up to defend himself.

The second innovation in military technology that weakened the feudal system was the firearm. This Chinese invention, using gunpowder to shoot stone or metal projectiles (see Environment

& Technology: Explosive Power in Chapter 14), completed the transformation of the medieval army. In the mid-fourteenth century, as Petrarch noted, "instruments which discharge balls of metal with most tremendous noise and flashes of fire [had] become as common and familiar as any other kind of arms"[9] (see Environment & Technology: Cannon).

On the battlefield the smoke and fire pouring forth from cannon may have been more useful in frightening the horses of advancing cavalry than the modest number of cannonballs were in causing damage. Large cannon, however, were quite effective in blasting holes through the heavy walls of medieval castles, ending the ability of their noble owners to withstand a royal siege. The first use of such siege artillery against the French, in the Battle of Agincourt (1415), gave the English an important victory. In the final battles of the Hundred Years War, French forces used heavy artillery to demolish the walls of once-secure castles held by the English and their allies.

With the English defeated, the French monarchs turned their armies on the duke of Burgundy, the most powerful remaining vassal, eventually seizing direct control of Flanders and Burgundy in 1477. During that struggle much smaller and more mobile cannon that could be fired more rapidly were developed. Made with greater precision and loaded with an improved gunpowder, these smaller cannon were nearly as powerful as the earlier behemoths. With only slight changes these weapons formed the basis of field artillery until the 1840s.

The final rout of the cavalry was due to improvements in hand-held firearms. By the late fifteenth century, projectiles shot from muskets could pierce even the heaviest armor, and the noise and smoke that muskets produced spooked the horses.

As a consequence of these changes in military hardware, armies depended less and less on knights and more on bowmen, pikemen, and musketeers, along with specialized artillery units. These new armed forces had to be financed from the royal treasury, not from feudal fiefs. Thus a third requirement of the new

Cannon

With some modifications the techniques and materials long used in the casting of bronze church bells were transferred to the casting of cannon. Europeans quickly surpassed all others in the qualities and quantities of cannon they produced. Until the mid-fifteenth century the tendency was for cannon to grow larger and larger. The largest, such as those used by the Turks to destroy the walls of Constantinople, were up to 15 feet (4.5 meters) long and so heavy that the German and Hungarian craftsmen who made them had to cast them on the spot. After firing stone projectiles 30 inches (76 centimeters) or more in diameter, such giants had to cool for hours before they could be fired again.

This illustration from the late fifteenth century depicts a large cannon being readied for use in blasting through a wooden rampart. As the scene shows, the cannon is not the center of the siege strategy. It is being used to supplement older forms of assault. Some of the attackers are attempting to scale the wall on a ladder. Note that none of the soldiers has a firearm. Most are armed with bows and arrows; a couple have crossbows.

Cannon, late fifteenth century (British Library)

monarchies was a system for financing a standing army.

Controlling the Purse and the Church

Rulers had not been slow to recognize the new revenue they could extract from the expansion of trade. Many of them taxed goods entering or leaving their realms. Some Christian princes and kings who gave Jewish merchants their protection taxed them heavily for the privilege. In addition, merchant towns were willing to make generous contributions to monarchs who freed them from the demands made by local nobles. Individual merchants curried royal favor with loans, even though such debts could be difficult or dangerous to collect. For example, the wealthy fifteenth-century French merchant Jacques Coeur gained many social and financial benefits for himself and his family by lending money to important members of the French court, but he was ruined when his jealous debtors accused him of murder and had his fortune confiscated.

Nobles were also willing to convert their feudal obligations to monarchs into money payments and to cough up taxes for wars they supported. For example, in 1439 and 1445 Charles VII of France (r. 1422–1461) won from his vassals the right to levy a new tax on land. The tax not only enabled him to pay the costs of the current war with England but provided the financial base of the French monarchy for the next 350 years.

Royal efforts to gain access to the wealth of the church met with greater resistance. When English and French kings tried to impose taxes on their clergy during the Hundred Years War, they set off major conflicts over the independence of the church from state control. In 1302 the outraged Pope Boniface VIII (r. 1294–1303) went so far as to assert that divine law made the papacy superior not just to monarchs but to "every human creature."

Issuing his own claims to superiority, King Philip "the Fair" of France (r. 1285–1314) sent an army to arrest the pope. After this treatment has-

tened Pope Boniface's death, Philip engineered the election of a French pope who established a new papal residence at Avignon in southern France in 1309. With the support of the French monarchy, a succession of popes residing in Avignon improved church discipline—but at the price of compromising the papacy's neutrality in the eyes of other rulers. Papal authority was further eroded by the Great Western Schism (1378–1415), a period when rival papal claimants at Avignon and Rome vied for the loyalties of Latin Christians. The conflict was eventually resolved by returning the papal residence to its traditional location, the city of Rome, but the long crisis broke the pope's ability to resist the rising power of the new monarchies.

By then, French and English rulers controlled all high ecclesiastical appointments within their realms and thus could use the wealth attached to such offices to reward their supporters. Other states secured similar control over the church appointments and finances in their territories. In so doing, the monarchs were not abandoning the church. Indeed, they often used state power to enforce religious orthodoxy in their realms more vigorously than the popes had even been able to do. But, as reformers complained, the church's spiritual mission could be subordinated to political and economic concerns.

One of the tragic ironies of the closer association of church and state was the fate of a young French peasant woman, Joan of Arc. Believing she was instructed by God to save France, she donned a knight's armor and rallied the French troops that defeated the English in 1429 just as they seemed close to conquering France. When she had the misfortune to fall into English hands shortly after this victory, she was tried by English churchmen for being a witch and was burned at the stake in 1431.

As a result of these complex dynastic and military struggles, by the end of the fifteenth century England and France stood unified under strong kings, and the nobility and the church had lost much of their independence. In future centuries nobles rebelled many times when kings were weak or unpopular, or when, as English dynastic rules permitted, a woman occupied the throne. But never again would the trend toward centralized rule be seriously deflected.

Iberian Unification and Exploration

The growth of Spain and Portugal into strong, centralized states was also marked by struggles between kings and vassals, dynastic marriages and mergers, and wars (though firearms were less important). But their story was also related to another form of territorial expansion in the Middle Ages: the crusade to expand the boundaries of Latin Christianity. Religious motives featured prominently in the wars to reclaim the lands of southern Iberia from the Muslims.

Such religious zeal did not exclude personal gain. The Iberian knights who gradually pushed the frontiers of their kingdoms southward knew that to the victors went the spoils. The spoils included irrigated fields capable of producing an abundance of food, rich cities of glittering Moorish architecture, and ports offering access to the Mediterranean and the South Atlantic. Victorious Christian knights were often rewarded with a grant (an *encomienda*) over the land and people in a newly conquered territory. The pattern of serving God, growing rich, and living off the labor of others became ingrained in the Iberian nobility.

The reconquest advanced in waves over several centuries; there were long pauses to consolidate the conquered territory and unify the Christian kingdoms. Toledo was taken in 1085 and made into a Christian outpost. The Atlantic port of Lisbon fell to a multinational assault in 1147. The beautiful cities of Cordoba and Seville succumbed respectively in 1236 and 1248, leaving only the Muslim kingdom of Grenada hugging the Mediterranean coast. Aragon and Castile's joint conquest of Grenada in 1492 secured the final piece of Muslim territory in Iberia for the new kingdom. The crusading mentality of this conquest showed in the order issued less than three months after Grenada's fall expelling all Jews from the Spanish kingdoms. That year was also memorable because of Ferdinand and Isabella's sponsorship of a voyage of exploration from Seville led by Christopher Columbus. The objective was to reach the riches of the Indian Ocean, but the eventual outcome was the extension of Spain's crusading system across the Atlantic.

The Atlantic kingdom of Portugal had driven Muslim rulers from its southern limits in 1249. After a long pause to colonize, Christianize, and consolidate this land, Portugal also set out on new conquests. In 1415 Portuguese knights seized the port city of Ceuta in Morocco. During the next few decades Portuguese mariners sailing out into the Atlantic discovered and colonized the island chains of the Madeiras and the Azores.

As in the case of their conquest of the mainland, Iberian maritime explorers were motivated by a mixture of religious and economic motives. When the leader of the assault on Ceuta and its first Portuguese governor, the young Prince Henry (1394–1460), returned to Lisbon to plan a far greater expansion south along the Atlantic coast of Africa, his goals were to spread the Christian faith, find allies against Muslim power, and secure wealth for his kingdom. The Azores became centers of fishing, sugar cane plantations were introduced into the Madeiras and other Atlantic islands, and a flourishing trade in gold and slaves was established with coastal Africans.

Portuguese overseas expansion depended on more than royal backing and a crusading tradition. New knowledge of world geography and improvements in sailing technology were equally important to success. From 1409 a Latin translation of a world geography attributed to Ptolemy, a second-century Greek, circulated widely in Europe. The geography was in fact substantially the work of medieval Byzantine and Arab scholars trading on Ptolemy's reputation as a geographer. One of the important contributions of this work was to teach European mariners how to compute their location on the open sea. In other respects maps attributed to Ptolemy were highly inaccurate. They represented the Indian Ocean as being enclosed by land at the bottom, they had no knowledge of the Americas, and they underestimated the earth's circumference and thus the distance westward from Europe to China. The last two mistakes were the reason why Columbus thought he could reach Asia by a relatively short voyage westward across the Atlantic instead of by sailing around Africa.

Not all Europeans were so in awe of the authority of "Ptolemy." Under the direction of Prince Henry of Portugal (later called "the Navigator"), detailed geographical information was collected from sailors and other travelers as part of a determined effort to overcome Europe's ignorance of the South Atlantic. Four years before Columbus first sailed west across the Atlantic, Portuguese mariners had completed nearly seven decades of careful exploration of the Atlantic coast of Africa and proven that, contrary to Ptolemy's *Geography*, there was a water passage around the southern tip of Africa into the Indian Ocean.

In 1498 Portuguese mariners reached India, and that same year Columbus, on his second voyage in the service of Castile and Aragon, touched the mainland of the previously unknown continents of the Americas. Immense new worlds to conquer to the east and the west had been opened up to the most expansive western Europeans. Already in 1494 an agreement brokered by the pope had divided the world between the Spanish and the Portuguese. Just behind them were merchants, mariners, and missionaries from other parts of Europe eager to continue the overseas expansion of the Latin West.

CONCLUSION

From an ecological perspective the later medieval history of the Latin West is a story of triumphs and disasters. Westerners excelled in harnessing the inanimate forces of nature with their windmills, water wheels, and sails. They excelled at finding, mining, and refining the mineral wealth of the earth as well, although localized pollution and deforestation were among the results. Their inability to improve food production and distribution as rapidly as their population grew created a demographic crisis that became a demographic calamity when the bubonic plague swept through Europe in the mid-fourteenth century.

From a regional perspective the centuries from 1200 to 1500 witnessed the coming together of the basic features of the modern West. States were of moderate size but had exceptional military capacity honed by frequent wars with one another. The ruling class, convinced that economic strength and political strength were inseparable, promoted the welfare of the urban populations that specialized in trade, manufacturing, and finance—and taxed their profits. Autonomous universities fostered intellectual excellence, and printing diffused the latest advances in knowledge. Art and architecture reached peaks of design and execution that set the standard for subsequent centuries. Perhaps most fundamentally, later medieval western Europe was a society fascinated by tools and techniques. In commerce, warfare, industry, and navigation, new inventions and improved versions of old ones underpinned the region's continuing dynamism.

From a global perspective, in these centuries the Latin West changed from a region dependent on cultural and commercial flows from the East to a region poised to export its culture and impose its power on the rest of the world. It is one of history's great ironies that many of the tools that the Latin West used to challenge Eastern supremacy had originally been borrowed from the East. Medieval Europe's mills, printing, firearms, and navigational devices owed much to Eastern designs, just as its agriculture, alphabet, and numerals had in earlier times.

Western European success depended as much on strong motives for expansion as on adequate means. Long before the first voyages overseas, population pressure, religious zeal, economic motives, and intellectual curiosity had expanded the territory and resources of the Latin West. From the late eleventh century onward such expansion of frontiers was notable in the English conquest of Celtic lands, in the establishment of Crusader and commercial outposts in the eastern Mediterranean and Black Seas, in the massive German settlement east of the Elbe River, and in the reconquest of southern Iberia from the Muslims. The early voyages into the Atlantic were an extension of similar motives in a new direction.

SUGGESTED READING

A fine guide to the Latin West (including its ties to eastern Europe, Africa, and the Middle East) is Robert Fossier, ed., *The Cambridge Illustrated History of the Middle Ages*, vol. 3, *1250–1520* (1986). Daniel Waley, *Later Medieval Europe* (1975), is briefer and emphasizes Italy. For the West's economic revival and growth see Robert S. Lopez, *The Commercial Revolution of the Middle Ages, 950–1350* (1976), and Harry A. Miskimin, *The Economy of Early Renaissance Europe, 1300–1460* (1975). Fernand Braudel provides wide-ranging global perspectives from 1400 onward in his *Civilization and Capitalism, 15th–18th Century,* 3 vols. (1982).

Students will find fascinating primary sources in James Bruce Ross and Mary Martin McLaughlin, eds., *The Portable Medieval Reader* (1977) and *The Portable Renaissance Reader* (1977). *The Notebooks of Leonardo da Vinci*, ed. Pamela Taylor (1960), show this versatile genius at work.

Technological change is surveyed by Carlo M. Cipolla, *Guns, Sails, and Empires: Technological Innovation and the Early Phases of European Expansion, 1400–1700* (1965); Jean Gimpel, *The Medieval Machine: The Industrial Revolution of the Middle Ages* (1977); and William H. McNeill, *The Pursuit of Power: Technology, Armed Force, and Society Since A.D. 1000* (1982). For a key aspect of the environment see Roland Bechmann, *Trees and Man: The Forest in the Middle Ages* (1990).

Charles Homer Haskins, *The Rise of the Universities* (1923; reprint, 1957), is a brief, lighthearted introduction; more detailed and up-to-date is Alan Cobban, *The Medieval Universities: Their Development and Organization* (1975). Johan Huizinga, *The Waning of the Middle Ages* (1924), is the classic account of the "mind" of the fifteenth century.

For social history see Georges Duby, *Rural Economy and Country Life in the Medieval West* (1990), for the earlier centuries; George Huppert, *After the Black Death: A Social History of Early Modern Europe* (1986), takes the analysis past 1500. Brief lives of individuals are found in Eileen Power, *Medieval People* (1924), and Frances Gies and Joseph Gies, *Women in the Middle Ages* (1978). More systematic are the essays in Mary Erler and Maryanne Kowaleski, eds., *Women and Power in the Middle Ages* (1988). Vita Sackville-West, *Saint Joan of Arc* (1926; reprint, 1991), is a readable introduction to this extraordinary person.

Key events in Anglo-French dynastic conflict are examined by Christopher Alland, *The Hundred Years War: England and France at War, ca. 1300–ca. 1450* (1988). Joseph F. O'Callaghan, *A History of Medieval Spain* (1975), provides the best one-volume coverage; for more detail see Jocelyn N. Hillgarth, *The Spanish Kingdoms,* 2 vols. (1976, 1978). Barbara W. Tuchman, *A Distant Mirror: The Calamitous 14th Century* (1978), gives a popular account of the crises of that era. P. Ziegler, *The Black Death* (1969), supplies a thorough introduction.

The Latin West's territorial expansion is well treated by Robert Bartlett, *The Making of Europe: Conquest, Colonization, and Cultural Change* (1993); Pierre Chaunu, *European Expansion from the Thirteenth to the Fifteenth Centuries* (1978); and, more narrowly, Bailey W. Diffie, *Prelude to Empire: Portugal Overseas before Henry the Navigator* (1960).

Francis C. Oakley, *The Western Church in the Later Middle Ages* (1985), is a reliable summary of modern scholarship. Kenneth R. Stow, *Alienated Minority: The Jews of Medieval Latin Europe* (1992), provides a fine survey up through the fourteenth century. For pioneering essays on the Latin West's external ties see Khalil I. Semaan, ed., *Islam and the Medieval West: Aspects of Intercultural Relations* (1980).

NOTES

1. Quoted in *The Portable Renaissance Reader*, ed. James Bruce Ross and Mary Martin McLaughlin (New York: Penguin Books, 1968), 75, 78.

2. Quoted in Marina Warner, *Alone of All Her Sex: The Myth and Cult of the Virgin Mary* (New York: Random House, 1983), 179.

3. Harry Miskimin, *The Economy of the Early Renaissance, 1300–1460* (Englewood Cliffs, NJ: Prentice-Hall, 1969), 26–27.

4. George Basalla, *The Evolution of Technology* (New York: Cambridge University Press, 1988), 144.

5. Geoffrey Chaucer, *The Canterbury Tales*, trans. Nevill Coghill (New York: Penguin Books, 1952), 32.

6. Ibid., 29.

7. Ibid., 25.

8. H. W. Janson, *History of Art* (Englewood Cliffs, NJ: Prentice-Hall, 1962), 272.

9. Quoted in Carlo M. Cipolla, *Guns, Sails, & Empires: Technological Innovation and the Early Phases of European Expansion, 1400–1700* (New York: Minerva Press, 1965), 22.

This guide provides pronunciation information for words in *The Earth and Its Peoples* that may be unfamiliar to you. Using this guide to pronounce proper names and other terms in the text should both aid your understanding of the material and build your confidence in speaking (and listening) in class.

To make the guide easy to read, the pronunciation for each word is spelled by syllable, with pronunciation symbols used for vowel sounds, as shown in the key below. The primary stress syllable in each word is capitalized, this shows which syllable should be emphasized in pronunciation.

Pronunciation Key:

a	h*a*t	ā	d*a*te	âr	d*are*	ah	f*a*ther
e	p*e*t	ē	f*ee*d	îr	p*ier*	ou	h*ou*se
i	s*i*t	ī	f*i*ne	ô	s*aw*	uh	*a*lone, h*er*
o	n*o*t	ō	s*o*	ûr	b*ur*n	œ	as in French, p*eu*
u	b*u*t	oo	n*oo*n	ŏŏ	f*oo*t		

The following references were used in compiling the pronunciations:

American Heritage Dictionary of the English Language, Third Edition (Boston: Houghton Mifflin Company, 1992)
Concise Cambridge Italian Dictionary (London: Cambridge University Press, 1975)
Ehrlich, Eugene H. and Hand, Raymond, Jr., *NBC Handbook of Pronunciation*, 4th ed. (New York: HarperPerennial, 1991)
The International Geographic Encyclopedia and Atlas (Boston: Houghton Mifflin Company, 1979)
The New Cassell's French Dictionary (New York: Funk & Wagnalls Co., 1962)
The New Century Cyclopedia of Names (New York: Appleton-Century-Crofts, 1954)
Papinot, E., *Historical and Geographical Dictionary of Japan* (Ann Arbor, MI: Overbeck Co., 1948)
Pronouncing Dictionary of Proper Names (Detroit, MI: Omnigraphics, Inc., 1993)
Spanish and English Dictionary (New York: Holt, Rinehart & Winston, 1955)
Webster's New Geographical Dictionary (Springfield, MA: Merriam-Webster, Inc., 1988)

A'isha AH-ē-shah
Abbasa ah-BAS-uh
Abbasid ah-BA-sid
'Abd al-Qadir AHB-d al—KAH-dēr
Abd al-Rahman AHB-d al—ruh-MAHN
Abd al-Wahhab ABD uhl—wuh-HAHB
Abu Bakr a-BOO BAK-uhr
Achaean uh-KĒ-uhn
Achaemenid a-KĒ-muh-nid
Acheh ah-CHE
Achilles uh-KIL-ēz
adat AH-daht
Adena ah-DAY-nah
Adowa AH-dŏŏ-wah
Aegean i-JĒ-uhn
Afrikaner af-ri-KAH-nuhr
Agamemnon ag-uh-MEM-non
Agincourt AJ-in-kort
Aguinaldo ah-gē-NAHL-dō
Agung of Mataram AH-gŏŏng ŭv mah-tah-RAHM
Ahaggar uh-HAG-uhr
Ahasuerus uh-HAZ-yoo-ēr-uhs
Ahhijawa uh-kē-YÔ-wuh
ahimsa uh-HIM-sah
Ahl al-Sunra wa'l-Jama'a AHL as—SUUN-uh wel—jah-MAH-uh
Ahmadabad AH-muhd-ah-bahd
Ahmose AH-mōs
Ahuramazda ah-HŎŎR-uh-MAZ-duh
Ain Jalut YYN jah-LOOL
Akkad AH-kahd
Akkadian uh-KĀ-dē-uhn
Aksum AHK-soom
al-Andalus al—AN-duh-lus
al-Ghaba al—GAH-buh
Ala-ud-din Khaliji uh-LAH—uh-DĒN KAL-jee
Alalakh UH-luh-luhk
Aleutian uh-LOO-shuhn
Algonquin al-GONG-kwin
Alighieri, Dante ah-lē-GYE-rē, DAHN-tā
alkali AL-kuh-lī
Allah AH-luh
alluvial uh-LOO-vē-uhl
Almoravid al-muh-RAH-vid
Alsace-Lorraine al-SAHS—lô-REN
Altai AL-tī
Amarna uh-MAHR-nuh
Amaterasu ah-mah-te-RAH-sŏŏ
ambergris AM-buhr-grēs
Ambon AHM-bôn
Amenhotep ah-muhn-HŌ-tep
Amitabha u-mi-TAH-buh
Amon AH-muhn

Amorite AM-uh-rīt
Anasazi ah-nuh-SAH-zē
Andalusian an-duh-LOO-zhuhn
anderun ahn-duh-ROON
Angra Mainyu ANG-ruh MĪN-yoo
Anjou AN-joo
Ankara ANG-kuhr-uh
Annam uh-NAHM
anthropomorphic an-thruh-puh-MÔR-fik
Antigonid an-TIG-uh-nid
Antioch AN-tē-ok
Anyang AHN YAHNG
Apache uh-PACH-ē
apartheid uh-PAHRT-hāt
apiru uh-PĒ-roo
Aquinas, Thomas a-KWĪ-nuhs, tō-MAHS
Aquitaine AK-wi-tān
Arafat ΛR uh fat
Aramaic ar-uh-MĀ-ik
Araucanian ahr-ô-KĀ-nē-uhn
Arawak AR-uh-wahk
Archangel AHRK-ān-juhl
Archilochus ahr-KIL-uh-kuhs
archipelago ahr-kuh-PEL-uh-gō
Ardashir ahr-dah-SHĒR
Argentina ahr-juhn-TĒ-nuh
Arianism ÂR-ē-uh-niz-uhm
Aristophanes ar-uh-STOF-uh-nēz
Arjuna AHR-joo-nuh
armillary AR-muh-ler-ē
Aro AH-rō
Arochukwu AH-rō-CHOO-kwoo
Asante uh-SHAHN-tē
Ashdod ASH-dod
Ashikaga ah-shē-KAH-gah
Ashurbanipal ah-shŏŏr-BAH-nuh-pahl
askeri AS-kuh-rē
Assiniboine uh-SIN-uh-boin
Astarte uh-STAHR-tē
Astrakhan AS-truh-kan
astrolabe AS-truh-lāb
Aswan AS-wahn
Atacama at-uh-KAM-uh
Atahualpa ah-tuh-WAHL-puh
Aten AHT-n
Athanasius ath-uh-NĀ-shuhs
atlatl aht-LAHT-l
auqaf OU-kahf
Aurangzeb OR-uhng-zeb
australopithecine ô-strā-lō-PITH-uh-sēn
Australopithecus africanus ô-strā-lō-PITH-uh-kuhs af-ri-KAH-nuhs
Avar AH-vahr
Averroës uh-VER-ō-ēz

Avicenna av-uh-SEN-uh
Avignon ah-vē-NYŌN
Awdaghost OU-duh-gust
awilum uh-WĒ-loom
Axum AHK-soom
ayatollah ī-uh-TŌ-luh
ayllu ī-LYOO
Azambuja, Diogo da ah-zahm-BOO-yah
Azcapotzalco ahs-kah-pô-TSAHL-kô
Azerbaijan ah-zuhr-bī-JAHN
Azores Ā-zorz

Babur BAH-buhr
Bactria BAK-tre-uh
Bahia buh-HĒ-uh
Bahrain bah-RĀN
Bajio bah-Ē-oh
Bal Tilak BAHL tē-LAHK
balam BAH-lam
Balboa, Vasco Núñez de bal-BŌ-uh
Balkh BAHLK
Baluchistan buh-loo-chi-STAN
Bani Hilal BAH-nē hē-LAHL
Baoyu BOU-yoo
Barbados bahr-BĀ-dōz
Barmakids BAHR-muh-kidz
bas-relief bah—ri-LĒF
Basque BASK
Bastille ba-STĒL
Batavia buh-TĀ-vē-uh
batik buh-TĒK
Batista, Fulgencio bah-TĒS-tah, fool-HEN-syō
Bayazid BAH-yah-zēd
Bayeux bah-YOO
Beauvais bō-VĀ
Begin, Menachem BĀ-gin, muh-NAH-kem
Behistun bā-hi-STOON
Beijing bā-JING
Bektashi bek-TAH-shē
Beltaine BEL-tān
Benguela ben-GĀ-luh
Berytus buh-RĪ-tus
biblion bi-BLE-ahn
Bight of Biafra BĪT of bē-AH-fruh
bilad al-Sudan bi-LAD uhs—soo-DAN
Bis im Pharrhof BĒS ēm FAHR-hôf
Blaise Diagne BLĀZ dē-AHN-yuh
blitzkrieg BLITS-krēg
Boccaccio, Giovanni bō-KAH-chē-ō, jē-uh-VAH-nē
bodhisattva bō-di-SUT-vuh
Bohai BŌ-HĪ
Bolívar, Simón bō-LĒ-vahr
Bologna buh-LŌN-yuh

Boniface BON-uh-fās
Bordeaux bor-DŌ
Bosch, Hieronymus BOSH, hī-RON-uh-muhs
Bosnia-Herzegovina BOZ-nē-uh—her-tsuh-gō-VĒ-nuh
Bosporus BOS-puhr-uhs
bourgeoisie bŏŏr-zhwah-ZĒ
Brahe, Tycho BRAH-hē, TĒ-kō
Brazza, Savorgnan de brah-ZAH, sa-vor-NYAHN
Brescia BRE-shah
Bruges BROOZH
Brunei broo-NĪ
Buenos Aires BWE-nôs Ī-res
Bukhara boo-KAHR-uh
burgess BÛR-jis
burgh BÛRG
Burgoyne, "Gentleman Johnny" buhr-GOIN
Burma BÛR-muh
Buyid BOO-yid
Byblos BIB-los
Byrsa BÛR-suh
Byzantine BIZ-uhn-tēn

Cabral, Pedro Alvares KA-brahl
cacao kuh-KĀ-ō
Caesar SĒ-zuhr
caesaropapism sē-zuh-rō-PĀ-piz-uhm
Caffa KAH-fah
Cahokia kuh-HŌ-kē-uh
Cakchiquel kahk-chē-KEL
caliphal KAL-uh-fuhl
Calixtus kuh-LIK-stuhs
Cambyses kam-BĪ-sēz
Camões, Luís de kuh-MOINSH
Cao Cao TSOU TSOU
Cao Xueqin TSOU SHOO-EH-CHIN
Caramansa kah-rah-MAHN-sah
caravel KAR-uh-vel
Cárdenas, Lázaro KAHR-dn-ahs, LAH-sah-rō
Carnelian kahr-NĒL-yuhn
Carolingian kar-uh-LIN-juhn
Carranza, Venustiano kah-RAHN-sah
Carthaginian kahr-thuh-JIN-ē-uhn
Cartier, Jacques KAHR-tē-ā
Casas, Bartolomé de las KAH-sahs
cassia KASH-uh
castas KAH-stahs
Castiglione, Giuseppe kah-stē-LYÔ-nē
Castillo kahs-TĒ-lyō
Çatal Huyuk cha-TAHL hoo-YOOK
Catalan KAT-l-an

Caucasian kô-KĀ-zhuhn
Caucasus KÔ-kuh-suhs
caudillo kô-DĒL-yō
Ceausescu, Nicolae chou-SHES-koo, nē-kô-LĪ
celadon SEL-uh-don
Celt KELT
Cernunnos KÛRN-yoo-nuhs
Cervantes, Miguel de suhr-VAN-tes
Cetshwayo ke-CHWĪ-ō
Ceuta sā-OO-tuh
Champagne shahm-PAHN-yuh
Champlain, Samuel de shahm-PLĀN
Chan CHAHN
Chandigarh CHUN-dē-guhr
Chang´an CHAHNG AHN
Charlemagne SHAHR-luh-mān
Cheka CHĀ-kuh
cheque CHEK
Chiang Kai-shek CHANG KĪ-SHEK
Chiapas chē-AH-pahs
Chihuahua chuh-WAH-wah
Chile CHĒ-le
chinoiserie shēn-wah-zuh-RĒ
Chishti CHISH-tē
Choctaw CHOK-tô
cinchona sing-KŌ-nuh
Circassian suhr-KASH-ē-uhn
Clairvaux klār-VŌ
Clemenceau, Georges klem-uhn-SŌ
cloisonné kloi-zuh-NĀ
Cluny KLOO-nē
Cnossus KNOS-uhs
Coeur, Jacques KÛR
Colbert, Jean Baptiste kôl-BÂR
Comanche kuh-MAN-chē
Comnenus, Alexius kom-NĒ-nuhs, uh-LEK-sē-uhs
Condorcanqui kon-dor-KAHN-kē
conquistadore kon-KĒ-stuh-dor
Constantinople kon-stan-tuh-NŌ-puhl
Le Corbusier luh kor-boo-ZYĀ
Cortés, Hernán kor-TEZ, âr-NAHN
costaria coh-STAH-rē-uh
Costilla, Hidalgo y Ē kōs-TĒ-yah
Coucacou koo-KAH-koo
courtiers KOR-tē-uhr
Creditanstalt crā-DĒT-ahn-shtahlt
creole KRĒ-ōl
Crimea krī-MĒ-uh
Crimean krī-MĒ-uhn
cruzado kroo-ZAH-dō
Cugnot coo-NYŌ
cuneiform kyoo-NĒ-uh-form
curia KYŎŎR-ē-uh
Cuzco KOOS-kō
Cyclopes sī-KLŌ-pēz

Cyrillic si-RIL-ik
Czech CHEK

Daedalus DED-l-uhs
Dahomey duh-HŌ-mē
Daiyu DĪ-yoo
Dalai lama DAH-lī LAH-muh
Daoist DOU-ist
Dardanelles dahr-dn-ELZ
Darius duh-RĪ-uhs
Date Masamuni DAH-tā mah-sah-MOO-nē
Daulatabad dou-LAT-ah-bahd
Davar dah-VAHR
Deccan DEK-uhn
Dehua DUH-HWAH
Deir el-Bahri DYYR uhl—BAH-rē
Delft DELFT
Delhi DEL-ē
Deshima DE-shē-mah
Deuteronomic doo-tuhr-uh-NOM-ik
devshirme dev-shēr-MEE
dhikr DIK-uhr
dhow DOU
Dhuoda doo-WOH-duh
Diderot, Denis DĒ-duh-rō, duh-NĒ
Dido DĪ-dō
Dienbienphu dyen-byen-FOO
dinar di-NAHR
Diodorus dī-ō-DOR-uhs
Dionysia dī-uh-NIZH-ē-uh
diorite DĪ-uh-rīt
dirham di-RAM
Djoser JŌ-sûr
Donatism DON-uh-tiz-uhm
Dravidian druh-VID-ē-uhn
dromedary DROM-i-der-ē
Druids DROO-ids
Du Bois, Eugene doo-BWAH
Du Bois, W. E. B. doo-BOIS
ducat DUK-uht
duchy DUCH-ē
Dur DOOR
Durkheim, Émile DÛRK-hīm, ā-MĒL
Dyula DYŎŎ-la

Ebla Ē-bluh
Eblaite Ē-bluh-īt
ecclesiastical i-klē-zē-AS-ti-kuhl
Ecuador EK-wuh-dor
Edessa i-DES-uh
Ekwesh EK-wesh
Elamites Ē-luh-mīt
emir i-MÎR
encomenderos en-kō-MĒN-der-ōs
encomienda en-kō-mē-EN-duh
Enkidu EN-kē-doo

ensete en-SE-tā
entente on-TONT
entrepôt ON-truh-pō
épée ā-PĀ
Epistle i-PIS-uhl
epoch EP-uhk
Epona e-PŌ-nuh
Equiano, Olaudah ā-kwē-AH-noo, ō-LOU-duh
Erasmus i-RAZ-muhs
Eritrea er-i-TRĒ-uh
Erythraean er-i-THRĒ-uhn
Eugenie œ-zhā-NĒ
eunuch YOO-nuhk
Euphrates yoo-FRĀ-tēz
Exchequer EKS-chek-uhr
Ezana ē-ZAH-nah

Faisal FĪ-suhl
Faiyum fī-YOOM
Falasha fuh-LAH-shuh
Faruq fuh-ROOK
fascisti fah-SHE-stē
Fatimid FAT-uh-mid
Ferghana fuhr-GAH-nuh
feudum FYOO-duhm
Fibonacci fē-bō-NAH-chē
fief FĒF
frater FRĀ-tuhr
Frumentius froo-MEN-shuhs
Fuggers FOOG-uhrz
Führer FYOOR-uhr
Fujiwara foo-jē-WAHR-uh
Fustat fus-TAHT

Gabriel, José gah-BRĒ-el
Gabriol GĀ-brē-uhl
Galilei, Galileo gal-uh-LĀ, gal-uh-LĒ-ō
Gallipoli guh-LIP-uh-lē
Gamal Abd al-Nasir gah-MAHL abd—uhn-NAH-suhr
Gandhi, Indira or Rajiv GAHN-dē
Ganges GAN-jēz
Gansu GAHN-SOO
Gath GATH
gaucho GOU-chō
Gaugemela GÔ-guh-mē-luh
Gdansk guh-DAHNSK
Ge Hong GUH HOONG
Gebel Barkal JEB-uhl BAHR-kahl
Genghis Khan JEN-gis KAHN
genista juh-NIS-tuh
Genoese JEN-ō-ēz
Gezer GE-zuhr
Ghana GAH-nuh
Ghat GAHT
Ghazan gah-ZAHN

Ghent GENT
Ghiyas al-Din GĒ-YAHS ad-DĒN
Ghurkhas GUHR-kuhz
Gila River HĒ-luh
Giotto JOT-ō
Girondist juh-RON-dist
Giza GĒ-zuh
glasnost GLAHS-nôst
Go-Daigo GŌ—DĪ-gō
Goa GO-uh
Gobi Desert GŌ-bē
Gomorrah guh-MOR-uh
Graeci GRĪ-kē
Gran, Ahmed GRAHN, AH-muhd
Guadeloupe GWOD-l-oop
Guangxu GWAHNG-JOO
Guangzhou GWAHNG-JŌ
Guangzi GWAHNG-SHĒ
Guatemala gwah-tuh-MAH-luh
guerrilla guh-RIL-uh
Guevara, Che guh-VAHR-uh, CHĀ
Guiana gē-AH-nuh
Guillaume gē-YŌM
guillotine GĒ-uh-tēn
Gujarat goo-juh-RAHT
gulag GOO-lahg
Guo Shijie GWŌ SHÛR-jē-yeh
Guomindang GWŌ MIN·DAHNG
Guyuk GUH-YOOK

hadith hah-DĒTH
Hafiz HAH-fiz
Hagia Sophia HĀ-jē-uh SŌ-fē-uh
Hainan HĪ-NAHN
Hajj Bektash HAH-jee bek-TAHSH
Hakkas HAHK-kahz
Hakra River HAK-ruh
halal hah-LAHL
Halevi, Judah hah-LĀ-vē
Halicarnassus hal-i-kahr-NAS-uhs
Hamadan ham-uh-DAN
Hammurabi HAM-uh-rah-bē
Hangzhou HAHNG JŌ
Hanoverian han-ō-VĪR-ē-uhn
Hanseatic han-sē-AT-ik
harem HÂR-uhm
harijan HAH-rē-jahn
Harkhuf HAHR-koof
Harun al-Rashid hah-ROON al—rah-SHĒD
Hatshepsut hat-SHEP-sŏŏt
Hattusha haht-tŏŏ-SHAH
hauberk HÔ-bûrk
Hausa HOU-suh
Havel, Vaclav hah-VEL
hectare HEK-târ
Heike HĀ-KEH
heknu HEK-noo

Heliopolis hē-lē-OP-uh-lis
Hellenes HE-lēnz
helot HEL-uht
Henan HŒ-NAHN
henequen HEN-i-kwin
Herat he-RAHT
Herero huh-RÂR-ō
heretical huh-RET-i-kuhl
Herodotus he-ROD-uh-tuhs
Heshen huh-SHUN
Heyerdhal, Thor HĀ-uhr-dahl
hieroglyphics hī-ruh-GLIF-iks
hijra HIJ-ruh
Himalaya HIM-uh-lā-uh
Himyar HIM-yuhr
Hippalus HIP-uh-luhs
Hittite HIT-īt
Ho Chi Minh HŌ CHĒ MIN
Hohenstaufen hō-uhn-SHTOU-fuhn
Hokulea hō-koo-LĀ-ah
hominid HOM-uh-nid
Homo erectus HŌ-mō I-REK-tuhs
Homo habilis HŌ-mō HAB-uh-luhs
Homo sapiens HŌ-mō SĀ-pē-enz
Hong Xiuquan HOONG SHĒ-Ō-choo-wan
Honglou Meng HOONG-lō MUNG
Houphouet-Boigny, Félix oo-FWĀ—bwah-NYĒ, fā-LĒKS
Huang Chao HWANG CHOU
Huang Da Po HWAHNG DAH PŌ
Huang He HWANG HUH
Huantar, Chavin de HWAHN-tahr, CHAH-vēn dā
Huaqing HWA-CHING
Huari HWAHR-ē
Huguenot HYOO-guh-not
Huitzilopochtli wē-tsē-lō-POCH-tlē
Hulegu HOO-luh-goo
Huna Capac WĪ-nah kah-PAHK
Husayn, Saddam hoo-SAYN, Sah-DAHM
Hwangnyang-sa HWAHNG-NYUHNG SAH
Hyksos HIK-sōs
Hystaspes his-TAS-pēz

Ibadan ē-BAH-dahn
Ibn al-Arabi IB-uhn ahl-AH-rah-bē
Ibn Battuta IB-uhn ba-TOOT-tuh
ibn Ezra, Abraham IB-uhn ĒZ-ruh
Ibn Khaldun IB-uhn khahl-DOON
Ibn Rushd IB-uhn RUSHD
Ibn Saud IB-uhn sah-OOD
Ibn Sina IB-uhn SĒ-nah
Ibn Tufayl IB-uhn too-FAYL
Ibn Tumart IB-uhn TOO-mahrt
Ibo Ē-bō

Il Duce il DOO-chā
Il-khan ĒL-KAHN
Iliad IL-ē-ad
indigénat in-di-jay-NOT
ingenio in-IĒN-yoh
Iolcus YOL-kuhs
Iona ī-Ō-nuh
iqta ik-TUH
Iranian i-RAH-nē-uhn
Iroquois IR-uh-kwoi
Isandhlwana ē-sahn-LWAHN-nuh
Isfahan is-fuh-HAHN
Ismail is-MAH-ēl
Iturbide, Augustín ē-tŏŏr-BĒ-dā
Ituri ē-TOO-rē
Izmir IZ-mēr

Ja'far JAH-far
Jacobin JAK-uh-bin
Jacquerie zhahk-uh-RĒ
Jagadai JAH-gah-dī
Jam'at-i Tabligh jam-AHT-uh tab-LĒG
Janissary JAN-i-ser-ē
Jeanneret, Charles Édouard Zhe-nuh-RAY
Jericho JER-i-kō
Jiang Qing JYAHN CHING
Jiménez hē-ME-nes
Jin JIN
Jingdezhen JING-DUH-JŒN
Jinnah jē-NAH
jizya JIZ-yuh
Juárez, Benito HWAH-res
Junta HŎŎN-tuh
Jurchen JUHR-CHEN
Juvaini JOO-VĪ-NĒ

Ka'ba KAH-buh
Kabul KAH-buhl
kaffiya kah-FĒ-uh
Kahlo, Frida KAH-lō, FRĒ-duh
Kaifeng kī-FUNG
Kaiser KĪ-zuhr
Kalahari kah-luh-HAHR-ē
Kalhu KAL-oo
Kamakura kah-mah-KOO-rah
Kanagawa kah-nah-GAH-wah
Kanem kah-NEHM
Kanem-Bornu KAH-nuhm—BOR-noo
Kangxi KAHNG-SHĒ
Kanishka ka-NISH-kuh
Kara-Khitai KARA—Kē-TĪ
Karakorum kahr-uh-KOR-uhm
Kashgar KASH-gahr
Kassite KAS-īt
Kathiawar kah-tē-uh-WAHR
Kazakh KAH-zahk
Kazakhstan KAH-zahk-stahn

Kepler, Johannes KEP-luhr, YO-hahn
Keraits KEH-RĪTS
Khadija ka-DĒ-juh
Khalifa kah-LĒ-fuh
Khan-balikh KAHN—BAH-lik
Khanate KAH-nāt
Kharijite KAHR-uh-jīt
Khartoum kahr-TOOM
Khayyam, Omar kī-YAM
Khedive kuh-DĒV
Khefren KEF ren
Khelat kuh-LAHT
Khitai kē-TĪ
Kho KŌ
Khoisan KOI-sahn
Khomeini, Ruhollah khoh-MAY-nee, ROO-hoh-luh
Khrushchev, Nikita KRUUSH-chyof
Khubilai KOO-buh-lī
Khufu KOO-foo
Khurasan kor-uh-SAHN
khuriltai KOO-ril-tī
Khwarasm KWAH-RAZ-um
Kiet Siel KAYT SEL
Kiev KĒ-ef
Kikuyu ki-KOO-yoo
Kitans KĒ-TANS
Kivas KĒ-vuhs
Kojiki KŌ-JĒ-kē
Kongjo KONG-JŌ
Koryo KOR-yō
Kosovo KÔ-sô-vô
Krac des Chevalliers KRAHK day shuh-vahl-YAY
Krishna KRISH-nuh
kulak KOO-lak
Kyrgyzstan KÎR-gē-stahn

Lab'ayu luh-BAH-yoo
labyrinth LAB-uh-rinth
Lahore luh-HOR
laissez-faire LES-ā FÂR
Lamaism LAH-muh-iz-uhm
Lambeyeque lam-bay-YAY-kay
Languedoc lahng-DÔK
Laos LOUS
lapis lazuli LAP-is LAZ-uh-lē
Lascaux la-SKŌ
Lebensraum LĀ-buhns-roum
legume LEG-yoom
Leiden LĪD-n
Leptis Magna LEP-tis MAG-nuh
Lesotho luh-SŌ-tō
Levant luh-VANT
Li Qingzhao LĒ CHING-JOU
Li Shizhen LĒ shûr-JEN
Liao LYOU
Liaodong LYOU-DONG

Liège lē-EZH
Liliuokalani lē-lē-oo-ō-kah-LAH-nē
Lima LĒ-muh
Lin Zexu LĒN zuh-SHOO
lineage LIN-ē-ij
Liuqiu lē-Ō-chē-ō
loess LES
Lucca LOOK-kah
Luddite LUD-īt
lugal LOO-guhl
Luo Guanzhong LÔ GWAHNG-JOONG
Luoyang LWŌ-yahng
Lusiads loo-SĒ-uds
Lusitania loo-si-TĀ-nē-uh
Lysistrata lis-uh-STRAH-tuh

ma'at muh-AHT
Ma Huan MAH HWAHN
Macao muh-KOU
Madeira muh-DĒR-uh
madrasa MA-dras-uh
Maharaja mah-huh-RAH-juh
Maharashtra mah-huh-RAHSH-truh
Mahayana mah-huh-YAH-nuh
Mainz MĪNTS
maize MĀZ
Malagasy mal-uh-GAS-ē
malam MAH-lahm
Malawi muh-LAH-wē
Malay muh-LĀ
Malinke muh-LING-kā
Mallia mahl-YAH
Manchukuo MAN-CHOO-KWŌ
manganese MANG-guh-nēs
Manichaean man-i-KĒ-uhn
Manichee MAN-i-kē
manikongo mah-NĒ-KÔNG-gō
manioc MAN-ē-ok
Mansa Kankan Musa MAHN-suh KAHN-kahn MOO-suh
mansab MAN-suhb
mansabdar man-suhb-DAHR
Mantua MAN-choo-uh
Manzikert MANZ-i-kuhrt
Mao Zedong MOU DZUH-DONG
Maori MAH-ô-rē
Maraga mah-rah-GAH
Maratha muh-RAH-tuh
mare librum MAH-rā LĒ-brum
mare nostrum MAH-rā NO-struhm
Mari MAH-rē
Marne MAHRN
Maronnage mah-ruh-NAHZH
Marquesas mahr-KĀ-suhs
Marquis mahr-KĒ
Marrakesh mar-uh-KESH
Martinique mahr-ti-NĒK

martyr MAHR-tuhr
Maruz muh-ROOZ
Mashhad mahsh-HAHD
matriarchy MĀ-trē-ahr-kē
matrilineal mat-ruh-LIN-ē-uhl
Maule MÔL
Mauritius mô-RISH-uhs
Maurya MORYA
Maya MAH-yuh
Mazzini, Giuseppe maht-SĒ-nē, joo-ZEP-pe
Mbuti uhm-BOO-tē
Mede MĒD
Medici MED-i-chē
Medoi MĀ-doy
Megara MEG-uh-ruh
Mehmed ME-met
Meiji MĀ-jē
Mein Kampf MĪN KAHMPF
Mejid, Abdul me-JĒD
Melanesia mel-uh-NĒ-zhuh
Melgart MEL-kahrt
Menes MĒ-nēz
Meroë MER-ō-ē
Merovingian mer-uh-VIN-juhn
mestizo mes-TĒ-zō
Metternich MET-uhr-nik
Mevlevi MEV-le-vē
Mexica MEK-si-kah
Michaelangelo mī-kuhl-AN-juh-lō
Michoacán MĒ-chô-ah-kahn
Minas Gerais MĒN-ahs JAYR-yys
Mindanao min-duh-NAH-ō
Minoan mi-NŌ-uhn
Minotaur MIN-uh-tor
Mitanni mi-TAH-nē
Mitsui mē-TSOO-yē
mitt'a MIT-uh
Moche MOK
Mochica mō-CHĒ-kuh
Moctezuma môk-ti-ZOO-muh
Mohenjo-Daro mō-hen-jō—DAHR-ō
monasticism muh-NAS-tuh-siz-uhm
Mongke MUHNG-KUH
monophysite muh-NOF-uh-sīt
Montpellier mōn-pel-YĀ
Mosul MOH-suhl
Mozambique mō-zam-BĒK
Mu'awiya moo-AH-wē-yuh
muezzin moo-EZ-in
Mughal MOO-guhl
muhtasib muh-TAH-sib
mulatto môo-LAH-tō
Muscovite MUS-kuh-vīt
Musqat MUS-kat
Mutsuhito moo-tsoo-HĒ-tō
Myanmar myahn-MAH

Mycenae mī-SĒ-nē
Mycenaean mī-suh-NĒ-uhn
myrrh MÛR
Mysore mī-SOR

Nabataean nab-uh-TĒ-uhn
Nabopolassar NAB-ō-pō-las-uhr
Najaf NA-jaf
Nanking NAN-king
Nantes NAHNT
Nanzhao nahn-JOU
Napata na-PĀ-tuh
naphtha NAF-thuh
Naqshbandi naksh-BAN-dē
Nasir al-Din NAH-zuhr ad—DĒN
nawab nuh-WOB
Nazi NAHT-sē
nazir NA-zir
Ndebele nn-duh-BĀ-lā
Neanderthal nē-AN-duhr-thôl
Nebuchadnezzar NAB-oo-kuhd-nez-uhr
Nefertiti nef-uhr-TĒ-tē
Nehru, Jawaharlal NĀ-roo
New Guinea new GIN-ē
Ngo Dinh Diem NGŌ DĒN DYEM
Nguni nn-GOO-nē
Nian NYAHN
Nicaea nī-SĒ-uh
Nineveh NIN-uh-vuh
Nishapur ni-shah-PŎŎR
Nizam al-Mulk nee-ZAHM ulh—MOOLK
Nkrumah, Kwame nn-KROO-muh, KWAH-mee
Novgorod NOV-guh-rod
Nuer NOO-uhr
Nyamwezi nn-nyahm-WĀ-zē
Nyasaland NYAH-sah-land
Nyssa NĪ-suh

oba Ō-buh
ochre Ō-kuhr
Oduduwa o-DOO-doo-wah
Ogodei UH-GUH-DĀ
Olduvai ol-DOO-vī
oligarchy OL-i-gahr-kē
Omani ō-MAH-nē
Ophir ō-FĒR
ordu OR-doo
Orinoco or-uh-NŌ-kō
orthopraxy or-thuh-PRAK-sē
Osiris ō-SĪ-ris
Oudh OUD

Páez, José Antonio PAH-es
pagani pah-GAH-nē

Pahlavi, Mohammad Reza PAH-luh-vē
Palenque pah-LENG-ke
Palmares PAL-muh-ruhs
Palmyra pal-MĪ-ruh
Palmyrene pal-MĪ-rēn
Pamir pah-MĒR
Pampas PAM-puhz
Panathenaea pan-ath-uh-NĒ-uh
papacy PĀ-puh-sē
papyrus puh-PĪ-ruhs
Paraguay PAR-uh-gwī
Pasha, Ibrahim PAH-shuh, ib-rah-HĒM
patriarchate PĀ-trē-ahr-kit
patrie PAH-trē
patrilineal pat-ruh-LIN-ē-uhl
Peng Yu PUHNG YOO
perestroika per-i-STROI-kuh
Pericles PER-i-klēz
Pernambuco PÛR-nuhm-byoo-kō
Petrarch, Francesco PĒ-trahrk, fran-CHES-kō
Phaistos FĪ-stuhs
phalanx FĀ-langks
Phnom Penh puh-NOM PEN
Phoenician fi-NĒ-shuhn
Phoinikes FOY-nē-kes
Phosphoric fos-FOR-ik
Piccolomini PĒ-kuh-lō-MĒ-nē
piety PĪ-i-tē
Piraeus pi-RĀ-uhs
Pisistratus pī-SIS-truh-tuhs
Pizarro pi-ZAHR-ō
Plateau pla TŌ
Pleistocene PLĪ-stuh-sēn
Po Zhuyi BŌ JOO-YĒ
pogrom PŌ-gruhm
polis PŌ-lis
Pondicherry pon-di-CHER-ē
pontifex maximus PON-tuh-feks MAK-suh-muhs
Prometheus pruh-MĒ-thē-uhs
Provençal prō-vuhn-SAHL
Ptah ptah
Ptolemy TOL-uh-mē
Pueblo Bonito PWEB-lō buh-NĒ-tō
Punt pŏōnt
Pygmy PIG-mē
Pylos PĒ-lōs
pyre PĪR
Pyrenees PIR-uh-nēz
Pythagoras pi-THAG-uhr-uhs
Pythia PITH-ē-uh

Qadiri KAH-duh-rē
Qairawan kyyr-ah-WAHN
qanat Kah-NAHT

Qatabah KA-tuh-buh
Qatar KAH-tar
Qianlong CHĒ-EN-LONG
Qiantang CHĒ-EN-TAHNG
Qin CHIN
Qing CHING
Qinghai CHING-HĪ
qizilbash ki-zil-BAHSH
Québec kā-BEK
Québecois kā-be-KWAH
Querétaro ke-RE-tah-rō
Quetzalcoatl ket-sahl-kō-AHT-l
quilombos kē-LŌM-bōs
quinoa KĒN-wah
quipu KĒ-poo
Quixote ē-HŌ-tē
Quran kŏŏ-RAHN
Quraysh kuu-RYYSH

Rabban Sauma RAH-BAHN
   SOU-mah
Rabelais, François RAB-uh-lā
rah RAH
Rai RYY
Rajput RAHJ-poot
Ramesses ram-i-SĒZ
Rashid al-Din rah-SHĒD ad—DĒN
Ravenna ruh-VEN-uh
raya RAH-yuh
Rayy RĀ
Re RĀ
Reichstag RĪKS-tahg
Remarque ri-MAHRK
Ricci, Matteo RĒ-chē, mah-TĀ-ō
Richelieu rē-shuh-LYŎŎ
rinji RIN-jē
Rio de Janeiro RĒ-ō dā zhuh-
   NÂR-ō
Rio de la Plata RĒ-ō dā lah
   PLAH-tah
Robespierre, Maximilien ROBZ-pē-âr
Roca, Julio RŌ-kuh
Romanesque rō-muh-NESK
ronin RŌ-nin
Rosas, Huan Manuel de duh RŌ-sahs
rouble ROO-buhl
Ruhr RŎŎR
Rwanda roo-AHN-duh

Saadi SAH-dē
Saarinen, Eero SAHR-uh-nuhn
Safavid SAH-fah-vid
Sahel SAH-hil
Said sah-ĒD
Sake SAH-kē
Salamis SAH-lah-mēs
Samaj, Brahmo suh-MAHJ, BRAH-mō
Samarkand SAM-uhr-kand

samorin SAH-muh-rin
samurai SAM-ŏŏ-rī
São Tomé SOU tō-MĀ
saqiya suh-KĒ-yuh
Saqqara suh-KAHR-uh
Saracen SAR-uh-suhn
Sarepta suh-REP-tuh
Sargon SAHR-gon
Sasanid suh-SAH-nid
sati su-TĒ
satrap SĀ-trap
satyagraha suh-TYAH-gruh-huh
sawahil suh-WAH-hil
Shechem SHE-kuhm
schism SKIZ-uhm
Schliemann SHLĒ-mahn
Scythian SITH-ē-uhn
Seine SEN
Sekigahara se-kē-GA-HAH-ra
Seleucid si-LOO-sid
Selim se-LEEM
Seljuk sel-JOOK
Semitic suh-MIT-ik
Senegalese sen-uh-gah-LĒZ
sepoy SĒ-poi
seppuku SE-poo-kŏŏ
Sesshu ses-SHOO
Seville suh-VIL
Sèvres SEV-ruh
Shaanxi SHAHN-SHĒ
Shahansha SHAH-han-SHAH
shahid sha-HĒD
shaitan shī-TAHN
Shalmaneser shal-muh-NĒ-zuhr
Shamir, Yitzhak shah-MĒR
Shang SHAHNG
Shari'a shah-RĒ-ah
Sharrukin SHAH-roo-kēn
shawabti shuh-WAB-tē
Shechem shuh-KEM
Shephelah she-FE-luh
Shi'a SHĒ-uh
Shi'ism SHĒ-iz-uhm
Shi'ite SHĒ-īt
Shiraz shē-RAHZ
Shuwardata shoo-wuhr-DUH-tuh
sian SĒ-ahn
Sichuan SECH-WAHN
Sidon SĪD-n
Siena sē-EN-uh
Sierra Leone sē-ER-uh lē-ŌN
Sijilmasa si-jil-MA-suh
Sikh SĒK
Sind SIND
Singhalese sing-guh-LĒZ
Sinhalese sin-huh-LĒZ
Sioux SOO
Socotra suh-KŌ-truh

Sodom SOD-uhm
Sogdian SOG-dē-uhn
Sogdiana sog-dē-AN-uh
Solzhenitzyn, Alexander sōl-zhuh-
   NĒT-sin
Son SUN
sorghum SOR-guhm
Sousse SOOS
Sri Lanka SRĒ LAHNG-kuh
Srivijaya srē-VI-juh-yuh
Sry Darya SHRĒ DAHR-yah
Steppe STEP
Strabo STRĀ-bō
Strachey, John STRA-chē
styrax STĪ-raks
Subudei SUH-BUH-DĀ
suffetes SOO-fētz
Suhrawardi suh-ruh-WAHR-dē
Sui SWĒ
Suleiman SOO-lā-mahn
Sumanguru soo-muhn-GOO-roo
Summa Theologica SŎŎM-uh thē-uh-
   LOJ-i-kuh
Sundiata soon-JAH-tuh
Surat SŎŎR-uht
suzerainty SOO-zuh-rin-tē
Suzhou SOO-JŌ
Swahili swah-HĒ-lē
Swidden SWID-n
Sylvius, Aeneas SIL-vē-uhs,
   in-Ē-uhs

Tabriz tah-BRĒZ
Tahert TAH-huhrt
Tahmasp tah-MAHSP
Tahyast TAH-yast
Ta sety TUH-SE-tē
Taika TĪ-kah
Taiping TĪ-ping
Tajik tah-JIK
Takla Makan TAH-kluh muh-KAHN
Talmud TAHL-mŏŏd
Tamburlaine TAM-buhr-lān
Tamerlane TAM-uhr-lān
Tang TAHNG
Tanganyika tahn-guh-NYĒ-kuh
Tangguts TAHNG-GOOTS
Tangier tan-JÎR
Tanit TAH-nit
Tarim TAH-rēm
Tashkent tahsh-KENT
Tassili ta-SEE-lee
Tawantinsuyu tah-wahn-teen-SOO-
   yoo
te TĀ
Techuacán te-choo-uh-KAHN
Tecumseh ti-KUM-suh
Temeh TĒM

Temüjin TEM-oo-chin
La Tene lah TEN
tenno TEN-NŌ
Tenochtitlán te-NÔCH-tē-tlahn
Tenskwatawa ten-SKWAHT-uh-wah
Teotihuacán tā-uh-tē-wah-KAHN
terik te-REK
Teutonic too-TON-ik
Téwodros tā-WŌ-druhs
Thar Desert TAHR
Theodosius thē-uh-DŌ-shuhs
Thermopylae thuhr-MOP-uh-lē
Theseus THE-sē-uhs
Thesmophoria thes-mō-FŌ-rē-uh
Thucydides thoo-SID-i-dēz
Tiahuanaco tē-uh-wuh-NAH-kō
Tiamat TYAH-maht
Tian TE-EN
Tibesti tē-BES-tē
Tien Shan TYEN SHAHN
Tiglathpileser TIG-lath-pi-LE-zuhr
Tigris TĪ-gris
Tikal tē-KAHL
Timur Lenk ti-MŎŎR LENK
Timur-i lang tē-MOOR—yē LAHNG
Timurid ti-MŎŎR-id
Tiryns TĪR-inz
Tito TE-tō
Tlaloc tlah-LŎK
Tlateloca tlah-tay-LOH-koh
Tlemcen tlem-SEN
Tocqueville, Alexis de TŎK-vil
Todaiji tō-DĪ-jē
Toghoril TŌ-guh-rul
Tokugawa Ieyasu tō-kō-GA-wa Ē-yeh-YAH-suh
Tongzhi toong-JÛR
tophets TŌ-fet
Topiltzin toh-PELT-seen
Tordesillas tor-duh-SE-yuhs
Toulouse too-LOOZ
Touré, Sékou too-RĀ, SĀ-koo
Transoxiana trans-ox-ē-AHN-ah
Trianon trē-ah-NŌ
Tripitaka tri-PIT-uh-kuh
Tripoli TRIP-uh-lē
trireme TRĪ-rēm
Trujillo troo-HE-ō
tsar ZAHR
Tsirinana, Philibert tsē-RAH-nah-nah
Tsushima TSOO-shē-mah
Tuareg TWAH-reg
Tughril TUUG-ruhl

Tunisia too-NE-zhuh
Tupac Amaru TOO-pahk ah-MAH-roo
Turkic TÛR-kik
Tuscany TUS-kuh-nē
Tutankhamun toot-ahng-KAH-muhn
Tuthmosis tuth-MŌ-sis
Tyre TĪR
Tyrolian Alps ti-RŌ-lē-uhn

Uaxactún wahsh-ahk-TOON
Ugarit OO-guh-rēt
Uigur WE-gŏŏr
ulamai OO-luh-mā
Umayyad oo-MĪ-ad
umma UM-uh
Upanishads oo-PAHN-i-shahds
Urartu ŏŏ-RAHR-too
Urdu ŎŎR-doo
Urugu YŎŎR-uh-gwī
Uruk OO-rŏŏk
Usuman dan Fodio OO soo mahn duhn FŌD-yō
Uthman uuth-MAHN
Uzbekistan ŏŏz-BEK-i-stan

Vairocana VĪ-rō-chah-nah
Vallon-Pont-d'Arc vah-LON—pon—DAHRK
van Eyck, Jan vahn ĪK, YAHN
Verde VÛRD
Versailles vuhr-SĪ
Vijayanagar vē-juh-yah-NAH-gahr
Vizier vi-ZĪR
Vladivostok vlad-uh-VOS-tok

Wafd WAHFT
Walesa, Lech wah-LEN-suh, LEK
Walpurga val-PŎŎR-gah
Wang Jinghong WAHNG JING-hong
Wazir wuh-ZER
Wehrmacht VĀR-mahkt
Wei WĀ
Weizmann, Chaim WĪTS-muhn, KHĪ-im
Whorl HWORL
Whydah HWĪ-duh
Wojtyla, Karol voy-TE-luh
Wu Cheng'en WOO CHUNG-UHN
Wu Jingzi WOO JING-zuh
Wu Zhao WOO JOU

Xanadu ZAN-uh-doo
Xavier, Francis ZĀ-vē-uhr

Xenophon ZEN-uh-fuhn
Xhosa KŌ-suh
Xi'an SHE-AN
Xia SHYAH
Xiang SHYAHNG
Xinjiang SHIN-JYAHNG
Xiongnu SHE-OONG-noo
Xu Guangqi SOO GWAHNG-CHE
Xu Wei SOO WĀ
Xuan de SHOO-WEN-DEH
Xuanzang SHOO-WEN-ZAHNG

Yahweh YAH-wā
Yang Guifei YAHNG GWĀ-FĀ
Yangdi YAHNG-DE
Yangzi YANG-ZUH
Yaqui YAH-kē
Yazdigird YAZ-duh-guhrd
Yazid ya-ZED
Yelu Chucai YEH-LŌ CHOO-tsī
yeni cheri YEN-i CHE-rē
yerba YÂR-buh
Yi Son-sin YE SUN-shin
Yongle YOONG-LŌ
Ypres E-pruh
Yuan Shihkai yoo-AHN shē-KĪ
Yucatán yoo-kuh-TAN

Za-ar ZAH—ahr
Zagros ZAG-ruhs
Zaibatsu ZĪ-bah-tsoo
Zaire zah-ER
Zarathushtra zar-uh-THOO-struh
zealots ZEL-uht
Zeng Guofan TSUNG GWŌ-FAN
Zhang Qian JAHNG CHE-EN
Zhapu JAH-poo
Zheng He JUNG HUH
Zhou JŌ
Zhu Shijie JOO SHÛR-jē-yeh
Zhu Yuanzhang JOO YOO-WEN-JAHNG
ziggurat ZIG-uh-rat
Zimbabwe zim-BAHB-wā
Zin CHIN
Zollverein TSOL-fer-īn
Zoroastrianism zor-ō-AS-trē-uh-niz-uhm
Zumárraga zoo-MAH-rah-gah
Zworykin, Vladimir ZWOR-i-kin, VLAD-uh-mír

Index

Shang dynasty *(cont.)*
(illus.); divination and, 69;
ceremonies and rituals of, 70
Shari'a (law of Islam), 298–300
Shawabtis, 81
Sheba, Israelite trade with, 111–112
Shelter, of early migrating peoples, 16–18.
See also Housing
Shi Huangdi (China), 182, 183
Shi'ite Muslims, 288; Khurasan rebellion
and, 291–292; Buyid family as, 294;
Egyptian rule by, 294; of Arabia,
443. *See also* Islam; Muslim(s)
Shikoku, Japan, 415 (map)
Shilla, Korea, 325
Shinto religion, in Japan, 326
Ships and shipping: in ancient Egypt, 47
(illus.), 55; of ancient Greeks, 86,
137; of Celtic peoples, 100;
Phoenician warship, 114 (illus.);
Athenian, 147–148; of India, 208;
maritime system and, 229–230; of
early Indian Ocean sailors, 230;
Song improvements in, 335; in
China and Southeast Asia, 406–408;
in Ming Empire, 410; in tropical
regions, 428; dhow and, 439, 440
and *illus.*; junks and, 439; European
trade and, 461. *See also* Exploration;
Indian Ocean region; Maritime
trade and routes; Navigation;
Navy; Portugal
Shiva (god), 198, 199
Shoguns and shogunates (Japan), 420;
Kamakura, 327
Shrines, Hindu, 199–200
Shudra class, in India, 194
Siam (Thailand), 210
Sicily, 116; Roman conquest of, 167;
Crusades and, 273; Islamic empire
and, 290
Siddhartha Gautama, 196. *See also* Buddha;
Buddhism
Sidon, 115
Sijilmasa, trade of, 237–238
Silk: in China, 186; trade routes for, 212. *See
also* Silk Road
Silk Road, 183, 186, 221, 223–228; camels
and, 224–226; spread of Buddhism
along, 227, 243; trade along,
227–228; Sasanid Empire and, 280,
282; Chang'an and, 310–313;
Beijing and, 402. *See also* Trade;
Trade routes
Sind region: of Pakistan, 55; Islamic empire
and, 289
Singapore, 210
Sixth Cataract, 80. *See also* Nile River region
Skin colors: changes in, 12; in Indian society,
194. *See also* Social class
Slash-and-burn agriculture, 210
Slaves and slavery: in Mesopotamia, 40; in
ancient Egypt, 52; in classical
Greece, 150; in Roman and Han
Empires, 169; in China, 183; Indian

Untouchables as, 194; in Germanic
kingdoms, 254; Christianity and,
263; Turks as slaves and, 294; in
Islam, 303; in Mongol Empire, 374;
in Africa, 447; in Delhi Sultanate,
447; uses of slaves, 447–448; blacks
in Renaissance art and, 470 (illus.)
Slavic languages, 250
Slavic peoples, Christianization of, 392
Slums, in Rome, 170
Smelting, of iron, 242
Smiriti, 48
Social class: in Mesopotamia, 38–39; of
priests, 42; in ancient Egypt, 52;
Celtic, 99; in Assyrian Empire, 106;
in Iran, 128–129; in Athens, 145; in
Roman Republic, 165–166; in
Roman Empire, 167–168; gender
and, 181; in China, 183, 184–185; in
India, 194; Hindu duties and, 200;
in feudal society, 255–257; in
Byzantine Empire, 265; in Korea,
325; in Japan, 327; Song elite and,
327–329; Chinese footbinding and,
329–330; in Mesoamerica, 342;
conflict among, in Teotihuacán,
345–346; in Moche, 361; in Yuan
China, 403; educated class as,
410–411; in Japan, 419–420; Indian,
and Islam, 447; in tropical societies,
447–448; women and, 448;
European, 454–456. *See also* Elite
class; Gentry
Social life, in Ice Age, 15–16
Social mobility, in western Europe, 463. *See
also* Social class
Social roles, of Indian women, 448
Society: creation myths and, 5; in Ice Age,
15–16; in Neolithic Age, 25–29;
matrilineal and patrilineal, 26;
early civilizations and, 32; in
Mesopotamia, 39–41; in ancient
Egypt, 52–53; of Indus Valley
civilization, 56; migrations and, 96;
of Celtic peoples, 99–100; Assyrian,
106; in Iran, 128; in classical Greece,
150–151; in Roman Republic,
165–166; in China, 179–180; in
Indian Vedic Age, 194; skin color in
India and, 194; Jainism and, 196;
women in Gupta, 206–208; in sub-
Saharan Africa, 239; feudal
European, 254–257; in western
Europe, 263; of Byzantine Empire,
265–266; decline of feudal, 273–275;
women in Islamic, 302–303; in
Tang Empire, 313–314; in East
Asia, 324–327; in Song Empire, 328;
Mayan, 346; Toltec, 350–351; Aztec,
352; in North America, 354–355; of
Moche, 361; of Tiahuanaco, 362; of
Incas, 364; in Central Asia, 374–376;
Mongols and European, 391–395;
in Eastern Eurasia, 399; of Yuan
China, 403; in tropical regions,

447–450; rebellion in Europe,
456–457; European civic life and,
463–465. *See also* Culture(s);
Gender; Lifestyle; Men; Religion;
Slaves and slavery; Women
Socotra (island), 230
Socrates (philosopher), 148–149; followers
of, 143; method of, 149
Sodom, 109
Sogdians, 221, 319; syllabic script of,
316
Soil: in China, 66; in tropical regions, 428.
See also Agriculture; Fertile
Crescent; Land
Solar system, *see* Astronomy
Solomon (Israelite): reign of, 111–112;
Temple of, 111 (illus.)
Solon, 145
Somalia, Israelite trade with, 112
Somali peoples, 239
Song Empire (China), 320 (map), 320–321
and *map*, 402; achievements of, 309;
elite life in, 327–329; footbinding of
women in, 329; women in, 329–331;
cities and towns in, 332; printing
in, 332–333; technological
explosion in, 333–335; Mongols
and, 399
Songhai Empire, slaves in, 448
Son of Heaven, Chinese Emperor as, 184
Sophists, 148
Sophocles, 148
Sound-based writing systems, 317
South America: maize in, 341; Andean
civilizations and, 359–367; Incas in,
363–367. *See also* Expansion and
expansionism; Exploration
South Arabia, 442
South Asia, between 1200 and 1500, 437
(map). *See also* Asia
South China Sea, trade across, 228
Southeast Asia, 209 (map); Indian
civilization and, 191–209;
geography of, 209–210; economy
and trade of, 210; land and
resources of, 210; early states in,
210–212; Funan in, 211–212;
language and culture in, 211–212;
Srivijayan Empire in, 212–214;
chronology in, 214; trade routes in,
221–223, 222 (map); maritime trade
and, 228; products traded from,
231; Tang Empire and, 310; Song
Empire and, 321; Annam in, 327;
Champa in, 327; Ming aggression
against, 406; tropics in, 426;
between 1200 and 1500, 437 (map);
Malacca in, 443–444. *See also* Asia;
East Asia
Southern China: migrations into, 332; Ming
Empire in, 405–409. *See also* China
Southern Song, *see* Song Empire (China)
South India, independence of, 438
Southwestern United States, desert cultures
in, 354, 355–356

Spain, 477–478; Celtic peoples in, 98; Phoenicians and, 116; Roman conquest of, 167; Visigoths in, 249; Muslims in, 274; Umayyad rule in, 293; Islam and, 294–295; religious groups in, 295; Aztecs and, 352, 353; Jews in, 463; exploration by, 477. *See also* Colonies and colonization; Empires; Exploration

Sparta, 144, 156; Peloponnesian War and, 151–152; Athenian defeat and, 152

Specialization: of crafts, 25, 27; in Mesopotamian cities, 36; in East Asia after Tang Empire, 319–335

Species, *see* Prehistoric peoples

Spirits, Jinns as, 285

Sports, Mesoamerican ball game and, 348 (illus.)

"Springs and Autumns Period," in Zhou China, 71

Sri Lanka, 192, 203; Buddhism and, 243. *See also* Ceylon (Sri Lanka)

Srivijaya Empire, 209 (map), 212–214; culture of, 213–214; religion in, 213 and *illus.*; maritime trade and, 231

Starvation, *see* Famine

States, *see* Empires; Nations (states)

Status: Chinese footbinding and, 329; of women in China, 329–330; of women in Korea, 329–330; of Indian women, 448. *See also* Elite; Social class; Women

Steel: in north China, 335; decline in Ming China, 410

Steppes, Mongolian, 65. *See also* Central Asia

Stirrups: impact of, 227; iron, 312 (illus.); in Central Asia, 376, 377

Stone Age, 13–15; divisions of, 14; American cultures and, 340. *See also* Tools

Stone Age peoples, 5–12; australopithecines, 7–9; *Homo erectus* and, 9; *Homo habilis* and, 9; dispersal of, 10 (map); *Homo sapiens* as, 11; modern species and, 12; history and culture in Ice Age, 12–18; African rock paintings and, 231–234

Stonehenge, 28; constructing, 29

Stone tools, *see* Stone Age; Tools

Strait of Gibraltar, Spain and, 294–295

Strasbourg Cathedral, 466 (illus.)

Strategic importance, of Southeast Asia, 210

Stratification, *see* Social class

Stress, environmental, 59, 374. *See also* Environment

Stupas (mounds), 197

Subcontinent, India as, 192, 193 (map)

Sub-Saharan Africa, 432 (map); farming in, 22; trade of, 64; impact on Nubia, 82; Carthaginian trade with, 118–119; cultural exchange throughout, 238–242; trade in, 238–242; environment and climate of, 239; cultural characteristics of, 239–241; iron and, 241; Bantu migrations and, 241–242;

languages in, 242; agricultural cultivation in, 428; Islam in, 431; Islam and literacy in, 445–446. *See also* Africa; Sahara Desert region

Sübüdei (Mongol military commander), 392

Sudan, 46; Mali Empire in, 431–436; Western (1375), 433 (map); changes in, 434–436

Sufi brotherhoods, 304, 388

Sui Empire, 310

Sulla, 168

Sultan, meaning of term, 297. *See also* Ottoman Empire

Sultanates, in India, 436–438

Sumanguru (Takrur king), 431

Sumatra, 209 (map); Srivijayan Empire and, 212; trade of, 443

Sumer, 121; cuneiform writing of, 38; Sargon and, 38

Sumerian culture and peoples, 35; kings of, 37–38; impact on Semitic peoples, 41; religion of, 41

Sumerian King List, 38

Summa Theologica (Thomas Aquinas), 468

Sundiata (Empire of Mali), 431

Sunni Muslims, 288; caliphs and, 294; in Egypt, 294; Turks as, 297; in Arabia, 443

Supernatural: in Celtic beliefs, 100; in Mesoamerican cultures, 342. *See also* Witches

Superstition, Christian church and, 257

Survival, human reproduction and, 16

Susa, 130

Swahili Coast, trade and, 440–441

Sweden, invasions from, 251

Swidden agriculture, 22, 210; of Maya, 346

Syllabic writing, 317; of Sogdians, 316. *See also* Written language

Symbols, written, 43

Synagogue, 113. *See also* Israel and Israelites

Syria: Mesopotamia and, 33; Egyptian battles against, 77; invasions of, 88; Phoenicians of, 96; Canaan and, 110, 114; cities in, 280; trans-Arabian trade and, 284; Islamic Empire in, 289; nomadic uprisings in, 297

Syriac script, Semitic, 316

Syria-Palestine region, 74; Egyptian expansionism and, 74. *See also* Middle East

Tabasco, Mexico, 342

Tahert (city-state), trade of, 237–238

Taika Reforms, in Japan, 325

Takla Makan Desert, 65

Takrur state, Islam in, 431

Talas River, Battle of, 319

Tale of Genji, The (Murasaki Shikibu), 317, 331–332

Tale of the Heike (Japan), 327

Tamerlane, *see* Timur (Mongol Empire)

Tamil Nadu, 192

Tamil peoples: kingdoms of, 202; culture of, 203; language of, 203; agriculture and irrigation of, 429

Tang Empire, 310–319, 311 (map); cavalry stirrup and, 228; culture of, 276; East Asia after, 309; Chang'an and, 310–313; Silk Road and, 310–313; Buddhism and, 313–314; impact of monasticism on families in, 314; society of, 314; trade in, 314–319; chronology of, 316; Turkic power and, 316; women in, 318 (illus.), 319; fragmentation of, 319; migrations in, 319; successor states to, 323; Tibetan battles with, 324. *See also* Uigur Empire

Tanggut Empire, 320, 402; ideology in, 321; of Minyak people, 323; Mongol attacks on, 401

Tanit (goddess), 119

Tanzania: hominid footprints in, 7 (illus.); Stone Age tools from, 14

Tarquinius Superbus, 163

Ta-sety, 78

Tashkent, 316

Tawantinsuyu, as Inca state, 363–364

Taxation: in Assyrian Empire, 104; in Persian Empire, 130; in Roman Empire, 172; in China, 178; in Song Empire, 332; by Mongols, 382–383, 399; clergy and, 476; by monarchs, 476

Tax farming, 382

Technology: human evolution and, 8 (illus.); food gathering and preparation tools and, 13–15; agricultural tools and, 21–22; irrigation and, 37; coinage and, 39; writing and, 42–43; in ancient Mesopotamia, 42–45; irrigation and, 43, 54–55; transportation and, 43–45; military, 45; in ancient Egypt, 54; of Indus Valley civilization, 57; spread of, 64; creation of bronze, 68; engineering and, 68; in Shang China, 68; in Egyptian New Kingdom, 74; Minoan influence on Mycenaean, 85; of Celtic peoples, 100; Assyrian Empire and, 103, 106; Phoenician alphabet as, 115; naval, 147; military, 152; in Roman Empire, 174–176; writing as, 180; of Qin dynasty, 183; in Han Empire, 185–186; in India, 205, 215; in sailing, 229–230; camel riding and, 235–236; metals in sub-Saharan Africa, 242; flow along trade routes, 244–245; and western European revival, 268, 269–270; diffusion of, 269; agricultural, 269–270, 269 (illus.); Muslim, 305; in China, 309; transfer of Chinese to Tibet, 323; printing and, 325, 332–333; in Song Empire, 332–335; timekeeping and, 333; Chinese